VOLUME 3

THE COLLECTED WORKS OF ARTHUR SELDON

Everyman's Dictionary of Economics

THE COLLECTED WORKS OF ARTHUR SELDON

VOLUME 1 The Virtues of Capitalism

VOLUME 2 The State Is Rolling Back

VOLUME 3 Everyman's Dictionary of Economics

VOLUME 4 Introducing Market Forces into "Public" Services

VOLUME 5 Government Failure and Over-Government

VOLUME 6 The Welfare State: Pensions, Health, and Education

VOLUME 7 The IEA, the LSE, and the Influence of Ideas (includes cumulative index)

Arthur Seldon

VOLUME 3

THE COLLECTED WORKS OF ARTHUR SELDON

Everyman's Dictionary of Economics

ARTHUR SELDON
and F. G. PENNANCE

Edited and with a New Introduction
by Colin Robinson

LIBERTY FUND, Indianapolis

This book is published by Liberty Fund, Inc., a foundation established to encourage study of the ideal of a society of free and responsible individuals.

The cuneiform inscription that serves as our logo and as the design motif for our endpapers is the earliest-known written appearance of the word "freedom" (*amagi*), or "liberty." It is taken from a clay document written about 2300 B.C. in the Sumerian city-state of Lagash.

Photo of Arthur Seldon courtesy of the Institute of Economic Affairs
Printed in the United States of America

09 08 07 06 05 C 5 4 3 2 1
09 08 07 06 05 P 5 4 3 2 1

Library of Congress Cataloging-in-Publication Data

Seldon, Arthur.
Everyman's dictionary of economics/Arthur Seldon; edited and with a new introduction by Colin Robinson.
p. cm.—(Collected works of Arthur Seldon; v. 3)
Originally published: London: Dent, 1976. 2nd ed. (revised, enlarged and reset).
Includes bibliographical references and index.
ISBN 0-86597-544-2 (alk. paper)—ISBN 0-86597-552-3 (pbk.: alk. paper).
1. Economics—Dictionaries. I. Title. II. Title: Dictionary of Economics. III. Robinson, Colin, 1932– . IV. Series: Seldon, Arthur. Works. 2004; v. 3.
HB61.S39 2005
330'.03—dc22 2004042971

LIBERTY FUND, INC.
8335 Allison Pointe Trail, Suite 300
Indianapolis, Indiana 46250-1684

CONTENTS

INTRODUCTION

Background and Editorial Approach

Everyman's Dictionary of Economics, which is the sole work in volume 3 of The Collected Works of Arthur Seldon, may seem an unusual book for a classical liberal economist to write: it not only surveys the ideas of like-minded economists, but, as a dictionary designed to help the layman understand the terms used by economists, it also covers a very wide range of economic thought. It is a major work about which, in the publicity for the second edition, the authors claimed quite reasonably that

> it explains all the terms and ideas that Everyman (and Everywoman) is likely to meet in the press, broadcasting, in public debate and private conversation. And all this in short essays written in plain English.

The first edition was published in 1965 by J. M. Dent,[1] famous for its Everyman series; the second edition, also published by Dent, appeared in 1975. The second edition, reproduced here, differs substantially from the first. In the intervening ten years there had been many developments in economics, and, in particular those years saw the beginnings of the "counter-revolution," which brought about a retreat from Keynesian economics and a revival of classical liberal ideas. Consequently, the new ideas had to be incorporated: the first edition, consisting of 225,000 words, was pruned and brought up to date, with the addition of almost 600 new entries and some 90,000 words.

Seldon was asked by Dent to compile the *Dictionary* in 1960, a time during his early days at the Institute of Economic Affairs when it was not possible

1. J. M. Dent, which was founded in 1888 and began its Everyman's Library of low-priced classic texts in 1906, no longer exists, having been purchased by Weidenfeld and Nicholson in 1988.

for him to devote the necessary attention to such a large project. Compiling a dictionary is a different matter from the composition of a specialized text. In writing for a lay audience, the author of a dictionary has a responsibility to carry out the necessary research across a wide range of economic ideas to ensure that the reader, consulting any given entry, finds it both enlightening and directed toward related ideas. To help him in that task, Seldon was fortunate to find a collaborator in his friend F. G. Pennance, who later became professor of land economy at the University of Aberdeen. In addition to Pennance, Seldon also had help from a number of specialist contributors (listed on pages xxiii–xxiv).

The prime editorial responsibility for the extensively revised second edition fell on Seldon, who also supplied about three-quarters of the entries. Pennance contributed entries on the economics of land, property, and related matters and also helped with editing. As Pennance remarks in the acknowledgments:

> Apart from some entries on specialist topics and general editing, the whole burden of revision, new writing, and compilation was undertaken with characteristic unselfishness by Arthur Seldon (p. xxii).

Pennance checked the manuscript on his return to the United Kingdom, but unfortunately he died just before the book was published.

The *Dictionary* received some enthusiastic reviews. For example, the late Patrick Hutber, a well-known and perceptive British economic journalist of the time, wrote in the *Sunday Telegraph:*

> If the layman could have only one book beside him to guide him through the economic maze, which should it be? Beyond a doubt the new edition of Everyman's *Dictionary of Economics*. . . . With this by your side there is no excuse for not understanding what economists are talking about . . . or what are the great issues of economic debate.

Subsequently, the *Dictionary* was translated into both Italian (*Dizionario di Economia,* Milan, 1979) and Portuguese (*Dicionario de Economia,* Rio de Janeiro, 1968).

Unlike many dictionaries of economics, *Everyman's* avoids unexplained jargon, which is not surprising, given Seldon's devotion to ensuring that IEA authors explain themselves "in plain English." He also edited the contributors' work for consistency to ensure that the entries could be understood by the layman.

For example, consider the entry for "Investment Appraisal" (p. 373–74), a subject that most dictionaries explain in mathematical symbols and technical language. First, there is a careful explanation of the elements of investment appraisal, including the basic equations for the net present value and internal rate of return approaches. But that explanation is followed by a conclusion that places methods of investment appraisal in context—namely, that the major issues are not the technical aspects of discounting and compounding but rather how to deal with uncertainty and how to quantify benefit and cost flows.

On an even more technical matter, take the entry for "Skedasticity." "Homoskedasticity" and "heteroskedasticity" are specialized terms in econometrics that often baffle students. The *Dictionary* describes skedasticity as a "fancy Greek term for variance" and goes on to explain briefly its significance as a measure of dispersion. Correlation and regression are similarly explained in nontechnical terms and placed in context by an explanation of the dangers of relying on statistical associations when the theoretical bases of the relevant equations are not clear.

Another feature of the book that is helpful for the general reader is the Related Subjects Index, which places each entry within one of fourteen categories (such as "Development of Economic Thought," "Industrial Structure and Organisation," "Money and Financial Organisation," and "Scope, Method and Sources"). This method allows the reader of one entry to refer to other entries in the same category, which is easier on the reader than the more usual dictionary method of adding a string of cross-references at the end of each entry.

Scope of the Entries

The scope of the *Dictionary* is ambitious. Seldon's aim, as explained in the introduction to the first edition (page xxi), is to reach

> every man who comes new to the subject: the scholar at school, the student at university or the maturer citizen.

Examples and applications are taken principally from the British economy, but they come also from the United States, continental Europe, and other parts of the world. The selected entries described below will help to illustrate the scope and nature of the book. In particular, they show how Seldon's view of economics—and, in particular, his classical liberal ideas—shine through the entries.

An important and fundamental feature of the book is the attention Seldon pays to the history of economic thought, for which there are more than 170 entries, about one-eighth of the total entries. There is even an entry on

"Economic Thought" (pp. 220–25), which briefly summarizes developments in the subject since the seventeenth century. Seldon has always been conscious of the dependence of present scholars on those of the past. Economic ideas have evolved over the centuries, from the writings of the Greek philosophers and scholars such as Thomas Aquinas to Adam Smith and his immediate forerunners to leaders on the subject today.

The *Dictionary* therefore devotes considerable attention to concise biographies of the most prominent economists, giving the reader a sense of how the economist has developed. The first edition deliberately eschewed listing any living economists, but the second edition includes many of the more-famous economists of the twentieth century. Thus, along with the great classical economists, there are entries for people such as John Maynard Keynes, Milton Friedman, Friedrich Hayek, Harry Johnson, Kenneth Arrow, Lionel Robbins, James Buchanan, George Stigler, Gary Becker, and many others. Each biography explains the essence of the economist's ideas, along with details of his or her professional career, and provides a list of major works.

The entry for Hayek, for example, explains the nature of his disagreements with Keynes and discusses his contributions to economic methodology, emphasizing his view that prices communicate indispensable information to consumers and producers.

Leading schools of economic thought (for example, the Austrian, Cambridge, Chicago, Manchester, and Virginia Schools) all have entries. Of the Austrian School, for example, the reader learns that its analysis is

> founded on price-changes as sources of empirical information about changing conditions that is not obtainable from other sources or by other methods . . . in sharp contrast to the aggregative (macro-economic) approaches of other schools which . . . neglect the market processes that determine *relative* prices and equilibria of different though interconnected goods. (p. 33–34, italics in the original)

The history of the Chicago School, "a group of disciples of liberal economic philosophy" (p. 102), is traced, and its approach is summarized as emphasizing

> the empirical testing of economic hypotheses, an approach not always shared by liberal economists elsewhere. (p. 102)

The principal characteristic that distinguishes *Everyman's* from a similar reference work compiled by a present-day economist is that, although Seldon is careful to set out the mainstream view on each topic, he goes further by also explaining the classical liberal perspective. A few examples from the entries will make the point clear.

First, consider the entry for "Competition." Economists differ significantly in what they mean when they refer to "competition," or "competitive markets." Neoclassical economists often equate competition with perfect competition—an abstraction from the real world in which the market contains very large numbers of buyers and sellers, in which the products of different firms are identical, and in which there is perfect knowledge (an assumption that ensures that such a market can never exist). In the long-run equilibrium of this kind of market, price is equal to long-run marginal cost and all "excess" profit is eliminated by the force of competition (though the model includes no description of the competitive process itself).

The definition of competition is much more than a technical matter: it influences the way economists see the scope for government intervention in the economy. If a "perfect" market is taken as the standard against which other markets should be judged, other "imperfect" (and, by implication less desirable) market forms are then identified, going under the technical titles of imperfect or monopolistic competition (where products are differentiated), oligopoly (with a small number of sellers), and monopoly (a single seller). Mainstream "welfare economics" treats these non-"perfect" forms of markets as departures from what is desirable, and it thereby provides an apparent intellectual justification for widespread government intervention. If market "perfection" is the aim, all real-world markets fall short of that ideal and so every market apparently becomes a suitable case for government action.

In addition to explaining these "perfect" and "imperfect" market forms in the entry for "Competition," here as elsewhere, the *Dictionary* is careful to show the reader that there are different points of view among economists. But it then goes on, as most other dictionaries do not, to discuss competition in the Hayekian sense, as a process of discovery:

> Competition in its fundamental social, dynamic purpose is a device for *discovering* demand and supply (in their everyday sense, i.e. what people want and how to give it to them) rather than merely *responding* to existing wants and techniques. (p. 130, italics in the original)

It is, as the *Dictionary* says, competition in this sense that is "most relevant to political debate on the desirability of a competitive economy" (p. 131). Competition not only provides incentives to discover and supply the wants of consumers and to improve efficiency but also provides a means of

> diffusing power and responsibility throughout the community and of continually widening the area of freedom and opportunity. (p. 131)

Seldon goes briefly through the problems that may arise in competitive markets—the so-called market imperfections and failures—such as monopolization and possible failures to take into account social costs and to provide public goods such as defense and law and order. But he is careful to direct the reader's attention to the fundamental idea that competition is a process of discovery and to explain the circumstances in which the competitive process can fulfill its social purpose:

> It requires a framework of law and institutions on property, contract, business organizations, etc., to direct private effort into channels that ensure public advantage. (p. 132)

"Market Forces" similarly sets out the classical liberal notion of the market. After explaining the mainstream view—that "the power of the state should be exerted to achieve results different from those that would emerge from market forces" (p. 425)—Seldon points to the liberal market idea that, "in general it is better policy to exert power so that it harmonizes with human proclivities (as expressed in market forces), not against them" (p. 426).

The entry for "Price Mechanism" explains how government and other controls have, in some cases, damaged the working of the price mechanism, which is the device for

> limiting to particular uses the use of resources and the consumption of goods with alternative applications . . . a means of guiding, controlling and "rationing" production and consumption. (p. 516)

"Profit" takes the reader through the views of the early classical economists (profit as a reward for risk-taking), and those of J. B. Clark (profit stems from change), to Frank Knight's theory that profit results from uncertainty, before explaining that profit is present in all kinds of economic activity and in any kind of economic system.

"Free Trade" traces the development from classical times of the doctrine that free trade allows best use of the world's resources and maximizes standards of living. Seldon also discusses the qualifications to the free trade case but concludes that they do not represent "a rebuttal of the underlying case for free trade." He explains the growth of protectionism, in public choice terms, as a result of the power of pressure groups that know that any benefits of protection will be concentrated on their members, whereas the diffused costs will be borne by the community at large.

"Individualism" summarizes the development of the idea that human institutions can successfully evolve without "a directing mind or deliberate design" and also presents the opposite view, which justifies "social engineering." Regarding the critique of individualism that markets are too often monopolized rather than competitive, Seldon says that individualists would answer that lack of competition is often the result of state action that tolerates or encourages monopoly.

Perhaps the best way to summarize the *Dictionary of Economics* is to say it has stood the test of time. Nearly thirty years after the second edition, and nearly forty years after the first, the *Dictionary* still provides the reader with a comprehensive view of the scope of economics and the meaning of the main technical terms. Moreover, it imparts a sense of how economic thought has evolved over the centuries and, in its refusal to accept the conventional view about the virtues of government intervention—a view even more marked when Seldon wrote the *Dictionary* than it is now—sets before the reader the challenge to that view from the great classical liberal scholars.

Colin Robinson

INTRODUCTION TO THE SECOND EDITION

The Second Edition is a revised and considerably enlarged version of the First, which was published in 1965. First, the original material, some 225,000 words, has been updated and pruned and then increased by 90,000 or so words of new matter. In conformity with the spirit of the First Edition in explaining and illustrating economic concepts rather than merely describing them, the up-dating has covered developments in economic thinking rather than historical detail. The latest information is inappropriate in a volume with an intended life of perhaps ten years and will in any case probably be out-of-date as soon as it is published, or even before in view of the lag of over a year between completion of writing and publication. Up-to-date statistics are in any event more appropriately sought in annual abstracts or statistical year-books. Where quantities have been thought desirable to indicate broad orders of magnitude, they have been conveyed in round numbers and for recent trends ("in the early 1970's," "by the mid-1970's, etc.") rather than for the latest year or quarter.

Second, many new entries have been added on economic concepts that Everyman might meet in the press or on television. These new terms include some that have come into use in everyday language only recently and are often used imprecisely and misleadingly.

Third, the opportunity has been taken to fill gaps in the First Edition's coverage which had to be left because of limited space. These new entries include many of especial value to students approaching the subject for the first time; and there has been a large expansion in their numbers in schools, polytechnics and universities since 1965. But they will also be of interest to adult newcomers to economics who want to know what economists are saying and why they differ among themselves.

Fourth, there are numerous new entries on concepts evolved in the last ten years in the development of economic thinking and theory. These are of several kinds. There has been continuing reappraisal of the Keynesian approach to economics and increasing doubt whether the Keynesians (i.e. economists who use Keynesian methods of analysis) are accurately reflecting what Keynes said or meant, or what he would be saying in the conditions existing in the 1970's. For these conditions are at the opposite end of the economic spectrum to those of the deflation and unemployment existing in the 1930's when he wrote his major work, *The General Theory of Employment, Interest and Money.* The informed general public and often the student, at least in Britain, is given or gathers the impression that economic thinking is still predominantly Keynesian, and that it has displaced the classical economic thinking. In Britain, Keynesian economists continue to exert a strong influence on economic teaching and policy; in the USA, classical and neoclassical economics contest much of Keynesian theory, and in some respects are displacing it. In Britain it is less generally known that the changing balance between Keynesian and classical economics is being redressed in favour of the latter.

There have also been developments in the economic theory of information, a new emphasis on the theory of property rights, refinement of the theory of costs and of the firm, a new interpretation of unemployment, and an extension of economic theory to areas of human behaviour and action not conventionally considered to be within the competence of economists; here a new section of the Related Subjects Index (No. 13) has been created to accommodate the main concepts in the application of economic theories to charity, crime, marriage, politics, revolution and other new topics.

Fifth, it has been decided to add entries on living economists whose contribution to economic thinking can be presented and appraised briefly. Living economists were intentionally omitted from the First Edition, but if Everyman is to understand the concepts and principles developed and debated by economists, he (or she) should know something of the main thinkers and theorists who have produced them in recent years. Over one hundred new entries have been added on living economists, some of whom are becoming household names through the medium of the press and television. Most of them are British, but there are also some in America and Western Europe, and several in Eastern Europe and the USSR.

Everyman's Dictionary of Economics differs from other works of reference by focusing on fundamentals of economics rather than on what may be fashionable and therefore ephemeral concepts, terms or meanings. These fundamentals change slowly; they are gradually refined and supplemented. But attempts to explain them to newcomers should not fail to indicate that economists differ, even about some fundamentals, although their differences are often over value-judgements about how society should be organised rather than about the material and language of economics.

Everyman's Dictionary of Economics also avoids being loaded with definitions of essentially financial, statistical, or technical terms which are better consulted in specialized works of reference.

Although increasing use is made of mathematics in teaching economics, the main principles are explained here in plain English, and mathematical symbols have been reduced to a bare minimum. They have been introduced in several entries on land and capital for the convenience of students.

It was thought that for a work of reference with a life of some ten years it would be inappropriate to include a list of readings which, like statistics, would become out of date after two or three years. The short list of classical texts has been retained, and students may pursue the subject further in Alchian and Allen, *University Economics,* International Paperback Edition, Prentice Hall, 1974.

September 1974 *A. S.*
F. G. P.

ACKNOWLEDGEMENTS

Thanks are due to Nathaniel Harris, who acted for the publisher and as critical general reader and literary mentor to the authors, not least for his timely admonitions to clarify the meaning for non-economists and for correction of errors; to Mr. Henry Smith, formerly Vice Principal of Ruskin College, Oxford, who, when time was running out fast, helped with notes for 45 entries on living economists; to Michael Solly for assembling biographical material and reading some early drafts; to Kenneth Smith for discovering sources and references with characteristic promptitude; to Jean Penfold for transforming increasingly tired longhand into coherent typescript; and, not least, to Marjorie Seldon for tolerating the unconventional working-hours and the unpredictable reactions during five months of intensive cerebrations and writing.

September 1974 *A. S.*

Professor Frederick George Pennance 1917–1975

Fred Pennance was only in the last two or three years becoming known as an economist with an acute, original, and courageous mind. He was, in my view, perhaps the best analyst of land economics in Britain, and his repute was extending to North America. He brought his insight into general economics, mature judgement, and scrupulous integrity to all he did—from the teaching of university students to his too rare writings and his appearances at conferences. Thousands of former students in industry and government owe him gratitude for their grounding in economic methods of thought.

His professional writings were mostly articles in economic and specialist journals and papers addressed to economists and laymen. *Everyman's Dictionary of Economics*, the longest work in which he collaborated, reflects his influence. He was persuaded to compile the First Edition with me, and when chance required the Second Edition to be prepared during his absence at the University of British Columbia his first task on returning was to scrutinize and amplify the revisions to ensure that the requirements of students were satisfied.

Fred Pennance was conscientious in thought and teaching to a degree that confined his analytical insights mostly to students, colleagues, and friends, but in his last years his professorial appointments in Aberdeen and Vancouver were making them more widely known.

This book embodies his qualities.

October 1975 *A. S.*

Inopportunely, the preparation of the Second Edition of *Everyman's Dictionary of Economics* coincided with a twelve-month absence from the UK which effectively prevented my undertaking more than a nominal share of the work involved. Apart from some entries on specialist topics and general editing, the whole burden of revision, new writing, and compilation was undertaken with characteristic unselfishness by Arthur Seldon, without whose energy and perseverance the publisher's deadlines could never have been met. Without relinquishing any share of errors of omission or commission that may remain, I gratefully acknowledge my very heavy debt to him. My thanks are also due to Professor Michael Goldberg and Mr. Ray Heung, University of British Columbia, for advice and research assistance.

October 1974 *F. G. P.*

INTRODUCTION TO THE FIRST EDITION

The purpose of this book is to explain shortly, and as far as possible in simple everyday language, the main ideas and concepts of the science of economics in current use by economists who teach them or who apply them to industry and public affairs. It is intended for every man who comes new to the subject: the scholar at school, the student at university or the maturer citizen. We have tried to include the ideas and concepts the reader is most likely to meet in books, newspapers or broadcasting. The book is therefore selective, but we have tried to make the omissions few.

To help the user interested in one of the broad subdivisions of the subject, such as banking, structure of industry, international trade, in which there are many entries, and to avoid frequent cross-references, we have tried to construct a framework of entries for each main subdivision. In the body of the book each entry bears the number of the chief subdivision into which it falls, although many entries are related to entries in other subdivisions. And in the Related Subjects Index the entries are listed together under their main subdivision. The subdivisions are themselves, of course, interrelated, and the reader may need to refer to the entries in more than one.

For readers whose interest in the subject is aroused we have compiled a reading list of books for the subject as a whole and for each subdivision, and prepared entries on "Sources, Statistical (economic)" and on "Associated Sciences" that have a bearing on economics.

Economics is a living science. Ever since it was systematized by Adam Smith in 1776, economists have evolved new concepts to replace old ones. The central content—markets which bring together buyers and sellers of goods and services and the prices which emerge from the interplay of supply and demand—remains at the heart of economic theory, but the approach and emphasis of economists and the tools of economic analysis have changed down the years. It may be that some concepts in this book will have fallen out of use in the next five or ten years and that new ones will appear.

To show how economic thought has developed, we have given generous space to concise lives of the main economists who have contributed to and influenced it since Adam Smith. These biographies are necessarily incomplete because we have had to omit some minor though interesting economists, and we have also omitted living economists mainly because their contribution is unfinished or changing and therefore especially difficult to assess. But we have included some economists whose main contribution was to economic policy and public affairs, and some living economists are referred to in other entries.

In the last thirty years economic thought has been profoundly influenced by the writings of the late Lord Keynes who, in a celebrated book in 1936, argued that the classical economic theory of markets, employment, interest and money related to the *special* circumstances in which all resources are fully employed and that his theory was a *general* one applicable to a world of either full employment or underemployment. Lord Keynes died in 1946. Since then his writings have in turn been increasingly reinterpreted as a special case both by some followers and by some economists who had not wholly accepted his writings. The content of economics is in a state of change, and this book is therefore not a final statement of economic doctrine.

Economics is in the last resort a technique of thinking. The reader will therefore need to make an intellectual effort, more substantial for some entries than for others, to get the most interest and value out of the dictionary.

We have drawn on a number of specialist contributors. Their drafts were edited to remove or minimize overlapping or inconsistencies and to achieve some continuity of prose style. It was not possible, nor would it have been desirable, to remove all differences in approach or emphasis, and the attentive reader will detect them. In particular, the contributors differ in the extent to which they reflect the Keynesian and the classical systems of economic thought. In many cases economists are generally agreed about the basic ideas; where there are wide or important differences of interest to the newcomer they have been indicated.

The examples and applications are drawn mainly from the British economy, but there are also illustrations from many other parts of the world. We hope therefore that the dictionary will be found helpful and interesting to readers in Commonwealth countries, the USA and Europe, and wherever English is read and understood.

In attempting to explain economics for the newcomer we have faced a difficult task. Some economists would say it was impossible or even undesirable. To attempt to simplify is to run the risk of over-simplifying. It may be that many entries will be too difficult for some readers and not sufficiently sophisticated for others. We claim only that we have tried to include the essential without over-simplifying to the extent of misleading the reader.

Where entries touch current affairs and public policy they inevitably tend to reflect the views or judgement of the writers. We have tried to avoid doing violence to the basic principles.

One final general caution may be desirable. Economics uses everyday words in a more specific sense than that in which they are used by the non-economist. "Demand," "supply," "cost," "market," "rent," and many other words do not mean the same to economists as they do in everyday usage.

It is over half a century since Palgrave edited the celebrated *Dictionary of Political Economy.* It would be difficult to emulate this work of scholarship, but in view of the increasing importance of economics in public affairs and everyday life it was felt there was need for an up-to-date work of reference with an analytical approach that emphasized the essentials of economic thought and showed its power to illumine public policy, the activities of industry and private action. This present attempt is the result. To help remove its imperfections and make it more valuable for readers, we should be grateful to them for comments, corrections and suggestions to bear in mind in revising it for further editions.

We should like to thank our fellow contributors whose names are listed below for their skill and ready co-operation in meeting our requirement to set down the elements of economics in a few words, and the publishers, in the person of Mr. E. F. Bozman, who conceived the project, for their understanding patience in the face of the ill-health and the pressure of other work that have repeatedly delayed completion.

June 1964 *A. S.*
F. G. P.

D. R. E. ABEL, B.A., Economic Historian; K. J. W. ALEXANDER, B.SC. (ECON.), Professor of Industrial Economics, The Royal College of Science and Technology, Glasgow; J. A. BATES, PH.D., B.A., Lecturer in Economics, University of Bristol; D. BURNINGHAM, B.SC. (ECON.), Business Economist, Industrial and Commercial Finance Corporation; the late PATRICIA BURTON, B.SC. (ECON.), Lecturer in Economics, University of Exeter; P. HANSON, M.A., Lecturer in Economics, University of Exeter; A. I. MACBEAN, M.A. (GLASGOW),

B.PHIL. (OXON.), Research Associate, Centre for International Affairs, Harvard University; A. L. MINKES, M.A. (OXON.), Staff Tutor in Economics, Department of Extra Mural Studies, University of Birmingham; K. J. PENNEY, B.A., Lecturer in Economics, University of Exeter; G. L. REID, M.A., Department of Social and Economic Research, University of Glasgow; A. J. STRUDWICK, B.SC. (ECON.), Professional Accountant; H. TOWNSEND, B.SC. (ECON.), Reader in Economics, University of London; D. WALKER, B.A., Economist, Queen's College, Cambridge.

RELATED SUBJECTS INDEX

A single entry cannot tell the reader all there is to know about its subject-matter, because it is related to other entries. The reader who wants to know the meaning and importance of the Bank rate will start by looking up *Bank Rate.* There he will find references to related ideas, or to institutions through which they work, or perhaps to economists who have developed them. Each entry is therefore part of a family of entries which form its setting. To understand Bank rate the reader needs to know something of the Bank of England, of the joint-stock banks, of interest rates, of banking in general, and even something of the economy as a whole. It is therefore desirable to lead him from the entry he consults to others related to it which help to explain it.

The method commonly used is to add at the end of each entry "*See also*"—and a string of other entries. Such a chain of cross-references seems untidy and tiresome, and it is necessarily incomplete. We have therefore tried to devise an alternative method to indicate the nature and size of the family or grouping of entries to which each entry belongs: a Related Subjects Index which divides the entries into fourteen groups.

The subdivisions are numbered from 1 to 14 and the numbers are added at the end of each entry. Thus the reader interested in Bank rate will find the number 8 at the end of the entry; 8 is the number of the subdivision "Money and Financial Organization"; under this subdivision are grouped the entries related more or less closely to Bank rate and banking.

Two cautions must be added in using the Related Subjects Index. First, each entry is listed only in the subdivision of which it seemed to form *chiefly* a part. But many entries could almost equally have been listed under other groups. For example, Infrastructure is listed under Capital (subdivision 1) but it might have been listed under Economic Growth (subdivision 11); similarly other entries might have been grouped equally into two or three subdivisions.

Secondly, the subdivisions are themselves related, and entries which seem closely connected may be listed under different subdivisions. For example, Trusts appears under Industrial Structure (subdivision 3), but Trust-busting under Economic Policy (subdivision 10); some aspects of public borrowing are listed under Money and Financial Organization (subdivision 8) and others under Public Finance (subdivision 12). The final subdivision 14 contains the entries that relate to the scope and method of economics as well as its sources.

This method of grouping related entries in an effort to help the reader to follow through a subject from one entry to another is therefore arbitrary to some extent since the lines between subdivisions are not always drawn rigidly—it takes the form of a number of marriages of convenience based on technical or institutional groupings between which the entries have much in common analytically. It is hoped however that readers who use the book frequently will soon find their way round it.

There is a list of readings on economics in general and of periodicals on pages xlvi and xlvii. (See note on Reading Lists on page xlvi).

A. S.
F. G. P.

Related Subjects Index

1. Capital

2. Economic Thought, Development of

3. Industrial Structure and Organization

4. International Economic Theory and Organization

(*Note:* international economic theory is in principle no different from economic theory as it applies to economic activity within one country, but it is convenient to list these entries separately to help the reader to find them.)

5. Labour

6. Land and Agriculture

7. Market Analysis and Practice, Including Marketing

8. Money and Financial Organization

9. National Income

10. National Economic Organization and Policy

Abortive Benefits
Affluent Society
Anarchism
Anarcho-capitalism
Anarcho-syndicalism
Anti-trust
Autarky
Beeching
"Beggar-my-neighbour"
Bounty
Bureaucracy
Cabinet Committee on Economic Policy
Capitalism
Ceiling
Central Planning
Central Statistical Office
Cheap Money
Christian Socialism
City (of London)
Closed Economy
Collectivism
Colonialism (Economic)
Command Economy
Common Carrier
Communism
Consumers' Sovereignty
Controlled Economy
Corporate State
Council of Economic Advisers
Coupon
Cunliffe Committee
Dear Money
Debasement (of Coinage)
Demand Management
Department of Economic Affairs
Depressed Areas
Development Areas
Development District
Disinflation
Economic Planning
Economic Policy
Expropriation
Fabian Socialism
"Feather-bed"
Fiscal Policy
Forecasting
Free Economy
Free Enterprise
Full Employment
Gosplan
Growth Point Theory
Growthmanship
Harmony
Incomes Policy
Individualism
Industrial Reorganization Corporation
Intermediate Areas
Intervention, State
Laissez-faire
Liberalism, Economic
Licensing
Market Socialism
Mercantilism
Mixed Economy
Monetary Correction
Monetary Policy
Monopolies Commission
National Board for Prices and Incomes
National Economic Development Council
National Plan

11. Population and Economic Growth

12. Public Finance

Consols
Consumption Tax
Customs and Excise Duties
Debt Conversion
Debt Management
Deficit Financing
Derating
Double Pricing
Double Taxation
Earmarking
Estate Duties
Excess Profits Duty
Excess Profits Levy
Excess Profits Tax
Exchequer
Exchequer Accounts
Exchequer Bills
Exchequer Return
Expenditure Tax
Floating Debt
Gifts Inter Vivos
Incidence of Taxation
Income Tax
Indirect Tax
Inheritance
Initial Allowances
Investment Allowances
Land Tax
Legacy
Legacy Duty
Matching Finance
National Debt
Negative Income Tax
Notional Income
Outlay Tax
Output Budgeting
"Pay-as-you-earn"
Poll Tax
Post-war Credits
Public Finance
Public Works Loan Board
Purchase Tax
Rate Deficiency Payment
Rate Rebates
Rate Support Grant
Rates
Road Fund
Sales Tax
Selective Employment Tax
Stamp Duty
Succession Duty
Sumptuary Tax
Surtax
Tax, Direct and Indirect
Tax, Income and Capital
Tax, Shifting and Incidence
Taxation
Taxonomy
Turnover Tax
Unearned Income
Value-added Tax
Ways and Means Advances
Withholding Tax

13. Charity, Political and Non-Monetary Markets

Aid
Altruism
Charity
Charity Market
Collective Choice
Common Access Facilities
Common Property
Conservation
Cost-benefit Analysis
Cost-effectiveness

14. Scope, Method and Sources

READING LISTS

In addition to the works referred to in the text, suggestions for further reading in a book intended for newcomers, from young people at school to adults who are specialists in other subjects or "general readers," may best be confined to lists of recommended books from which individual readers will select those that suit their capacities, temperaments and interests. Some of the books are simple introductions, others more advanced texts. Readers will find it helpful to taste chapters from several to discover which author or authors they find easiest to follow and most enlightening. They are also advised to read several authors and compare—or contrast—their approaches, methods and conclusions.

A. S.
F. G. P.

Economics in General

Modern Texts

Alchian, A. A. and Allen, W. R. S.: *University Economics,* International Paperback Edition, Prentice Hall 1974.
Benham, F. C.: *Economics.* Pitman 1973.
Cairncross, A. K.: *Introduction to Economics.* Butterworth 1973.
Carter, C. F.: *The Science of Wealth.* Edward Arnold 1973.
Croome, H. M.: *The Approach to Economics.* Christophers, 8th edition, 1964.
Hague, D. C., and Stonier, A. W.: *A Textbook of Economics.* Longmans 1972.
Hicks, Sir J. R.: *The Social Framework.* Oxford University Press 1971.
Lipsey, R. G.: *An Introduction to Positive Economics.* Weidenfeld & Nicolson 1973.
Morgan, E. V.: *First Approach to Economics.* Pitman 1973.

Pigou, A. C.: *Income: An Introduction to Economics.* Macmillan 1955.

Robbins, L. C.: *An Essay on the Nature and Significance of Economic Science.* Macmillan 1935.

Roche, J. W., and James, G. R.: *Getting and Spending.* Longman and Institute of Economic Affairs 1971.

Samuelson, P. A.: *Economics: An Introductory Analysis.* McGraw Hill 1973.

Scitovsky, T.: *Welfare and Competition.* Unwin University (Paperbook) Books 1971.

Williams, Lady Gertrude: *Everyday Economics.* Pelican Books 1970.

Classic Texts

Malthus, Thomas: *Essay on the Principle of Population.* Dent, 2 vols., 1973.

Marshall, Alfred: *Principles of Economics.* Macmillan 1961.

Ricardo, David: *Principles of Political Economy and Taxation.* Dent 1965.

Smith, Adam: *The Wealth of Nations.* Dent, 2 vols. 1964.

Periodicals

Banker (monthly), Banker Ltd., London.

District Bank Review (quarterly), District Bank Lts., Manchester.

Economic Journal (quarterly), the journal of the Royal Economic Society. Macmillan & Co. Ltd., London.

Economic Trends (monthly), HMSO, London.

Economica (quarterly), London School of Economics and Political Science, London.

Economics (quarterly), The journal of the Economics Association, London.

Economist (weekly), Economist Newspaper Ltd, London.

Journal of Industrial Economics (three times a year), Basil Blackwell & Mott Ltd, Oxford.

Journal of Law and Economics (twice a year), University of Chicago Law School.

Lloyds Bank Review (quarterly), Lloyds Bank Ltd, London.

Manchester School of Economic and Social Studies (three times a year), The Manchester School, University of Manchester.

Midland Bank Review (quarterly), Midland Bank Ltd, London.

Moorgate and Wall Street (quarterly), Hill Samuel & Co. Ltd, London.

National Institute Economic Review (quarterly), National Institute of Economic and Social Research, London.

National Westminster Bank Review (quarterly), National Westminster Bank Ltd, London.

The Public Interest (quarterly), National Affairs Inc., New York.

Scottish Journal of Political Economy (three times a year), Oliver & Boyd Ltd, Edinburgh.

Three Banks Review (quarterly), National and Commercial Banking Group, London.

Times Review of Industry (monthly), Times Publishing Co. Ltd, London.

Everyman's Dictionary of Economics

A

A fortiori, "with all the more force," Latin term used occasionally by economists. For example, suppose it is argued that a 4 per cent general increase in national income will tend to raise incomes generally and so probably lessen resistance to the legal discouragement of restrictive trade practices; then *a fortiori* a 5 per cent annual increase will make it still easier to outlaw restrictive practices. [14]

A priori, Latin term used to describe a proposition the truth of which is known in other ways than from experience. The validity of *a priori* propositions is either accepted by intuition (as when a statement is said to be "true by definition") or the result of logical reasoning from such statements. The Quantity Equation in the theory of the value of money is an example of an *a priori* proposition. [14]

"A" Shares. *See* SECURITIES.

Ability to Pay, (*a*) the principle that taxes should be related to the income or wealth of the taxpayers. The implication is that the richer should be required to pay higher taxes than the poorer. This would cover not only progressive but also proportional and even some regressive income tax systems. (*b*) in American unionism, the ability of firms to give pay increases in accordance with their profitability. (*c*) the principle of charging what the traffic will bear, e.g. an exporter setting relatively higher prices in markets where he has little competition. These ideas imply an element of "fairness" or "justice" whose meaning in economics is ambiguous. [12]

Abortive Benefits, term applied to social benefits that do not achieve their intended purpose of redistributing income from better-off to worse-off. It began to be used in Britain during the 1960's with the increasingly searching questioning by some economists of the assumptions and effectiveness of the welfare state. This was done through statistical analysis of the sources of finance (taxes and social insurance contributions) and the destinations of benefits (in cash—pensions, family allowances, education grants, etc., or in kind—mainly education and medical care). The growth in the size of social benefits and relative equalization in income have spread the cost of social benefits down the income scale, so that increasingly people with middling and lower incomes have been paying in taxes (indirect if not direct) more or less as much as they receive in benefits. For more people the difference between the two has been decreasing, so that the system of taxes and benefits has become increasingly "abortive." Some economists have even argued that it transfers income from relatively poor to relatively rich. [10]

Above-the-Line, that part of the government's budget embodying revenue (mainly from taxation) and expenditure. Until recently the annual Financial Statement presented by the Chancellor of the Exchequer as part of the budget contained information about two accounts: (1) revenue from taxes and other current income, and current expenditure (i.e. broadly, the revenue account or current account of the government); (2) receipts and payments on capital account. The distinction was not drawn sharply: some capital payments were met out of revenue, and some non-capital payments out of borrowed funds. Therefore a distinction grew between (1) budget revenue (principally from taxation) and expenditure to be met from taxation—the "above-the-line" statement, and (2) receipts related to the redemption of debt (i.e. interest and repayment of loans) and expenditure to be financed by borrowing (i.e. all Government expenditure not covered by taxation)—the "below-the-line" statement.

The distinction frequently appeared arbitrary and could not be compared exactly with the distinction in business between the income (or revenue) account and the capital account. Many capital items were charged to revenue: those expected to recur annually in roughly similar amounts (e.g. the cost of government offices) were placed above-the-line. And items normally charged against revenue or income account (e.g. part of the accumulated deficit of the British Transport Commission) were placed below-the-line since they were regarded as permanent and met by borrowing.

The distinction between "above-the-line" and "below-the-line" was originally legal, designed to facilitate parliamentary control. After World War II it became functional as part of the general policy of using the budget for controlling the economy. It passed out of use in the early 1960's. [12]

Absentee, (*a*) normally a landlord who lives away from his estate. In this sense it is usually implied that the estate is neglected. The most familiar instances in British history are the Irish landlords living in England, particularly in the eighteenth and nineteenth centuries. (*b*) more recently, an employee not at work for any reason other than ill health. [5]

Absolute Advantage, specifically the superiority in efficiency (and therefore cost) of one country over another in producing a commodity or service, in contrast to the *comparative* advantages that economists have used to explain the bulk of exchange (trade) between individuals and regions, as well as between countries. The gains to both parties of exchange of commodities or services in which each has an *absolute* advantage over the other are self-evident: Lancashire exchanges (sells) cotton goods for Kentish fruit because the moist atmosphere of Lancashire and the soil of Kent give each county an *absolute* advantage over the other. Comparative cost advantage widens the scope of trade because it yields gains even where one party has an absolute advantage in the costs of all commodities and services. For such a party there are no absolute gains from trade, but there is a comparative advantage in undertaking some activities rather than others; the gain comes from its ability to concentrate (specialize) on activities in which it has a comparative advantage. Thus, in individual exchange, a shopkeeper may wrap parcels better than his shop assistant (absolute advantage), but it benefits both for the shop assistant to wrap parcels so that the shopkeeper can concentrate on shopkeeping in which his advantage in skill is even more (comparative advantage). Similarly a town, county, region or country may gain from importing a commodity or service it can produce more cheaply than another town, county, region or country (absolute advantage) because it can pay for it by producing a commodity or service in which it is even more efficient (comparative advantage). [4]

Abstinence, a term describing the way in which capital can be accumulated. It was first used in this sense by Nassau Senior.

Capital accumulation consists of the production of capital goods (buildings, machinery, raw materials, etc.) which are used with other factors of production to produce consumer goods. The production of capital goods requires the use of factors that could have been employed to produce consumer goods. Current consumption is therefore reduced in order to increase the output of consumer goods in the future. The capital goods could not have been produced if the community had used all its income to satisfy its current wants. Capital accumulation therefore requires the sacrifice of some current consumption in favour of future consumption.

Senior defined abstinence as "the conduct of a person who either abstains from the unproductive use of what he can command, or designedly prefers the production of remote to that of immediate results." There are two elements in this definition. First, capital accumulation consists of the conversion of current income into future income; but if the loss of current income is permanent, the "abstinence" is said to be the psychic (i.e. imagined) cost or disutility of saving. Secondly, capital goods have varying rates of turnover; their products take different lengths of time to produce or mature. In this context there is "waiting," that is, foregoing present consumption in the expectation of enjoying increased consumption in the future. It is this "abstinence" that is used in economics to indicate the "waiting" required for the accumulation of capital. It is not "abstinence" in its everyday sense of disutility or moral abstemiousness. [1]

Abundance, a situation in which human needs for goods and services can be met fully: the opposite of scarcity. It would require unlimited supplies of almost all conceivable commodities. The existence of a price is evidence of scarcity: goods available in abundance (like air) can command no price. Abundance is impossible as long as people's wants are not limited. Since it is hard to conceive of productive resources capable of meeting unlimited needs, and since the demand for leisure would also have to be fully met, it is not clear how production would take place at all. There may often be an abundance of particular goods or services, but the underlying condition of scarcity seems likely to be present always in the human environment. Utopias, such as those of Sir Thomas More and Karl Marx, imply abundance in the full sense of the word, i.e. the complete disappearance of scarcity. [7]

Acceleration Principle, an economic "law" which states that changes in the demand for finished goods produce larger changes in the demand for the capital equipment used to make them. The reason is that the demand for capital is determined by (*a*) the replacement of the parts (if any) used up in production and (*b*) extensions to increase output (if demanded). Suppose a television factory uses capital valued at £50,000 to produce (in a year) receivers valued at £10,000, and that 10 per cent of the capital, or £5,000, is worn out in the process. If demand remains unchanged, £5,000 worth of capital has to be replaced each year. If the demand for receivers grows by 10 per cent to £11,000, the demand for capital is (*a*) £5,000 for replacement, plus (*b*) £5,000 new capital to produce the £1,000 of additional output, total £10,000. Thus an increase of 10 per cent in the demand for the finished consumer goods "accelerates" to 100 per cent the demand for the capital to produce it.

The relation between the changes in the two demands is based on the durability of the capital equipment. The larger the proportion that needs to be replaced, the larger the acceleration, and *vice versa*. The key to the principle is that, since capital is durable, the change in the demand is concentrated on the small proportion renewed each period. This "durability" is economic, not merely technical. Although only 10 per cent of equipment may wear out each year, it may be necessary to replace 20 or 30 per cent if an invention has made some of it obsolete.

The acceleration principle helps to explain why the demand for capital fluctuates more widely than the demand for final commodities. It operates markedly only in certain conditions: first, when durable equipment is important relatively to materials and labour; secondly, when stocks of finished goods cannot be varied easily (otherwise the increased demand can be met out of the cushion of stocks); thirdly, when there is little or no unused capital equipment; fourthly, when the existing equipment cannot be used more intensively, e.g. by using labour in shifts to work round the clock; fifthly, when the increase in demand is expected to continue, otherwise producers will not expand their productive capacity; sixthly, when there is a general increase in demand (due to an increase in the amount of money in circulation, or to an increase in its velocity of circulation) and not merely a switch of demand from some products to others (in which case the degree of acceleration would depend largely on the importance of durable equipment in the production of the goods for which demand had changed). [9]

Accelerator, the process described in "Acceleration Principle."

Accepting House, a finance house (generally a private company, sometimes a partnership) most of whose business is to finance home or overseas trade by accepting bills of exchange.

An accepting house provides buyers or sellers with the assurance that finance will be available by giving them a "letter of credit." This signifies that when the business is completed, the trader may draw bills of exchange which the accepting house "accepts" by signing and so undertakes to pay the money on a given date. The trader can then take the bills to the discount market where a discount house will buy them at the best ruling market rates. The trader is thus paid immediately.

A credit "line" may also be arranged to cover a series of shipments or a seasonal movement of goods. If the sums required are large, several accepting houses form a syndicate to supply them jointly.

Some accepting houses also conduct banking business, deal in foreign exchange, handle investments for their customers (e.g. pension funds, college endowments), etc. Some act as issuing houses, engage in the bullion market, handle insurance, and/or own merchant companies developing export trades, provide (with the joint-stock banks and the Export Credits Guarantee Department) medium-term finance for exports of capital goods, finance orders placed by overseas owners with British shipbuilders and develop interests in the Commonwealth.

Seventeen accepting houses in the City of London constitute the Accepting Houses Committee, which transmits to its members messages from the Treasury, the Chancellor of the Exchequer, or the Governor of the Bank of England. Members must be financially strong, as testified by the willingness of the discount market to buy its acceptances at the lowest rates and of the Bank of England to take its acceptances from the market. [8]

Accepting Houses Committee. *See* ACCEPTING HOUSE.

Accessibility, nearness. The term is widely used in explanations of the patterns of land use, rents and prices observed in urban areas. R. M. Hurd (*Principles of City Land Values,* 1911) developed the notion that the values of properties depended on their "nearness" (convenience of location), although Alfred Marshall had suggested a similar explanation at a much earlier date. R. Turvey (*Economics of Real Property,* 1957) argued that individual urban commercial property values were dependent on the property's *general accessibility* (nearness—in terms of travel cost rather than physical distance—to all other buildings of the town) and on its *special accessibility* (nearness to other land uses which are complementary to it, e.g. other shops in a shopping district). [6]

Account Day. *See* SETTLING-DAY.

Accounting, the method of recording the money value of business transactions—sales, purchases, receipts, payments, etc.—in order to show their effect upon the financial position of the firm or person conducting them. Accounts are prepared to perform three main functions:

(1) To reveal the financial position.
(2) To enable the income tax computations to be prepared.
(3) To provide management with information it requires to control its affairs efficiently.

Double entry is the system of book-keeping and accounting commonly used: it recognizes that each business transaction has a twofold aspect, receiving and paying. Each amount—payment or receipt—is placed to the debit of one account and the credit of another. The advantages of double entry are (*a*) a complete record of each transaction, (*b*) full information concerning the business, (*c*) an arithmetical check.

In practice, all except the very smallest businesses keep some kind of records. These vary from the very incomplete book-keeping of small retail shops and the like to the complex accounting systems of the large industrial groups based on computers and other electronic equipment. In recent years there has been much development in cost accounting and management accounting.

Limited liability companies have been required by a long succession of Companies Acts to keep books of accounts and prepare Profit and Loss Accounts and Balance Sheets, which have to be audited. Most other businesses prepare accounts because, apart from any other purpose, they are required by the Inland Revenue as the basis of the income tax assessments. Economists differ on the amount of information that the law should require companies to show. Some argue that disclosure should be limited to information that would not weaken the trading position of the firm. Others argue that fuller disclosure is required in a competitive economy if the relative capacity of individual firms to use capital profitably is to be judged by investors so that it is directed to its most efficient employment; they would have company accounts published more frequently than annually and in more detail (value of sales, subsidiary companies' contribution to profits, purchases and sales of fixed assets, market value of investments quoted on the Stock Exchange, directors' holdings of shares and interest in contracts placed with other companies, and others).

Firms of professional accountants are usually engaged to prepare the final accounts of firms too small to employ full-time accountants. They also usually negotiate the tax assessments with the Inland Revenue. For larger firms with full-time accountants the independent accountant's work is usually confined to the audit.

Accounting plays an increasingly important part not only in commerce and industry but also in local and national government, including the nationalized industries. Detailed accounts are published by government departments dealing with various aspects of the financial and economic position of the public sector of the economy. Social accounting, the recording of transactions determining the economic position of the nation as a whole, has developed extensively since World War II. [8]

Accounting, Management. *See* MANAGEMENT ACCOUNTING.

Acquisition Costs, (*a*) the difference between the purchase price of a commodity and the immediate selling price. The acquisition cost of a car that costs £1,000 to buy and would sell for £900 is £100. This is a form of fixed or sunk cost. It is the cost of acquiring the object: once acquired the cost is "fixed" on the owner; it is irrevocable and therefore "sunk." [7]

(*b*) the time, effort, etc. spent in buying goods or services. It may be worth paying more for purchases if acquisition costs are lower, e.g. a meal in a restaurant that is served promptly, a cinema show that can be seen without queuing, medical care that does not require waiting, etc. The reasons are that the satisfaction is lessened if acquisition costs are high, e.g. a meal served after an hour's delay may be less satisfying than if served when it is wanted; or the character of the demand may have changed, e.g. a chronic non-urgent condition like varicose veins or a cataract may become acute and serious; or the opportunity costs are less, e.g. time saved in travelling from London to Glasgow by air rather than train may be worth more in other activities so that the *total* "price-time" price is lower by air. Where acquisition costs are significant a below-market clearing price will produce a queue so that the supply is rationed by time as well as price. [7]

Active Balance of Trade. *See* BALANCE OF TRADE.

Active Money. *See* DISHOARDING.

Activity Rate, the proportion of the population of working age that is employed or seeking employment. It is obtained (for the country as a whole, or for a region or district) by dividing estimates of the number of employees, and would-be employees (unemployed), by the estimate of the total population of working age (aged sixteen and over). The resulting activity rates vary between males and females, between regions, and with the degree of urbanization. [5]

Acton, Lord. *See* INDIVIDUALISM.

"Actuals." *See* COMMODITY MARKET.

Ad Hoc, "for this specific purpose"; Latin term commonly used by economists when discussing a concept or device created for a defined and perhaps unique purpose. [14]

Ad Valorem, "according to value." Thus an *ad valorem* tax is one levied on a percentage of value. It is contrasted with a *specific* tax which is levied at a given sum per unit of a commodity. The economic interest in the difference is that an *ad valorem* tax remains the same proportion if the price of the commodity changes, and a specific tax rises as a proportion of price if the price falls and falls if the price rises. Thus if the prices of imports generally rise, specific taxes are less "protective" than *ad valorem* taxes. [12]

Adjustment Costs, (*a*) the costs to an individual, household, firm or government of adapting itself to changes in the underlying conditions of demand or supply tending to a new equilibrium. Examples are the costs of writing off obsolescent plant or skills, of acquiring information about new market conditions, of shifting mental attitudes, moving physical equipment to new situations or sites, adapting machinery, retraining labour, negotiating new contracts, etc. Conventional textbook theory was apt to ignore adjustment costs or tacitly assume that they were too small to be significant in analysing the new equilibrium or the transition to it. The comparatively recent attention paid to information and other adjustment costs, especially by American economists, has been a major development in economic theory. [7]

(*b*) the time, effort, etc. spent in altering prices to equate changing supply with changing demand. If the goods are perishable and cannot be held in stock, prices may be adjusted from hour to hour, as in a soft fruit market. If the market price is low, price adjustment may be impracticable. If the goods are not physically perishable but are seasonal, and costs or risks of carrying stock are high, as with crackers on Christmas Eve or fireworks on Guy Fawkes Day, the price will be adjusted rapidly to clear stocks. Prices of some goods are not adjusted with every passing change in supply or in demand if it is desirable to hold stocks from which buyers may choose, e.g. homes which buyers could not change, or fashion clothes they could not buy, unless stocks were held in reserve. Such stocks are not necessarily wasted on under-used resources: in a world of certainty in which future requirements could be predicted, they would be superfluous; but given unpredictability, they are a cheaper and more convenient way of obtaining information about new purchases than inspecting the purchases made by others and in use by them (and therefore not such good sources of information). They also provide the home or the clothes with less expenditure of time. There may therefore be good reasons for adjusting prices instantaneously in some goods and not in others. [7]

Administered Pricing, milieu in which market forces of supply and demand are replaced by governmental or industrial management in setting prices. It is therefore possible where competition is excluded by economics of scale which create dominance by one or a few producers, or by government action to confine production to a government department, corporation or other "public" body. Prices are thus (apparently) "administered" from above rather than decided from below. Some economists have tended to regard administered pricing as a long-term accompaniment of large-scale industrialization, and others see it as shorter-lived because dependent on government acquiescence in or encouragement of large producing units for political or "social" rather than efficiency reasons. "Public utilities" have come to be regarded as desirable or unavoidable in Britain and Europe but not in the USA. Administrative pricing is encouraged by national wage-bargaining with government or government-owned or regulated industries. It tends to be shorter-lived in private industry where concentration of power in a large firm, or agreement between a small number of firms, tend to be dissolved as a result of technical innovation. [3]

Advance, in everyday language, a prior payment or loan; in economics a loan or overdraft by a joint-stock bank to a customer. Advances of the British joint-stock banks form about half of total deposits and are the least liquid and most profitable of bank assets, although in a sense loans at call and other highly liquid loans are also a form of advance.

Advances may be of two main types:

(1) For an *overdraft* the customer is permitted to "overdraw" his current account by cheque up to a stated limit, at times and in amounts to suit his convenience. Collateral security may be required, but overdrafts are frequently granted on the banker's estimate of the credit-worthiness of the borrower. The advantage of the overdraft is that interest is paid only on the amount by which the customer is overdrawn in the period for which the interest is calculated, e.g. if a person has overdraft facilities for £1,000 but is overdrawn only by £100 he pays interest on £100.

(2) For a *loan* the borrower usually places security with the banker and in return an account is opened to his credit, a loan account is debited with the equivalent sum, and the interest charged on the whole sum.

In recent years there have been two innovations: (*a*) the Personal Loan, granted to an individual for a specific purchase or group of purchases; repayment is by agreed regular instalments. (*b*) Term loans, common in the United States, but still relatively uncommon in Britain.

Except for the term loan, it has long been a feature of British banking (unlike German, Italian and some other continental banking) that advances are normally for short periods (up to six or twelve months), after which they are reconsidered. British banks thus supply mainly "circulating" or "working" as distinct from fixed capital. In practice renewal of advances is often automatic and much bank lending that is nominally short term may continue for long periods. [8]

Adverse Balance of Trade, another name for passive balance of trade.

Advertising, the methods employed by buyers or sellers to draw attention to their products or services (or the record or reputation of a firm). It implies that there is freedom of choice between alternatives, and that potential buyers need to be made aware of them. It grew with the emergence of industrialization, which created free markets in which competing sellers vied for the attention of consumers and which led to localization of industry producing goods for widespread, distant markets. In the middle of the nineteenth century there was a big increase in advertising by retailers; later, as newspapers were more widely read, individual manufacturers bypassed their distributors (wholesalers, retailers) and used advertising to impress consumers directly with the merits of their products, for which they established brand names to facilitate recognition and identification.

Advertising expenditure in Britain was about 2 per cent of net national income in 1938; it fell to 1.3 per cent in 1948 (owing to shortage of commodities, which made advertising less necessary) and returned to 2 per cent in the 1960's and 1970's. This compared with about 3 per cent in the USA. Broadly the percentage seemed to vary with living standards in different countries.

Over half of the total is spent by manufacturers advertising direct to the public, and smaller percentages by retailers, by people offering services and individuals offering goods to the public; in all, about three-quarters of the total is consumer advertising. The remainder is "trade" advertising to industry, the professions, etc., and advertising by firms for employees, which they have used increasingly rather than recruit through government employment exchanges.

Since the advent of large-scale industry, economists have been interested in advertising for its effects on costs and prices. They have divided advertising broadly into "informative" (or "constructive") and "persuasive" (or "combative") advertising. The former, they argued, gives consumers information about commodities and services, helps them to choose better between the alternatives offered, keeps suppliers and sellers on their toes and so makes markets *more* "perfect." The latter "differentiates" products, varieties or single brands from one another by emphasizing (or exaggerating) differences between them, creates consumer loyalty for each product, variety or brand, establishes an "institutional" or "reputation" monopoly for it which enables its producer or seller to raise its price beyond the competitive level, and thus makes markets *less* "perfect."

This distinction has recently been questioned. Some economists argue that the purpose of *all* advertising is persuasive, but that the method is to use information to a larger or lesser extent according to the consumers aimed at, the kind of buying appeal employed and so on. Information, which must necessarily be limited to the main facts it is to convey in a newspaper or on a television screen, may be less useful to the consumer than a personal trial of a product or service, which he may be induced to make by having his attention drawn to it by "persuasive" advertising. The more "persuasive" an advertisement, the more "informative" it may be ultimately, because it replaces description by personal experience. Consumers may prefer to act on the advice of a retailer or the reputation of a manufacturer; if the retailer's advice or the manufacturer's advertising is misleading, there are laws to give the victim redress, information services to advise him and competition to enable him to avoid making a mistake twice. These laws could be strengthened, the information services extended and competition made more effective.

Advertising can be used to create monopoly for an individual supplier if applied to products whose intrinsic worth is difficult to judge, particularly in the short run. In the long run few products can maintain an appreciable hold on the consumer by deceptive advertising because new competitors will invade the market, unless prevented or discouraged by law, as in some forms of transport, or fuel. The larger the deception the larger the inducement to a new producer to enter the market or to a competitor to develop demand for a new product. They can use advertising to do so. While advertising can create partial or sectional monopolies in the short run, it can help to break them down in the long run.

The economic claims made for advertising are not universally accepted by economists. The main one, that it is essential for the development of large-scale production and so reduces costs and prices, is difficult to support by evidence. Technical invention, improving transport and increasing education would have produced mass production in any event, although advertising may have accelerated the *rate* of development. Much advertising is wasteful because it misses the market, is unnecessarily extravagant or cancels out other advertising. Even if an effect on sales can be traced, the *cost* of advertising may be higher than that of some alternative marketing method (commercial travellers, wholesalers, price reductions, etc.).

Advertising is claimed to increase production by stimulating demand, evening out fluctuations in it, guiding it into fewer channels, by displacing more costly methods of marketing and by sharpening competition. The power of advertising to increase demand is probably over-estimated; advertising cannot normally increase demand unless the basic social and environmental conditions (income, social habits, fashion, etc.) are favourable, although it can accelerate an expansion arising from favourable conditions and retard a decline arising from unfavourable conditions. Although advertising can (at a cost) reduce fluctuations in demand (e.g. stimulate demand for ice-cream in the winter), it can equally amplify the fluctuations by being intensified when conditions are favourable and being discontinued when they are unfavourable because the cost of "sailing against the wind" might be too high. Similarly, while advertising can be used to concentrate demand on a narrower range of varieties (as in chocolates, toothpaste, beer) it can also be used to multiply variety. Advertising sharpens competition in the long run by helping to introduce new products, but in the short run it can be used to keep them out. It could stimulate excessive innovation and so divert factors of production from other uses which consumers might prefer. That people buy advertised goods in preference to unadvertised goods means that they have chosen the goods they know, not necessarily that they prefer them to the unknown. In the long run, however, a competitive market would throw up fresh choices, and advertising could not for long substantially distort demand for products in general.

The claim that advertising is a guarantee is generally true of *quality,* since a brand name is taken to indicate known ingredients, but not necessarily of *value,* unless it is supposed that if the consumer goes on buying A although it seems to be inferior, or dearer, than product B, he is nevertheless getting better "value."

Advertising is an incentive to increase effort and output to the extent that it encourages people to work for the products or services advertised. Even in the western countries, there is a long way to go before man enjoys all the material objects that would make life easier or more pleasurable, or reduce labour or pain.

Many of the economic issues in advertising must remain unresolved because it is difficult to judge its effects. By its nature the information is difficult to assemble because many factors are affecting sales at the same time. The judgment must in many respects remain tentative. [7]

Affluent Society, an economy with high output and living standards. Adam Smith used "opulent" in much the same sense. The term was popularized in the 1960's by Professor J. K. Galbraith in a book with that name, but less in an analytical than in a pejorative sense to emphasize the contrast between "private affluence and public squalor" in capitalism, at least in the USA. He argued that the production of consumer goods had reached such a large volume that resources should be shifted from the private to the public (government) sector of the economy to expand the quantity and improve the quality of public (government) services—schools, roads, amenities, etc. The term and the theme caught the fancy of the communications media but the argument did not have much influence on economic thinking. Many American and other economists did not accept the view that consumer wants had virtually been satisfied, or the implication that a transfer of resources from the market to government would necessarily be preferable to their use in accordance with consumer preferences. An echo of the argument came some years later with the increasing attention by some British economists, notably E. J. Mishan in *The Costs of Economic Growth* (1967), to the effects of market decision on the environment. This kind of critique, and its implications for the scope of government activity, have been contested by other economists, notably Gordon Tullock in *Private Wants, Public Means* (1970). [10]

Agency for International Development (AID), section of the US State Department which administers non-military aid under the US foreign assistance programme. It was created in 1961 following growing criticisms of the administrative cost and waste, especially in "defence support," of aid programmes. New emphasis was put on development aid and "self-help," with aid provided mainly in commodities, technical services by US experts, and training in the USA and other countries. AID encourages and promotes US business investment and helps develop private enterprise in the countries aided. [14]

Agglomeration, the tendency for men and enterprises to concentrate in urban areas. The resulting economies of production and consumption are thought to be important reasons underlying the faster growth rates of larger cities. The American economist E. M. Hoover has classified agglomeration factors as (1) economies of large-scale production, which accrue to individual firms as they grow in size; (2) economies of localization, which accrue to all the firms in an industry in a location as it expands its output; (3) economies of urbanization, which accrue to all firms in all industries consequent upon the growth of population, income and wealth in an area. Although the first class of economies depends on size rather than on location, the ability of firms to continue to grow also depends heavily on the availability of inputs (of labour, specialized services, transport facilities and capital). Economies of localization thus interact with the individual economies of large-scale production that firms can achieve for themselves. As new units of production come into existence they tend to gain economies of localization by "agglomerating" round established production points and tapping the advantages of existing supply sources, auxiliary lines of production, and markets for labour and goods. Economies of urbanization are not easily distinguished from these economies of localization. They might be described as economies of localization on a large scale. But additionally they embrace economies in the production of social capital and services such as roads, public utilities, fire and police protection, communication services and the like. In turn the growth of urban facilities increases the attractiveness of an area as a consumption centre for managers, skilled personnel and capitalists, so that only when pronounced diseconomies (of congestion, relatively high costs) emerge are the forces of agglomeration likely to be weakened. Although such a "balance of forces" would seem to indicate an optimum size of city, the quest for a general underlying theory has not so far been successful and the economic discussion of agglomeration tends to remain largely descriptive. [6]

Aggregate, the sum or total of individual items (such as income, expenditure, output, sales, spring mattresses, fertilizers). Aggregates yield averages when the total figure is divided by the number of items, e.g. income or expenditure per head of population. Aggregate and average statistics have always been employed in economics, more particularly in econometrics. [14]

Aggregated Rebates arise in the practice of totalling rebates for purchases of a specified regularity or amount in order to "tie" customers, that is, ensure their custom. The practice was investigated by the Monopolies Commission in its *Report on Collective Discrimination,* 1955, and condemned in principle (by a majority) as contrary to the public interest by suppressing competition. [7]

Aggregation, the collecting of items or variables into a smaller number of classes to simplify presentation, understanding, explanation and analysis. Index numbers such as the retail price index provide an example. All economic models employ aggregation in varying degrees; e.g. a model of the housing market might classify all dwellings as either rented or owner-occupied. At the other extreme, National Income and Expenditure models employ a very high degree of aggregation, compressing total national spending into a very few categories such as consumption, investment, government and foreign spending for the purpose of expressing and testing relationships between these "variables." Highly aggregated economic models of this kind are loosely classified as *macro-economic;* those employing a low degree of aggregation (a high degree of disaggregation) are classified as *micro-economic,* although the classification of all economic models into one or other group is itself a form of aggregation. [14]

Agricultural Mortgage Corporation, set up under the Agricultural Credits Acts 1928 and 1932 to provide long-term finance to agriculture in England and Wales. The original capital was provided by the Bank of England and the joint-stock banks (which also act as agents for loan applications). The Agricultural Mortgage Corporation has power to borrow against Government-guaranteed debentures up to a stated limit. Loans made are of two types: (*a*) on first mortgages of agricultural land, (*b*) for major farm improvements on the security of a rent charge created against the improvement. Repayment terms are half-yearly instalments over sixty years for mortgage loans, over forty years for improvement loans. The rate of interest is fixed for the whole term and reflects the rate at which the Agricultural Mortgage Corporation borrows. Unlike private mortgage loans, they cannot be called in or disturbed. Valuation for mortgage loan is conservative (two-thirds of long-term agricultural value); the Agricultural Mortgage Corporation reserves the right to assess the adequacy of other farm capital, including the ability of the farm tenant. [6]

Agricultural Support Policy, the methods and aims pursued by national or regional governments in maintaining the income of the agricultural community above that it would receive if it was exposed to free markets, including free imports. Agricultural incomes may be supported by subsidies, or less directly by price guarantees or restrictions on imported food and agricultural raw materials. The normal consequence of support is to maintain agricultural population and output at a higher level than they would otherwise have reached. Such policies are operated in Britain, some other EEC countries, the USA and elsewhere.

In the UK the main agricultural products were imported without tariffs or other restrictions from the Commonwealth, and since their prices were lower than those that would have to be charged by British producers to cover their costs, there was a subsidy to the UK farmer to close the gap between the (lower) world or free market price and the (higher) guaranteed support price. (Together with other subsidies to agriculture, they have cost the British Exchequer a sum roughly the same as the total addition to the national income from the agricultural industry.) The result was that the price of home grown food to the consumer was lower than it would be in a free market but taxes were higher. In the Common Market countries farmers are subsidized (more in Germany than in France) by duties on imports which go to them directly or indirectly (for improvement in equipment and methods or subsidies on exports of surplus production). Since Britain joined the Common Market her method of agricultural support has changed from subsidies to import duties and this has tended to raise prices.

The primary reason for agricultural support in many countries is thought to be political—although it often seems that political parties in western countries over-estimate the strength of farmers' votes—and military: to disperse the population and ensure a supply of food in time of war. In Britain it is also argued that agricultural support saves imports and thus helps the balance of payments. In India, where about 70 per cent of the population are in agriculture (but produce only 50 per cent of the national income), price support means that 30 per cent of the population help to support the rest and it produces over-expenditure by the government by stimulating budget deficits and inflation. In the USA the cost of agricultural price support is borne by the large bulk of the industrial population and is therefore not politically obvious, but it has provoked problems of disposing of the growing stock-piles of agricultural produce and curbing production by farmers. For economists the question is whether the real or supposed advantages of agricultural support policy are brought at too high a price. [6]

Aid is analysed in the economics of giving by persons to others (charity, philanthropy), by governments to persons or institutions (welfare state), or by government to government (overseas aid to developing countries in general and to other countries in emergencies). It is also studied in the political and charity markets. [13]

Alchian, Armen Albert (1914–), American academic economist, born in Fresno, California. He has been Professor of Economics at the University of California, Los Angeles, since 1946. He mostly specializes in general economic theory and economic systems, and monetary theory and institutions. Apart from contributions to learned journals he has written (with William R. Allen) *University Economics* (1964, third edition 1972), an unusually perceptive and readable introductory textbook for students and laymen. A cheap edition was published in Britain in 1974. [2]

Allen, George Cyril (1900–1982), Emeritus Professor of Political Economy at the University of London. Educated at the University of Birmingham, Allen was Lecturer in Economics at the Higher Commercial College, Nagoya, Japan (1922–5), and has studied the Japanese economy ever since. He served at the Board of Trade during the Second World War, and was a member of the Central Price Regulation Committee (1944–53).

Allen made an extensive study of the development of British industry, especially of monopolies and restrictive practices (he was a member of the Monopolies Commission, 1950–62). He is the author of *British Industries and their Organization* (1933, revised edition 1970), *The Structure of Industry in Britain* (1961, revised edition 1970), and *Monopoly and Restrictive Practices* (1968). He has written several authoritative studies of the Japanese and Far Eastern economy. [2]

Allen, Sir Roy George Douglas (1906–83), British economist and statistician, a pioneer in the application of mathematical techniques to economic analysis. He was educated at Sydney Sussex College, Cambridge, and became reader in Economic Statistics at the London School of Economics (1939–44) and since 1944 has been Professor of Statistics at the University of London. An early contribution was an article, with Sir John Hicks, in *Economica* (1934) which demonstrated the use of indifference curves based on ordinal utility as an analytical tool in the theory of consumer behaviour. Other publications include: *Mathematical Analysis for Economists* (1938), *Statistics for Economists* (1949), *Mathemat-*

ical Economics (1956) and *Macro-Economic Theory—A Mathematical Treatment* (1967). Allen was Chairman of the Committee of Enquiry into the Impact of Rates on Householders (1963–5). [2]

Allocation, apportionment of (scarce) resources (labour, capital, time, etc.) between (alternative) uses. It is the central preoccupation of economic analysis and the central task of all societies, capitalist, socialist, communist, syndicalist or corporative. The task can, in theory, be performed by markets with private ownership of resources, markets with government ownership of resources, direction by governments with private ownership of resources, or direction by governments with government ownership of resources. Economists differ on the relative efficiency of these methods. The first is used mainly by capitalist countries in peacetime, the second has been attempted on occasion by some communist countries (Yugoslavia, Hungary, etc.), the third by capitalist countries in wartime or other emergencies, while the fourth is used by most communist countries. Socialist, syndicalist and corporative societies have used mixtures. The effectiveness of the methods depends on the consistency with which they are employed (markets are commonly restricted in operation for political, social or military reasons; while the larger the country the more difficult it is to enforce government directives). The results vary: some yield rising output with political and civil liberties, others faster economic growth with fewer liberties, some cultural cohesion or social stability with relatively slow growth and minimal liberties. [7]

Allocative Efficiency, the effectiveness with which (scarce) resources are apportioned between (alternative) uses. In a market system rules have been evolved for defining maximum conceivable efficiency (which is not in practice necessarily attainable). The maximum conceivable situation is when total output would not be enlarged if the resources were rearranged between the uses; in this situation they are yielding equal marginal products in all uses. Another measure is named after Pareto ("Pareto optimality"): the allocative efficiency is not maximized if reallocation would make some people better off (because they prefer the new to the original arrangement) but no-one worse off. The analysis of allocative efficiency has been described as Welfare Economics. [7]

Alloidal Tenure. *See* FREEHOLD.

Alternative Cost. *See* OPPORTUNITY COST.

Alternative-use Cost. *See* COST.

Altruism, concern for others as the primary purpose of activity; absence of self-interest. Since it is not universal, it is a scarce attribute of mankind and therefore can be analysed by the tools of economics. Hence D. H. Robertson argued that economists were concerned to devise an institutional framework within which individuals, singly or collectively, could reach their objectives without over-dependence on disinterestedness—altruism. Hence the interest of economists since Adam Smith in institutions—markets or "market forces"—that seem to yield desirable results through the human pursuit of personal self-interest.

Self-interest is commonly thought to be synonymous with selfishness, but "economic man" may rationally allow for the interests of others in earning and using the proceeds of his work. In his economic activities he may take into account the effects on others since it might be short-sighted and damaging to himself in the long run if he did not. And he may use the proceeds for a wide range of purposes from personal consumption ("self-interest" for himself, his family or friends) at one extreme to giving to third parties or causes (hospital, school, the church, people in need, etc.). The relevance of economic analysis does not depend on whether resources are sold or given but on whether they are scarce. If they are, giving as well as selling can be analysed by economic rules on maximizing utility and productivity. Giving can be combined with selling if the object (or service) is provided at less than its market price.

An important question is whether the existence of selling in markets discourages or destroys altruistic giving. It has been argued (by the late Professor R. M. Titmuss) that this is, or would be, true of blood. Some economists have doubted this proposition; they have argued that people who give blood are not necessarily deterred by the existence of others who accept payment. [13]

Amalgamation. *See* COMBINATION.

Amenity, an omnibus term for a satisfaction or benefit received in kind rather than cash, often jointly with others as well as individually, and possibly in a form not easily measured. Thus the amenities of a residential property might include (in addition to the services provided by the dwelling itself and its grounds) neighbourhood facilities such as shopping centres (commercially provided), public amenities such as schools, parks, recreational facilities and roads, and intangible items such as pleasant views and peace and quiet. [6]

American Economic Association, the main US association of individuals interested in economics and related subjects. It was formed in 1885, consisting largely of academic economists, but has increasingly attracted members from business and other professions. Its main purposes are to encourage economic research, especially the historical and statistical study of industry, to promote freedom of economic discussion, and to publish economic studies. Its publications are the *American Economic Review* (first published in 1911), the *Papers and Proceedings* of the annual meetings, and the *Journal of Economic Literature.* Occasional monographs on economic subjects are issued as supplements to the *Review.* The headquarters are in Evanston, Illinois. [14]

American Economic Review. *See* JOURNALS, ECONOMIC.

American Enterprise Institute, research and educational organization in Washington, D.C., that publishes works on public policy mostly by economists and other academics. It is much smaller than the (nearby) Brookings Institution, which presents studies broadly reflecting Democratic Party sympathies. The American Enterprise Institute represents roughly the opposite viewpoint. It publishes works by American economists who are generally sceptical of the efficacy of government intervention in economic policy, and more inclined to believe in progress through the improvement and refinement of market institutions. [14]

American Federation of Labor–Congress of Industrial Organizations (AFL-CIO), a federation of autonomous labour unions, established in 1955 by the merger of the American Federation of Labor, representing mostly craft unions, and the Congress of Industrial Organizations, representing mostly industrial unions. The AFL-CIO does not engage directly in union bargaining but collects and provides information for its members and presents economic analyses to the US Congress and government for the labour movement as a whole. It has established standards on ethical practices, racial equality and jurisdictional matters binding on affiliated unions. Failure to observe the code has led to expulsions, notably of the Teamsters union in 1957. [14]

Amortization, the gradual repayment of a debt or redemption of securities by periodic payments (an *annuity*); also the process of writing off an asset over a period of years (usually its expected working life).

Where, e.g., a debt is amortized by equal periodic payments the annuity instalments comprise (*a*) *a sinking fund contribution,* a periodic contribution that will accumulate at compound interest to a sum equal to the original debt by the end of the loan term, (*b*) *interest* on the debt. Together the two elements constitute a series of payments sufficient to accumulate to a sum whose present (discounted) value is just equal to the original debt. [1]

Analysis, collective name for the methods used by economists to break down a situation into causes and consequences. There are six main kinds. (1) *A priori* hypothesis, the process of drawing deductions from realistic assumptions and rigorous logic. (2) "Empirical" analysis of the past, which is not conclusive because the past may not be repeated in the future. (3) The use of econometric models which may make it possible to project the past into the future. The difficulty is that the information fed into the models may itself be defective; and projections adjusted by judgement (guesses) as to changes in trends may make the whole exercise subjective rather than objectively scientific. (4) Comparisons with other places (e.g. international comparisons). These may be misleading because elements common to two countries may be influenced by outside factors that are not common to both. (5) Experimentation, which may indicate consequences that cannot be learned any other way. But it must be conducted on a scale large enough and for a period long enough to apply to the real world—and this may be costly. (6) Creation of hypothetical ("surrogate") demand schedules and curves for alternative goods or services with a series of realistic prices, as developed in the 1960's by the Institute of Economic Affairs for state and private education and medical care. Here the difficulty is that people may not act in practice as they say they will.

Ideally all these methods would be used to check one another. For example, if a deficiency of funds for a state medical system was being analysed, *a priori* deduction could yield a hypothesis about the causes and solutions for testing by historical analysis, by econometric projection of state, private and mixed financing, by comparisons with other countries that have state and private financing, by local experimentation for a period, and by research into the hypothetical demand for state medical service (financed by taxes and/or social insurance) and private services (financed by fees and charges met from out-of-pocket cash and/or private insurance). In practice it might be possible to put both systems to the test by offering both in a market, which would then be used as a technique for discovering which method of organizing or financing medical care was preferred to the other, or which combination of both. [14]

Anarchism, the theory that economic (and other) affairs are best conducted by man without control, regulation or any other form of intervention by government. ("Anarchy" is normally used to describe the state of chaos resulting from the absence of law and order enforced by government.)

Anarchists share the socialist view that individual freedom is endangered by monopoly and concentrations of private power; the socialist would replace private power by state power, the anarchist would overthrow all power. In this sense he is nearer the liberal who would confine government to activities that individuals could not organize more efficiently or at all through competitive markets.

The anarchist movement originated with the French Encyclopaedists and was developed by Pierre Proudhon (1809–65), who denounced property as theft and argued that order could be maintained by individual self-control. Mikhail Bakunin (1814–76) is regarded as the leading teacher of anarchism. Others were Prince Kropotkin and Count Leo Tolstoy. [10]

Anarcho-capitalism, a synthesis of anarchy (as minimal or virtual absence of government) and capitalism (as maximal private ownership), advocated in recent years in the USA by economists in reaction against over-government. They go further than the liberal economists of the Chicago School and elsewhere in the UK and Europe in arguing that most of the supposedly essential functions of government—defence, the courts of law, the police, etc.—as well as functions conventionally but not necessarily performed by government—education, medical care, roads, etc.—could be and should be run by private arrangements between individuals and firms making voluntary contracts, enforced by private systems of arbitration in a free market. Their view (e.g. as put forward by David Friedman in *The Machinery of Freedom: Guide to a Radical Capitalism,* Harper & Row, 1973) is that government is "legitimized coercion" paid for by taxes that are a form of extortion or theft. [10]

Anarcho-syndicalism, a system that combines minimal (or non-existent) government with control of industry by syndicates of employees (roughly comparable to trade unions). The movement began in the early years of the 20th century in France, lost ground to communism in the 1920's, but spread to Spain in the 1930's where it was suppressed during the Civil War. It did not provide solutions to the problems of valuation of goods and services or of allocation of scarce resources, and has not been tried for periods long enough to test its efficacy. [10]

Anarchy. *See* ANARCHISM.

Anderson, Benjamin McAlester (1886–1949), American economist who severely criticized the fashionable economic policies of his day—the New Deal and others espoused by American Democratic Party critics of laissez-faire capitalism in the inter-war years, who were described as "liberal" rather than socialist but whose thinking reflected the socialist critique of capitalism. Anderson was the economist of the Chase National Bank (1919–39) and editor and sole author of the *Chase Economic Bulletin* and later of the *Economic Bulletin* published by the Capital Research Company. Here and elsewhere he analysed the policies he condemned and when they failed showed what could be done to mitigate their consequences. He criticized easy money, credit expansion and inflation, the abandonment of the gold standard, unbalanced budgets, Keynesian "pump-priming," spending on public works, price controls, subsidies, tariffs, etc., mainly on the grounds that they would necessitate further intervention by government and destroy the capitalist system. He assembled his economic critique and philosophy in *Economics and the Public Welfare, Financial and Economic History of the United States, 1914–1946,* in which he also wrote on Britain, France and the economy of the Western world. [2]

"Annual Abstract of Statistics." *See* SOURCES, STATISTICAL.

Annuity, a sequence of periodic payments, usually equal, made at equal intervals of time, e.g. rent payments, life assurance premiums, pensions, instalment payments. Originally the word referred to annual payments, but modern usage includes payment intervals of any constant length. When the *term* of an annuity (the time from the beginning of the first to the end of the last payment interval) is fixed, it is called an *annuity certain;* when the term depends on an uncertain event such as the death of a person, it is called a *contingent annuity.* If payments are made at the ends of payment intervals, the annuity is called an *ordinary annuity,* if at the beginnings an *annuity due.* The *present value* or purchase price of an annuity depends on the rate of interest used in the calculation. If the amount of the annuity is A per period for n periods and the rate of interest (expressed as a decimal) is i, the present value of an ordinary annuity (V) is given by the expression:

$$V = A \cdot [1 - (1 + i)^{-n}] / i \qquad (1)$$

and the annuity for n periods equivalent to a present capital sum of V when the rate of interest is i is given by the expression:

$$A = V \cdot i / [1 - (1 + i)^{-n}] \qquad (2)$$

Similarly, the amount (S) of an annuity payment of R per period (i.e. the amount due at the end of the term that would be regarded as equivalent in value to the annuity) is given by the expression:

$$S = R \cdot [(1 + i)^{n} - 1] / i \qquad (3)$$

and the periodic payment necessary to accumulate over n periods at a rate of interest i to an amount (S) is given by the expression:

$$R = S \cdot i / [(1 + i)^{n} - 1] \qquad (4)$$

The value A in expression (2) is the periodic payment necessary to *amortize* a sum V (say a mortgage loan) over a term of n years when the rate of interest is $100i$ per cent. The value R in expression (4) is the sinking fund contribution per period necessary to accumulate to an amount S over n periods when the rate of interest is $100i$ per cent. [1]

Anti-trust, American term for laws designed to combat the growth of monopoly—to "bust the trusts," and hence "trust-busters." [10]

Applied Economics, the use of economic theory to examine practical problems or policies and reach conclusions. Some economists specialize in the study, teaching and development of economic theory usually at universities; most use theory in applied economics in industry, commerce, government or international organizations. [14]

Appraisal, an estimation of the value of an asset. An appraisal of real property (real estate) is an estimation of the capital value of the specific rights attaching to that "parcel" of real property at a given time and for a defined purpose. Appraisal for some purposes, e.g. for property taxation or compensation for compulsory acquisition (condemnation, expropriation in North America) tends to follow formal rules either laid down by statute or established by legal precedent. Appraisals for market transactions such as sale or purchase are based on analysis of comparable transactions or on capitalization of estimated income flows to be derived from the property or on knowledge of original cost and estimated depreciation (or appreciation) since acquisition. Estimates of capital value invariably involve a degree of subjective assessment based on professional expertise and knowledge of specialized markets. [1]

Appreciation, a rise in the current value, as measured by market price, of company plant and equipment, stocks, buildings and land, financial investments or other assets. The opposite of depreciation. Current market value is distinguished from "book" value in the company accounts, i.e. original value adjusted downward for wear and tear or upward by revaluation for rising value owing to changes in supply or demand or inflation. Economists are usually critical of accounting practice in failing to bring book values up to date with changing market conditions, mainly because the significant figure for replacing used assets is not book value but current cost. [3]

Appropriation Account. *See* OUTLAY.

Aquinas, St. Thomas (1225/6–74), generally regarded as the most eminent medieval philosopher-theologian. The economic ideas of the Middle Ages were influenced by St. Thomas's Christian "humanism"; he believed that goods should be shared to satisfy human needs. Together with medieval views on a "just" price, the sin of usury in taking interest except as a return for risk, etc., this philosophy ran counter to the appeal to self-interest underlying the market philosophy, and has been revived in recent decades. [2]

Arbitrage, the process of making a profit out of differences in the prices of commodities or currencies in different places (countries). It performs a similar function in minimizing price differentials over *space* to that performed (in normal markets) by speculation in minimizing price differentials over *time.*

Commodity and currency markets constitute the points of contact through which international trade takes place. Specialized dealers and traders in these markets ensure by arbitrage operations (buying in "cheaper," selling in "dearer" markets) that prices of an internationally traded commodity in two countries do not differ by more than the cost of transport and handling; by similar trading in currencies and short-term income-bearing financial assets *arbitrageurs* tend to eliminate differentials in currency exchange rates that are inconsistent with underlying conditions of supply and demand, expectations and interest rates. [7]

Arbitration, the procedure by which the parties to a dispute submit it to a third party for settlement. Submission may be voluntary or imposed by law. For example, in Great Britain disputes over wages and conditions of the employment of about six million workers in public and private employment may be referred to the Industrial Court, a permanent body created in 1919, or to an arbitrator appointed by the Ministry of Labour, or to an independent arbitrator. Reference is usually voluntary, and the arbitrators' awards are not legally enforceable. Under landlord and tenant legislation the terms of new tenancies must be fixed by the County Court if agreement cannot be reached by negotiation. Legislation on the compulsory acquisition of property by public bodies requires the compensation to be assessed by the Lands Tribunal in the absence of agreement between the parties. The rents payable under protected farm tenancies may, failing agreement, be referred to arbitration by the landlord or tenant, and the other party cannot refuse.

Involuntary arbitration makes use of complicated rules for ascertaining values and tends to distort the free market pattern of values. They reflect the restrictions placed by statute law on the free movement of resources and on freedom of contract. Arbitration cannot arrive at decisions (wage rates, compensation, etc.) very different from those that would emerge in a free market. For example, if wages rates are fixed much lower than they would be in a free labour market, some workers will reject them and move to other employers and recruiting will tend to fall away; if they are fixed much higher, wage costs will tend to rise, sales may fall, labour may be replaced by machinery, and some employees may be dismissed. Some economists argue that wage arbitration should try to reproduce the wage rates that would emerge in a free market for labour.

Arbitration to settle disputes in courts of law has long been a function of government. In the USA increasing delays have led to private arbitration, used especially by firms engaged in international trade and liable to be involved in complex issues of international law. Private arbitration can be cheaper and quicker than arbitration in government courts of law. The difficulty in private arbitration, that of enforcement, could, it has been argued, be met by lodging sums to cover the penalties under the contract or by credit rating to encourage acceptance of the arbitration decision, with the sanction of blacklisting firms that did not accept the decision. It has been argued that if government courts deteriorate, private arbitration will grow, as private activity has grown in other American government services like the delivery of mail, the police, etc. [5]

Arithmetic Mean (AM), an average value. The AM of a set of values of a variable is their sum divided by the number of items in the set. Unless otherwise qualified, the word "mean" is usually interpreted as arithmetic mean. [14]

Arrow, Kenneth Joseph (1921–), American academic economist, born in New York City. He has been Professor of Economics at Harvard University since 1968. He studies general economic theory, economic planning theory and policy, and the economics of technical change in industrial organization. He has contributed widely to learned journals. [2]

Articles of Association, the rules governing the internal workings of a company. By the Companies Act 1948 every limited liability company must have Articles of Association. *Inter alia* they specify the powers and duties of the directors, the procedure for the transfer of shares, the issues of capital and the conduct of meetings, etc. A model set of Articles of Association is provided by Table A of the Act, and many companies adopt Table A with modifications to meet their requirements. The Articles may be changed with the shareholders' consent. A copy must be filed with the Registrar of Companies. [8]

Assessment, the formal process of establishing a tax base. The basis of assessment for local rating purposes is the *rateable value* of real property, generally the same as the property's *net annual value*—the rent at which it might "reasonably" be expected to let from year to year if the tenant bore the usual rates and taxes and costs of repairs and insurance. Alternatively, a *gross value* is first ascertained (it differs from net annual value in assuming that the landlord, not the tenant, bears the costs of repairs, insurance etc.) and a net annual value is derived by making "statutory deductions" from it. The amount of local rate payable on a property is arrived at by applying a *rate poundage* to the rateable value. [12]

Assessmentism. *See* INSURANCE.

Assets, the resources of an enterprise used in conducting its activities. They are tangible (plant, etc.) or intangible (goodwill, patent rights, licences to trade, franchises to manufacture, etc.); current (i.e. liquid or readily convertible to liquidity—cash, bank deposits, accounts due or almost due for payment, saleable stocks, saleable investments, etc.) or non-current (i.e. fixed—land, buildings, long-term investments or other assets that are eventually saleable but not immediately so without disrupting the enterprise). [3]

Associated Sciences. Economics is explained in this book as the study of the principles that man employs or applies, consciously or unconsciously, in using the limited means at his disposal to give the largest possible total satisfaction. He can be regarded as beginning by taking the outside physical world and himself and other human beings as he finds them. At its simplest, therefore, economics is found at the meeting-place of the physical and human social worlds: technology and psychology. Economic principles are determined or affected by, and in turn determine or affect, many branches of knowledge in the physical and social sciences. The main ones are: Technology—the natural and physical sciences (geography, geology, physics, mechanics, biology, chemistry, etc.); Law; Psychology; Logic; Mathematics, Statistics; Politics, Sociology, Ethics; History.

Technology relates to man's physical environment—both the natural world and the modifications of it wrought by the scientist. Some technical facts the economist must take as given and as unalterable: the coal below the surface in South Wales cannot be "wished" to Ireland or Iceland; to mine it and transport it there involves a cost. On the other hand, the properties of the water in Burton, Edinburgh and other places which led to the establishment of breweries there to brew particular kinds of beer can to some extent be reproduced elsewhere, although again at a cost. The burst of invention in the last two centuries has transformed economic relationships. For example, the revolution in transport has "annihilated distance": by reducing costs it has made possible the change from small manufacturing units to large units which can produce much more cheaply because they can exploit the economies of scale. Eventually the replacement of coal by atomic power would possibly bring equally fundamental changes in economic relationships.

A source of much misunderstanding among laymen has been the confusion—mainly by the physical scientists—between technological and economic decisions and judgments. The definition of economics in terms of the application of scarce means (with alternative uses) to numerous possible ends makes this distinction clear. The decisive characteristic of an economic decision is that it involves a choice on the basis of a comparison of cost and benefit. A technical decision rests solely on physical properties and is not concerned with complications of cost. In building a house the choice of materials is a technical decision in so far as it depends on, say, the soil, the prevailing wind and rainfall, and the kind of heating to be installed. It is an economic decision in so far as some materials may be technically superior to others but are not thought worth the higher cost they would involve, part of which could go to provide, say, better interior fittings.

In the real world technical decisions normally affect but do not take precedence over economic decisions. Bananas can be grown under glass in Scotland; but they are not normally grown there because the climate is such that they can be grown much more cheaply in, say, Jamaica, so that it pays to import them and pay for them by goods which Britain, in turn, can produce more cheaply because of its natural, acquired and/or human advantages. Again, the trams that used to adorn or disfigure the main streets of Western cities no longer do so not because they were technically incapable of carrying passengers but because new means of passenger transport were devised that were more comfortable, flexible, faster and/or cheaper. But if economic criteria normally predominate over technical criteria, they sometimes take second place to political, military or strategic criteria (*see* below).

Law. Economic activity has to work not only within physical but also within man-made conditions as reflected in law and the institutions they create. Probably the most important is the law governing the ownership and use of property. In the western democracies most property is privately owned; a system of competitive markets and private initiative rests on this substructure. The law governing the formation and conduct of business units—companies, partnerships and so on—is a second. That on contracts is a third. The law may enforce some contracts, permit but not enforce others and prohibit the remainder. The difference in the law on company organizations and contracts in Britain, the USA and Germany go far to explain the differences in their industrial organization and trade practices. In the USA, Federal anti-trust laws since 1890 have maintained markets in a more competitive condition than might otherwise have been the case. In Germany the law enforced contracts in restraint of trade and thus fostered the growth of cartels in which the member firms agreed on prices or output quotas. In Britain the equivocal attitude of the law before the war produced restrictive agreements on a large scale; more recently a change in attitude has produced new anti-monopoly legislation.

Psychology. The way in which men react to varying conditions, difficulties and opportunities will affect their economic decisions. Economics does not rest on the assumption of "economic man"—one who in his everyday business relationships is concerned only to achieve the largest possible material advantage for himself. Men sometimes act impulsively, perhaps against their true interests; or with public spirit, again perhaps contrary to their personal interests; or they may prefer to give rather than sell. But these conflicting motives for human behaviour can be taken into account in economic analysis, and they do not disturb the theories or the findings of economics. The only assumption that economics needs to make about the way men act is that they do so in order to satisfy some purposes before others, that they have a "scale of preferences" which will govern their choices. Whether the order of preference indicates that a man is wise or foolish, selfish or altruistic, rational or illogical, is not the business of economics. Nor does economics depend on the assumption that a man will put material motives above others: a man's actions may be subjected to economic analysis whatever the order in which he puts wealth, profit, power, esteem, fame, the urge to serve his family, his trade union, his church, his village, his political party, his country, a cause or any other aim.

Nevertheless it is convenient to begin by assuming that man is a rational animal with clear aims: the complicating motives can then be introduced one by one, and the conclusions about how he is likely to act in a given situation modified accordingly. Economic analysis uses models in which men are assumed to buy in the cheapest market and sell in the dearest. This assumption does not always fit the facts of modern life, but it is a useful starting point for analysing complex situations. In practice men may pay more than they could elsewhere, or accept a price lower than they could obtain elsewhere, partly as a method of giving, either at less than the market price or wholly "free" at nil price.

Many of the laws of economics, which concern the behaviour of people in markets and therefore their reaction to varying conditions of supply and demand and to changes in price, could not be made unless people were by and large ready to prefer the better of two bargains if they had a free choice. Men seeking goods and services and housewives shopping do not confine themselves only to price, quality, etc.: they are affected by habit, custom, pride, prejudice, by what business colleagues or rivals or neighbours will consider "fair" and "right," and so on. But to suppose that people are irrational altruists is even further from the truth than to suppose that they are rational egoists. In wartime patriotism is a powerful motive, although even then business men, trade union negotiators and ordinary shoppers put their personal material interests high in their scale of preferences. But in peacetime ordinary personal motives come to the fore. And attempts to create new social institutions on any other assumption have displayed periodic weakness. For example, the argument that miners and railwaymen would work better when they were working "for the nation" under nationalization has not been supported by events.

Logic. In its analysis of events, economics follows the logical methods of reasoning used in all the "empirical" sciences, that is, those conducted by experiment. An event can be said to be scientifically (causally) explained or established by demonstrating cause and effect, when its occurrence can be deduced from a universal statement ("law," "theory," "hypothesis") in conjunction with a statement about a particular event. For example, a causal explanation of boiling water requires a hypothesis about the boiling-point of water in terms of heat required, and a particular statement about the heat applied in the given instance. From the universal statement or hypothesis a prediction can be made that the water will boil at a stated temperature. The statement which completes the causal explanation is that the temperature was reached. Broadly, the particular statement describes the "cause" of the occurrence, and the specific prediction or deduction describes the "effect." All empirical sciences are thus systems of hypotheses from which a picture of the world can be obtained by pure deduction. The progress of scientific knowledge as a whole consists of an endless intuitive search for hypotheses which have increasingly larger powers to explain and which are capable of being tested, since it is only by its ability to stand up to repeated critical tests without being refuted that the accuracy of a theory or an hypothesis can be judged.

Economics similarly seeks to establish statements that are universally applicable and which will both support explanation and be capable of being tested.

For example, from hypotheses relating to total demand and the distribution of wealth in the form of different kinds of asset in the economy it is possible to deduce specific predictions or conclusions about inflation and the general level of interest rates. Events discipline such speculations by forcing them to submit to the test of observed facts. Disagreement between speculation and event would refute the premise from which the conclusions were derived or indicate weaknesses in the logic used in the theory.

There are differences of degree between the natural sciences and economics (and other social sciences). Controlled experiments can often (not always) be used to test the theories of the natural sciences, but not to the same extent in the social sciences. The laboratory of the economist is the complex real world of interrelated events, where any one set of events cannot usually be isolated. For example, to examine the effect of a change in price on the quantity demanded of a commodity it is necessary to assume no change in all other influences which may simultaneously affect demand—such as personal incomes and preferences, quality, the weather. The theoretical constructions of the economist are therefore necessarily abstract "models" of real life, and they invite the criticism that the conclusions he draws from them derive entirely from the artificial assumptions and definitions with which he began. Such criticism would be justified if the economist were concerned only to develop a theory, and then juggled with the assumptions and definitions so that it always "fitted the facts." Economics is not, however, an intellectual exercise in deductive reasoning pursued for its own sake. Its merit, as that of any other empirical science, lies entirely in the light it throws on the practical problems of the everyday world. The safeguard against useless theorizing lies in the continued testing and criticism of theories in the light of observed fact *wherever possible.* In this respect the progress of economic theory is no different from that of any other scientific discipline. In periods when the critical attitude is lacking scientific advance languishes, and conversely.

This view underlines the basic purpose of all scientific knowledge to provide guide lines for human action. The laws of science are best regarded as general prohibitions telling us what man *cannot* do, rather than as positive statements telling us what he *can* do. They set upper limits to what can be achieved by man with the fund of knowledge at his disposal. The laws of economics are basically no different. They provide a guide for policy by indicating the *direction* which the unintended consequences of actions may take. The theory of money, for example, does not try to say that if the quantity of money is increased by x per cent, prices will rise by y per cent, but that it is impossible (other things remaining the same) to increase the quantity of money in the economy without it exerting *some* effect on the level of employment, or prices, or the level of interest rates. Such a statement, and the use to which it can be put, constitutes an addition to the stock of human knowledge.

Mathematics, Statistics. Economics is concerned with quantities, or rather with changes in them at the margin. A characteristic problem is, "What will be the effect on the demand for labour of a (small) change in wages?" Thus, simple mathematics is implied in economic reasoning. The language and techniques of advanced mathematics are useful in deductive reasoning, although their use in economics may tempt the economist to sacrifice clarity for elegance and to push ahead too far by making assumptions that are correct on paper but are useless for practical purposes. Statistics—the science of arranging quantities to show important relationships or trends by expressing them systematically in the form of averages, index numbers, etc.—is used increasingly by the economist; it is a substitute for the controlled experiments he cannot undertake because social phenomena cannot be isolated.

Mathematical and statistical methods are increasingly being applied to economics; the resulting technique is known as econometrics. This makes it more possible to analyse and study the real world as it is because it enables the economist to handle a number of changing quantities. Thus, in studying movement of trade, it is necessary to examine productive capacity, stocks, new orders, unfilled orders, sales and so on. These categories not only affect employment and demand but also one another. The larger the number of quantities that change ("variables") the more difficult it is to reduce them to words; hence the increasing use of mathematical formulae similar to those used by the natural scientists. In some respects econometrics is similar to the science of meteorology, the study of movements in the phenomena of the atmosphere. And just as meteorology makes possible limited forecasts in the weather, so econometrics is making possible limited forecasts in business conditions. Thus the Econometric Institute of New York was able to foresee with some accuracy the recessions of 1953 and 1957. But owing to the unpredictable human element, forecasting is not likely to be as feasible in the social as in the natural sciences. Econometric techniques are being refined but there is a tendency (not unnatural, since economists are human) to run ahead of the statistical material they must use. The most common temptation is to over-"formalize" human conduct in macro-economic laws, rules, tendencies or generalizations by losing sight of the unpredictable differences in "micro-economic" individual behaviour. In particular, macro-economic forecasting sometimes tends to overlook the limitations of "models" into which estimates with wide margins of error are fed. And, in the "management" of demand by government, short-term forecasts are used that are rarely accurate, except by accidental cancelling-out of comparable but opposite errors.

Politics, Sociology, Ethics. Politics is the science of the relationships between citizens and the state. Sociology is the study of human society in groups—families, communities, institutions. Ethics is the science of the moral nature of human character and conduct.

A course of action that may be indicated on economic grounds (a comparison of costs and benefits) may be judged unwise on political, sociological or ethical grounds. For example, Adam Smith in *The Wealth of Nations* declared: "Defence is of much more importance than opulence"; protection for agriculture raises the price of food to home consumers but it may be regarded as an insurance premium in the event of a war cutting off outside supplies; the Premium Bonds have stimulated saving in a period of inflation, but they may be considered immoral by giving official blessing to a form of gambling.

Economics is a behaviourist, not a normative, science: it is concerned not with what *should be,* but with what *is,* and *why.* It studies the behaviour of man in activities which find expression in the market, that is, in prices and values. The essence of economics is explanation of the phenomenon of value. But it is not concerned with value judgements—with saying what should be. That is the province of politics or sociology or ethics. Politically or morally it may be desirable that all men shall be fully employed; ethically a school may be judged preferable to a cinema or a public house. These are value judgements with which economics is not concerned; its concern is only with the causes and repercussions of over-full or under employment, with the relative cost of building schools, cinemas and public houses and the value of their services.

Economics measures and compares values and costs as shown in the market, in so far as they reflect general consumer preferences. The economist can show which means of achieving given ends is the most "economic," i.e. involves the least cost or sacrifice of other things; but he does not say, *as an economist,* that the most economic method *should* be adopted: economy is only one purpose of human conduct, and it may conflict with what is considered good or beautiful or true. But economics does help the best value judgements to be made, because it reveals the real relative cost of, say, preferring beauty to economy, or economy to security. The economist may have value judgements of his own, e.g. he may think it unwise to sacrifice cheap food in peacetime to the doubtful risk of war, but he has no authority in economics for his view, although his science may enable him to arrive at a more dispassionate and more informed judgement than some other people.

History. Economics as the study of mankind in business life has its counterpart in the economic history which describes the development of farming, manufacturing, transport, banking and so on. Economics as the science of the human disposal of scarce resources has its counterpart in the developments produced by scarcity down the ages. This approach to history studies, say, the inventions of the late eighteenth and early nineteenth century not as technical developments (this is the history of science), or for their effects on company structure (legal history), or the extension of the franchise (political history), but for their effects on the supply of and the demand for the factors of production that went into their manufacture and the supply of and the demand for the goods and services they produced. The newest reinterpretation of history by economists reflects the analysis of the distinction between private and social costs and benefits; it examines the development of institutions and property rights that create incentives for individuals to bring the private benefit or rate of return from economic effort closer to the social benefit or rate of return. Thus it argues that by the eighteenth century property rights had developed in England and the Netherlands that created the incentives for sustained growth, not least to encourage innovation and investment in industrialization. On this view the industrial revolution was not the *source* of industrial growth but the *result* of raising the private rate of return ("profit") on technical innovation (e.g. the celebrated spinning jenny) and applying it to industrial production. International competition induced other countries to adapt their institutions to provide similar incentives for growth and so bring about the spread of the "industrial revolution."

Both Adam Smith and Karl Marx saw that the development of effective rights in property, that is the fruits of innovation and investment, were prerequisites for economic growth. But Marx thought that industrial growth ("capitalism") would inevitably produce communism, without recognizing that growth was not inevitable. Smith inveighed against mercantilism and its obstruction of the required development of property rights, and saw that the distinction between private and social returns might require some government functions, but did not analyse the property rights required or how governments could devise and maintain them. [13]

Assumptions, simplifying propositions about human nature and technical conditions used by economists in establishing "laws." If oversimplified they are abandoned or changed to approximate more closely to reality as the analysis becomes more refined. For example, it is commonly assumed that individuals try to maximize utility in earning and spending, and that firms profit in organizing production; but in some circumstances these assumptions may not be realistic. [14]

Atomistic Competition, another name for pure competition. [7]

Attribute, statistical term used to denote a *qualitative* characteristic of an individual or item, as distinct from a *variable* or *quantitative* characteristic. Thus housing might be classified according to tenure attributes (rented or owner-occupied) and according to variables or quantitative characteristics such as size (number of rooms). [14]

Auction, a public sale in which would-be buyers compete by making progressively higher bids until one offers a price no other bidder is prepared to exceed. In a "Dutch auction" the seller progressively lowers the price at which the commodity is offered until a bid is made. The competitiveness of bids at auctions may be limited by bidders' "rings," i.e. by agreements among bidders to act in concert and refrain from competition. The gain to the ring is discovered or agreed later, either by a further (private) auction or some other method, and is shared by agreement among ring members. [7]

Audit Office, in the UK the department of the Comptroller and Auditor-General, an official independent of the executive who is responsible for the annual audit of the accounts of government departments. The work is performed in the name of the House of Commons and is closely linked with the work of the Treasury. [12]

Austrian School, a group of late nineteenth-century economists at the University of Vienna. They include Carl Menger (1840–1921), Friedrich von Wieser (1851–1926) and Eugen von Böhm-Bawerk (1851–1914). Their work is thought to form a separate "school" largely because their methods were directly opposed to the prevailing inductive or "historical" approach in Germany and Austria. Menger engaged in a long controversy with Gustav Schmoller (the leading exponent of the historical school) over the relative virtues of inductive and deductive methods. Apart from methodology, their main contribution to economics lay in the subjective theory of value. With Walras and Jevons, Menger was one of the first to formulate the theory of marginal utility. His work in this field, first published in *Grundsätze der Volkswirtschaftslehre* (1871), was developed and disseminated by Wieser and Böhm-Bawerk. [2]

The Austrian teaching was developed by von Mises, F. A. Hayek, Gottfried Haberler, F. Machlup and others who studied at Vienna, and the tradition is continued by Professors L. M. Lachmann of Johannesberg and Israel Kirzner of New York, and by a growing number of younger economists mainly in the USA. The first American Economics Conference was held in South Royalten, Vermont, in 1974. The "new" Austrians are emphasizing the methodology of the school: social structures are analysed theoretically from the individual elements in human *action* (as opposed to human *design*) regarded as the sole source of knowledge. The Austrian analysis is founded on price-changes as sources of empirical information about changing conditions that is not obtainable from other sources or by other methods. The emphasis on individual prices underlies the Austrian view of capital as a structure of heterogeneous but interrelated capital goods. This approach is in sharp contrast to the aggregative (macro-economic) approaches of other schools which concentrate on *general* equilibrium and neglect the market processes that determine *relative* prices and equilibria of different though interconnected goods. [2]

Autarchy. *See* AUTARKY.

Autarky, the policy of economic self-sufficiency, as opposed to trading with other economic groups. A country, region or enterprise is said to behave autarkically if it tries by restricting imports and stimulating internal production to eliminate reliance on trade with other countries, regions or enterprises. The outstanding example in recent history is that of National Socialist Germany between 1933 and 1945. It is also practised by Soviet Russia and other Communist countries and in milder form by other countries that attempt to direct their economic systems through centralized state regulation. [10]

Automation. *See* DIVISION OF LABOUR.

Autonomous Investment, investment that responds to underlying indirect influences such as scientific discovery or invention rather than to direct market conditions such as the price of capital (interest rates), increased demand for goods and services produced by the investment, or changes in the relative efficiency of capital and labour. D. H. Robertson and other economists have pointed to changes in technical innovation as possible origins of cyclical fluctuations in economic activity. [3]

Autonomous Stabilizer, a built-in mechanism for restoring equilibrium to an economic system. The notion has developed since the Great Depression in the 1930's, President Roosevelt's use of large-scale government expenditure, and J. M. Keynes's theoretical support for counter-cyclical public expenditure to offset fluctuations in private expenditure. In particular social insurance has been used in Britain, the USA and elsewhere as a stabilizer; the contributions can be raised in a boom and the benefits (pensions, unemployment pay, etc.) in a recession to even out purchasing power and demand. The difficulty is that this use of social insurance weakens it as insurance and makes it an ancillary tax mechanism. More generally, government expenditure on the "infrastructure"—roads, schools, hospitals, telecommunications, etc.—can be varied to remove or reduce fluctuations in demand, economic activity and output. In Britain (and elsewhere) these attempts produced the derogatory term "stop-go" because they overshot the target of equilibrium ("flation"—neither deflation nor inflation) by *over*compensating for the fluctuations they were supposed to neutralize. "Fine tuning" was a form of monetary control to restore equilibrium. Dissatisfaction with 10–15 years of "stop-go" led to an attempt in Britain in the early 1970's to escape from the alternation by "going for growth" through tax incentives and (when, after about eighteen months, they seemed to have failed) by monetary inflation.

Probably too much was expected of government skills in offsetting fluctuations. But this meant that the stabilizers were not truly autonomous if they were dependent on political judgement, pressures from industry and trade unions, and electoral considerations. Yet the more general counter-cyclical policies may have contributed to shortening and shallowing the "trade cycle" since the Second World War. A residue of fluctuation in activity, short-term and long-term, may be unavoidable because of changing attitudes and technical innovation; and it may be preferable to government attempts to entirely flatten out fluctuations—attempts that are over-effective and end by making the fluctuations more violent than would otherwise have been the case. [12]

Availability. *See* CAPACITY, UNUSED.

Average, a summary statistic, in some way representative of a set of values of a particular variable. As ordinarily used, the word refers to the *arithmetic mean* of a set of values; but it may also embrace other average values such as the *median* or *mode* or *geometric mean* of a set. [14]

Average Cost. *See* COST.

Avoidable Costs. *See* SUPPLEMENTARY COSTS.

B

Babeuf. *See* SOCIALISM.

Backward Countries, another name for poor or under-developed countries. It is a less neutral term than "under-developed." "Backwardness" implies immaturity which is politically unacceptable to under-developed countries. The search for euphemisms to describe these countries illustrates the emotive quality of words and the political dynamite which these economic problems represent. More recently the word "developing" is being preferred to "under-developed."

In some textbooks "backward countries" is used to describe countries with economically backward populations, that is, where the quality of the labour force is relatively low, as shown in unwillingness to move between jobs or regions, in subsistence rather than specialized production, in ignorance of economic possibilities, and in lack of enterprise. The level of labour productivity is low, so that five or even ten workers are required to produce the same output as a worker in the same occupation in an advanced country. The causes are generally low standards of health, malnutrition, illiteracy, disinclination to sustained work, shortage of capital, and lack of the entrepreneurial capacity and readiness to run risks. Economic discussion of the needs of under-developed countries has moved in emphasis from capital investment to training and education and most recently to the institutions—a monetary and banking system, laws of property, contract and business organization and conduct—required to nurture the entrepreneurial qualities of initiative, enterprise and risk-taking that underlie economic advance in the western countries. Economists, and through them other people, have become more aware that aid given direct to governments may be misused for political purposes and may therefore not help their peoples to become more self-supporting. [11]

Backward Integration. *See* INTEGRATION.

Backwardation. (*a*) On the Stock Exchange a percentage charge paid by the seller of securities for the right to delay delivery. For example, if a bear has "sold short," and the price does not fall within the period of the Stock Exchange Account, he may pay a backwardation to carry his bargain forward to the next settlement in the hope that the price will fall as expected. (*b*) In a commodity market, the amount by which the spot price (and the costs of carrying the commodity over time) exceeds the forward price. [8]

Bad Money Drives Out Good. *See* GRESHAM'S LAW.

Bads, objects (tangible or intangible) of which man prefers less rather than more. The opposite of goods. [7]

Bagehot, Walter (1826–77), English economist, lawyer and banker. Educated at London University, called to the bar in 1852, but soon afterwards joined his father in banking. From 1860 to 1877 he was editor of *The Economist,* and his *Lombard Street* (1873), based on a collection of articles he wrote for that magazine, is an observant examination of finance and banking. His other main works, *Universal Money* (1869) and *Postulates of English Political Economy* (1876), show him as a moderate critic of the methodology of the classical school of political economy. His concept of a psychological cycle of optimism and pessimism was an early attempt to explain the trade cycle. [2]

Bakunin, Mikhail. *See* ANARCHISM.

Balance of Payments, part of the nation's accounts that shows payments by residents and their receipts from foreigners resulting from international transactions. Most payments and receipts are for goods or services provided by the citizens of one country to those of others; some payments are "unrequited" transfers such as gifts and loans. The items are therefore divided into several broad categories. This may be helpful in deciding economic policy, because the remedies for a balance of payments deficit or surplus will differ according to the causes, which may emerge from study of the items. The main components are shown in Table 1. Of these,

(1) "Visible exports" are the receipts from sales to people in other countries of commodities produced in or re-exported from Britain. "Visible imports" are the payments to them for the goods they export to us.

(2) The "invisibles" are the receipts from the payments for shipping, insurance and banking services, interest, profits and dividends, tourism, migrants' funds, gifts and legacies.

(3) The capital account shows the balance of lending between Britain and the rest of the world. It includes loans between the UK and other governments as well as long-term and short-term private investments by British citizens in other countries and by them in Britain.

(4) Transfers of gold and convertible currency are called "accommodating movements" because they result from and reconcile the decisions to import, export, borrow and lend taken by people in Britain and other countries. Surpluses or deficits on the total balance of payments cannot continue indefinitely because no country has infinitely

Table 1. The Balance of Payments (imaginary quantities)

	Current Account			
	Receipts		Payments	
		£ million		£ million
(1)	Visible exports	100	Visible imports	120
(2)	Invisible exports	30	Invisible imports	25
	Capital Account			
(3)	Borrowed	50	Lent	55
		180		200
(4)	Accommodating monetary movements (change in gold and foreign currency reserves)	20		—
		200		200

large reserves, and a surplus for one country implies a deficit for one or more other countries. Sooner or later a country which is in deficit has to take action to stop the outflow of its reserves. This means either reducing its payments to people in other countries, increasing its receipts from them, or both. Many ways of achieving this objective are available to governments, at least in theory. First, devaluation of the exchange rate may stimulate exports and reduce imports; if the domestic economy can produce sufficient exports and substitutes for imports without causing inflation, devaluation may solve the problem. Secondly, internal deflation may cure the trouble by restricting demand for imports and exportable goods and stimulating exports.

The words balance of payments surplus or deficit are often applied to the current account section of the balance of payments. In this sense both can continue for a long time; e.g., if a country earning a large current account surplus is willing to lend it abroad it can carry on earning the surplus without placing its trading partners in difficulties. Britain followed this policy in the nineteenth century and Western Germany for several years after World War II. [4]

Balance of Trade, the current account section of the balance of payments, measured by the difference between a country's receipts for visible and invisible exports and its payments for visible and invisible imports.

When exports exceed imports the difference is described as a balance of trade surplus or "active" balance; when imports exceed exports the difference is a deficit or "passive" balance. These terms do not necessarily imply approval or disapproval, for without further information it cannot be said whether a surplus or a deficit is good or bad. An under-developed country borrowing heavily from international institutions and foreign countries will run a current account deficit for a long time, as it uses the loans to pay for imports of capital goods that will assist its development and eventually enable it to replace some imports by home-produced substitutes. A country receiving reparations payments must run a current account deficit, otherwise it may prevent the paying country from earning enough foreign currency or gold to make the payments. But if a country cannot expect an inflow of capital to pay for its excesses of imports over exports of goods and services, or if (like Britain) it wishes to be on balance a lender to the rest of the world, a continuing deficit may be serious. One likely cause is too high a level of monetary demand at home, so that the pressure of demand for goods and services diverts them from export markets to the home market and stimulates imports. This situation, together with the obligation or wish to lend capital to the rest of the sterling area and to under-developed countries, appears to have been the main cause of Britain's difficulties in external payments after the end of the Second World War. If the obligation to lend to overseas territories is unavoidable, the remedy would appear to be the reduction of internal demand by (*a*) credit restriction, (*b*) cuts in government expenditure, (*c*) increases in taxation, or combinations of these measures. Since they may lead to some unemployment and check investment in industry, the government is in difficulty because the solution of the external problem creates unwelcome problems in the internal economy. It is largely as a result of this dilemma that the British economy was in the 1960's subject to the much criticized "stop-go" policy of imposing restrictions on demand when a balance of payments crisis appeared, and easing them when unemployment figures rose and perhaps before the external difficulties had been removed, so that another crisis soon recurred. In the early 1970's an effort was made to break out of "stop-go" by "going for growth," first by encouraging investment and output by tax concessions and refusing to subsidize inefficient or declining firms, and then, when this policy was thought to have failed after about eighteen months, by monetary expansion coupled with an incomes policy to avoid inflation. This too failed owing to trade union opposition into the mid-1970's. [4]

Balanced Budget, equalizing income with out-go; for a country's budget, tax plus other revenue with expenditure. Conventionally budgets were balanced annually as a restraint on political irresponsibility. Some economists have argued for long-term balancing to even out economic fluctuations, by running deficits of government income relatively to out-go in times of low or falling activity and surpluses in times of high or rising activity. Since Keynes's *General Theory* it has been thought that raising taxes to produce a surplus (or diminish a deficit) is deflationary by reducing purchasing power, and lowering taxes inflationary by expanding it. In the 1960's and 1970's the growing use of trade union power to raise gross pay when higher taxes reduced "take-home" pay was effective because governments feared higher unemployment and therefore inflated the money supply and enabled employers to absorb higher wage costs by passing them on in higher prices to consumers. The limitations of government control in practice, as distinct from their apparent efficiency in theory, is seen from the disturbing (inflationary or deflationary) effects of attempts to balance the budget: because the individual distribution of income between spending and saving is beyond government control, a change in taxes or expenditure to balance a national budget may simply unbalance family budgets and spark off compensatory changes; for example, a rise in taxes may be offset by dissaving in order to maintain customary household expenditures. [12]

Baltic Exchange, the Baltic Mercantile and Shipping Exchange, like many City institutions, originated in the London coffee-houses, but is now in St. Mary Axe; the largest market for shipping in the world. It has two main functions: (1) A commodity exchange, specializing in the grain trade, with a specialized "futures" market comprising expert operators who buy cargoes of grain when dispatched and sell an equivalent amount on the market, that is, "sell forward," buying back the grain on delivery, thus protecting themselves by "hedging" against price fluctuation. (2) The shipping market, in which almost any business connected with ships and cargoes is transacted: merchants who want to ship cargoes "demand" shipping space and charter it usually through ship-brokers from shipowners who are represented in the market by agents. Often the cargoes are shipped between two ports in other countries, so that the "Baltic" is a source of earnings for invisible exports. Since the end of World War II the "Baltic" has accommodated a market for cargoes transported by air. In the mid 1970's the Exchange had approximately 2,200 members. [7]

Bank Advances, generic term for a wide range of loans. Loans to banks in Britain have traditionally been for working capital (e.g. payment of wages before goods were sold) for six months; but the period has tended to grow longer. In Germany and other countries in Europe, banks have lent industry money for much longer periods and have become involved as risk-sharers by owning part of the equity. Other forms of advances are personal overdrafts, personal loans, etc. [8]

Bank Deposits. *See* DEPOSITS (BANK).

Bank for International Settlements (BIS), a central bank for central banks founded at Basle in 1930, when its main functions were to secure co-operation among central banks, to provide facilities for international payments and aid the transfer of reparations from Germany under the Young Plan. Central banks and banking groups in Belgium, France, Germany, Italy, Japan, the UK and the USA provided most of the share capital. It has been partly replaced by the International Monetary Fund. Later the BIS was closely associated with post-war European monetary institutions, especially the Intra-European Payments Agreement of 1948 to 1950 and its successors, the European Payments Union and the European Monetary Agreement, which it manages. [4]

Bank Interest, paid and charged automatically by the joint-stock banks on money deposited with or borrowed from them. Until the early 1970's two per cent less than Base rate was normally paid on deposit accounts; 1 per cent more than Bank rate was normally charged on overdraft borrowing. But the encouragement of competition in banking led to a situation in which interest on overdrafts has varied from one to about five per cent depending on customers' creditworthiness. [8]

Bank Loan. *See* BANK ADVANCES.

Bank-note, paper currency carrying the promise of a bank to pay a stated sum of money to the bearer on demand. The issue of bank-notes is strictly regulated by law; in England only the Bank of England may issue notes; Scottish banks may issue notes if backed by holdings of Bank of England notes. Such notes are usually legal tender.

In Britain the note issue is regulated by the Currency and Bank Notes Act of 1954, which authorizes the Bank of England to issue a stated amount of notes against securities held, called the fiduciary issue ("fiduciary" from "faith," that is, money not backed by gold).

Up to 1914 the currency principle, enshrined in the Bank Charter Act of 1844, was widely accepted. It argued that, since gold was the ultimate source of cash and the volume of bank deposits depended on the supply of cash, the supply of notes should be tied strictly to the supply of gold.

After 1939 the gold reserve played no part in determining the size of the note issue, in time almost entirely fiduciary and regulated by the Treasury and Parliament according to the "need" for notes. British bank-notes are thus not convertible into gold (coin). The printing of bank-notes has been expanded by successive British governments to finance public expenditure, and underpinned the accelerating inflation from 1969. [8]

Bank of England, the central bank of Britain. Established as a joint-stock company by Act of Parliament in 1694 primarily to deal with the Government debt created by Charles II. A group of individuals subscribed £1,200,000 at 8 per cent to fund the debt; in return they were given a charter of incorporation with the right to receive deposits and lend at interest. In 1709 the Bank received the monopoly of corporate bank-note issue within a sixty-five mile radius of London. The Bank Charter Act of 1844 gave it a virtual monopoly of note issue. In 1946 it was nationalized and its capital acquired by the state. It is now governed by a Governor, a Deputy Governor and sixteen directors (of whom four are full time).

Under the 1844 Act the Bank was divided into two departments, the Issue Department to hold the gold reserve and be responsible for the note issue, and the Banking Department to conduct general banking business. The division is now of little practical importance.

Each week the Bank issues a balance sheet (*see* Table 2) called the Weekly Return, which shows in summary its functions, operations and responsibilities.

The balance sheet of the Issue Department shows the issued note liabilities of the Bank and their countervailing assets or "backing." Gold coin and bullion, once assets of importance, are now trivial. Almost the whole of the note issue is now "fiduciary," backed by government securities. (This large holding of government securities is important for the Bank's management of the National Debt and monetary policy.) The asset item "government debt" has been unchanged since 1833; it is merely a book entry.

On the liabilities side the Banking Department accounts show "capital," now held by the Treasury and unchanged since 1833, and "rest" (reserves and retained profits). These items are of no economic significance.

The item "public deposits" represents sums standing to the credit of government departments, including the Exchequer, National Debt Commissioners, the Post Office Savings Bank, etc.

"Bankers' deposits" refer to the joint-stock banks' credit balances at the Bank, and are regarded by them as part of their cash reserves. Since the joint-stock banks regulate their lending policy by reference to the size of their cash reserves, the Bank of England can control the supply of money by manipulating these bankers' deposits, and changes in this item therefore provide an indication of changes in monetary policy. "Other accounts" are the balance of accounts of ordinary customers (a few private individuals and companies, plus other governments and foreign and Commonwealth banks); this item remains fairly constant and has no monetary significance.

On the assets side, the main item again is "government securities," consisting of Treasury bills and other securities. The size and composition of this item may be changed at any time on the initiative of the Bank by purchases and sales in the discount market and stock exchange ("open market operations").

Table 2. Bank of England Weekly Return (illustrative figures in round numbers)

Issue Department			
	£ million		£ million
Notes issued:		Government debt	20
In circulation	4,000	Other Government securities	4,075
In Banking Department	100	Other securities	2
		Coin other than gold coin	2
		Fiduciary issue	4,099
		Gold coin and bullion	1
	4,100		4,100
Banking Department			
	£ million		£ million
Capital	15	Government securities	240
Rest (undistributed profits)	3	Discounts and advances	40
Public deposits	12	Other securities	20
Bankers' deposits	250	Notes	50
Other accounts	70	Coin	1
	350		350

"Discounts and advances" may be of three kinds—bills discounted for the Bank's customers, advances made by the Bank to its customers and advances made to discount houses in its capacity as "lender of last resort."

"Other securities" consist of non-government securities bought by the Bank on its own initiative.

"Notes" represent merely a cross-entry from the Issue Department, "coin" represents silver coin held for issue to joint-stock banks as required.

These accounts reveal most of the Bank's main domestic functions. It acts not only as banker to the government but also manages the National Debt. As a bankers' bank it provides a source of notes (which it issues itself), coin (which it buys from the Royal Mint) and credit (which it provides either directly as lender of last resort to the money market or indirectly by "open market" dealings in bills and bonds. In these ways it can influence the level and the structure of interest rates and the supply of money in the economy.

The Bank also conducts transactions between Britain and the rest of the world. It manages the Exchange Equalization Account, administers Foreign Exchange Control, maintains relations with foreign and sterling area central banks and monetary authorities, and participates in the work of international financial institutions—the International Monetary Fund, Bank for International Settlements and others. [8]

Bank of Issue. *See* BANK OF ENGLAND.

Bank Overdraft. *See* BANK ADVANCES.

Bank Rate, the rate of interest at which the Bank of England will lend to the banking system. In practice it is the minimum rate at which the Bank of England stands ready as "lender of the last resort" to provide cash to a discount house with access to the discount office of the Bank, either by rediscounting first-class ("eligible") bills or by lending against their security or against short-dated government bonds.

Bank rate is announced every Thursday morning by the Court of Directors of the Bank of England.

Short-term interest rates are geared to Bank rate through the banking system; they rarely move far below Bank rate and tend to move in step with it. Long-term interest rates, though not directly geared to Bank rate in the same way, also tend with modifications and time lags to move in the same direction. The extent of this sympathetic movement of long-term rates depends on expectations about possible future changes in Bank rate and on the ability of lenders and borrowers to switch between long-term and short-term markets.

When the monetary authorities are trying to make Bank rate effective, it becomes the key interest rate in the economy, influencing all other rates in some degree.

The use of Bank rate as an instrument of monetary policy is usually intended to have two main effects. One effect is on the rate of investment and capital expenditure. If borrowing is made more expensive by raising Bank rate it is argued that business men will be deterred from spending, and that the level of activity in the economy can thus be reduced. There is some controversy among economists over the effects of such a policy, some arguing that small changes in interest rates have little effect and others that changes are more effective than business men admit and that high taxation and other causes have made them less effective than they could be. The second effect is on the attraction of short-term funds from overseas lenders: if short-term interest rates are higher in Britain than in other countries, overseas lenders will transfer funds to Britain. Such a result may be temporarily advantageous in the event of a balance of payments deficit.

The monetary authorities make Bank rate "effective" by the use of open market operations, the effect of which is to change the supply of money by changing the volume of deposits in the joint-stock banks. If the monetary authorities are to make a high Bank rate effective they will sell securities, thus reducing deposits and causing the joint-stock banks (if they are to maintain their proportion of cash reserves to deposits) to call in loans from the discount market. The discount houses, if they are unable to borrow the short-term funds from elsewhere, are therefore forced to apply to the Bank of England for assistance, which the bank, as "lender of the last resort," is always ready to give. By charging a *penal* rate above the market rate, and thereby increasing the rate at which the houses borrow, the Bank of England forces the discount houses to put up the rate of interest for money which they lend (i.e. they increase the rate of discount by reducing the price they tender for Treasury bills offered for sale) in order to retain their profit margin. In this way, by keeping money short, the authorities can make high Bank rate effective.

For nearly twenty years, from 1932 to the end of 1951, Bank rate was kept down at 2 per cent in order, by making money "cheap," to stimulate borrowing and economic activity generally after the great depression of the early 1930's. But by being kept down during the war and after it, when economic activity was high and the economy fully employed, the Bank rate and "cheap money" became inflationary. The use of monetary policy was restored in 1951; in the following years Bank rate was raised and lowered frequently; its highest point in the 1950's was 7 per cent in 1957. During the 1960's and into the 1970's it rose with inflation until it reached unprecedented double figures. But it seemed to have almost lost its power as a deflationary device, since expectations of continuing inflation made industrial and private borrowers willing to pay very high interest for loans for investment and private consumption. [8]

Bankers' Clearings. *See* BANKS, CLEARING.

Bankers' Deposits. *See* BANK OF ENGLAND; DEPOSITS (BANK).

Banking, the business of holding deposits and lending money. The organization and functions of modern banking depend on credit: the system of credit is possible largely because of the development of the banking system.

A banker may be regarded as one who deals in debts—his own and other people's. A bank's "debts" (that is, money deposited with it which forms its liabilities) are generally acceptable to the public in payment of people's debts; e.g. by buying securities with his deposit liabilities, the banker is exchanging his I.O.U.s, which have the characteristics of money, for other instruments of debt which do not. He is "creating" money.

The British banking system may be divided into three main parts, of which the first two represent the mechanism through which credit is created and the financial system controlled:

(1) The Bank of England.
(2) The joint-stock (or "commercial") banks.
(3) Savings banks and other banking institutions.

Banking in Britain originated in the lending of money by wealthy individuals to merchants who wished to borrow; but it was not until the seventeenth century that some form of deposit banking grew with the custom of depositing money for safe keeping with goldsmiths. The goldsmiths discovered that only a small proportion of the money (usually gold) was required to meet current withdrawals and demands, and so developed the profitable practice of lending at interest the surplus that experience showed was not required. Other individuals then entered this profitable trade, and there grew up the practice of issuing notes payable to the bearer on demand. The foundation of the Bank of England in 1694 began the development of the banking system proper, but progress was slow and many private banks failed. There were two opposed schools of thought at the beginning of the nineteenth century—the banking school, which held that the issue of notes could be left to the bankers who would limit the issue to meet the needs of business and trade, and the currency school, which argued that bank-notes were merely convenient substitutes for metallic money and not instruments of credit and that issues should be limited to the amount of gold backing. The Bank Charter Act of 1844 was a victory for the currency school: it restricted the note issue to the Bank of England and a few existing issue banks, in order to ensure that it was convertible into gold. Subsequent changes of legislation have removed the requirement of gold backing for the currency. The Bank of England was nationalized in 1946; it is now legally the agent of the government but retains substantial authority of advice and action.

The fundamental importance of the joint-stock banks is that they provide a mechanism by which transactions can be carried out without the need to pay in coin or notes. In so doing the banks "create" money. There are two main sources of money in circulation in Britain: bank deposits (including deposits at the Bank of England), a smaller amount of Bank of England notes in circulation, and a much smaller amount of coin.

Bank money has accounted for about four-fifths of the total supply of money. Bank deposits are liabilities of the banks, which are balanced by the corresponding assets of cash, security or loan. If an individual wishes to borrow from the bank, he offers it an asset (e.g. a security, such as a life assurance policy, share certificates, the deeds of a house, or often merely a promise or guarantee that he will be able to pay interest and repay the principal); the bank creates an account for the borrower, that is, it offers in return a book debt in the form of a bank deposit. Thus in return for his asset the individual obtains purchasing power or *money,* which was not previously available to him; and the operation therefore adds to the total supply of money. In the words of the banking maxim, "Every loan creates a deposit." Similarly the acquisition of an asset by the bank creates a deposit. The principal assets of a joint-stock bank are loans and overdrafts (or "advances"), bills discounted, investments (or securities) and cash. Thus a bank's purchase of securities, which are paid for by crediting an account for the seller (either in the bank making the purchase or in another bank), will also create a deposit. Whatever the method of creation, the bank exchanges *claims* with the individual: the individual acquires a claim against the bank in the form of a deposit; and the bank acquires a claim against the individual in the form of a security or a promise to pay. The significance of the transaction is that the claim acquired by the individual is money.

The basis of these banking operations is confidence by the general public that the money created will be accepted in payment of debts. In the past in Britain (and more recently in some other countries) there have been occasions when banks have been unable to pay in full all depositors wishing to exchange deposits for cash, and there have been "runs on the banks." To avoid such loss of confidence, the banker holds sufficient reserves of cash and assets which can quickly be realized or turned into cash ("liquid" assets) to enable him to pay out any *likely* withdrawals by depositors. (No modern banker is ever able to pay *all* his liabilities in cash.) But since the banker earns his living from the profits made on advances and investments, there is a conflict between *profitability* and *liquidity*. In Britain the banks therefore customarily hold their assets in approximate proportions which experience has indicated; these proportions are not necessarily held at any one time, but they are the ideals which bankers achieve in the long run:

	Percentage of Total Deposits
Cash in hand and at Bank of England	8
Liquid assets (cash; loans at call and loans to the discount market; bills)	30
Advances (to firms or individuals) and investments (mostly Government bonds)	70

In Britain these ratios are adhered to by custom and experience (from time to time the banks have been allowed to lower the liquidity ratio to make more purchasing power available at holiday times, etc.); in the USA and other parts of the world minimum legal reserve ratios are enforced by law. The ratio of cash to total deposits is known as the "cash ratio," that of liquid assets to total deposits as the "liquidity ratio."

The banking system is controlled in most western countries by the central bank in cooperation with the Treasury or finance ministry. The two together, usually referred to as the monetary authorities, can use direct compulsion, persuasion and legally required reserve ratios to influence and change the monetary situation.

In recent years in Britain, special deposits and directives setting broad limits to bank lending have been used as supplementary direct controls, but the two main weapons of monetary control are:

(1) Operation of the central bank as "lender of the last resort" by variations in the Bank rate. If the central bank is always willing to lend to commercial banks, there need be no difficulties from lack of confidence; in most modern banking systems the central bank acts in this way. This assistance also provides the central bank with the opportunity of controlling the banking system; it may impose stringent conditions to dissuade the commercial banks from using central bank facilities as a substitute for prudent lending policies. Central bank lending is usually restricted to assistance of the commercial banks by the purchase of short-dated securities. In Britain commercial banks by tradition do not seek such "accommodation" direct; instead, by calling in loans to the discount market they force the discount houses to apply to the Bank of England; but the net results are the same as if the banks applied direct. Such assistance is also normally available only at rates of interest higher than market rates of interest, and penal terms further discourage recourse to the central bank. This rate of interest is called Bank rate.

(2) Open market operations. By buying or selling securities on the open market, the central bank has been able to influence interest rates and the level of commercial bank deposits, and so the supply of money. When it sells securities the deposits of the commercial banks with it are reduced, because the central bank is reducing its debt to them, and they in turn have reduced their lending to industry.

Control of the monetary situation *via* the banking system therefore depends largely on the maintenance by commercial banks of their cash ratio and liquidity ratio. If the banks wish to add to their earning assets (which are, in order of profitability, advances, investments and liquid assets), they will increase their total deposits and the cash ratio will fall. Absolute cash reserves may also fall as the public starts to demand increasing quantities of cash to finance the growing economic activity and volume of transactions following an increase in advances, etc.

Subject to the supply of cash, the banks have complete control over the volume of deposits; but if they maintain a fixed cash ratio effective control over the responsibility for the volume of deposits lies with the central bank, which can control the supply of cash. Control over the supply of cash is exercised through open market operations, that is, by the central bank controlling its liabilities—cash and deposits—by rearranging its assets.

The essence of the banking system has thus been that banks are commercial institutions dealing in *claims;* on the liabilities side of their balance sheets are claims against the banks; on the asset side are claims by the bank against the public. By control over the total and composition of these claims the banking system has controlled the total supply of money and to that extent the level of economic activity. [8]

Banking, Branch. *See* BANKS, JOINT-STOCK.

Banking School, a group engaged in the controversies on the note-issuing policies of the English banking system in the period 1825–60. The name seems to have been coined by Samuel Jones Loyd in evidence before the Committee on Banks of Issue in 1840. Prominent members of the group were Thomas Tooke, John Fullarton, James Wilson and J. W. Gilbart. They opposed the views of the currency school, which advocated the automatic regulation of the note issue. They argued that the volume of currency was not determined solely by the quantity of gold and paper notes in existence, but included bank deposits and bills of exchange. Therefore regulation was impossible, and control would produce undesirable consequences. They maintained that individual banks should be free to decide how many notes to issue, subject to the control that they should be convertible into gold on demand. In these circumstances, they argued, the total number of notes in circulation would be regulated by competition between banks, and would vary according to the state of trade and the needs of the public. The Bank Charter Act of 1844 reflected the views of the currency school. [2]

Banking, Unit. *See* BANKS, JOINT-STOCK.

Bankruptcy, one of several legal processes aimed at enabling an unfortunate but honest debtor to escape from a dead-weight of debts he could never repay and start afresh. It also punishes the dishonest debtor and divides his property among his creditors. The test of insolvency in English law is whether the debtor is unable to pay his debts when they become due; whether assets exceed liabilities is generally irrelevant. Insolvent corporate bodies are dealt with under separate legislation.

Statistics of bankruptcy and the liquidation of corporate bodies are sometimes used as a measure of business failures, but they may be misleading. The Bankruptcy Acts extend to persons who are not engaged in business on their own account; and some bankruptcies are due to private claims arising outside business activity. Bankruptcy among small firms is a means of removing inefficiency from the economy. [7]

Banks, Clearing, the commercial banks that are members of the London Bankers' Clearing House. They do most of the banking business of England and Wales. Banks present claims against one another as a result of their daily transactions; instead of settling them in currency they draw a cheque on their balances at the Bank of England; if in a day's "clearing" one of the banks owes to others, the balance is conveniently settled by cheque rather than by cash. In Britain the main economic importance of these banks is their behaviour as joint-stock banks. [8]

Banks, Industrial, comparatively recent name in Britain for firms that finance hire purchase. Members of the Industrial Bankers' Association hold at least 75 per cent of their assets in the form of hire-purchase "paper," claim to act as bankers because they receive money on deposit account from the public and use it to give credit in the form of hire-purchase finance. The security for their advances lies in their ownership of the goods named in the hire-purchase agreement. The number of such banks is large, but most are relatively small, with offices outside London. Unlike joint-stock banks proper, they did not hold deposits on demand or short notice or provide short-term credit or other banking services but used fairly long-notice deposits to supply medium-term credit that was repaid by the hire purchasers more or less regularly so that there was a constant return of funds. More recently, some have moved into other forms of personal finance and have opened "money shops" in competition with the clearing banks. [8]

Banks, Joint-stock, banks whose principal function is to receive deposits and make short-term loans, mainly for working capital. Also described as commercial banks.

Until the nineteenth century commercial banking in Britain was conducted by several hundred private banks, each with unlimited liability (that is, the partners were entirely responsible for the debts of the banks). These banks proved inadequate to finance the rapidly growing British economy. In 1826 joint-stock company banks were permitted, although the principle of limited liability was not extended to them until 1858. The functions of joint-stock banks comprise (*a*) *ordinary banking business:* the exchange of cash for bank deposits, and *vice versa;* the transfer of deposits between individuals or businesses by the cheque system; the exchange of bank deposits for securities (bills of exchange, government bonds, etc.); the advance of credit to customers, and the consequent exchange of bank deposits for promises or collateral security; (*b*) *ancillary services:* e.g. executor and trustee services, Stock Exchange transactions, custody of valuables, foreign currency transactions, income tax advice, etc. In the 1970's they tended to expand services to personal customers by more flexible forms of loans, insurance advice, etc.

The typical joint-stock bank in Britain has numerous branches throughout the country; this is "branch" banking. In the USA by contrast a system of "unit banking" predominates under which a bank comprises a single office or at most a few branches in a small area. The advantages of branch banking are principally those of large-scale operation, specialization and division of labour and the spreading of risks. The corresponding disadvantages of unit banking are to some extent overcome by the system of correspondent banks, which allow one another deposit and other banking facilities, and by the provision of many facilities by the central bank.

An important consequence of the development of the branch banking system in Britain is the small number of large banks. The most important English joint-stock banks are usually referred to as the clearing banks, since they are members of the London Clearing Bankers' Association. The "big four" banks (Barclays, Lloyds, Midland and National Westminster) have branches in most towns and their resources account for most of the total.

The Scottish banks are nominally separate from the English banking systems. There are also several Northern Ireland banks. Scottish and Northern Ireland banks have the right to issue notes, but most of the issue has to be covered by Bank of England notes. In Scotland there are proportionately considerably more branch banks than in England, and there is a traditional emphasis on the collection of small savings.

Although there are some differences in operation, for most practical purposes the Scottish banks can be considered part of the British banking system as a whole, subject to the same general conditions and control.

The balance sheet of the London clearing banks conveniently summarizes the operations of joint-stock banks.

On the liabilities side, with the exception of a relatively small amount of "capital" liabilities to shareholders (which accounts for about 3 per cent of liabilities and is omitted from the balance sheet), the main item is "deposits," which consist of debts owed to customers and which can be used as money by them. About four-sevenths are in the form of current accounts (deposits encashable on demand) and the rest deposit accounts encashable at seven days' notice. No interest is normally paid on current accounts; on deposit accounts the rate of interest is customarily 2 per cent less than Base rate.

On the assets side, a minor item (accounting for about 1 per cent of assets and omitted from the balance sheet) is "bank premises." The remaining assets may be classified in order of liquidity and reverse order of profitability, ranging from completely liquid assets (with zero earning power) to relatively illiquid assets which yield high returns.

The most liquid asset is *cash,* either in the form of notes or coin or balances with the Bank of England (shown as "bankers' deposits" in the latter's balance sheet). The cash item is conventionally held at approximately 8 per cent of total deposits, but this figure is not always a reliable guide to the total liquidity position of the banks, for if reserves fall below it they can easily be restored by recalling short-term loans. Thus the total "liquid assets" ratio (i.e. ratio of cash plus other liquid assets to total deposits) is considered the more important indicator. These remaining liquid assets, which are usually held at approximately 30 to 35 per cent of total deposits, are: (1) *money at call and short notice*, consisting mainly of day-to-day loans to the Discount Market which earn relatively low rates of interest; (2) *bills discounted*, including some commercial bills, but mainly comprising Treasury bills bought from the discount houses when partly matured.

Special deposits at the Bank of England have been employed to reduce the liquidity of banks in order to reduce their lending.

The remaining "earning assets" are: (1) *Investments* consist mainly of British government securities. British banks concentrate largely on holding bonds with less than ten years to run to maturity. Investments are therefore relatively illiquid and, as their prices may fluctuate sharply, they are also of uncertain value, although readily saleable. To minimize this possibility of capital losses through the enforced sale of longer-term bonds at times when their prices are falling, the banks aim to hold a proportion of bonds with early maturity dates. (2) *Advances* are the least liquid but most profitable of the assets. Bank advances (with some exceptions) are formally repayable on demand but in practice many are renewed repeatedly. [8]

Bargaining. (*a*) Individual: process of higgling and haggling to arrive at an agreed price between buyer and seller. More common in imperfect than in perfect markets, where there is more knowledge of prices in other parts of the market, and where products are identifiable by branding or grading. Thus more common in the market for second-hand than for new furniture, and in Eastern than in Western markets. The final price in imperfect markets after bargaining is probably not too far from the price in more perfect markets, because if it is thought that the buyer will bargain the seller begins with a price he is prepared to reduce, and vice versa for the buyer. [7]

(*b*) Collective, *See* Collective Bargaining. [5]

Barrier, price, economic or financial obstacle between would-be buyer and the commodity or service wanted. Its existence was emphasized by Beveridge in his celebrated 1942 report on the social services, and subsequently by British sociologists and social administrators, as the central difficulty of developing the welfare state. It can be removed either by providing education, medical care, etc., without price, "free" (at the time of service), or by supplementing low incomes to enable all to pay the price (out of pocket or with the help of insurance). Each method has merits and defects. Some economists have argued that providing "free" commodities or services means, for an increasing proportion of the population, indirect payment through taxes or social insurance premiums without the "consumer sovereignty" of direct payment; it also requires high taxation (with adverse effects on incentives), entails universal distribution to people who could pay directly if they did not have to pay indirectly, and narrows the choice of service and of method of financing. Sociologists and social administrators generally have argued that providing "free" services is administratively simpler, tends to create social cohesion or "parity of esteem" through equality of access, and removes the need for means tests. Some economists have replied that administrative simplicity requires a large bureaucracy, that means testing can be avoided by reverse taxing, and that removal of rationing by price entails rationing by administrative decision or judgement of social utility (e.g. in allocating scarce kidney machines to people whose lives are most worth saving), by time (waiting, queuing), by proximity (to schools, hospitals, etc.), or by political or other influence. The central economic difficulties are, first, that if resources are scarce they must be rationed somehow (if not by price then by other methods); and, second, that price is regressive, i.e. it takes a larger proportion of a lower than of a higher income. "Barriers" are therefore unavoidable, and if they are not economic (financial, price) they are political, administrative or cultural. [7]

Barter, the direct exchange of goods and services without the use of money. Barter is common in primitive societies, but may also appear in a developed money-using economy during rapid inflation (hyper-inflation), when the value of money is falling so drastically and quickly that people are unwilling to hold notes or coin. The main disadvantages of barter are that it requires a "double coincidence" of wants between the two parties (each wanting what the other offers), and that in the absence of money there is no common measure of value. If notes and coin are not available, or after the emergence of barter in inflation, there is a tendency to use a commodity as currency. For example, after World War II when the German mark had shrunken in value, coffee and cigarettes were widely used as currency. Modified barter between countries may also occur in the form of bilateral trading agreements in which there is barter of commodity for commodity or value for value. International barter arises as a modification of attempted self-sufficiency (autarky) or when the mechanism of international currency payment has been disrupted by war. [7]

Base, a value or magnitude used as a reference in comparing other values or magnitudes. Index numbers are measures not of the absolute value of items but of their values relative to a base value. If unemployed male adults numbered 1 million in an initial (base) period and 1 ½ million at a later (or earlier) date, this second fact might be expressed as 1.5, or as 150 of the base value expressed as 100. [14]

Base Period, a point or period of time from which changes in prices, output, etc. are calculated by index numbers or other methods. It must therefore be, in a sense, "normal" rather than exceptional. Even so, it may not remain relevant for long if conditions of supply or demand change. The "basket" of goods bought by the "typical" family or household may change so that it becomes irrelevant as the base for a measure of changes in an index of retail prices or the "cost of living." For example, much less is spent on bread and the cheaper cuts of meat as incomes and living standards rise, and new commodities or services—smoked salmon, manicures, slimming treatment—may enter into the expenditure of the "typical" family or household. [14]

Base Rate, the basic rate of interest for joint stock bank lending, to which a second rate is added according to market conditions, the price of money and the creditworthiness of the borrower. Rates paid by borrowers on overdrafts thus amount to the base rate plus a varying percentage. [8]

Basing-point, a point in space from which distance to the buyer is measured for the calculation of transport costs, which are then added to the basic price to yield the final price. A celebrated example is "Pittsburgh-plus" for steel, in which the price in Pittsburgh was supplemented by the cost of transport from the basing-point to the buyer. Pittsburgh could be, but was not necessarily, the point from which the steel was despatched (it might have gone from Chicago or any other place with steel mills). The system has also been used for chemicals. It has been applied where transport costs are a high proportion of the price to the buyer. More than one basing-point could be used. The advantage was fixed, known and stable prices, which could be valuable to suppliers with heavy fixed charges for capital equipment, and possibly to buyers. The main disadvantage was the suppression of price competition, which could tend to discourage innovation and newcomers. The system was favoured by suppliers because new customers could be supplied without prices to old customers being reduced, and this semi-monopolistic-discriminating price system could be maintained because economies of scale made the industry one of large plants, few in number, which rendered competition in any event difficult or costly. [7]

Bastable. *See* TAXATION.

Bastiat, Frederic (1801–50), a French writer on economics. He was orphaned at an early age and soon afterwards contracted tuberculosis. He studied at a university and tried business and agriculture, but failed at all three. Failure and idleness turned his thoughts to economics, where he used ridicule with devastating effect. He was an ardent free trader and rose to prominence with his article, *De l'influence des tarifs français et anglais sur l'avenir des deux peuples* (1844), which was followed by other *Sophismes économiques.* In 1848 he was elected to the National Assembly, but poor health caused him to retire to Pisa, where he died. His satire was popular with the liberals of his time, and some is worthy reading in our day, though his work had little fundamental effect on economic thought. [2]

Bauer, Peter Thomas (1915–2002), Professor of Economics, with special reference to economic development and under-developed countries, in the University of London (London School of Economics) since 1960. He was born in Hungary and educated in Budapest and at Gonville and Caius College, Cambridge, where he afterwards taught. He is a specialist in development economics: he argues from analysis and example that private entrepreneurship by traders and farmers in developed and developing countries is likely to yield more growth in living standards than inter-government aid. He therefore advocates free trade, international investment and a minimum of interference with the operation of market forces. He is particularly critical of planners who rely too explicitly upon the capital/output ratio, arguing that while the accumulation of capital may be a condition (indeed a result) of economic progress, the creation of capital resources, particularly if they are out of step with the growth of management capacity, can itself do very little for economic development. His publications include *The Economics of Under-developed Countries* (1957, with B. S. Yamey), *Economic Analysis and Policy in Under-developed Countries* (1958), *Indian Economic Policy and Development* (joint, 1961), and *Dissent on Development* (1972). [2]

Baumol, William Jack (1922–), American academic economist with a Ph.D. from the London School of Economics (1949); Professor of Economics at Princeton University since 1954. His main work has been in the development of cost-benefit analysis. Publications include *Business Behaviour, Value and Growth* (1959), *Welfare Economics and the Theory of the State* (1952) and (with William G. Brown) *Performing Arts: the Economic Dilemma* (1966). [2]

Bear, a stock exchange speculator who expects the price of securities to fall and accordingly sells securities in the hope that he may close the deal by buying them at a lower price. If the bear does not possess the securities he sells, he is said to have "sold short"; if he does, he is known as a "protected" or "covered" bear.

By operating within the Stock Exchange Account (i.e. closing the deal before payment is due on "settling day"), a bear can make a profit without paying for the securities. [8]

Bearer securities, those of which the ownership may pass from one owner to another merely by handing over the securities themselves. They usually have dated interest coupons which are detached and presented for payment. [8]

Becker, Gary Stanley (1930–), American economist, senior research staff member at the National Bureau of Economic Research after 1957, and later Professor of Economics at the University of Chicago. His main research interests have been in human capital and the valuation of time. He has written *Economics of Discrimination* (1957) and *Human Capital* (1964). "A Theory of the Allocation of Time" in *The Economic Journal* of September 1965 challenged conventional assumptions about the valuation of productive and leisure time. Becker argued that households are producers as well as consumers, producing commodities by combining inputs of goods and time according to the cost-minimization rules of the traditional theory of the firm. The theory led to new interpretations of empirical data, e.g. a new approach to changes in hours of work and "leisure," integration of the idea of "productive" consumption into economic theory, and analyses of the effect of income on the quantity and quality of commodities consumed. Becker is also a pioneer in extending economics to non-money-using markets, as in the economic theory of marriage. [2]

Beeching, the name of a British industrialist (and Chairman of the British Railways Board), and now a general term for pruning of uneconomic dead wood. The Beeching Report of 1963 strongly recommended the closure of uneconomic rail services and concentration on those in which rail could carry passengers or freight more cheaply than by road, sea or air. (One third of rail mileage was carrying 1 per cent of traffic, 50 per cent of the stations were used by less than 5 per cent of the traffic.) The Report was generally accepted as valid, though in 1968 government grants were arranged to enable British Rail to continue "socially necessary" branch lines, etc. Differences about accounting methods of measuring uncompetitive rail services and political pressures from railway unions and their political supporters prevented the fuller implementation of the Report. In general the railways were probably run down more slowly than envisaged. Increasing road congestion was also cited by the supporters or defenders of the railways. On a small scale, uneconomic branch lines were bought and run profitably by private companies. [10]

Beggar-my-neighbour, name given to remedies for unemployment by reducing imports at the expense of other countries, e.g. by higher tariffs or currency depreciation. The argument was that the consequent fall in imports raised the demand for home-produced output and therefore employment and incomes. The method might be serviceable in emergency if accepted as such by other countries whose trade would thus be damaged unilaterally. Apart from retaliation by them, in the long run reduced imports might tend to reduce demand for exports, visible or invisible, and provoke economic nationalism. [10]

Behaviourism, the study of the economic activity of individual units—consumers, families, firms, politicians, public officials, government departments—

and their motives. Traditionally economists have supposed that individuals and families maximize utility, and that firms maximize profit, but behaviourist studies have suggested other hypotheses. Bureaucracies (government or private) have been analysed as economic entities, and one hypothesis is that their maximand is the budget at their disposal. Economists have also described the effects on behaviour of uncertainty and expectations (ex-ante investment describes what people intend, ex-post what occurs) and the high cost of acquiring information. Others have re-examined the firm on the hypothesis that it maximizes not profit but sales, or capital size, or some other indicator of power for the operators (directors, executives, employees) rather than the owner-shareholders.

The classical theory of profit-maximization remains the most serviceable working hypothesis. It would be even more valid if shareholders regained authority over their directors and other employees. The activities of individual businessmen may also be analysed as a search not for maximum monetary reward (especially where taxation is high) but for fame, satisfaction of vanity, power, influence, reputation for public service or charitableness, etc. But again the monetary element is a serviceable general hypothesis even where it has to be qualified or refined in individual cases. [14]

Behaviourist Economic Laws. *See* Law, Economic.

Below-the-Line. *See* Above-the-Line; Budget.

Benefit-cost analysis. *See* Cost-benefit Analysis.

Benefit-cost ratio, a measure of relative desirability used in the evaluation and comparison of alternative investment schemes. The B.-C. ratio for a project is simply the ratio between the sum of the expected benefits and its costs. Four varieties of B.-C. ratio are used. The *undiscounted B.-C. ratio* measures benefits and costs at their face value, ignoring the question of *when* they occur. The *discounted B.-C. ratio* adjusts the values of benefits and costs to allow for their timing, on the principle that the value today of a sum due next year is higher than that of an identical sum due the year after next. The longer the benefit flow expected from an investment, the more it is therefore necessary to use the discounted version of the B.-C. ratio, if distortion of choice is to be avoided. Further, both versions have what may be termed a *"gross"* and a *"net"* form. In the gross version benefits are calculated without allowing for depreciation of the capital assets providing the flow of benefits, and the sum of benefits is divided by the cost of the project or investment. In the net version depreciation is deducted in calculating benefits. [1]

Benefit Theory, embodies the precept that taxes are prices paid for government services or benefits. In Britain local taxes (rates) are levied on the size of homes (or "hereditaments") as a rough measure of the use made of some local government services—street lighting, fire-fighting, refuse collection, police protection, etc. The principle is more difficult to apply where services are "public goods" provided for groups from which it is difficult to exclude any individual, so that all must pay for it by compulsory levy or taxes, or some would leave payment to others (or to none)—defence, a system of law and (more arguably) arbitration. Toll charges, licences for dogs, broadcasting, fishing, etc. can be regarded as prices for government services rather than taxes. Some economists have argued in favour of direct charging for education, medical care, water, fire-fighting, refuse collection, seaside facilities, libraries, museums and art galleries, etc. as a means to encourage care in use and economy. Others—mainly in the USA—have argued that direct charging for private, competing services in legal arbitration, police protection, etc. are feasible and desirable for similar reasons: to reduce political and bureaucratic influences and to raise standards by creating choice between competing services. [12]

Benelux, initially a form of customs union between Belgium-Luxemburg (whose economic union had been virtually completed before World War II) and the Netherlands. First proposed in London in 1944 during the wartime exile of these governments and established in 1948. The Convention of 1944 aimed at free trade between the three countries and a common tariff policy towards the rest of the world (excluding Dutch and Belgian territories overseas). It was envisaged as a first step towards the final objective of full economic union, with common fiscal, monetary and exchange policies.

Tariffs between the members were abolished in 1948 and a common external tariff adopted, although internal Benelux trade remained hampered by the far more important quantitative import restrictions then in force. Many of them were in turn abandoned or reduced in 1949 and subsequent trade between the members expanded. The economies of Belgium-Luxemburg and the Netherlands are largely, though not wholly, complementary, and the treatment to be accorded to competitive products there presented numerous difficulties, which were largely met by agreements restricting some exports.

Although many of the wider problems of full economic union, e.g. fiscal and social questions, the harmonization of agricultural policies and others, await complete settlement, continuous progress towards full economic union has been made. A final treaty of economic union was promulgated in 1958 and ratified in 1960. Benelux has, in effect, provided a pilot scheme and object lesson for the wider European Economic Community of which the Benelux countries became members under the founding Treaty of Rome, 1958. [4]

Bentham, Jeremy (1748–1832), English philosopher, social reformer and economist; educated at Westminster School and Queen's College, Oxford. He was primarily a philosopher in the tradition of the eighteenth century, and translated its system of thought into a comprehensive programme of social reform that had much influence on legislation. *Defence of Usury* (1787), his first essay on economics, was an extremely logical application of Adam Smith's principles. His later economic works included *Principles and Morals of Legislation* (1823) and *Manual of Political Economy* (1825). All follow the principle of laissez-faire, for which Bentham envisaged a structure of institutions in which otherwise free action would create the good society; he envisaged a cabinet with ministers for preventive services (police, fire, etc.), interior communications, indigence relief, education, health, trade and finance, etc. Bentham's utilitarian calculus of pleasure and pain had much influence on economists of succeeding generations. [2]

Bernstein, Edward (1929–), American economist. He worked for the US Treasury (1940–46), where he produced the plan for international finance which became the framework of the Bretton Woods agreement. His plan was similar to Keynes's scheme in aiming to eliminate exchange controls and restrictive financial practices, with fixed rules for changes in rates of exchange; but it differed in setting definite limits to the obligation of creditor nations to provide funds for the relief of debtor nations. He also provided for an international bank, an idea which blossomed into the World Bank (Bank for International Construction). [2]

"Best Buys." *See* Consumer Education.

"Best Fit." *See* Regression Analysis.

Betterment, a windfall increase in the value of land and buildings arising from the actions of public authorities in carrying out public works or improvements or in imposing restrictions on the use of land elsewhere. For example, street improvements may confer additional value on adjoining or nearby property: zoning ordinances may improve the amenity of a residential area and thus increase values. The term is also sometimes used to describe a charge levied on an owner of property who has benefited from such an increase in value.

From time to time attempts have been made to recover betterment from the owners of property (i) by *direct assessments,* (ii) by *set-off* of betterment against compensation payable for adjacent land owned by them, or (iii) by *recoupment*—the purchase and resale by a public authority of land adjoining a public improvement and likely to be increased in value by it.

Any systematic attempt to recover betterment faces two major difficulties: first, betterment may accrue to others than property owners; secondly, identifying and isolating betterment due to one specific cause from improvements in value due to general influences is difficult. The urge to recover betterment arises in, first, the feeling that publicly created value is an unearned increment and should properly be taxed, and, secondly, the feeling that as long as land planning involves the payment of compensation for the reduction of private values by public actions in other directions, the recovery of betterment ought to help balance the books. Apart from the "hit-and-miss" nature of betterment levies, the second argument is suspect because a better use of land is not likely if the economic cost of planning decisions is disguised. For if all improvement value in land were to go to the state, compensation could be confined to the value of land in its use at a given date; and the incentive to economize in the use of scarce land resources might be impaired. [6]

Beveridge, William Henry (1879–1963), English economist, educationalist and public servant. Knighted in 1919; raised to the peerage in 1946. His main influence on economic thought was in the labour market and social insurance. His writings led to the establishment of employment exchanges by Winston Churchill in 1909, and his report *Social Insurance and Allied Services* in 1942 led to the enlargement of state welfare services to cover the whole population. He was also a member of the Royal Commission on the Coal Industry (1925), chairman of the Unemployment Insurance Statutory Committee (1934–44), chairman of a subcommittee of the Committee of Imperial Defence on Food Rationing (1936) and chairman of the Broadcasting Committee (1949–50). He was the Director of the London School of Economics (1932–7), Liberal Member of Parliament (1944–5) and Master of University College, Oxford (1937–45). His main publications were *Unemployment—a Problem of Industry* (1909), *Full Employment in a Free Society* (1944), *Voluntary Action* (1948). Towards the end of his life he had apprehensions about the effects of comprehensive social insurance on the scope for voluntary provision and about the effects of inflation on the value of social benefits. [2]

Bias, (*a*) technical, inherent tendency to overstate or understate, e.g. in a forecast because of excessive or inadequate emphasis on one or several elements. Experience should reduce a technical bias, but the difficulty of judging new elements may prolong it. It has been argued that short-period forecasting by the British Treasury tends to be technically biased by overcaution or other subjective influences. Bias may be unavoidable in so far as judgement is involved in interpreting statistics and indicators, yielding overshooting or undershooting of targets and objectives, as in "stop-go."

(*b*) philosophic, value judgements imported into economic analysis or its applications. Economists differ on whether economics is, or can be, free of value judgements (*wertfrei*). Behavioural (or positive) economics analyses "what *is*," normative economics "what *should* be." Since economists are closely concerned with public affairs they are likely to form views and preferences. It is probably best for value judgements to be stated (otherwise they tend to remain hidden); the reader is then forewarned, and there is less danger of mistaking opinion for analysis. Economists can be more easily independent than purely objective. An economist once said, "The man who says he is impartial is a prig." Since most important biases are unconscious, any attempt at self-eradication is foredoomed: the best protection against bias, according to Sir Karl Popper, is adequate publicity and competition, which at least will help bring biases into the open. [14]

Big Business, colloquialism for large-scale industry, or merely "large" firms, with little distinction between those that rest on economies of scale and others that are created by political privileges, such as tariffs, subsidies, discriminating taxation, or by limited liability. [3]

Big Four Banks, the largest of the clearing banks in England: Barclays, Lloyds, Midland, National Westminster. [8]

Bilateral Monopoly, a market situation in which a dominant supplier is confronted by a dominant buyer. An example is a government department, a nationalized industry, or a public corporation faced by a sole supplier of equipment. Since there is no free competitive market the price would be indeterminate within a range set at the lower limit by the profitability of the seller's resources in other industries and at the upper limit by the ability of the buyer to produce more cheaply by organizing production itself. [7]

Bilateralism, exchange of goods and services between two countries. The economic effects are similar to those of barter between persons: international division of labour is restricted and total world output made smaller than it would have been in a system of multilateral exchange.

The increase in bilateralism in world trade dates largely from the world depression of the early 1930's and the efforts of individual countries to insulate themselves from outside events. It was extended by wartime controls which disrupted the channels of international trade. Its growth was further encouraged after World War II by state trading, international commodity control schemes, and by the fear of economic instability which subordinated international trade to national full employment. It has receded with the increasing efforts to remove the barriers to international trade such as those under the General Agreement on Tariffs and Trade. [4]

Bill Broker. *See* DISCOUNT HOUSE.

Bill of Exchange, a transferable order, drawn by a creditor on a debtor, payable on a stated date; an IOU; a form of near-money that is easily changed into cash, at a discount or small reduction off its full value. (In law "an unconditional order in writing, addressed by one person to another, signed by the person giving it, requiring the person to whom it is addressed to pay on demand or at a fixed or determinable future time a certain sum in money to or to the order of a specified person or bearer.") The bill may be "accepted" by the person to whom it is addressed by signing his name across its face; if the acceptor's (or debtor's) name is good enough, the person drawing the bill (the creditor) may be able to exchange the bill for cash.

A first-class bill, which will receive most favourable discount terms (become "eligible paper") and be readily exchangeable, requires a second signature or acceptance of high standing. Such bills are accepted by banks, others by accepting houses or merchant banks who specialize in this kind of transaction. (They account for about a quarter of all bills outstanding.) Once a bill has been accepted it may be discounted in the London discount market.

A bill may change ownership several times during its currency (usually three to six months) and is thus a convenient financial instrument, but commercial bills accepted by London banks are not usually discounted before maturity.

Commercial bills of exchange are used mainly as a device for financing goods in transit and transactions that may take some time to complete. Most bills are drawn in connection with overseas trade (mainly in the commodity markets); some relate to trade conducted outside Britain; there is also some financing of internal trade, mainly in trade connected with imports, but also through hire purchase finance companies. During the twentieth century the inland bill of exchange has declined in importance, and most of the short-term business of the discount market is now in Treasury bills. [8]

Bill of Lading, a document in which a shipper acknowledges receipt of a consignment of goods and undertakes to deliver them to the consignee at the port of destination. It is widely used by exporters as evidence of the value of goods in transit, and therefore as security for borrowing until payment for them is received. [4]

Bill of Sale, a document which evidences the sale (or mortgage) of personal "chattels" but which does not transfer possession from the assignor to the purchaser (or mortgagee). A bill of sale is normally used as security for a loan. If the interest due is not paid, or the loan not repaid, the creditor may at law seize and sell the goods. [7]

Bimetallism, a system of currency under which the monetary unit is defined by law in terms of two metals (usually gold and silver) in a specific ratio. Each metal is accepted in unlimited quantity for coinage, and each coinage is legal tender. The main difficulty of the system is that of maintaining the ratio between the metals in the face of fluctuations in their market price; another is that the undervalued metal would tend to drive the other out of circulation. The system was used in America and on the continent of Europe in the nineteenth century largely because it was thought that dependence on only one metal risked deflation if its supply did not keep pace with growing economic activity. It tended to break down when the values of the two metals in world markets differed because the metal with higher value tended to be exported, leaving the metal with the lower value. When metal was replaced by paper currencies in the twentieth century the need or argument for bimetallism became weak. [8]

Black Market, a free market that forms spontaneously when forbidden by law. When the maximum price of a commodity, a service or a factor of production is fixed by administrative decree, and buying or selling above the fixed price is outlawed, there will usually be economic pressures that induce people to break the law.

Such a decree on prices is frequently used with rationing in wartime, that is, with the allocation of supplies according to coupons and not money. If the law is broken, the transactions at the illegally high prices form the black market. The economic pressure tending to create a black market comes into being because the price at which supply and demand would be in equilibrium in a free market tends to be above the legal maximum. Therefore if demand exceeds supply at the (low) fixed price, it cannot be wholly satisfied and supplies are allocated either by some form of rationing or on a "first come, first served" principle or by preferences for known or influential customers. Frustrated buyers thus tend to offer higher prices to obtain supplies in spite of the law. The economic pressure to create a black market may be contained by a sense of common purpose that restrains people from buying and selling at market prices or by strong administrative controls and heavy penalties. The former was effective to some extent in Britain during the Second World War (but much less after it); the second method is used in state-directed economies such as Russia, China, Poland and others where black (free) markets persist on a large scale in spite of them. [7]

Blanket Mortgage, a mortgage covering several properties or sites. To secure finance for a comprehensive development a developer may mortgage it as a whole and arrange to free each property from the "blanket" mortgage as it is sold by a "release schedule" clause inserted in the mortgage which specifies a release price for each property. By this means the marketing of properties is facilitated and transaction costs of terminating and renegotiating mortgages are minimized. The practice is more widespread in North America than in Britain. [6]

Blocked Balances. *See* Sterling Balances.

Blue Book, colloquialism for the annual *National Income and Expenditure* prepared by the Central Statistical Office following the closer attention paid to macro-economic statistics in wartime government. The best known statistics, Gross National Product ("GNP"), and associated aggregates have been criticized as misleading indicators of wealth unless used with awareness of the micro-economic elements of which they are composed, and also because they largely ignore the environmental and social costs of producing the GNP. [14]

"Blue Chip," colloquialism for the safest of equity shares, i.e. the least risky of risky investments. The largest and best known companies are considered to have blue chip equities. [8]

Blue Collar, colloquialism for wage-earners, as distinct from white collar salary-earners. [5]

Böhm-Bawerk, Eugen von (1851–1914), Austrian statesman and economist. He studied law at the University of Vienna and became a member of the Austrian government, where in fifteen years he was Minister of Finance three times. In 1904 he was appointed Professor of Economics at Vienna, and soon came to be one of the best known representatives of the "Austrian School." Böhm-Bawerk's main contribution to economics lies in his theory of capital. In *Capital and Interest* (1884) he criticized earlier theories of interest, and in his *Positive Theory of Capital* (1889) he applied the theory of marginal utility more closely to the theory of interest, using the Anglo-German productivity and wages fund theories. The resultant concept of "time preference" had considerable influence on economic thought. [2]

Bolton Report, on small firms, published in 1971. It found that small firms were falling in number, were playing a smaller part in the economy, and were less important than in other industrial countries. Among the reasons given were economies of large-scale marketing technique and financing, improved transport which enabled large firms to penetrate further into local markets, and the growing role of government financed by rising taxation. The Report recommended government provision of better statistics for small firms and general governmental benevolence but not (yet) special treatment. It thought small firms important as origins of new industries and competition. Of central interest for the economist is whether the decline of the small firm is explained by the superiority of the larger firm or by unintended, arbitrary discrimination against it because of administrative convenience in government town planning (siting of shops, small factories, etc.), or other causes not connected with the relative efficiency of small and large firms. [3]

Bond, a certificate issued by a government, municipality or company as a promise to repay money borrowed over a generally long period. It is a security on which interest is paid at a fixed rate and is repaid when due ("maturity") at face value. A wide variety of bonds is possible: e.g. they may be secured or unsecured, maturity dates may be near or distant and so on. Bonds with less than five years to run are often termed short or short-dated. Bonds may also be undated and irredeemable. [8]

Bonded Warehouse, depot for storing imported goods that are liable to pay duty but on which it has not (yet) been paid. If the goods are intended for use or sale in the country, the duty is paid when the goods are "taken out of bond"; if they are re-exported the duty is not paid. [4]

Bonus Shares, shares which are issued by a limited company without any charge to the existing shareholders with the object of putting reserves into capital when the issued capital of the company differs markedly from the capital employed (i.e. the amount subscribed by the shareholders, plus undistributed profits and reserves). They are also known as "capitalization issues" (*see also* Rights Issue and Scrip, which are virtually synonymous). It was common for this differentiation to be made between issued and employed capital after the Second World War, when profits were often retained and "ploughed back." Bonus shares are issued to existing shareholders using undistributed profits and reserves. Thus the dividend would be stated as 18 per cent of the issued capital if the profit recommended for dividend in any year represented 6 per cent of the capital employed by a company as shown in the following example:

	£	£
Issued Capital		200,000
Capital Reserve	250,000	
Revenue Reserve	125,000	
Profit and Loss Account	25,000	400,000
Total capital employed		600,000

This misleading position was removed when bonus shares brought nominal capital more into line with the market value of the net assets as reflected by the current market price of the shares. [8]

Book value, the original market or buying price of company assets, adjusted only for "wear and tear" but not for changes in their market price to indicate the cost of replacing them. Much of British industry was slow to pass from "book value" to "replacement value" in its accounts, so that profits did not accurately show the earnings on the capital. More generally the acceleration of inflation in the early 1970's was only very slowly reflected in accounting practice. [8]

Boom, a peak in fluctuations in economic activity, when the economy is employed at full stretch; also an expansion of business activity. The general level of economic activity, employment and income has a tendency to fluctuate; during the nineteenth century and until the outbreak of the Second World War major fluctuations of this kind tended to occur with some regularity. The fairly regular pattern of alternations of "boom" and "slump" was called the trade cycle. The main characteristics of the trade cycle were that both expansions and contractions of employment were cumulative; but the upward movement eventually lost momentum (at or near the top of the "boom"), for psychological, monetary or political reasons, and the downward movement similarly tended to slow down; after a time the "slump" ended and activity began to grow again.

The term is also used more narrowly for peak periods of activity in security exchanges (e.g. Stock Exchange boom). These frequently coincide with and reflect fluctuations in employment and general economic activity, and the ending of such booms in crises has frequently coincided with the onset of a depression. The Wall Street crash of 1929 is a good example of a security boom ending in a crisis, but there were several lesser booms in the London Stock Exchange in the 1950's and 1960's, usually connected with general feelings of optimism in the security markets about the expected course of economic activity. Since World War II the trade cycle has become shorter and milder, so that booms are more frequent and less pronounced relatively to slumps (renamed recessions). [9]

Bosanquet, Charles (1769–1850), writer on economic problems. A member of a family of successful London merchants. Became Governor of the South Sea Company. He wrote many works, mainly concerning the West Indian sugar trade, but is best known for his *Practical Observations on the Report of the Bullion Committee* (1810), in which he took issue with the committee's recommendation that the Bank should resume cash payments, and with Ricardo's *High Price of Bullion,* condemning both as "highly theoretical." His contention that fluctuations in prices were caused by taxation and vagaries in the corn trade was generally thought to have been brilliantly refuted by Ricardo in *A Reply to Mr. Bosanquet's Observations.* [2]

Bottleneck, in economics an obstacle or difficulty which slows down the flow of output of a commodity or service below the desired level. A common bottleneck is caused by inadequate or inelastic supply of a factor of production so that the output of a commodity cannot be expanded rapidly. Such bottlenecks are frequently short-lived because the scarce factor can be diverted from other uses, new supplies (e.g. by training additional labour) can be arranged, or a close substitute may be devised or discovered.

Bottlenecks may arise in any economic situation, but they are most common and are felt most acutely when there is rapid expansion of demand for a product or range of products as in the early part of a war. In normal commercial conditions a bottleneck problem can be studied with the aid of the normal tools for price analysis (e.g. elasticity of supply and cross elasticities of supply and demand), and is removed in time if markets are free so that supply and demand can react to changes in each other. In emergencies, as in war, when the primary need is for swift action to provide essentials, and the freedom of consumers or producers is secondary, the difficulties are handled to some extent outside the price mechanism by state controls, direction of private producers or direct production by the state, for example in government arms factories. [3]

Bounty, subsidy given by the state to merchants or manufacturers to encourage particular branches of production. The historic example was the parliamentary bounty on the export of corn. Export-stimulating bounties on goods whose trade might otherwise have languished because of relatively inefficient production and high prices were given on a wide range of manufactures during the era of Mercantilism. Such bounties were severely criticized by Adam Smith in *The Wealth of Nations* for, *inter alia,* forcing trade into less advantageous channels and raising home prices. [10]

Bourgeoisie, term commonly used, from the mid-nineteenth century, for the upper-middle class of business and professional men that developed during the Guild System and emerged as the source of entrepreneurial skill during the Industrial Revolution. It was used in a pejorative sense by Karl Marx to refer to middle-class people with substantial property. The *petit bourgeoisie* were small-scale merchants, traders and shopkeepers. [8]

Bourse, a stock or similar exchange. The word is French, but is commonly used to describe the major continental exchanges. The Paris Bourse is the French equivalent of the London Stock Exchange; there are also several provincial bourses. Commercial exchanges are also called bourses. In France bourses are of two kinds—commercial exchanges (*bourses de commerce*) and stock exchanges (*bourses des valeurs*). [8]

Bowley, Sir Arthur. *See* MODELS, ECONOMIC.

Boycott, the collective refusal of customers, workers or firms acting as suppliers or buyers to deal with other individuals or firms (from Captain C. C. Boycott, an English land agent with whom the Irish refused to deal in the land tenure disturbances of 1879–81). An economic sanction used for political, trade union or monopolistic reasons. Political boycotts, e.g. by British merchants of Icelandic fish as a protest against the extension of Iceland's fisheries limits, are rare and can be only partially effective if those boycotted can buy or sell elsewhere.

Trade unions occasionally refuse to handle "black" goods supplied by a firm with which a labour dispute is taking place. Consumer boycotts of a firm's products have occasionally been urged by trade unionists to overcome its opposition to union organization. On rare occasions trade unionists have sent a fellow worker "to Coventry" for refusing to join a union.

Firms organizing boycotts have generally done so to enforce restrictions on competition. "Black-listing" a distributor by suppliers in order to impose resale price maintenance was made illegal by the 1956 Restrictive Trade Practices Act.

Arrangements for similar action to support other restrictions have to be registered and justified before the Restrictive Practices Court.

The economic arguments against collective refusals to deal with others rest mainly on objections to the restrictive practices they are intended to enforce, such as resale price maintenance, but such collective action in itself is likely to obstruct manufacturers or distributors experimenting and trying out different ways of conducting business. It may occasionally help to maintain standards of service, preserve common prices which facilitate exchange of technical information or protect small firms from the monopoly power of large organizations. But in general economists tend to be critical of restrictive arrangements such as boycotts, because although on paper they can be used for acceptable purposes, in practice they lend themselves to abuse and misuse for objectionable purposes. [7]

Branch Banking. *See* Banks, Joint-stock.

Brand, Lord (1878–1963), economist, business man, public servant. Member or chairman of government economic and financial committees and missions: Macmillan Committee (1930–1), British Ford Commission to Washington (1941–4), British Supply Council in North America (1942 and 1945–6), UK delegate at the Bretton Woods and Savannah Conferences, and others. In general a liberal economist who followed the classical tradition of economic thought. [2]

Brand. *See* Advertising; Monopoly.

Brassage, the charge made by government for coining bullion, with no allowances for a surplus over the cost of coining ("profit"). [8]

Break-even, term applied to the point at which a deficit or a loss has been avoided and a surplus or profit not yet attained. The break-even point for a factory may be 100 cars a month; at 99 it makes a loss, at 101 a profit. [14]

Bretton Woods, international conference attended by forty-four nations held at Bretton Woods, New Hampshire, USA, in 1944. The Bretton Woods Agreements Act which followed in 1945 provided for the establishment of the International Monetary Fund and the International Bank for Reconstruction and Development. [4]

Bridging Loan, a short-term bank advance to enable the customer to pay for a purchase before his receipt of the proceeds of a sale. Commonly applied to purchase and sale of homes. The rate of interest is considered worth paying by the borrower to avoid loss of the home he wants and to anticipate sale of the home he owns. [8]

Broker, an intermediary between two or more persons in a business transaction. His fee is called brokerage. Unlike a dealer, he does not buy or sell. For example, a stockbroker acts as an agent paid by commission for the general public buying and selling Stock Exchange securities (the public are not permitted into the Stock Exchange to deal themselves). On the London Stock Exchange brokers do not deal with each other, but through jobbers.

Other types of brokers include import brokers, issue brokers, insurance brokers, bullion brokers, foreign exchange brokers, etc. [7]

Broker, Bill. *See* DISCOUNT HOUSE.

Brokerage. *See* BROKER.

Bronfenbrenner, Martin (1914–94), American economist, Professor of Economics at the Carnegie-Mellon University since 1962. His writings include a "Survey of Inflation Theory" (*American Economic Review*, September 1963); "Das Kapital for the Modern Man" (*Science and Society*, Autumn 1965); and "Economic Miracles and Japan's Income-Doubling Plan" (*State and Modern Enterprise in Japan*). His research has concentrated mainly on the theory of income distribution. [2]

Brookings Institution, wealthy American research, education and publishing organization that specializes in economics, government, foreign policy and the social sciences. It seeks to bridge the gap between the academic and non-academic worlds, to bring new knowledge to decision-makers, and to give scholars a new insight into practical problems. As a centre for the study of public affairs it brings together research specialists from government, the universities, etc. It grants research fellowships to advanced graduate students for study at Brookings, and research professorships to teachers of economics or business; guest appointments are extended to visiting scholars. Its research claim is that of independent analysis and criticism, and it is committed to publishing its findings, though it has been described as "the Democratic [Party] intelligentsia in exile." Among Brookings' books is *Britain's Economic Prospects* (1968) by Richard E. Caves and Associates. The Institution's headquarters are in Washington, D.C. [14]

Brutzkus, B. *See* CALCULATION, ECONOMIC.

Buchanan, James McGill (1919–), American academic economist, Professor of Economics and Director of the Thomas Jefferson Center for Political Economy at the University of Virginia (1956–68) and Professor of Economics at the University of California (1968–9). He has been Professor of Economics and Director of the Center for the Study of Public Choice at Virginia Polytechnic Institute since 1969. Buchanan has been a pioneer in the development of economic theory, and in particular of the theory of the economics of democracy, based on his study of finance and the allocation of public goods. His main publications are *The Calculus of Consent* (1962, with Gordon Tullock), *Public Finance in Democratic Process* (1967) and *Demand and Supply of Public Goods* (1968). [2]

Buchanan Report, so called after Colin (later Sir Colin) Buchanan, the chairman of the Ministry of Transport's Study Group on Long Term Problems of Traffic in Towns, whose Report, *Traffic in Towns,* was published in 1963. The Report was an attempt to foresee the impact of an expected rapid increase in the growth of traffic in towns over forty to fifty years, and to reconcile two conflicting objectives—the efficient and convenient movement of traffic and the preservation of urban amenity. The Report, which attracted considerable attention, emphasized that traffic, and the buildings which generate traffic, are two sides of the same urban problem and required to be approached through the common mechanism of Town Planning—whether regulatory or in the form of comprehensive urban redevelopment. It foresaw the need to undertake a gigantic programme of urban redevelopment in order to reconcile traffic growth with the preservation of urban amenity and (in most urban areas) to control the ability of traffic to enter and use urban central areas. A number of the report's assumptions, conclusions and recommendations received considerable criticism from economists who thought that its estimates of traffic growth were not well-based, and that its conclusions and recommendations were inadequately supported by economic analysis. [6]

Bucket Shop. (*a*) Originally a place where bets were made on the price of securities on the Stock Exchange or on the price of commodities bought and sold in commodity markets; the transactions were usually in the nature of wagers or bets, the "betters" not trading themselves in the securities or commodities. (*b*) Firms not members of the Stock Exchange dealing in stocks and shares, particularly the more disreputable "share pushers" eliminated from the (legal) scene by the Prevention of Fraud (Investments) Act 1939 which requires dealers in stocks and shares to have a Board of Trade licence unless specifically exempted. [8]

Budget, a formal estimate of income and expenditure over a period; in business and government it usually includes an indication of the policy to be pursued to achieve stated objectives.

(1) In industry budgets are accounts drawn up in order to plan the financial, commercial and production policies of a business. They usually comprise, in addition to a master budget, a series of detailed or subsidiary budgets relating to sales, production, cash, capital expenditure, plant utilization, etc.

Budgetary control consists of the comparison of achieved results with budgeted results in order to ascertain or ensure that the objects of policy are achieved or to provide a basis for revision.

(2) The national budget is similar in nature to a business budget; it is an account of the past and future activities of the government in financial terms. In the annual budget statement to the House of Commons the Chancellor of the

Exchequer reviews the government's income and expenditure for the past year, forecasts them for the coming year, and introduces changes in taxation needed to bring about the expected results and help achieve government policy.

The budget provides two main pointers to government policy: the expenditure side reflects policy on defence, the social services, subsidies, the nationalized industries, etc.; the revenue side reflects policy on taxation and the distribution of incomes. In all the budget is a convenient annual summary of fiscal policy and, when seen against a background of general economic policy, reflects in some degree the approach of the government to economic problems in general.

The Financial Statement (commonly known as the Budget White Paper), which is available at the end of the Chancellor's speech, assembles all the figures relevant to his report. It sets out what is usually described as the budget proper: the figures of revenue and expenditure to 31st March of the previous financial year and the estimates of revenue for the succeeding financial year based on changes in taxation and other policies proposed and the corresponding estimates of expenditure.

A condensed version in approximate round numbers of the statement of revenue and expenditure for an imaginary year, and the estimates for the following financial year, is shown in Table 3. The statement has been divided into two parts: Above-the-line and Below-the-line accounts.

(A) "Above-the-line" revenue from taxation was in three parts: (1) "Inland revenue" comprised income tax, surtax, profits tax, death duties, stamp duties, etc. (or, broadly, the proceeds from direct taxation). (2) "Customs and excise duties" levied on goods such as alcoholic drinks and tobacco and including purchase tax on motor cars, furniture, etc. Customs duties levied on goods from abroad, excise duties on home-produced goods (broadly these comprise the proceeds from indirect taxation). (3) Taxes on motor vehicles (a relatively small proportion of the total).

"Other revenue" included receipts from the GPO, receipts from loans, surpluses on government trading services and a large and varied miscellaneous group of revenues, none very large.

On the expenditure side government spending was in two main parts. (1) The "Consolidated Fund services." The Consolidated Fund was established in 1787 to ensure that the revenues previously earmarked for particular expenditures should go into one central fund from which all regular annual public expenditures should be paid. Parliament decides by statute which expenditures shall be met from the Consolidated Fund and not from the annual supply votes. The main charge on the Consolidated Fund was National Debt Interest and Management (although some National Debt Interest was charged "below-the-line"

Table 3. The Budget

	£ million						
	Year 1		Year 2		Year 1		Year 2
	Estimate	Achieved	Estimate		Estimate	Achieved	Estimate
			ABOVE-THE-LINE				
Revenue				*Expenditure*			
Inland Revenue	3,600	3,650	3,700	Consolidated Fund Services	800	850	750
Customs and Excise	2,500	2,600	2,700	Supply: Defence	1,650	1,700	1,700
Motor Duties	150	140	150	Civil	3,550	3,700	3,900
Total Tax Revenue	6,250	6,390	6,550	Total Supply	5,200	5,400	5,600
Other Revenue	250	260	200	Total Expenditure	6,000	6,250	6,350
				Surplus	500	400	400
Total Revenue	6,500	6,650	6,750		6,500	6,650	6,750
			BELOW-THE-LINE				
Total Receipts	500	550	600	Total Payments	1,050	1,150	1,100
Net Payments	550	600	500				
	1,050	1,150	1,100				

and balanced by interest received on Exchequer loans). Other charges include payments to the Northern Ireland Exchequer, Civil List payments, expenses of parliamentary elections.

(2) "Supply services" are financed by annual votes of Parliament. Approximately one-third goes to Defence and two-thirds to the Civil Services: Central Government, Home Department, Commonwealth and Foreign Estimates, Education, Health, Housing, Local Government, Trade, Labour, Supply, Works, Agriculture, Transport, Pensions, National Insurance, etc.

(B) Below-the-line receipts were in two groups: (1) interest received on loans and (2) repayments of principal of such loans by local authorities, nationalized industries and others.

Below-the-line payments consisted mainly of loans to local authorities, the Public Works Loans Board, nationalized industries, the GPO, New Towns and the Colonial Development Corporation, plus some non-recurring items such as Post-War Credits, War Damage Payments, etc.

It is unlikely that revenue and expenditure will balance exactly in any one year. Thus surpluses and deficits may arise, usually as a result of deliberate government policy. After the Second World War an Above-the-line surplus was common, achieved by making revenue exceed expenditure. This meant that purchasing power was taken from the private sector of the economy (private individuals and privately owned businesses). The size of such a surplus or deficit could be altered by changes in taxation or expenditure.

An Above-the-line surplus was frequently matched, however, by a Below-the-line deficit, that is, payments below the line exceeded receipts. For example, the Above-the-line surplus of £400 million in "Year 2" was exceeded by net payments below the line of £500, the difference between the two of £100 million representing the total deficit to be met by borrowing. [12]

Budgetary Control. *See* BUDGET.

Buffer Stocks, held to reduce fluctuations in the prices of "primary" products. Prices tend to move frequently and sharply because (*a*) the output of agricultural products fluctuates widely with weather conditions, diseases and pests, (*b*) the demand for them (particularly for raw materials) fluctuates with changes in the level of economic activity in the industrial countries which buy them, (*c*) there are technical difficulties and time lags in trying to increase or decrease the output of primary products, which is thus inelastic—e.g. rubber trees produce rubber seven years after planting. The purpose of the buffer stock is to adapt the supply of commodities coming on to the market to the current demand for them in order to narrow the movement in prices. Usually a "ceiling" and a "floor" price are chosen and the authority operating the scheme is required to sell from stock when prices reach the ceiling and to buy when they drop to the floor. When demands seem high the supply in the market is increased by running down the stock, and when supply seems excessive the authority buys.

The success of such schemes depends on the size of their funds and stocks, the width of the gap between the buying and selling prices, and most important the correct prediction of the long-run trends in demand and supply. If the authority running the scheme wrongly estimates the long-run average price for the commodity and sets its price range too high, its buffer stock will grow very large. If it then moves its price range down to a more realistic level it can unload stock only at a loss. It will also have encouraged over-production. Producers who would have been discouraged by lower prices will have maintained production: new producers will have been attracted into the industry. The inevitable readjustment may prove more difficult and painful when it is ultimately made than it would have been if made earlier in the absence of the scheme.

These failings are common in producer-run schemes. They tend to be too optimistic about the trend in demand for their product; or they may take the short-sighted view that by using the stockpile to reduce the supply reaching the market they can raise their incomes, ignoring the effect of high prices in stimulating new producers to enter the field and perhaps other producers to offer synthetic substitutes, both of which reduce demand for their output in the long run. Partly for this reason the United Nations has recommended that consuming nations should be represented on such schemes.

The need for the commodity to be suitable for storing cheaply and with little risk of deterioration sets narrow limits to the range of products for which buffer stock schemes can be used. The principal example of a buffer stock scheme in operation in recent times is in tin.

These weaknesses are common to all buffer stock schemes, but especially in those run by, and for the sole benefit of, producers. The larger schemes set up under international agreement now usually provide for consumer representation; but this has not proved sufficient to ensure success. [7]

Building Lease. *See* LEASEHOLD.

Building Society, an institution that makes mortgage loans to (mainly) house purchasers. The funds are derived from the savings of the public, who invest in deposits and in "shares"; the latter are not transferable and are more like deposits themselves but carry a higher rate of interest because they are less liquid. Deposits may be withdrawn as cash at short notice; the societies make a compound settlement of tax due from investors and therefore pay interest free of tax. Most of the money on deposit is in small holdings, the average being under £1,000; holdings over £5,000 account for only a small percentage.

The building society movement is peculiar to Great Britain. It is over two hundred years old, but the fastest growth has been since the end of the Second World War. The assets of building societies are made up of balances due on mortgages, with some investments and a small amount of cash and other assets.

As financial institutions, building societies are thus essentially illiquid: most of the assets are long term and the liabilities nominally short term; that is, individual investors can withdraw them with little notice. But in practice the deposits and "shares" are looked upon by holders as long-term savings. Also, although the assets are individually long term, they are self-liquidating as a whole since mortgages are being repaid regularly. Assets are therefore more liquid than they may appear. Flows of funds into and out of building societies have generally been fairly regular.

Rates of interest paid to depositors and by mortgage holders do not necessarily follow movements in other interest rates in the short run, but in the long run they must tend to approximate fairly closely to trends of long-term rates if investments are to be attracted but not in larger amounts than can be lent profitably. Short-term adjustment between inflow and outflow of funds is often achieved by an unofficial but effective rationing of advances according to type of property, amount of advance and income of borrower. Rationing may continue over long periods of time if funds fall behind the demand for them, and if interest rates are not raised to restore equilibrium. In the 1970's the building societies ran into difficulties when it became politically embarrassing to raise interest rates to depositors as much as other institutions such as banks were able to do. They accepted a loan from the government in order to maintain mortgage lending at lower-than-market rates of interest at the expense of becoming further exposed to political influence.

The conduct of building societies is controlled by Building Societies Acts and supervised by the Registrar of Friendly Societies to protect the public against fraudulent management. Some economists believe the societies need more freedom to enable them to act commercially in a competitive market for savings.

In 1960 there were 726 building societies in Britain, but amalgamations had reduced this number to less than 450 by the mid-1970's and most mortgages are arranged by twenty of the largest. [8]

"Built-in Stabilizers." *See* STABILIZATION, ECONOMIC.

Bull, on the Stock Exchange a speculator who believes that the price of securities will rise and accordingly buys in the hope of selling later at a profit; in a more restricted sense a speculator who has bought shares in the hope that their price will rise soon enough for him to take a profit before he is called on to pay. This is made possible by dealing within the Stock Exchange Account period or by carry-over transactions. [8]

Bullion, ingots or bars of the precious metals. Silver bullion is traded for industrial use and personal decoration. Gold bullion is traded between banks and governments as a means of payment. It is also held as a stock of wealth and as a backing for paper currency. [8]

Bullion Broker. *See* BROKER.

Bullion Market, a financial centre in which gold bullion is bought and sold. In Britain the business is conducted by five firms of bullion brokers which meet daily to fix an official price; other dealings are carried out between banks and authorized dealers. All business is done for cash. [8]

Bureau of the Census, part of the Social and Economic Statistics Administration of the US Department of Commerce. It conducts ten-yearly censuses of population and housing, and five-yearly censuses of agriculture, business, government, manufacture, mineral industries and transport. It also compiles detailed statistics on US foreign trade. The Bureau's sample surveys are widely used. It also processes data for other government agencies and makes tabulations of its data for many users. [14]

Bureaucracy, rule by officials (or, literally, people in offices). Frequently used slightingly to label a system of administration as unwieldy, inefficient or corrupt. With a similar intention the word may be used in a concrete sense to denote a group of administrators. Bureaucracy is often equated exclusively with governmental administrative work in advanced economies, which tends to grow with increasing government intervention in economic affairs, but there are also "bureaucratic" tendencies in very large firms. Schumpeter used the word to describe the giant industrial enterprises in which economic and technical change is "routinized" and the importance of the individual *entrepreneur* has disappeared.

In recent years economists have been analysing bureaucracy more closely, as an aspect of the economics of politics. Until the 1960's, the academic study of bureaucracy was largely dominated by political scientists from Max Weber to C. Northcote Parkinson. The only important exception was Ludwig von Mises' *Bureaucracy* (1944). In the 1960's two of the pioneers of the economics of politics produced book-length studies: Gordon Tullock in *The Politics of Bureaucracy* (1965) and Anthony Downs in *Inside Bureaucracy* (1967).

In 1971 a new approach to the economics of bureaucracy came in William A. Niskanen's *Bureaucracy and Representative Government.* The central argument was restated in 1973 with comments by former British government ministers and civil servants in *Bureaucracy: Servant or Master?* (Institute of Economic Affairs, 1973). Niskanen analysed the bureaucracy as a firm—the determinants of its size, output and efficiency, its maximand as a competitor or monopolist, its "product," and the incentives and motives operating within it. His main conclusion was that bureaucracies tend to be too large and that excessive size might be corrected by competition and quasi-profit incentives to contain costs, by developing market alternatives to bureaucracies, and by political re-organization to make bureaucracies more sensitive to pressure from consumers, taxpayers and public opinion. [10]

Burke, Edmund. *See* INDIVIDUALISM.

Business, originally activity (busy-ness), specifically industrial and commercial activity. It implies initiative as well as routine; hence "business man," more common in the financial and commercial world than "entrepreneur." More emotive versions of "business man" are (with approval) "captain of industry" and (pejoratively) "tycoon." [3]

Business Cycles. *See* TRADE CYCLES.

Business Ethics, journalese for the moral standards of business men, with the possible implication that they are lower than elsewhere because the prospect of financial gain overrides all other considerations. Where information on the composition or performance of commodities is technical and beyond the ordinary consumer, he can be deceived; similarly where he cannot judge the effectiveness of services or skills, or where the seller rapidly changes his stock or moves frequently from market to market. Such situations arise with a variety of commodities from expensive clothes to street-market goods. The consumer can defend himself by the law, by asking advice, and by shopping around to compare prices and quality. The profit motive may encourage short-run exploitation of consumers, but it would be a short-sighted policy for business men who depend on their customers returning to buy (or suppliers or employees returning to sell or work). Scope for short-run "business ethics" can also be created by the lag between technical change and law reform, so that for a period consumers of new products or materials are not protected by law, though in general standards and values are normally maintained by competition. [14]

Bust, colloquialism for a collapse in economic activity, more formally "slump" or "severe recession." [9]

Buyers' Market, one in which producers are willing to produce, or sellers willing to market, larger amounts than buyers are currently willing to pay for at existing prices. Stocks pile up, prices are forced down, suppliers cut or stop production and buyers gain from the lower prices (unless their wealth or incomes are reduced by the state of such markets).

In manufacturing firms will minimize their losses by continuing to produce until specialized plant wears out so long as prices at least cover out-of-pocket ("marginal") expenses and make some contribution towards overheads. In agriculture self-employed farmers may even increase production when falling prices reduce their incomes because they cannot easily or do not wish to change their employment.

Buyers' markets are characteristic of slumps. They also occur in individual goods at times of full employment because of the slow adjustment of capacity to shifts in demand, over-estimation of demand, installation of excess capacity by firms in ignorance of one another's plans or in full knowledge but with the intention of eliminating rivals, and the unpredictability of harvests.

Buyers' markets may last for only a few hours (as when a bumper catch of fish is landed) or for a decade or more (as when there are large stocks of durable goods such as houses). When a buyers' market is caused by excess capacity its duration depends upon the specificity, durability and age of the plant. As plant is often specialized and its life usually exceeds the time it takes to build, buyers' markets with over-capacity generally last longer than the corresponding sellers' markets with under-capacity. For example, the buyers' market in cotton goods persisted throughout the inter-war years as Lancashire mills went slowly out of production; but the sellers' market which followed the disruption of production in Europe and the Far East in the Second World War lasted for only some six years. [7]

Bygones Are Bygones, dictum indicating that value-creating attitudes and decisions are not influenced by the past. Values derive from present—and prospective future—evaluations. A commodity or service is valuable because subjective attitudes make it so, not because it embodies materials that were valuable, or attitudes that gave it value, in the past. That is why prices are not determined by costs. Newspapers and other sellers that attempt to explain or justify higher prices by reference to higher raw material, labour, transport or other costs are thus being naive: these are the pretexts for higher prices which consumers would not have to pay if competition were brisker and provided lower-priced substitutes, or if inflation had not raised personal money incomes or enabled industrial buyers to pass higher prices on to consumers. [14]

By-product, incidental yield of a production process. It may be material or an idea. The residue of industrial process formerly regarded as waste is increasingly being used again or treated ("re-cycled") for eventual re-use (repulping of waste paper, re-use of glass bottles, etc.). Anxiety about "dumping" (e.g. of industrial discard) is encouraging research and scientific innovation to transform it into by-products. [3]

C

Cabinet Committee on Economic Policy, a USA group of presidential advisers established by President Nixon in 1969, to discuss and make recommendations on economic policy. It includes the President, the Vice-President, the Chairman of the Council of Economic Advisers (who co-ordinates the work of the Committee) and the secretaries of the Treasury, Agriculture, Commerce, Labour and Housing and Urban Development. The Cabinet Committee considers a broad range of business and economic issues and reviews the findings of sub-committees appointed to study specific problems. [10]

Cairncross, Alexander K. (1911–98), British economist. He was educated at Hamilton Academy and Glasgow and Cambridge Universities. He was a university lecturer from 1935 to 1939 and then a civil servant from 1940 to 1949 and Economic Adviser to the EEC from 1949 to 1950. In 1951 he returned to university teaching as Professor of Applied Economics at the University of Glasgow until 1961. After further government and advisory posts he became Master of St. Peter's College, Oxford, in 1969. During the war he wrote a standard text-book, *An Introduction to Economics* (1944).

Cairncross is a tool-user rather than a tool-maker. Most of his writings exhibit a sceptical and pragmatic attitude based on observation, experience and practical wisdom rather than formal analysis. He is mainly concerned with the practical problems of the effective use of fiscal and monetary policy in steering the economy, and more widely with the difficulties, conceptional and administrative, of making economics useful. He distrusts too much reliance on monetary policy as an instrument of control on the grounds that the statistics and definitions are very imperfect, and that, in the light of experience, there are too many ways round controls. His work conveys a strong sense of the importance of the texture of a society for which the economist is to prescribe.

Cairncross's main writings are *Home and Foreign Investment, 1870–1913* (1953), *Monetary Policy in a Mixed Economy* (1960), *Factors in Economic Development* (1962), and *Essays in Economic Management* (1971). [2]

Cairnes, John Elliot (1823–75), Irish-born economist educated at Trinity College, Dublin. He began his career as a journalist but later became Whately Professor of Political Economy at Dublin in 1856, at Galway in 1859 and at London in 1867. Cairnes was one of the last "classicists"; his main works, *Character and Logical Method of Political Economy* (1857) and *Some Leading Principles of*

Political Economy (1874), gave an orthodox account of the essentials of the classical system. The first was part of a long controversy with Mill and Senior over the scope and method of economics. [2]

Calculation, Economic, (*a*) generally, the consideration by a consumer (or a producer) of the alternatives open to him in spending and saving a personal income (or running a business). A consumer must decide how much of his income to spend on alternative or complementary commodities and how much to save. A business man must decide what products to make, what size of output to aim at, and what methods to use. To provide a starting-point in framing theories in economics, these calculations are assumed to be consistent. Thus the consumer may be thought of as mentally balancing the utility of minutely differing combinations of goods and services until the combination that gives the largest total utility for a given expenditure is reached.

(*b*) specifically, a method of determining values not in markets by competition but by a process of calculation by a centrally directing authority using techniques of mathematical economics. The idea was stated in general terms by the early socialists, who wished to find an alternative to the method of determining value by markets in which there was competition between sellers who offered goods and services produced by privately owned resources. In the English-speaking world the American economists F. M. Taylor and W. C. Roper and in England H. D. Dickinson attempted to show that, if there were perfect knowledge of all the relevant information, the economic theory which explains the formation of prices and the distribution of productive resources between alternative goods and services in a competitive system could also be used in a centrally directed socialist society without a free pricing system to decide the values and the quantities of the alternative commodities to be produced. The debate has continued for over fifty years with B. E. Lippincott (USA), Oskar Lange (Poland), A. P. Lerner (USA), the late E. F. M. Durbin (Britain) and others claiming that "socialist calculation" was possible and preferable to "capitalist competition," and Max Weber (Germany), N. G. Pierson (Holland), B. Brutzkus (Russia), L. von Mises (USA), F. A. Hayek (Britain) and others arguing that it was impracticable or inefficient. [13]

Call, part of the nominal value of a share the shareholder is asked to pay. Often the purchaser of a share pays part of the purchase price when he applies for them, a further part when (or if) they are allotted to him, and the remainder in one or more subsequent calls. [8]

"Call Birds." *See* Loss Leader.

"Call Option." *See* Option Dealing.

Cambridge School, originally a pre-war group of economists at the University of Cambridge, England, who reflected the "classical" teaching of Alfred Marshall and his pupil, A. C. Pigou, and later of D. H. Robertson, with its emphasis on micro-economic supply and demand analysis, and value and distribution theory; although Robertson also worked on money, where he differed from the more influential J. M. Keynes, for long the dominant economist at Cambridge. More recently, although economists at Cambridge are not all agreed, the term has been mostly applied to the post-Second World War economists who look to their origins in Ricardo and Marx and/or who follow Keynes, and have interpreted and applied his macro-economic thinking (mainly Joan Robinson, Lord Kahn, Piero Sraffa, Nicholas Kaldor). They have had much influence both on academic economic teaching and on the policy of British Labour governments (and governments abroad). The Cambridge (UK) School has conducted an intense debate with the Cambridge (Massachusetts) School of neo-classical economists (Samuelson, Solow, etc.) who generally follow Pareto and Walras.

The School has been criticized on the grounds that, in its emphasis on macro-economic concepts and models, it has tended to lose sight of the micro-economic foundations of economic behaviour, i.e. that individuals (persons, families, firms) cannot be assumed to act in the way required for formal macro-economic laws, rules, tendencies or generalizations applied to the behaviour of large groups (a country, an economy, or a society as a whole). The School differs from other schools in its conclusions on incomes policies, the management of economic growth, the conditions of technical progress, and the monetary and fiscal measures required to resist inflation. [2]

Cambridge School (Mass.). *See* CAMBRIDGE SCHOOL.

Cameralism, an older name for the study of public administration and finance. [12]

Cannan, Edwin (1861–1935), British economist. He was educated at Balliol College, Oxford, and became Lecturer in Political Economy at the University of London. He played an influential part in building the tradition of the London School of Economics, where he was appointed professor in 1897. His first major work, *A History of the Theories of Production and Distribution* (1893), the result of extensive research into the works of earlier economists, established his reputation in economics. Throughout his career Cannan was mainly concerned with the history of economic doctrines, and his edited version of *The Wealth of Nations* (1904) became a standard edition of that work. For a period he was regarded as a severe critic of the classical economists, but his *Wealth* (1914) and *Review of Economic Theory* (1929) modify this view. His definition of economics as the study of material welfare was later questioned by Lord Robbins, F. A. Hayek and others. [2]

Canons of Taxation, the rules or aims advocated by economists at various times for designing an ideal system of taxation. Adam Smith's (in *The Wealth of Nations*) were four: equality (according to individual ability to pay), certainty, convenience and economy. On economy he said: "Every tax ought to be so contrived as both to take out and to keep out of the pockets of the people as little as possible over and above what it brings into the public treasury of the state": it should not require "a great number of officers," "it may . . . discourage the people from applying to certain branches of business which might give maintenance and employment to great multitudes," "it may frequently ruin . . . by forfeitures and other penalties . . . those unfortunate individuals who attempt unsuccessfully to evade the tax," and it should not "subject the people to the frequent visits and the odious examination of the tax-gatherer [and so] expose them to much unnecessary trouble, vexation and oppression. . . ."

In our day, when in Britain taxation takes 45 per cent of incomes, the emphasis is not only on simplicity, efficiency, ease of collection and "fairness" but also on avoiding discouragement to effort, industry and output. Economists would generally agree that beyond a point the use of taxation to redistribute income conflicts with its effects in inhibiting the growth in total incomes, although they differ on the points at which the conflict emerges in different taxes. The appearance of a tendency to blur the moral distinction between tax avoidance (legal) and tax evasion (illegal), as in some countries in the south of Europe, is regarded by some economists as evidence that the limits of taxation are being reached. Others believe that for purposes approved by tax-payers, such as benefits for pensioners and other people in need, it could go higher. [12]

Cantillon, Richard (?–1734), British economist. Very little is known about him except that he was born in Ireland, probably about 1680. For some time he lived in Paris, where he established a banking business, but eventually he moved to London, where he was murdered. His contribution to economics is embodied in his *Essai sur la nature du commerce en général;* probably written about 1725, but not published until 1755, it was a vigorous analytical work ahead of its time—one of the first works to show that currency is, at best, only a measure of wealth, which is itself derived from production. Cantillon's contention that only agricultural enterprises yield a surplus over the costs of production gave rise to the Physiocrats' concept of "produit net," and his thoughts on the circulation of wealth undoubtedly influenced the later work of Quesnay. [2]

Capacity, Unused, (*a*) efficient use of resources or (*b*) waste, depending upon the reasons for its existence. Some capacity is left unused because the cooperating factors required to exploit it are more productive elsewhere; e.g. jungles, swamps, deserts and highlands are uncultivated, the oil sands of Canada undeveloped and thin seams of coal unmined. Similarly capacity may be left unused, e.g. canals and branch railways, because of technical change which has discovered better methods. Some unused capacity consists of facilities available to meet fluctuations in demand. It yields a flow of "availability" in the same way as a dinner suit in the wardrobe or a pen in the pocket; power stations are kept in service to satisfy the peak demand on only a few days in the year. Finally, some excess capacity may arise because firms acting independently overbuild to provide for a growing market. They may be aware of what is happening but each hopes to be more successful than the others. In so far as the firms that survive (in the absence of monopoly) are said to be the most efficient, the excess capacity may be regarded as the cost of the competitive process of discovering their identity.

There are two main circumstances in which unused capacity represents waste. First, in periods of depression: all the co-operating factors needed for production are available and failure to use them reflects the breakdown of the economic mechanism for co-ordinating them. Secondly, capacity may be kept idle by a monopolist in order to gain higher profits from higher prices with a lower turnover. [3]

Capital, (*a*) in economic theory, the stock of resources available to help satisfy future wants. In this main sense capital may refer to (1) a community's stock of material wealth (plus its claims against and minus debts owing to people in other countries); (2) that part of the stock intended for use in further production (plus net claims against people in other countries); or (3) an individual's private assets (which include claims against his countrymen and government as well as material objects and claims against people in other countries).

In the past capital has also been used to refer not to a *stock* but to a *flow* of savings in such terms as "the supply of capital" and "the amount of free or floating capital." The act of postponing or foregoing consumption, a necessary but not sufficient condition for capital formation, would now be called saving rather than supplying capital; and free or floating capital, that is, money intended by its owner to build up material wealth or to lend to others, would be called loanable or investible funds.

Society's stock of man-made material wealth, plus net claims on people in other countries, is the most inclusive concept. It is used for comparisons of the power of different societies to satisfy wants. The average worker in the USA or Britain enjoys a higher standard of living than the average worker in an Asian developing country largely because he works with much more capital. It consists of houses and other buildings, durable producers' goods such as machinery and equipment, stocks of raw materials, semi-finished goods and products held by manufacturers and distributors, net claims against other countries and stocks of goods held by householders. Household stocks range in durability from foodstuffs consumed in a short time, through semi-durables such as clothing, to "consumer" durables such as furniture, cookers, refrigerators and motor-cars.

It is usual to exclude household stocks from capital, partly because their purchase calls for a separate explanation from that for capital goods intended for further production and partly because household stocks are difficult to value. The exclusion is arbitrary, since there is no difference in principle between the real income in the form of amenities that a house yields to its owner and that which is yielded by his furniture; moreover it leads to anomalies; e.g. motor-cars are counted as capital when owned by firms and used for business but not when owned privately for pleasure.

The capital stock intended for use in further production may be divided into two kinds, fixed and working (or circulating). Fixed capital consists of instruments of all kinds, including buildings, improvements to land such as drainage works and harbour installations, and machinery and equipment. Working capital consists of goods in the process of being prepared for consumption: raw materials, semi-finished goods and finished goods in the hands of manufacturers, wholesalers and retailers. This distinction is made for two main reasons. First, the income yielded by fixed capital may for long periods depart from a current market return on replacement cost because the capital is usually specialized and takes time to increase or decrease in amount (its supply is inelastic). In the meantime its income depends upon the demand for its product and the quantity of fixed capital in existence. Working capital can be quickly adjusted if its yield departs from the market return on replacement. Secondly, industries supplying fixed capital goods are subject to large fluctuations in demand because durability allows discretion in the timing of replacements, and additions to fixed capital are not usually made at a regular rate.

The stock of goods making up a nation's capital might in principle be listed in a vast stock-taking. Valuing this capital is more difficult. The value of a capital good depends upon the net receipts which will be earned over its life discounted back to the date of valuation. Future earnings can only be estimated, and the life of an asset is not a physical but an economic quantity depending upon obsolescence (due to unforeseeable change in fashion, etc.) as well as physical breakdown.

(*b*) of an individual, stocks and shares, his bank deposit and other titles to property all form part of personal capital; but not to the community. These pieces of paper are merely evidence of indebtedness; whatever A is owed by B, B owes to A, and for the community as a whole (apart from debt owed to it by people outside it) such debts cancel out. The concept of personal capital as applied to an individual, that is, paper claims as well as real assets, is important, however, because decisions made by individuals about the *form* in which they will hold their personal wealth affect the pattern of asset prices and interest rates in the economy at a given time. [1]

(*c*) of a company, the authorized, nominal or registered amount of share capital indicated in documents establishing a company, as required by company law. [3]

Capital Allowances, deductions from business income allowed for calculating income liable to tax. They are a recognition that fixed assets are gradually used up in producing output and that taxable income is overstated if their wear and tear and obsolescence is not taken into account. The attitude of the British government has always been against permitting business men to charge annual depreciation (for tax purposes) at the rates they found most suitable for their individual businesses: annual capital allowances have traditionally taken the form of fixed percentages of asset cost. In recent years there have been (selective) changes in this attitude: to encourage investment in areas of unemployment "free" depreciation allowances (i.e. at a rate of the firm's own choosing) were introduced in 1963 for new investment in Development Districts. Other annual permitted rates of capital allowance on industrial buildings, plant and machinery and so on were also increased to more "realistic" levels. But capital allowances were still not permitted for commercial buildings, although the distinction between "industrial" and "commercial" buildings has no clear economic significance. [12]

Capital Budgeting. *See* INVESTMENT APPRAISAL.

Capital, Circulating. *See* ADVANCE.

Capital Co-efficient, the relationship between the capital employed in production and the output. It indicates the amount of new capital required to produce an additional ("marginal") unit of output; hence "marginal capital co-efficient." The co-efficient varies widely from "heavy" industry like iron and steel, petroleum, coal and paper, with high co-efficients, to furniture and clothing etc. which have low co-efficients because they have a high content of skilled labour. The co-efficient can also be used to assess the prospects for industry and for expansion of output in countries with relatively scarce capital but abundant labour supply. [1]

Capital Consumption. *See* INVESTMENT.

Capital Flight, investment finance removed from countries in social, financial or military upheaval. Sometimes known as "hot money." It can disrupt the international exchange markets and provoke balance of payments crises by "speculation" and by weakening general confidence. Export of capital for these reasons was usually expected (though it did not always occur) on the advent of left-wing governments in capitalist countries. Post-war institutions, such as the International Monetary Fund, have provided for loans to deal with temporary balance of payments disturbances. [4]

Capital Gains, profits or gains made otherwise than in the course of normal trade or business. Examples are profits on the sale of investments and property, or arising from the sale of the goodwill of a business, or from isolated transactions. Individuals may realize capital profits by selling their private houses or cars or through Stock Exchange dealings. There are many cases where it is difficult to decide whether or not a gain is capital or not, such as compensation payments for loss of employment. Broadly the distinction is that if a gain is made on an isolated transaction, such as the sale of a private house, it is a capital gain; if the isolated transaction is followed by others and becomes regular the gain is income. [12]

Capital Gains Tax, a tax on an increase in capital value. The main argument for it is that since an individual's purchasing power and standard of living in a given period depends not only on his income but also on the increase, if any, in the value of his capital, tax should be levied not only on income but also on capital gains in the period. It is argued that capital gains tax also reduces or stops avoidance of income tax by switching from activities that earn income to those that offer the prospect of (untaxed) capital gains. Counter-arguments are that the resort to capital gains as a means of increasing income is partly the result of the high taxation of incomes, and that it would decline if the taxation of incomes were lower; that capital gains arising out of inflation only partly reflect real gain because they are partly nominal, and that a capital gains tax does not reach more elusive forms of tax avoidance such as payment in kind (or cash not recorded in income tax returns).

Capital gains are taxed in most developed countries. Britain introduced a tax on short-term capital gains in 1962 and a more comprehensive capital gains tax in 1965. It applies to gains realized on all kinds of assets, subject to exemptions, chiefly private residences, "chattels" (goods apart from real estate) worth less than £1,000, and private motor cars. National Savings Certificates, life assurance policies and gambling gains are outside the scope of the tax and gains from the disposal of British Government securities are exempt. [12]

Capital Gearing. *See* GEARING.

Capital Goods. *See* DURABLE GOODS; INVESTMENT.

Capital, Human, present value of future flow of an individual's services. There is no market for the sale and purchase of people who are "free" (as there once was for slaves), so there is no market in which the capital value of a human being can be identified (or exchanged). In practice an approximation to an individual's capital value can be obtained in the life assurance market in which the value of his future services can be assessed and ensured for his dependants. Future services can also be sold for a period—e.g. in the market for entertainers and sportsmen; the buyer can safeguard himself by accident insurance or life assurance against loss of services by illness, deterioration of talent or skill, or death. By sale for a period an individual can "capitalize" on his future earnings. [1]

Capital Intensive, term applied to a productive process that combines relatively large input of capital with other factors of production, e.g. a brewery, a paper mill, an oil refinery and other plants that are highly mechanized and approach the "push-button" stage. Industry has become more capital-intensive with technical innovation. The scope for substituting capital for labour sets a limit to the power of trade unions to push wage-costs above the marginal productivity of labour. Increasing capital-intensity has initially lowered wage-rates but ultimately raised living standards. Developing countries have wished to follow the developed countries by installing large-scale, heavy, capital-intensive plant like steel mills, but they require managerial, financial and technical skills that take time to develop. Economists have therefore tended to advocate education, technical training and intermediate "middle-scale" technology for Asia and Africa. [3]

Capital Issues Committee, a non-statutory body created in Britain by the Borrowing (Control and Guarantees Act) of 1946 to decide whether new issues of share capital accorded with the public interest. The Act empowered the Treasury to control borrowing and capital issues: from 1947 to 1959 no more than £50,000 (£10,000 from March 1956 to July 1958) could be raised in a year without Treasury consent. The Capital Issues Committee recommended the Treasury to give or withhold consent, and worked under broad guidance from the Treasury. After 1959 restrictions were relaxed. By the mid 1960's only persons and firms abroad that wished to borrow on the British capital market required the Committee's consent. The period of stringent control by the Committee gave rise to considerable growth of alternative non-market forms of financing, e.g. the cash sale of real property in shops coupled with a "lease-back" arrangement, which limited the effectiveness of control and made it arbitrary. [8]

Capital Levy, a tax on capital. Although often advocated in post-war periods as a means of taxing wealth acquired during the war, it has been used only once in the UK, in 1948, in the form of the "once-for-all" Special Contribution. Although based on investment income, the levy had to be met out of capital. It was described as a tax on capital based on the amount of income. The Special Contribution was levied on incomes above £2,000 where investment income exceeded £250. For investment income of £5,000 or more the levy was 10*s*. in the £.

The arguments for a capital levy were revived in the early 1960's and again in the mid-1970's in the form of a wealth tax. The two main ones were that it would reduce the inequalities in the ownership of wealth, and tax away for the benefit of the community part of the rise in capital values in a period of inflation. The arguments against were that the increase in capital values was in part the outcome of high taxes on income which shifted economic effort from activities yielding higher income to those yielding higher capital values; a tax on capital would discourage investment in risky enterprises; the official Inland Revenue statistics of estates were misleading; the distribution of capital/wealth often reflected accumulation by the owner as well as inheritance; private ownership of wealth independent of the state was politically advantageous in decentralizing power and providing plural sources of finance. Capital is taxed in Germany and some other countries. [12]

Capital, Marginal Efficiency of. *See* PROPENSITY TO INVEST.

Capital Market, the collection of financial institutions that canalize the supply of and demand for longer-term financial loans or claims. It brings together lenders and borrowers (suppliers and demanders of newly created claims on wealth) as well as dealings in the existing stock of financial claims. Many of the institutions are intermediaries that bridge long-term and short-term markets, act as "wholesalers" in the issue and sale of new claims, or as "processors" in adapting the supplies of financial claims to meet demands. They are thus like the specialist suppliers that comprise any large modern industry. The "products" in which the capital market deals are financial claims of all sorts and sizes, new and second hand. The "firms" include the central and commercial banks, the discount houses, merchant banks and new issue houses, the Stock Exchange, mortgage, and innumerable ancillary organizations.

Shorter-term loans are negotiated in the "money market," but there is no clear dividing line between "short" and "long" or between the "capital market" and the "money market." [8]

Capital Recapture Rate, the return or recovery *of* invested capital, expressed as an annual rate. It is applied to wasting assets (e.g. buildings, equipment, plant machinery) and to property rights for a limited term (e.g. lease-holds), i.e. with a finite economic life. The rate of return *on* capital invested in such assets is the sum of (*a*) the interest rate on capital invested, and (*b*) the capital recapture or *sinking fund* rate which will permit the investor to recoup the original sum invested by the end of the life of the investment. [1]

Capital Recovery Rate, another term for capital recapture rate.

Capital Tax. *See* TAX, INCOME AND CAPITAL.

Capital, Working. *See* ADVANCE, CAPITAL.

Capitalism, the social system in which capital is owned by private persons and work is undertaken, not as a customary duty or in response to commands, but for individual reward under a system of free contract. The word may be used to describe the system of production in a particular sector of an economy or, more loosely, an economy in which part of the productive capital may be owned by the state or by co-operatives but in which private ownership of capital is predominant. Capitalism differs from socialism in its private as opposed to socialized (normally state) ownership of capital; it differs from the feudal system in its extensive use of free contract between employer and employee in place of status.

The term is used widely to cover strikingly different social and economic systems. The early capitalism of sixteenth- and seventeenth-century Europe was particularly associated with trade and finance and with relatively small units of production. The importance of religious and other factors in the early development of capitalism has been debated by historians, sociologists and theologians (such as Weber, Troeltsch, Tawney and others). With further technical progress and accumulation of capital it became possible to argue, as Marx did, that capitalism created a propertyless, wage-earning proletariat exploited by a class of property owners or capitalists who played no part in "production" but expropriated the "surplus value" created by labour. Marx argued that "internal contradictions" in capitalism would lead to its destruction. He predicted, among other things, a growth in monopoly power and worsening crises of overproduction, with the "proletariat" increasing in size and coherence as a group while its standard of living was forced down by increasing exploitation. These and other developments would create the preconditions for a socialist state; socialism, and then communism, would replace capitalism first in the more advanced countries and then everywhere.

The development of capitalism has not so far favoured the Marxist prophecy. The evidence does not support the expectation of increasing concentration in industry; the standard of living of wage and salary earners in the advanced capitalist economies has risen; and capitalist development since Marx has tended to blur the distinctions between "proletariat" and "bourgeoisie" rather than aggravate them.

Changes in capitalist economies during the present century have led to a further discussion of the nature of capitalism. Attention has been focused on the large limited liability company, which differs from the one-man firm or private partnership of the earlier nineteenth century since its owners are numerous and exercise no continuous or unified control over the company's affairs, while the salaried directors who wield control are frequently not sizeable shareholders. Hence the "divorce" between ownership and control. The tendency towards "bureaucratization" in this type of capitalist firm has been treated by Schumpeter and others as part of a more general development into a different type of society. Other economists and social scientists, such as Walter Lippmann, F. A. Hayek, Lionel Robbins and others, have emphasized the responsibility of the legal framework on companies, contract, etc., for the forms of monopoly that have developed within capitalist economies.

In the 1970's a difference of approach developed between economists who favoured capitalism over socialism: some would use government to modify capitalist market-pricing institutions to spread wealth and equalize incomes, others would free them from government restrictions and let them raise incomes and extend wealth more widely.

Capitalist activity has persisted in the communist economies, where it is tolerated for political reasons or alternately encouraged and suppressed when centralized direction of the economy has weakened incentives and reduced production. Much private enterprise is permitted in Russia, Poland, Yugoslavia and other economies in which the main means of production are owned by the state. [10]

Capitalist Accumulation. *See* MARX, KARL.

Capitalization, the process of converting an annuity, in the form of an annual stream of income, into a single capital sum. In economic and investment analysis (including real property valuation) the values of income-bearing property rights (capital assets) are established and measured by calculating the equivalent *present value* (at the date of valuation) of the future streams of income the assets are expected to generate over that period. In traditional valuation terminology, the multiplier applied to an annuity to arrive at its capital value is known as its (number of) Years' Purchase, and indicates the capital sum that a "representative" investor would be prepared to pay at the valuation date for the right to receive the forecast income over the period.

The Years' Purchase applied to an investment income stream depends on the rate of return expected by a "representative" investor on capital invested in assets of that type and risk. For example, ignoring income tax, if an investment with a ten-year life were of a type and risk such that a "prudent" investor would expect a rate of return of 10 per cent on capital to persuade him to acquire the asset, its capital value is obtained by applying a Years' Purchase multiplier of 6.1446 to the expected annual net income stream. If the net income stream was £100 per annum this would be sufficient to provide interest at 10 per cent on an investment of £614.46 and also to allow a sinking fund to accumulate at 10 per cent to produce an amount of £614.46 in ten years, thus allowing the investor to recapture his capital at the end of the asset's life. [1]

Capitalization Issue, an issue of "bonus" shares to existing shareholders which distributes accumulated profits and reserves, so that the total issued capital more truly reflects the capital employed by the firm. Capitalization issues do not themselves necessarily increase the total value of the shares in the hands of shareholders. [8]

Capitalization Rate, the rate at which a stream of annual income is discounted or capitalized to ascertain its present value or "worth." It is a combination of (*a*) interest rate on the capital sum invested and (*b*) a capital recapture or sinking fund contribution rate which, when applied to the original sum invested, would permit an investor to recapture his capital investment at the end of the asset's life. (Where the asset or investment is "non-wasting," e.g. freehold property, it is not necessary to provide for capital recovery and the relevant income stream would be capitalized "in perpetuity" so that the capitalization rate would consist of element (*a*) only.) Thus in the example in Capitalization, the Years' Purchase of 6.1446 was arrived at by taking the reciprocal of the sum (0.1 + 0.062745). The first figure is the interest rate of 10 per cent expressed as a decimal; the second is the sinking fund constant or rate of capital recapture contribution, also expressed as a decimal, which if allowed to accumulate at an interest rate of 10 per cent for ten years would amount to 1.0. [1]

Capitation Tax, a tax levied equally on each person irrespective of income, wealth or any other criterion. Also known as a poll tax. [12]

Captive Consumer, term developed mostly by critics of advertising to describe buyers of consumer goods held "captive" by intensive advertising. This may be true for some goods for a period, or in a localized region, until alternative sources of supply enter the market. More generally, the term applies to consumers of goods or services produced by monopolies. Investigations by the Monopolies Commission have demonstrated that industries or firms can most easily hold customers captive if new suppliers are excluded by law, e.g. by patents. Captivity in this sense is more common, and long-lasting, for consumers of goods or services produced by central or local government monopolies—education, medical care, rail transport, fuel, police, libraries, etc. [7]

Cardinal, term applied to the measurement of utility once thought necessary in the theory of consumer demand. *See* Indifference Analysis, Ordinal Ranking. [14]

Cartel, specifically a joint marketing organization created by firms which would otherwise sell in competition with one another. The syndicate or central bureau fixes selling price and output quotas for the member firms, which thus cease to compete (openly) in price. Competition is subsequently channelled into devices that might support a claim for larger quotas from the cartel. The term is also applied to looser types of association that limit competition by fixing prices or sharing markets.

In the full sense of selling syndicates, cartels grew to prominence in Germany at the turn of the century. A typical example was the Rhenish-Westphalian Coal Cartel, formed in 1893, which acted as the selling agent for most of the Ruhr mines, allocating output quotas and sharing profits between the member firms. Production was left under the control of the individual mining companies. By the 1930's there were some 3,000 cartels in Germany, and they were used by the Nazi government in its central direction of the economy. Since 1945 German cartels have been subject to more stringent legislation limiting their functions, but many remain active. The successors to the Rhenish-Westphalian Cartel, for example, were engaged in repeated and inconclusive litigation with the High Authority of the European Coal and Steel Community for the first ten years of the Authority's life.

In Britain the earliest cartel is thought to have been the Newcastle Vend in the seventeenth century. There were minor cartels before the First World War, e.g. in salt and sewing thread, but reliance on export markets and the absence of protection against imports made cartel selling arrangements difficult to organize. During the inter-war years several cartels were formed with government assistance or insistence, e.g. in coal, hops, milk and potatoes. After World War II central control of selling was tightened by nationalization in coal, gas, electricity, railways, steel, etc. In the main, however, British firms have relied on looser arrangements to limit competition. Cartels are criticized because they help to keep inefficient units in production, limit the output of efficient firms, and therefore maintain prices at levels higher than in competition. They are sometimes defended as a means of securing an orderly concentration of production in efficient firms (rationalization was intended to accompany the British coal cartels of the 1930's, although by relieving the pressure on mining companies' profits the cartels probably hindered rather than helped reorganization), facilitating exchange of technical information and guaranteeing the quality of products.

In the absence of government assistance to make membership compulsory, cartels are difficult to maintain because of the competing interests of member firms. Highly mechanized firms with high fixed costs are more anxious than firms with lower fixed costs to keep output up even if prices are driven down; growing firms seek more favourable quotas; and firms well placed for home sales object to a cartel disposing of too much output abroad at relatively low prices. If a cartel is successful in raising members' profits their customers may be induced to produce for themselves and new firms may be encouraged to set up in the industry. Cartel agreements take many forms: they may refer to price levels, price determination, supply quotas, standardization of products or services, cost calculation, trading discounts and rebates and other aspects of potential competition.

Cartels were subject to increasingly intensive scrutiny in Britain after the Second World War, under legislation on monopolies and restrictive practices.

Broadly the difference between cartels and trusts is that cartels are intended to be temporary and trusts permanent. [3]

Cash, any widely-accepted form of money, usually in the form of legal tender coins and notes. In banking cash may also be considered as anything accepted by a joint-stock bank as perfectly "liquid" or a ready alternative to coin and notes. Thus bankers' deposits at the Bank of England are considered cash because the Bank is always able to offer its notes in exchange for deposits. Cash in this sense is thus a debt or liability of the central bank. In the balance sheet of joint-stock banks, therefore, the two items "Coin, notes, etc." and "Balance with the Bank of England" are considered as cash, and are customarily held at approximately 8 per cent of total deposits (the "cash ratio"). [8]

Cash Flow, the amounts received and expended by a person or enterprise during an "income reporting" period. In investment appraisals cash flows in the form of income receipts, operating expenses, debt service charges, etc. are counted when they are received or expended (or forecast to be received or expended). They differ from the "income and expenditure" statements derived from accrual methods of accounting, in which "income" for normal accounting purposes is adjusted to reflect periodic increases or decreases (appreciation, depreciation) in asset values since these changes contribute to the net worth of an enterprise. But unless and until assets are disposed of, these items do not appear in a statement of cash flow. The distinction is important for two reasons: first, knowledge of the true cash flow position may prevent the emergence of situations in which firms, despite showing good accounting profits, are forced into liquidation for want of liquidity (cash) to meet immediate and pressing commitments; second, for investment appraisal purposes involving the use of *capitalization* or *discounting* techniques, the timing of receipts and payments is important and may be crucial for choice among investment alternatives. [8]

Cash Ratio (banks). *See* BANKING, CASH.

Cassel, Gustav (1866–1945), Swedish economist. During his early career he came to England and was much influenced by Alfred Marshall. He became Lars Hiertas Professor of Political Economy at the University of Stockholm in 1904. His main publications, *Grundriss Einer Elementaren Preislehre* (1899) and *The Nature and Necessity of Interest* (1903), made important contributions to the theory of interest and the analysis of the trade cycle. He became widely recognized for his *Theory of Social Economy* (1918) and for his contribution to the discussion of monetary policy during and after the First World War. [2]

Catallactics, the science of exchange. Richard Whately coined the word in his *Introductory Lectures on Political Economy* (1831), and argued that it would have been a better name than "political economy" since economics can deal only with commodities in the process of exchange and not with systems in which the economic problem is met in some other way—as on Robinson Crusoe's island.

F. A. Hayek described catallactics as the theory of the catallaxy, the spontaneous market order which *discovers* human purposes, as distinct from the economy, which organizes resources to serve *prescribed* purposes. Economics as catallactics was described by Aristotle as *chrematistike,* the science of wealth, and is in part a return to the older definition of economics as the study of mankind and its endeavours to improve its condition. [14]

Catallaxy (from Greek *katallatein* or *katallassein,* "to exchange," "to make an enemy into a friend"), a market order produced spontaneously, not by deliberate arrangement. Thus it is distinguished by F. A. Hayek from "economy," the organization of resources to serve given purposes, as in a family, firm, government, nation or any other unit of organization. A catallaxy or spontaneous order produced by a market cannot be made to behave like an economy because its objectives are not known in advance and therefore cannot be laid down by organization from above; hence it cannot be judged by its failure or success in achieving *pre*-designed purposes, e.g. equality, "social justice," or the objectives of "welfare economics." The catallaxy works by competition, a mechanism for *discovering* desired purposes that are not foreknown. This view of economic behaviour differs from the (Robbins) definition of economics as the study of the allocation of scarce means to *given* ends, in which sense economics refers only to the pure logic of choice, the "economic calculus" of a family or firm or country in which the ends are pre-arranged or agreed in advance. [14]

Caveat Emptor, Latin for "let the buyer beware," common in economic analysis of markets which create or facilitate "consumer sovereignty" but require him to inform himself of the properties of purchases and to take the risk of bad buys. In practice the consumer is, or can be, helped by laws requiring goods to be suitable for the purposes they are intended to serve, providing for guarantees and warranties, and laying down penalties for fraud and misrepresentation, etc. The consumer may also buy advice on technical or scientific goods or services. In practice, if competition is active it is often the most effective safeguard because it provides alternative sources of supply so that a bad buy does not have to be repeated. "Caveat emptor" is therefore in practice virtually inoperative in a market dominated by a monopoly, e.g. a local garage, or a large firm in an industry with economies of scale, or a nationalized industry, since the buyer is effectively deprived of choice. [7]

Caveat Venditor, Latin for "let the seller beware." Strictly the opposite of caveat emptor, i.e. the seller is responsible for ensuring that he sells on the most favourable terms available in the market. This may be difficult if he sells to a monopsony (single buyer) or has few alternative buyers. More generally, the phrase can mean that sellers should beware of making a short-sighted profit but damaging their reputation or losing public goodwill, i.e. in the common phrase "making a sale but losing a customer." [7]

Ceiling, a maximum price, wage, profit, output, etc. allowed by government. Ceiling prices may be fixed in wartime; ceiling wages or ceiling rates of increases in wages in a peacetime wages policy; ceiling dividends or increases in dividends in an incomes policy; ceiling output in agricultural policy or in quotes for members of a commodity agreement. Ceilings may be effective for a time but usually require widening controls to make them work when market conditions of supply and demand change. [10]

Census, a count of population, output, processes. It has long yielded more than accurate estimates of numbers. The censuses of ancient states such as Rome and Persia were used to determine, *inter alia,* the taxable capacity and military potential of the state: twentieth-century censuses are concerned with a wider range of social and economic matters.

The modern census dates back to the seventeenth century; the first British census was in 1801. UK population censuses have been taken, with occasional breaks, every ten years since that date. Censuses of production and of distribution have also been introduced in the UK, the USA and other countries in recent years. They obtain information on the number of enterprises of particular kinds and deal with employment, equipment and output.

In the British census of population information is obtained by enumerators who visit all houses and institutions in areas assigned to them, distribute and later collect questionnaire forms, and check on the accuracy and completeness of the answers. The scope of census questions has been reduced since the nineteenth century; the most important information now obtained is of total population (which cannot be so accurately determined from the data on births, deaths and migration) and of its distribution by age, sex, marital status, occupation, employment, education and place of residence, and also of some aspects of living conditions.

The results are valuable because they make it possible to analyse the population not merely into groups according to age, employment and so on, but into subgroups such as total married female clerical workers within age group and area. Subgrouping is possible because information under many heads has been collected simultaneously for each individual. Census information is used in policy-making by national and local government.

Other censuses of economic interest are those of production (at intervals since 1907) and distribution (number, size, turnover, etc., of shops and retail outlets for hairdressing and other services); the first was in 1950. [11]

Census of Distribution. *See* CENSUS; SOURCES, STATISTICAL.

Census of Production. *See* CENSUS; SOURCES, STATISTICAL.

Central Bank, a banking institution that is the focus of the financial system of a country, usually controlled wholly or partly by the government as the principal regulator of credit.

The fundamental task of a central bank is to control the commercial or joint-stock banks so as to support the government's monetary policy: it must therefore remain a distinct part of the monetary system, and does not usually (with minor exceptions) undertake ordinary banking business.

The functions of a central bank are mainly in four groups:

(1) Control of the note issue. It usually has a monopoly of the note issue (the Scottish banks have the right to issue notes provided they are "covered" by Bank of England notes). In Britain the note issue is regulated by an Act of Parliament which empowers the Bank to issue a stated amount of notes backed by securities and an unspecified amount backed by gold. The amount backed by gold is small and the authorized note issue is therefore issued virtually entirely against securities. This issue unbacked by gold is known as the fiduciary issue ("issued in faith"), the volume of which is fixed by Parliament in accordance with what are thought to be the needs of the economy.

(2) The banker's bank. A central bank stands in a similar relationship to commercial banks as the commercial banks to their customers. Commercial banks hold deposits with the central bank which they regard as cash; they may also look to the central bank either directly or indirectly (as in Britain through the recall of loans to the discount market) for temporary accommodation (loans) if there is a shortage of cash reserves. Thus, by providing these services for commercial banks the central bank is the ultimate source of cash. It is through this control that the bank is able to influence the volume of credit.

(3) The government bank. The central bank of a country usually conducts the ordinary banking business of the government. In Britain the Bank of England is owned by the government; in some countries the government owns a large interest; in the USA the Federal

Reserve Board is private but is controlled by the state through the appointment of Governors.

(4) Other functions: A central bank also usually conducts foreign exchange business (buying and selling foreign currencies, operation of exchange control, etc.); undertakes open market operations; acts as a "lender of last resort" and fixes the official Bank rate or rate of discount, often in conjunction with the government. [8]

Central Place Theory, originated in the work of the German economist Walter Christaller during the nineteen-thirties (*Central Places in Southern Germany,* English translation by C. W. Baskin, 1966) and refined and developed by economists, geographers and others, which postulates a hierarchy of urban areas related by size and distance from one another. Cities and towns are regarded as centres of market-oriented activities, each kind of activity tending to have an optimum sales area defined by (*a*) transport costs, (*b*) the extent of possible economies of large-scale production, (*c*) the minimum scale of demand (the "demand threshold") necessary to generate the activity at all. Thus corner shops are found everywhere, department stores only in larger towns; family doctors in small towns, neurologists only in major centres along with central government agencies, foreign embassies, major cultural services and the like. The provision of goods and services with approximately the same threshold size, transport costs and scale economies in production tends to be located in the centre of a market area, and on the principle that "big fleas have lesser fleas" a system of "central places" tends to emerge with small central places and their market areas included in those of the larger. An urban hierarchy thus tends to emerge with possibly a single capital city at the top, thousands of villages at the bottom, and a well-defined rank-size distribution of urban areas in between. Although well-defined statistical regularities of this kind can be observed in most countries, the theory is subject to qualifications that limit its power as an all-embracing explanation of the size and growth of urban areas. [6]

Central Planning, (*a*) the regulation of resources by government in which labour is "directed" and capital "conscripted" by law. Central planning can make official use of markets to a degree: very small in countries with no long traditions of civil and political liberty, such as Russia and China, more in countries with independent local traditions, as in Yugoslavia, Poland and Hungary. Where markets are proscribed officially they tend to spread unofficially as "black" or "grey" markets. Central planning can be effective in war or other emergencies where it can operate more quickly than free markets to transfer resources from less to more urgent uses, e.g. from consumption to armaments, or from trading to agriculture. If they do not use markets internally, central planners can to a lesser degree assess relative values of goods and services from external (international) markets.

(*b*) In Western democracy central planning takes milder forms such as *indicating*, rather than *directing*, the desirable use of resources, as in French indicative planning and the short-lived British National Plan (1965–6), or, more loosely, setting targets for private industry in output, exports, investment, etc.

(*c*) the term does not normally refer to the conduct of government machinery or nationalized industry. [10]

Central Statistical Office (CSO), British government office that coordinates and collects statistics from British government departments for the guidance of Ministers in forming policy. It originated in the Second World War when national accounts of income, expenditure, etc. were assembled to facilitate wartime economic controls. It has thus concentrated largely on macroeconomic quantities (totals and averages). [10]

Ceteris Paribus, Latin for "other things being equal." Logical device commonly used by economists to isolate the subject of study so that changes external to it need not be considered, even though they would affect it in the real world. Thus in examining the effect on demand of a change in price, other influences on price—income, season, fashion, etc.—are assumed to remain unchanged. In examining the effect on employment or unemployment (demand for labour) of a change in wages (price of labour) other influences on the demand for labour—rising demand for the product from abroad, technical innovation that would reduce the demand for labour, etc.—are supposed unaltered. If the device is not applied strictly, wrong conclusions may be drawn, e.g. if a higher tax on cars is followed by larger sales of cars, it does not follow that the demand for cars rises with their price: the larger demand may have been caused by *other* influences that had *not* remained unchanged. [14]

Chamberlin, Edward H. (1899–1967), American economist. He first taught at the University of Michigan and then at Harvard, where he was Professor of Economics from 1937. He became best known for *The Theory of Monopolistic Competition* (1933), which coincided in time and outlook with Joan Robinson's *The Economics of Imperfect Competition* (1933). Both emphasized the "institutional monopoly" created by the artificial "differentiation" of products from one another by branding, packaging, advertising, etc., and both developed the geometry of marginal and average revenue and costs. Chamberlin argued that industry was not best analysed by the theory of competition or of monopoly because it operated as a mixture of both, each firm with a "monopoly" of its product(s) competing with other "monopolies." A criticism of this approach, which has influenced economic thinking for forty years, has been that it is too static and short-period, and that in the longer run the more characteristic aspect of a dynamic economic system and structure of changing markets is that constant movement in supply and demand tends to break down local, partial and temporary "institutional" (or other) monopolies. [2]

Chance, in economic theory, means probability. Decisions made in conditions of uncertainty have been an important object of study in economics. Uncertainty can be treated by assuming that chances or probabilities of particular events are weighed up, that is, in the process of decision a future event is assigned a rough mathematical probability and the course of action is influenced by it. A different view was taken by Professor G. L. S. Shackle, who analysed uncertainty as "potential surprise." In this analysis it is not assumed that the chance of a particular outcome is weighted according to its (approximate) mathematical probability.

In a more general sense, taking business chances or risks which are not insurable may be regarded as the essence of the entrepreneurial function and the reason why realized profits may be higher or lower than the expected rate of return on the capital used in the enterprise. [14]

Characteristics, Demand for, a new approach to the theory of consumer behaviour, first adumbrated in 1966 by the British economist K. Lancaster and further developed in his *Consumer Demand, A New Approach* (1971). He postulated that consumers value the characteristics inherent in goods rather than the goods themselves, that the number of goods and the number of characteristics need not be equal (each good will generally have more than one characteristic and in mature economies the number of goods will generally exceed the number of characteristics), and that goods consumed in combination may give rise to attributes which do not exist when the goods are consumed in isolation. From these basic postulates Lancaster developed a perceptive theory of demand that transformed goods into characteristics. Although highly suggestive, the theory has proved difficult to apply in practice. [7]

Charging What the Traffic will Bear. *See* PRICE DISCRIMINATION.

Charity, the voluntary transfer (i.e. not in response to coercive power) of income, goods or services to another individual, or other individuals, directly or through an agency, at a price ranging from less than the market price to nil. It does not necessarily imply giving with no price—"free"; that *part* of the value of the object (or service) between the price charged and the market price is the "free" gift. Transfers made through the political market are not voluntary, except in the sense that individuals may voluntarily agree to compel themselves to give others medical care, etc. through the political market on the ground that, unless all give, none or only few will give (which may or may not be true). The political process implies coercion of some or many, unless 100 per cent agree voluntarily to compel themselves; but 51 per cent can compel 49 per cent to give against their inclinations. Personal charity is direct; "collective" charity is dispensed indirectly through a collecting and distributing intermediary. The motives behind the two kinds of charity differ: T. R. Malthus wrote of the extremes of motives, "In the great charitable institutions supported by voluntary contributions . . . the subscriptions . . . are sometimes given grudgingly, and rather because they are expected by the world . . . than because they are prompted by . . . genuine benevolence . . . But it is far otherwise with that voluntary and active charity which makes itself acquainted with the objects it relieves; which seems to feel, and to be proud of, the bond that unites the rich with the poor . . ." [13]

Charity Market, the newest market studied by economists (mostly in America, more recently in Britain), in which people give goods or services with no apparent return. The private market, in which individuals and firms exchange goods and services with one another against money, has been studied increasingly since Adam Smith in the second half of the eighteenth century. Its strengths and weaknesses, although still debated, are known in detail. The political market, which organizes the production of "public goods," has been studied since the 1950's, although its strengths and weaknesses have yet to be clarified or defined. But study of the charity market began systematically only in the 1960's. The little analytical or empirical research so far done is mostly by American economists, but the Institute of Economic Affairs' *The Economics of Charity* (1973/4) incorporated an analysis by A. J. Culyer of York University.

The neglect of the economics of giving may be explained by the economist's traditional view of man as rationally materialistic and therefore reluctant to contribute to private "good causes" or to the cost of public goods. But to a larger or lesser degree man is influenced by a wide range of motives to give, for both public goods and private goods for other individuals. Furthermore, the demand for gifts exceeds the supply, so that resources for giving are scarce. Economists can therefore analyse the charity markets as a mechanism for financing and allocating resources that is distinct from the private and political markets but in which laws on maximizing/optimizing utility and returns can similarly be applied. The motives for charitable giving may vary from pure benevolence, through hope of indirect benefit (prestige, fame, etc.), to desire to influence people or policies. [13]

Cheap Money, the policy of low interest rates to stimulate the borrowing of money. A low Bank rate and extensive open market dealings in securities by the monetary authorities are two essential methods. It has also been known, especially in the USA, as easy money.

In Britain the cheap money launched by the War Loan Conversion of June 1932 was continued throughout both the depressed and the boom war and post-war years until 1951. Bank rate was kept down at 2 per cent during this period. As a wartime measure, cheap money turned conventional monetary policy upside-down. Normally, high interest rates would be called for to restrain inflationary demand. Its success in smoothing diversion of the country's resources to the war effort depended on maximum use of taxation, direct controls and patriotic appeals as complementary measures to restrain "non-essential" demands for resources. The post-war efforts of the Labour Government to continue and intensify cheap money without inflation failed mainly because these complementary measures were unavailing in peacetime boom conditions. After 1947 long-term interest rates rose to more "realistic" levels, and since 1951 "dear money" policy, including higher Bank rate, has been used to help restrain spending during boom periods especially after the acceleration of inflation in the 1970's, when interest rates rose to unprecedented heights (although after allowance was made for rates of price inflation of 15 or 20 per cent or more, real as distinct from nominal or money rates of interest were generally around 3 to 4 per cent). [10]

Check Trading, financing purchases by a voucher ("check") to be used for immediate purchase from undefined sources and to be repaid by instalments with interest. The voucher is encashed less a discount. Check trading originated in nineteenth-century industrial England and is still conducted mainly among wage-earners. It has increasingly had to compete with new, more extensive methods of credit-trading, such as hire purchase, but it has also benefited by escaping the post-war fluctuations in governmental regulation of hire purchase in the effort by government to control economic activity by "stop-go." [8]

Cheque, an instrument or document by which bank deposits are transferred between individuals. A written order authorizing a banker to pay a specified sum of money to the person named in the order. When one person pays another by cheque the drawer's bank balance is reduced by the amount of the cheque, the payee's is correspondingly increased.

Cheques originated in the late seventeenth century and grew rapidly in volume in the nineteenth century, especially after the 1844 Bank Charter Act, which limited the note issue. They form the main part of the means of payment in Britain: in the 1960's and 1970's about 90 per cent of payments, and cash about 10 per cent. The development of credit cards, at first as a competitor of bank money (cheques based on deposits), was used by the banks in the late 1960's and 1970's to supplement their cheque business. Cheques (and credit cards) are also in common use in the Commonwealth and in North America and Europe but less elsewhere. [8]

Cherry-picking. *See* Loss Leader.

Chicago School, a group of disciples of liberal economic philosophy, working at the University of Chicago. It was founded by the late Henry C. Simons and Frank H. Knight in the 1920's, fortified by F. A. Hayek in the 1950's, and continued by Professors Milton Friedman and George Stigler and others. They follow the tradition of the English classical economists in their emphasis on the economic progress and political liberties afforded by free markets as the central allocative mechanism, with its two instruments of competition between sellers and choice for buyers. Friedman is also the leader of the Chicago Monetarist School, which regards money and the control of its supply (or miscontrol by governments and central banks) as the determinant of economic instability and inflation. Hayek emphasized the power of trade unions to induce government to inflate the money supply to avoid the unemployment that would otherwise follow wages pushed above the value of the marginal product. The philosophy of the Chicago School in its free market and monetarist aspects is assembled in Friedman's *Capitalism and Freedom,* which also puts the argument for two Friedman discoveries (or rediscoveries), education vouchers and a negative income tax. The School also emphasizes the empirical testing of economic hypotheses, an approach not always shared by liberal economists elsewhere, some of whom remain sceptical of historical/mathematical macro-methods in economics. [2]

Choice, the act of preferring one course of action to others. It lies at the centre of the economic problem; economics is very largely concerned with the principles explaining how choices are made. Human beings have to decide how to use limited resources to attain the largest possible satisfaction of their wants. Since wants cannot be satisfied completely and the available means can be used to obtain different ends, and given ends in different ways, there must be choice between ends and between means.

Decisions on how people are to earn their living, how they are to distribute their spending, how goods are to be produced—all aspects of the basic problem of choice—may be decided in several ways. In one society choice may be guided almost exclusively by custom: people work in different occupations according to their social origin, and consumption and production are organized in conformity with traditional patterns. In another society choice may be exercised by only a small ruling group, work being done under orders rather than for material reward, and consumption goods allocated from above by the state. In a third type of society choice may be guided predominantly by a price system. It is with this last type of society that economics is chiefly concerned. Economic theory is useful wherever choice is or can be expressed in varying degrees through a price mechanism in capitalist or communist countries. [14]

Christian Socialism, philosophy originated in mid-nineteenth century England by Charles Kingsley and Frederick Maurice. It modified the theory of state socialism by emphasizing Christian ethics and substituting voluntary co-operation for nationalization of industry. It envisaged the replacement of self-interested private profit by disinterested mutual aid, but differed from state socialism in emphasizing the supremacy of the human spirit and individual liberty. It has made less headway than state socialism, except in local communities for short periods, perhaps because mutual aid is not a sufficient inducement to effort unless enforced by the state, although it remains an element in all societies, capitalist and communist, as an expression of man's humanity to man. [10]

CIF, "cost, insurance, freight." The name given to the system of payment for goods shipped when the costs of insurance and freight are included in the price. [4]

Circulating Capital, working, current, "unfixed" capital in contrast to fixed assets; i.e. stocks of partly or wholly completed goods, in contrast to plant and equipment. [1]

City (of London), the square mile centred on the Bank of England and containing the main institutions that finance British and much of the world's trade and industry: the Stock Exchange, Lloyd's (insurance), the headquarters of the four clearing banks, the merchant banks, many stockbrokers, discount houses, money and commodity markets, insurance companies, shipping companies, etc. It is thus the site of those activities that produce the invisible exports (financing, insurances, transport, merchanting of trade in or between other countries) that in the past made London the financial leader of the world and still pay for much of the visible imports. The City's invisible earnings were questioned by several British economists in the late 1950's and early 1960's but more recent developments indicate that they underestimated their importance. [10]

Clark, Colin (1905–89), English economist. He was educated at Winchester and Oxford and graduated at the Universities of Oxford and Cambridge. He showed early interest in politics by standing as a Labour candidate in 1929, 1931 and 1935. His first teaching post was as Lecturer in Statistics at the University of Cambridge (1931–7). He soon established a reputation by four books which showed his original mind by pioneering private work that pre-dated government national income macro-statistics: *The National Income, 1924–31* (1932); *National Income and Outlay* (1937); *The Conditions of Economic Progress* (1940); and *The Economics of 1960* (1942). In 1945 he traced a statistical correlation between taxation and inflation that Keynes accepted. During the 1950's he inspired a re-examination of the economic rationale of the Welfare State by *Welfare and Taxation* (1954). He wrote *Growthmanship* (1961) and *Taxmanship* (1964) for the

Institute of Economic Affairs, *The Economics of Subsistence Agriculture* (with M. R. Haswell; 1964), *Population Growth and Land Use* (1967), and frequent articles in the learned journals. After the war he lectured widely in Universities in Australia and round the world and advised many governments. From 1953 to 1969 he was Director of the Oxford Institute for Research in Agricultural Economics. He returned to Australia in 1969 as Research Fellow at Monash University. [2]

Clark, John Bates (1847–1938), American economist. Educated at Brown University and Amherst College, followed by a period at the University of Heidelberg. On his return to the USA he began an academic career at Carlton College, finally becoming Professor at Columbia University. Although his early interest was philosophy, he became convinced that economics was of vital importance to mankind; yet his studies left him with a feeling that the subject was deficient in many respects. He tried to remedy the deficiencies in *Philosophy of Wealth* (1885) by reformulating the postulates of the classical economists. Apart from *Essentials of Economic Theory* (1907), he is best known for his *Distribution of Wealth* (1899), in which he extended the marginal principle into the analysis of production and distribution and introduced the concept of the "marginal product." [2]

Clark, John Maurice (1884–1963), American economist; son of J. B. Clark. He taught at Columbia University from 1915 and succeeded to his father's chair in 1926. His treatment of overhead costs based on contemporary American market conditions in *Economics of Overhead Costs* (1923) was important in the development of dynamic analysis. He also developed and introduced the concept of the *acceleration principle*, i.e. the relationship between the rate of growth in the demand for consumers' goods and the rate of growth in the demand for producers' goods. In 1936 he published the *Essays in Preface to Social Economics.* [2]

Class Struggle, a doctrine developed by Karl Marx that economic change reflected and was motivated by conflict between (in the nineteenth century) the bourgeoisie and the proletariat. It was a powerful explanatory device that has considerably influenced economic and political thinking and policy. Critics of the theory, mainly economists, have argued that there is both conflict within each class (e.g. between highly organized and unorganized wage-earners, between large established industries and new emerging industries) and collusion between classes (e.g. employers and employees in an industry who combine to press for tariffs or other privileges or to resist competition). [14]

Classical Economists, the academics and men of affairs, philosophers and economists, Englishmen and Scotsmen who between 1750 and 1850 formulated the principles of the new science of economics and the theory of economic policy which it yielded. The most prominent were David Hume, Adam Smith,

David Ricardo, Thomas Malthus, Robert Torrens, Nassau Senior, John McCulloch, James Mill, John Stuart Mill, Jeremy Bentham and John Elliot Cairnes.

For many years in the nineteenth and twentieth centuries historians and political theorists, such as Sidney and Beatrice Webb, the Hammonds, G. D. H. Cole and others, regarded them as apologists for the developing system of industrial capitalism and for the widespread pauperism and large profits that went with it. Some commentators went further and discredited them as the tools of industrialists and the opponents of social reform, and claimed that they preached the system of laissez-faire in which the state stood aside and allowed the strong to dominate the weak. A different interpretation of their writings and the policy they advocated has been presented in the writings of Lord Robbins, F. A. Hayek, Ludwig von Mises, Wilhelm Röpke, W. H. Hutt and others. This view is that the dominant impression given by the writings of the classical economists—that they were opposed to governmental action in principle and in favour of complete freedom in economic activity—must be explained by the circumstances of the time: they were essentially reformers writing to expose the defects of the restrictive mercantilist institutions and habits of thought which lingered from the seventeenth and eighteenth centuries. They were concerned with current political controversies and were addressing themselves to their contemporaries, not to posterity. It was natural, therefore, that they should emphasize the liberating aspect of their theories. But their writings show that they contemplated not laissez-faire, in the sense of non-interference by government in economic activity, but an active state in which man-made laws and institutions enabled the market economy to work to the social advantage.

Adam Smith spoke of ". . . the duty of erecting and maintaining certain public works and certain public institutions, which it can never be for the interest of any individual or small number of individuals to erect and maintain; because the profit could never repay the expense to any individual or small number of individuals, though it may frequently do much more than repay it to a great society." Jeremy Bentham formulated a structure of institutions that would coordinate action so as to create what he thought was the good society: his *Constitutional Code* provided for a cabinet with ministers for elections, legislation, army, navy, preventive services (police, fire, etc.), interior communications, the relief of poverty, education, health, foreign relations, trade and finance. They were to be served by administrative machinery he outlined in detail: the President of the Board of Trade, for example, was instructed to bear in mind the need to revise regulations following changes in the value of money produced by changes in its supply relatively to the quantity of goods. McCulloch, Senior, J. S. Mill and other classical economists discussed the functions of the state in a "liberal" society.

Where it was not possible to perfect the framework of laws and institutions so that spontaneous activities promoted the general interest, e.g. where competition was not practicable, the classical economists envisaged direct state intervention. Adam Smith favoured assistance for infant industries; J. S. Mill advocated assistance for backward peoples, an upper limit on inheritance and a tax on the increment of land values; McCulloch argued for limitation of the dividends of public utility companies. These and other "interferences" were designed to fit into the system of economic freedom in order to increase opportunities and knowledge, or reduce excessive power, so that the market economy worked for general good.

The attitude of the classical economist to social conditions was often different from that suggested by their traditional critics. Smith and Malthus wanted subsidized schools. Senior (in the Report on the Handloom Weavers) said: ". . . both the ground landlord and the speculating builder ought to be compelled by law . . . to take measures which shall prevent the towns they create being centres of disease." With the exception of Ricardo, all the classical economists opposed truck (payment of wages in goods); Ricardo thought that Robert Owen's experiment at New Lanark might benefit from a truck shop. They supported the Factory Act restrictions on the employment of children. Senior favoured restrictions on the employment of women in mines. Some of the classical economists thought that most women should be treated as men; the reason put by J. S. Mill was that they would then be allowed access to industrial employment as a means of emancipation. Torrens wanted compensation for handloom weavers displaced by machinery.

The classical economists were generally opposed to minimum wage-fixing because they considered it would reduce the demand for labour. Most of them supported trade unionism, but with misgivings about the effects on the workers; J. S. Mill wrote: "There must be some better mode of sharing the fruits of human productive power than by diminishing their amount. Yet this is not only the effect but the intention of many of the conditions imposed by some unions on workmen and on employers. All restrictions on the employment of machinery, or on arrangements for economizing labour, deserve this censure. Some of the union regulations go even further than to prohibit improvements; they are contrived for the express purpose of making work inefficient; they positively prevent the workmen from working hard and well. . . ."

The classical economists foresaw the development of the social services. They saw them as a helping hand that would teach people in time to help themselves. John Stuart Mill, for example, said: ". . . government aid . . . should be so given as to be as far as possible a course of education for the people in the art of accomplishing great objects by individual energy and voluntary co-operation." Nassau Senior, who inspired the Poor Law Amendment Act of 1834, said in a memorandum on popular education submitted in 1861 to the Royal Commission on Education under Lord Newcastle: "We may look forward to the time when the labouring population may be safely entrusted with the education of their children; . . . the assistance and superintendence . . . of the Government for that purpose . . . [is] . . . only a means of preparing the labouring classes for a better, but remote state of things . . . in the latter part of the twentieth century . . . when that assistance and superintendence shall no longer be necessary."

The classical economists made assumptions about man and his environment: first, that man sought his own interest (which meant not self-interest but the interest of any whom he chose to benefit by his efforts); secondly, that while the world was getting richer, it was still poor and that all had to be given incentives to contribute to the common good. Hence the need for machinery that would gear self-interest to the social advantage. The classical economists thought that only a market economy could reconcile these objectives with personal freedom.

Interest in the teaching and judgements of the classical economists continued into the 1970's with the intensifying debate between economists and economic historians on the effects of industrialization on living standards and social conditions. Broadly the "pessimists," notably E. J. Hobsbawm and E. P. Thompson, who saw deterioration and immiseration, especially before the 1840's, tended to criticize the classical economists for arguing against state action to alleviate and ameliorate social conditions. The "optimists," notably Max Hartwell, and to a lesser degree G. E. Mingay and others, saw the system of economic freedom advocated by the classical economists as the necessary condition for general economic and social advance. [2]

Clay, Henry (1883–1954), British economist, born in Germany, educated at Bradford Grammar School and University College, Oxford. He was early and widely known for *Economics: An Introduction for the General Reader* (1916, second edition 1942), which established his reputation in Britain and the USA for its lucidity and homely illustrations of economic principles. He taught at the Universities of Oxford and Manchester until 1930, when he joined the Bank of England. He was a member of the Royal Commission on Unemployment Insurance in 1930–1. He helped to organize the Economic Section of the Cabinet Secretariat and the Central Statistical Office, and did other war work. In 1944 he became Warden of Nuffield College, Oxford, and he was knighted in 1946. [2]

Clayton Act. *See* Trust Busting.

Clearing Banks. *See* Banks, Clearing.

Clearing House, (*a*) a regional association of banks through which claims between banks arising from the issue of cheques, etc., are settled. In Britain the chief clearing house is in London (it was established in 1775): there are others in the main provincial centres which deal with local bank clearings; cheques outside a given radius are cleared through London. The business of clearing inter-bank indebtedness in London comprises Town Clearing (relating to the City financial district) and General Clearing, which deals with the remainder. (*b*) any organization through which deliveries of goods, services or financial facilities are made, e.g. the London Clearing House for the International Air Transport Association provides periodic settlements by airlines; the Railway Clearing House settles inter-regional accounts, passenger traffic arrangements, lost luggage recovery, etc.; a clearing house associated with the New York Stock Exchange arranges delivery of securities. [8]

Clipping (coins). *See* COINAGE, DEBASEMENT.

Close Company, defined for tax purposes as a business controlled in practice by up to five shareholders and in which the public own 35 per cent or more of the ordinary shares. The 1965 Finance Act introduced corporation tax to forestall avoidance of surtax (by shareholders who had ploughed profits back into the business) by requiring most trading profit (and investment income) to be distributed unless essential for the development of the business. [3]

Closed Economy, a self-sufficient economic system. Primarily a simplifying teaching device to remove external complications in analysing internal changes in micro-economic conditions of supply or demand or in macro-economic government revenue or expenditure, etc. No economy is completely closed. Britain and some other western countries have exported up to a fifth of their national product to pay for imports. Communist countries conduct a relatively small external trade with capitalist countries, sometimes in barter deals controlled by the state. [10]

Closed Shop, a place of work in which all employees are required to be members of a trade union, or, in its strictest form, of one trade union. It tends to be most common where "craft" unions are in a strong bargaining position, as in printing; inflation, and the sellers' market for labour it tends to create, has encouraged efforts to create closed shops. A trade union would argue first that, since all employees benefit from its efforts in collective bargaining, all employees should be members, otherwise non-unionists secure the advantage of unionization without being members or paying a subscription; secondly, 100 per cent unionism strengthens a trade union's disciplinary power over members, so that there are few unofficial strikes and a more orderly method of collective bargaining. Some economists reply first, that the closed shop curtails the employer's right to hire whom he likes, since he is unable to hire non-unionists, and this restriction impairs efficiency; secondly, that an employee who does not wish to join a union is excluded from some opportunities of employment, so that the trade union ceases to be in practice what it is in law, a voluntary organization; thirdly, that the trade unions are able to enforce closed shops only by the increase of powers granted by law, such as the 1906 Trade Dispute Act, when their bargaining power was weak, and that these powers have become exceptional privileges that should be withdrawn.

In the middle 1960's a court ruled that strikes to enforce a closed shop could be "torts" (civil wrongs), which made trade union officials liable to heavy damages. This led trade union leaders to demand a change in the law to protect the officials and some economists, lawyers and others to argue that a new trade union law should deal also with closed shops, demarcation rules and other restrictive practices in particular, and the individual liberty of employees in general.

The 1971 Industrial Relations Act required unions to register in order to retain their privileges, which were thus not removed but changed from unconditional to conditional. Registration entailed accepting the condition that no qualified worker should be excluded from membership of a union, i.e. the closed shop became impossible if a union registered. Because of this and other conditions, i.e. quid pro quos for the retention of union privileges, many unions did not register. The 1971 Act was repealed in 1974 and the closed shop restored to its former legal status. [5]

Coase, Ronald H. (1910–), British economist. He was educated and taught at the London School of Economics in the 1930's and 1940's, then went to the USA in 1951. He was Professor of Economics at the Universities of Buffalo, Virginia, and, from 1964, Chicago, where he was also editor of the *Journal of Law and Economics*. He has been a seminal contributor to economic theory and indirectly to policy. "The Nature of the Firm," in *Economica* (1937), delineated the firm as the province in which resources were allocated outside the market by direct orders or commands. *Broadcasting, A Study in Monopoly* (1950) revealed that the monopoly of the BBC rested not on unavoidable technical conditions but on avoidable political decisions. "The Problem of Social Cost" (*Journal of Law and Economics*, 1960), which has influenced economic thinking fundamentally, showed, in the developing theory of "externalities," that private and social benefits were not necessarily in conflict but could be reconciled by redefining property rights. [2]

Cobb-Douglas Production Function, a technical relationship between factors used in production and output, such that the returns to scale are constant. It was developed by the American economists Cobb and Douglas in 1928 as a hypothesis to explain the relatively unvarying share of wages (roughly 80 per cent) in the USA national income in the early years of the century. Empirical evidence so far seems to support the hypothesis, although there has been some change in the shares within the total of wages going to highly-organized and unorganized wage-earners. [5]

Cobweb Theory, name given to "cobweb" movement of some prices in growing or shrinking in recurring cycles. Classical market equilibrium suggested that prices would return to equilibrium. The Cobweb Theory indicates that if the elasticity of demand for the product equals the elasticity of supply, the price (and output) will fluctuate regularly; if the elasticity of supply exceeds the elasticity of demand the "cobweb" grows larger and equilibrium is not reached unless the elasticities change; if elasticity of demand exceeds elasticity of supply the "cobweb" shrinks to an eventual equilibrium. (An early version of the theory was the "pig cycle" demonstrated by R. F. Fowler.) The simplifying assumptions were that producers ignored the reaction of other producers, ignored expectations of change, and overlooked past errors. But it may still help to explain price disturbances in some markets where these assumptions apply in some degree. [7]

Co-efficient, mathematical device used in economics as a number that qualifies (multiplies or divides) a quantity, known or unknown. [14]

Coin, money made of metal stamped with a usually intricate and recognizable design as a protection against fraud and forgery. Nowadays the only coins in circulation in most countries are of small denominations made of bronze, nickel silver and other alloys. They are "token" coinage, i.e., their intrinsic metallic value is less than the face value in contrast with standard coinage (e.g. the gold sovereign), whose face value is equal to its intrinsic value. [8]

Coinage, money made of metal. Money that circulates, "currency," has taken the form of coinage since its use in Greece and China about 700 B.C. Minting coins as a medium of exchange spread to England in the second century B.C. (a century before the arrival of Caesar). Modern methods began with milling under Elizabeth I. Before that, coins—including the gold pound, the unit of English coinage—were made by hammering two handcut dies between which metal had been placed. (The pound became known as a sovereign because gold was thought the royal or "sovereign" metal.) The first coin sovereign was hammered under Henry VII in 1489, four years after he came to the throne, the first silver shilling under Edward VI (1548–53), and the first silver sixpence and threepence under Elizabeth I (1558–1603).

Hammered coins were not perfectly circular and could easily be clipped and forged. Hammering was superseded by the "milled" coin: the metal from which the coins were produced was converted to a strip of uniform thickness by heavy rollers driven by a mill—hence "milling."

During the Republic (1649–60) emergency coins of rough-shaped silver were made in besieged towns. The return of monarchy saw a new series of coins with the familiar shape and design—round, with the monarch's head on one side, etc. While the designs were being prepared, coins were made by hammering, but milling recommenced in 1662, two years after the Restoration of Charles II. The coins included a "guinea" piece, so called because much of its metal came from Guinea. The Caroline series of coins continued until the next great reform of the coinage in 1816 under George III. Coins were further remodelled in 1927. The twelve-sided threepenny piece appeared under George V (1910–36). Silver coins were discontinued in 1946. The only silver coins still struck are Maundy money, coins of one, two, three and four pence distributed by the Queen on Maundy Thursday to old men and women of a number equal to her age in years: Maundy money coins are legal tender currency. In 1972 the pounds-shillings-pence coinage was replaced by a new relationship of £1 equal to 100 new pence. [8]

Cole, George Douglas Howard (1889–1959), English economist, university teacher, social reformer, prolific writer and novelist. He was born in Cambridge and educated at Oxford (Balliol). He soon embraced socialism as "a way of life," became an ardent Fabian, and advocated guild socialism and syndicalism or "workers' control" of industry.

G. D. H. Cole was the first research secretary of the Labour Party but resigned in 1924 in protest over communist influence. He was also the first full-time tutor and organizer of the Workers' Educational Association from 1921. In 1925 he was appointed University Reader in Economics at Oxford, with which he retained a close connection for the rest of his life (chairman and director of Nuffield College Social Reconstruction Survey, 1941–4; Chichele Professor of Social and Political Theory from 1944).

Cole's forte was not economic theory but practical analysis and interpretation, mostly within a socialist framework. He admired Russian planning but as a libertarian rejected the rigidity and dogmatism of Soviet philosophy. He popularized socialist ideas, often in social histories. In *Principles of Economic Planning* (1935) he espoused complete socialist planning as essential to the construction of a socialist democracy.

Cole was a member of the Economic Advisory Council created by Ramsay MacDonald in 1930.

A series of books followed the Second World War, including *The Intelligent Man's Guide to the Post-war World* (1947) and *The Post-War Condition of Britain* (1956). The first volume of his massive *History of Socialist Thought* was published in 1953, the fourth in 1958. Between 1923 and 1942 he collaborated with his wife in detective novels and short stories. [2]

Collateral, assets added as secondary support for a loan. Banks may require securities, home deeds, or life assurance policies, etc., to support a borrower's personal standing. [8]

Collective Bargaining, negotiation between a group of employees as a unit and an employer (or employers) on terms and conditions of employment. Before the Industrial Revolution an employer usually made an individual bargain on wages and conditions of employment with each worker, but as the factory system developed and the craftman's skill became much less important the bargaining power of the employer increased. He employed large numbers of employees and it was usually easy to replace an employee who demanded better terms. Groups of workers therefore banded together to bargain collectively, and it was from these early attempts to safeguard employee rights that collective bargaining developed.

Effective collective bargaining requires several conditions: first, an appropriate unit of employees and an agent to carry out the bargaining: trade unions fulfil this function; secondly, the employer must recognize both unit and the agent: in Britain trade unions are generally recognized as "bargaining agents" (this is not legally required in the USA and Canada, and some British employers still refuse to recognize unions); thirdly, a procedure by which the parties can meet for discussion and exchange views; fourthly, a readiness by both sides to approach negotiations in good faith and make a genuine effort to reach agreement. Since collective bargaining in Britain is voluntary, it can be easily frustrated by either side.

There are several "levels" of collective bargaining in Britain, and the pattern of bargaining is complex. There is national bargaining, in which a union or federation of trade unions negotiates with an association of employers for all the members of the union. The most important national bargaining structure is in the engineering industry. National bargaining generally covers only minimum wages, hours of work and holidays with pay. It lays down a broad framework and leaves particular issues to district or local bargaining, perhaps between a union district committee and a group of employers. These bodies can take into account local conditions, and can graft on to the national agreement additional provisions to cover special circumstances. Finally there is plant bargaining between the management of a single firm and employee representatives, often a shop stewards' committee from several unions. Since anything affecting union-management relations or working conditions is a subject for collective bargaining, plant negotiations have wide scope to determine the conditions of employment of groups of workers.

These types of bargaining do not exist in all industries. In practice the process is less formal, especially in local and plant bargaining where a collective agreement, which in some other countries is a detailed legal document, may not even exist. Often bargaining results only in an informal understanding between the two sides. That a collective agreement is not enforceable by law illustrates the voluntary nature of British industrial relations. It is regarded as a gentleman's agreement; it depends for its successful operation on its acceptance by both sides. Many students of industrial relations hold that an unwritten understanding can have as much force as a written agreement.

As well as wages and conditions of employment, collective bargaining often covers the settlement of disputes by laying down a procedure to be followed. Disputes may occur either over the interpretation of an existing agreement, which may in the last resort go to arbitration, or in negotiations of new conditions of employment, which may be assisted by the Department of Employment's conciliation services. But, except in special circumstances, a dispute can be ended only with the consent of the parties.

How bargaining proceeds and on what basis depends on the institutions and circumstances. The alternative for collective bargaining as a system is either a return to individual bargaining or complete state control. Some critics of large-scale collective bargaining between nation-wide employers' organizations and employees' trade unions have argued that employees and employers have little inducement to show sufficient regard for the consumer interest. Others have argued that the solution is an effective law against restrictive practices by both employers' and employees' organizations and monetary and budgetary policy which prevents inflation so that employers and trade unions cannot combine to raise costs and pass them on to the consumer in higher prices. [5]

Collective Choice, ideally the machinery of "the political process" through the ballot box by which majorities decide between policies by voting for parties presenting lists of policies on "public goods." It has been increasingly analysed in the recent development, especially in the USA, of "the economics of politics" and electoral (majority and other) voting systems. This approach indicates that collective choice may not yield clear-cut preferences or a stable government capable of satisfying them, and that democratic majority voting may frustrate preferences. If the choice is between parties offering *lists* of policies, preference for no *single* policy can be recorded (except by referendum). If the lists of policies are confined to "public goods" (defence, etc.) rough preferences can be indicated, recorded and satisfied. If the lists include "private goods" (medical care, etc.) the system is not necessarily capable of satisfying individual preferences. [13]

Collectivism, centralized planning of an economy by the state. It is a means of obtaining a number of collective ends, socialist (equality, social justice, etc.), fascist (national aggrandizement) or any other, through state action. It denotes the opposite of economic and political liberalism.

Two older meanings were: first, that of socialists who opposed Marx and Marxism towards the end of the nineteenth century on the ground that Marxian doctrine prescribed a powerful central government; they called themselves collectivists as opposed to communists and included Bakunin and his followers. In this sense collectivism was closely associated with anarchism. The collectivists favoured the abolition of government as well as of private ownership of the means of production, though not of personal property, and advocated a free association of communes.

Secondly, collectivism was used to mean state socialism with centralized authority, as opposed to guild socialism and co-operation.

In current writing collectivism tends to be used loosely as an equivalent of state socialism. It implies a system in which capital used in production is owned by the community and operated by the state while individuals retain a right to personal property. It is thus contrasted with capitalism and includes communism.

During the 1930's there was extensive discussion among economists of the ways in which a collectivist or socialist economy might deal with the fundamental economic problem of scarcity and choice. The principal issue was whether a collectivist economy could in principle allocate resources efficiently. This was denied by Ludwig von Mises on the grounds that markets and therefore prices could not be formed, and that rational allocation without prices was impossible. The possibility of an efficient collectivist economy was argued by Barone in a theory, since developed by F. M. Taylor, Oskar Lange, A. P. Lerner and others, that envisaged accounting prices for the factors of production to be prescribed by central authority and rules to be applied by the managers of plants for equating marginal cost and price. Some "collective" economies have in some respects appeared to be successful, for various reasons in which collectivism is thought among the least important.

The movement for collective ownership of capital has lost some of its force in Western Europe but it influences some developing countries. A number of advanced western countries (France, Britain) have experimented with voluntary central planning within a broadly capitalist framework, and the collectivist countries (Yugoslavia, Hungary, Poland, Russia) are using market mechanisms in varying degree. [10]

Collectivists. *See* COLLECTIVISM.

Collusion, agreement between legally separate firms or other organizations to act together to increase their bargaining power in the market, e.g. by agreeing on prices they charge or offer, output quotas, etc. Such agreements are monopolistic in intention and therefore discouraged or outlawed by legislation on monopolies and restrictive practices. They also suffer strain as market conditions of supply or demand change and one or more of the participants finds it more profitable to withdraw. [3]

Collusive Tendering, collaboration by firms to submit tenders on agreed terms. The agreement might be that each would quote the same price (level tendering), that one would offer a lower price than the rest (allocating contracts), that some would quote prices above the rest (cover prices), that proposed tenders would be submitted to a central office to "adjust" "unreasonably" low ones, or that each would raise his tender by an amount sufficient to cover the costs of preparing tenders in all the firms and the firm securing the contract would reimburse the others for these costs.

Level tendering was an extension of price agreements into industries where sales are made by submitting tenders. The constructors of heavy electrical equipment, for example, at times agreed to tender at fixed prices and to limit competition to their comparative technical efficiency in fulfilling contracts. Where firms shared markets in agreed proportions as well as fixed prices, they nominated the one to submit the lowest tender for each contract. This system was used for some years before the Second World War in the sale of metal windows. The selling power obtained by manufacturers of electrical machinery by level tendering may have offset the buying power of their few large customers. The short-lived system of allocating contracts in the metal window industry did not reduce competition from wooden windows.

The practice of letting rivals know the cover price and of submitting "dummy" tenders at these prices was said to exist in the British building industry. Building contractors argued that in order to maintain their places on architects' lists they were forced to submit tenders even when too busy to do the work; a cover price enabled them to submit a realistic tender with safety. Collaboration on cover prices could extend to tacit agreements on contract prices. Builders' conferences in various parts of Britain had arrangements to register proposed tenders and "adjust" those thought "unreasonably" low. It was argued that this practice protected developers inclined to accept the lowest bid from inefficient contractors quoting unprofitable prices out of anxiety to secure a contract and then trying to recoup their position by skimping the job. Reimbursement of tendering costs was also arranged by building conferences. Tendering costs were invariably a sore point with contractors. When a tender was not accepted they appeared as wasted expenditure. They were, however, simply a cost of securing business, and there was no substantial difference between firms recovering these costs individually as part of their overheads and collectively in a reimbursement scheme. The London Builder's Conference was investigated by the Monopolies Commission, which found that its tendering arrangements had little effect in restricting competition. [3]

Colombo Plan, scheme devised by the USA, Canada, the UK, Australia, New Zealand and Japan to promote the economic development of countries in South and South-East Asia after the Second World War, mostly by supplying technical advisers, equipment and training. [4]

Colonialism (Economic), broadly the theory that trading relationships with developing countries have benefited only the advanced countries. An extreme version is that international trade has hindered growth in the developing countries by emphasizing the division in their economies into an export sector developing with trade and commerce and a large subsistence sector which continues to stagnate.

It is difficult to show that the developing countries have grown more slowly than they otherwise would have done because of their trading contacts with the advanced nations, but the association may have brought them less gains than they might have hoped or expected. The chief interest of foreign investors in these countries is in the production and export of raw materials, oil and tropical food products. It is argued that foreign companies have controlled and organized production and export, employing few local workers and then only in unskilled capacities; they have shown little interest in developing production for the home markets and given little help to spread western capital and "know-how" into the interior. Dependence on trade with the advanced countries has grown and invites description as a "colonial" pattern of trade such as that between Britain and the American colonies under the Mercantilist system in the eighteenth century. It is also argued that a long-term fall in their export prices compared with their import prices has robbed the developing countries of much of the benefits of trade. There is some truth in these assertions, but these countries are likely to need all the foreign exchange earnings they can get by exports to pay for imports of the capital goods, technical knowledge and general education they require to develop their internal economies. Even more they may need to learn or import entrepreneurial faculties and judgement in recognizing and running risks and in allowing for uncertainties that basically underlie western economic development.

A striking exception to economic colonialism developed in the early and mid-1970's when the oil exporting countries, mostly in the Middle East, sharply raised their prices and curtailed supplies, especially to countries they regarded as politically unfriendly. The question was whether they had over-played their hand by stimulating the industrialized countries, mainly the USA, Europe and Japan, to accelerate the development of other oil fields, as in the North Sea, and other fuels such as natural gas. [10]

Combination, (*a*) the act or result of joining two or more previously independent firms into a single organization; also referred to as amalgamation, merger or take-over. It is important as a method by which firms may grow and diversify their interests, the main means by which the control of resources in manufacturing has been concentrated in comparatively few hands, a way of achieving monopoly power, a preliminary to the organized removal of excess capacity, and a source of profit to financiers.

Industrial combination in Britain dates mainly from the 1880's. It is the offspring of the Companies Acts, improved methods of communication and large-scale techniques of production and administration. The right to organize industrial concerns as joint-stock companies with limited liability enabled ownership in companies to be united by the simple expedient of an exchange of shares, and it provided lucrative opportunities for company promoters.

The first widespread merger movement occurred at the turn of the century when such combinations as the Wall-Paper Manufacturers (embracing 31 firms representing 90 per cent of the trade), the Calico Printers Association (46 firms with 830 of some 1,000 printing machines) and Associated Portland Cement Manufacturers (27 firms with 45 per cent of the trade) were formed. All these combinations aimed at securing a monopoly of their trades. But amalgamation is an expensive method of arranging a monopoly. It is in the interests of each firm to be the odd one outside the combination able to sell all it produces or wishes at prices maintained by the combination's restrictions on output. Hence firms may have to be brought in on terms that represent their nuisance value rather than their value as operating parts of the combination; this is the reason why combinations seldom achieve 100 per cent control of a trade. Monopoly power is also difficult to preserve if entry of new firms cannot be barred. The more successful a combination is in maintaining prices and profits, the stronger the encouragement to new entrants. The Wall-Paper Manufacturers' combination engaged in further bouts of acquisition in 1915 and 1934, and its share of the trade has tended to decline again since 1935. Associated Portland Cement engaged in further amalgamations in 1912 and 1931.

Another motive for many of the early combination movements was the lure of profits to be earned from the sale of shares in the united undertakings to optimistic investors who were often prepared to pay prices far in excess of the current value of the assets of the combines. For example, when Watney & Co., Combe & Co., and Reid's Brewery Co. were amalgamated in 1898 the £15 million of shares sold in the new combination was £6 million more than the sum of their individual values.

During the inter-war years the number of combinations continued to grow. At first they were regarded as a means of ensuring supplies and combating the anticipated raw material shortages of the post-war years (as in the iron and steel industry). Subsequently they were seen as a means of softening the effects of competition in a period of declining demand and shrinking world markets. Hence the name "rationalization" given to the policy of "orderly" elimination of excess capacity by concentrating production in the most efficient plants. The Lancashire Cotton Co-operation, established in 1929 with the help of the Bank of England to buy up and scrap excess spindle capacity, was a leading example of officially blessed movements of this kind. Imperial Chemical Industries (1926), Associated Electrical Industries (1929) and Unilever (1929) were all products of this period of competition-eliminating amalgamations. By 1935 over half the total employment in manufacturing industry was concentrated in less than 2,000 business units.

Since 1951 there has been a fresh phase of combinations. Some of them appear to have been effected for "traditional" reasons—to secure continuity of component supplies, rationalize production and marketing arrangements, and for fuller exploitation of technical and other economies of large-scale production, e.g. British Motor Corporation in 1952, Courtaulds-British Celanese in 1957, the ICI bid for Courtaulds and the *Daily Mirror*-Odhams Press take-over in 1961. Extensive combination ("re-grouping") within the aircraft industry in 1959 is a post-war example of rationalization of production encouraged officially in the face of a shrinking government market for conventional defence aircraft. Many combinations, however, were induced by the post-war fiscal and monetary policies pursued by the authorities until the end of the 1950's. Profits taxation which favoured retained profits and policies of dividend limitation helped to create wide differences between company share prices and asset values and encouraged takeover bids: the bidders bought the shares and so acquired ownership of assets worth much more.

In the USA combinations which substantially lessen competition or tend to create monopoly are prohibited under an amendment to the Clayton Act made in 1950. In Britain combinations may be investigated by the Monopolies Commission if they control one-third or more of the production of an industry. [3]

(*b*) term applied in the eighteenth and early nineteenth centuries to trade unions, outlawed as conspiracies by the Combination Acts, notably those of 1824 and 1825. [5]

Comecon, Council for Mutual Economic Assistance, created in 1949 by Russia and the communist countries of Eastern Europe, for co-operation to promote economic development, probably as a political counter to Marshall Aid for Europe. It has strengthened the bargaining power of the communist countries by joint bulk buying from capitalist countries, and their political influence by aid to the developing countries of Africa and Asia. Comecon's population is roughly comparable with that of the Common Market (250–300 million). [4]

Command Economy, an economic system directed by government. The strictest command economy is the USSR, the least centralized probably the USA or Australia or Switzerland. In war many countries introduce varying degrees of command economy, as the fastest way to mobilize labour and capital for war production, by direction of labour, conscription of capital, rationing, licensing, price controls, etc. [10]

Commercial Banks, another name for joint-stock banks.

Committee on Public Accounts, a select committee of the House of Commons which receives the report of the Comptroller and Auditor General. The report has two main purposes: to ensure (1) that expenditure has been approved by Parliament, (2) that it has been spent on the objects specified by Parliament. [12]

Commodity, comprises articles which are perfect substitutes for one another and therefore between which the cross-elasticity of demand is very high (in theory, infinite). This meaning is narrower and more precise than that of popular usage. For example, in everyday language one would refer to butter as a commodity, but consumers are not indifferent between English, New Zealand, Danish, Dutch and blended butters, and in economics they are therefore regarded as five different commodities. Similarly Danish butter in Denmark is not the same commodity as Danish butter in Britain, and Danish butter in June is not the same commodity as Danish butter in December. In addition to being distinguished from one another objectively by quality, distance and time, commodities may be further differentiated subjectively (but not less significantly) by packaging, branding and advertising.

Commodities are defined in this narrow way because demand conditions and often supply conditions are different for goods which are not perfect substitutes and in consequence their outputs and prices must be explained separately. For example, standard record players and hi-fi equipment both reproduce sound; but they are demanded by people in different age groups with different incomes and different tastes, and they are supplied by firms using different production techniques and distributive channels and retail outlets. [7]

Commodity Agreements, international arrangements to stabilize the prices of primary products (sugar or other foods, rubber or other materials) or the earnings of their producers, to reduce fluctuations in the export of food to industrialized countries, and so on. They were adopted in the 1930's to mitigate the effects of the Great Depression, and again in the 1960's. They have tended to be favoured especially by developing countries dependent on one or two commodities, e.g. Brazil (coffee), Bolivia (tin), Ceylon (tea). The methods used are regulation of output by quota, buffer-stocks and stock-piles, bulk sale contracts, marketing boards, compensation for falls in earnings, etc. Restriction of output can work best, at least for a time, if the producers are few and all of them participate (otherwise some will drop out as market conditions change), or if the arrangement is supported or enforced by government, or if demand is not elastic (otherwise total earnings are *smaller* at a higher than a lower price).

The general criticism of commodity agreements by economists is that they have subsidized the least efficient producers and penalized the most efficient; that they have not always achieved even their immediate purpose because they could be manipulated for political reasons by governments that themselves caused most of the major price disturbances; and, most fundamentally, that they have not strengthened the primary producing countries or producers in the long run because they tackled symptoms rather than causes and resisted rather than accepted change. Price fluctuations are basically unavoidable, and may be helpful by acting as signals of changing market conditions. Ultimately primary producers and countries, it has been argued, are best helped by enabling them to accept and adapt themselves to change by learning to anticipate it through development of the entrepreneurial qualities of judgement in recognizing, running and responding to risk (by saving, insurance, forward contracts, diversification, etc.). Steadily rising living standards in industrial countries would also expand demand for primary products. Reduced tariff, quota or other measures to protect agriculture and extractive industries in the developed countries, as in the Common Market, would open markets for the primary producers. And generally less government/political action and more encouragement of private/voluntary action would remove price and other fluctuations provoked by uncertainty about the often arbitrary and unpredictable reactions of government. [4]

Commodity Exchange, a market in which contracts are made for immediate ("spot") or future delivery ("futures") of commodities all over the world. Most trading is in futures, which even out price fluctuations by facilitating trading at a known price. London has commodity exchanges for coffee, cotton, furs, metals, tea, wool, etc. The main US exchanges are for coffee, cotton, corn, sugar, wheat, etc. Sales are by auction from sample or (increasingly) by direct purchase from the primary producers. [7]

Commodity Market, generally, a market in which commodities are exchanged; particularly the international markets for food and raw materials, cocoa, wheat, tin, wool, etc. For many of these products the market is more or less world wide: prices for uniform grades of, say, wheat, tend to move closely together in all the main trading centres. London and New York are important among the centres in which world commodity transactions are concentrated. In each centre the market may be housed in a building or it may be a "telephone" market. Deals are normally made between buying and selling brokers acting for users and producers respectively. If the goods are closely classified according to internationally agreed standards, it may not be necessary for buyers or sellers to inspect them in warehouses; or if such agreed standards do not exist (as in wool) storage and inspection may be necessary, and sales will often be made by regular public auctions such as in the London Wool Exchange.

Commodity markets may deal in "actuals" or "futures." Trading in the "actuals" market may be for "spot" (current) supplies or for "forward" delivery at a future date. In either case a wide variety of individual grades and qualities of commodity are traded: "forward" transactions will also embrace a wide variety of delivery times and conditions. Both need to be distinguished from the market in "futures" contracts which many organized commodity exchanges provide. Unlike transactions in "actuals" markets, "futures" transactions are usually in a standard grade of the commodity and the contracts traded are also highly standardized. The purpose is to provide a smooth market to facilitate the "hedging" of risks of price changes so that, for example, a merchant carrying stocks of a commodity can, by selling "futures" when he buys "actuals" (and buying in "futures" when he eventually sells his stocks of the commodity), "hedge" any risk of undesirable gains or losses due to price changes. Since price movements in the "actuals" and "futures" market will tend broadly to be related, the merchant's loss or gain on his "actuals" transactions will tend approximately to be balanced by an opposite gain or loss in the "futures" market. A smoothly working "futures" market thus enables the risks of price changes to be interchanged between traders whose interests in price changes are opposite. [7]

"Commodity Shunting." *See* EXCHANGE CONTROL.

Common Access Facilities, another term for *public goods.* They are facilities open to all because the costs of excluding non-payers by making direct charges to users are prohibitively high. Financing such facilities thus calls for collective payments such as initiation fees, club dues, membership subscriptions, etc. where the facilities are privately owned (e.g. golf, yacht clubs), or taxes where they are government owned (e.g. parks and recreation areas). Tax financing of common access facilities raises problems in the distribution of the tax burden among the income classes who use them, and regarding the basis on which decisions to expand or contract them are made. [13]

Common Carrier, a seller given the privilege of protected trading by law and required, as a *quid pro quo,* to sell to all comers without discrimination. Railways, taxis, omnibuses and licensed premises ("pubs" and hotels) have been examples in Britain. [10]

Common Market, an organization proposed at the Messina Conference in 1955 and established in 1958 under the Treaty of Rome, 1957, for the economic integration of Belgium, France, Germany, Italy, Luxemburg and the Netherlands. In 1973 it was joined by Britain, Ireland and Denmark to become the "nine." (Norway was expected to join but voted against in a referendum.) Narrowly defined, the Common Market is a customs union committed to the gradual elimination, over a "transition period," of all internal tariffs and trade restrictions and the erection of a common external tariff on goods imported from outside. In its wider context, the Rome Treaty is more properly regarded as a political instrument for the progressive unification of Europe; it envisages the ultimate removal of all barriers to the movement of goods, persons, services and capital, and the harmonization of the economic, financial and social policies of member countries embracing a total population of 250 millions.

The underlying philosophy of the Common Market was that despite the achievements of the post-war General Agreement on Tariffs and Trade and the Organization for European Economic Co-operation in liberalizing trade, something more than the prescriptions of free trade was needed to achieve and maintain the maximum benefits of large stable markets. The optimum economic exploitation of larger trading areas was considered more likely if there were assurance that trading barriers would not be reimposed and if other economic barriers between countries were broken down. Hence the need for a comprehensive and "irreversible" economic community with common economic, financial and social policies. These views were originally not acceptable to other members of the OEEC, who preferred a politically looser European Free Trade Area as a logical extension of the achievements of GATT and OEEC.

The permanent executive organ of the OEEC is the Common Market Commission, consisting of thirteen members chosen by the member-countries. Policy decisions rest with a Council of Ministers (one from each member-country). Commission and Council are supported by a Consultative Economic and Social Committee. The European Parliamentary Assembly, composed of 142 members appointed by member-states in agreed proportions, is a deliberative body exercising general supervision.

Later, the original programme for the abolition of tariffs and quotas and the co-ordination of the Common Market's external tariff was accelerated. Eventually the common external tariff was to average the existing duties of individual members, although provision was made to keep the general level as low as possible—particularly on raw materials—to co-operate in further moves towards free trade within the framework of GATT and the eventual elimination of quotas with the rest of the world. Price support for agriculture was to supplant protection by tariffs and quotas. Tariff preferences extended by members to each other were to apply similarly to overseas territories.

Discussion of these general principles underlying the Common Market were intensified in the early- and mid-1970's when the "six" were enlarged to "nine" and a new British government in 1974 asked for the terms to be "re-negotiated." Throughout its life since 1958 the fundamental economic questions arising from the Common Market have been, first, whether a large free trade area with more than the population of the USA or the USSR would raise living standards in Europe and thus make her independent of aid from the USA and too strong to be undermined by the USSR; second, whether it would be "outward" or "inward-looking," i.e. gradually reduce trade restrictions with the rest of the world or try to become self-sufficient and protective of European interests such as the small farmers; third, whether the liberal intentions of the Treaty of Rome would resist the bureaucratic tendencies of the political and administrative organizations in Brussels or elsewhere; fourth, whether the decentralizing forces of diverse interests and the difficulties of organizing and managing the bulk of Europe from the top would resist the political tendencies and economic interests making for centralization; and thus whether harmonization would make much headway against the national, regional, cultural and other local differences making for diversification. [4]

Common Pricing, (*a*) fixing identical prices by agreement between competing firms selling through wholesale and retail channels, or (*b*) contracting by several firms for single projects such as a bridge or power-station ("level tendering"). The economic implications may be different in the two cases.

In the first the alternative is not usually active price competition. Price agreements are most easily reached when there are only a few competitors—in "oligopolistic" markets. Price competition is then unstable: a price reduction by one firm which others did not meet would have a marked effect on their sales. A price cut may thus start a price "war." To avoid it firms are likely to hold prices at a level thought "reasonable." Prices fixed by agreement are presumed higher than they otherwise would be, although this is only a probability. In inflationary periods agreed prices may be adjusted upwards more slowly than competitive prices because of delays in negotiations. But the resulting waiting lists may be no more desirable for consumers than the exclusion by higher prices of would-be buyers.

The identical prices tendered for single projects may depart more clearly from what would be expected in the absence of common pricing. Economists would expect that firms tendering for "bespoke" work would be differently placed for fulfilling particular contracts so that their prices would differ if there were no price agreements. The common price is therefore likely to be higher than would yield normal profits to some of the firms. [3]

Common Property, a resource owned by no identifiable individual, firm or government, and used by all with free access. No individual therefore has an incentive to protect, conserve or improve it. On the contrary it invites users to "exploit" it without regard for other users. Over-grazing, deforestation, over-fishing are common examples in many countries. The solution is usually appropriation to an identifiable individual, group or government with exclusive ownership so that it will have an interest in, and can be held responsible for, protection and conservation. The environment in general is a common property resource that no individual or other entity has an interest or inducement to preserve. The ambiguity of property rights, some economists argue, is therefore the main economic origin of environmental pollution. [13]

Common Stock, another expression for Ordinary Shares or Equities. [8]

Commonwealth Preference, the advantage of lower tariffs levied on imports from Commonwealth countries than on imports from other countries. The practice was systematized in the 1932 (bilateral) Ottawa Agreements. It conflicts with the 1947 General Agreement on Trade and Tariffs (GATT), which enshrined the principle of *non*-discrimination in the most-favoured nation clause, and it has become less important since Britain joined the Common Market in 1973 because UK exports to Commonwealth countries have been falling as a proportion of her total overseas trade. [4]

Communism, a body of doctrine and a political movement originating from Lenin's interpretation of the writings of Karl Marx. It is the official doctrine of the political parties controlling the USSR and the "People's Republics" of China and Eastern Europe and of political parties with varying degrees of support in other countries.

Communist doctrine is clearly Marxist in teaching that human society is evolving towards a situation without class barriers; there is no exploitation of man by man, and indeed no state power over the individual; productive resources are owned communally; scarcity has been overcome and there is an "abundance" of material wealth. Marx did not say, but Lenin asserted, that the "inevitable" change from capitalism must be brought by revolution. The Russian Bolshevik Party, which took power in 1917, was inspired by the Leninist interpretation of Marx.

Lenin held that a small and tightly knit party could carry through a revolution, as in Russia, without the support of the majority of the population, and could then rule the country in the name of the proletariat ("dictatorship of the proletariat"). During the dictatorship, called socialism, in which people would be paid according to *effort,* bourgeois elements from the previous, capitalist, society would disappear, and the nation and its economy would be developed, with particular emphasis on heavy industry, in preparation for the final stage of "communism," in which distribution would be according to *need.*

For economists the central interest of this doctrine lies in the implicit assumption (or explicit assertion) that communism could abolish scarcity. If this were true, its claims to distribute according to "needs" rather than according to "work" could be satisfied. In this sense communism approaches the early Christian and later perennial socialist teaching of selflessness. In the USSR scarcity remains after 60 years (since 1917) and distribution according to work or effort continues. J. K. Galbraith has argued that superabundance has arrived in some consumer goods in the capitalist West. More orthodox economists, including Keynes, have welcomed the prospect of a society in which men could turn from coping with scarcity to contemplating the higher life. The outcome will turn on how far human demands keep pace with the increased productive capacity made possible by advances in technology.

"Communism" may also be used to describe societies or doctrines in which communal ownership of capital and egalitarianism are thought essential for religious, humanitarian or traditional reasons. [10]

Company, a form of industrial organization created by the Companies Acts, of which the first was in 1855, and subject to its provisions which lay down its powers (e.g., to raise money from shareholders and to borrow money) and obligations (e.g., to publish accounts showing stated information). Company legislation is revised and reformed periodically as economic conditions change. Up to the Companies Act of 1948 it has required increasing information to be disclosed, mainly to protect creditors and (existing) shareholders. In 1962 the Jenkins Committee proposed further disclosures, but its proposals did not go far enough, since the purpose of disclosure is not only to prevent abuse and enable (existing) shareholders to control their company more fully, but more fundamentally to enable potential shareholders to judge the efficiency with which capital is employed by individual companies so that they can invest in those that employed it more efficiently as measured by its earnings. [3]

In the 1970's a debate developed on the "social responsibilities" of the company to employees, customers and the environment in general as well as to the shareholders. In the short run, and insofar as legislation lags behind technical change and public opinion, companies may be able to neglect wider "social" interests. In the long run, some economists argue, the company is best confined to the pursuit of profit, which it can measure; but it will have to take into account the wider interests of all with whom it deals if the legal framework is suitably revised to keep pace with change. [3]

Company Union, an organization of employees of a firm. It is more common in the USA than in Britain, where it is criticized or condemned as weakening the bargaining power of labour, because trade unions speaking for *all* members of a trade can more effectively deny labour to an individual employer. [5]

Comparative Advantage. *See* COMPARATIVE COST.

Comparative Cost (Comparative Advantage), the principle that under given technological conditions the increased product obtainable from specialization and exchange rather than from a policy of self-sufficiency and economic isolation will be maximized when each country or region specializes in the production of those goods and services in which its relative advantage is largest (that is, its comparative cost of production is least). Although first clearly stated by Ricardo in developing the theory of international trade, the doctrine can be applied to all forms of specialization, or "territorial division of labour," and exchange, whether between persons, businesses or nations.

There are three kinds of differences in costs: *absolute, comparative* and *equal.* They may be illustrated by simple examples of two countries, A and B, producing the same two commodities x and y. If A and B are differently endowed with resources, their production costs are likely to differ. Suppose a given quantity of resources could produce the following amounts of x and y in the two countries:

(1) A $100x$ or $50y$; B $50x$ or $100y$

Example (1) indicates that country A has an absolute advantage in the production of x, country B an absolute advantage in the production of y.

(2) A $100x$ or $80y$; B $50x$ or $60y$

Example (2) indicates that country A has an absolute advantage in the production of both x and y, but a comparative (relatively larger) advantage in the production of x. Country B is at an absolute disadvantage in both lines of production, but her comparative advantage (relatively smaller disadvantage) is in the production of y.

(3) A $100x$ or $80y$; B $50x$ or $40y$

Example (3) indicates that country A has an absolute advantage in the production of both goods but that there is no comparative advantage for either country. The cost differences are equal in both lines of production x and y and in both countries.

Comparison of the three examples suggests that the gain from specialization and exchange flows from *comparative* advantage, that is, from differences in comparative cost, rather than from *absolute* advantage. Thus, assuming that if the two countries do not specialize they will divide their resources equally between x and y production, comparing total "world" production with and without specialization in each of the three examples shows:

	Total Production	
	Without Specialization	With Specialization
(1)	$75x + 75y$	$100x + 100y$
(2)	$75x + 70y$	$100x + 60y$
(3)	$75x + 60y$	$100x + 40y$

Specialization obviously pays in (1) since larger amounts of both x and y are produced. It also pays in (2) if it can be shown that the loss of $10y$ is more than compensated for by the gain of $25x$. That it does is confirmed by comparing the ratios of production costs in A and B: in A $25x$ has the value of $20y$; in B $25x$ has the value of $30y$. But specialization does not pay in example (3) despite A's absolute advantage, for $25x$ has the value of $20y$ in both, so that there is no net gain from specialization: the gain in x no more than compensates for the loss in y. Thus whether or not there is an *absolute* cost difference does not matter. What is important is that there must be a *comparative* cost difference, and where there is none, as in example (3), there is no gain from specialization and exchange.

The doctrine can be restated in this form: other things being equal, specialization and exchange according to the principle of comparative advantage will pay only if the ratio between production costs differs in the two countries. The qualification is necessary since in real life specialization itself may cause cost ratios to change, increasing or reducing the gain from exchange. Also if the goods produced in each country are not completely identical, trade may be worth while even though relative cost ratios are the same. With these qualifications the principle can be extended to deal with more complex examples of many countries and many commodities.

The general principle of comparative cost provides an economic explanation of specialization, but by itself it is not a sufficient argument for free trade between nations, since it makes no allowance for the effects of free trade where economies are growing or where factors are immobile within one or both countries or where there is monopoly power. But it embodies fundamental economic truth. [4]

Comparative Statics, a method of economic analysis. Hypotheses in economics may be developed and analysed by examining hypothetical situations or "models." The relationships between changing elements ("variables") in these models may be investigated in either a "static" or a "dynamic" setting. Comparative statics is the method of analysis in which the characteristics of the model in different situations of equilibrium are compared. In dynamics the path of adjustment from one equilibrium to another is itself studied. [14]

Compensation, the payment made to persons, groups or institutions as indemnity for injury, loss or damage. Adjustments of this kind between private persons are governed by the general law on damages in contract and tort. Economic interest centres largely on the question of compensation for the compulsory acquisition of private property by a public authority or for loss of value due to the action of a public authority in limiting the uses to which private property may be put.

The compensation code on compulsory acquisition first emerged in Great Britain during the railway building era in the middle of the nineteenth century: later legislation on housing, nationalization measures and town and country planning have affected it. The central economic question is: What is "adequate" compensation? There are three possibilities: the value to the owner, the cost of "equivalent reinstatement" and "open-market" value. The first of these provides full economic compensation but rests on a personal judgement of value that cannot readily be measured. Equivalent reinstatement cost provides a next-best alternative but is just as indefinite unless physical reinstatement is possible. Open-market value can be ascertained more readily, but it under-compensates owners other than those who would have sold at that value in any case.

Open-market value forms the central basis of compensation for compulsory acquisition under the British Town and Country Planning law. In establishing open-market value, however, the question of how far it should include elements of "public" value created by the activities of the public authorities themselves has never adequately been settled. Alfred Marshall, for example, considered the larger part of urban land value to derive from its situation and surroundings, and thus to be "public" value of this kind. The code relating to compensation for compulsory acquisitions deals only partially with this aspect; but compensation for loss caused by planning restrictions on the permitted use of property reflects it more fully. The latter compensation is strictly limited and excludes compensation for "good neighbour" restrictions, that is, prohibition of uses which have come to be regarded generally as against the public interest. More recently, the British government has significantly extended the scope of compensation to include compensation payments for depreciation in the value of property affected by the use of public works such as new motorways; hitherto the owner of affected property could neither claim compensation nor bring an action at common law to seek redress for nuisance if the use in question was one which was sanctioned by statute. [6]

Compensation Principle, a method of easing the achievement of the social optimum in economic welfare by compensation from people benefited by change to those harmed by it. If the former gain despite paying the compensation, the change can be judged desirable. The principle was advanced by Nicholas Kaldor in 1939. Since comparisons of this kind involve subjective valuations and it is impossible to compare them for different persons (how to measure A's liking for cakes against B's liking for ale?), situations in which some people are made better off at the expense of others cannot strictly be assessed at all. Kaldor argued that it was possible to overcome this defect and to regard one position as superior to another if people benefiting from a change could compensate those harmed by it yet still derive a net benefit themselves.

Later discussions of the compensation principle have produced several qualifications, have shown that it can produce ambiguous results and that it is necessary to make assumptions about the relative desirability of the distribution of the community's real income in the two situations being compared. Criticisms of this kind have in recent years led to some abandonment of the principle, which could not in any event provide a practical guide for economic policy since compensation is rarely practicable. [14]

Compensatory Finance. *See* DEFICIT FINANCING.

Competition, in economics, market situations, forms of activity or a social process.

(1) Competition is used in a technical sense to classify market conditions according to the degree of control over prices exercised by producers or consumers. The situations depend on the numbers of suppliers and customers, the uniformity of the goods and the freedom of entry for potential suppliers. They range from (*a*) pure and perfect competition, in which there are many producers so that none is able to influence the price and newcomers are free to produce on the same terms as existing producers; through (*b*) imperfectly competitive markets in which individual producers can influence prices to an extent depending upon numbers of producers in relation to total demand, the degree to which products are differentiated in quality, design, style and location, and the degree of freedom of newcomers to produce close substitutes; to (*c*) pure monopoly, in which a single seller of a single product with no close substitute has complete control over price. These market forms can also be applied by buyers: e.g. monopsony is a market situation in which there is a single buyer.

This technical language may cause confusion because the adjectives "perfect" and "imperfect" seem to imply a moral or ethical judgement of desirability. But economists use them in the same sense as physicists who refer to perfect and imperfect vacuums. Some of the technical market imperfections are physical facts of life, such as space and consequent variety in locations (e.g. in retail trade); others would be generally considered desirable, such as product improvements or variations in response to differing requirements of customers; yet others, such as sales promotion and advertising, represent in part efforts to inform consumers, or to persuade them to try new commodities or services so that they can inform themselves, which may or may not be economically wasteful or ethically objectionable.

The analysis of real-life market situations in terms of varying degrees of competitiveness helps to explain the pattern of prices and outputs and to suggest reasons for differences in producers' responses to changes in the conditions of demand or cost. The simple situation of perfect competition in the production and sale of one commodity may be generalized to cover an entire economy in order to demonstrate the interdependence of all kinds of economic activity. It can be argued that the properties of such a perfectly competitive economy provide a set of standards for government policies designed to secure an efficient allocation of resources. Although formally valid, the significance of such an approach is debated by economists. Since governments are concerned with developing events it would seem that study of the ways in which adjustment takes place in a changing competitive economy is likely to have more importance for the optimum allocation of resources.

(2) In its sense of activity, competition refers to the ways in which firms vie with one another for custom, when they may not only adapt themselves to given market conditions but also attempt to change them. This is close to the common meaning of competition, defined by Dr. Johnson in his *Dictionary* as "the action of endeavouring to gain what another endeavours to gain at the same time." The main difference is that there need be no winner. Firms compete by making their products attractive, striving to secure lower costs than their rivals and attempting to get more resources to work with. Competition in its technical meaning of market situations embraces only impersonal adaptations to given conditions; competition as activity is strictly personal, comprising the acts of production managers, sales managers, workmen and so on.

Economists use competition in the sense of activity when investigating industrial research, innovation, location of economic activity, scales of production, sizes and types of organizations, and the principles determining choice between alternative possibilities. It is in this sense also that meaning can be attached to terms like "cut-throat" and "wasteful" competition. "Cut-throat" competition is often the weak participants' term for vigorous competition; but some activities, such as selling "fighting" brands temporarily at less than even direct costs solely in order to eliminate competitors, are different in kind from a firm's more usual attempts to do better than its rivals. "Cut-throat" competition is intended to be short-lived and to end in the destruction of competition. "Wasteful" competition may refer to activities which add to an industry's costs without improving its service to consumers or changing the relative standing of the firms involved. Some advertising which simply offsets that of rivals, as in detergents or cosmetics, may fall under this head.

(3) Competition in its fundamental social, dynamic purpose is a device for *discovering* demand and supply (in their everyday sense, i.e. what people want and how to give it to them) rather than merely *responding* to existing wants and techniques. Successful activities strengthen firms and unsuccessful ones weaken or ruin them. Taken altogether, these activities result in a social process which constitutes competition in its third sense. This is the process by which products that people are not prepared to pay for, high cost methods of production and inefficient organizations are weeded out and opportunity is given for new products, methods and organizations to be tried. By selecting and rejecting alternative uses of resources, the competitive process spreads the knowledge through-

out society for the better satisfaction of individual wants. It provides a means of "discovering" the most wanted products and the least cost methods and scales of production (which are usually taken for granted in technical analyses of competitive market situations).

Competition not only governs existing organizations but also destroys them and creates new ones. This is the form it takes in the real world rather than the price competition used as a teaching device in text-books which came under apparently severe and damaging criticism from Joan Robinson in the UK and E. H. Chamberlin in the USA in the 1930's. In practice, as they said, competition is not merely in price but in quality and sales effort, with advertising and other marketing arts used to create "product differentiation," so that each brand has a monopoly, and competition becomes imperfect or monopolistic. The debate among economists is which kind of competition "counts." The other view, put by Schumpeter, is that "in capitalist reality . . . it is not that kind of competition . . . within a rigid pattern of invariant conditions, methods of production and forms of industrial organization . . . which counts but the competition from the new commodity, the new technology, the new source of supply, the new type of organization—competition which commands a decisive cost or quality advantage and which strikes not at the margins of the profits and the outputs of the existing firms but at their foundations and their very lives. This kind of competition is much more effective than the other as a bombardment is in comparison with forcing a door, and so much more important that it becomes a matter of comparative indifference whether competition in the ordinary [price] sense functions more or less promptly; the powerful lever that in the long run expands output and brings down prices is . . . made of other stuff" (*Capitalism, Socialism and Democracy,* Allen & Unwin).

It is competition in the third sense that is most relevant to political debate on the desirability of a competitive economy. To some the competitive process represents the basis of a liberal society; to others it appears as a ruthless chaos of "devil take the hindmost."

Competition provides a means of diffusing power and responsibility throughout the community and of continually widening the area of freedom and opportunity. On the strictly economic plane it provides spurs to efficiency, incentives to seek out and supply the varied wants of consumers, a method of sharing the benefits of technical progress in lower prices and higher incomes, and a means of discovering what, how and for whom to produce.

Competition is no panacea. The freedom it provides may be used to concentrate power, as has been evident since the growth of the large joint-stock companies, trade associations and trade unions. Monopoly power may also result from the superiority of large-scale techniques. Even where the competitive process is unimpeded, it selects according to the distribution of purchasing power, and its results are good or bad only in terms of the prevailing distribution of wealth and income, although inequalities can be lessened by redistribution through government (or private) giving of income or wealth outside the competitive process, and by voluntary (partial) giving of goods or services at less than their market prices within it. Social costs, such as the noise, dirt and congestion of urban living, and social benefits, such as the pleasure provided by good architecture, may not always enter into market prices and so may fail to influence the competitive process, although government can to a degree "internalize" social costs by pollution charges (on agencies, private or governmental, that cause pollution), or by requiring pollution-preventing devices to be fitted. Some wants such as defence and law and order, are collective in nature, and others, such as some forms of education, medicine, roads and parks, may be most effectively provided collectively. If these wants were left to be satisfied by competition they might be provided inadequately. Finally, a competitive economy if left unregulated may be subject to booms and slumps. Whilst there is much to be said for a competitive economy, therefore, the competitive process is not sufficient alone to provide a satisfactory social system. It requires a framework of law and institutions on property, contract, business organizations, etc., to direct private effort into channels that ensure public advantage. [7]

Competition, Atomistic, another name for pure competition.

Competition, Imperfect. *See* IMPERFECT COMPETITION.

Competition, Monopolistic. *See* MONOPOLISTIC COMPETITION.

Competition, Perfect. *See* PERFECT COMPETITION.

Competition, Pure. *See* PURE COMPETITION.

Competition, Workable, a form some way between intensely active and sluggish competition. It favours established producer interests at the expense of consumer interests. It attempts to avoid the disruptive effects of intense ("pure") competition, and may be easier for government to provide within legal institutions; but in practice it tends to degenerate into protection for established firms. [7]

Complementary Goods, those which must be used in combination in order to satisfy a want, in contrast to competitive goods. Consumers are generally faced with a wide variety of goods from which to satisfy their wants. Some wants can be satisfied with more than one good, that is by competitive goods which are substitutes for one another. For example, ball-point pens are good substitutes for fountain pens, but less good substitutes for typewriters. But other wants require more than one good to be satisfied. The collection of goods needed to satisfy them are complementary to one another. As an individual uses more of one good, he must use more of the goods that are complementary to it, e.g. motor-cars and petrol, electricity and electrical appliances, cigarettes and matches. There are differing degrees of complementarity. In most cases the quantities of the complementary goods needed to satisfy the want can be varied. But in the most extreme cases the goods must be used in a one-to-one ratio: e.g. one left and one right glove, one lock for each door, and one driving wheel for each car.

The relations between competitive and complementary goods are important in the theory of consumers' demand. With competitive goods, such as detergents, a fall in the price of one brand will cause a fall in the demand for competing brands. With complementary goods the effect is generally opposite; if the price of electrical appliances is reduced, the demand for them will increase and therefore the demand for electricity. [7]

Composite Demand, applies to a commodity or service with more than one use, in which the elasticities in response to price may differ. Sheep are demanded for meat to eat and wool to wear. A woman may be demanded as wife, adviser, banker, co-author, research assistant. An increase in the demand for sheep as meat will, *ceteris paribus,* reduce their supply for wool, raise their price to people who want wool, and reduce the demand for wool. [7]

Composition, Fallacy of, the logical error of supposing that what is true of a unit is true of a group comprising a number of units, or in economics that the behaviour or reactions of an individual indicate the behaviour or reactions of the economy as a whole. D. H. Robertson once wrote that an individual who lost a coin through a hole in the floor was poorer by its value, but if all individuals lost coins none would be poorer because the reduction in the quantity of money in circulation would lower the prices of goods proportionately so that the smaller amounts of money would buy the same quantity of goods as before.

The proposition that a group or country, or the economy, is larger than, or differs from, the sum of the units that comprise it also underlies the claims of macro-economics to yield truths in economic analysis not revealed by micro-economic analysis of individuals. The opposing view held by other economists is that macro-economic analysis (national income, national outlay, national output, national consumption, national investment, national exports or imports, average prices, average costs, etc.) cannot properly be understood except by understanding its component elements—ultimately individuals, families, firms, etc. They argue that much macro-economics can reach unreal, erroneous and misleading conclusions by neglecting the micro-economic foundations. Some economic problems cannot be analysed by macro-economics and require micro-economic analysis: for example, the "shortage" of water supplied without a price ("free") is a meaningless concept in economics, because individuals would vary the quantities of water they used according to its price. The solution may therefore be not the costly process of desalinizing sea-water but a system of charging prices for water (possibly by meters). [14]

Compound Amount, the final amount realized when interest is added to an original sum invested (the *principal*) and the new sum is used as the principal for the next time-period and interest added to that, the process being repeated for a number of periods. The difference between the compound amount and the original principal is called *compound interest.* If P stands for the original principal, i is the interest rate per period, and n is the number of periods involved, the interest earned during the first period is Pi and the amount at the end of the first period is $P + Pi$ or $P(1 + i)$; that is, the amount at the end of the first period is $(1 + i)$ times the principal at the beginning of the period. Similarly the amount at the end of any period will be $(1 + i)$ times the principal during that period, so that the amount at the end of the second period will be $P(1 + i)(1 + i) = P(1 + i)^2$. Proceeding in this manner shows the final compound amount (S) after n periods will be:

$$S = P(1 + i)^n$$

Using the algebra of geometric progressions enables this formula to be extended to find the compound amount of a constant payment per period (an *annuity*). If R is the annuity payment, its compound amount after n periods when the rate of interest is i will be:

$$S = R[(1 + i)^n - 1]/i$$

The use of compound amount tables, which give values of $(1 + i)^n$ and $[(1 + i)^n - 1]/i$ greatly facilitates calculations involving compound interest. [8]

Compound Interest. *See* COMPOUND AMOUNT.

Compounding, the process of adding compound interest to an original amount to arrive at a final compound amount. [8]

Compulsory Acquisition, the compulsory purchase of real property rights by government bodies, usually for public purposes. The term is British and is widely used in other countries that have been subject to British legal and administrative influences. In USA the practice is called *eminent domain,* in Canada and some other countries *expropriation.* The power of government to acquire rights from its citizens in order to carry out its duties has always been recognized, but the procedures to be followed and the compensation to be paid for purchase have always been and still are hotly debated. In Britain at present the basis for these is contained in the Land Compensation Act, 1961, the Compulsory Purchase Act, 1965, and the Land Clauses Act, 1845. [6]

Comte, August. *See* POSITIVISM.

Concentration, the degree to which an industry is controlled by one or a few firms, i.e. monopoly or oligopoly. The proportion so calculated is the concentration ratio, e.g. 90 per cent, 70 per cent. It is difficult to calculate accurately and unambiguously, since "industry," "product," "control" and "firm" are themselves difficult to define in the *economic* sense, although easy in a *technical* sense. In particular, competition from products that are technically dissimilar may be underrated, *potential* competition that would be activated if concentration raised prices is by definition unknown, and concentration among buyers (manufacturers, merchants, retailers, importers) might be stimulated. [3]

Conciliation, the process of persuading the parties to a dispute to discuss it in the hope of finding a solution acceptable to both (or all). It is commonly used in trade disputes between employers (singly or in groups) and trade unions. In Britain the Department of Employment tries conciliation, which has no legal sanction, as a stage before arbitration, which has. [5]

Condillac, E. B. de. *See* Economic Thought.

Condominium, North American term denoting a form of real property tenure which provides for individual freehold ownership of a specific apartment or similar space, not necessarily at ground level, together with an undivided interest in the land or other parts of the structure which is held in common with other owners. In Britain known as *flying freeholds.* [6]

Confederation of British Industry (CBI), the main national industry organization in Britain, created in 1965 by the amalgamation of the British Employers' Confederation, the Federation of British Industry and the National Association of British Manufacturers. It has some thirty committees covering most aspects of business. New committees formed in 1968 were "Europe Steering," "NEDC Liaison," "Public and Private Sector Relationships" and "Small Firms." Twelve Regional Councils cover the UK.

Two constitutional features distinguish the CBI from its predecessors. Full membership is confined to firms engaged in "productive and manufacturing industry," construction and transport, and organizations representing them. A new category of membership—commercial associate—is provided for organizations such as banks, finance houses, advertising agents, regional or local organizations concerned with industrial problems, and organizations representing the distributive trades. A third category—industrial associate—has accommodated the main nationalized industries; it carries the rights and obligations of full membership but not representation on the governing body. Since its establishment the CBI, in defending its members' interests, has been faced with increasing state intervention in the economy. There has been criticism that it has too readily co-operated with interventionist measures and, most fundamentally, that it has urged government policy on industry rather than industry's opinion on government. The leadership has thought its choice was either to co-operate—as in the 1965 "Joint Statement of Intent" designed to curb prices and incomes and increase output—or have much the same measures imposed by law. The Labour Government after 1964, and the Conservative government after 1970, appeared also to hold out to the CBI the prospect of a major share, with the TUC, in determining economic policy. The CBI leaders have been under pressure to "act responsibly in the public interest." Such collaboration creates the danger of a corporate state dominated by producer interests. It has been argued that the attitudes of the CBI since the early 1960's, when it assisted Conservative Government national planning, suggest doubts whether some British "capitalists" understand the nature or principles of the capitalist system. [3]

Congestion, in economics an imprecise term implying pressure, discomfort and more-than-normal or desirable use of capacity (especially of social capital). The economic implication of congestion is that it may reach a stage where, although it is within no one person's competence to do anything about it, all would benefit by a reduction. This paradox can arise when use of a common access facility or public good, such as a road, increases to the point where the inflow of further users imposes more cost on the *totality* of users (in reduced quality of service, waste of time, discomfort) than the benefit to new users. But because an individual user, in deciding whether or not to make use of it, considers only the costs and benefits to himself, use of the facility is likely to expand beyond the level which would be desirable socially (from the viewpoint of the community as a whole). These notions have led to suggestions that the levy of a *congestion tax* related to the *congestion costs* currently borne by users would be beneficial from the viewpoint of the community of users as a whole. Such a tax would raise the effective "price" to users of the service or facility and would discourage its use. This would increase the benefit (or reduce the disbenefits) of people continuing to use the facility despite the tax (they clearly value the service higher than the tax and other costs they have to meet; otherwise they too would stop using it). Even if the tax proceeds were paid to those encouraged to stop using the facility there would still be a reduction in its use because of the higher "price," so that from a community viewpoint the tax would seem justified. The argument is attractive and has been urged as a solution to congestion of roads, housing, office and industrial space in particular areas of Great Britain (the South-East, for example). But the argument is incomplete and cannot easily be tested because of the difficulty of identifying and measuring the costs and benefits involved. [6]

Congestion Costs. *See* CONGESTION.

Conglomerate, American term for a large firm comprising subsidiaries producing technically dissimilar products. Its growth by takeover or other means is often determined by economies of large-scale financing or management, a desire for diversification to increase market power or to guard against declining demand for some of its products, or the capabilities or ambition of a dominating personality. [3]

Conservation, an imprecise term commonly used in public discussion. In precise economic terms it refers to the investment of current resources, in the form of consumption forgone, in order to increase the amount of a resource available at a future date. Conservation thus implies a *deferment* of resource use rather than an indefinite preservation. If resources are owned privately and owners enjoy exclusive rights to their use, private benefit will dictate the rate of use through time. Forests will be cut, minerals mined and buildings utilized in accordance with the preferences of owners and the demands of the market for the services of resources. If property is not appropriated privately, or if enforcement of private property rights is costly and difficult (the resources of the sea and the atmosphere are examples), there is unlikely to be any strong incentive to conserve even though a smaller or zero rate of exploitation might be in the interests of all. And even if property rights are well-defined and cheap to enforce, a private owner's view on the best rate of use of a resource may not coincide with the rate that would be optimal from the viewpoint of the community as a whole. Taxes and/or subsidies may help reconcile divergences of this kind between private and public interests: most countries have fiscal policies relating to forestry and mineral extraction and planning restrictions governing the use of land that are (in principle) geared to reconciling such divergences. The knotty problems of resource use refer to the exploitation of resources with only ill-defined or no property rights (sea and air), solution of which calls for international co-operation. [13]

Consolidated Fund Services, British government expenditure made direct from the Consolidated Fund. It does not come under the annual review of Parliament. The Civil List of the Crown, the salaries of the judges, the payment of interest on the National Debt are charged in this way by permanent Acts of Parliament. [12]

Consols, an abbreviation of "Consolidated Stock." Various sums of public money borrowed at different times by the government were consolidated in 1787 into one debt called the Funded Debt. The sources of revenue were consolidated at the same time and the consolidated funds were pledged as a security for the payment of the interest, fixed at 2½ per cent. Strictly, Consols are not a loan, since the government need not repay the money. An investor in Consols is really buying the right to a perpetual annuity or annual payment of interest on his money, but he can sell them at prices reflecting the yield on securities of comparable security. [12]

Conspicuous Consumption, ostentatious use of goods to yield satisfaction by demonstration of superior wealth. Term coined by the American economist, Thorstein Veblen. [7]

Conspiracy, a combination to harm others unlawfully. It was a charge against early trade unions that they were conspiracies in restraint of trade. [5]

Constraint, fashionable synonym for limitation, e.g. budgetary constraints are limitations on government spending set by its capacity to tax or borrow (its capacity to print money is usually less constrained). [14]

Consultation, Joint, in industry the practice by which employers inform and invite the opinion of employees (in practice their spokesmen or representatives) on business problems or intentions; hence *joint* consultation. In Germany *Mitbestimmung* is arranged in a two-tier system of boards; consultation takes place in the lower tier, and decision-making in the upper. [5]

Consumer Council, (*a*) in general, bodies created under various names for the nationalized transport and fuel industries in Britain in the effort to ensure that the consumers' opinions or complaints were heard. They are more effective as safety valves for consumer dissatisfaction than in changing policy. Insofar as these industries are subsidized at the expense of the consumer, consumer opinion cannot be taken into account if its adoption would remove the subsidy. If the Council's function is to supply information about consumer preferences, this could also have been obtained (and probably more accurately) through market research than through representatives.

(*b*) specifically, a body created by the British Government in 1963, following the recommendation of the Molony Committee on Consumer Protection, as a state-financed but independent body to protect, advise and guide consumers. It was considered desirable because consumers cannot judge modern materials used for clothing, household goods, etc., rising incomes are enabling them to buy more higher-priced durable goods, advertising makes claims they cannot easily test, salesmanship plays on fundamental human feelings and inhibits judgement, and the gap between consumers and manufacturers is not always filled effectively by retailers with reliable advice and guidance on shopping. The Council was abolished in 1971 but followed by the National Consumer Council in 1975.

As the economist sees it, such activity would help consumers by making them better informed and manufacturers more sensitive to criticism. What remains essential is effective rewards for giving consumers good value and effective penalties for giving poor value. Better informed consumers could supply these rewards and penalties by buying from sellers who gave good value and bypassing those who did not. To do this consumers would need to have a choice of competing sellers. The consumer's fundamental protection would then lie in the maintenance of competition wherever possible. [7]

Consumer Credit. American for hire purchase. [8]

Consumer Durables, goods bought by consumers which yield a flow of services to the buyer over a period of time, such as furniture, in contrast to goods used once and for all, like food. In practice attention is usually focused on durable goods whose price is high relatively to the consumer's income, such as houses, cars, refrigerators, washing machines, furniture. Consumer durables are important in economic analysis because expenditure on them may fluctuate widely according to the general economic situation, people's expectations and other influences, and because the analysis of demand for them raises special problems, e.g. durability means that existing stocks of goods are large relatively to new production coming on to the market; prices of new and second-hand consumer durables are interrelated; demand is affected by replacement booms; and so on.

Because their price is high in relation to the income of many consumers, consumer durables are commonly bought by hire purchase or other methods of spreading the payment over a period so that each instalment is not a large proportion of income. [7]

Consumer Education, information and advice for the consumer on the composition, qualities and performance of consumer goods and services. Its economic significance is that by making consumers better informed and more discriminating in buying and by shifting interest from brand names to performance it helps to make markets more perfect and more competitive.

Organized consumer education based on laboratory tests of competing brands began in the USA with the foundation of Consumer's Research in 1929 and Consumers' Union in 1936. In Britain it was thought that the law of libel prevented publication of the results of tests. But *Shopper's Guide* was founded in 1957 by the Consumer Advisory Council of the British Standards Institution and *Which?* by the independent Consumers' Association. *Shopper's Guide* ceased publication in 1963, partly it was thought because its independence was uncertain in view of the association of manufacturers with the British Standards Institution, partly because it was written in technical language, and because it was not advertised sufficiently. *Which?* has continued to grow to a membership of 500,000 in the middle 1960's but thereafter remained more or less unchanged into the mid-1970's. It has also produced two offshoots; the Research Institute for Consumer Affairs, which claims to investigate commercial, professional and public goods and services, and the Advisory Centre for Education, which offers advice on education.

Which? publishes information and advice (in the form of "best buys") derived from objective laboratory testing and/or subjective panels of people who try the products. Its problems, on which it has attracted some criticism, have been to ensure that the samples it tests are typical and representative of the whole range available to consumers, otherwise its findings are misleading or incomplete. A further difficulty is to avoid judging goods by standards that are too high, since imperfections are unavoidable if repeated testing and changes in products to anticipate misuse by consumers are not to drive up costs and prices beyond the reach of many.

Differences in individual preferences make it difficult to offer advice on which most or many people can act. Information may also be of limited value if individuals differ markedly. Ultimately the best source of information is individual experience. It is the most reliable source for goods and services of low unit value, especially if bought frequently and so tested by trial and error. For goods of high value, especially if bought infrequently like furniture or motor-cars, the personal experience of other people and laboratory testing cut the cost of experimenting with unknown purchases and help to avoid "bad buys" but are probably less certain guides to "best buys." [7]

Consumer Loyalty. *See* ADVERTISING.

Consumers' Sovereignty, an economic system in which consumers "direct" producers through a free, competitive market. By refusing to buy straw hats, consumers have forced the hat industry to make trilby and bowler hats; by preferring packaged to draught beers, they have induced brewers to sell more beer in bottles and cans; by preferring to ride in buses, charabancs and cars, they have made the railways shut down some branch lines. Broadly, the more competitive the market the greater the power of the consumer; the larger the element of monopoly, the more he is at the mercy of the producer.

Man is both consumer and producer; but his interest as producer is immediate and obvious, his interest as consumer distant and diffuse. The two conflict sharply: the interest of consumers is to replace uneconomic coal-pits by profitable pits or by other sources of power; the interest of miners is to keep all mines working whatever their cost or efficiency. The case for consumers' (rather than producers') sovereignty is that, to safeguard his interest as producer, man would be tempted to stultify change by suppressing invention, new methods and ideas; the result would be stagnation and ultimately impoverishment. In the 1960's and 1970's there was increasing resistance to change, especially from trade unions but also from other producers. Reluctance to move jobs and (still more) homes was largely responsible for the persistence of wide differences in regional unemployment, which induced post-war governments to inflate the economy in general to prevent a rise in unemployment in some regions.

There are possible dangers in consumers' sovereignty. (1) Consumers may be ill-informed or persuaded by advertising into making bad choices. The solution is general education, information and advice (as supplied by consumer organizations), protection by common law (implied warranty that goods are fit for the purpose for which they are bought) and statute law (Sale of Goods Act, Merchandise Marks Acts, Weights and Measures Acts, etc.), voluntary advice (solicitors, stockbrokers, insurance brokers, etc.). To the extent that consumers buy for "non-rational" motives of emulation or other subjective reasons, the "artificial" distinctions between products give consumers real satisfaction and make them willing to pay higher prices for wider choice and variety. (2) Consumers' preferences may be frustrated by monopoly or imperfect competition. Market imperfection can be limited by legal penalties on restrictive practices and measures to maintain free entry by new producers; any remaining monopoly due to "natural" or other unavoidable causes can to some extent be controlled by law or public opinion. (3) Consumers can "distort" the industrial system by making it produce luxuries rather than essentials. If this is a criticism of consumers for preferring, say, television to tea-cloths, it opens up again the question of personal preference and education. If it refers to the disproportionate influence exerted by the more wealthy, it is a criticism of the distribution of income rather than of consumers' sovereignty. Inequality of income is itself the result partly of consumers' sovereignty, since those with abilities in wide demand (film actors, playwrights) or producing goods that sell well will earn high incomes. If the inequality of income is considered excessive, it can be tempered by progressive taxation. (4) Consumers can be considered the best judges of their needs and preferences and therefore best capable of making choices most likely to satisfy themselves only if they can learn by trial and error what to avoid and how to choose better. Choice by trial is easy in many goods and services but not where purchases are made infrequently (a house, furniture, etc.) or where the effects or performance of a commodity are not immediately or soon apparent (tobacco, medicines, etc.). Here consumers' sovereignty may need to be restricted by authority or strongly influenced by disinterested advice unless consumers show they are aware of the experience of other consumers in learning of the properties of commodities or services they are unable to test themselves. [10]

Consumer's Surplus, a concept generally associated with the name of Alfred Marshall. It is based upon the observation that consumers seldom pay the price for a commodity that they would be prepared to pay rather than go without it. Because of the law of diminishing marginal utility further units of a commodity will be bought only if its price falls. Conversely, the price which will clear the market of supplies of a commodity will be determined by its *marginal* significance to consumers, not by its *total* significance. The total satisfaction derived from buying a given quantity of a commodity at a price is thus larger than the loss of satisfaction represented by the total amount of money spent. The measure of a consumer's surplus is the excess of the money he would be *willing* to pay, rather than go without the amount bought, over the amount of money he *does* pay.

The concept of consumer's surplus is used at several points in economic analysis. For example, it introduces an important qualification into the theory of price: although willingness to pay the price for a commodity or service indicates that the community values it more than possible alternatives, the converse need not follow from unwillingness to pay a *uniform* price. There may be a commodity or service that could not at any *uniform* price attract sufficient demand to cover its cost of production; it would therefore not be produced at all. But charging discriminating prices, tapping consumers' surpluses by charging most those who receive the largest benefit, may enable it to be produced and the costs to be covered. Again, the concept suggests that the increases in price due to outlay taxation cause losses of consumer satisfaction. If the only consideration were to minimize such loss it would be better to levy income taxes rather than to tax commodities: income taxes reduce incomes but leave consumers to adjust themselves to the cut in income by paring expenditure all round in a way that keeps individual losses of satisfaction to a minimum; commodity taxes, by selectively raising prices, result in the loss of large chunks of consumer's surplus *regardless* of consumers' individual preferences. But here again economists differ about the meaning and measurement of consumer's surplus.

More generally, the notion of consumer's surplus has been used as an indicator of changes in social welfare. All policy decisions on the use of resources benefit some people and harm others. If it can be shown that gainers could compensate losers and still be better off as a result of a change, the change could be said to be worthwhile. Implementation of this rule requires an attempt to compute losses and gains of consumers' surpluses. The concept thus provides a theoretical foundation for cost-benefit analysis (although it has proved to be precarious in practice). The applicability of the concept has been criticized by a number of economists: one outspoken critic, Dr. I. M. D. Little, in his *Critique of Welfare Economics* (1957), concluded that consumer's surplus was a "totally useless theoretical toy." [14]

Consumption, the process of deriving utility from a commodity or service. More generally, it describes the business of acquiring commodities and services in order to obtain satisfaction directly from them; or it indicates the amount of expenditure on them.

In economics, "consumption" does not necessarily imply the physical destruction of the commodity "consumed." Food is consumed, but so are objects such as pictures, which are not destroyed in yielding utility or satisfaction. Consumption is therefore not necessarily a tangible process: an audience may be said to "consume" the services of actors or musicians.

Economists have come to regard utility less in terms of the satisfaction derived from goods and services and more in terms of the degree to which goods and services are desired. They have correspondingly tended to shift their use of the word "consumption" to mean the process of acquiring goods and services, and the amount of expenditure on them, where the purpose is to derive utility.

It has thus become customary, in considering the total spending that generates the community's flow of production of goods and services, to distinguish between consumption demand and investment demand, the latter representing demand for capital goods desired not for their utility but because they add to the future productive capacity of the community. If consumption is regarded as closely related to output and income, investment then becomes the decisive element determining the level of total demand and thus the level of total production in the economy. [14]

Consumption Function, a name for the general relationship between income and consumption. J. M. Keynes originally called it "the propensity to consume." It shows what expenditure consumers will wish to make on consumers' goods and services at each possible level of income. Keynes thought that, because of a "fundamental psychological law," consumption would rise with, but less than, a rise in income, because some of the increase would be saved. (This relationship might not apply in poorer countries where a rise in income could lead to a proportional rise in consumption of essential goods.) Studies of the relationship of income to consumption tend to suggest that income exerts a significant influence on consumption, though there is less evidence that, as income rises, the percentage that goes on consumption falls. Though there seems little evidence in the short term to suggest a relationship between consumption and income, when they are measured in longer-run averages (five to ten years), a closer relationship emerges. This indicates that factors other than income influence consumption expenditure, such as wealth and availability of credit. The evidence also suggests it would be advantageous to use more than one consumption function, e.g. one for year-to-year changes, one for decade-to-decade changes, etc. [14]

Consumption Tax, a tax sometimes imposed not primarily to raise revenue but as an instrument of economic policy. It has been used in wartime when it was desired to reduce output over a wide range of consumer goods and where it is not practicable to impose production controls or consumer rationing. The reduction in consumption may be more important than the amount of tax collected. Purchase tax when originally imposed in 1940 was a tax in this class though it was retained after the war because it was raising large amounts of revenue and because it could be used to regulate demand and consumption good expenditure; it was replaced by VAT in 1973. [12]

Contango, a charge paid by a buyer or seller of securities to continue a transaction by postponing a transfer. The first day after the ending of a Stock Exchange account is "Contango" day, on which speculators who do not wish to transfer securities may postpone the handing over. For example, if a bull's securities have not risen during the account as expected, he may wish to carry over the bargain into the next settlement. Normally bull contango applies, with bears in effect lending bulls money by not delivering the security sold. When "uncovered" bears with no goods to deliver outweigh bulls, so that bulls are technically lending securities to bears, there is said to be backwardation. The sum of money paid to bulls by bears for this privilege is also known as backwardation. [8]

Continuation, another name for contango.

Continuous Variable, a quantity that changes by imperceptible amounts and thus virtually without "gaps," so that there is an infinite number of values. [14]

Contract Curve, the line of optimal positions in exchange (of given stocks of two goods) between two transactors. Starting from a position of trade somewhere off the contract curve, a movement towards the curve will improve one transactor's position without worsening that of the other. This device is based on a construction by F. Y. Edgeworth and applied in the analysis of bargaining strategy and welfare economics. [7]

Contracting Out. *See* Disintegration; Farming Out; Pension; Trade Union.

Controlled Economy, a system managed or directed by government. [10]

Convenience Goods, normally stocked at numerous points for the convenience of the consumer, so that no effort is required in "shopping." Confectionery and groceries are familiar examples stocked in village stores, corner shops, in large stores, railway stations, airports. [7]

Conversion, replacement of a loan or security by another carrying a smaller rate of interest. During the cheap money period organized by Dalton after World War II, holders of British government securities were asked to convert them into new loans at lower interest rates or receive their market value in cash. [8]

Convertibility, a situation in which the currency of a country can be exchanged for foreign currencies. It requires that the currency can be freely bought and sold in the markets for foreign exchange. A currency may be convertible at a fixed exchange rate, or within a narrow range of exchange rates, or it may be free to find its own price according to supply and demand in the market.

The modern meaning of convertibility is wider than the old. In pre-war textbooks on economics convertibility meant convertible into gold. Convertible currencies were "on gold," i.e. they could be exchanged for gold at a fixed parity.

Convertibility is necessary for the development of international exchange. If major currencies are inconvertible, barriers are placed in the way of free trade. Potential customers are forced to obtain import licences or central bank approval in order to get hold of the foreign currency they need to buy imports from countries whose currencies are scarce. Their freedom to buy goods from the cheapest sources is limited by the inconvertibility of their home country's currency. The free flow of capital between countries is also limited by inconvertibility. Permission is required before the investor can obtain the foreign currency required to buy shares in other countries.

The price paid for convertibility is that it increases the risks of balance of payments crises. The danger of flights of "hot money"—movements of short-term capital from one financial centre to another—become larger when the mechanism of exchange control is dismantled. The question is whether these risks are worth running in order to remove obstacles to international economic intercourse. Economic analysis indicates the alternative possible policies; it is for politicians or the community at large to make the choice. [4]

Conveyance, legal term used for the transfer of property from seller to buyer. In Britain conveyancing has become one of the largest and most remunerative sources of income of solicitors as rising incomes have increased the number of people who own their own homes from four million in 1948 to around nine million in the middle 1970's. Since conveyancing costs, together with estate agents' fees, stamp duties and other costs raise the cost of transactions in the housing market, they have been the subject of considerable debate. Conveyancing and agency work increase the efficiency of the market: the debate therefore turns on what constitutes a competitive reward for such services and how to combine more cost-efficiency with safeguards for buyers and sellers. [8]

Co-operative Societies, may be producer or consumer co-operatives, voluntary or state-assisted. The essence of co-operative societies is that groups of consumers (or producers) control and share the profits of organizations that sell to (or buy from) them. The success of voluntary co-operatives depends primarily on their relative efficiency. If the services they provide are more costly or of lower quality than those provided by competing enterprises, they rarely succeed unless fostered and protected by the state. The efficiency of voluntary co-operatives tends to vary between countries, regions and kinds. They tend to flourish wherever competition is sluggish or weak so that unorganized consumers or producers are exploited. They then stimulate competition.

Producer co-operatives are common in many countries, particularly in agricultural production and distribution; where they are voluntary their existence is economically justified, that is, it may be presumed that they are preferred to possible alternative arrangements. Many, however, are state supported or depend for success on the state suppression of competitors. In British agriculture voluntary producers' co-operatives have been less successful than in many countries mainly because they have been overshadowed by compulsory co-operatives in agricultural Marketing Boards created by Act of Parliament in milk, potatoes, hops and other products.

Consumer co-operation has been more successful in Great Britain. Organizations engaged in production and distribution are formed by groups of people in accordance with the Industrial and Provident Societies Acts. The members jointly own the capital of the societies and are in law the sole controllers. The size of individual shareholdings is limited. The trading surplus is normally distributed quarterly to members in proportion to their purchases, with the rate of dividend approved by a general meeting. In some cases there is only a nominal charge for membership. Policy is determined and staff appointed by an elected committee.

The retail societies are federated in the Co-operative Wholesale Society, which they in turn control by the election of directors and by quarterly general meetings. The CWS is grouped with other co-operative organizations in the Co-operative Union, which holds the annual Co-operative Congress at which general policy decisions for the Co-operative movement as a whole are taken. The running of the Co-operative Union is in the hands of a Central Board and Central Executive. Co-operation has spread in this country from retailing to wholesaling, production, banking and insurance, but remains more prominent in retailing than in other activities.

Since the Second World War co-operative societies in the UK have accounted for about one-eighth of total retail sales and have had about ten million members. The failure to achieve much further growth in their share of the market has drawn attention to defects in organization. Some economists argue that the suspicion of highly paid executives, hostility to loss of sovereignty by small societies and a general reluctance to try new ideas in marketing may be traced to the "uncommercial" philosophy of the movement and the absence of profit and loss incentives and disciplines. Others believe that these disadvantages may not be inherent in co-operation as such, and that its rapid growth and the more recent achievements of co-operative production in countries such as Sweden suggest that co-operative societies can be efficient and enterprising if they satisfy changing consumer demands.

In Denmark, India, Japan and other countries co-operation has been fostered by the state in agricultural capital and credit. [3]

Co-ownership, worker participation in ownership as well as in control and profits of a business. [3]

Co-partnership, generally, a system of production in which employees share under a formal agreement in the profits of the firm; in particular, where they do so as shareholders of the company. Co-partnership need not imply workers' control of management, though it may be associated with it. It is distinguished from consumers' co-operatives because it does not distribute profit to customers.

An early example of co-partnership in the UK was in the Yorkshire collieries. From 1865 to 1874 Henry Briggs, Son & Co. Ltd ran a scheme in which shareholders were recommended to share equally with the company's workers distributable profits above 10 per cent on capital. Later experiments went further in giving (or selling on favourable terms) shares to workers; this practice is now normally regarded as essential to co-partnership.

Co-partnership was often advocated as a way of increasing material incentives and cutting costs, and in its early history was fostered by employers as an alternative to unionism. The development of bonus and piece-rate payments, work study and trade unions has weakened these arguments for it. It is not common in British industry, but it exists in a number of firms, large and small, where it is thought to contribute to a sense of solidarity between management and workers. [3]

Copyright, the exclusive right to reproduce an original literary, dramatic or musical work in a material form, perform it in public, publish, broadcast or cause it to be transmitted to subscribers of a diffusion service, and make an adaptation of it, or to authorize other persons to perform any of these acts. The author of a work is usually entitled to the ownership of the copyright, but it may belong to his employer, e.g. newspapers, government departments, the person who has commissioned a particular work. Copyright lasts for the author's lifetime and for fifty years thereafter. It also applies in sound recordings, cinematograph films and television and sound broadcasts. The terms of copyright are set by the Copyright Act, 1956.

The main economic interest in copyright lies in the monopoly power it confers which may prevent works becoming available in cheap reproductions. Copyright provides a means for authors to secure remuneration for their work and protection from competition. But as a means of paying authors it is haphazard because a writer of original ideas may find his work quickly superseded by books for which he has provided the groundwork. Some economists believe the period of copyright is longer than necessary to provide protection of the initial investment in a publication. [3]

Corn Exchange, essentially a "wholesale" market specializing in corn, fodder, fertilizers and seeds, cattle foods and cattle cake. It was founded in 1749 in Mark Lane in the City of London. Membership totals about 3,000, embracing 200 firms. Business hours are from noon until 3 P.M. to ensure the best light for judging the colour and texture of grains. Samples of products can be inspected on the stands. Stand holders buy on "CIF" terms and sell to customers at home on ex-ship ("delivered") terms. Corn brokers sell to millers, merchants and stand holders on the parallel "retail" exchange, the Baltic. [7]

Corner, the act of buying up the entire stock of a commodity in order to resell at a higher price. A commodity must satisfy some stringent conditions before it is suitable for cornering. The quantity supplied must not be able to expand rapidly in response to an increase in its price, i.e. it must be produced by specialized resources and the production cycle must extend over a long period of time. The quantity demanded must contract less than proportionately with an increase in its price: if not, the proceeds from resale will be less than the total cost of purchases. This means that the commodity must have no close substitutes. Before the world became linked by rapid means of transport these conditions were satisfied in local markets for many agricultural products. Today supplies are drawn from many sources, quantities traded are large and the range of substitutes has increased so that corners are unlikely. The last notorious attempt to corner a market occurred with pepper in the 1930's, but the speculators were bankrupted with some two years' supplies on their hands. [7]

Corporate State, a system, similar to guild socialism, in which the major segments of the national economy are grouped in a single "corporation" with extensive powers over cost, price and output. The corporations are in theory autonomous but in the "corporate states" of Italy, Portugal and elsewhere have been themselves subject to the power of the state, which is in turn organized as a single, closed corporation.

In principle the corporations contain representatives of employers, employees and consumers, while the state corporation is an oligarchy of picked men ruling in theory in the best interests of the nation but in practice usually forming a party organization with autocratic power.

The notion of the corporate state figured prominently in fascist theory. It was the logical outgrowth of an ideology that opposed both communism and liberalism; it did not involve state control of the economy as a means to economic progress and social change, as in Leninism; on the other hand individualism was as contemptible as Marxism to Fascists since it allowed men to pursue economic gain instead of the holy or heroic selfhood that could be attained in serving the national cause; so there was no room for the freely functioning market economy or for private enterprise as a form of economic organization.

In Britain there have in recent times been political difficulties in the use of market incentives (high profits, salaries, and wages; low taxes) to promote growth and of market disciplines (bankruptcy, liquidation, redundancy) to restrain inflation. British governments therefore resorted to policies—from National Planning in the 1960's to statutory incomes policies in the 1970's—in which they offered organized employers and organized workers an increasing say in running the economy. This collaboration of leaders, spokesmen or representatives of economic interests could lead to a form of corporative state. [10]

Correlation, statistical technique used in economics which establishes a relationship between an economic quantity and one or more others on which it is dependent. Thus saving (dependent variable) may be related (correlated) to income (independent variable). Correlations in this way help in testing hypotheses and in forecasting. If one dependent variable is related to two or more variables, the correlation is multiple. The main (relatively) independent variables are GNP, industrial production, disposable income—only relatively, because they are dependent on other elements. The correlation establishes a relationship that could be accidental; it does not indicate a causal relationship. Thus two dependent variables may have a high (direct) positive or (indirect) negative correlation with an independent variable: hair grows grey with age; eyesight becomes weaker; but there is no causal link between greying hair and weakening sight. To establish causes requires a theoretical analysis of causes and consequences. [14]

Cosmos, Greek for a spontaneous order; in economics a market order, which discovers human purposes by competition rather than serves pre-decided ends. The contrast is with (Greek) *taxis,* which describes a deliberate arrangement of resources to serve *given* ends, e.g. a family, a firm, a government. [14]

Cost, in earlier treatises on economics was explained in terms of real effort and sacrifice—the "toil and trouble" entailed in producing goods and services. The approach to cost generally accepted in our day is in terms of opportunities or alternatives forgone ("opportunity cost," "alternative-use cost"). This approach regards the cost of acquiring goods as the forgone enjoyment of other goods. If resources are used to produce one thing they cannot be used to produce others; therefore the cost of the one is the value of the alternatives forgone. The cost of using farm land to grow, say, barley is the value of the alternative crops that could have been grown on it instead.

The concept of opportunity cost makes possible a more rational choice between alternatives than the everyday notion of costs as the money outlay necessary to buy something. The reason why is not readily apparent, for if the money laid out on the hire of factors reflects the prices that have to be paid to attract the factors from alternative occupations, and if those prices reflect the value of the alternative goods the factors were capable of producing, then money costs and prices would correctly reflect opportunity cost. In real life this equivalence is distorted for a number of reasons:

First, because money prices determined competitively may be altered by individuals or groups powerful enough to "rig" markets and prices in their own interests: if factors of production are thus prevented from moving into these privileged lines of activity their money rewards (prices) are artificially limited and no longer reflect the value to consumers of the alternatives they could produce.

Secondly, because the costs or prices on which *individuals* base their decisions may not correctly reflect the alternatives sacrificed by the *community as a whole.* Economists have long argued that, for example, a smoky factory may involve widespread sacrifice of alternatives by imposing additional cleaning and renewal costs on the community at large; these are not normally considered as part of the costs of the firm concerned, although some economists argue that they could be taken into account by those who move near smoky factories or in areas where smoky factories could be built.

Thirdly, because alternatives forgone are not always clear-cut. If production were everywhere organized so that factors of production could always be hired in "penny numbers," and if the factors of production were always readily and immediately adaptable to alternative uses, there would be no problem. But modern production processes are complex, using large amounts of highly specialized and durable capital equipment which (*a*) can often be bought only in expensive "lumps" and (*b*) once acquired has no alternative use (except perhaps to another producer in the same line of production). A firm's accountant allocates the money costs of durable equipment to current output as overheads in the form of depreciation charges. But in terms of opportunity cost this practice has no significance for current decisions on what or how much output to produce. In the past the price paid for equipment may *at that time* have reflected the alternatives forgone in producing it; but this "historic" cost is irrelevant for two reasons. First, since "bygones are bygones," the recovery of historic cost has no economic meaning. The only question of economic relevance is, "Will the value of the output of equipment during its life be sufficient to cover its *current* replacement costs?" Secondly, if it had no alternative use at all, and was wholly unadaptable to any other line of production, then its opportunity cost would be zero; and whether or not it was currently "earning its keep" (other than covering current maintenance charges) would not matter. It might just as well be used as not. The question is therefore relevant only to decisions about renewal or replacement.

Thus the period under consideration, the adaptability or otherwise of the factors and their method of payment all serve to make money costs (unless interpreted as opportunity cost) an imperfect basis for economic decisions even by individual producers. The economist is concerned with the principles that determine decisions on the use of scarce resources, which are necessarily about what to do tomorrow, not yesterday. Hence his interest is in the costs which actions *will* incur rather than in the expenses which past actions *have* incurred. His concern with cost as a whole derives from his interest in the question of how much of a commodity is likely to be supplied (produced) at any price. The answer requires consideration of exactly what costs are relevant to production decisions.

Economics analyses the following categories of production costs:

Fixed costs are those which do not vary with output. A better term might be *constant costs,* since they refer to the cost of fixed factors of production, those whose quantity employed (and thus cost) is a constant. Strictly speaking it is necessary to add "over some range of output." What is regarded as fixed cost thus depends on the period of time and the range of output. If a sufficiently long period and wide range is taken, no factors are fixed and all costs are variable.

Variable costs are those which vary with output. They refer to outlays on factors of production the quantity of which varies with output, e.g. power, raw materials. The longer the period and the wider the range of output, the more factors fall into this category. In the long run all costs are variable.

Supplementary and prime costs are an alternative classification which to a large extent overlaps fixed and variable costs. In some textbooks no attempt is made to distinguish between the two pairs. Broadly, supplementary cost refers to the costs of staying in business, even if output were zero. Prime cost refers to the direct expenses incurred in producing output: they thus cover variable costs plus that part of fixed cost that might be avoided by not producing the output. Supplementary costs are the remainder of fixed costs. The distinction between prime and supplementary costs, as between fixed and variable cost, is not absolute, but varies with the organization of the firm. The essence of the distinction is that, however distinguished, prime costs are those that revenue *must* cover if output is to continue: if they were consistently not covered it would be more profitable to keep plant idle or to close it down.

Average cost refers to the cost per unit of output; hence it is sometimes referred to as *unit cost.* It consists of average fixed cost plus average variable cost. Average fixed cost will fall as output expands. Average variable cost may fall, remain constant or increase as output expands, depending on the technical conditions of production. Economic theory relating to factor combination suggests that average variable cost will first fall and eventually rise. Thus average (total) cost can similarly be assumed first to fall and then to rise as output expands. In the long run, when all factors and costs are assumed to be variable, the same sequence of fall and rise is presumed for long-run average costs, because of the increasing and decreasing returns to scale.

Marginal cost refers to the additional cost of increasing output by a small amount, say one unit. Since fixed cost by definition does not change with output, marginal cost refers to the change in total variable cost as output changes. It will in practice be the behaviour of marginal cost that determines the course of average variable cost and thus average total cost, for if the additional cost of additional output is rising it will be dragging average variable cost up too, although more slowly. This relationship is easy to see in terms of cricket scores: a better-than-average cricket score will drag up the seasonal average. A falling marginal cost will thus pull average variable cost down too. [7]

Cost, Avoidable. *See* SUPPLEMENTARY COSTS.

Cost-benefit Analysis, a procedure for assessing the full "social" costs and benefits of an economic activity, whether undertaken by private enterprise or by government. It differs from the more familiar private calculations of the costs and benefits of activities, which are generally regarded as taking into account only "internal" costs and benefits—i.e. the costs and the benefits to the decision-makers—by also taking into account "external" or "spillover" costs or benefits which the activities impose on third parties who have had no part in the decision to undertake it. For example, expenditure on a third London airport would affect people and buildings for miles around it: trade and employment opportunities would be enhanced; noise, atmospheric pollution and congestion on approach roads would be increased. Cost-benefit analysis tries to identify, measure and bring into account all such costs and benefits from the wider viewpoint of the community as a whole.

In principle the notion of bringing into account all the costs and benefits involved in any decision about the use of resources, and not only the costs and benefits to the decision-taker, is unexceptionable. In practice it is difficult, if not impossible, to quantify all the elements involved. Assumptions have to be made about key elements in the reckoning, for example what rate of interest to use in *discounting* or *capitalizing* flows of (future) benefits and costs; how to value intangible costs and benefits such as personal frustration from noise or the amenity afforded by views of unspoilt countryside; how to deal with uncertainty.

Estimates of social costs or benefits may therefore in practice degenerate into rough forecasts, projections, predictions, estimates, "guesstimates" (hardly disguised guesswork). At worst, the process may encourage the quotation of figures that are difficult to check (or refute) but that lend a spurious accuracy, precision or objectivity to the estimates. A small difference in such estimates may decide whether a large investment should be undertaken or be scrapped.

Conceptually the distinction between the internal and external effects of decision-taking seems to be a truism that yields relatively little of practical value for policy. In a general sense every form of activity by an individual, family, firm, or government exerts external as well as internal effects. Attempts to trace every external effect and to compensate people affected adversely or to tax those affected favourably could exhaust themselves by chasing elusive detail and run into the sand. The external effects of many activities are foreseen as risks and voluntarily or spontaneously taken into account ("internalized") in private transactions. A man who buys a house in a town knows he risks noisy neighbours and may offer less for it than if he thought there were no risks; in the countryside he knows he risks losing a view by a new school or road; and so on. Further, individuals and firms do not necessarily consider only themselves and their immediate interest, or take decisions based solely on "self-interest": they are often aware of the interests of others and would prefer to avoid the adverse effect of antagonizing them; i.e. they are concerned with wider issues than just their own advantages, non-monetary as well as monetary, long-term as well as short-term. Moreover, some "externalities" can be internalized by government: motor car manufacturers are required to fit seat-belts (to reduce the external cost of accident injuries on medical services) or filters to exhausts (to reduce fumes and their external effects on pedestrians, residents, and buildings). Social benefits are usually urged by industries or governmental interests that ask for a subsidy: for example, that Concorde would encourage high technology and raise the standard of scientific research and engineering skills in the aircraft industry in general and in the economy as a whole. Such claims are often vague, difficult to establish (or disprove), and usually neglect the social opportunity *costs* of subsidies, e.g. the goods or services that could otherwise have been produced if the large subsidies for (e.g.) Concorde had been withheld. [13]

Cost-effectiveness, a measure of the relative cost of alternative methods of achieving a purpose where a cost-benefit study becomes too difficult or nebulous because values cannot be attached to costs or benefits. Thus, since the individual benefit from expenditure on defence cannot readily be assessed, a cost-effectiveness study may be able to examine the "effectiveness" of alternative weapons or weapon systems relatively to their cost. Similarly calculations can be made for government expenditure on education, health services, libraries, recreational facilities, etc. A cost-effectiveness study (as in the Roskill Report on a third London airport) cannot by itself demonstrate a conclusive case for (or against) a projected investment or scheme, because it is concerned only with possible alternative costs and cannot show whether the costs exceed or are exceeded by prospective or potential benefits. [13]

Cost of Living, the expense needed to maintain a standard of life. The prices of goods and services change over time for various reasons; it is therefore useful to investigate changes in the cost of buying the combination of goods and services typically bought by members of the group whose cost of living is being investigated. There is no single and constant measure of the cost of living for a whole community since the spending habits of individuals differ and change through time. Indexes of "the" cost of living are therefore to be understood as more or less faithful measures of *general* trends in prices affecting a *group* of people. In the UK the official Index of Retail Prices is a measure of changes in prices of goods and services bought by wage-earners and earners of moderate salaries. Separate indexes would be needed to represent changes in the cost of living for either the poorer or the better-off sections of the community. Periodic inquiries into household expenditure by the Department of Employment reveal changes in spending habits so that measures of this type can be revised periodically. Some wage rates vary with the Retail Price Index.

Constructing a cost of living index requires investigation into the expenditure of a representative sample of households belonging to the group whose cost of living is to be studied. It shows the expenditure on each commodity and each service within the period by the members of the group as a whole. When the importance of each good and service in the consumers' budget is known, the prices can be "weighted" in the index so that a given price change in a more important commodity or service has more effect on the index than the same change in a less important commodity or service. Thus if consumers spend ten times more on bread than they do on cabbages, and cabbages are assigned a "weight" of one, bread is given a "weight" of ten. The prices of the commodities or services in the "base-year" are taken as equal to 100. If there are only two commodities, bread and cabbages, the index can be calculated as shown in Table 4.

If the average were not weighted, the index of the cost of living would have risen, since the increase in the price of cabbages would have outweighed the more important fall in bread prices.

Cost of living indexes become less valuable over time if the weighting is not brought up to date because consumption habits change, and the weights given to commodities in the base year will cease to represent the importance of the items in the consumers' budget. In particular there is a tendency to shift expenditure towards things whose prices have fallen most or risen least. Over a long period consumption patterns may alter markedly, especially where new products, such as television sets, appear on the market, or rising incomes enable people to move from cheaper food like fish and chips to dearer food like smoked

Table 4. Cost of Living Index

	Price		Weight	Expenditure-relatives (price index multiplied by the weight)	
	Year 1	Year 2		Year 1	Year 2
Bread	100	50	10	1,000	500
Cabbages	100	200	1	100	200
Total			11	1,100	700
Cost of living index (total expenditure-relatives divided by total weights)				100	63.7

salmon, or developments in techniques of production cheapen prices and cause demand for formerly expensive products, like chicken, to expand. [9]

Cost, Opportunity. *See* OPPORTUNITY COST.

Cost, Overhead. *See* OVERHEAD COSTS.

Cost, Prime. *See* COST.

Cost Pull. *See* COST PUSH.

Cost Push, the theory that inflation is caused by employers passing on increases in wages and wage-costs "pushed up" by trade union pressure. The argument against the theory is that cost push cannot be effective unless government expands the money supply so that higher prices are willingly paid by consumers. Otherwise employers faced by a higher price for labour (wages) will *reduce their labour supply* until its marginal product rises to the new higher wage. It is fear of the resulting unemployment (a political motive) that induces government to inflate the money supply. Therefore, it is argued, inflation is caused by politicians, and the trade unions cannot be blamed.

Professor F. W. Paish argued that in late 1969 inflation changed from "demand-pull" (an upward effect on prices caused by monetary inflation) to "cost-push," because trade union pressure increased. This may have happened because the real value of net pay after tax and other deductions ("take-home pay") had been eroded by increases in taxes and national insurance contributions in the previous three to four years, and the unions began to use their monopoly power more strongly; and perhaps because the incomes policy (to hold wages down) had collapsed shortly before in the summer of 1969. Paish argued that cost push inflation could be controlled by tax reductions, by deflation through tighter monetary or fiscal (budgetary) controls, or by direct action to restrain the rate of rise in wages by an incomes policy. If an incomes policy proved politically or administratively impracticable, he supported the proposal (made by Professor Sidney Weintraub of the University of Pennsylvania) for a progressive tax on wages and salaries to increase the cost of, and therefore encourage more resistance by employers to, increases in pay. He thought such resistance might be strengthened by government financial assistance to firms suffering losses from strikes precipitated by refusal to meet excessive wage demands.

Other views on resisting cost push inflation, whether induced by direct economic effect on employers (cost push proper) or by indirect political effect on politicians (government push, politician push) have been diverse. Taxes and national insurance deductions should be reduced, expectations of inflation should be weakened, perhaps by indexing, to remove a bargaining-counter of the unions in driving wages higher, workers should be retrained for new or expanding industries to reduce government anxiety about unemployment. Raising taxes should be avoided by increasing government revenue by charging more for government services supplied at a price less than the market price (some postal services) and by charging for government services hitherto supplied "free." Not least, the economy should be made more competitive so that higher wage-costs could not easily be passed on to consumers in higher prices. [7]

Cost, Sunk. *See* SUNK COSTS.

Cost, Supplementary. *See* SUPPLEMENTARY COSTS.

Cost, Unavoidable. *See* SUPPLEMENTARY COSTS.

Council of Economic Advisers, a three-member board which advises the US President on national economic policy. It was established in 1946. Its primary role is "to develop and recommend to the President national economic policies to foster and promote free competitive enterprise, to avoid economic fluctuations . . . and to maintain employment, production and purchasing power." Each January it publishes the *Annual Report to the President by the Council of Economic Advisers.* In the early and mid-1970's while under the chairmanship of Professor Paul McCracken it was criticized for failing to advise against the controls of pay and prices introduced by President Nixon in 1971, or to recommend sufficiently strong monetary discipline against inflation. [10]

Countervailing Power, Theory of, the notion, suggested by Professor J. K. Galbraith in *American Capitalism* (1957), that private power is held in check by the countervailing power of those who are subject to it. Thus the trend towards concentration of industrial enterprise in a relatively few firms encourages the emergence of strong buyer groups as a defence against exploitation; monopoly buying power among firms generates countervailing power on the part of trade unions; retail chain stores with massive buying power counteract the selling power of large food manufacturers; and so on. Galbraith believed that competition among individual suppliers, which has always been regarded as promoting efficiency and the satisfaction of consumers, had in effect been superseded in this respect by the operation of countervailing power across the market. [3]

Coupon, (*a*) a form presented to obtain a money payment, commodity or service. An example is the detachable part of a bearer bond which states the interest due to the holder. When the interest becomes payable, the coupon is cut from the bond and presented for payment. The derogatory term "coupon clipper" is sometimes used to denote a person living solely from interest on bonds. Coupons have also been used in government rationing schemes: a coupon would enable the holder to buy a stated quantity of a commodity in a stated period. Books of coupons were issued to the population of the UK during, and for some time after, the Second World War, when most foodstuffs, clothing and basic raw materials were allocated by a system of rationing instead of through the price mechanism. When goods are sold with detachable slips that entitle the holder to a "bonus" offer of free or cut-price goods or services, the slips are often called coupons. [7]

(*b*) earmarked purchasing power issued by government to ensure that the recipients buy and are able to pay for specified commodities or services. Other names are "tickets" (as applied to education by W. E. Forster in 1870), "stamps" (as applied in the 1960's to food in the USA), "vouchers" (as applied to education by Milton Friedman in the 1950's). [10]

Coupon-clipper. *See* COUPON.

Coupon Rate of Interest. *See* YIELD.

Cournot, Antoine Augustin (1801–77), French mathematician and economist. He became Professor of Mathematics at the University of Lyons in 1834 and later Rector of Dijon Academy. He was distinguished mainly for his knowledge of science and his contributions to mathematics, but in his work on economics he was perhaps the first to have a competent knowledge of both economics and mathematics. His main works include *Recherches sur les principes mathématiques de la théorie des richesses* (1838), *Principes de la théorie de richesses* (1863) and *Revue sommaire des doctrines économiques* (1877), in which he built up an apparatus of supply and demand "functions" which he used to show how price was formed under conditions of pure monopoly, duopoly and perfect competition. These attempts to use mathematical techniques in the analysis of economic problems have caused him to be considered the founder of mathematical economics. [2]

Cover Prices. *See* Collusive Tendering.

Covered Bear. *See* Bear.

Cowboy Economy, expression adopted by Professor Kenneth Boulding to describe the reckless, exploitative economic philosophy he considered characteristic of the American economy in particular and which in his opinion was based on the twin premises that there are always more resources just over the horizon and nature has an infinite capacity to absorb garbage. These premises may have had some validity in the frontier economy of the "Wild West" but not in a modern world in which the limits of resources and the capacity of the biological environment to absorb "waste" are more readily discernible. In place of an unheeding quest for growth and maximum "throughput" (the conversion of resources into artifacts and rubbish) as conventionally measured by gross national product, Boulding proposed a "spaceman economy," in keeping with the notion of "Spaceship Earth" (a system of finite resources and fragile biological life-support processes) whose central concern would be to *minimize* the throughput needed to achieve a stable stock of goods consistent with desirable stability of the environmental systems upon which life depends. Quality would be emphasized rather than quantity, communication rather than physical movement of men and material, production of non-resource-using services rather than resource-using goods, the preservation rather than the elimination of options about future uses of resources that affect the quality of life. [6]

Credit, the grant of permission by one body to another to obtain possession of something owned by the former (e.g. an asset, cash or service) without payment at the time of receipt; any transfer of goods, services or money in exchange for goods, services or money to be received at a future date; or, in most advanced form, a transfer of money in return for a promise to pay in the future. Original meaning is belief or trust (Latin *credere,* to believe).

Since few business transactions are settled in cash at the time, modern society rests largely on credit, or on confidence and trust.

The essence of a credit transaction is the promise to pay at a future date. Such promises may be formal and written (as in banknotes, bills of exchange, cheques and other promissory notes) or may take the form of book debts and loans (as in credit sales made in the normal course of trade or bank "advances," sums placed at a person's disposal in the books of a bank). Industry and commerce make extensive use of such book entries, relying heavily on a smoothly working system of credit. In Britain this system is provided by the banking system plus a large network of related and subsidiary institutions that act as financial intermediaries (merchant banks, finance houses, the Stock Exchange, the discount market, insurance companies, building societies and others).

The principal function of credit is to finance production in anticipation of demand, i.e. to marry the ownership of productive resources with producers' demands for them. The credit mechanism also economizes the use of currency, permits a more flexible planning of expenditures over time and acts as gathering ground and channel for society's small savings.

Credit generates current spending power. It is always possible that over-expansion of credit in an economy may lead to inflation. For this reason the monetary authorities in post-war Britain from time to time in the 1960's restricted the volume of credit by taking measures to raise its cost (thus reducing demand) and/or reducing its supply. In the early 1970's credit was expanded by government in the hope of breaking out of the cycle of "stop-go" and "go-ing" for growth. It did not last long: growth accelerated for about a year but inflation developed, the attempts to control it by "incomes policy" disrupted production; and growth turned into recession. [8]

Cross-elasticity of Demand, a measurement of the degree of responsiveness of the demand for one commodity to a change in the price of another. It is measured by dividing the proportionate change in the demand for the one commodity by the proportionate change in the price of the other. A high-valued measurement would indicate that the commodities were close substitutes; a low one would indicate that they were remote substitutes. [7]

Cross-section Analysis, the study of a series of recordings of economic data for different individuals (or firms or countries) at the same moment or in the same period of time. A method of investigation and research commonly used by economists. The best known examples are censuses of population and production in many countries; in Britain the Department of Employment has recorded the expenditure of a sample of 3,000 households in two consecutive weeks every year; and so on. A cross-section analysis of household income and expenditure may reveal that households with different incomes allocate different proportions of it to food, housing, clothing, entertainment, holidays, insurance, saving, etc. It can then be deduced that if the income of a household rose it would probably distribute it in the same way as the average household with the higher income, or that if total income in a country rose spending or saving would change in the ways indicated by the habits of the higher income households. There is some confirmation of this tendency in recent years in the USA. These deductions are not certainties but *a priori* probabilities depending on the assumption that no other changes that might affect spending and saving habits have taken place. Cross-section analysis can sometimes be checked by time series. [14]

Csikos-Nagy, Bela (1915–), Hungarian economist. He was born in Szeged and graduated in Social Sciences in Szeged University in 1937. He was granted the title of Docent at the University of Pecs in 1942, has lectured at the Karl Marx University of Economic Science since 1959, and was given the title University Professor in 1964 and the academic rank of Doctor of Economic Sciences in 1967. He has developed the theory and practice of pricing in a socialist market economy by university lecturing and by acting as Chairman of the Hungarian Board for Prices and Materials. In 1967 his lecture to a British audience at the Institute of Economic Affairs on the 1968 price reforms was amplified and published as *Pricing in Hungary* (IEA, 1968). It seemed to reflect the effort to make more use of incentives for state "enterprises" without creating personal or private profit, although part of the profit made by enterprises might be allocated to benefits (rather than cash sums) for managers and other employees. The socialist market economy was using prices as signals to supply and demand but not as forms of payment. Professor Csikos-Nagy developed his thinking in *Socialist Economic Policy* (1974). [2]

Cum Dividend, term used with description of a share or in a list of share prices to mean that the buyer takes the next dividend. (*Cum* is Latin for "with.") [8]

Cumulative Preference Shares. *See* PREFERENCE SHARES.

Cunliffe Committee, appointed to examine the problems of currency and foreign exchanges expected to arise after the First World War and to suggest steps to restore "normal conditions." The chairman, Lord Cunliffe, was Chairman of the Bank of England. A. C. Pigou was a member. The 1919 report was noted in particular for its support of the gold standard: "The adoption of a currency not convertible at will into gold or other exportable coin is likely in practice to lead to over-issue and so to destroy the measure of exchangeable value and cause a general rise in all prices and an adverse movement in the foreign exchanges." This view contributed to Britain's return to the gold standard in April 1925. It fell out of favour, especially since the gold standard had to be abandoned in 1930, although largely because the pound had been over-valued in relation to gold and other currencies. Economists who favour "managed" paper currency have rejected the Cunliffe view. The experience of inflation during and after the Second World War has caused some economists to restate the case for linking the currency to gold or for devising some other method of taking it out of the authority of politicians. The "floating" of sterling in 1972 was followed by accelerated inflation. [10]

Currency, the official medium of exchange or money of a country. ("Currency" because money runs or passes from person to person.) The currency in circulation in Britain consists of coin and bank-notes; about one-sixth is held by banks, the remainder by the public. Bank deposits are nowadays a much more important part of the total money supply, accounting for about four-fifths of the whole, currency for only a fifth. Table 5 shows the currency circulation of Britain as it was in the mid-1960's before the "Great Inflation" of 1969.

Each sovereign state has a currency (e.g. the American dollar, the French franc); a payment from one country to another requires to be made in terms of a rate of exchange between their currencies.

A variation in the rate of exchange between two currencies is known as depreciation or devaluation of the currency which becomes cheaper as a result of the appreciation of the others.

Rates of exchange between currencies basically depend on the demand for them and their supply. These in turn depend upon: (1) underlying trade conditions; e.g. if British demands for French goods and services were exceeding French demands for British goods and services, more pounds sterling would be on offer for exchange into francs than francs for exchange into sterling, and in a free market in currency and commerce the pound price of francs would rise and sterling would depreciate; (2) international movements of capital, i.e. the import and export of securities and similar financial claims.

Like other prices the foreign exchange rate can be manipulated. Most governments intervene in the currency market to protect agreed "pegged" rates of exchange against what are considered as undesirable fluctuations arising from the ebb and flow of trade, unpredictable capital movements or speculative currency dealings. The agreed exchange "parities" of the seventy or so member countries of the International Monetary Fund have been pegged in this way. They may impose positive restrictions on some transactions, such as control imports or capital movements, or operate buffer-stock schemes to supplement free market demand for and supply of currencies to help counter temporary insta-

Table 5. Currency Circulation in Britain (in round numbers)

Notes and Coin outstanding	£ million	Holdings	£ million
Coin	200	Bank of England reserve	30
Bank of England notes	2,300	Scottish banks	130
Scottish bank-notes	130	Northern Irish banks	10
Northern Irish bank-notes	10	London clearing banks	320
		Total held by banks	490
		Estimated circulation with the public	2,150
Total	2,640		2,640

bility (in Great Britain this is the task of the Exchange Equalization Account). But as most domestic policy measures have international "spillover" effects (e.g. high interest rates in Britain tend to attract foreign funds to London), it is often difficult in practice to isolate the precise effects of state intervention.

An international currency is one widely accepted internationally in the settlement of debts. During the nineteenth century and up to World War II sterling was widely accepted as the major international currency; for about fifteen years after the war the major international currency was the dollar; for a time the strongest currency was the Deutsch mark (DM) introduced by Erhard in 1948, and at some periods the Japanese yen, because of the strong demand for Japanese and German exports, and therefore for their currencies to pay for them. Various international monetary institutions (of which the International Monetary Fund is the largest and best known) were created to help maintain an orderly supply of national currencies and hence to ensure an adequate quantity of international currency.

"Soft" currencies are those for which international demand is weak, "hard" currencies those for which international demand is strong. When the dollar was strong after the war, and there was a dollar "shortage" or "gap," some economists thought it would remain so for many years, but it became "soft" in the early 1960's when the American balance of payments ran into deficit. [8]

Currency School, a group of economists, financiers and statesmen engaged in the debates on monetary policy in the second quarter of the nineteenth century. They included Lord Overstone, G. W. Norman, R. Torrens and W. Ward. Their main doctrines were referred to as the "currency principle" by William Ward in 1832, but were probably formulated by Thomas Joplin in *Outlines of a System of Political Economy* in 1823 and by Henry Drummond in *Elementary Propositions on the Currency* in 1826. The period was one of violent business fluctuation: short periods of prosperity were interrupted by business failures and financial crises. It was generally felt that these crises were aggravated by mismanagement of the currency by the banking system in its note-issuing capacity. Although there were differences between members of the currency school (many modified their views under criticism), they nearly all felt that the primary duty of the banker, and especially the Bank of England, was to maintain a sufficient reserve of bullion to safeguard the stability of public credit. They argued that the total volume of metallic currency varied with inflows and outflows from abroad, and if credit were to remain stable a mixed currency should work in the same way, the volume of paper notes being kept in strict proportion to the amount of gold in the banking system. The Bank Charter Act of 1844 reflected their views rather than those of the Banking School. [2]

Current Account. *See* Deposits (Bank).

Customs and Excise Duties, indirect taxes (that is, collected not directly from individuals but through importers, manufacturers, distributors or other intermediaries) in the form of customs duties (on imported goods) and excise duties (on home-produced goods and services). The principal sources of customs and excise revenue, accounting for some two-fifths of British Government tax revenue have been: tobacco duty, purchase tax (20 per cent), hydrocarbon oils duty, and beer, wines and spirits duties. Of the remainder, protective duties have accounted for just over a half, betting, television and various licence duties for the rest.

Purchase tax, betting, television (advertising) and some protective duties have been levied *ad valorem* (that is, as a percentage of value): the other duties levied have been *specific* (that is, so much per pound of tobacco or per gallon of spirit of given proof strength, etc.). The theoretical economic interest of indirect taxes such as Value-Added Tax is that they are regressive. They are administratively difficult to refund. So tax rebates are normally confined to income tax. [12]

Customs Union, a single customs territory within which tariffs and other trade restrictions are eliminated between member countries of the union and a *common* external tariff is maintained against other countries. It contrasts with a free trade area, which provides for free trade between member countries but permits *separate* national tariffs against third countries. Because of its common tariff policy and the tendency to some integration of fiscal and monetary policies of the member countries, a customs union also calls for some degree of political union. Examples are Benelux and the Common Market.

A customs union both diverts and creates trade. It *diverts* trade to the extent that it turns the demand for imports from outside countries towards higher-cost producers in member countries who can undersell outside competitors only because of the tariff. This tends to impair the efficiency of specialization. It also *creates* trade to the extent that the removal of restrictions between member countries creates opportunities for more efficient specialization within the union because low-cost producers are encouraged and high-cost producers discouraged. This trade creation is likely to be the smaller the less alike are the economies of the members and therefore the smaller the degree of competition between them. The widening of the market is also likely to produce economies of large-scale production, especially in such aspects as research and design. Additional trade and a more efficient pattern of specialization, depending on the degree of political and economic integration achieved, may also result from the widening of the market in which government and other public contracts, normally confined to domestic producers, can be placed.

The net gain in economic welfare in the customs union depends on the balance between these contrasting tendencies. Trade diversion will tend to cause some loss of economic welfare to other countries, unless the creation of the union causes such an expansion of trade and income within its area that its total imports from outside countries rise despite the diversionary effects of the common external tariff by a larger amount than they would otherwise have done. Initially, at least, destruction of trade is likely to result in some distribution of world income away from outside countries. In the longer run the effect depends on the degree to which the customs union is part of wider forms of economic integration with which it may be associated or to which it may lead. Even so a customs union may be economically inferior to more universal arrangements for widening the scope of free trade. [4]

Cycle, Business. *See* Trade Cycles.

Cycle, Inventory Investment. *See* Inventory Investment Cycles.

Cycle, Trade. *See* Trade Cycles.

D

Dalton, Edward Hugh John Neale (1887–1962), English economist and politician. He was educated at Eton and King's College, Cambridge, and taught public finance at the London School of Economics (Lecturer 1919, Reader 1920–36). He was Labour M.P. from 1929, and the first Chancellor of the Exchequer (1945–7) in the post-war Labour Government, responsible for the financial and economic policy of reconstruction largely worked out in the 1944 White Paper on Employment Policy. Hugh Dalton was the architect of "cheap money" policy (a continuation of successful wartime orthodoxy), which reduced first the short-term and later the long-term rate of interest from 3 to 2½ per cent. His pursuit of cheap money was based on a belief in its beneficial social effects in encouraging redistribution and stimulating production. (He frequently quoted Keynes in his defence when criticism of his policy began to grow.) The policy engendered severe inflationary pressure, the danger of which he did not recognize until late 1947 (cheap money and associated policies had been framed out of fear of deflation). Neglect of monetary policy, and failure to deal with the sterling balances, contributed to the severe balance of payments crisis of August 1947, and forced him to introduce a degree of deflation in his autumn budget, the first post-war budget to restrain consumer demand. [2]

Dated Securities, those with a stated date (or range of dates) for the cash repayment (redemption) of the nominal or face value. The redemption date(s) may be near (short-dated securities) or distant (long-dated). [8]

Days of Grace, (*a*) the additional days allowed for paying a bill of exchange; in England three. The effect is of an interest-free loan. (*b*) the additional time allowed for paying an insurance premium, usually fourteen days. [8]

Deadweight Debt. *See* DEBT; NATIONAL DEBT.

Dealer, a trader who buys and sells goods, services or financial claims. He operates in organized commodity or other exchanges. His description varies with the product: in commodities he is a "merchant" or "wholesaler"; in stocks and shares a "stock-jobber" or "jobber"; in bills of exchange the operator of a "discount house." [7]

Dear Money, a government policy of maintaining a high price for borrowing money by maintaining high rates of interest. The intention is generally (*a*) to resist inflation by reducing borrowing, demand and economic activity; or (*b*) to reduce an outflow of funds and therefore pressure on the foreign exchange rate of the currency and strengthen the balance of payments; or (*c*) both. Dear money is also known as Tight Money. It is an aspect of "fine tuning" about which economists differ. [10]

Debasement (of Coinage), depreciation or reduction in value of a standard coinage. The cause may be government issue of coins below the prescribed weight (a practice common in medieval times), or interference after issue, e.g. "clipping" (cutting away small portions), "sweating" (by the use of chemicals) or abrasion (shaking coins together in a bag and removing small particles). It largely died out as coins lost their intrinsic value and became token money. [10]

Debentures, securities issued by joint-stock companies in return for long-period loans, usually ten to forty years. They may be "redeemed" (repaid) before the final date if the borrower wishes; or they may be irredeemable. Debentures are a debt of a company and not part of its capital. They are normally secured by a mortgage on its fixed property or by a floating charge on some or all of its assets. Debentures therefore form a suitable form of finance for companies earning steady profits and owning large fixed assets which may be pledged as security, e.g. breweries.

A holder of debentures is entitled to a fixed rate of interest each year whether the company is earning profits or not. If a company is unable to pay the interest due, the debenture stockholders may force it into liquidation or appoint a receiver and manager to run it in their interests.

The market price of debentures depends upon the general level of interest rates and the trading risks of the company. Since they do not share in profits, debentures provide no hedge against inflation: their yield in times of prosperity is therefore usually higher than the current yield on ordinary shares (equities). [8]

Debt, a sum of money, goods or services owed by one person or organization to another. Modern economic society rests largely on debt—short-term or long-term. Relatively few transactions are paid in cash. Credit is used for buying homes, and other buildings, durable consumer goods, industrial plant and machinery, clothes, food, and so on. Shakespeare's "neither a borrower nor a lender be" (Polonius to Laertes in *Hamlet*) would bring a modern economy almost to a standstill.

Debt is sometimes divided into "living" (used to finance current economic activity) and "deadweight" (which was used to finance past wars). [8]

Debt Conversion, the issue by any organization but particularly by the government of new securities to replace existing or maturing debt. A government conversion issue merely represents a switch by debt-holders in general from one gilt-edged security to another and does not raise new money. More generally, conversions are a part of debt management technique which tries to vary the supply of debt to suit the changing preferences of the public for various kinds of security so as to minimize the total interest cost. [12]

Debt Management, government conduct of the National Debt to maximize its utility to the community and minimize its cost as conditions in the money and capital markets, especially interest rates, change. In recent years British governments have been criticized for putting Debt Management by low interest rates, which stimulate inflation by making borrowing cheap, before management of the economy to avoid inflation. By deferring the date of maturation of an issue of securities, government can remove cash and liquidity from the economy and exert an anti-inflationary influence. A shift to short-dated issues can be used to stimulate the economy. [12]

Decreasing Returns. *See* RETURNS TO SCALE.

Deduction, a method used in economic analysis to evolve general rules, principles or laws by beginning with a set of assumptions or premises about the conditions of supply and demand and proceeding by logic to consider the effects of a new influence on them. For example, a change in Bank rate is assumed to take place in given conditions and its effects are deduced by reasoning. For this deduction to be applied to the real world the premises must be realistic and the logical reasoning accurate. In practice the premises may at first have had to be oversimplified to make the process feasible; the deductions will then have to be modified to allow for the difference between the premise and reality. Deductions can thus be tested by empirical data obtained by research. [13]

Deferred Rebate, another name for Aggregated Rebates.

Deferred Shares, customarily issued as fully paid to founders or promoters of a company; although usually few, they often had considerable voting power and carried the equity of the company. They were used more before than after the Second World War. [8]

Deficiency Payment, the difference paid by government to producers when the free market price falls below the level guaranteed. Deficiency payments are usually used as a form of subsidy to farmers. The UK system from 1954 until 1973, when Britain joined the Common Market, comprised an annual price review and a Government White Paper presenting the guaranteed prices for the year. The government was then committed to financing from the Exchequer the difference between receipts from farmers' free market sales and the value of their output at the guaranteed prices (which could vary to reflect seasonal fluctuations of supplies throughout the year). The individual farmer received a payment equal to his saleable output multiplied by the difference between the guaranteed price and the average national price received in the market. If he had luck or skill in selling and obtained more-than-average prices, his deficiency payment per unit would be larger than the gap between his individual realized price and the guaranteed price. Conversely, this gap would not have been covered had he sold at less-than-average prices.

Guaranteed minimum prices were used to subsidize British agriculture from 1947, and applied to over three-quarters of total agricultural output. Agricultural support by deficiency payments was open to the criticism that it encouraged over-production, propped up the inefficient farmer, promoted inflexibility in the farming structure, and was an undesirable form of "open-ended" budget expenditure. Whether it was a price worth paying for a larger agricultural industry than the taxpayers were prepared as consumers to support in a free market was a political, military, aesthetic or other non-economic question. The method of agricultural support changed after 1973. [6]

Deficit, an amount, usually expressed in money terms, by which one sum is smaller than another to which it is related; usually measured as an excess of liabilities over assets. For example, a balance of payments deficit is an excess of voluntary imports of goods, services and financial claims over similar exports; a budget deficit is an excess of government expenditure over revenue, or total government payments over receipts in a financial year. [8]

Deficit Financing, also described as "compensatory finance" or loosely as "pump-priming," large-scale borrowing to meet an unusual situation requiring large expenditure; more specifically a policy employed by a government to finance a budget deficit incurred to alleviate unemployment during a business depression or otherwise to stimulate the economy. Such financing would normally entail borrowing against the issue of government securities, that is increasing the National Debt.

The case for deficit financing derives from macro-economic or employment theory. To the extent that large-scale unemployment in a business depression is due to a fall in incomes and purchasing power, most economists believe that one way of alleviating it is to inject more purchasing power into the economy by government spending than is collected in taxation or other revenue. This injection requires a budget deficit.

With the general growth of government expenditures, particularly in investment, deficits have now become a fairly regular feature of Exchequer budgets in Britain, USA and elsewhere even in times of normal employment.

The British Exchequer has three main sources of borrowing: (*a*) internal (surplus National Insurance funds, sterling capital of the Exchange Equalization Account); (*b*) non-market borrowing (Savings Certificates, Defence Bonds); (*c*) market borrowing, by sales of quoted marketable securities, Treasury Bills, etc.

Total government borrowing at any one time will not necessarily measure the extent of deficit financing since it includes borrowing for other purposes (e.g. the capital requirements of the nationalized industries).

Economists have been deeply divided over the desirability or efficacy of deficit financing, the two extreme positions being reflected in the teaching of the Cambridge (England) and Chicago Schools. [12]

Deflation, (*a*) a situation in which the value of the monetary unit is rising as a result of falling prices. In theory, the value of money may rise as a result of increased productivity if money incomes rise less than proportionately. Supply of goods and services would then exceed demand, and prices would have to fall if the amount of goods and services bought was to be equal to the amount available for sale. In practice, deflation is a situation in which falling total monetary demand is causing reduction in the output of goods and services, in the demand for factors of production, in money incomes and in the general price level. There can be several reasons for a fall in monetary spending or outlay. Initially the fall in demand may be internal or external. Government expenditure may be reduced, or the level of private consumption expenditure may fall, or the business world may reduce its investment expenditure. Overseas demand for a country's exports may decline. Whatever the reason, reduced expenditure means unsold goods and the accumulation of unwanted stocks. If the reduction in demand persists, output will be reduced, unemployment will rise, and wages and prices will fall.

Especially since Keynes's *General Theory* it has been accepted by economists that a rise in taxation is *deflationary* by reducing net income and therefore expenditure and demand. When monopoly trade unions can push pay above output and governments are apprehensive of unemployment, some economists have argued, a rise in taxation can be *inflationary* by reducing take-home pay and inducing trade unions to push government into expanding the supply of money to avoid unemployment at the higher rates of pay.

An important contributory factor in the extent of deflation and the rate of growth of depression is the psychological. Once optimism is replaced by pessimism, *entrepreneurs* plan for reduced output, fears spread and tend to produce the state that is feared. When there is a general fear of falling incomes, there is a tendency to be cautious and to reduce expenditure. Moreover when prices are expected to fall, there is an increased demand for liquidity in the form of money, in the hope of buying later when prices will be lower. As with inflation, deflation tends to be cumulative, and monetary demand may continue to fall until an "external" event provides an impetus to recovery, the central government reflates the economy or stocks and capital equipment are run down to the point at which replacement is needed to sustain even the low slump level of production and thus provides an "internal" impetus to recovery. [9]

(*b*) the correction of an economic quantity, e.g. income, for a rise in price to indicate its real (as distinct from its nominal or money) value. [14]

Demand, the quantity of a commodity consumers wish, and are able, to buy at a given price in a given period. Demand in economics thus goes beyond the everyday notion of "desire" or "need": unless the desire is made effective by ability and willingness to pay it is not demand in the economic sense.

The amount of a commodity that a consumer will be prepared to buy in a given period depends upon the price charged, the quality of the commodity, the service supplied with it, the prices of related (substitute or complementary) commodities, his preferences between alternative commodities, his income and his expectations (of future income and prices). To relate quantity demanded to so many "variables" at once is not practicable: the economist therefore attempts to isolate what he considers (either intuitively or from observation of events in the market) to be the most important variable and to relate the quantity demanded to changes in it, assuming all other things constant. In this way demand is generally expressed in relation to price. Observation of behaviour of buyers in the market then yields the following basic generalization or "law" of demand: "The higher the price the smaller the quantity demanded; the lower the price the larger the quantity demanded." But demand can also be expressed as a "function" of quality, service, income, expectations or the other variables.

It is instructive, and helpful in more refined analysis, to express this law in a chart or graph. If price is measured vertically and quantity horizontally, so that the "boundaries" of the graph appear like a capital L, then if price is assumed to change continuously by small amounts, the law of demand given above would yield a smooth "demand curve" inside the L, falling from left to right. Starting at any relationship between price and quantity as indicated by a point on the curve, a fall in price would produce an "extension" of demand to a new point lower down the curve to the right; a rise in price would produce a "contraction" of demand to a new point higher up the curve to the left. The *extent* of the "extension" or "contraction" indicates the (price) elasticity of demand, that is, the responsiveness of demand to changes in price.

To obtain this relationship between demand and price all other variables were assumed to be unchanged. In turn they can be supposed to vary and their effects analysed. Thus if income rises (or falls) a consumer will tend to buy more (or less) of a commodity *at any given price* than before, the amount of increase (or decrease) depending on the pattern of his preferences. In a graph, this relationship would be represented by a shift of the whole demand curve to the right (or left). It is thus possible to measure the "income elasticity of demand," that is, the responsiveness of demand to changes in *income*. Similarly if the price of a substitute commodity falls or if tastes change in favour of other commodities, the demand curve would again shift bodily to the left, indicating that at each price a smaller quantity of the commodity would be demanded.

The introduction of expectations complicates the analysis. A rise in price may not lead to a smaller amount demanded if buyers expect the price to rise further still; they may *increase* their purchases for a time. This possibility is best considered as the total effect of two simultaneous effects: first, a price rise inducing a normal contraction of demand; secondly, a shift to the right of the whole demand curve due to the change in expectations produced by the price change. The apparent contradiction of the basic demand law is thus explained.

Another apparent contradiction is the case of "inferior" goods. If at low income levels a large part of a consumer's total spending has to go on, say, bread to sustain him, then a marked fall in the price of bread may release income for spending on other goods to such an extent that the demand for bread *falls* as it is replaced by more palatable and nutritious forms of food. For any *one* consumer this response to a fall in price may be feasible: for *all* consumers considered together it does not appear likely. It is true that a fall in price might in this way induce *some* people to buy less of a commodity rather than more; but it would also encourage others to buy more who could not previously afford to buy all they would have liked at the higher price.

This introduction of *market* demand, that is demand from all consumers, reinforces the basic law, for reductions in price not only encourage existing buyers to extend their purchases but also bring into the market new customers who previously could not buy any of the commodity at all. Conversely, a rise in price causes contraction in the demand of existing buyers, some to the point of buying none at all.

The basic "law" of demand could be derived from observation of markets in real life. A more satisfactory (that is, more general) theory of consumer demand can be derived from basic assumptions: first, that consumers always act to maximize the total satisfaction (utility) they obtain from spending a given income; secondly, that the more of a commodity a consumer possesses relatively to other commodities, the smaller the additional utility he derives from further units of it (the principle of diminishing marginal utility). It can then be deduced that a consumer will at all times tend to distribute his income among various commodities available at given prices in such a way that the marginal (additional) utility he derives from a unit of expenditure is the same for every commodity. If then the price of one commodity falls, the marginal utility per unit of expenditure on it will then rise. To restore equilibrium will call for a shift of expenditure to it from others until the marginal utilities per unit of expenditure on all commodities are again equal. This process leads once more to the basic law of demand that the lower the price the larger the quantity demanded, and conversely. [7]

Demand, Cross-elasticity of. *See* CROSS-ELASTICITY OF DEMAND.

Demand Curve, the chart drawn from the demand schedule for a commodity or service. It is a series of *points* showing *alternative* relationships between price, conventionally measured on a vertical axis, and quantity demanded, measured on a horizontal axis. It is not a continuous line or curve showing movement over time, i.e. it is a collection of snapshots, not a moving picture or histogram (although in practice, over *short* periods with *small* price changes, the demand curve may serve as a rough histogram). It normally curves down from left to right, indicating that the lower the price the larger the demand: exceptions are prestige and inferior goods. [7]

Demand Deposits. *See* DEPOSITS (BANK).

Demand, Elasticity of. *See* ELASTICITY OF DEMAND.

Demand Function, the relationship between the quantity of a good (or service) a consumer wishes to purchase and the factors which determine its quantity: its price, the prices of all other goods, the consumer's income, the availability of credit, individual taste, etc. Many demand functions can be obtained by isolating one factor, e.g. the consumer's income, assuming all the others remain unchanged and examining changes in quantity demanded with changes in income. The most common form of demand function is the relationship between price and quantity demanded, all other factors being held unchanged. It yields the demand curve, which almost invariably slopes down from left to right, indicating that, for almost all goods, the lower the price the higher the quantity demanded would be: the so-called "law of demand." The exceptions occur where the quantity demanded would be higher, the higher the price: these are prestige goods, of which the price is taken as an indication of quality; and inferior goods. [7]

Demand Management, government manipulation of the demand for goods and services by monetary, fiscal or other policies. Largely a product and legacy of Keynesian economic thinking. In the 1960's and 1970's a debate developed between Cambridge and Chicago economists as the leaders in the argument on how far demand could be managed and which methods were desirable. [10]

Demand Pull, the process by which inflation at some periods since World War II has been said by some economists to have been caused or intensified by an excessive amount of money in the economy. They have argued that the fundamental responsibility has been that of government for failing to restrict the flow of money through the banking system and in other ways, with the result that it grew faster than output, so that the general level of prices rose. They have therefore absolved the trade unions from pushing up costs by using their strong bargaining power in a seller's market for labour—the opposite theory of "cost push." Other economists have combined the two theories by arguing that demand has been pulled up by government under pressure from the unions. In this case government is at fault for exposing itself to union influence, although the *instrument* or *mechanism* of inflation is the supply of money. [7]

Demand Schedule, a two-column list of quantities of a commodity or service bought in a given period or point of time at nearby alternative prices. "Nearby" because if the alternative prices are very different the real income of the buyers can be affected by the difference in expenditure and the demand can be affected by the change in real income. "Alternative" (not successive in time) because the schedule shows what the demand *would* be *if* price were different, not how it *will* change *when* price changes. The demand schedule for an individual buyer or for all buyers, i.e. the market as a whole, provides the information for the demand curve. [7]

Demarcation Rules. *See* RESTRICTIVE PRACTICES.

Democracy, Economic Theory of, derived by extending the "self-interest" axiom from the analysis of exchange in the market to the analysis of exchange between votes and benefits in the political process. The theory postulates that governments and politicians as "entrepreneurs" pursue policies to attract maximum votes in competition with potential governments that could be formed by opposition politicians. The theory has developed from the original analysis by the American economist Anthony Downs in *An Economic Theory of Democracy* (1957), followed by Duncan Black's *The Theory of Committees and Elections* (1958).

The theory indicates ("predicts") that in a two-party democracy the parties will converge in policy because they assume that their extremists will prefer their party to the other, as "the lesser of two evils." Political rationality thus leads the parties to make their policies ambiguous in order to attract as wide a range of voters as they can.

Such political competition is usually highly imperfect because information about the products—policies—is difficult or costly to gather. Moreover there is little inducement to exert much trouble or expense in obtaining the information because the reward is relatively small, an individual vote in the political market is practically without effect unless joined with enough others to form a majority; and since both parties offer a large number of policies in each election package (manifesto) it is difficult to demonstrate that a majority vote for a party indicates decisive support for any specific item in the package.

Not least, in political elections producer interests normally prevail over consumer interests. Producer interests are concentrated, they are more easily crystallized, and their beneficiaries are identifiable (they can also generally charge their costs against income tax). Although, for example, an increase in benefit may go to relatively few, the increase is more apparent to the few than the cost (in higher taxes) to the many, who in any event cannot easily trace the reason for higher taxes. Organized groups, such as importers asking for a tariff, employers for a subsidy, or employees for a grant, are encouraged to form pressure groups by party democracy. [13]

Demography, the study of populations. In particular it means the statistical investigation of trends in the influences on the composition, size and distribution of populations, such as birth rate, mortality rate, average age at marriage and size of family, migration, etc., from the study of which demographic "laws" may be derived. Modern demography relies heavily on information obtained in censuses, but demographic studies were made by William Petty in Britain in the seventeenth century, when parochial registration of births and deaths was the main source of information. [11]

Demonstration Effect, the effect of evidence on behaviour. Specifically it has been applied to the effect on a consumer of seeing a larger or superior selection of goods and raising his expenditure on them without his income or other conditions of demand having changed. If correct it would modify the Keynesian consumption function: a consumer might raise his expenditure after inspecting superior goods, or might not reduce it if his real income fell. The Demonstration Effect has also been applied internationally: extended trade and communications, or international advertising, might cause consumers in Africa or Asia to change their consumption habits and buy superior goods from Europe and America, and perhaps reduce savings. (If sufficiently strong it could thus affect a country's balance of international payments.) [14]

Demurrage, the payment to a shipowner by a shipper who detains the ship in port for discharging or loading beyond the stated time ("lay" or "lie" days). The demurrage is paid when the ship is ready to sail. It also refers to similar railway charges for detaining rolling-stock. [4]

Department of Economic Affairs (DEA) (1964–9), a British government department of historical interest. It was created by the Labour Government to stimulate economic growth by government planning. In 1965 it published a five-year "National Plan" for the growth of the economy based on a 4 per cent per annum expansion of the Gross Domestic Product. As some critics predicted, this rate proved too high. (The average annual growth rate of national income between 1950 and 1965 was 2.4 per cent.) The "National Plan" was abandoned in 1966, but the rise in money incomes it encouraged led to devaluation in 1967. In 1969 the DEA published the more humble "The Task Ahead, an Economic Assessment to 1972," which postulated rather than prognosticated growth. The

DEA was wound up in 1969; some of its work, especially prices and incomes policy, was transferred to other departments. [10]

Deposit Account. *See* DEPOSITS (BANK).

Deposits (Bank), an entry in the book of a bank stating that customers have claims of given amounts against it.

Deposits in joint-stock banks may be of two kinds: demand deposits (or current account balances), which are repayable in cash on demand, and time deposits (savings deposits, or deposit account balances), which require notice of withdrawal, normally seven days. The economic importance of commercial bank deposits is twofold. First, subject to the requirements of prudence and control by the monetary authorities, the volume of deposits may be varied at will by the banks simply by acquiring assets. Second, demand deposits, being transferable by cheque and encashable on demand, are just as much money as are notes and coin.

Deposits in the Bank of England are of four kinds. (1) *Public deposits*—the balance of the main accounts of the British Government (including the Exchequer, the National Commissioners, Savings Banks, etc.). These deposits are in some ways like the deposits of private individuals with joint-stock banks, and reflect the role of the Bank of England as the government bank. (2) *Banker's deposits*—the balances of joint-stock banks at the Bank of England, which the banks may draw on by cheques on the Bank. They are regarded by the joint-stock banks as a basic part of the platform of liquid assets on which their pyramid of credit rests: their size thus provides a bell-wether. (3) *Other deposits* refer to balances of private individuals, foreign governments and overseas banks with the Bank of England. (4) *Special deposits* represent joint-stock bank balances temporarily "frozen" as a measure of restriction by the monetary authorities.

The total volume of bank deposits in the economy depends on a number of factors, some of which may be influenced by the monetary authorities. First, the monetary authorities (the Treasury and the Bank of England) can directly influence the budgetary position of the government, the structure of the National Debt and thus the pattern of bond prices, interest rates, and the supply of cash and liquid assets available to the money market. Such action will influence the volume of deposits. Secondly, the joint-stock banks themselves can affect the level of deposits by their attitude towards advances, their ideas on what constitutes "satisfactory" ratios of cash and liquid assets to deposits and their willingness to hold bonds. Thirdly, the general public can influence the volume of deposits by its inclination to hold cash, use bank advances and hold bonds. The volume and level of general business activity and the level of prices also affects the volume of deposits, since at times of high activity and prices the demand for money rises. [8]

Depreciation, (1) continued decrease in quantity, quality or value of an asset because of passage of time, wear and tear, obsolescence, fall in market prices or other causes.

Depreciation allowances are charges against the income of a business (before profits are calculated) and represent the benefits the business has derived from the use of the assets: they reflect the principle that the use or consumption of an asset must be included as a charge for running the business.

Methods of dealing with depreciation include (*a*) the *Straight Line Method,* under which the original cost, divided by the expected number of years of life, is charged as an annual cost: this method has the advantage of simplicity; (*b*) the *Diminishing Balance Method,* under which a fixed percentage is deducted each year from the diminishing balance of the cost of the asset: the chief advantage is that depreciation charges are highest in the early years of the life of the asset when maintenance and repair charges are small; (*c*) the *Annuity and Sinking Fund Methods* take account of the interest which the capital invested in the asset is assumed to earn. Under the annuity method the asset is valued at cost price plus interest and then written off on the straight line method; a regular sum is thus set aside each year sufficient when invested to accumulate at compound interest to provide an eventual sum equal to the cost of the asset. A variant of this method is to make like annual payments as an insurance premium.

All these are forms of *Book Depreciation*—the setting up of arbitrary reserves or allowances for cost accounting and income tax calculation purposes. They may bear little relation to depreciation in value suffered.

The ideal method of depreciating an asset would provide the sum of money required to replace it when worn out or obsolescent. This purpose has not always been facilitated or permitted by governments, which have other objectives in the short or middle run—maximizing tax revenue, minimizing tax avoidance, equalizing tax burdens, maximizing the electoral appeal of tax policy in general.

(2) a change in the value of a currency by which the currency becomes cheaper (i.e. has a smaller exchange value) in terms of foreign currencies. [3]

Depressed Areas, a term (like "distressed areas") coined in the 1920's for parts of Britain with staple industries (coal, iron and steel, and shipbuilding) which bore the brunt of unemployment, rising to three million in the early 1930's. South Wales, Northern England and central Scotland specialized in export and/or capital goods and were therefore more severely hit than other areas by the decline in world trade. Unemployment rates in the depressed areas rose to 25 to 35 per cent (15 per cent in London and the South-East). In 1928 the government initiated "regional policy," which tried to take workers to the work (outside the depressed areas) by grants and loans, and by setting up re-training centres. These measures were insufficient in scope (not necessarily in principle) to meet the large demand for assistance, supported by political pressure, and in 1934 the government instituted the second type of regional policy, moving work to the workers. The "depressed areas," periodically redefined, were in time replaced by "special areas" (from 1934), "development areas" (from 1945), "development districts" (from 1960), "development areas" (from 1966). [10]

Depression, a situation in which output per head of population in an economy is low compared to the level attainable at full capacity. There is generally said to be a depression or recession when there are idle resources, especially labour, not being used in production. In trade cycle theory the term is often extended to cover the "depression phase" of the cycle during which total output, the rate of employment and other "indicators" of economic activity are falling. The word "depression" is commonly reserved for relatively large falls in output and employment; the word "recession" is used for less severe reductions.

Depressions or recessions are part of the trade cycle process which is common to industrial, capitalist societies, where they are recognizable and measurable in terms of output, employment, etc., and to non-capitalist systems where they may be suppressed and not measurable because statistics are not published. Before World War II the cyclical process was an alternation of prosperity with depression over a typical, though not regular, period of seven to ten years. Since the war alternation has been more frequent but shallower. The causes of this phenomenon have been studied by economists and substantial agreement now exists on important points.

In a depression total demand in the economy falls short of the output of which it is capable when fully employed. Measures to cure depression therefore concentrate on increasing total demand by increasing private consumption (e.g. by reducing income tax), stimulating private investment (lowering interest rates) or increasing government spending without equivalent increases in taxation ("deficit spending"). [9]

Derating, in British local taxation, the reduction in rates payable on real property. It may be partial or complete.

The basis of rateable value (on which rate poundage is levied) is the net annual value (NAV) at which a property might be expected to let. For practical reasons, derating has taken the form of reductions from the NAV rather than a reduction from the poundage payable. Agricultural land, railways and canals have had derating relief in varying degrees since 1875. In 1929 agricultural land and buildings (other than farmhouses) ceased to be assessed for rating. From 1929 to 1959 factories, workshops, mines, docks, canals and railways received relief of 75 per cent of their NAV, between 1959 and 1963, 50 per cent. Between 1957 and 1963 commercial properties received relief of 20 per cent. Residential properties had relief until 1963 to the extent that their assessments were based on 1939 values, which were usually much less than current values. All derating reliefs other than agricultural and charitable ended in 1963.

Derating has been regarded as a method of reducing the burden of taxation of particular kinds of activity. It may be considered in this sense as part of the general policy of government support for agriculture, and in 1929 it was also seen as a method of encouraging industry. The actual reduction of costs of production secured in this way is doubtful since part at least of the relief from rates tends to be absorbed in higher rents payable for premises. Derating in effect reduces the independent resources of local government revenue; its counterpart has been an increase in grants from the central Exchequer to local authorities. One result has been the growth of central control over local government finance. The effect of derating on the distribution of the rate burden between different classes of property has varied with each derating Act. Economists are less concerned with the distribution of the rate burden between properties than between persons, and this is conjectural since local rates are a form of indirect tax which individuals can affect by varying the amount of house property they own or occupy but which may affect them even when paid by owners or occupiers of industrial or commercial property who can pass on rates to the consumer in higher prices (or lower quality) if the demand for their products or services is inelastic. Policy since the mid-1960's has tended to reflect these views. Where relief from the burden of rates has been given it has taken the form of *rate rebates* related to the means and needs of individual households: these are in effect a form of personal grant towards the payment of rates. [12]

Derived Demand. *See* WAGES.

Determinism, Economic, generally the theory that developments are determined by economic institutions, not by men; specifically that the conditions of work decide human thought and activity. Originated by Marx ("It is not the consciousness of men that determines their existence, but . . . their social existence that determines their consciousness"). This view has generally had more influence on political action than on economic theory. Non-Marxist economists generally place more emphasis on thinking and ideas. [2]

Detriments, external costs or harmful effects on third parties not associated with a contract between buyer and seller. [13]

Devaluation, reducing the value of the home currency in terms of foreign currencies. In 1949, for example, the British government devalued the pound sterling in terms of the USA currency. The value of the pound fell about 30 per cent in terms of dollars. Before devaluation £1 could buy approximately $4; after it could buy only $2.8. Sterling was devalued several times in the 1960's and floated in 1972.

The effect of devaluation is to cheapen the exports of the devaluing country to people in other countries, which should normally lead to increased demand for them, and to raise the price of imports into the devaluing country in terms of its currency, and thus divert demand in it away from imports towards home-produced substitutes. For example, apart from transport costs and tariffs, a British car selling at £1,000 might cost a US citizen $2,400 before devaluation but only $1,800 after a 25 per cent devaluation. This is likely to switch American demand towards British cars and other exports in place of home-produced goods which compete with them. Within Britain the sterling price of imports from America would have risen and this would tend to switch British citizens' demand away from imported goods towards home-produced substitutes. If these switching effects are large enough they may bring about an increase in export earnings and a decline in payments for imports of goods and services, so that the balance of trade is improved.

For a devaluation to cause an improvement in the balance of trade, there should also be slack or flexibility in the economy of the devaluing country to enable it to increase the supply of goods for export and of substitutes for imports. If output cannot be increased, the additional pressure of demand caused by the devaluation will create inflation. The most unfavourable situation in which to devalue is thus when the country is suffering from inflation, for then there is little or no slack in the economy. The most favourable situation is where there is some unemployment and under-utilization of capacity, so that the additional demand generated by devaluation puts the idle resources to use.

When a country has a high level of employment, devaluation tends to produce strong inflationary pressures not only on the demand side but also on the cost side since devaluation raises import prices. For example British imports are very largely food and raw materials. Increases in their prices raise the cost of living, which encourages trade unions to demand wage increases to compensate their members for a fall in their real incomes. If demand for consumer goods and other final products is high, manufacturers are likely to concede these claims and pass on the increase in their costs to consumers by raising prices. Unless the government then cuts demand, the wage-price spiral can continue. Devaluation thus affords no easy escape route from domestic inflation. At best it only buys time for other, more stringent, policies to be implemented. [4]

Developer, a person who (or enterprise which) develops or "improves" land by subdividing it, providing basic "services," constructing buildings or improving existing buildings, or by other activities designed to shift land to more valuable uses. Because much private development of residential real property is undertaken in advance of housing demand it is often termed "speculative" and the undertakers "speculative developers." In the climate of intense demand for urban land and tight land-use controls characteristic of recent times in Britain and other countries, the term "speculative developer" has been used pejoratively rather than objectively. [6]

Developing Countries, name for countries formerly described as backward or under-developed. [11]

Development Areas, in general, regions which qualify for government help in overcoming local unemployment, helping to maintain industrial "balance," refurbishing staple industries, running down declining industries like coal, etc. Specifically the term was introduced in 1945 to replace "special areas," and again in 1966 to replace "development districts," the successive terms being redefined to include new regions for new purposes. Employment prospects in these localities can be improved in various ways. The Department of Industry has been able to acquire land and build factories for letting at low rents or make building grants to industrialists; the purchase or hire of plant and equipment and working capital for new projects might be assisted by loans and grants; the attractiveness of a district to industry might be improved by acquiring and clearing derelict, neglected and unsightly land; grants might be made for resettling key workers and for improving basic services (e.g. local roads and bridges). The refusal of Industrial Development Certificates to firms wishing to build in congested areas was also thought to help steer development to areas of high unemployment.

Economists differ about the relative consequences of "taking work to workers" and "taking workers to the work." Since the end of World War II the absolute and relative expansion of industry and employment in the "over-crowded" south and the "loss of social capital" (transport, schools, hospitals, etc.) in the north has provoked the need to choose between the two policies. If industries are encouraged to settle where there happens to be a large unemployed labour force but where other production costs are high and the costs of reaching markets at home or abroad are higher than they need be, the whole economy may suffer. Hence the argument for allowing industries to settle where their costs are lowest, leaving it to the market to prevent overcrowding by rising labour, land, capital or transport costs. Employees might be more willing to move to areas where labour was relatively scarce and relatively better paid if collective bargaining did not maintain labour costs at a higher level in development areas, if a free market in housing encouraged builders to build more houses for letting, if rent restrictions did not discourage older people from moving out of rented homes, and council housing did not give "squatters' rights" to people who might otherwise have moved. On the other hand if the "social" costs of overcrowding were reflected more clearly in the money costs of producers the relative attractiveness of the south of England might be lessened. The debate turns on a balancing of economic, political and social considerations. [10]

Development District, an area in the UK of "high and persistent" unemployment designated under the Local Employment Act, 1960, and qualifying for official assistance under it (and earlier Acts). For policy purposes on the distribution of industry they replaced the much wider "development areas" defined by the Distribution of Industry Acts of 1945 to 1958. Districts could be added to or removed from the official list as thought necessary. Some districts were small and unable to support long-term policies of rehabilitation. Several economists criticized the 1960 Act on this score and urged a "regional approach." Development districts were replaced by Development areas in 1966, which covered 40 per cent of the land area and 20 per cent of the population of Britain. Incentives in the form of "free" depreciation and plant allowances against profits were replaced by investment grants in cash, in turn replaced by tax allowances in 1970. [10]

Devise. *See* LEGACY.

Diagonal Integration. *See* INTEGRATION.

Dickinson, Henry Douglas (1899–1969), British economist. He was educated at King's College School, Wimbledon, and the University of Cambridge, and taught at the London School of Economics, the University of Bristol (Professor of Economics, 1951–64, then Emeritus Professor), and Queen's University, Belfast (1964–5). In *The Economics of Socialism* (1939) Dickinson summarized the long debate in the 1930's on the determination of product and factor prices in a socialist society, in which the main protagonists had been Mises, Hayek, Lange and Lerner. It was clearly reasoned, and argued that there is nothing incompatible between the operation of a rational pricing system, based on accepted logic, and the complete public ownership of productive resources. [2]

Dictatorship of the Proletariat. *See* COMMUNISM.

Differentiation, Product. *See* TRADE MARK.

Diminishing Marginal Utility, a law describing the rate at which the satisfaction derived from a commodity (or service) varies with its quantity. The purpose of economic activity is the production of goods and services to satisfy human wants. Such goods and services are said to have "utility." The utility of a commodity is the satisfaction which the owner (or prospective owner) derives (or expects to derive) from owning or consuming it; it does not imply moral, aesthetic or other judgement or standards. It is subjective, it exists only in the mind of the individual, not objective or intrinsic.

As an individual acquires further units of a commodity the total satisfaction or utility he derives from it increases, but not proportionately; it increases at a diminishing rate, possibly reaching an eventual maximum. Beyond this point further units would yield no utility or even disutility, i.e. they could get in the way, or be a nuisance or obnoxious. One dog can be a welcome acquisition to a family, but it might be desirable to pay someone to take the eighth away.

The law of diminishing marginal utility expresses these ideas. It is based upon the observation that, at any given moment of time, wants are satiable, so that the additional (or "marginal") ability added by succeeding units falls and may become negative. The law of diminishing marginal utility, expressed in general terms, states that as an individual's consumption of one commodity increases relative to his consumption of other commodities (all other things being equal), its marginal utility to him will decrease relative to the marginal utility of other commodities.

The law helps to explain why more of a commodity is generally bought at lower prices. An individual's expenditure on different goods reflects his scale of preferences for them and for his income. It follows from the law of diminishing marginal utility that total utility from the expenditure of a given income will reach its maximum when expenditure is distributed among goods and services so that a unit of expenditure (a penny or a pound) yields *equal* additional (marginal) utility from all of them, or more precisely (since prices of goods differ), so that *relative* marginal utilities are *proportional* to relative prices. If this were not so, total utility could be increased by redistributing expenditure until marginal utilities were equal (or rather proportional to price).

This is the condition of equilibrium for the individual. The equilibrium would be disturbed if the market price of one commodity were, say, to fall, while all others remained the same. The ratio of marginal utility to price would then, because of the fall in price, be larger for that commodity than for others. To restore equilibrium expenditure would have to be switched from other commodities until once again relative marginal utilities were everywhere proportional to relative prices. This "substitution effect" of a change in the price of a commodity invariably tends to increase the purchases of a good when its price falls relative to others. The substitution effect is normally reinforced by the income effect, i.e. a fall in the price of a commodity really increases the income of the consumer: the same amount of it can now be bought with the sacrifice of less income. Since income has increased, consumers will tend to buy more of all goods, including the commodity in question. Normally this "income effect" of a change in price is unlikely to be significant unless the price changes are large and the commodity bulks large in consumers' expenditure. When the commodity is an "inferior" good, the income effect of a price change becomes important, since it may work in opposition to the substitution effect instead of reinforcing it, and, if strong enough, may outweigh it, thus leading the individual to buy *less* of a commodity when its price falls. [14]

Diminishing Returns. *See* VARIABLE PROPORTIONS, LAW OF.

Direct Tax. *See* TAX, DIRECT AND INDIRECT.

Disamenities, adverse external effects in the environment; for example, the impairment of a view by a new farm building in the country, or stable noises or smells. [13]

Disbenefits, another name for external costs or detriments. [13]

Disclosure, specifically the degree of detail shown in company accounts. The tendency has been for government to require more information (on major shareholdings, on shares owned by directors, etc.), and publication by more firms (private as well as public). Some firms have also issued accounts more frequently than required by law and in more detail as an advertising and confidence-winning device. [3]

Discontinuity, the relationship (in time or space) between economic quantities which change by relatively large amounts. Economic theory usually assumes that the relationship is continuous, i.e. connected without a break: e.g. that quantities of goods demanded and supplied and their prices change by infinitely small amounts, so that a fall in the price of a commodity by the smallest possible amount will cause a correspondingly small expansion in the quantity bought. In a demand curve infinitely small differences in prices are shown on the vertical axis and the accompanying small differences in the quantities demanded on the horizontal axis. In practice very few goods can be bought in infinitely small amounts, and many are highly indivisible. For example, one must buy a whole washing machine, although it may be shared with a neighbour, or with many neighbours in a launderette; a business man must buy a whole boiler; a firm may have to engage a "whole" legal or economic adviser, although it may buy part of his time by paying him as a consultant. A graph of the demand curve for such commodities or services would show sharp jumps or breaks instead of the "continuous" smooth curve yielded by changes taking place by small quantities. Real life illustrations of economic laws are usually discontinuous; but continuous relationships are used in theory because their geometry and mathematics are simpler.

Frequently the assumption of continuity does not upset the conclusions drawn from a piece of analysis based on it. Thus in the general law of demand (which states that, other things equal, more will be bought at a lower price) no serious errors arise if the relationship between price and quantity is treated continuously rather than discontinuously. But sometimes discontinuity affects the conclusions. Thus, as the price of a commodity with two uses falls, more of it may be bought to satisfy one use until saturation is reached. A slight fall in price might induce no further demand; the fall might have to be large before more units were bought to satisfy the second use. The demand curve of such a commodity would have a sharp break between the two prices.

To grasp the essentials of economic ideas and concepts it is best at first to think of them as concerned with quantities between which the relationships are continuous. When the principles have been worked out allowance can be made for discontinuities. [14]

Discount, (1) the amount deducted from the face value of a bill of exchange or other promissory note for cashing it in advance of the date when it matures. The importance of a bill of exchange is that it can be readily discounted and rediscounted, and is therefore readily negotiable. The rate of discount varies with the time to maturity, the credit standing of the parties, etc.

(2) the surplus of the face value of a security or nominal value of a currency or commodity over its market price.

(3) a deduction made from an account or charge, frequently as an allowance for prompt payment, e.g. trade discount. [8]

Discount House, (1) a member of the London Discount Market. The major houses (or bill brokers) form the London Discount Market Association. A discount house borrows money from banks and other institutions on short terms and uses it to buy and hold bills of exchange (mainly Treasury bills) and short-dated government bonds. They live by borrowing money more cheaply than they lend it, and to a much smaller extent from jobbing profits and commissions.

They enjoy privileges at the Bank of England, including the right of recourse to cash if in need. [8]

(2) a commercial organization which sells goods, particularly consumer durables, at reduced prices (or discounts). The practice has spread from the USA to Britain since resale price maintenance was abolished in 1964. [3]

Discount Market, the London discount market consists of major discount houses and similar small institutions. Its business consists of dealings in bills of exchange, mostly Treasury bills, but increasingly in short-term government bonds. In effect the market lends to the government by buying Treasury bills and government bonds. About half of the funds of the market are borrowed from London clearing banks, and most of the remainder comes from the commercial banks and overseas banks.

Traditionally the clearing banks do not buy bills themselves, partly because the banks (to remain liquid) prefer bills with less than two months to the date when they mature, partly because the discount houses group bills into parcels maturing at the same time. Other financial institutions compete with the discount houses for the weekly "tender" of bills.

When a bill broker buys a three-month bill he does not borrow for the same terms, but finances the bill by borrowing from day to day. His profit lies in the very narrow margin between his lending and borrowing rates of interest. If these loans are "called in" simultaneously by all banks, the discount houses may find it difficult to finance their bills, and they may have to borrow from the Bank of England, which will traditionally always help the market at a price (*see* Bank Rate). In these circumstances the market is said to be "in the Bank."

The discount market is a feature of the financial system peculiar to Britain; other countries have short-term money markets, but only Britain has institutions which specialize entirely in such dealings. From time to time the need for them has been questioned. In particular, the "syndicated bid" which the discount houses make for the weekly Treasury bill tender is criticized by some economists and others as a restrictive practice. Some observers also consider the Treasury bill system unnecessary and would confine government short-term borrowing to ways and means advances from the Bank of England. The monetary authorities have considered that the discount market plays a useful role in providing a smooth and flexible market in bills and short-term bonds. [8]

Discounted Cash Flow (DCF), procedure for calculating the net present value of a capital investment project which involves a flow of benefits and costs over time. Cash flows rather than accounting profits are discounted to the present to compare alternative investment projects or to determine the worthwhileness of a project. As the term implies, the practice is based on the notions of *cash flow* and *discounting*. The first is a notion that has only in comparatively recent years become generally used by accountants; the second has been widely used by economists, actuaries and valuers for many years. [3]

Discounting, (1) allowing for expected changes in security prices, commodity prices, rates of exchange, etc. For example, when a fall in the value of a security is anticipated for some reason, large numbers of holders may decide to sell before the fall takes place; such large sales may depress the value of the security in advance, so that when the expected event occurs part of its effect has already been "discounted" by the market. Changes in the values of securities may be expected because an expected change in Bank rate would affect the price of fixed-interest securities, and speculators would buy or sell depending on whether they expected a fall or a rise in Bank rate. Expectation of the dividends on the shares of quoted public companies will affect their price. Anticipated scarcities in commodities may induce purchasers to buy larger stocks than they otherwise would, so increasing the price in advance. An anticipated change in an exchange rate between currencies may stimulate purchases and sales of them, bringing the market rates nearer to the expected rates.

Such discounting of news is common in money markets, foreign exchange markets, commodity markets and security markets; one of the incidental advantages is that it tends to reduce the severity of day-to-day fluctuations in market prices and to bring about more gradual adjustments than would otherwise occur.

(2) the opposite of *compounding*. The process of calculating the present value of a sum to be received at a future date or of a stream of future payments. The present value depends on the rate of discount or interest applied. Thus if funds can be invested in similar rights to earn, say, 10 per cent, the present value (PV) of the right to receive £1 in 3 years' time will be 75.1p, since 75.1p allowed to compound at 10 per cent would amount to £1 in 3 years' time. Similarly, the PV of £1 due after 2 years will be 82.6p, and the PV of £1 due at the end of 1 year will be 90.9p. The sum of this series, i.e. the present value of an *annuity* of £1 per annum for 3 years when the rate of discount is 10 per cent, is £2.49. Formally expressed, if S is the amount due at the end of n periods, i is the interest or discount rate, then the present value P of the amount S is given by the expression:

$$P = S(1 + i)^{-n} \qquad (1)$$

Expression (1) can be extended to find the present value of an annuity. If A is the annuity payment per period, n the number of periods, and i is the rate of interest or discount, then V, the present value of the annuity A, is given by the expression:

$$V = A \cdot [1 - (1 + i)^{-n}] / i \qquad (2)$$

Discretionary Purchasing Power, left to a household after contractual payments that cannot be avoided in the short run have been made. Over the years discretionary purchasing power has increased as expenditure on the customary or staple items of food, rent, etc. have declined as a proportion of income. [8]

Discrimination, Price. *See* PRICE DISCRIMINATION.

Discrimination, Trade, trade-diverting or trade-reducing policies which shift production between regions so that buyers cannot buy in the cheapest markets. The result is invariably a less desirable pattern of international specialization. Trade discrimination may be practised by a country expressly to influence world prices so that the gains from trade are redistributed in its favour. It is more generally pursued to correct disequilibrium in a country's balance of international payments with the minimum of disturbance to employment, income and prices at home. Before 1914 the international gold standard provided a semi-automatic mechanism that corrected disequilibrium in a country's balance of payments in a non-discriminating fashion, proximately by capital movements, ultimately by changes in domestic employment and price levels. After World War I many countries refused to accept the movement in home prices and employment that would follow such adjustments and tried to isolate themselves from international economic events by alternative policies designed to maintain international balance—e.g. exchange rate manipulation, tariffs, quotas, exchange control, bilateral trading. Most of these alternatives were discriminatory and tended to reduce or distort world trade.

Exchange rate depreciation need not be discriminating. But loss of capital by export, high elasticities of demand for imports and retaliatory currency depreciation by other countries tend to reduce its effectiveness and compel resort to other measures. Tariffs to reduce demand for foreign goods and currencies can be made to discriminate against countries with which a deficit in payments is largest, either directly (differential rates of duty) or indirectly (by manipulating tariff descriptions). Direct limitation of imports by quotas, increasingly resorted to during the 1930's, are discriminating. Even when quotas are allocated uniformly (e.g. in proportion to countries' exports in a base period) they tend to freeze trade in channels that reflect the situation in the base period, ignore changes in the cost conditions of various suppliers and inhibit new sources of supply. Exchange control, another child of world depression, restricts demand for foreign currencies—including demands to finance capital movements. To combine conservation of "scarce" currencies with maximum use of other currencies with which there is no unbalance, foreign exchange may be limited in convertibility and allocated with varying degrees of rigour among different countries and according to the uses for which it is required. Discrimination may also be reinforced by multiple exchange rates varying according to the type of import or export, by combinations of export subsidies and tariffs, by commodity agreements and by state trading. One result of these and other measures of discrimination is to force trade and capital flows away from multilateral into bilateral channels.

The post-war growth of international organizations such as the International Monetary Fund, the International Bank for Reconstruction and Development and the General Agreement on Tariffs and Trade reflected a general movement away from the economic lawlessness of the inter-war years towards international conduct designed to minimize the use of discriminatory measures and promote a more desirable pattern of multilateral world trade while minimizing the domestic disadvantages of the gold standard in requiring a deflationary movement in prices to correct an adverse balance of payments. [4]

Diseconomies of Scale, the conditions inside or outside a firm that explain the rise in (average) costs resulting from an increase in the scale of operations. Economies of scale leading to reduced cost per unit of output arise largely because a firm as it grows can take increasing advantage of "indivisible" factors of production such as highly specialized machinery. Long-run unit costs do not continue to fall indefinitely because after a point conditions inside or outside the firm give rise to *diseconomies* of scale which slow down or reverse the fall in unit costs.

Some economists have argued that diseconomies of scale eventually occur mainly because of growing difficulties in management. For example, as a firm run by a single head expands, it will become more difficult for him to know what is happening and to take decisions. If there is one unit with a works manager and a further unit is set up with a second works manager, a general manager will be needed to co-ordinate the two units.

Up to a point there may be gain from increasing scale as the opportunity arises to employ good executives and advanced management techniques. But as the organization grows a disproportionately large number of people is involved in management, and the effective span of control of individual managers is limited because control and accountability become difficult; inertia and vested interests hamper initiative; and communications become more costly.

Other economists have argued that diseconomies can be offset by delegation and decentralization, and that there is no necessary limit to size. It is true that improvements in management aids and methods can increase the size which is most efficient, and there is a trend towards larger average size in many industries. But business is increasingly exercised by the problems of coping with size.

Diseconomies that are "external" to individual firms may also ultimately raise unit costs. If an industry as a whole is expanding, its growing demand for the factors of production may eventually drive up their prices: regional expansion of a number of industries may bring congestion and bottlenecks in supplies of factors and the distribution of goods. Where firms supplying components run into internal diseconomies they appear as external diseconomies to the firm supplied by them. The continuing existence of small firms in engineering, building, farming, retailing and elsewhere is explained in part by diseconomies of scale. [3]

Disequilibrium, a state of unbalance between economic forces leading to change. If a small disturbance is introduced into a given situation, and if after the introduction the original equilibrium is restored, equilibrium is said to be stable. Equilibrium is unstable if a small disturbance does not restore the original situation. Disequilibrium occurs when forces exist in the situation which cause it to change. Thus demand and supply are in equilibrium when the quantity demanded equals the quantity supplied at a given price. If the conditions of demand, or supply, or both, change, there is disequilibrium for a time. A disturbance has been introduced which will normally cause movement to a different position of equilibrium. [14]

Disguised Unemployment, the use of labour in employment at less than its maximum economic value. Employment can be "full" or "high" if all who want work are technically "employed" but they are *unemployed* insofar as the economic value of their output is less than it could be. [5]

Dishoarding, the desire to hold fewer assets in the form of money. Hoarding and dishoarding are basically related to the demand for money, which, in the language used by Keynes, is part of the liquidity preference theory.

Hoarding and dishoarding are now usually defined in terms of "idle" balances of money held by people. A distinction is made between "active" money in circulation and financing current transactions and "inactive" money held in idle balances. An increase in dishoarding means that the community wants to hold a smaller quantity of money in idle balances, so it increases its purchases of goods and services out of idle balances (without changing its expenditure out of current income).

In the loanable funds theory of the rate of interest dishoarding is an important part of the supply of loanable funds. An increase in dishoarding, with no change in the demand for loanable funds, will cause the rate of interest to fall. The dishoarded money constitutes an increase in the demand for securities, causing their prices to rise and the rate of interest to fall.

In Keynesian theory this case would be described as a reduction in liquidity preference to satisfy the speculative motive. [8]

Disinflation, government policy designed to remove inflationary pressures from the economy and maintain the value of the monetary unit. Methods employed in post-war years have included direct restrictions on consumer expenditure by rationing, hire purchase controls, a budget surplus (to "mop up" purchasing power), raising interest rates, credit squeezes, incomes policies (voluntary or statutory), and other measures to check spending out of borrowed funds.

There is no secret about the cure of inflation: either the supply of goods and services must grow without a parallel increase in money earnings, or total monetary demand must be reduced. Rationing and price controls tend to suppress rather than to cure inflation; if such measures are general and absolute, they can be enforced only by stringent penalties. There are two difficulties in working disinflation policies. They may for a time reduce the amount of employment far below the level that is politically acceptable: this calls for better public understanding of the alternatives and an awareness of the need to choose between evils. There is also the danger that disinflation will become deflation, i.e. that the measures will go too far; the solution here lies in more knowledge of the economic system and how it is reacting to economic policies, and this in turn calls for more up-to-date information about the key "indicators"—output, prices, investment, stocks, orders, etc. The need for disinflationary measures is eased to the extent, on the supply side, that productivity rises. Total monetary demand may be reduced by (1) an increase in private savings, (2) an increase in taxation relatively to government spending (although there is some doubt whether it is disinflationary if strong unions can induce government to expand the money supply in order to avoid the unemployment that might accompany higher wages to offset the rise in taxes), (3) specific measures to reduce consumption and investment expenditures, (4) a reduction in government expenditure relatively to taxation. [10]

Disintegration, hiving-off processes or products and buying them from external suppliers; also called "contracting out." More generally it is the situation in which firms obtain all that they need for the manufacture or sale of a product through the mechanism of the market. The limit of disintegration would be reached if all transactions were individual and there were no co-ordination within firms (a firm is essentially a device that supersedes the price mechanism, although there has been a tendency to re-create it by "internal" or "transfer" pricing). The less integration there is within firms, the more the prices of their inputs, i.e. the services of the factors of production they buy, are determined by the play of market forces.

Integration takes place for reasons of cost, quality control, security of supplies and spreading of risk. But conversely it may be cheaper to buy materials or components from specialist suppliers. If, for instance, there are advantages in producing a component on a larger scale than the user requires for himself, he is more likely to buy it in rather than produce more than he wants and face the additional problems of selling off surpluses. The same principle applies to selling to a wholesaler who can carry a range of goods rather than going into direct dealing with retailers. Quality control is often easier for the firm if it makes the product itself, but other means may be as effective: making part of its supplies as a method of control, buying to precise specification, buying from competing suppliers.

Security of supply and definite delivery dates are important, but they can often be assured by the eagerness of suppliers in a competitive market to retain the custom of the buyer. If a service such as road transport is wanted to fulfil particular requirements and schedules, it is possible to arrange it on a contractual basis thus ensuring availability as and when required. If the firm depends on external suppliers, they undertake the necessary investment in fixed assets, have to hold stocks, and bear part of the strain of any decline in demand for the main product. Subcontracting is a good example of disintegration, specialization and division of labour, which frees the main contractor from some tasks and releases his resources for others which may be more profitable for him. [3]

Disintermediation, a contraction in the lending and deposits of the financial intermediaries, such as building societies, because of higher interest rates offered on investments elsewhere. In the UK building societies (and in the USA the savings and loan associations) have lost deposits and investment in recent years because of higher yields on some central government or local authority bonds and their inability or unwillingness to raise the interest rates they paid lenders or depositors. In both countries, government funds were made available in order to maintain the supply of mortgage money. In Britain the building societies have been under government pressure to keep down the interest on money borrowed by house purchasers. [8]

Dismal Science, The. *See* MALTHUS, T. R.

Disposable Income, the purchasing left for expenditure or saving after deduction of taxes on income (including national insurance contributions). Known colloquially as "take-home" pay. It is private income in contrast to "the social wage." [5]

Dissaving, the excess of expenditure over disposable income. It entails drawing either upon wealth accumulated by past saving, or on loans guaranteed against future income. The subtraction of total dissaving from gross saving gives net saving, often used in national income statistics. Dissaving can be stimulated by inflation or by rising taxation, which give rise to the fear that in the future consumption will be more costly or disposable income reduced. [8]

Distribution, the theory concerned with the forces underlying the rates of reward (i.e. the prices) of factors of production (resources). In classical economics distribution theory was primarily concerned not only with *rates* of reward but also with the forces determining the relative *shares* of the broad categories of productive resources—land, labour, capital and enterprise—in the total wealth arising from productive activity. Modern economic theory has never been able satisfactorily to solve this problem of the determination of relative shares. Although interest in it continues, the term distribution without qualification usually refers to the theory dealing with the more limited problem of the determination of factor *prices.*

Like other prices, those of productive factors are determined by demand and supply. The demand for a factor by a business enterprise is a derived demand. It is derived from, first, the change in output (product) attributable to the employment (or non-employment) of a unit of it and, secondly, from the resulting change in sales revenue. The variation in product depends on the amount of co-operating factors with which the factor is combined; if they are held constant the law of variable proportions (diminishing returns) comes into play, that is, as increasing amounts of one factor are combined with fixed amounts of others, the additional (marginal) physical product attributable to each successive unit added will eventually begin to diminish. The variation in sales revenue will depend on the conditions of market demand for the product, that is, on what happens to selling price per unit of output as more is produced and marketed.

These two features explain the demand of an individual firm for a factor of production. If selling price per unit of the product remains unchanged throughout, the marginal physical product of the factor will eventually fall as more of it is employed; therefore (at constant product prices) the additional revenue to be derived from the sale of the marginal physical product will also fall. In short, as increasing amounts of the factor are used, the value to the firm of successive units becomes less and less. To persuade a firm to employ more of the factor, a reduction in its rate of reward or price is therefore necessary: conversely, the higher the factor price, the less will be demanded.

An industry's demand for the factor at a given price will be the sum of all the firms' demands at that price, except that as more of the factor is employed (thus producing more output to be marketed) the selling price of the output—hitherto assumed to be constant—will probably have to drop to persuade the market to take up the additional supplies. This is a further reason why the demand for a factor of production is likely to expand when its price falls and contract when it rises.

Given the conditions of demand, the equilibrium price of a factor will depend on its supply. It will be such as to induce a total demand from all employers just sufficient to clear the market of the factor supply called forth by it. At that price, if there is competitive behaviour, all units of the factor will receive a rate of reward just equal to the value of its marginal product. If any firm were paying less than this it could, by definition, increase its profits by hiring more of the factor; if it were paying more it could expand profits by hiring less. Competition among the factor units—or their owners—would ensure that all units received the same rate.

Under certain assumptions, this theory can be generalized to show that in competition *all* factors of production (including management) would receive a rate of reward equal to their marginal products, and that this would be consistent with the requirement for a general theory that the total of such income payments would precisely exhaust the total value of the products. The formal proof of this proposition is complicated: in simple terms what it amounts to is that if every hired factor is paid a reward equal to its marginal product, any residual must go in profits; but if in long-run competitive equilibrium no firm will be earning profits in excess of the minimum necessary to keep it in production (i.e. equal to the marginal product of management), the sum of the marginal products must precisely exhaust the total product.

It is in this sense that the marginal productivity theory can be said to form a general theory of factor prices. It has two major weaknesses. First, it takes the overall total of factors as given and says nothing about the forces determining the long-run supply, e.g. of labour. Secondly, its practical usefulness as an explanation of the demand for resources—especially labour—is limited because it is difficult to define and measure marginal product. But within those limits the theory helps to explain the "prices" or rewards of the factors of production. [7]

Disutility, the opposite of utility, i.e. the ability of a commodity or service to cause discomfort, inconvenience, or even pain. The utility of a commodity is the satisfaction it yields to the consumer. The law of "diminishing marginal utility" explains how the total satisfaction or utility he derives from additional units increases, not proportionately but at a diminishing rate, eventually reaching a point at which an additional unit no longer yields utility and begins to yield disutility. Theoretically, an individual would have to be paid to consume a good which yielded disutility. Thus, whereas short periods under a hot sun might be pleasant and beneficial, further exposure may cause pain through skin damage which may require payment for lotions to repair. With a "free" good, such as sunshine, hypothetically the individual can be expected to consume it till the marginal utility is zero; but the disutility of scarce goods that cost money is less likely to be reached because the individual would prefer to spend his money elsewhere. In classical economic theory the utility of the wage when a given volume of labour is employed is equal to the marginal disutility of the amount of employment. Thus the wage serves to overcome the disutility of working. Since work tends to yield increasing disutility, overtime rates are usually above the "normal" hourly rates of pay. [7]

Diversification, the spread of a firm's activities over several apparently disconnected products but in which there are economies of combined production, financing, marketing, or risk-reduction (sometimes, for example, to forestall declining demand in a long-established market). It is thus an ambiguous term because there is no economic reason why a firm should specialize in one product, or in physically similar products (e.g. motor cars of varying engine power or fittings), if there are economies in combining physically dissimilar products, e.g. beer and confectionery or tobacco and chemicals. Diversification is more difficult to judge if its purpose is not economies of combined production but market power, i.e. higher profits by supplying a larger share of the market. This tendency can become most undesirable when other firms are acquired (e.g. by merger to form holding companies or "conglomerates") with surplus funds withheld from shareholders to enlarge the authority of "empire-building" boards of directors. [3]

Dividend, a share in the profits of a joint-stock company expressed as a percentage of the nominal value of the ordinary shares of stock held, or in money yield per share.

In most companies the directors recommend the dividend, which is then declared at general meetings of the shareholders. Dividends may be paid only out of profits, either of the current year or undistributed profits of past years. An interim dividend is one paid before the end of the financial year or period as part payment of the total dividend to be paid for the whole year.

A dividend calculated as a percentage of the *nominal* value of the shares is often misleading; it should be related to the market value of the capital employed. Thus:

A. B. C. Limited

Share Capital	
£1 Ordinary Shares	£150,000
General Reserve	50,000
Profits retained in business	100,000
Capital employed	£300,000

A dividend of 20 per cent on the nominal capital of £150,000 is only 10 per cent of the real capital employed (£300,000). Even this figure is not correct unless the fixed assets of the company have been revalued at current market prices; in a period of rising prices, such as after World War II, book values based on original cost may be meaningless.

The terms *ex* dividend and *cum* dividend denote that the Stock Exchange valuation of the shares are exclusive or inclusive of dividend.

The term dividend is also used to describe payments of interest on Government and public authority stocks, and payments received from a debtor's estate in bankruptcy or from a company in liquidation. [3]

Division of Labour, a basic characteristic of the modern economy; also described as specialization. Specialization not only enables every individual and region to take advantage of different endowments of skill and natural resources; it creates and accentuates such differences; and even where no differences exist it encourages large-scale production by permitting (and requiring) a large volume of activity.

Adam Smith (in *The Wealth of Nations*) illustrated the advantages of specialization and division of labour by describing a pin factory in which one man working entirely alone would produce a small number of imperfect pins a day, whereas several men each specializing in a single stage of production could produce several thousand perfect pins a day.

In the primitive stage of economic life each man works to satisfy his wants directly; in time he delegates jobs to members of his household. As an exchange economy develops he specializes in one or a small number of goods or services, and in time this specialization develops into trades and crafts. A later stage of development is the co-operation of groups of individual specialists under one employer in return for wages. Still later it is found advantageous for individuals to concentrate on single processes or stages of production. From this it is a relatively simple step to specialization into industries; and, as this process develops further, it is accompanied by specialization and division of labour into regions, which economists call the localization of industry or the territorial division of labour.

Division of labour as we know it came to Britain with the Industrial Revolution of the eighteenth and nineteenth centuries, with the organization of factory trades and the increasing use of machinery, which is a concomitant of specialization.

Machinery increases man's command over the manipulation of resources, his work is lightened, the work is faster and frequently more accurate, output can be increased at reduced cost, and standardized production becomes possible. Inventiveness and skill, developed by the use of machines, facilitate still further developments. On the other hand there is a boredom, a loss of individual craftsmanship and (even if temporary) displacement of labour. Automation is in principle a further development of these tendencies.

For the individual worker division of labour has several advantages: hours of work may be shortened and earnings increased; the work is usually lightened, though strain may not be diminished; trades are usually learned more easily and quickly; skill and dexterity in one or two jobs is usually acquired more easily than in several. On the other hand there are a loss of skill and pride in the job, monotony, and reduced mobility of labour and difficulty in finding alternative employment if the conditions of demand or supply change. A mitigation of monotony is that repetition makes work automatic and may free the mind to range over the other interests.

For production as a whole the main advantages are: an increase in output at reduced unit cost; the increased use of machinery; the increased possibility of improvement and supervision of the product; and the saving of time and tools through the avoidance of the need of labour to pass from one occupation to another or to own the necessary equipment. On the other hand division of labour and specialization increase the complexities of administration and the danger of "having all one's eggs in one basket" for society as a whole.

Specialization has usually brought progress and development. The modern technological advance on which society increasingly depends could not continue without division of labour. Increasing productivity and real incomes also depend on specialization. Some economic historians have said that the factory system was seriously abused in the nineteenth century, that labour was dehumanized and treated merely as a factor of production, and that these evils were remedied only by state legislation and the trade unions. Others maintain that the factory system enabled legislation to improve working conditions that had been bad under the previous "domestic system" (in which people worked at home), and that labour has benefited basically more from competition for it, particularly in full employment, than from trade unions. Some economists emphasize the dangers of over-standardization and the creation of "mass culture"; others the rising standards of living and the growing capacity for discrimination. Since specialization brings interdependence, it was considered that it must render an economy susceptible to large-scale economic fluctuations, although the trade cycle has become less severe and violent than it was before World War II.

The extent of division of labour is ultimately limited by the extent of the market, which must be large enough to absorb the increased output. Extension of output by this or any other means can be profitable only if the market can absorb the product at a price that covers costs. On the supply side the division of labour is limited by the onset of decreasing returns beyond given levels of output. [3]

Dobb, Maurice H. (1900–1976), British economist. He was educated at Charterhouse and Cambridge (Pembroke), taught economics at Cambridge and elsewhere, and was Emeritus Reader in Economics and a fellow of Trinity College. Dobb was profoundly influenced by Marx, but was not a doctrinaire Marxist. He wrote authoritatively and with objectivity on the economic development of the Soviet Union and the economic systems of East Europe and made extensive contributions to the development of the economics of socialism and to welfare economics. Perhaps his main contribution to analytical economics was in *Capitalist Enterprise and Social Progress* (1925), where he developed the relationship between "pure" profit and economic uncertainty in a direct line from the work of Knight. He also worked closely with Sraffa on the definitive edition of Ricardo's writings. His other main works were *Russian Economic Development since the Revolution* (1928), *An Essay on Economic Growth and Planning* (1960), and *Welfare Economics and the Economics of Socialism* (1969). [2]

Dollar Area, term formerly used after World War II when freedom to convert sterling into dollars was limited by the Government. It comprised countries whose sterling in accounts with UK banks was convertible into dollars, and included the USA and its dependencies, Canada and "American Account" countries: the Philippines and fourteen Latin American republics.

After the end of the 1950's there was a general tendency towards increased convertibility of sterling and the term dollar area lost its former precise meaning. Official returns of overseas holders of sterling group non-sterling countries by broad regions in which the former "dollar area" has been replaced by "North America." [4]

Dollar Gap, dollar shortage provoked in the early post-war period by pent-up demand from Europe for capital and consumer goods that only the USA could provide. The continuing dollar gap resulted from the rigidity of foreign exchange rates and/or domestic price and income levels.

Although the problem of the dollar gap attracted most attention for several years after World War II, rigidities of exchange rates and prices have characterized world trade since World War I. Demand for American foodstuffs and essentials outstripped Europe's weakened capacity to export immediately after the 1914–18 war, and the resulting dollar shortage was covered by loans and credits and by running down Europe's gold reserves. Later in the 1920's many countries stabilized their foreign exchange rates on paper in terms of gold (but in practice in terms of the major world currencies, sterling and dollars). The rates chosen, however, bore little relation to the underlying conditions of demand and supply, and a precarious balance between dollar demand and supply was maintained only by the coincidence of high demand for imports and foreign securities in the USA and (in Great Britain) by deflationary measures to keep down domestic prices and import demand. The US depression exposed the underlying disequilibrium and precipitated the foreign exchange crisis of 1931. During the later inter-war years efforts to insulate national economies from American depression led to trade and exchange controls to avoid balance of payments deficits.

The dollar gap reappeared in 1940 with the high wartime demand for American goods, and was temporarily plugged by the massive sale of British overseas investments and strict exchange controls. The wartime Lend-Lease Agreement between USA and the Allies postponed the problem from 1941 until the end of the war, when it re-emerged in acute form. In Britain the situation was complicated by the reduction in income from overseas investments, shipping and insurance, which had offset normal deficits on visible (commodity) trade.

In the post-war political climate the problems were too large for correction by adjustment of exchange rates, prices or incomes by debtor countries, or by the institutions created under the Bretton Woods Agreements to facilitate international balance of payments. Exchange controls were intensified everywhere, but despite American assistance and dollar loans, it was not until the Marshall Plan for US co-operation in European recovery that the dollar gap was brought under control. Marshall Aid ended in 1951–2 but the trade supply of dollars to

Europe and after that to the rest of the world, was augmented by military and economic assistance from the USA and by considerable US private investment abroad. In most post-war years the USA had a large visible trade surplus, but her continued outflow of capital caused a net deficit on her international accounts. This outflow was reflected in the growth of productive capacity and of the gold and dollar reserves of the rest of the world, in the partial relaxation of trade and exchange controls, and in the gradual recovery in world trade.

A British economist forecast that the dollar gap would remain, but in the 1960's short-term capital exports from the USA tended to produce a "reverse" dollar gap, i.e. a superfluity, which led the US to reduce the supplies of dollars coming on to world markets. [4]

Domar, Evsey David (1914–97), American economist born in Poland. After studying at Harvard and the Universities of California and Michigan, he was appointed Professor of Economics, Massachusetts Institute of Technology, in 1958. He became known chiefly for original work on the dynamics of economic growth. The resulting Harrod-Domar model was independently originated by Domar in the USA and Sir Roy Harrod in Britain. It attempts to "dynamize" the static Keynesian theory of the determination of income by allowing for changes in saving and investment, and shows that the "warranted" rate of economic growth will be determined by the marginal propensity to save the incremental capital-output ratio. This relationship has been criticized by some economists, notably Colin Clark, for ignoring qualitative criteria (human abilities, education, etc.), being based on Keynesian solutions to unemployment (of human beings) when the post-war problem has been over-full employment, ignoring the imperfections in the data, and overlooking the possibility that marginal capital-output ratios can fall as well as rise. Domar's main published work is *Essays in the Theory of Economic Growth* (1957). [2]

Domestic Credit Expansion (DCE), a recent name for the change in the total supply of money after allowing for changes in government borrowing abroad and in the reserves of foreign exchange. Broadly interpreted, DCE represents the sum of (*a*) increase in the money supply and (*b*) deficit in the balance of payments. It was used in the late 1960's after an undertaking by the British Government to the International Monetary Fund that domestic money and credit would be controlled strictly in exchange for IMF assistance. [8]

Doomsters, term applied to (mostly) non-economists and some economists who reflected or stimulated widespread anxiety by foretelling exhaustion of world energy supplies because of over-rapid exploitation of oil, etc. and environmental amenity in general. Their conclusions were that materials should be recycled where possible and, more fundamentally, that the rate of use of resources accompanying high rates of growth should be slowed down, if necessary by government action.

Economists were divided, more by their value-judgements on the relative importance of natural environmental resources and economic growth than on the economic analyses of the effects of growth. Those who criticized the "doomsters" replied on two grounds. First, natural resources and the environment were not absolutes to be preserved at all costs, and a small sacrifice of environment was worth paying for the advantages of economic growth, such as high living standards, more assistance for the relatively poor, the developing countries, etc. (Professor Wilfred Beckerman). Second, the non-economists who prophesied "doom" overlooked the effects of rising costs and prices of coal, oil, etc. in disciplining demand (thus avoiding over-consumption) and in stimulating research in new fuels, and the potential effects of pricing the environment, where possible, to yield these effects (Professor Colin Robinson). Robinson argued that "alarmists" in the 1860's who foretold the exhaustion of British coal had similarly overlooked the effects of working deeper coal-seams on costs, prices and consumption. On the other hand he argued that government action or international governmental co-operation was necessary to deal with the effects of rising energy consumption on the climate, a fundamental aspect of the environment, and to prevent or protect people against accidents in nuclear power production: these two consequences or risks could not be dealt with by the market through the pricing process. [11]

Double Coincidence (of wants). *See* BARTER.

Double Pricing, is used of the attachment of two prices to a contract, a lower price for payment in cash (or kind), a higher for payment by cheque. The practice spread in Britain in the early 1970's. The tax evasion implied in a payment in cash (or kind), which is easier to conceal from formal accounting and therefore omitted from tax returns, is a reaction to rising taxation. Double pricing is comparatively recent. Other forms of tax evasion have been commonly practised in Europe, especially in the southern countries, for decades. The economist's interest in double pricing is in the division between the buyer and seller of the tax evaded. [12]

Double Taxation, the application of two separate taxes or tax systems to a source of income or capital. For example, corporation tax may be levied on a company's profit which is later liable to income tax when it reaches shareholders in the form of dividends. Some forms of income may also be taxed by the country where they originate and by the country where the recipient lives. A recent form of double taxation is Value-Added Tax on goods or services (e.g. in restaurants) that have borne customs or excise taxes. [12]

Dow Jones, name given to the oldest American index of thirty share prices by Dow Jones & Co., publisher of the *Wall Street Journal.* Three other Dow Jones indexes are for twenty transport firms, fifteen public utilities, and for the total of sixty-five share prices. With time the indexes have become increasingly imperfect measures of absolute prices, but they are still used to indicate *changes* in them. The indexes are recalculated for publication each hour. [14]

Downs, Anthony (1930–), American economist. He was Assistant Professor of Economics and Political Science at the University of Chicago (1959–62), and from 1959 economic analyst and senior vice-president of the Real Estate Research Corporation. His original theoretical research has led to the development of the economic theory of democracy and a new branch of economics which seeks to explain the relationship between governmental budgets and the performance of bureaucratic institutions, and the effects on the public in political voting. His major publications have been *An Economic Theory of Democracy* (1957) and *Inside Bureaucracy* (1967). [2]

Drawback, an amount paid back from a charge, more specifically an amount of excise or import duty remitted when the commodities on which it has been paid are exported. Most drawbacks are paid on imported materials made up into finished goods. [12]

Dummy Tender. *See* Collusive Tendering.

Dumping, a form of monopoly price discrimination: selling goods abroad at prices below those in the exporter's home market (after allowance for transport and other costs).

Producers adversely affected often apply the term as a criticism to *all* low-price competition, whether or not there is price discrimination between domestic and foreign markets, particularly where low prices can be traced to the use of cheap foreign labour. This is not dumping in the true sense, although in some cases it could be construed as a form of it (as where monopoly power in another country is exercised by employers to keep wage rates in the export trades below those in the rest of the economy). It is difficult in practice to distinguish between this case and labour which is cheap simply because of the relative abundance of foreign labour as a whole. Both may result in low prices for the goods they produce, but to protect home producers against competition from abundant labour would mean a loss of the benefits of world specialization and trade based on the principle of comparative cost.

True dumping, i.e. price discrimination, may be either persistent or temporary. Persistent or long-term dumping arises where the demand conditions facing a producer differ in home and foreign markets, so that his profits are increased by charging different rather than identical prices in the two markets. To maximize profits he will charge a lower price in the market where the elasticity of demand is higher (usually the export market). Such dumping is unintentional in the sense that if demand conditions in the two markets were similar prices charged would be identical after allowing for transport costs, etc. In the country receiving dumped products consumers gain (as they do from any kind of dumping): competing producers are faced with long-term problems of adaptation similar to those arising out of "genuine" low-cost competition from overseas. Protection for aggrieved domestic producers is not justified on economic grounds, although there may be other grounds for it, as the desire to maintain small farmers in production for political or military reasons.

Temporary or intermittent dumping may be deliberately used as an aggressive weapon to eliminate competing domestic producers in the export markets. It may also arise from a desire on the part of producers in other countries to dispose of temporary surpluses without upsetting the home market price structure. These forms of dumping tend to dislocate domestic production in the export market while conferring only temporary gains on consumers. A better case can be made out in theory for protection against this kind of dumping; but even here it is politically difficult to limit it so that it does not become general protection against all kinds of foreign competition.

Dumping is excluded by the Treaty of Rome of the Common Market, and the Kennedy Round of trade negotiations (between North America, the Common Market, and the European Free Trade Association) agreed on rules to control dumping. [4]

Duopoly, a market situation in which there are only two sellers. The theory of duopoly, originally associated with Antoine Augustin Cournot (1801–77), forms a special case of the theory of oligopoly, which is applied to the situation, some way between monopoly and perfect competition, in which the number of sellers is not large enough to make the influence of any one on the price negligible. A monopoly exists when there is only one seller, oligopoly when there are few sellers; the simplest case of oligopoly is that of two sellers, duopoly.

Duopoly provides a simplified model for showing the main principles of the theory of oligopoly: the conclusions drawn from analysing the problem of two sellers can be extended to cover situations in which there are three or more sellers.

If there are only two sellers producing a commodity a change in the price or output of one will affect the other; and his reactions in turn will affect the first. Thus each seller realizes that a change in his price or output will set up a chain of reactions. He has to make assumptions about how the other will react to a change in his policy. The essential characteristic of the theory of duopoly is that *neither seller can ignore the reactions of the other.* The two sellers' fortunes are not independent; neither can take the other's policy for granted, because it is in part determined by his own.

Under pure competition, or monopoly, price or output can be decided by reference to the conditions of demand and cost that face individual producers. But there is no simple answer in duopoly. It will depend upon the assumptions made by each seller about the reactions of the other. The answer is in this sense "indeterminate." Two limiting solutions are possible. Both sellers may charge the monopoly price as a result of agreement or independent experience. This supposes that both sell identical products and have the same costs, and that consumers are indifferent between them when both ask the same price. If a duopolist moves his price above or below the monopoly price he will be worse off because profits are maximized at the monopoly price. The two thus behave as a single monopolist, and the market is shared between them. The other possible solution occurs when, as a result of a price war, each seller is making only normal competitive profits. Price is then fixed at the competitive level. Between these two limits there is an indeterminate number of possibilities about which theory can say little. [7]

Duopsony, the market situation characterized by two dominant buyers. The analogue of duopoly. [7]

Dupuit, Arsène Jules (1804–66), French economist. He was trained as a civil engineer and began his career in the service of the French government. In supervising the construction of roads and waterways he reflected on their advantage to the general public, and his efforts to measure this advantage led him to develop a theory of utility. His views were published in the French technical journal *Annales des ponts et chaussées* in 1844 and 1849. In these papers Dupuit devised a means of measuring utility with the aid of geometrical diagrams, and developed a theory very similar to Marshall's "consumer's surplus." He was one of the first to use the concept of the demand curve. [2]

Durable Goods, commodities that yield a stream of services over time. They include consumer durables and producers' or capital goods. The phrase occurs particularly in the "over-investment" theories of the trade cycle where durable goods play a strategic role in explaining economic fluctuations.

Capital-goods industries and industries producing consumer durables are, by and large, more severely affected than other industries in the downswing of the trade cycle. It is argued that during the period of prosperity the capital-goods industries expand more rapidly than consumer-goods industries, because of the operation of the "accelerator." Since an expanded output of the capital-goods industries can be sustained only if the rate of increase of demand for consumption goods is maintained, the basis of prosperity in the capital-goods industries is precarious. A tendency for consumption demand to level out may produce sharp falls in their output which may indicate the end of an upswing and the onset of recession and subsequent depression. Consumer durables are also included in this analysis, since they too can be regarded as subject to the accelerator principle. [9]

Durbin, E. F. M. *See* CALCULATION, ECONOMIC.

Dutch Auction, a public sale in which the auctioneer, the owner/seller's agent, opens with the highest price he can expect and reduces it until a bidder indicates he will buy. The owner may thus receive from a bidder with consumer's surplus more than what would have been the free market price. The form of auction more usual in Britain invites bidders to make bids beginning with the lowest and ending with sale to the highest. [7]

Dynamic Analysis. *See* DYNAMIC STATE; STATIC ANALYSIS.

Dynamic State, a condition in which the relationships between economic phenomena are changing. The dynamic approach to economic problems was originally associated with the writers of English classical political economy: Adam Smith, Ricardo, Mill, etc. Their works attempt to analyse the growth and development of the nation's economy. This is typified in the Malthusian theory of population, which was concerned with the diverging rates of growth of population and food supplies. The classical economists were concerned, too, with the approach of the stationary state. Their writings discuss the paths along which they believed the economy was moving towards it. During the twentieth century there has been considerable revival of interest in dynamics, but the approach is much narrower and less ambitious than the broad approach of the classicists.

Static analysis is the name usually given to the method of dealing with economic phenomena which attempts to determine the relationships between them at a given moment of time. All economic forces and the relations between them are the results of preceding relationships between economic phenomena. And these relationships are influenced by what may happen in the future.

Economic dynamics relates economic phenomena at different points of time. Methods of analysis which take into account past and expected values, time-lags and rates of change constitute economic dynamics. Dynamics is thus the study of economic phenomena in the context of preceding and succeeding events: the analysis of the process of change. Any economic problem may be analysed in this way. The problems of a stationary state may be analysed by a "sequence analysis" which relates economic phenomena belonging to different points of time. An historically changing process may be treated in a static manner, each of its changing positions being studied and compared as successive points of equilibrium. It is the method of analysis which gives an economic problem its dynamic nature. There has been much development of economic dynamics in the study of business cycles and in price theory in the last forty years. [14]

E

"Ear-Bashing," a persistent and forceful form of ear-stroking. [13]

"Ear-stroking," term coined by D. H. Robertson for the preaching by politicians to industry to behave differently from the way market conditions indicate to be in their best interests. It has been much in evidence in voluntary incomes policies or "indicative planning" in Britain and the USA since the early 1960's. The scope for such persuasion is created by uncertainty or lack of precise knowledge about the optimum quantities buyers should buy or sellers sell, and about the optimum prices. The limits to successful prolonged ear-stroking are nevertheless narrow, since after a probably short time, perhaps nine to fifteen months in wage restraint, changing market conditions intensify market forces in favour of change: employers either find ways round restrained wages or lose employees to employers who ignore the appeals, perhaps by agreement with the employees. Politicians in communist economies practise ear-stroking with sanctions when they require or order managers of state plants to sell at marginal cost. (Economists also practise ear-stroking when they urge politicians to act differently from the course indicated by maximum electoral advantage!) [13]

Earmarking, term applied to resources or funds assigned to stated purposes, specifically government revenue assigned, "dedicated" to or "hypothecated" for a named function or service. The celebrated (or notorious) British example is the 1909 Road Fund, financed by a tax on petrol and vehicles that was assigned to expenditure on roads and ultimately diverted to other purposes. Occasionally the managers or employees of state services, e.g. the British National Health Service, ask for government funds to be earmarked solely for health expenditure (and controlled by them). Governments in financial straits are prone to raid earmarked funds. In theory no British taxes are hypothecated to stated services or purposes; governments and politicians generally dislike earmarking funds because it would restrict their range of manoeuvre in switching money from "surplus" to "deficit" purposes. National insurance contributions are strictly not earmarked funds because they are nominally insurance premiums and not general tax revenue. But in practice they have become barely distinguishable from income tax as seen by British employees in deductions from gross pay; they are increasingly treated as taxes in national income and government statistics; and in the USA they are explicitly described as social security taxes. [12]

Earned Income, drawn from work (manual or mental) in varying forms (wages, salaries, profits, fees, charges, commissions, royalties, etc.) in contrast to property (dividends, interest, rent, etc.). The distinction is legally drawn by government to explain or justify differential rates of taxes—higher on unearned than on earned income. But in economics the distinction is less clear: "unearned" income is not earned *currently* by the present owner of property; but it may be derived from property accumulated by the work of others in the recent or distant past. [5]

Earnings Yield. *See* YIELD.

Easement, the right to make limited use of real property owned by another, e.g. rights of way, drainage rights or rights to carry water across another's land. [6]

Easy Money. *See* CHEAP MONEY.

Ecology. *See* ECOSYSTEM.

Econometrica. *See* JOURNALS, ECONOMIC.

Econometrics, numerical economics; the branch of economics in which economic theory, mathematics and statistics are fused in the analysis of numerical and institutional data. Econometrics presents economic theories in a form in which they can be tested statistically against observed events. One major aspect is the application of scientific methods of inquiry to the observed facts and statistical data of economic history. Econometric studies are a comparatively recent development in economics. The Econometrics Society was formed in 1930 to encourage them, with the aim of making economics more "scientific."

Economists have long debated the value of econometric studies, but the extent of such studies has increased in recent years: articles in learned economic journals increasingly use the language of econometrics, and mathematics forms an increasing part of economics teaching. Econometricians are for the most part aware of the difficulties inherent in attempts to capture the intricacies and uncertainties of the economic world in formal forecasting models; but they consider the attempt useful and tend to scorn analyses which they think fail to make explicit the assumptions on which they are based. On the other hand some critics consider that the formal garb and pseudo-precision of econometric models may mislead even its own practitioners. The continuing debate illustrates forcefully the enormous difficulties of testing even simple hypotheses in economics. The search for more rigorous methods is likely to continue and is just as likely to attract criticism; both aspects reflect the essential trial-and-error method of advancing scientific knowledge.

One aspect of the debate tends to be overlooked. Because economics is one of the main social sciences, touching ordinary life at many points, there is widespread industrial, political and general interest in its teachings. It must therefore be able to explain itself to "outsiders" in language they can understand if it is to continue to exert an influence on events or policy. This view probably underlies the reaction among some economists against the proliferation and use of mathematics where it is not essential, and its tendency to replace the language of prose. [14]

Economic and Social Council of the United Nations, formed in 1945, comprises eighteen members elected by the General Assembly for three years. It is responsible for advancing higher living standards, full employment and conditions of economic and social progress and expansion, world co-operation in cultural and educational matters, universal respect for, and observance of, human rights, and the fundamental freedoms for all peoples whatever their race, sex, language or religion. [4]

Economic Base Theory, urban economic base theory seeks to explain and predict urban income, employment and growth in terms of the degree to which an urban area specializes in "exports," i.e. the production of goods and services supplied to other areas. An increase in "export" trade generated by demand from "outside" will lead to faster growth in the urban area. The first step is to identify activities within the urban area as either *basic* (orientated towards exports) or *non-basic* (service, i.e. oriented towards satisfying the "service" needs of the inhabitants of the area). In theory, such a classification could be based on data relating to income, employment, sales or value added in production: in practice the lack of local data means that employment statistics are generally used for this purpose. The next step is to calculate relevant ratios such as that of employment in basic activities to total employment in the urban area (the *base ratio*) or the ratio of employment in basic activities to that in service activities (the *basic-to-service ratio*). For example, a town of 40,000 people with 20,000 employed—10,000 in basic activities, 10,000 in service activities—would have a base ratio of 0.5 and a basic-to-service ratio of 1.0. If, because of increased export demand, basic employment were to increase to 11,000, service employment remaining at 10,000, this would cause both the above ratios to rise slightly. The crude economic base theory would then suggest that total population and employment would increase until the ratios had been restored to "normal": this would happen when an additional 1,000 jobs had been created in service activities.

Although the crude form of theory has undergone refinements, it remains an oversimplification of reality and a relatively ineffective predictor of urban growth or decline. A more refined approach utilizes Keynesian multiplier theory to examine the effect on an urban economy of an injection of new spending generated by "export" demand: the resultant total expansion of spending and economic activity then depends on the community's marginal propensities to save and to import goods and services from other areas. Together these propensities determine the extent of leakages from each round of income-generating expenditures within the urban area. But as with the crude economic base theory, urban multiplier theory has not proved to be a good predictive tool. [6]

Economic Commission for Europe (ECE), an agency of the United Nations created in 1947 to consider regional economic questions. A non-United Nations member, Switzerland, is consulted. Sub-commissions deal with single industries (e.g. coal), services (housing, etc.) and trade development. [4]

Economic Development, generally this term means simply economic growth. More specifically it is used to describe not the quantitative measures of a growing economy (such as the rate of increase in real income per head) but the economic, social or other changes that produce the growth.

Economic development requires changes in techniques of production, in social attitudes and in institutions. Such changes may produce economic growth; conservatism and repression of change is likely to inhibit growth. The opposition to change and the conditions that will produce the fastest rate of growth will vary from society to society. In some developing countries growth requires strengthening the central government and enforcing existing laws; in others it may require changes in social customs relating to the kind and amount of property that individuals may accumulate or the kinds of food they may eat. In industrial countries economic development is seen in industrial innovation—new products and new methods or machines for producing them, but its underlying conditions are the attitudes of management and workers to the prestige of managerial occupations, the importance of efficiency, technological unemployment, the preservation of amenities and so on. Some societies may reject the fastest attainable rate of economic development as the objective of economic policy, since it may require the present generation to exert itself in order that future generations are bettered. Economic development has often been achieved at the cost of bad housing, ill health, sweated labour, maldistribution of income. Democratic societies may not wish to pay the costs of joining in a race to raise indexes of economic growth such as production or investment that do not necessarily indicate real standards of living, particularly if the growth is directed by politicians with little reference to the preferences of consumers, as in some countries in Africa and Asia. [11]

Economic Dynamics. *See* DYNAMIC STATE.

Economic Efficiency, relates to output per unit cost of the resources employed; contrasted with *technical* efficiency, which measures output of energy per unit of energy applied. The difference is that economic efficiency is concerned with cost and value. A machine may produce a product that satisfies technical, chemical or engineering criteria, but it is economically inefficient if its costs are so high that no one will pay the price sufficient to cover them. A technically perfect car would incorporate the ideal materials; but no one would buy it.

A labour force may be fully employed in the *technical* sense that it is engaged in work (exertion, physical or mental), e.g. making ships, digging coal, running trains, building aircraft, airfields or tunnels, but not in the *economic allocation* sense that its contribution to output, as valued by consumers, is maximized; i.e. could not be enlarged by being applied elsewhere.

The concept of allocative efficiency (efficiency in the economic use of resources) lies at the core of economic theory and a large part of theory and empirical investigation has been devoted to the impact of e.g. barriers to competition in the form of monopolistic practices and discriminatory and exclusive policies on allocative efficiency. In recent years some economists have questioned the value of these studies, arguing that the effect of such practices and policies in reducing allocative efficiency is trivial compared with the much more important and widespread types of inefficiency that are endemic in all forms of economic activity but which allocative efficiency largely ignores. Because these comprise a number of elements, the notion has been termed "*X-efficiency*" or "*non-allocative efficiency*": neither individuals nor firms work as hard, or search for information as effectively, as they could. The argument is that economists in the past have spent too much time discussing and researching the causes of allocative inefficiency: the gains to be achieved are probably small relative to the gains from an increase in X-efficiency. [3]

Economic Flow. *See* Flow, Economic.

Economic Friction, the influences that impede the full or rapid operation of economic "laws." For example, if labour is completely mobile between jobs and areas, seeks the highest return for its services and knows of changes in pay and conditions offered throughout the economy, men will shift their occupations in such a way that there is a tendency for the net advantages in jobs of a given grade of skill to be equal. In practice, ignorance of opportunities or obstacles to movement, such as an inefficient market in housing or trade union restrictions, produce the friction which restricts and slows down the adjustment to new or changing conditions.

In the physical sciences analysis of a world without frictions is made more realistic by introducing them and observing their effects. In the social sciences this method is impracticable since an economy cannot easily be dissected in order to examine parts of it one at a time. [14]

Economic Good, a commodity for which the supply falls short of the demand, so that it is scarce and can command a price. Air is not an economic good where it is plentiful but an economic good where it has to be conveyed at some cost, e.g. in a deep mine. Water is not an economic good in a rainy country but is an economic good in the desert. [7]

Economic Growth, generally means economic development, more specifically it may be used to describe the outward evidence of the process of economic development. "Growth" is then measurable and objective: it describes expansion in the labour force, in capital, in the volume of trade and in consumption. And "economic development" can be used to describe the underlying determinants of economic growth, such as changes in attitudes and institutions.

There are various ways of defining and measuring economic growth. An increase in total real national income over a long period is one ("real" and "long period" because changes in the value of money due to inflation or deflation and cyclical swings in output must be allowed for). But an increase in real national income might be accompanied by even faster growth in population, so that less would be available for each person and the (average) standard of living would have been reduced. A second measure of growth is therefore to divide the increase in national income by the increase in population, so that the indicator of economic growth becomes the increase in income per head. But difficulties remain. If all the increase in national income went to a small and relatively well-off section of the population, and the share of income going to the rest remained the same while their numbers grew, most of the population would be both relatively and absolutely worse off than before. If economic growth is to be regarded as a process which raises the real standard of living of a community as a whole, a third indicator of economic growth is income per head supplemented by information on the distribution of income and on the extent to which national resources are being used to satisfy the preferences of consumers as a whole.

This meaning of economic growth requires value judgements on what is a desirable or undesirable change in the distribution of income. The main objective of economic growth, to raise standards of living, is generally a very long-term objective that may require living standards to be depressed in the short run, e.g. by saving to accumulate capital or to build national defences. To avoid "social welfare" judgements, and for simplicity, many economists use the figure of real national income as the measure of economic growth. If required, adjustments for increase in population can then be made separately.

The weaknesses in the attempts to define economic growth and compare it in different countries arise from the difficulties in measuring national income over time, particularly in under-developed countries where statistics are often little better than informed guesses. The use of statistics such as Gross National Product (GNP) or National Income (NI) to measure growth or social welfare has come under the more fundamental criticism that neither economists nor other social scientists know what constitutes the well-being of populations as a whole, or the rate of growth in well-being or the means of promoting the rate of growth. This view is that an individual can define his personal welfare and its rate of growth, but that it is pretentious to measure total or social welfare or its growth by gross or national statistics. Such totals are based on arbitrary geographical divisions, they exclude goods and services that do not enter into the market (the services performed by members of a family or larger group for one another), they include government output and services at fictitious rather than market prices reflecting consumer valuations, and they exclude goods consumed directly by their producers (e.g. farm produce, especially in the developing countries). Furthermore, some goods, such as investment goods, are consumed in the process of obtaining or expanding social welfare rather than as part of it. Finally there is the doubt whether economic growth can be measured in material terms; the West Indian economist Professor Sir Arthur Lewis has put the point thus: "The advantage of economic growth is not that wealth increases happiness but that it increases the range of human choice . . . control over [the] environment"; and this cannot be measured by statistics of total output or income. [11]

The relationship between economic growth and property rights is discussed in Economic Organization. [14]

Economic History, the aspect of history that analyses the efforts of man to make the most of, safeguard or improve the human and physical environment. It can thus be regarded as concerned with man as the creation of material conditions (Marx), with human activity in relation to material concerns (Cannan), with the deployment of scarce resources to serve given ends (Robbins), with discovering new or better means and ends (Hayek). The latest developments are the application to economic history of rigorous statistical empirical testing and the re-interpretation of western economic history in terms of the refinement of property rights. [2]

Economic Imperialism, theory of the exertion of authority by an economically stronger over an economically weaker country. It was developed by Karl Marx to describe, or explain, the search for markets and investments and thereby for political influence by capitalist countries in less developed countries. More recently the phenomenon has been applied generally to the relationship between the larger advanced countries and the smaller, relatively backward countries. The largest communist country, the USSR, is also often described as behaving imperialistically towards smaller communist and non-communist countries. [4]

Economic Indicators, key measurements of the most characteristic or fundamental economic activities. They are supposed to show how the economic system as a whole is behaving or will react to internal or external developments in the immediate or more distant future. Thus orders for industrial equipment can be expected to indicate the trend in industrial activity. The number of people in employment, hours of work, etc., may be thought to rise and fall with output. Changes in the output of steel, which is used in a wide range of goods from office blocks to motor cars, could show how the economy is moving. And prices could reflect the general "sentiment," attitude or expectations of buyers (of consumer goods, investment goods, labour, etc.). But at the time it is never (or rarely) possible to know the point on the upward or downward slope of economic activity at which the indicators are being marked or judged. (If it were, the future would be known, and could be influenced or prevented!) Even broad "trends" cannot invariably be discerned from indicators. The Scottish economist, Professor Sir Alexander Cairncross, has written (1964)

> "A trend," to use the language of Gertrude Stein, "is a trend
> is a trend,"
> But the question is: will it bend?
> Will it alter its course, through some unforeseen force,
> And come to a premature end?

But when delayed consequences are derived from rigorous economic analysis of causes and consequences, perhaps supported by example (from the not too distant past, otherwise circumstances may have changed so that no conclusions can be drawn), recent policy may yield indicators to future events. Thus if a change in the rate of increase in the quantity of money takes six to nine months to change the rate of increase in money income and output (Friedman claims this delayed consequence has been found in the USA, Canada, Japan, Israel, India and South America), and a further six to nine months to raise prices, the rate of increase in money supply is an indicator to the rate of inflation twelve to eighteen months ahead. Once the monetary circulation has been expanded inflation is to be expected: it cannot be stopped (at least in a short term and without drastic measures). And if an inflation cannot end except by the failure of firms that were made profitable by it, as was argued by Professor F. A. Hayek and other economists, monetary inflation is itself an indicator of the state of the economy and the probability of recession and unemployment in the future. It is not as precise in time as the monetary circulation indicator, though it may be more reliable since it rests on economic analysis and not on the evidence of history, which indicates past sequences but may not repeat itself. [14]

Economic Interpretation of History. *See* DETERMINISM, ECONOMIC.

Economic Law. *See* LAW, ECONOMIC.

Economic Life, of an asset is the period over which it is expected to be capable of economic use, i.e. to yield a rate of return on capital invested in it competitive with that obtainable from similar investments of comparable risk. In effect, this means that when the expected returns from an asset, less running costs, have a net present value less than its current sale value, the asset will be sold. It will still have an economic life for the new owner, who will repeat the process of assessing economic life. When the asset's net present value becomes less than its scrap value, its life will be ended. The economic life of a building, for example, will be governed by the net income it is thought capable of yielding, relative to what the cleared site could earn if available for alternative development. [6]

Economic Man, concerned with the immediate aim of obtaining the largest possible command over resources with the minimum of sacrifice. Economic man is a convenient abstraction, useful in discussing economic affairs, but not intended as a description of man in modern society. The study of economics does not require men to be supposed selfish, self-centered or concerned only with money or material things.

It is seldom necessary in economic theory to regard individuals as identical, so that we can analyse the behaviour of a number of "economic men" differing in tastes and abilities.

Men seek more purchasing power for numerous reasons: to benefit themselves, their families, friends, churches, schools, clubs, political parties, etc. But their *purposes* are not relevant. A philanthropist's behaviour in acquiring wealth illustrates the notion of economic man: only the immediate aim (of maximizing wealth) is relevant to the economist, not the use made of it. Many other influences affect people even in their ordinary economic affairs and must be brought in when a theory is being elaborated and applied to reality; but it is often useful to leave these influences out in the early stages of the theory. This procedure is valid if, in the words of John Neville Keynes (the father of J. M. Keynes), "in economic affairs the desire for wealth exerts a more uniform and an infinitely stronger influence among men taken in the mass than any other immediate aim."

Economic analysis can also be applied to the disposal of income or wealth, whatever the motives. If resources are scarce, the theory of choice between alternative uses and the economic rules or laws of equalizing marginal products, etc. can be applied whether goods and services are traded or given away ("free" or below the market price that could have been obtained). [14]

Economic Method. *See* Analysis.

Economic Models. *See* Models, Economic.

Economic Morphology, the classification and study of the different pure market forms of which actual markets may be composed. A small farmer may use his own labour and consume part of his own produce: to this extent his economic activities are representative of a *subsistence economy* with no trade. He may swap equipment and produce with neighbouring farmers and mirror a *simple barter* economy. He may sell vegetables and buy seed in highly *competitive markets:* he may sell some output (e.g. liquid milk) and buy some inputs (e.g. electricity) in *monopolistic markets:* he may sell some (e.g. fat stock) and buy (labour) in *imperfectly competitive markets.*

The construction and study of the properties of abstract "models" of the main types of market enables economists to see how general principles are modified in their application to each situation. The apparent complexities of real life are thus explained. [14]

Economic Nationalism, the policy of national self-sufficiency bolstered by tariffs, quotas, currency restrictions and other means of excluding imports. It was widely applied in varying degree in the inter-war years for various reasons—to maintain employment, conserve currency reserves, foster local industries out of national pride, build up war industries, etc., by countries ranging from pacific Ireland to aggressive Nazi Germany. Since the end of World War II economic nationalism has given way to varying degrees of international economic liberalism in many parts of the world outside the communist countries.

Some communist countries, most notably Yugoslavia, but also Czechoslovakia, Hungary and Poland, have also developed their trade with other countries, although the scope for expansion is relatively small because large or variable imports could disrupt national state planning. [11]

Economic Organization, the creation of institutions and laws (on property, contract, monopoly, etc.) to provide inducements that will channel individual economic activity to serve the general (social, public) interest. In the economics of externalities and politics, this principle is formulated as the creation of incentives to individual activities that bring the private rate of return (the earnings or yield or benefit to the individual from a given activity) close to the social rate of return (the total benefit to all individuals in the community as a whole). The history of the western world has been re-interpreted by this neo-classical approach in economic theory, which examines the evolution of institutions and property rights to close the gap between private and social benefits (Douglass C. North and Robert Paul Thomas, *The Rise of the Western World,* 1973). This interpretation is based on the work of modern economists who have developed and refined the distinction drawn by A. C. Pigou between marginal private and marginal social net product; on the writings of economic historians and economists who have written on economic history such as Marc Bloch, Carlo Cipolla, Maurice Dobb, John U. Nef, M. M. Postan and Joseph Schumpeter; and on the classic legal and constitutional studies of Pollock and Maitland and Stubbs. Basically it is a re-interpretation of the history of economic growth in terms of developing property rights. Countries such as Britain, Germany and Holland succeeded sooner or later in evolving the property rights required for economic development; others, such as Spain, Latin America, Asia and Africa, failed. The re-interpretation is also a syntheses of the classical liberal approach of Adam Smith and of the revolutionary approach of Karl Marx, both of whom saw that economic growth depended on the evolution of effective property rights. [14]

Economic Planning, in present-day, fashionable usage, means national or regional government direction or "guidance" of the economy, directly or through agencies. It entails centralized decisions on what ought to be produced and in what quantities, and may require decisions about prices, costs, location and the development of productive capacity. Such "economic planning" differs from the use of general fiscal and monetary policy to regulate total money flows in the economy without conscious discrimination, and from other forms of government intervention in the economy—e.g. redistribution of capital wealth or income by taxation and legal restrictions on monopoly power. Some economists say that the creation of a legal and institutional framework for an otherwise free market economy is no less a form of planning. Individual consumers or business men may also be said to plan in so far as they try to assess future wants and the means of fulfilling them and act accordingly.

All the advanced industrial countries "plan" in these several senses in varying combination. Plans may vary in extent, detail and status. The *extent* of government planning may be only a narrow public sector. Even here, in planning the future mileage of roads or output of atomic power stations, the planners have to make a broad assessment of the prospects of the economy as a whole, and the decisions taken centrally on output, prices and capacity in the public sector will affect decisions taken in the private sector of the economy. Central planning may be carried out in more or less *detail,* leaving less or more decisions to be taken by those concerned with day-to-day management. The formal and the effective powers to take decisions need not coincide. Where a very large number of decisions are in theory taken by a small group of planners "at the top," it is in practice likely that effective decisions will be made lower down because human capacity to control large units is limited. The *status* of a plan also varies. The French Commissariat du Plan tried to co-ordinate general government plans and those of private firms whose rewards are determined not by their adherence to the plan but primarily by the market, although they may be encouraged or induced by tax incentives and access to capital to "toe the line." Soviet planning, on the other hand, takes the form of directives or commands that are binding on all citizens; the rewards of state enterprises depend officially on fulfillment of the plan, although in practice it may be circumvented by private arrangements between their managers.

Extensive, detailed planning and the use of directives are the opposite of planning or co-ordinating the use of resources through the price system. The main economic argument for detailed planning is that it may be able to accelerate development, at least in the short run, especially where there are significant external economies; but its long-run effects, especially in a country dependent on international exchange, are less certain because changes in imports may disrupt the plan. Extensive voluntary planning can be consistent with the maintenance of a market economy and may be compatible in practice with rational allocation of resources in accordance with consumer preferences, since prices and profits continue to exert pressure to sell in the dearest market and buy in the cheapest.

The chief advantages claimed for extensive voluntary planning of the French type were that it promoted smooth and rapid growth by enabling firms and government departments to identify and remove bottle-necks in future development and by reducing uncertainty about trends in the economy. French experience after 1947 made some of these claims at least plausible, but it did not avoid, and may have caused, balance of payments difficulties and devaluation of the franc. The danger lies in the pressure to resort to stricter controls and more positive planning to ensure that plans or targets are fulfilled.

National planning has long had wide support in Britain and elsewhere as an objective because it seems to aim at replacing the disparate activities of many separate organizations or firms by a more coherent, better integrated and more informed effort to use national resources to satisfy agreed purposes or "priorities." It had some success in wartime and the post-war siege economy, perhaps because the general purposes or "priorities" could be indicated more or less effectively by democratic political means—the ballot box, public discussion, etc. It seems to be more difficult to organize national planning in peace-time, perhaps because diverse and conflicting private purposes and "priorities" are given more emphasis or there is less agreement on broad general purposes and objectives. [10]

Economic Policy, (*a*) the means by which a government tries to regulate or modify the economic affairs of a nation and (*b*) its aims in so doing. The aims will depend on the group of people for whose benefit economic policy is made: a single autocratic ruler or, at the other extreme, all members of the population. In practice economic policy is usually the outcome of a political process in which different interest groups manoeuvre to achieve their aims, the influence of long-term principle depending on whether statesmen and politicians follow or lead public opinion.

In the western democracies policy is generally directed to a number of objectives, many of which are accepted, although in varying degree, by the major political parties in Britain and most other western countries. The first is that of a high and stable level of employment—in other words, a low level of unemployment. This requires that the government should use fiscal and monetary policy to help maintain a high level of total demand and avoid recessions. A second is that national living standards should rise at a desired rate. This is a matter of controversy among economists since it is not clear what part the state should play in securing "growth." The state can ensure that the goods and services produced in the public sector, e.g. electricity and roads, come in amounts consistent with the smooth and rapid development of the economy as a whole; it can also manipulate taxation to encourage capital accumulation; and it may make more use of "planning"—e.g. by the voluntary co-ordination of public and private sector plans. A difficulty is that people may prefer growth in the form of leisure or quality or variety or choice rather than in physical output.

A third objective is the avoidance of inflation, which may be seen as an end in itself or as subordinate to a fourth—stability in the balance of payments. Where inflation is treated as a nuisance solely because of its effects on the balance of payments the requirement need be only that inflation should not proceed faster than in other countries. Balance of payments stability is normally an objective of prime importance. The avoidance of inflation may be sought also because of internal injustices and distortions: inflation erodes the value of money savings and may in time undermine the will to save; it arbitrarily redistributes income from those groups living on incomes relatively fixed in terms of money to others. A fifth objective of economic policy is that governments try to curb exploitation by monopolies within the economy. Sixth, they may seek a more "just" distribution of real income by taxation and providing subsidized goods and services.

The main problem is to balance the different objectives against one another and against other aims, since pursuit of all of them at once may lead to conflicts—e.g. between growth and price stability.

In the 1970's it seemed that economic growth had become the main objective of government in Britain, and other objectives, not least the mastery of inflation, had been put second. It is not clear that this was the order of preference of the population at large, or of individuals or families. Field research seemed to indicate that their first priority was the control of inflation, especially as it accelerated from 5 to 15 and then to 15–20–25 per cent a year by the mid-decade. [10]

Economic Power, command over resources conferred on an individual, a group or a country by monopoly or political authority. Economic resources range from goods and services used in consumption to factors used in production or in commerce.

Economic power exists at various levels. In a free enterprise economy it rests nominally in the hands of business men unless it is disciplined by competition. If competition is weak or non-existent, the economic power of a single business man or a group may be strong. Part of the socialist case for nationalization is that it is designed to transfer economic power from private individuals to the state in the hope that resources are used to the best advantage for the country as a whole. The nationalization of several British industries since the Second World War shifted economic power in them from private enterprise to public corporations. In practice the problem is whether the community can discipline power better by making the power competitive, or by strengthening state controls devised by politicians in Parliament and administered by public officials.

The term is frequently applied to the position of individual countries or groups of countries (often termed "blocs") in the world economy. The important constituents of a country's economic power are its natural resources, its accumulated capital stock and the state of production techniques, the current flow of production and volume of trade, and the size and quality of its labour force. Frequently unexploited resources are taken into account in the concept of a country's (or bloc's) "potential" economic power.

A further distinction came increasingly into public discussion in the 1970's: economic power resting on private ownership of wealth (and/or high income) and economic power derived from the strategic market power to restrict output by withholding supplies of materials or labour. Some economists calculated that despite higher taxes on inheritance, capital gains, etc., wealth was still concentrated in relatively few hands. Others emphasized the power of trade unions to influence not only incomes but also industrial policy, especially where firms used large-scale specific plant that could not be put to other use (like shipbuilding yards) or produced perishable goods that could not be held in stock (like newspapers), and government itself. For economists interest lies in the extent to which ownership of wealth confers economic power (and how to disperse wealth if it becomes too concentrated), and how far economic power can rest on bargaining power in the market without ownership of wealth. [13]

Economic Rent, (1) economic surplus. The earnings of a factor of production in excess of the minimum sum necessary to keep it in its existing use and prevent it moving to other uses (its "supply price"). This minimum sum will depend on employment opportunities available to the factor elsewhere: hence it is also described as "opportunity cost" or "transfer earnings." These will be larger (and thus the element of economic surplus in earnings smaller) the more adaptable the factor, the longer the period of time considered, the more narrowly alternative occupations are defined and (with human resources) the more similar people's attitudes are towards uncertainty.

The use of a factor of production which is completely specific (adaptable to only one use) requires no alternatives to be foregone: its opportunity cost is nothing, and the whole of its earnings are economic surplus as defined above, the amount depending on the extent of the demand for the available supply of the factor. If all possible uses of land are regarded as one kind of employment, the earnings of the fixed supply of land are entirely economic rent: it has no supply price; it would still be there whether it earned anything or not. Hence the term rent is used to describe (by analogy) the earnings of any factor that is limited in supply and adaptable to only one use. The earnings of most factors include elements of economic rent, especially in periods of time so short that existing supplies can be neither adapted to other uses nor easily enlarged in response to falls or rises in demand.

The doctrine of economic surplus or rent has been used to support arguments for fiscal policies aimed at taxing incomes regarded as "unearned" in this sense, particularly land rents and land values. In theory the effect of such taxation of the supply of, for example, land forthcoming for economic use would be nil (since it is a tax on pure surplus); but in practice the effects on the *pattern* of land use could be significant and the distribution of the tax among individuals uncertain. Moreover economic rent is now recognized as an element likely to enter into the incomes of all factors to some extent, rather than as a separate category of income earned only by one type of factor.

(2) the term is also often used in the property market to mean a full market rent, i.e., a rent for residential, commercial or other real property sufficient to yield a rate of return on the capital at least equal to the return currently earned on other investments of comparable risk. It is sometimes used by local authorities that provide subsidized housing to mean the rent that would be sufficient to cover either actual or average annual loan charges and other outgoings. Alternatively, it is the rent currently being paid in the open market for similar (unsubsidized) accommodation. [6]

"Economic Review." *See* SOURCES, STATISTICAL.

Economic Sanctions, an instrument for weakening or damaging a country economically (its industry, trade, finance, exports). A refusal to trade is the most pacific but possibly most effective form of sanction, though not with Rhodesia in the 1960's. The threat of using force against would-be suppliers is the most warlike form of sanction. The difficulty is to obtain agreement among all the countries concerned, some of which would gain from the withdrawal of others as suppliers or customers of the intended victim. In the short run stocks, and in the longer run (higher-cost) substitutes, may enable the victim to hold out. In the Second World War Germany lived on *ersatz* materials that replaced a wide range of goods. The sanctions imposed by the Middle East oil exporting countries in 1973 which interrupted and transformed the economies of some major oil-importing countries affords probably the most striking example of the use of economic sanctions in recent years or ever in peacetime. [4]

Economic Self-sufficiency. *See* Economic Nationalism.

Economic Theory, the study of the system of relationships between the parts of the economic system. It yields generalizations or principles or laws that indicate how individuals or families or firms or governments react to given conditions. The methods of analysis are described briefly in Analysis. The main method is *a priori* deduction by logic from assumptions made about the nature of human beings and the environment.

The two main branches of economic theory are behaviourist (or positive) theory, which traces the consequences that would follow a given event or situation if all other elements remained unchanged, and normative (or welfare) theory, which analyses the way in which the economic system could be arranged to serve stated moral purposes or value-judgements. There is debate between economists who believe only the former is properly regarded as economic theory and economists who believe that economic theory cannot avoid value-judgement. The possible harm to the scientific standing of economics might be avoided if the value-judgements were stated clearly so that the student or reader could allow for them.

Economic theory is essentially a study of the results that *would* follow given conditions, *if* they could be isolated. For example, if there is a rise in the demand for soccer players, or nurses, opera stars, secretaries, printers, editors, or economists, their price (wages, salaries, fees, commissions, bonuses, royalties) will *tend* to rise. Economic theory does not say their price *will* rise, for events elsewhere in the economy may also affect their price: if the increased demand for secretaries leads to the invention of dictating machines and other office equipment that mechanize some secretarial functions, their price (salary) may not rise. Thus economic theory does not forecast. But if events turn out differently from what economic theory indicates *would* happen *if* other circumstances did not change, it is not proved wrong if circumstances *do* change: the logical link that it has traced between cause and result may remain true. "Facts" therefore cannot disprove "theory." But if the "facts" (the empirical evidence, history) repeatedly show results different from those suggested by the theory, the theory should be re-examined. It may be found that the assumptions were not true (there was no increased demand for girls as secretaries but only as shorthand typists); or that the logic was faulty. But alternatively it may be found that all the factual cases contained an element that was excluded by the theory. In that event the theory is formally still correct but, to make it more realistic and useful in "prediction" in real life, its assumptions should be refined to provide for the recurring element it has excluded.

Economic theory based on realistic assumptions and rigorous logic applies to all economic activity, private, familial, industrial or governmental, to giving as well as trading (exchange), to all economic systems, whether capitalist, mixed, socialist or communist, and to any form of ownership or property-rights in goods and services. The differences between systems are (in this respect) of degree rather than kind. Under capitalism property-rights are largely private, but there is extensive public property. Under communism property-rights are largely public, but personal property is usually private (and there is some private property in goods used in production). [14]

Economic Thought, a short history. The study of economics is a relatively modern development compared with the history of other sciences. Some aspects were discussed in the works of early Greek philosophers and medieval moral theorists, but the study of man in his economic environment did not begin in earnest until rigid feudal society was replaced by the growing social freedom of modern times. The period in history known to economic historians as the "mercantilist" era produced some economic writers and theorists of note, including Sir William Petty (1623–87) and Thomas Mun (1571–1641); but perhaps the first to single out the subject for rigorous analysis were Fernandino Galiani in *Della Moneta* (1751) and Richard Cantillon in his *Essai sur la nature du commerce en générale* (1755). The latter was followed in France by the school known as the "Physiocrats." Under their leader Quesnay (1694–1774) they examined the origins and distribution of wealth. Most of their views are to be found in Quesnay's *Tableau économique* (1756), which traces the flow of wealth from its origins (according to Quesnay) in the agricultural sector through the other classes in society. The work of the "Physiocrats," or "les économistes" as they were known to their contemporaries, was important mainly because it focused attention on the production of wealth and recommended increased liberalization in the economic policy of the state.

It is generally considered that the major landmark in the history of economic thought was the publication of *An Enquiry into the Nature and Causes of the Wealth of Nations* in 1776. Its author, Adam Smith (1723–90), was a contemporary of the Physiocrats and agreed with their views on the liberty of the individual in economic society, but disagreed with their theories of the origins of wealth. Adam Smith believed the individual was always striving to better his economic position and knew best how to spend his time and money, and that the wealth of a nation was the sum of all the "productive labour" of the individuals in it. It seemed to follow that harmony existed in the economic community. Man had only to follow his self-interest and he would be led by an "invisible hand" to benefit the rest of society. The manufacturer in search of profit necessarily provided the goods desired by the rest of the community in the right quantities and at the right prices, while factors of production (labour, capital, land) seeking the largest possible earnings would flow into the occupations where they were most wanted.

The time seemed right for Adam Smith. The period was the Industrial Revolution in Great Britain, but the emerging commercial and manufacturing classes were bound, at least nominally, by numerous regulations left over from the "mercantilist" period. The automatic, "natural" mechanism outlined by Adam Smith seemed to indicate that these controls should be swept away and replaced by "laissez-faire," or confining the economic role of the state to that of maintaining competition. Adam Smith's influence was profound; he was one of the first "academic" economists, bringing together a vast amount of material, producing from it a systemic analysis and making policy recommendations that have remained unrivaled in their impact.

The next forty years or so saw the rise of the "classical" school of economics in Great Britain. Its main ideas tended to be refinements of Adam Smith's thinking, but they were based on a theory of human behaviour developed by the philosopher Jeremy Bentham (1748–1832) and embodied in his "utilitarian calculus of pleasure and pain." The distinctive flavour of "classicism" was largely the work of Thomas Malthus (1766–1834) and David Ricardo (1772–1823). In his *Essay on the Principle of Population* (1798) Malthus discussed the possibility of population outrunning the available means of subsistence, thereby introducing a note of gloom into the optimistic atmosphere created by Smith's theories of growth. The tendency was maintained by Ricardo. His theory of rent seemed to indicate that in time landlords would benefit at the expense of the labouring and manufacturing classes. This hint of class conflict was taken up by the socialist school of economics in Britain and on the continent, culminating in the works of Karl Marx (1818–83).

Ricardo was also largely responsible for the methodology of classical economics. While Smith and Malthus had tended to be descriptive in their approach, he preferred to isolate economic activities in an abstract world and devise conclusions that could then be compared with events in the real world. This "deductive" approach set the pattern of economic investigation in Britain for many years.

After Ricardo, most of the energies of the classical school were devoted to the labour theory of value, vaguely formulated by Adam Smith and developed by Ricardo. The theory maintained that the value of a commodity varied with the quantity of labour used in its production. It was widely criticized but not replaced until the "full cost" theory of John Stuart Mill (1806–73) that the value of a commodity depended on the amount of all the factors used to produce it.

On the continent the history of economic thought in the early years of the nineteenth century took a slightly different course. On the whole, European economists remained aloof from discussions of the labour theory of value and tended to follow the subjective or "utility" concept, that value depended on the personal satisfaction yielded by a commodity, developed as early as 1776 by Condillac in *Le Commerce et le Gouvernement considérés relativement l'un à l'autre.* The main differences from English classical thinking occurred in Germany, where discontent with the "deductive" method produced the "historical" school. Wilhelm Roscher (1817–94) provided the link between the classical and historical schools of thought. In his *Outline of Political Economy according to the Historical Method* (1843) he expressed the need to infuse the study of historical facts and opinions into economic analysis. He was followed by Bruno Hildebrand (1812–78) and Karl Knies (1821–98). The "historical" movement reached its climax with the great debate (*methodensreit*) between Gustav Schmoller (1838–1917) and Carl Menger of the "Austrian School" (1840–1921).

In the 1870's there was a landmark in the development of economic thought. The "subjective" theory of value emerged into prominence due to the work of three men, Carl Menger in Austria, Leon Walras (1834–1910) in Switzerland and William Stanley Jevons (1835–82) in Britain. Each of them, working independently, produced the theory that the value of a commodity depended on the "utility" of a "final" ("marginal") unit. This theory of marginal utility, which lent itself to mathematical treatment, was refined and developed by Wieser and Böhm-Bawerk in Austria. In Britain, however, Jevons's principle met with some opposition from academic economists still deeply imbued with the classical approach, and it was not finally accepted until the publication of Alfred Marshall's *Principles of Economics* in 1890.

Marshall (1842–1924) had developed the marginal utility theory independently of Jevons, but had been reluctant to publish his findings because of the mathematical form in which they were couched. His caution earned reward, for when the *Principles* was published it soon came to hold a position almost rivalling (at least in academic circles) that held by *The Wealth of Nations* over a century before. Marshall brought together what had formerly been two competitive streams of thought, and fitted them into a precise theory of value and distribution: "cost of production" explaining the forces of supply, and "utility" those of demand. The detailed scheme of analysis and many of the tools developed later had considerable influence on the development of economic thought.

In the early years of the twentieth century the existing body of knowledge was steadily refined. In America John Bates Clark and Frank Hyneman Knight, like

Knut Wicksell in Sweden, tended to follow in the tradition of the Austrian school, while Vilfredo Pareto in Italy, Frances Ysidro Edgeworth and Arthur Bowley in Britain and Irving Fisher in the USA developed the mathematical techniques. In the British tradition important contributions were made by J. R. Hicks, who placed Marshall's subjective theories on a more objective foundation, and by Joan Robinson and E. H. Chamberlin (of the USA) in imperfect competition.

In the 1930's Lionel Robbins redefined the content of economics as the principles determining the allocation of scarce resources. This was a break with the traditional view that economics was concerned with the material part of human activity. Robbins argued that economics was concerned with an *aspect* of *all* activity.

The most important twentieth-century event so far is thought to be the work of John Maynard Keynes (1883–1946) on the theory of employment. Despite the recurrence of economic fluctuations and periods of depression, economists since the time of Malthus had assumed that there could never be general employment provided the market mechanism was allowed to work freely. This assumption derives largely from the work of the French economist Jean Baptiste Say (1767–1832), the first to formulate the doctrine that "supply creates its own demand" (Say's Law). In *The General Theory of Employment, Interest and Money* (1936) Keynes developed new tools of analysis and argued that the economic system could be in equilibrium when resources were underemployed as well as when they were fully employed. His system of analysis profoundly affected the development of economic thought. Although the terminology and method he developed were soon adopted by economists, the impact of his work was mostly felt in public policy. The tone of the *General Theory* indicated that it was the duty of the state to maintain full employment. This increased interest in fiscal and monetary policy among academic economists. Keynes's use of total demand "equations" prompted the beginning of social accounting.

Despite some doubts at the time, Keynes's policy recommendations were heeded by politicians, and depression has largely been mastered. The cost of full employment has however been persistent inflation, and although the analysis of the *General Theory* provided for this as well, such measures have proved to be less popular politically than those recommended to cure depression. The inflationary tendency in part has been reflected in the theories of some modern economists who assume that inflation is desirable or will necessarily continue. While it can never be certain that depression will not return, the tendency in some academic thinking and governmental policies to take Keynesian analysis too far (itself criticized by Keynes) is resisted by economists of the classical tradition who emphasize the dangers of inflation and the need for a reserve of productive capacity and a mobile labour force if the economy is to be dynamic, progressive and to satisfy the political requirements of a democratic society.

Keynes's thinking as presented in the *General Theory* continues to influence—often to dominate—academic teaching, especially in the University of Cambridge and in some universities in the United States. It also still dominates practical policy in almost all countries, not least Britain, where politicians, business men and journalists reflect Keynesian thinking, often unconsciously. The power of his ideas remains strong after four decades or more. (He once said that "Practical men, who believe themselves to be quite exempt from any intellectual influences, are usually the slaves of some defunct economist.") But it is not clear what Keynes would have said thirty, or forty, or fifty years after his *magnum opus*—whether he would have remained a "Keynesian" when he saw the consequences of applying Keynesian thinking in a changing world contending with inflation rather than deflation. And it is difficult to judge how far his followers have correctly interpreted or developed his theories and teaching. Nor is it known how he would have reacted to criticisms of his work, or its interpretation by some of his followers, in the 1960's and 1970's.

A long-standing main doubt about Keynes's work is whether, as he claimed, it was a major departure from classical economics. The neo-classical school of economists at Cambridge, Massachusetts, and elsewhere (e.g. Sir John Hicks at Oxford) have argued that Keynesianism was consistent with classical economics, although their view was contested by, among others, the Israeli economist Don Patinkin of the University of Jerusalem. A root and branch critique of Keynes by the English economist W. H. Hutt was written in 1938–9 but not published until 1963. In 1968 the American-Swedish economist Axel Leijonhufvud of the University of California wrote a critique, *On Keynesian Economics and the Economics of Keynes,* in which he maintained that the theoretical propositions and prescriptions for policy frequently advanced as "Keynesian" bore little resemblance to Keynes's thinking. Another challenge to Keynes emerged from historical research by American monetary economists who favour the neo-quantity theory of money, e.g. Friedman and Schwartz. Their work suggests that the Great Depression of 1930–3 was sparked off by the failure of the banks to maintain the supply of money and was not the outcome of inexorable "real" forces such as the exhaustion of investment opportunities. And it was ended not by Keynesian budgetary policies for government spending and lower taxes but by natural recovery, expedited by development of the war machine. Keynes thus appears as less of an intellectual giant than he has been made to appear, but he remains the outstanding economist of the twentieth century. Recent developments in economic thinking have been economic dynamics (largely associated with Sir Roy Harrod), the application of statistical techniques to economic models (econometrics), and the economics of the political and charity markets, and of other markets that do not use money but in which scarce resources are allocated, or of non-market behaviour: crime, fertility, leisure, marriage, racial discrimination, revolution. [2]

"Economic Trends." *See* SOURCES, STATISTICAL.

Economics can be defined in two ways, in terms of scarcity or material welfare. An example of the first is Lord Robbins's "Economics is the science which studies human behaviour as a relation between ends and scarce means which have alternative uses." An example of the second is Alfred Marshall's "Economics . . . examines that part of individual and social action which is most closely connected with the attainment and with the use of the material requisites of well-being."

The scarcity definition relates economics not to any particular kind of human activity but an aspect of *all* activity—that of scarcity and choice. This clearly separates "economic" from "technical," "historical," "political" or other aspects. The problem of how best to build a house with given resources is technical; the problem of choosing the best combination of differently priced resources to build a house, or the problem of allocating given building resources between a farmhouse, barns and cattle-sheds are economic, since they require choice between alternatives. F. A. Hayek has recently remarked that the scarcity definition is misleading because it suggests that economics is concerned with the logic of choice between *given* ends, which applies only to the internal economics of a family or firm or a centrally-directed country. Where the ends are not predefined or known to individuals engaged in economic activity (or to the economist studying it), its function is to *discover* the ends that individuals wish to serve, which they do by using the economic system as a laboratory in which particular ends are tried and either retained or rejected and replaced by others.

One field of study undertaken by economists, and expressly excluded from the scope of economics by the scarcity definition, is that of welfare economics—the study of the economic conditions under which the economic welfare of a community might be maximized. Such study necessarily involves comparisons between the economic welfares of individuals, as, for example, in considering the economic desirability of policies that will bring economic gain to some people but economic loss to others. This kind of analysis is "normative," i.e. it requires the use of standards or norms relating to "what *ought* to be," rather than "positive," "behaviourist" and neutral, i.e. requiring only analysis of "what *is.*" At some point in the course of welfare economic analysis, ethical judgements ("value judgements") about these norms must be imported from "outside." It can thus be argued that such studies lie outside the proper scope of "pure" economic science, rather as astrology lies outside the field of pure astronomy, without at the same time denying that they may be of use in relation to economic policy. Although the scarcity type of definition would seem to confine economics to scientific propositions of a positive nature, the distinction between positive and normative is not always easy to draw in practice. The great value of the scarcity definition is that it indicates the essence of economics whereas the material wealth type of definition tends to exclude rather arbitrarily many kinds of activity that have an economic aspect.

Economics is a scientific study in the sense that economists try to build up economic laws of general validity by analyzing data and by formulating and testing theories about the relationships between various phenomena of social life. This distinguishes it from disciplines such as literary criticism, whose chief aim is the cultivation of sensitivity and judgement in particular kinds of human experience. Economics has so far produced only a small body of scientific knowledge compared with that of the physical sciences. There are regularities in economic phenomena but also irregularities, since human beings can respond in different ways to the same stimuli by learning from experience and thus trying to alter the stimuli themselves. Analysing the regularities is difficult because controlled experiment is impossible. Some economists think there ought to be more use of statistical materials and methods of analysis, others that the scope for such methods is limited because they are too rigid and run on "tramlines."

Economics is valuable because, first, it builds up a number of economic laws; secondly, it has developed terms which make possible classifications of economic events that assist discussion of economic policy by eliminating the vagueness and resulting *non sequiturs* of ordinary usage; thirdly, it may also, like literary or other "non-scientific" studies, inculcate judgement and practical wisdom. [14]

Economies, External. *See* External Economies.

Economies, Internal. *See* Internal Economies.

Economies of Scale, the gains in output and/or costs from increasing the size of plant, firm or industry.

Given the prices at which a firm can buy the factors of production, there are economies of scale if a less than proportionate physical input is required for a given proportionate rise in output. Alternatively, costs per unit of output may decrease because the prices of factors fall if they are bought in larger quantities.

The nature of the gain from scale can be explained by simple arithmetic. For example, a field 20 yards square and 400 yards in area requires a perimeter fence of 80 yards or half as much as a field 40 yards square and *four* times this area, or 1,600 square yards. Generally, large "indivisible" units of, e.g. capital equipment or expert advisers or education, market research or other highly specialized departments in a firm, can be employed with maximum profitability only if the scale of activity is large enough to occupy them fully. Benefits from lower prices may result from bulk buying. If the scale of production is not large enough to justify the big units of capital, etc., a smaller plant or firm is a more economic unit. In other words, even if there are gains from larger size, it does not follow that they will be realized at every possible output in each scale of operations unless the product can be sold. In this sense marketing may be more important than production.

Economies of scale may be internal or external. The former result largely from imperfect divisibility of the factors of production, the latter from expansion of the industry as a whole. Internal economies influence the size and the number of firms in the market. They also influence the relative ease or difficulty with which firms can enter an industry and hence the potential as well as actual competition within it. If the most economic scale of production is large, the firms will tend to be relatively few and large. If there are large indivisible requirements in, say, capital for starting up an enterprise, entry will be difficult, and existing firms will be protected from additional competition. Entrants, if any, will tend to be firms already established elsewhere that wish to use their resources to diversify their interests.

Economies of scale, by limiting the number of firms, is thus one of the reasons for monopoly and oligopoly. Examples are electricity generating, in which much larger generating units have been introduced in recent years; steel-making, in which large blast furnaces and rolling mills are installed in technically integrated works; the motor industry, in which there are big technical economies in large-scale assembly-belt production. Technical economies lead to the building of large factories; where the main economies come from, say, bulk buying or massing of skills, the factories may be small but the firm (comprising a number of factories) large. [3]

Economist, a social scientist who specializes in theoretical or applied economics. Since economics requires judgement, intuition, experience and other subjective qualities, the economist requires art as well as science and is an "artist" as well as a scientist. Economists are usually concerned with policy as well as with analysis, and they usually evolve value-judgements which reflect their opinion. As with other social scientists, an economist's personal opinions need to be distinguished from his analytical skill and judgement. [14]

Economistes, Les. *See* Economic Thought.

Economists, Austrian. *See* Austrian School.

Economists, Cambridge. *See* Quantity Theory of Money.

Economists, Classical. *See* Classical Economists.

Economists, Keynesian. *See* KEYNES, J. M.

Economy, (*a*) the optimum use of resources, so that a given amount yields the maximum satisfaction or a given amount of satisfaction is derived from the smallest possible amount: the total amount of satisfaction is the largest possible when a given amount of resources is applied to several uses in such proportions that the loss of utility following the withdrawal of a marginal unit of resources is the same in all uses. (*b*) the economic system of an area, region or country. [7]

Ecosystem, the physical, chemical and biological relationships that exist between all living organisms (including man) and their environment. Ecology is the study of the ecosystem, as economics is the study of the social institutions determining how resources are organized to satisfy man's wants. Until recently the two studies proceeded separately but developments within economics related to externalities and the environment have focused attention on the interaction between economic organization and the ecosystem. Problems of pollution in the "biosphere"—the atmospheric, land and water system in which man exists—have been related to population pressure, resource depletion, property rights and prices, so that a wide area of common interest has now developed between economists and ecologists. [14]

Edgeworth, Francis Ysidro (1845–1926), Anglo-Irish economist. He was educated at Trinity College, Dublin, and Oxford University, reaching economics *via* mathematics and ethics. He became Professor of Political Economy at London University in 1890 and at Oxford in 1891. Most of his work consists of articles in learned journals (collected in 3 vols., *Papers relating to Political Economy,* 1925), but his *Mathematical Psychics* (1881) was his first major contribution to economics. In it he developed the concept of the indifference curve and its relation to contract curves. With his other works, *Theory of Monopoly* (1897) and *Theory of Distribution* (1904), this book established Edgeworth as a pioneer in the use of statistics and mathematics in economic theory. [2]

Efficiency, Economic. *See* ECONOMIC EFFICIENCY.

Efficiency, Technical. *See* ECONOMIC EFFICIENCY.

Elasticity of Commodity Substitution. *See* ELASTICITY OF SUBSTITUTION.

Elasticity of Demand, the concept that describes the responsiveness of demand to a change in price. More precisely it measures the relative change in the demand for a commodity when its price changes by a small proportion.

Elasticity may be defined as the proportionate change in the quantity demanded divided by the proportionate change in price. If a 1 per cent decrease in price results in a 2 per cent increase in the quantity demanded, elasticity is said to have a value of two. (This value will, strictly speaking, be a minus quantity since as demand increases when price decreases and *vice versa,* the numerator and denominator of the elasticity expression will have opposite signs and thus the whole expression will be negative. In non-mathematical economics the minus sign is usually ignored.) There are five categories of elasticity. First, perfect elasticity, where an infinitesimal change in price leads to an infinitely large change in demand. Secondly, relatively elastic demand, where a change in price will result in a more than proportionate change in demand. Thirdly, unitary elasticity, where a change in price results in exactly proportionate change in demand. Fourthly, relatively inelastic demand, where a change in price results in a less than proportionate change in demand. Fifthly, perfectly inelastic demand, where a change in price results in no change in demand. These are graduations in a complete range from nil to perfect elasticity.

Elasticity of demand depends principally upon the availability of substitutes. If at the ruling price a commodity has close substitutes, a change in price will probably affect demand considerably. One brand of butter is on the whole a good substitute for another brand, and an increase in its price, other things being equal, will cause consumers to buy other brands. The percentage fall in the quantity demanded will be larger than the percentage rise in price. If a commodity has no or few close substitutes at the ruling price, the increase in price will result in a less than proportionate decrease in the quantity demanded. Since, in the long run, effective substitutes can be found for most commodities, it follows that the long-run elasticity of demand for most commodities is also likely to be high. (This is an important "natural" limitation of the power of monopoly sellers to rig the market in their favour.) The proportion of income spent upon a commodity will also affect the elasticity of demand for it. Generally, when a consumer spends only a small proportion of his income on a commodity, he is relatively insensitive to price changes. Even a large increase in the price of drawing pins is not likely to cause much change in the quantity demanded.

The foregoing relates to *price-elasticity* of demand. Unless qualified, this is the usual interpretation of the term "elasticity." The quantity of a commodity demanded responds to other things than price. For example, when incomes change consumers normally redistribute their expenditures. As their incomes rise people will buy more of some goods and less of others. Changes in quantities demanded may therefore usefully be expressed in relation to changes in income as well as to changes in price. The resultant measure is called *income elasticity* of demand. If demand changes more than proportionately when incomes change, it is said to be income-elastic, and *vice-versa.*

A practical application of the elasticity concept is in relation to commodity taxation. Ignoring other considerations (which in practice may be of equal or more importance) a Chancellor would ideally try to levy taxes on commodities with a low price-elasticity of demand (thus minimizing consumers' shifts to other commodities) and a high income-elasticity of demand (so that the revenue from taxes on commodities keeps pace with changes in national income). [7]

Elasticity of Factor Substitution. *See* ELASTICITY OF SUBSTITUTION.

Elasticity of Substitution, a measurement to indicate the ease or difficulty of substitution (by consumers) between commodities or (by producers) between factors of production. The *elasticity of commodity substitution* is measured by dividing the proportionate change in the ratio in which two commodities are combined by the proportionate change in the ratio of their marginal utilities. A high value, indicating that large changes in the proportions combined would produce little change in relative marginal utilities, would indicate a high degree of substitutability, and conversely. The *elasticity of factor substitution* (sometimes referred to as *technical elasticity of substitution*) is measured by dividing the proportionate change in the ratio in which two factors are combined by the proportionate change in the ratio of their marginal physical productivities. Again, a high value would indicate a high degree of technical substitutability between factors, a low one poor substitutability. The measure indicates how far substitution of one factor for another (induced, say, by a lowered price of one) could advantageously proceed before being nullified by changes in the relative productivities of the two factors. *See* CATALLAXY. [7]

Elasticity of Supply, the concept used to measure the response of the quantity of a commodity supplied to changes in its price. More precisely, it is the proportionate change in the quantity supplied divided by the proportionate change in price. If a 1 per cent rise in the price of a commodity results in a 2 per cent increase in the quantity supplied, elasticity of supply is said to have a value of (plus) two.

There are five broad categories of elasticity of supply. First, perfectly elastic supply, where an infinitesimal change in price will cause an infinitely large change in the quantity supplied. Secondly, relatively elastic supply, where a change in price results in a more than proportionate change in the quantity supplied. Thirdly, unitary elasticity, where a change in price results in an equal proportionate change in the quantity supplied. Fourthly, relatively inelastic supply, where a change in price results in a less than proportionate change in the quantity supplied. Fifthly, completely inelastic supply, where a change in price results in no change in the quantity supplied.

Elasticity of supply reflects the ease or difficulty of changing the volume of production. If, as price rises and production expands, the quantity of some factors of production is fixed, increased production will require available factors to be substituted for the fixed factors. The cost per unit of output will tend to rise, the rise being larger the less easily the factors can be substituted for one another. The swifter the rise in costs the smaller will be the increase in output in response to a price rise. Substitution will become easier the more time there is in which to adapt productive methods and to allow new firms to enter production. Normally, therefore, elasticity of supply increases with time.

Elasticity of supply is usually lower for downward changes in prices than for upward changes where overhead costs represent a large proportion of total cost of production, because output will tend to be maintained in the face of a fall in price so long as revenue is slightly more than sufficient to cover prime costs, i.e. payments for labour and raw material, and there is some contribution, however small, towards overhead costs so that profits are higher or losses smaller than if production were curtailed. [7]

Electoral/Political Cycle, the post-war fluctuations in British economic activity, induced or accentuated by government to synchronize with General Elections. The term was used by the British economist Peter Donaldson of Ruskin College, Oxford (*Economics of the Real World,* 1973). He argued that the political influence had been "deeply built into the trade cycle or the cycle itself has been modified to fit in with the idiosyncracies of the British electoral system." This hypothesis was tested by the economic history of the 23 years from 1948 to 1971 and a high correlation was found between the acceleration in two indicators, earnings and GNP, and the election years 1950, 1951, 1955, 1959, 1964, 1966 and 1970. The coincidence could be explained by a sequence: an outgoing government inflated (or reflated) the economy to wipe out unemployment and raise incomes; the incoming government inherited a booming economy; rising demand sucked in imports and put the balance of payments into deficit; the new government, with the prospect of five years of power, imposed unpopular but politically safe monetary restraint, restrictions on borrowing and deflationary fiscal policy in the form of higher taxes and budget surpluses (in the first year of office); unemployment reappeared, the growth in incomes was halted or put into reverse, and pressure on the exchange rate was removed or the exchange rate was devalued (the second year); the economy was then reflated by easier credit and the lower taxes promised at the previous General Election (and the increased exports following the devaluation) in preparation for the next General Election (the third year). In the fourth year timing is delicate; British governments rarely go the full term, and advantage can be taken by the incumbent government in the fourth year if a favourable turn in events strengthens the chances of an extension of office at an early General Election. Sluggishness in the economy (perhaps because private industry, having been repressed, lacks the confidence in government to expand investment in response to the expansionist mood because of uncertainty about its duration) is promptly removed by monetary and fiscal expansion to avoid stagnation in the run-up to the General Election. In its anxiety to avoid recession government reflates and adds inflationary fuel to the reviving economic embers it had damped down in the second year. Rather than aim too low, the government aims too high, the next inflationary stage of the cycle is set in motion, and the cycle is completed.

This hypothesis would seem to fit the policies of several governments as seen particularly by their Chancellor's policies in their final months of office: Butler in 1955, Maudling in 1964, Barber in 1973, Healey in 1974. The incumbent government runs the risk that it may have to contend with its own inflation if it returns to office, but it can alter the timing of both the inflation and the General Election to optimize its electoral prospects.

The hypothesis of a synchronization between economic activity and political elections fits in with the recently developed Virginia theory of the economics of democracy. It also illustrates the central theorem, that Government cannot be assumed to exercise powers in "the public interest." The new instruments of economic control developed by the Keynesian techniques of monetary and fiscal measures to inject monetary demand into the economy to restore high activity and full employment, or any other instruments devised for central control by government, such as Friedman's optimum quantity of money, can be used either for the purpose for which they were designed or for the purposes that suit their controllers. In this sense, economists as social scientists are no more able to decide the use of their discoveries than natural scientists are. [13]

Eligible Paper. *See* Bill of Exchange.

Embargo, originally an order forbidding ships of a foreign power to enter or any ships to leave a country's ports; it has come to mean any suspension of a branch of commerce, e.g. an embargo on foreign lending, or on the export of strategic commodities to unfriendly countries. If a country does not have a monopoly of a commodity when it places an embargo on its export to another, its purpose may be frustrated because its former customers are able to buy from other suppliers. [4]

Eminent Domain, the power of a government compulsorily to deprive an owner of private property required (in its judgement) for "public" purposes in return for compensation. In Britain and other western countries a common use of this power in the mid-nineteenth century was the appropriation of land for railways and in the twentieth century for laying North Sea gas pipes. The politico-economic aspect of most interest is the compensation (i.e. price for loss of use) paid for property of varying appropriateness for the purpose. [13]

Empirical Testing, checking the validity or usefulness of a theory or hypothesis by comparing its prediction with the outcome in practice. The limitation of this test is that the assumptions of the theory may not have been satisfied in the test conditions. For example, the hypothesis that an injection of money will sooner or later raise prices if it is spent is not disproved if prices do not rise because the new money is hoarded. Failures of predictions are not *necessarily* disproofs of hypotheses. But a hypothesis or theory *is* disproved if a superior logic can demonstrate that the prediction does not necessarily follow from the assumption (the logical or praxeological test). [14]

Empiricism, the view that knowledge is derived from experience. A thoroughgoing empiricist would deny that there was such a thing as *a priori* knowledge. In the development of economic thought there have been cleavages (for instance, between the American "Institutionalists" and the main body of neoclassical doctrine) between those who appealed primarily to experience and those who relied mainly on deductive logic. Both deductive reasoning and empirical methods (collecting data and checking hypotheses against experience) are common in economics. [14]

Casual empiricism is the general observation of everyday events that suggest rules of human conduct or tendencies in the relationship between man and the environment. Thus, even if there were no *a priori* reasoning, or first principles, which suggested that man prefers more to less (in goods, services, leisure, etc.), casual empiricism, the observation of people in everyday life, seems to indicate that the general tendency is for more to be preferred to less. There may be exceptions, but a broad trend seems to emerge. And it seems to be consistent with the law of diminishing marginal utility (which also explains why, beyond the point at which additional units add no utility, i.e. are a nuisance or disutility, less may be preferred to more). The general tendency to prefer more to less is studied neutrally by economists, whose competence is confined to analysing its consequences. [14]

Employment, use of resources such that the output exceeds the input of effort, time or opportunity cost (loss of other work, sacrifice of leisure, opportunity for study, etc.). The economic sense of employment is thus basically different from the *technical* or *physical* input of effort and time without regard to the resultant output in value of goods or services. It may be rational for man to work if the alternative is idleness; hence the argument for "making work" as a hobby or exercise for unemployed people, so removing their sense of uselessness (assuming, of course, that economically productive work could not be found). And Keynes argued that in a slump men out of work should be employed making and filling holes or building pyramids if that provided an excuse to pay them and thereby increase total purchasing power and demand. But otherwise, and more generally, employment is a waste of effort, time, etc. if it does not satisfy the wants of consumers prepared to pay at least as much as the effort, time, etc. would be worth in alternative employment. [5]

Employment Exchange, an office to which employers notify job vacancies and workers their availability for employment. It thus helps to make the labour market work by acting as a clearing-house of information about employment.

Employment exchanges were first established in Britain in 1909 on the advice of Beveridge. In Britain there are now about 900 employment exchanges, which act as the local offices of the Department of Employment. They collect statistics of employment and unemployment, keep registers of unemployed and lists of unfilled vacancies, pay unemployment benefit and provide other forms of assistance to unemployed workers.

Some economists have argued that labour exchanges should be more active in matching the demand for particular types of labour with its supply in different parts of the country. But the sellers' market for labour produced by full employment and inflation and the general upgrading of jobs has increased the use made by employers of advertising in order to attract people in employment, and of specialist private employment agencies for senior managerial, technical and scientific staff, office workers, domestic staff and so on. Such methods probably fill more vacancies than do the official employment exchanges. [5]

Empty Economy. *See* OVERLOADED ECONOMY.

Enclosure, the creation of private property rights over land formerly used in common. When land was abundant relatively to population, it could be used in common without the danger that its supply would be reduced by over-use or neglect. When population grew and it was desirable to increase the supply of food, it became necessary to avoid over-use of land by over-grazing and to encourage more productive methods of farming. Attempts to avoid over-grazing were made by "stinting" (voluntary agreement to limit the number of grazing animals), but it was difficult or costly to enforce, partly because of the natural opposition from owners of animals who depended on them for their livelihood. Gradually over two or three centuries the pressure of population enforced agreements to restrict the common use of land until exclusive property rights were created and made possible the Agrarian "Revolution" in farming technology which culminated in eighteenth-century England. Enclosure brought immediate hardship to many and created scope for abuse by the new land-owning farmers. Economists and historians have long debated how far the enclosure movement was necessary or represented the best way of improving agricultural production.

A modern analogue of the enclosure movement is the compulsory acquisition of private holdings of real property in urban central areas for the purpose of comprehensive redevelopment of an area which would apparently be to the advantage of the community but would not be undertaken by private interests (because of the costs and difficulties of private land assembly and the problems of combining private and public land uses). As with agricultural enclosures, economists are divided on the merits of such procedures. [6]

Endogenous, internal. An endogenous influence originates within the economic interrelationship or system being analysed. For example, the familiar statement that as price rises the quantity demanded of a commodity will tend to decrease, expresses a simple relationship between two variables, price and quantity demanded. If this relationship were the only one under consideration it would constitute a "model" in which quantity demanded was the *endogenous* or the "explained" variable. The model would not explain *why* price changed: price in this model would therefore be an independent variable whose value was determined by influences outside the model, or *exogenously.* [14]

Engel's Co-efficient, measure of the relative fall in food consumption as income rises, originated by Ernst Engel, German statistician (1821–96). More recently the notion has been applied to other basic or staple purchases such as clothes and housing. As incomes rise these items could change from "luxuries" to "necessaries" (e.g. fashion clothes, houses with modern comforts and amenities); but broadly it remains true that as income rises a higher proportion is available for less essential purchases. [7]

Engrossing. *See* FORESTALLING.

Entrepôt, a commercial centre (e.g. City of London, Liverpool, Hull) where goods are brought for distribution; mart or place where goods are deposited—free of import duty—for re-exportation. The continental *entrepôt* is analogous to the British bonded warehouse, where dutiable goods are stored duty free until required for sale, or until re-exported (in which event they do not pay duty at the *entrepôt*). *Entrepôt* trade is re-export trade: a country's trade in the products of other countries. [4]

Entrepreneur, (*a*) in industry, one who ventures on or undertakes an enterprise; sometimes applied to a firm or more generally to entrepreneurship as decision-taking. Increasingly business men have ceased to be individual *entrepreneurs* in the sense that they risk their capital and own their businesses. Whether the present-day top executive should be called an *entrepreneur* is debatable. Individual *entrepreneurs* founded and developed many business enterprises in the nineteenth century. Some present-day firms are also run by energetic men who bear risks and co-ordinate resources. In the large public company, however, the board of directors and the senior executives who take the major decisions are not risk-bearers: they do not venture their capital in their own business. The ownership by shareholders is largely separated from executive control.

The entrepreneurial function is nevertheless a central concept in economics since uncertainty implies risks in organizing production. It consists in the task of co-ordinating the flow of resources to produce and sell an output, and it is essentially concerned therefore with decisions which establish and change the direction of the firm. These decisions concern borrowing, investment, price policy, markets, appointment of senior staff. The single *entrepreneur* would have to assess likely markets and demand structures, forecast the trend of costs, and, in competition, raise capital in the market at the prevailing rates. In the large firm many of these functions are undertaken by executives; decisions about distribution of profits to shareholders or retention within the business are made by the board. This division of decision illustrates the separation of ownership and control. Since the executives are not wedded to the firm in the same sense as an individual owner, it is sometimes argued that they are administrators rather than *entrepreneurs,* and that there may be a distinction between their personal interests and the interests of the firm as a whole.

These relationships are studied in the economics of the firm as an organization. Although the function of entrepreneurship is located in an executive board rather than an owner/controller/risk-bearer, it revolves around essentially the same kind of decisions. And the board does not face risks identical with those of the "entrepreneur," but its future is intimately associated with the survival of the firm. It is not entirely free from shareholders' pressure, or from the possibility of a takeover. [3]

(*b*) in politics, one who organizes groups or parties to offer benefits in exchange for power. This is the new economic interpretation of political entrepreneurship. *See* Democracy, Theory of. [13]

Environment, Economics of, the theory that postulates neglect of the physical environment as an external cost of growth through market activity or government policy. It supplements the older theory that forests, seas, etc. were despoiled because there were no property rights in them. A third approach is that environmental "degradation" is the outcome of population concentration, growing affluence and advancing technique.

A large economic literature developed in the 1960's, the most influential and prolific author in Britain being Dr E. J. Mishan. Some economists concluded that the solution was prohibition or strict government regulation of some private and government activities (e.g. manufacture of detergents which polluted rivers by discharge of chemical effluent; government airports which polluted the surrounding countryside by noise and congestion). Others, e.g. Professor Wilfred Beckerman, argued that, like other amenities and goods generally, a healthy, attractive environment and absence of pollution were not absolutes that should be "bought" at any price, however high: that they were worth a sacrifice of some but not all economic growth: and that there was a "trade-off" between desirable features of the environment and growth.

This debate led to a consideration of ways to preserve the environment from pollution not by absolute prohibition of some activities but by a system of pollution charges (e.g. to factories that burned smokey coal) and other devices (e.g. a law requiring filters for motor car exhausts) to "internalize the externalities," i.e. make the producers of pollution, private or governmental, bear the costs. A difficulty is that the costs may easily be passed on to people who do not benefit from the pollution-creating growth; and furthermore competitive industry may not be able to pass them on in higher prices as easily as government can in higher taxes, so that the pollution-creating activity of government is not discouraged.

Some economists have strongly criticized the "doom-school" of ecologists (e.g. in the Club of Rome) and other modern Malthusians, who have forecast exhaustion of the world's reserves of energy or other resources. They argue that the natural scientists who take this view ignore the effect of rising cost in moderating demand and so lengthening the life of known reserves until new forms of energy are discovered. In the 1860's W. S. Jevons similarly dismissed as unfounded forecasts that Britain's coal would be exhausted by the 1960's, which also ignored the impact of price. Ecologists respond that ultimately the limits to growth will be set by the disruptive effects on climate of the eventual reappearance as heat in the environment of all the energy being consumed: this is a problem of resource use rather than of diminishing supplies of fuels, which they see as an inevitable consequence of growth. The assertion (which rests on long-term extrapolation of trends which are themselves open to some dispute) may or may not be true: it is not a hypothesis easily testable. [6]

Envy, an important source of economic incentives, constructive or destructive, and an aspect of welfare economics, inequality and redistribution. For example, in the form of a desire to emulate, envy may be an inducement to effort, improved efficiency, risk-taking, saving and investment. In the form of resentment of others, it may encourage the urge to redistribute rather than to enlarge production. British economists have differed on the causes and extent of inequality. Some have strongly emphasized the inequality of wealth by inheritance and argued that much of the redistribution in recent decades has been from the very rich to the rich rather than from the rich to the poor. Others have questioned the statistics (mainly Inland Revenue estates levied for death duty), and argued that they have aroused envious expectations from redistribution of wealth that cannot be satisfied by further taxation. The economics of envy are discussed by a German economist and sociologist, Professor Helmut Schoeck of the Johannes Gutenberg University, Mainz, in *Envy: A Theory of Social Behaviour* (1969). [14]

Equal Pay, the principle of paying a given rate for a given job irrespective of the worker's nationality, colour or sex. In Great Britain equal pay is discussed mostly in relation to sex. Trade unions, especially those with predominantly female membership, have argued for "the rate for the job," but there are many difficulties in applying this principle. Many industrial jobs are exclusively male; where both men and women are employed there is the problem of deciding whether their jobs are similar and comparable. Even if they are, "equal work" requires equal output, but women may produce less or work less efficiently. Arguments for equal pay seem strongest in the non-manual occupations and in the professions like teaching, where the work and the degree of efficiency are likely to be the same for men and women. A counter-argument is that female employees are less likely to work continuously for long periods, since on marriage most leave for a time at least, and the employer has to recruit and train replacements more frequently than with men. Another economic argument against equal pay is that at existing levels of payment there seems to be no shortage of women workers, but the same is not true of men; the supply price of female workers is lower than that of male. Since a central purpose of price is to attract supply, equal pay may attract fewer men and more women than are required.

Equal pay is, however, being accepted in some jobs, notably the public service and education. Its long-term effects cannot yet be assessed. If it were to be universally accepted over the whole economy, the effect on women's employment opportunities might be adverse: many employers would prefer to employ a man rather than a woman at the same rate of pay. Equal pay might also raise costs in industry, where they would be paid partly by the consumer in higher prices, and in government service, where they would be paid by the taxpayer. [5]

Equilibrium, the condition in which there is no inducement to change. Equilibrium in a market for commodities, or capital, or labour, is reached when the supply coming on to the market at any given price is equal to the demand at that price. Since the number of units bought at a price must necessarily equal the number sold at that price, supply and demand in this sense must be equal at *every* price. But there is only one price at which there is equilibrium in the sense that at that price the amount that suppliers *wish* to supply is just equal to the amount that consumers are freely prepared to buy. At a lower price suppliers would supply less than this number and consumers would want to buy more than this number so that the price would tend to rise; at a higher price suppliers would supply more and consumers buy less so that the price would tend to fall. Only at the equilibrium price are the two equal; only at this price are buyers' preferences consistent with those of sellers.

Much economic analysis of what determines prices and quantities of commodities and services consists of establishing the conditions of equilibrium on the basis of certain assumptions. For example, to explain the quantity of a commodity demanded at any price requires a statement of the individual consumer's conditions of equilibrium. This follows from two basic assumptions: (*a*) that individuals always spend their incomes in such a way that utility is maximized; (*b*) that relative to other goods the additional utility from additions of a commodity diminishes the larger the quantities possessed. Given the prices of all commodities, a consumer may be said to be in equilibrium when he is distributing his income among various commodities so that an additional (small) unit of expenditure would yield the same additional (marginal) utility from all of them. Full market equilibrium further requires that for each commodity price is such as will generate just enough demand to clear the market of supplies forthcoming at that price. On the supply side, given the basic assumption that individual producers try to produce and sell in such a way as to maximize their net profit, the conditions of equilibrium depend on the assumptions made about the behaviour of production costs and sales revenue as the output of an individual producer is changed. Again, full market equilibrium for a commodity requires the further condition that the price is one at which every producer is in equilibrium but also the total of output is sufficient to satisfy the total demands of all consumers at that price.

The conditions of equilibrium will vary according to the time period under consideration. There are three time periods relevant to supply: (*a*) *momentary,* in which equilibrium conditions relate to the disposal of a given stock of a commodity; (*b*) *short run,* in which the equilibrium output (as a scale of flow) is related to a given number of producers operating with given stocks of equipment; (*c*) *long-run,* in which the number of producers and the scale of equipment at their disposal are assumed to be variable.

Similarly, in the markets for factors of production, equilibrium price and quantity conditions are related to considerations of factor productivity (underlying the demand behaviour of producers) and psychological attitudes (e.g. towards income and leisure as alternatives) underlying supply. With labour as a whole, however, the statement of "long-run" equilibrium conditions is confined to the rate of utilization of a given stock, since long-run variation in the size of the total supply of labour (population) is not necessarily related to its "price" or reward in any systematic way.

Equilibrium may be stable or unstable. If there is a tendency for the original equilibrium to be restored whenever price or output is slightly disturbed, equilibrium is said to be stable. If equilibrium is stable, any change in the conditions of demand or of supply will start up a process of adjustment towards a new equilibrium situation. If, however, an accidental disturbance of either price or output produces no such equilibrating tendencies, equilibrium is said to be unstable, and there is no certainty that a change in the conditions of demand and supply will result in a movement towards a new equilibrium. The examination of unstable conditions is important in dynamic analysis.

Equilibrium may also refer to either particular ("partial") or general equilibrium. Particular equilibrium assumes that all other prices and quantities in the economy are constant while the equilibrium conditions relating to one commodity or sector are examined. General equilibrium is concerned with the conditions under which there will be a simultaneous equilibrium of prices and outputs in all the markets of the whole economic system. [7]

Equities. *See* EQUITY.

Equity, the amount or value of a property over and above liens or charges outstanding against the property. If 70 per cent of the purchase price of a house is financed by mortgage, the buyer may be said to have acquired a 30 per cent equity in the house. The capital which the buyer invests in his equity position is risk or venture capital; he has no guarantees of either yield or capital recapture.

By analogy, the ordinary shares of limited companies are called equities. Their holders bear the residual risks of the enterprise; the shares carry the rewards of good, and the penalties of bad, trade. The equity of a company is the value of its net assets as represented by the ordinary shares. The Stock Exchange price of equities takes into account dividends paid and expected to be paid as well as market opinion on the accuracy of asset values shown in balance sheets. Other things equal, equity prices tend to rise as the value of money falls: for this reason equities have been regarded as a good hedge against inflation; but this view need not always hold good. In the mid-1970's equity prices fell severely while prices rose markedly: other things did not remain equal; in particular taxes rose on "unearned" income and on company profits while profit expectations themselves were reduced by trading difficulties.

Many rights issues, bonus issues and takeover bids have used non-voting shares. This allows the shareholders (if they so desire) to sell their bonus shares without losing voting rights. Such shares are usually quoted at slightly lower prices than the voting shares. Non-voting shares have been severely criticized on the grounds that it is wrong to require equity shareholders to undertake risk without having representation as voters. An opposite view is that there is no objection if equity shareholders knowingly entrust the directors and the management with their money, and voluntarily dispense with the control they could exercise through the vote. [8]

Escalator, device increasingly adopted to adjust values in accordance with rising prices in a period of inflation. Since the 1960's long-term contracts (for example to build houses or ships) or leases have incorporated escalator clauses which provide for increases in the contract price by reference to an index of costs or prices. (The alternative is to reduce the length of contracts so that they are renegotiated more frequently.) In essence escalation has also been built into British social security benefits, which in the 1970's were adjusted annually to take into account rising prices. In collective bargaining some wage rates are automatically varied with prices as reflected in the cost of living indexes.

In Brazil (and some other countries) government bonds, company assets, and other items are adjusted frequently by a system of "indexation" or "monetary correction," which is intended to direct attention from monetary to real values and so gradually slow down the pace of inflation. [8]

Estate Duties, taxes on property passing at death. First imposed by Sir William Harcourt in 1894. Of the seven introduced since then, only the Estate ("Death") Duty remains. Of the remainder, the last to be abolished were the Legacy Duty and the Succession Duty in 1949.

The 1894 Estate Duty marked the real beginning of the progressive principle in the British tax system. It was charged at rates rising with the net value of the estates. The rates of duty, the degree of progressiveness, the period for which transfers before death are not taxed, the property included or excluded or taxed at lower rates, etc. have been changed periodically since 1914. The general tendency has been to increase death duties on the grounds that inheritance has produced wide differences in the ownership of property, with undesirable economic, social and political consequences, and that it is least painful to tax it when it passes from the dead to the living.

For economists the interest in estate duties is to find out how far they prevent the transmission of inequality, whether there is a conflict between equalizing wealth and the general economic advantages of capital ownership and accumulation of capital, the effect on industry of taxing the owners of private as distinct from public companies, how avoidance of estate duties by gifts develops, and how far gift or wealth taxes are practicable or desirable. To encourage a dispersal of ownership and avoid increasing control of property by the state, some economists have advocated that the tax should vary according to the size of the individual legacy or inheritance (and according to the legatee's income or other means) rather than the size of the total estate. [12]

Estate Duties Investment Trust ("Edith"), an investment trust formed in 1953 to buy and hold minority shareholdings in family businesses and small public companies. Used by executors and trustees holding shares in such companies and faced with estate duty liabilities who wish to avoid selling out or losing control. [8]

Ethics, Relation to Economics. *See* Economics.

Euclidean Zoning, so named after the town of Euclid, USA, where the practice was first successfully tested in the courts in the early part of the twentieth century. It was a system of land use control by rigid district zoning which has since fallen into disfavour and has been largely replaced by more flexible zoning ordinances which do not require particular types of land use to be married to specific districts. For this reason, the more flexible type of modern zoning is sometimes referred to as "non-Euclidean" zoning. [6]

Euler, Leonhard (1707–83), a Swiss mathematician whose work has been used by economists. "Euler's theorem" has been applied to the analysis of production and distribution. It makes simplifying assumptions about the way in which factors of production may be combined to produce a commodity, and shows how the marginal productivity theory explains the best combination of factors and the distribution of income between factors. This application of Euler's theorem disposed of the "adding-up problem" which troubled early marginal productivity theorists who had been unable to demonstrate conclusively that the sum of factor rewards determined by the marginal productivity of the factors added up to the total product, no more and no less. A second important contribution to economics derived from Euler's work concerns dynamic economic models, particularly of trade cycle fluctuations. [2]

Euro-currency. *See* EURO-DOLLAR.

Euro-dollar(s), private (that is, non-government) dollar balances held in European commercial banks. They are dollars accumulated from large US overseas net lending and spending. They comprise a stock of international currency ("liquidity") additional to officially recorded gold and foreign currency reserves of European central banks or official agencies. Because of increased international convertibility of most major national currencies since 1958, they also constitute a fund of international short-term capital which tends to flow to borrowers in the country offering the highest interest rates (after allowing for international lenders' risk of possible exchange rate adjustments during the period of a loan).

If US banks pay lower interest rates on foreigners' deposits, and/or charge higher interest rates on loans to foreigners than do European banks, these dollar balances will be held in European rather than American banks and a separate international market in them will tend to emerge. Rate discrepancies of this kind were largely responsible for the growth of Euro-dollar transactions in the 1960's.

The dollar is not the only currency to have lent itself to the development of an external market in this way. In theory, any generally acceptable currency will tend to develop a separate (external) market if foreign holders of bank deposits in the country concerned are subject to discriminatory treatment, e.g. charged special withholding taxes or subjected to interest limitation. Foreign depositors will then be encouraged to transfer their deposits to financial intermediaries in other countries. The US dollar was the first, and is still the most important, currency to be treated in this manner. By analogy, similar markets in other currencies are termed Euro-currency markets. [4]

European Coal and Steel Community, also known as the Schuman Plan, after the French Foreign Minister who suggested the idea in 1950. An association of Belgium, France, Germany, Italy, Luxemburg and the Netherlands established in 1952 to create a common European market in coal, iron ore, scrap and steel. Its executive organ is the High Authority and its headquarters are in Luxemburg. A Common Assembly of seventy-eight members from the participating countries is elected annually. The High Authority (for coal and steel) abolished frontier-barriers among the six members, and eliminated customs duties, quotas, double-pricing, currency restrictions and discriminatory freight rates. A common market for coal, iron ore and scrap came into being in 1953, followed shortly by steel. There are internal through rates for cross-frontier rail traffic. [4]

European Common Market. *See* COMMON MARKET.

European Economic Community (EEC). *See* COMMON MARKET.

European Free Trade Area, the free trade area that was proposed to be formed by association of the European Economic Community with the UK and other members of the Organization for European Economic Co-operation. Following the Venice conference of 1956, it was the subject of two years of negotiation which finally broke down near the end of 1958. Major barriers to agreement were protectionism within the EEC, Imperial Preference and the opinion within the EEC that participation in a multilateral agreement dealing essentially with the freeing of trade might endanger the wider objectives of the Community. Following the breakdown in the negotiations, seven of the non-EEC countries formed a European Free Trade Association (EFTA) among themselves as a second best to the abortive wider agreement and in the hope of building a bridge between themselves, the EEC and other members of OEEC. [4]

European Free Trade Association (EFTA), "little" Free Trade Area established in 1960 following the breakdown of negotiations for a wider European Free Trade Area embracing the European Economic Community, the UK and other members of the OEEC. It comprises the original "outer seven" countries—Austria, Denmark, Norway, Portugal, Sweden, Switzerland and the UK, with the subsequent addition of Finland. Under the EFTA Convention the seven undertook to abolish trade barriers (tariffs and import restrictions) among themselves over a ten-year period (subsequently reduced to six years) beginning in 1960—roughly similar to the timing of tariff reductions between EEC countries. Unlike the Common Market of the EEC, there was to be no common external tariff against imports from the rest of the world: member-countries retained autonomy in deciding their separate national tariffs.

EFTA represented a "second best" arrangement to stimulate trade between the seven while preserving the original ultimate aim of a single European Free Trade Area. Viewed narrowly it could be regarded as a reply to the trade discrimination of the Common Market, and therefore likely to increase discrimination in European trade. [4]

European Monetary Agreement. *See* EUROPEAN PAYMENTS UNION.

European Payments Union (EPU), a regional payments organization, sponsored by the Organization for European Economic Co-operation (OEEC) and formed in 1950 to encourage multilateral trade among member-countries. It replaced the Intra-European Payments Agreements (IEPA) arranged under the European Recovery Programme (ERP) in 1948, a similar scheme but dependent on dollar aid.

EPU allowed member-countries to offset payments surpluses and deficits with each other and provided (within limits) for automatic credit. Members reported monthly net balances of current account transactions to the Union's agent, the Bank for International Settlements in Basle, where individual balances were related to one another, leaving members with net liabilities to or claims on the Union. The currencies of OEEC members (and their related monetary areas) were thus made convertible, within limits beyond which claims and liabilities were settled in gold. The limits were set by quotas for each country, the proportions of each member's monthly balance to be settled in gold or adjustment of credit with the Union depending on the relation between its balance and its allotted quota.

These arrangements did much to lessen the need for trade restrictions to counter temporary trade deficits. When the currencies of most OEEC countries were made convertible by non-residents in 1958, the EPU was replaced by the European Monetary Agreement, a scheme adapted to conditions of convertibility which includes a fund to provide short-term credit. [4]

European Recovery Programme (Marshall Plan). *See* ORGANIZATION FOR EUROPEAN ECONOMIC CO-OPERATION.

European Social Fund, created by the Common Market to help in re-settling workers made redundant by its operations or more generally by economic change. The regions intended to benefit were such as the Mezzo-giorno of Southern Italy. When Britain joined the Common Market in 1973 she hoped for subsidies from the Social Fund for the development areas of Scotland, North-East England, South Wales, etc. [4]

Ex Ante, a term first employed by Professor Gunnar Myrdal and now much used, especially in macro-economics, meaning literally "from beforehand." Hence "*ex ante* definitions" of income or saving mean income or saving as they are *expected* to be in the future in the light of present plans. *Ex post,* or realized, income or saving may diverge from the expected in so far as they include unplanned or unexpected elements. [14]

Ex Dividend, term used with the price of a share to mean that the seller takes the dividend. [8]

Ex Post, actual or realized, usually in contrast to *ex ante,* meaning planned or intended. Some economists have pointed to differences between *ex ante* and *ex post* savings and *ex ante* and *ex post* investment as being important in determining changes in the level of national output. [14]

Excess Capacity. *See* Capacity, Unused.

Excess Profits Duty, a tax imposed during World War I on excess profits arising out of the war, particularly those of the armament industries. It was similar in concept to the excess profits tax of World War II. [12]

Excess Profits Levy, a tax on "excess" profits imposed by the Finance Act, 1952, to prevent excess profits being made from the rearmament programme. Excess profits levy was imposed on companies and applied to the amount by which current profits exceeded "standard" profits, the average profits for two of the three years 1947–9, subject to a minimum of £5,000. Excess profits levy was payable at the rate of 30 per cent of the excess profits or 15 per cent of the total profits, whichever was less. It was not allowed as a deduction against income tax. It was abolished after 1953. The yield in the three years ending 1954–5 was £155 million. [12]

Excess Profits Tax, a tax on "excess" profits arising from the 1939–45 war. It applied from 1939 to 1946 to all trades and businesses in the UK (but not to professions) and was charged on the amount by which the profits exceeded the standard based on past profits. The rate was 60 per cent up to 1940, 100 per cent until 1945, and 60 per cent thereafter. A refund of 20 per cent for the period when the tax was 100 per cent was made after the war. These refunds were subject to income tax and had to be used for developing or re-equipping the trade or business. National defence contribution (later profits tax) was chargeable instead of excess profits tax if its assessment exceeded that of excess profits tax. The average yield of excess profits tax for the period 1941–2 to 1945–6 was just under £400 million per year. [12]

Exchange, generally in economics the transfer of a commodity or service from one person or institution to another in return for a commodity, service or money (an "exchange economy" is one in which the use of money is widespread); specifically, a market in which transactions of a particular type take place, as in "stock exchange," "corn exchange," etc.

Economics analyses the structure of exchanges of goods and services under a system of free contracts which are the outcome of willingness to exchange on both sides. Exchange may take the form of barter, in which goods and services are exchanged directly, or it may be made through the medium of money. In modern non-Marxian economics the value of a commodity is thought of as its value in exchange, that is, the rate at which units of it are exchanged against units of other commodities, services or money. Value in this sense exists only in exchange as a result of the interacting forces of supply and demand, and not as inherent in the physical nature of the commodity.

Exchange takes place because both individuals, firms or other parties to it benefit from it; they do so because they specialize as producers. If each individual (or family or group) were self-sufficient, producing all he or it wished to consume, there would be no exchange. Specialization, in turn, depends on the opportunity for exchanging the surplus of each person's (or group's) specialized output for commodities or services he (it) does not produce. [7]

Exchange Control, one method by which the monetary authorities can directly influence the balance of payments. Exchange controls can be applied to the use of foreign exchange for buying goods and services or for transferring capital. Sometimes exchange control covers only the second. If exchange control is in operation the currency is not fully convertible. The freedom to exchange it into foreign currencies is limited by the requirements laid down by the authorities that must be satisfied in order to obtain the exchange for making payments to foreigners. Exchange controls enable the authorities to discriminate against imports from particular countries. If dollars are scarce and francs and lire plentiful, the authorities can ration dollars to reduce imports from USA while leaving citizens free to buy from France and Italy. A balance of payments deficit with one country may thus be corrected without inflicting on third countries the difficulties resulting from general measures that do not discriminate between them, such as devaluation, deflation or restrictions on imports.

But exchange control also has disadvantages. First, it directly restricts the free choice of countries in which individuals may buy or invest. Secondly, it may provoke retaliation by countries discriminated against. (Most international organizations such as the International Monetary Fund and the General Agreement on Tariffs and Trade frown upon such intervention with free trade.) Usually it creates a "black market" in the scarce currencies. Particularly in less developed countries but also in more advanced countries it may lead to corruption of officials.

When exchange controls are intended only to restrict movements of capital, some control of the use of foreign exchange for buying goods is also necessary, otherwise the regulations can be circumvented by "commodity shunting"—the use of foreign exchange to buy goods that are then sold to obtain the currency of a country in which it is desired to invest. [4]

Exchange Economy. *See* EXCHANGE.

Exchange Equalization Account, in Britain a department of the government; in other countries its functions are carried out by central banks. The main purposes are to place the international monetary position of the country under government control, stabilize the exchange rate and cushion the impact on the internal monetary system of inconvenient changes in the balance of payments. The British Exchange Equalization Account holds reserves of gold and convertible currencies, particularly dollar assets, and has large sterling assets in the form of "tap" Treasury bills. It can thus enter the market for foreign exchange as a buyer or a seller of sterling, and limit movements in the price at which sterling is bought and sold in foreign currencies (the exchange rates).

The system works as follows: the commercial banks obtain the gold and dollars, etc., they require to satisfy a net deficit on Britain's external transactions by selling some of their Treasury bill holdings to the government. When there is a surplus in the balance of payments they sell their receipts of foreign exchange for interest-yielding bills. [4]

Exchange Rate, generally the terms on which one commodity will exchange for another, specifically the price of one currency in terms of another, "spot" (current) or "forward" (future). Like other prices, in a free market it would be determined by the supply of and demand for the two currencies, and would vary—"float"—to bring supply and demand into equilibrium. Many countries do not allow the exchange rate of their currency to move freely but control it by various devices and in varying degrees—from fixing it by regulation, with occasional changes, to influencing it by government buying or selling in the open market to remove the wilder fluctuations (as through the "exchange equalization" account operated in Britain).

After much criticism in the 1960's of the fixed exchange rate of sterling for "gearing" the British economy to overseas influences and enforcing a succession of "stop-go's," sterling was "floated" in the 1970's. Under fixed exchanges the control on internal inflation is a loss of gold and other reserves as exports are priced out of overseas markets and imports increase, with a resulting deficit on the balance of payments that can be met only by loss of reserves or borrowing. Under floating exchanges the control on internal inflation is a gradually sinking exchange rate. The question is which of these controls is the more effective.

Several economists—Haberler, Houthakker, Meade and others—have tried to devise techniques that would combine the advantages of both systems without their main disadvantages. The most widely-discussed was a "crawling-peg" in various forms and under various names: moving-parity, etc. [4]

Exchange of Shares. *See* COMBINATION.

Exchequer, the department of the public service that receives government revenue. In Britain the Exchequer originated in the reign of King Henry I; the name is derived from the Latin *scaccarium* (chess-board): a chequered cloth was used to cover the table in order to simplify the counting of money. The Upper Exchequer (Exchequer of Account), now merged in the Queen's Bench Division of the High Court, sat originally as a court to hear cases relating to Crown revenues. The Lower Exchequer (Exchequer of Receipt), originally a small group of administrative officials who collected revenue, has developed in modern times into Her Majesty's Treasury.

The Treasury is the central department of the British civil service; subject to the approval of Parliament, it imposes and regulates taxation and the collection of the revenue, controls public expenditure through the preparation of estimates for Parliament, arranges the provision of funds for the public service, initiates and carries out measures affecting public debt, currency and banking, and prescribes the manner in which the public accounts shall be kept. The traditional function of the Exchequer—the control of expenditure from public revenue, and its responsibility initially to the sovereign and in modern times to Parliament—has been performed since 1866 by the Department of Exchequer and Audit, presided over by the Comptroller and Auditor General, who is independent of the government and responsible only to the House of Commons. Under the Exchequer and Audit Departments Act of 1866 the revenues of the Post Office, the Inland Revenue, the Customs and Excise and other public money payable to the Exchequer are paid into "The Account of Her Majesty's Exchequer," the balance of which at any time represents the Consolidated Fund.

In common practice therefore the term Exchequer has come to be treated as synonymous with the Consolidated Fund, from which public expenditures are made.

The Chancellor of the Exchequer is the chief financial minister of the Crown and Second Lord of the Treasury (traditionally the Prime Minister is First Lord). His duties are to advise the Cabinet on financial and fiscal matters and to state government financial policy in the House of Commons, the most important occasion being the annual budget. [12]

Exchequer Accounts, the accounts at the Bank of England into which moneys collected by the fiscal officials—Inland Revenue, Customs and Excise, Post

Office, etc., and the proceeds of Government borrowing—are paid. These accounts can be drawn on only by the sanction of the Comptroller and Auditor General on the authority of Parliament. [12]

Exchequer Bills, promissory notes formerly issued by the Treasury, usually in multiples of £100, for three-, six- or twelve-month periods, to raise money for temporary purposes in the same way as Treasury bills. Once part of the floating debt. [12]

Exchequer Equalization Grant. *See* RATE DEFICIENCY PAYMENT.

Exchequer Return, the weekly Treasury statement showing the ordinary revenue and expenditure for the week and the cumulative figures for the financial year. It also shows other receipts and issues from the Exchequer for such items as Defence Bonds, National Savings Certificates, etc., and details of the floating debt—Treasury bills and Ways and Means advances. [12]

Excise Duties. *See* CUSTOMS AND EXCISE DUTIES.

Exclusionary Zoning, a form of land-use control applied by many North American municipalities which have adopted ordinances that carve up the area into "use" districts and restrict development in each to specified uses. Ostensibly this permits segregation of industrial, commercial and residential uses for the benefit of the community as a whole; but it also permits total exclusion of particular uses and the restriction of others in a highly discriminatory fashion that often identifies community benefit with that of existing residents. For example, multiple-family dwellings and mobile homes, apartments and town houses may be excluded from areas restricted to single-family residences: this effectively raises the costs of housing to poorer families and excludes them from the area. Minimum density zoning which specifies a minimum area of site per dwelling has a similar exclusionary effect, as do over-rigorous building, housing and fire codes. Restrictive Town Planning regulations tend to produce similar effects in Britain. [6]

Exclusive Dealing, limitation of the distributors to whom a manufacturer will sell, or of manufacturers from whom a distributor will buy, or limitation by manufacturers and distributors acting collectively of each other.

A single manufacturer may confine his sales to sole agents, e.g. as motor cars, petrol, beer, ice-cream. These arrangements do not prevent competition from other manufacturers selling through other outlets; but where the bulk of the trade outlets are tied to particular manufacturers, the entry of newcomers may be difficult.

Exclusive dealing arrangements may also be made by associations of manufacturers and distributors. They are defended as measures to preserve standards of service to the public, and criticized because of the barrier they raise to new competition in production and distribution. Exclusive dealing agreements between manufacturers and/or distributors have to be registered and approved by the Restrictive Practices Court. [3]

Executor, a person appointed by a testator to administer his estate. He has no power to act until the High Court grants "probate," i.e. proof that the will is valid and the authority to all concerned to recognize the executor. A trust corporation may act as an executor. If there is no will, or if for any reason probate is not granted, administrators are appointed who derive their powers from a grant of letters of administration by the court. [8]

Exogenous, external. An exogenous influence originates outside the economic "model" or system being analysed. For example, in most economic models of consumer behaviour, consumer tastes or preferences are assumed to be exogenously "determined." (*Endogenous* variables are "determined" within the system.) Thus a family's consumption of beef sausage (the quantity demanded) might be regarded as "determined" by the price of beef sausage in the light of the household's income, tastes, and the prices of other competitive and complementary goods. The quantity demanded would be an endogenous variable, explained from "within" the model: the prices of sausages and other goods, household income and tastes would be treated as exogenous variables, "determined" from outside, not by the model. All analytical models consist of a set of endogenous variables expressed in terms of exogenous variables: the more general the model the larger the number of variables that are "explained" or "determined" by the model, i.e. are endogenous. Models of National Product, for example, treat National Product, consumption spending, investment spending and the rate of interest as endogenous variables; government spending, foreign spending, and the quantity of money as exogenous variables. If the values of the exogenous variables are known, together with the set of statistically-determined constants which link the several variables, the outcome is a set of simultaneous equations in which the number of endogenous variables whose values are to be determined is equal to the number of equations. The mathematics of simpler models of this kind are straightforward: the difficulty lies in attaching values—to the exogenous variables and to the strategic constants—that are significant for forecasting. No amount of mathematical manipulation of hindsight will provide foresight. [14]

Expectations, the attitude to the future that influences decisions in the present. The consumption and production of commodities requires time. Their prices and the quantities bought and sold depend not only upon existing preferences and available resources but also upon expectations about future prices. The quantity which people are willing to buy and sell depends upon current prices and what people believe to be their probable tendency. Expectations about the course of prices, therefore, influence economic decisions by individuals, business men and public authorities, and thus the pattern of economic activity.

The development of dynamic methods of economic analysis during the twentieth century, with the emphasis on the interdependence of economic forces through *time*, has led to the incorporation of expectations into economic theory. The decisions of *entrepreneurs* to buy and sell take into account current and expected future prices. As the price of a commodity rises, *entrepreneurs* speculate about its future course. If they think the rise will continue, more of the product will be produced. This decision will affect demand for factors of production. Sellers who expect the future price to exceed the current price will tend to delay sales. Similarly, sellers who expect the future price to be less than the current price will try to sell as much as possible at the current price.

Expectations are especially important in the liquidity preference theory of the rate of interest. The demand for money to satisfy the speculative motive depends fundamentally not upon the current rate of interest but upon expectations of changes in it. If the current rate is "low" (and the prices of securities are therefore "high"), as judged by experience, people will expect the prices of securities to fall. They will wish to hold money rather than securities because the cost of holding money is low and they are anxious to avoid capital losses if security prices fall. Similarly, if the rate of interest is considered to be "high," the prices of securities will be expected to rise and people will prefer to hold securities instead of cash because the cost of holding money is high, and capital gains would be made if security prices rose. Expectations about the future rate of interest thus help to determine the current rate of interest.

Similarly, the current price of a commodity which costs little or nothing to store, i.e. carry through time, will tend to reflect expectations regarding its future price. Where costs of carrying stock are significant, they will complicate the relationship between current (or spot) and expected future prices.

Expectations help to determine current prices, but it is difficult to know what determines expectations. They are presumably governed by experience, but the interpretation of experience varies widely between individuals. [14]

Expenditure Tax, a tax on personal expenditure. Its advocates claim it would be more equitable than income tax because it would tax all moneys spent (including capital) and not merely income, and thus tend to equalize purchasing power more than does income tax. Taxpayers would be assessed directly (as with the existing income tax). The basis of assessment would be: initial balance of cash, etc., *plus* receipts during the year, *minus* end-of-year balance and any investments made during the year. Since it would be a direct tax its rate could be adjusted to the scale of expenditure in similar manner to income tax. It would, however, be difficult to administer, particularly if levied on payments for services. It would have to be comprehensive if a low rate were levied, and this would mean taxing food, which accounts for over a quarter of personal consumer expenditure in the UK. [12]

Exploitation, (*a*) the profitable use of human or natural resources—from a voice for singing to a reservoir for yachting. [7]

(*b*) a payment for a service or commodity that is less than its value. Karl Marx popularized the term in his argument that capitalists exploited workers by paying wages that were less than the value of their output. By controlling the capital equipment and the means of subsistence they could force workers to accept wages no more than they required for subsistence, the "surplus" value being the measure of the exploitation. George Bernard Shaw objected (in a letter to a journal in about 1885) that competing capitalists would sell the product for less and less until the price approached the wage, so that the exploitation or surplus value would be reduced or virtually wiped out. (Competition among capitalists for labour would also drive wages up, and the main beneficiaries of the lower prices would be the workers.)

Modern Marxist economists, e.g. Joan Robinson, have formulated a more precise definition in present-day economic terminology—that the measure of exploitation is the difference between a wage and the value of the worker's marginal product. [5]

Export Base Theory. *See* Economic Base Theory.

Export Multiplier, the net effect on a country's level of national income of an increase in its receipts from exports arising out of a shift in world demand from the goods of other countries. In the simplest case, if two countries only, A and B, are considered and a shift occurs in "world" demand from B's to A's goods, the total increase in spending and income in A will be the sum of (*a*) the initial increase in export spending, *plus* (*b*) any induced domestic consumption spending, *minus* (*c*) any induced spending on imports from B, *plus* (*d*) any further "induced spending" by B on A's goods arising out of (*c*). The size of (*b*) will depend on A's marginal propensities to consume and save; that of (*c*) will depend on A's marginal propensity to import; that of (*d*) will depend on both A's and B's marginal propensities to consume and save and B's marginal propensity to import. [4]

Exports, sales abroad of a country's goods and services, some "visible" (goods), others "invisible" (services).

Historically, "sales" should include the exchange of goods not only against money but also against other goods—barter. The Greek and Phoenician merchants would not part with their goods for the currencies of other countries, for they were interested in the direct exchange of goods for goods. In the Middle Ages new centres of export trade developed in Europe and merchant capitalism gradually became important in government policy, especially in England and France. These developments led, in the seventeenth century, to the establishment of the "mercantilist system," according to which exports were the only way of attracting precious metals to a country and building up a "favourable" balance of trade. The Industrial Revolution and the paramount importance it gave to Great Britain in international trade provided the ground on which free trade ruled for many years.

In opposition to mercantilism, the free play of supply and demand in world markets became the main object of trade policy and competition for individual profit (or avoidance of loss) was relied upon to ensure the flow of goods, services and precious metals leading to a favourable balance of payments. The working basis of the system was the gold standard. In the early 1930's free trade and the gold standard collapsed for various reasons, in part the strain of accumulated changes in industrial conditions brought about by the Industrial Revolution itself. In recent times rising exports are thought desirable not only as earners of precious metals but also as a source of and demand for the rising level of goods and services produced to maintain full employment. Export promotion has thus become one of the major aims of economic policy in most parts of the world.

Britain exports about a fifth of her domestic output to pay for food and raw materials. This dependence on overseas imports limits the extent to which she can pursue economic policies such as national planning which would be disrupted by the free flow of exports and imports. [4]

Exports, Invisible. *See* Balance of Payments.

Exports, Unrequited. *See* Unrequited Exports.

Exports, Visible. *See* Balance of Payments.

Expropriation, the confiscation, denial or restriction of private property rights by the state. Whether the expropriation is regarded as legal or illegal turns on the adequacy of compensation offered (if any). Most states have well-established legal codes governing the occasions when property may be *taken* and the compensation payable, e.g. the law of eminent domain (USA), expropriation (Canada), compulsory purchase (Britain). The law relating to the *restriction* of private property rights is less well signposted: many Town Planning restrictions on land use in Britain attract no compensation, but if damaging enough may give an owner the right to demand that the state acquire the whole interest and pay compensation. Usually, expropriation with nominal or no compensation is a measure reserved for foreign-owned interests in a country, especially where the likelihood of retaliation in kind is small, e.g. the assets of mining and petroleum companies in some African and Asian countries. [10]

External Economies, the economies of scale that result from the growth of an industry, or from industry in general. They are a result of increasing size and its increased division of labour (specialization) and better use of large indivisible factors of production.

In a highly industrialized country all firms benefit from well organized and efficient transport services, from a stable monetary system and from other specialized services. Similarly the growth of an industry can produce economies of scale for its firms. Thus, the growth of manufacturing industries leads to the development of the machinery industries, and *all* manufacturing enterprise can use their specialist goods and services. As the motor industry grew, rubber manufacturers specialized in the production of tyres, which are supplied to all motor firms. Frequently the expansion of industry in an area leads to the emergence of a skilled labour force, and all firms within the industry benefit. [3]

Externalities, term used increasingly in the 1960's and 1970's for the third-party, neighbourhood or spillover effects of private activities in the market or of government action. The concept is thought to have been originated by the British economist A. C. Pigou (in *The Economics of Welfare,* 1920) to analyse the divergence between the marginal private net product and marginal social net product of economic acts, although there is an earlier echo of the distinction in an analysis by George Bernard Shaw of differences between private and social costs in 1908. The simplest example of an external cost or detriment is factory smoke or railway engine smoke that spreads soot and grime over the surrounding countryside, people, clothes, etc. for which those adversely affected cannot make the factory owner or government railway corporation pay. An example of an external benefit is the building of a new shopping centre or motorway which benefits people living nearby more than others more distant, although both groups pay the same prices at the shops and the same taxes for use of the road.

Much of the development of economic theory in the 1960's and 1970's grew from the closer and more refined analysis of externalities into consumption externalities (e.g. "infilling" in a suburb that increases road traffic and congestion on the approaches to railway stations) and production externalities (e.g. benefit derived by a firm from training received by its employees at their previous jobs). How far this analysis and such examples are valid depend on whether the external effects are *anticipated* or reflected in costs or prices after the event. If "infilling" is seen as a possibility in suburbs in which some houses have large gardens bordering on roads, the prices of other houses will be lower than if "infilling" is thought to be unlikely, or less likely. If some firms are known to have good training schemes, untrained men will in time tend to accept lower pay in order to learn skills they can use in other firms, from which they will expect (and receive) higher pay. In time the market can thus anticipate and absorb many forms of consumption and production externalities and reflect them in prices.

Those it cannot anticipate or absorb may require action by government to close the gap between private and social benefits or detriments. Pigou and other economists advocated a system of taxes to discourage activities that generated external detriments and subsidies to encourage and extend activities that generated benefits. The main difficulty here is that taxes and subsidies cannot accurately be adjusted to external detriments and benefits because the latter cannot usually be measured with much refinement. Also in countries such as Britain where government controls or regulates a large part of the economy, and therefore itself generates a large part of total externalities, it is not likely to be as restrictive of detriment-creating government action as of private activities, or as liberal in subsidizing benefit-creating private as government activities, and might therefore in practice introduce further distortions in the use of resources. Government may be more successful in "internalizing" the externalities by statutory enforcement of standards, e.g. requiring that motor cars that emit noxious fumes shall be fitted with filters or suppressors, or that medicines with harmful side-effects shall not be manufactured or consumed unless the effects are prevented.

Almost all economic activities, private or governmental, have external effects, and attempts to prevent, or calculate and compensate for them would probably make the economy seize up. In many instances the effort to prevent or control them may be more costly than their effects, and it may be better to tolerate some of them as unavoidable consequences of human fallibility.

The theoretical analysis of the distinction between private and social effects has been contested by the British economist Professor R. H. Coase and the Chinese-American economist Professor Steven Cheung, both working in the United States. They have argued that the gap could be closed or removed by appropriate re-definition of property rights. This approach has been applied to the re-interpretation of history by North and Thomas (*see* Economic Organization). [13]

Extrapolation. *See* Regression Analysis.

F

Fabian Socialism, the theory that the essential of socialism was public property in land because private appropriation of land was the source of unjust privileges that socialism would remove. The impressive supporting economic analysis was the (Ricardian) classical theory of the rent of land: that since the supply of land was fixed, increased demand for its product with the growth of population would not enlarge its supply but drive up rents.

The main early theoreticians of Fabian Socialism, George Bernard Shaw and Sidney Webb (founder of the London School of Economics), were acute thinkers who have had more influence than the academic economists. The private ownership of land was also criticized by the classical economist John Stuart Mill (in 1859) and nationalization was advocated from 1882 by the unorthodox American critic Henry George, who influenced Shaw.

As the 19th century went on, the supply of land was extended. The repeal of the Corn Laws enlarged the supply to meet the growing demand for food. Free trade made land and wheat cheap. The Fabians had over-estimated rent as an element in national income. They included the rent of buildings; the rent of all land was probably about 5 per cent of income, not the 16–17 per cent estimated by the Fabians in the 1880's. Rural rents were also falling absolutely from the 1870's, and as a share of national income from the time of the Napoleonic Wars.

Shaw and Webb tried to widen the criticism of private property in land by assimilating capital with land and including interest on capital with rent on land. By "land," the classical economics meant not only the soil but all natural resources that could not be reproduced; in their sense land was only a small part of the total capital, which was highly liquid in form and reproducible and expandable in quantity.

The Fabians tried to apply the theory of rent to the "rent of ability" of superior workers, whose relatively high earnings were attributed to the "monopoly" of education among property-owning families. The main difficulty with this analysis was that people were not fixed in supply.

The Fabians criticized capitalism for generating unequal incomes. Shaw argued there was no objective basis for distributing income but equality (some economists have argued that competitive markets measure objectively the value placed by consumers on the produce of different kinds of labour); and that unequal income led to unequal consumption (logically this is an argument for increasing consumption by people with low incomes, rather than for equality of incomes among people with unequal requirements).

Economists have differed on the validity of Fabian Socialism but it has had much influence for almost a century on British economic and political thought. The Fabians advised gradual introduction of socialism by parliamentary persuasion, not by violent revolution. Fabius Cunctator was a Roman general who employed delaying tactics because he judged time was on his side. [10]

Face Value, or nominal value, the value stated on the face of a security as distinguished from the market value. It represents the amount at which a security is due to be redeemed or repaid when it matures. [8]

Factor, (*a*) in trade, a specialist who collects normal trade debts and finances their owners. He is paid by commission for recording and monitoring debts and for taking the financial risks by buying the goods and re-selling them to the purchasers. [7]

(*b*) in statistics, an element in an equation. [14]

Factor of Production, a source of scarce services which contribute towards valued output; i.e. factors are services the demand for which would exceed supply if the price were nil. Some essential ingredients of production, such as air or gravitation, are free goods and do not enter into economic calculations; they are therefore not considered to be factors of production. As production of most goods involves a large number of stages from agriculture and mining through manufacturing to distribution, the output of one stage is often a factor of production in a later stage; e.g. wool is a product from the standpoint of sheep-farmers, but to the spinning industry it is a factor of production.

Members of industrialized economies own and control a wide range of factors of production, including their personal potentialities and tangible property. They were classified traditionally into three broad categories, land, labour and capital, which earned income called rent, wages and profits. Land consisted of all gifts of nature which yield income: unimproved agricultural and building land, mines, fisheries, etc. Labour meant people of every kind, with all their varied physical and mental powers and skills. Capital meant all man-made resources. In modern economic theory rent, wages and profits no longer call for separate explanation, and this broad classification has little significance for production. There is little point in lumping together bureaucrats and butcher's knife-hafters as labour, distinguishing between original and man-made properties of land, or grouping together as capital such diverse factors as shops, lorries and lubricating oil. All labour is human, and all aspects of employment therefore receive special attention in labour economics. The three categories are usually retained in broad economic surveys of a country's resources (especially with regard to under-developed areas), and some theories of economic growth have been built up in terms of capital/output, capital/head and capital/acre ratios.

In economic analysis, however, it is more enlightening to group together all factors, whether acres, workers or capital goods, that can be considered as a separate factor of production. Each unit of any given factor is then a perfect substitute for any other unit. This method gives a large number of factors of production; but it permits generalization about the principles on which factors are combined and incomes shared out amongst their owners. The main uses of the concept of factor of production in economic analysis are in the theory of production, which has been developed to explain choices made between alternative combinations of resources, the theory of factor prices, which together with ownership determine the distribution of income, and the theory of costs of production, which depend upon the combinations of resources chosen and the prices that have to be paid for them.

The important distinctions are thus between specific and versatile (non-specific), fixed and variable, and divisible and indivisible factors. Specificity and versatility are in practice matters of degree. The sharp distinction drawn in economic analysis is enlightening however, because with a completely specific factor the economic problem of its use is the simple one of deciding whether its unique product has value, whereas versatile factors pose the more complicated problem of ensuring that they are not used for any purpose which is less highly valued than alternatives. Fixed factors are those whose cost is constant over a range of output, e.g. a bridge or a machine; variable factors are those whose quantity employed and cost vary continuously with output, as raw materials. This distinction is important in explaining why firms that have "sunk" costs in fixed factors may choose temporarily to work at a loss (in the sense of covering amortization charges incompletely) so long as the costs of the variable factors are covered. Divisible factors are those whose input may be adjusted to output finely. Indivisible factors are available only in minimum sizes. Hence indivisibility helps to explain economies of large-scale production, which are reaped when output is large enough to employ indivisible factors more fully. [3]

Fair Rent. *See* RENT RESTRICTION.

Fairness, not an economic term but increasingly in the 1960's and 1970's applied by non-economists in non-economic discussion, e.g. to a distribution of income different from that generated by the market. It is a modern echo of the medieval notion of the "just price."

Society may erect any criteria of morality or justice it wishes for the conduct of its working life, but economists must observe that if people as individuals do not voluntarily respond to what they, or a majority, or a small number of rulers and advisers, have laid down as "fair" for the remuneration of different kinds of work—nurses compared with nurserymen, miners compared with mechanics, teachers compared with telephonists—they must be induced by other means than monetary rewards in a free market: by law, or threats, or ultimately by force. The market yields "differentials" in pay according to the preferences of consumers for the products of varying kinds of labour. If these market-created (i.e. consumer-created) differentials are regarded as "unfair," efforts can be made, as by the Pay Boards in the early-mid-1970's, to establish "relativities" that will reflect different notions of morality or justice. In the early-mid-1960's "incomes policies" were based on an attempt to confine market wages or salaries to the value of the total output of goods and services in order to prevent inflation. The introduction of moral criteria of "fairness" in the mid-1970's would have overlaid the market distribution of incomes by the application of different criteria, or replaced it by a mixture of idealistic and realistic criteria based on the practices, traditions and power of varying groups of workers in trade unions. Incomes would have been determined by relative skills and other qualities, customary wage-differentials, a desire to help the relatively low-paid, the unorganized or disabled, etc.

The alternatives to the market, which reflects general consumer preferences on where labour should be employed and how much it should be paid, are the simple "fair" rule of equality, which in practice may require private agreement or compulsory direction of labour to enforce, or the relative market or legal power of employers and employed and of well-organized and unorganized workers. In practice a compromise would be to accept a market distribution of incomes in order to allocate workers between industries without compulsion and to modify it by redistribution of income outside the market through social benefits.

The consequence of replacing the market too much by "morality" ("fairness") is that beyond a point the effect on total output outweighs the "fairer" distribution. If wages/salaries are to be distributed not by the consumer market but by government-endorsed rules of "fairness," the same process may have to apply to other forms of income, to wealth and property in all its forms as well as to income, and to economic activity in general. [5]

Fallacies (in Economic Thinking), propositions which seem to be true but are not. Economic fallacies embrace three main elements: time, composition and other "variables."

The fallacy involving time frequently occurs in economic propositions which do not make clear that they are subject to a time factor. It is not true, for example, that in a growing economy subject to various shocks and influences the major variables, wages, profits, prices and costs, *will* always find their level; but it is true that they are always *tending* to find their level. This fallacy frequently arises in modern dynamic economics, where it is often asserted that elements in the economic system will grow at an equilibrium rate; all that is meant or can be said is that the rate will *tend* to move towards that which is the equilibrium.

The fallacy of composition derives from the practice of using terms collectively in one part of an argument and individually elsewhere. This type of confusion affects a large number of the popular errors which economic science has attempted to dispel, in which what is true of a part is, on that account alone, alleged also to be true of the whole. For example, it is often asserted that what is prudent behaviour for an individual or a single firm must be prudent for the country as a whole. If all members of a nation try to save more (spend less), it does not follow that the total level of savings will rise: it may fall. Older fallacies relating to wages and employment come under the same heading; e.g. the "Luddite" notion of making more work for men by breaking machinery is plausible only as long as attention is confined to the interest of the particular individual who may thus obtain a job. Those who argue in favour of customs unions or free trade areas are not altogether free of this fallacy if they ignore the distinction between the interest of a particular country or a group of countries and that of the world as a whole.

Finally, many mistakes have been made when variable quantities have been treated as fixed. The former "Iron Law" that wages tend to sink to the point of bare subsistence is an instance of this fallacy. Marshall, at the turn of the century, did much to expose this kind of fallacy and introduced into economic theory a new sense and understanding of the way in which different factors mutually determine one another. [14]

Family, in economics, the unit of earnings (until children become independent), expenditure, decision-making on consumption versus savings, inheritance, and inequality. Government has to decide when the unit for public policy is the individual or the family (immediate or extended), or the household (which may include non-family members). [14]

Farm Price Review, annual revision since 1947 of British agricultural subsidies (and some special grants for drainage, etc.) based on guaranteed prices to farmers. Subsidies are calculated as the difference between market and guaranteed prices (at agreed quantities, otherwise the subsidy could be enlarged by farmers simply producing more). In some years in the 1960's and 1970's the subsidies were comparable to the total value of agricultural output.

In this system British consumers have subsidized agriculture through taxes rather than through above-market prices, as in the Common Market, where an import levy (tax) raises the price on the home market to the amount required for the subsidy to farmers. If production rises above the supply that maintains the required price, the EEC may buy to reduce the amount coming to the market (or subsidize exports). British adhesion to the EEC in 1973 was therefore criticized for tending to raise food prices, though less was heard of the corresponding reduction in taxation for the "deficiency payments." For economists interest lay in the comparative effects on consumers, taxpayers and others as well as farmers of the two forms of subsidy (by taxation and by above-market prices). [6]

Farming Out, arranging for part of a process of production or an ancillary service to be performed by an independent specialist. Also referred to as contracting out. The advantages of integration under one control are thus exchanged for the advantages of specialization. Further advantages are that the work is costed separately, thus providing a check on internal costs; the firm can be smaller than it would otherwise have to be; risks can be shared (but also rewards); and a temporary shortage can often be more easily overcome by buying in from several suppliers outside. [3]

Favourable Balance of Trade, another name for active balance of trade.

Feather-Bed, to cushion a group, occupation or industry against competition by methods that "spoil" or "pamper" rather than merely or formally subsidize. In Britain farmers are a commonly-quoted example, in the USA trade unionists. Farmers are said to have been feather-bedded by subsidies, grants, low-interest mortgages, import tariffs, quotas, free information and advice, etc., trade unionists by limitations on entry to occupations and jobs, as in overmanning in publishing, filming, music-playing, shipbuilding, and dock loading and unloading. [10]

Federal Housing Finance Institutions, in the USA, a number of agencies directly affect the provision of finance for housing. They include (*a*) the *Federal Home Loan Bank System,* established in 1932 and comprising District banks that lend to member financial institutions such as Savings and Loan Associations, and the *Federal Home Loan Bank Board,* an administrative agency that grants charters to Savings and Loan Associations and regulates the activities of member institutions in the system; (*b*) the *Veterans Administration* (VA), an agency set up during the Second World War to guarantee loans to veterans (ex-servicemen) secured against real property; (*c*) *The Housing and Home Finance Agency* (HHFA), established in 1947 to co-ordinate various Federal activities with respect to housing; its principal constituent bodies are the Federal Housing Administration (FHA), the Public Housing Administration (PHA), the Federal National Mortgage Association (FNMA) ("Fanny May"), the Urban Renewal Administration and the Community Facilities Administration. Some of these, especially the FHA and FNMA, were agencies of long standing, created in the 1930's, the FHA to insure lending institutions against loss in the financing of mortgages, "Fanny May" to provide a unified secondary market in insured mortgages which would give more flexibility to smaller financing institutions and provide a vehicle for financing high risk housing (e.g. slum clearance programmes, reconstruction in disaster areas) which might otherwise have difficulty in raising finance. The PHA administers federally aided low-rent public housing programmes. [6]

Federal Reserve System, the central bank of the USA. All national banks (or incorporated commercial banks) in the USA are members of the system; state banks (unincorporated banks doing business under state rather than federal laws) have the option of being members. Nearly 7,000 banks (accounting for about 85 per cent of total deposits) make up the membership. The system comprises a Board of Governors, an Open Market Committee, an Advisory Council, twelve federal reserve banks (representing the twelve federal reserve districts) and member banks. The capital of each of the reserve banks is subscribed by the member banks of the region, which also elect directors on their boards. Reserve banks account for such a large part of the banking system that they can control the quantity of money.

Fundamental banking operations are under the control of a central body—the Board of Governors of the Federal Reserve System, which acts as the central bank of the USA. The Board of Governors has final authority over discount rates (corresponding to the British Bank rate) and other interest rates in the system; it can preserve legal minimum cash ratios for member banks; it supervises foreign business; it prescribes rates of interest on time deposits; and it appoints one-third of the directors of each federal reserve bank. The Open Market Committee, consisting of the Board of Governors and five representatives of the reserve banks, may require any federal bank to engage in specified open market operations.

Member banks have direct access to the central bank as lender of last resort, and cash and liquid asset ratios are prescribed by law. In most other essential respects the Federal Reserve System works in much the same way as the British banking system: in both the main actions of the central bank are aimed at controlling the supply of money, and the Bank depends for this control on its position as the ultimate source of cash. The "Fed" has been criticized by American economists for inefficient management of the money supply. [8]

Federal Trade Commission Act. *See* TRUST BUSTING.

Fee Simple, an alternative expression for Freehold. [6]

Feudal Tenure, a system of real property ownership under which ownership is vested in a sovereign who grants lesser interests in return for loyalty or service. Contrasts with alloidal tenure (freehold). [6]

Fiat, money that has value because the public has "faith" that it will be accepted as legal tender in exchange. The contrast is with money that has intrinsic value because it is made of precious metal. The value of fiat money—usually made of paper or low-value metals like copper or cupro-nickel—thus depends on restriction of its supply: if inflated by government or a private bank its value would decline. British bank notes and Treasury notes are examples of depreciating fiat money. Since the Second World War economists have criticized governments for feeding inflation by excessive printing of fiat money. [8]

Fidelity Bond, bond posted as security for the discharge of an obligation of (usually) personal services. [8]

Fiduciary Issue, the issue of notes unbacked by precious metal, i.e. issued "in faith."

In most countries the central bank has a monopoly of the right to issue notes because it must have full control over the quantity of paper money if it is to play a decisive part in monetary policy. In the UK the Bank of England has a virtual monopoly of the note issue (some Scottish banks issue notes).

This power is regulated by rules going back over a century. The Bank Charter Act of 1844 introduced the rule that all notes except a limited amount (£15 million) known as the fiduciary issue had to be backed £1 for £1 by gold. The fiduciary issue itself was backed by Government securities. This remained the system of regulation of the note issue until the 1914–18 war. During World War II the Treasury also issued 10*s*. and £1 notes unbacked by gold. In 1928 the two note issues were fused, the fiduciary issue was increased to £260 million by the Treasury, and all notes were again issued by the Bank of England.

Since 1931 holders of Bank of England notes have not been entitled to demand gold for them, though a large part of the country's gold reserve was held in the Issue Department of the Bank of England. On the outbreak of World War II the entire gold holdings of the Issue Department (with the exception of an insignificant quantity that scarcely figures in the Bank's returns) were transferred to the Exchange Equalization Account. The issue of notes by the Bank of England has no longer any connection with the amount of gold it holds. The only regulator of the note issue is the level at which the fiduciary issue is fixed by the government under the provisions of the Currency and Banknotes Act, 1954. In practice the monetary authorities can vary the note issue as they think fit, subject to parliamentary approval. By the mid-1970's the fiduciary issue had risen to over £5,000 million. Its quantity is regarded by the monetary authorities as of secondary importance to the supply of other forms of money, namely, bank deposits. [8]

Filtering, the change of occupancy and status of housing that occurs as the housing formerly occupied by one income group becomes available to the next lower income group as a result of a relative decline in its price or rental value. As incomes rise, relatively higher-income groups may find they prefer newer, larger, or better-quality housing and move home; the vacated dwellings become available to the next income class in relative terms, and so on. Attempts by economists to present a theory of filtering in more rigorous terms have not been very successful, although the association between age and condition of buildings and the income level of their inhabitants is well known and appears to offer some support for the notion; also the assumption of a preference for newer and better-quality housing as household income expands seems to be supported by empirical studies which have shown the demand for housing to be elastic in response to changes in income. The importance of the filtering notion for policy is that if the housing market can and does work in this way, it is not necessary to build specifically for lower-income groups to improve their housing condition: any growth in the available stock of housing will have much the same effect as housing "filters down." [6]

Final Goods, those used or consumed directly (like motor cars). The contrast is with intermediate goods, which are consumed indirectly by being embodied in final goods. [3]

Finance Corporation for Industry, founded in Britain in 1945 to supply larger firms deserving encouragement but unable to raise the money through the capital market with loan capital in the form of advances of £200,000 or more. The share capital of the Finance Corporation for Industry was supplied by the Bank of England, insurance companies and investment trusts. The need for the Finance Corporation for Industry was based partly on the fear that the special risks of the post-war period might make it difficult for some firms to raise money from the public through the new issue market or from the banks, and partly on the more traditional view that the joint-stock banks should not lend money for long periods and thus become involved in the fluctuating fortunes of individual firms. Whatever the circumstances in the capital market immediately after World War II, there would seem to be a less strong case for such an institution in the competitive capital market of the last decade or two. [8]

Finance Houses Association, British trade organization of the firms financing hire purchase. Founded in 1945.

Financial Intermediaries, the secondary banks, together with building societies, hire purchase finance companies, insurance companies, superannuation funds, investment and unit trusts that developed after the Second World War. They were judged by the 1959 Report of the Radcliffe Committee on the Working of the Monetary System to be frustrating government regulation of the economy by supplying liquid resources that were a close substitute for money. This view was almost immediately contested in a book published by the Institute of Economic Affairs, *Not Unanimous: A Rival Verdict to Radcliffe's on Money* (1960). Further criticism emerged in the 1960's. Professor Norman Gibson argued that the failure of monetary policy was not due to the financial intermediaries but to the authorities' efforts to manipulate the supply of money in order to maintain the market price of gilt-edged securities and so facilitate servicing of the National Debt and raising new loans for government expenditure. He further argued that the financial intermediaries had assisted in the efficient allocation of resources, but they were not perfect substitutes for the banks or bank credit, and could not therefore offset monetary policy. [8]

Financial Investment. *See* Investment.

"Financial Statistics." *See* Sources, Statistical.

Fine Tuning, changing the quantity of money, gradually and allowing for time lags, to offset other forces causing instability or disequilibrium. It was advocated by some monetarists on the grounds that the quantity of money and income (and therefore, indirectly, demand) determine economic activity and hence stability.

Other monetarists, notably Milton Friedman, argue that the connection between money supply and income is close on average and ultimately, but that it is not precise or mechanical. Since government and the monetary and banking authorities deal with individual cases and not with average general relationships, they cannot allow in each case for the looseness ("slippage") in the relationship. Fine tuning may thus overshoot or undershoot the target in attempting to neutralize the causes of instability, as it did in the USA by over-compensating for inflationary factors in 1929 and thus causing the 1929–33 Great Depression (and the 1970 acceleration of inflation). Hence discretionary fine tuning is likely to fail. The better monetary policy is automatic or semi-automatic month-by-month, year-by-year expansion in the supply of money corresponding broadly to the growth in output. (This explains the revival of the Quantity Theory of Money, in a refined form, by the Chicago School of Economics.) The required rate of monetary expansion will vary from country to country according to the rate of growth of output (and the demand for money to hold: if it increases, the amount of it in circulation falls, so that the supply used to pay for output must be enlarged).

Some monetarists may thus put too much emphasis on the control of money supply by fine tuning at the discretion of the political and banking authorities: i.e. they over-react against the under-emphasis on monetary policy by the followers of Keynes. The monetary critics of fine tuning claim that the more or less regular, automatic monetary growth they prefer would not wholly remove instability but it could help towards maximum growth with minimal inflation. [8]

Firm, in economics not a legal entity but a unit of control and decision. As a first approach the firm can be regarded as a combination of fixed factor services. If it ceased to employ its labour and materials it could continue for a time, but if it failed to replace its plant and equipment, if its controlling management departed, it would cease to exist. In this sense it is the *fixed* factors which define its existence; or, in another way, the costs of the fixed factors must be covered by earnings in the long run if the firm is to continue. But there is no one long run for all factors of production: executives change, plant is modified and replaced. In recent times economists have come to regard the firm as a device that supersedes the price mechanism. This idea sees the firm as the co-ordinator of activities which would otherwise be brought together by the price mechanism. Within it decisions and transactions are co-ordinated by an individual (or a committee). If it can make a component more cheaply than it can buy it in the market, it will incorporate the task of co-ordination within the boundaries of the firm rather than through the market.

Thus the firm appears as a unified area of planning, as an "island of conscious power" within the price mechanism as a whole. In its little island it supersedes the price mechanism in co-ordinating inputs and outputs. This approach helps to explain the essential economic difference between a free or market economy, in which many small firms or planning units are co-ordinated by prices, and a planned economy, which (on paper at least) consists of one vast firm.

Within a single firm the network of decisions is co-ordinated by a management authority. It takes policy decisions that determine or alter the direction of the enterprise by establishing and varying its procedures, settle its choice of markets and its investment expenditures, and select its top staff. The administrative apparatus and structure of communications exist to absorb information, take and execute decisions, operate routines as standing orders and correct mistakes.

The firm comes into being, in principle, because it can produce or buy and sell a commodity or service more cheaply than it can be obtained through the price mechanism. In the first instance it is the product of men, ideas and capital. Sometimes one man or several men possess the two other requisites. At other times the separate elements may be brought together from a number of directions. Some firms are single product and single process, others are multi-product and multi-process. Firms are as varied as their originators and the ideas which inspired them. The simplest form of organization is the one-man business. One man does all the work and "departmentalizes" the functions within himself. He is perhaps more accurately termed "self-employed," but the one-man business may refer to the firm owned by one person which employs a number of people. This is not widespread in industry as a whole in Britain; nor are the systems of partnership in which two or more people are associated (or limited partnership which limits liability for a sleeping partner). The major form of private business organization is the joint-stock company with limited liability. It may be a private company (shareholders limited to fifty) or a public company. Private companies are more numerous, but in terms of capital public companies are dominant. They have grown up as an effective means of mobilizing large quantities of capital both by attracting funds from shareholders through the capital market and by large-scale reinvestment of profits. A joint-stock company need not be large, but it lends itself to the development of large enterprises in which decisions are taken by managerial executives formally accountable to the shareholders, on paper, although not always effectively in practice, because shareholders are usually content to leave the direction of their company to the board of directors. An increasing number of "institutional investors" (insurance companies or mutual offices, pension funds, unit trusts and others) are bringing a change here: although they may not wish to be involved in business management they cannot be uninterested because they may not easily be able to dispose of their shareholding if they are dissatisfied with the conduct of the companies in which they invest.

In recent years some economists have argued that the firm, or its directors and executives, attempt to maximize not necessarily profit but size, sales, market share, or some other manifestation of power and prestige. This analysis is based on an earlier distinction (Berle and Means, 1932) between the ownership of a firm by its shareholders and its control by directors and executives. The new interpretation is that although profit could not be neglected, since enough had to be earned and distributed in dividends to satisfy shareholders and maintain the market value and standing of the shares, there was wide scope for taking a "long" view of profit and for the argument that shareholders and their capital values would be best served by developing size, by mergers, diversification, etc. even if in the short or middle run profits were not as high as they could be. These new analyses of the objectives and "maximand" (the measure to be maximized) of the firm seemed to explain why the firm acted differently—retained rather than distributed profits, had larger outputs, higher selling costs, acquired unconnected undertakings, operated more uneconomic units, spent more on prestige, etc.—from the way it would have done if it had sought to maximize profits. An even more unconventional view is that the firm does not attempt to maximize profits, sales, assets, market shares, rates of growth, etc. but that it emphasizes the efficiency or smooth running of its management, administration and general organization. It is true that profit can often be promoted in the long run by ignoring it or putting it second, third or fourth in the short or medium run, e.g. by generous terms to consumers with complaints, high expenditure on staff amenities, building up goodwill with suppliers of raw materials or distributors at home and abroad, etc. And imperfect competition gives directors and executives scope to put their judgement, which may not be disinterested, before the interests of shareholders. But the development of institutional shareholders closely interested in the efficiency and profitability of the firms in which they invest, the refinement of anti-monopoly legislation, and international competition for investment capital, basically impel firms to look to their profitability. [3]

First In, First Out (FIFO), a principle of accounting by which the valuation of a firm's stocks is based on the assumption that goods are used in the order of purchase, so that those bought earliest ("first") are used earliest ("first"). It is thus the opposite of Last In, First Out (LIFO). The effect of FIFO is to measure the cost of goods used during the period by the cost of the original units. In a period of general rising prices FIFO therefore overstates the value of stocks at the end of the accounting period, and in a period of general falling prices understates it. Since overstating the value of stock also overstates profit, FIFO inflates the tax on profit during inflation and deflates it during deflation. To minimize tax the tendency would be to use FIFO during deflation and LIFO during inflation. [8]

Fiscal Drag, the inhibiting effects on private economic activity of the automatic growth in government revenue taken from its income and cash resources. Some economists have argued that, when government revenue in inflation rises from unchanged tax rates levied on rising money incomes, part should be returned as a "fiscal dividend" (directly in tax reductions or indirectly through increasing government spending on the products of private industry) in order to maintain general economic activity and stability. In so far as this policy is a form of "fine tuning," the monetary economists, notably Milton Friedman, hold that it relies on necessarily defective forecasting of output, employment and prices, and attempts adjustments too refined for the uncertainties and tardy statistics inevitable in conditions of imperfect knowledge. [9]

Fiscal Illusion, the effect produced by government in making taxes seem lower and social benefits larger than they are. Fiscal illusion has had more scope as government revenue raised and spent has grown in proportion to total national income. The illusion is created by expenditure on current rather than capital expenditure (sickness cash benefits to the neglect of hospital building), supporting insurance benefits from general taxes so that the benefits seem generous relatively to insurance contributions, raising tax revenue by inflation rather than by increases in tax rates, etc. Such devices are not necessarily evidence of government incompetence or cynicism but symptoms of the conflicting pressures on them to reduce taxes and enlarge benefits. *See also* DEMOCRACY, ECONOMIC THEORY OF, and entries in [14].

Fiscal Policy, government management of the economy by varying the size and content of taxation, public debt, public expenditure, government fund, etc. When incomes are falling, and the economy is depressed, relief of taxation may help stimulate recovery by injecting purchasing power and so increasing activity; when purchasing power is excessive, as in inflation, taxation may be increased to decrease it. In addition, automatic changes in tax and other revenue receipts occur with fluctuations in income and employment; e.g. under the PAYE system of income tax a person who is unemployed receives automatic tax refunds that help to maintain his purchasing power; in general, government tax revenue tends to rise when national income rises and vice versa. Public works, welfare expenditures and other spending of public money may be used to stimulate the economy in times of depression or to reduce inflationary pressure. To be successful these changes in expenditure require careful timing.

There are three main aims of fiscal policy: (1) to counter the effects of booms and slumps ("counter-cyclical" policy); (2) to raise the general level of real incomes and demand, which some economists think requires a long-run increase in government expenditure but others a long-run policy to reduce taxation in order to sharpen incentives and widen individual choice; (3) to redistribute incomes and resources by taxing high incomes and wealth and transferring them to others by tax reliefs, subsidies and other government expenditure up to the point where the weakening of incentives to effort reduces production and national income.

As long as fiscal policy was limited to balancing annual revenue and expenditure, the scope for influencing the economy by fiscal means was limited. With the acceptance in recent decades of the Keynesian view that deficient or excessive spending in the private sector of the economy calls for government action to counter deflation or inflation by budget deficits or surpluses, the possibility and range of fiscal policy have been increased. This view still prevails: that an increase in taxation is deflationary and a decrease inflationary. But it is being questioned by some economists who doubt its applicability in times when government seeks above all to maintain full employment or economic growth. Government is then likely to inflate the money supply in order to avoid unemployment when wages are raised to compensate for higher taxes that reduce take-home pay. In these circumstances higher taxation may be inflationary, not deflationary.

Fiscal policy in general also lost some support as attention in the 1970's shifted to the importance of monetary policy and the control of the money supply in combining maximal growth with minimal inflation. [10]

Fiscal Therapy, term coined by Spanish economist Jesus Alfonso ("*fiscoter-*

apia") for the use of taxation as the remedy for diverse economic ailments, i.e. a remedy verging on a panacea. Higher taxes have long been regarded, especially since the 1930's, as the main remedy for inflation when the economy is *over*-heated. More recently, in so far as higher taxes reduce take-home pay and precipitate wage demands that are passed on in higher prices (as they seem to have done after 1969), higher taxes could be a means of stimulating expenditure in an economy that is *under*-heated. Higher taxes are advocated as a means of financing public goods (defence etc.) that individuals *cannot* provide by individual payment. They are also said to be desirable to ensure private goods (education etc.) that it is thought people *will not* provide for themselves. Higher taxes to finance redistribution by social benefits are the common means for *equalizing* income and/or wealth. They are also thought necessary to ensure that gifted children or adults can be given *differential* opportunities to develop exceptional gifts. These conflicting approaches are the result of either differences in economic analysis or political value-judgements; they also arise from a fashionable tendency in semi-informed thinking to look to government and its instruments of taxation as the remedy for economic and social ills. [8]

Fiscal Zoning, a form of exclusionary zoning: the manipulation of zoning processes by municipalities (especially in North America) to exclude all forms of land use that municipal officials feel will require more tax revenues to service than they return in taxes. Since the cost especially of educational services is largely met out of property taxation in North America, fiscal zoning tends to be highly discriminatory against poorer and larger families. [6]

Fiscalist, economist who emphasizes fiscal policy (government conduct of the budget by taxation, spending and borrowing) as more important than government monetary policy for the management of the economy. [9]

Fisher, Irving (1867–1947), American economist. He began his education at Yale University, where he showed aptitude for mathematics and spent two years studying in Berlin and Paris. In 1890 he returned to Yale as tutor in mathematics, eventually becoming Professor of Political Economy in 1898. Fisher was the author of numerous books and articles but his main contribution to economics is to be found in *Nature of Capital and Income* (1906), *Rates of Interest* (1907), *Purchasing Power of Money* (1911) and *Theory of Interest* (1930). All these works are mathematical and place him as a pioneer in the development of mathematical economics and econometrics, but they also made significant contributions to the theories of capital, interest and value.

Fisher originated, or powerfully refined, the celebrated Quantity Theory of Money represented by the formula MV = PT. M is money (quantity of), V is the velocity with which it circulates, P is prices, T is the volume of transactions.

M multiplied by V, said Fisher, must equal P multiplied by T. This formula was a centre-piece of economic theory before Keynes's *General Theory* of 1936. It then fell out of fashion for several decades because it was thought the Great Depression showed that the quantity of money (M) was ineffective in regulating the economy, at least during a depression. It has lately returned to favour because the monetary economists have seemed to show that the Great Depression was caused, or worsened, by monetary policy. Fisher's teaching has thus been revived. [2]

Fixed Capital. *See* INVESTMENT.

Fixed Cost. *See* COST.

Fixed Trust, an investment company using a "fixed" list of securities in which its funds are invested. Shareholders buy units of capital representing known proportions of the securities. The fixed trust originated in the USA. The advantages for the small investor are that it reduces the cost of buying and selling individual shares, it evens out fluctuations in dividend yield, and spreads the risk, and offers some insurance against mismanagement of the trust. In practice the insurance may prove illusory because the fixed list of securities restricts the freedom of manoeuvre of efficient managements. [8]

Flat Yield. *See* YIELD.

Flation, word sometimes used jocularly to indicate an economic condition in which there is neither inflation nor deflation, particularly in general price indices. In essence it is the objective of most economists' prescriptions, although some have argued that gently rising prices create buoyant activity and expectations. Others have maintained that, as productivity rises in Western countries by 3 to 4 per cent a year, prices would gently fall if the supply of money were held constant. [8]

Flexible Exchange, another name for floating exchange rates. [8]

Flight, abandonment of a currency by heavy selling on the foreign exchange market. Such currency may be described as "hot money." [8]

Floating Debt, the debt of the central government incurred by short-term borrowing against Treasury bills and (to a relatively small extent) by Ways and Means Advances. In the mid 1970's the Floating Debt amounted to about £6,300 million compared with £850 million in 1937, and formed an eighth of the internally held National Debt in 1939, between a quarter and a third in 1945, and a fifth in recent years. About one-half of the Floating Debt is held by banks and financial institutions operating in the money market, and forms an important part of their liquid assets. For this reason some economists have regarded the continued high level of the Floating Debt in post-war years and its impact on the general liquidity of the economy as a contributory cause of post-war inflationary pressures. In recent years the monetary authorities have to a limited extent funded the Floating Debt, i.e. converted it into longer-term debt, thus making it less liquid and less akin to money. [12]

Floating Exchange Rate (at which domestic currency exchanges for gold or foreign currencies), one which is allowed to fluctuate according to supply and demand in the foreign exchange markets. The exchange rate is rarely completely free-moving. Normally the central bank or Exchange Equalization Account uses its reserves to buy or sell in the market to at least moderate day-to-day or week-to-week variations in demand and supply, but the intention is usually that the external exchange rate should reflect the long-run conditions of supply and demand for the currency. Such adjustments of the external rate might be expected to act as an automatic regulator of the balance of payments, restoring equilibrium whenever it is disturbed. For this reason a floating rate has many advocates among economists. Others argue, first, that a freely fluctuating exchange rate increases uncertainty and may discourage trade (this can be insured against at a cost by covering transactions in the forward exchange market). Secondly, it may increase speculation, causing flights of "hot money" when the rate begins to depreciate. Thirdly, small changes in an exchange rate may have insignificant or even adverse effects on the balance of payments because of time-lags and frictions which reduce the elasticities of demand for exports and imports—i.e. the responsiveness of consumers to price changes. Fourthly, in even mildly inflationary conditions, depreciation of the exchange rate may spark off increases in cost and demand that will worsen the inflation. Not least, the discipline on government to resist inflation may be weaker under floating than under fixed exchanges because it faces no embarrassing and widely publicized loss of gold or other reserves. If a government floats the exchange rate of its currency it must not inflate (unless other countries also cannot resist inflation); if it inflates, the currency will not float, but "sink," as sterling tended to do in the early and middle 1970's. [4]

Floating Value, a concept developed in the Final Report of the Expert Committee on Compensation and Betterment (the Uthwatt Report), 1942. The Report argued that potential development value in land which is created by the expectation of development tends to be spread ("floats") over a much wider area than is likely to be required for development in the near future, if ever. Because it is impossible to predict with accuracy where the "float" will settle as sites are actually required for development, piecemeal acquisition of development rights by government would result in over-valuation for compensation payment purposes as each landowner over-estimated the likelihood of development settling on his land. Accordingly, the Report recommended the acquisition by the government of all development rights in non-urban land, to be paid for out of a global compensation fund for the whole country that would "rinse out" any element of over-valuation. The concept appeared to be based on a serious misapprehension of how markets deal with uncertainty: it received scant support and generated much opposition from economists and professionals concerned with land transactions, although it became enshrined in the Town and Country Planning Act of 1947, since amended in many respects. [6]

Flotation, the process of raising capital for a new company (or new capital for an existing company) by issuing shares to the public. [8]

Flow, Economic, the movement of a commodity or service or security to or from a market or within the economy as a whole. For example, the current production of goods such as coal, steel and wheat involves flows on to the markets as distinct from stocks, or their amount or volume accumulated at a point in time. The concept of economic flows in a country as a whole, as of consumption, investment and production and variations in them, are used in modern theories of employment and the trade cycle. [14]

Flying Freeholds. *See* CONDOMINIUM.

FOB, "free on board," the name given to the system of paying for goods shipped from or to another country when the amount is sufficient only to cover the value of the goods and excludes insurance and freight. [4]

Food and Agriculture Organization (FAO), established in Washington in 1945 as a special Agency of the United Nations. Its aims are to improve world nutrition and living standards and the labour conditions of rural populations, and to promote efficiency in the production and distribution of food and other agricultural, marine and forest products. It has headquarters in Rome. [4]

Forced Saving, the enforced reduction in consumption that takes place when a government creates money to finance its activities. It works as follows: the government prints new currency which it uses to pay for armaments, development projects, etc. The effect is to draw capital, labour and raw materials away from the production of goods and services for the private sector to produce for the public sector. But demand in the private sector will not have fallen, although the quantity of goods available to satisfy it has been reduced, so prices tend to rise until demand and supply are made equal at a new higher level of prices. Private citizens have thus been forced to reduce their consumption because they can no longer pay for the goods and services they formerly bought, and resources have been released to carry out the tasks required by the government.

This technique for appropriating resources has generally been associated with wars and defence, but in recent times it has been used for development projects in under-developed countries in peacetime. The political and administrative difficulties of raising revenue by taxation in such countries are usually formidable. "Forced saving" by inflation is thus an attractive method of avoiding them. But if it generates inflationary pressure it may create more difficulties than it solves: it provokes political stresses because poor people are hurt by the rise in prices and foreign investors may be frightened off.

In economic theory, the concept of forced saving dates back to at least the early nineteenth century, and during the twentieth century it was prominent in over-investment theories of the trade cycle. These theories envisaged an equilibrium, or "natural," rate of interest which equates voluntary savings with investment in capital goods and prevents fluctuations in output and employment. If other things remain the same and the level of savings is increased the equilibrium rate of interest will fall. At the lower rate of interest the level of investment will rise to the new level of savings. The economic resources released by the fall in consumption (the increase in savings) will be re-employed by the increase in investment resulting from the lower rate of interest. In a money-using economy, however, the money (or market) rate of interest can be influenced by changes in the quantity of money. An expansion of bank credit can supplement savings, cause the money rate of interest to fall below the equilibrium rate and increase investment expenditure. There is then no reduction in the demand for consumer goods, and so no release of economic resources for investment. The increase of investment expenditure is a net addition to total monetary outlay, and the economy will thus be subject to expansionary and inflationary pressure whenever the money rate of interest is less than the equilibrium rate, or, alternatively, whenever investment exceeds the level of voluntary savings appropriate to the money rate of interest. To the extent that the excess monetary demand causes prices to rise, real incomes fall, consumption in real terms is reduced and forced saving takes place to release resources for the production of capital goods.

The term forced saving could be applied to the saving of governments. By securing a budget surplus on current account through taxing more than is required for public expenditure, a central government can extract funds from the public which can be used to finance investment in roads, equipment for coal mines, railways. It can be said that the community has been made to yield forced saving measured by the amount of the budget surplus. [9]

Forces of the Market. *See* MARKET FORCES; TIME.

Forecasting, predicting the direction and extent of economic change from knowledge of the present and the past. Some long-term projections of needs, resources and levels of output extending ten and more years have been made on assumptions about the future size of the population, the proportion of the population in the work-force, the number of hours worked per year per man, productivity per man-hour and so on. These long-term projections may be useful in providing a setting for government policies, suggesting opportunities or needs for total demand to grow, and helping businesses such as oil companies and electricity undertakings which invest in very durable plant. But most forecasting is short-term, seldom extending beyond a year. As it takes time to assemble, process and publish statistics, they are necessarily out of date, so skill is required to judge from the recent past what is happening at any moment in the present.

Methods of forecasting fall into four main groups. First, a number of unsophisticated methods, such as listing the factors which are favourable and unfavourable to a particular development, and judging from the list where the most probable outcome lies or projecting trends into the future. The troubles with factor-listing are that it ignores interconnections between the forces at work and depends on intuition to assign "weights" to the different factors. The mechanical projection of trends breaks down at the point where an accurate forecast is most needed, i.e. before a turning-point and a change of trend.

Secondly, "barometric" methods try to identify changes which usually precede the change to be forecast. The prices of ordinary shares are a commonly used "barometer" because they often fall some time before a business recession and begin to rise in advance of recovery. But share prices are subject to fluctuations which are independent of the state of business and may be in advance of general changes by varying periods. Other "barometers" have been open to similar objections; but the extensive work done on "barometric" statistical series by the National Bureau of Economic Research in the USA has provided indicators which usefully supplement other forecasting methods.

Thirdly, there has been an extensive development of opinion polling. In economic forecasting the most important poll is that carried out by the Confederation of British Industry inquiring whether members' orders are up or down, whether they expect to authorize new expenditure on plant and machinery, whether stocks and work in progress are up or down, whether the most important shortages are of orders, skilled labour, unskilled labour or capacity, and whether profit margins per unit of output are up or down. Such inquiries provide an indication of the direction of change, but they provide no clear basis for estimating its extent. Further, there is difficulty in assembling a representative sample of firms prepared to volunteer information.

Fourthly, there are methods of forecasting the likely performance of the economy as a whole which are based on national income theory and accounting. These methods range from intelligent guesses at the main totals of expenditure—the balance of trade, consumption, investment and government spending on goods and services—and checks that these totals are compatible with one another and add up to a likely gross national product, to forecasting models in which the components of national expenditure depend upon sets of mathematical equations estimated statistically. The latter mix economics and statistics and are termed macro-models. These models have also been used to forecast the behaviour of individual segments of the economy, such as future sales of durable consumer goods.

Forecasts can be judged only partly by their accuracy. A forecast which is right because inaccurate estimates or judgements happen to cancel out or for reasons the forecaster did not expect is likely to lead to bad guidance later on. Again, a forecast based on trend will be right so long as events follow a continuous pattern, but will be wrong when new plans and decisions are most needed at a turning point, such as a change in taste or technique which is difficult to foresee. In addition to the requirement of accuracy, forecasts need to be understood easily if they are to be used, must not take too long to prepare, and must not be more costly to produce than the value of the contribution they make to the better use of resources or the avoidance of waste.

The techniques of economic or near-economic forecasting are still often crude and untried in Britain, the USA and Europe. In business firms economists are increasingly expected to attempt forecasts, though their forecasts do not necessarily rest entirely on economic analysis. Errors in forecasting within individual firms are likely to be limited by their effects on costs and profits. Forecasting on a national scale in Britain by governmental departments, agencies or committees in atomic energy and coal, the demand for doctors, the size of the population, the costs of national insurance benefits, the output of and the demand for steel, etc., have caused waste of resources that are more difficult to control.

Short-term forecasting has been used increasingly by government, in Britain by the Treasury and by the National Institute of Economic and Social Research. It has also been criticized by some economists as rarely of sufficient accuracy to guide government policy. [10]

Foreclosure, the enforcement by a mortgagee (the lender of money secured against real property) of his security following default by the mortgagor (the borrower). A court order for foreclosure vests the mortgagee with absolute ownership of the property, but prevents him claiming further payment from the mortgagor. Alternatively, the court may direct a sale of the property, redeeming the mortgage out of the proceeds of sale and paying any residue to the mortgagor (if the sale proceeds are insufficient to redeem the debt outstanding, the mortgagee has the right to sue for the deficiency). [6]

Foreign Balance, another name for the balance between payments to people in other countries and receipts from them. The balance may be described as active or passive (surplus or deficit). Apart from its effect upon the gold or other reserves, an active or passive balance affects the domestic economy. An active balance tends to have the same effect as an increase in domestic investment (e.g. house or road construction): i.e. it increases demand, employment, incomes and prices, and in turn imports, and so tends to restore equilibrium to the foreign balance. A passive balance tends to reduce employment, incomes and prices, and cuts demand for goods generally, including imports, thus releasing goods for export and tending to restore equilibrium to the foreign balance. [4]

Foreign Exchange, the currency of other countries. It is required by individuals and institutions to buy goods and services from and to make gifts or loans to people in other countries. At the same time they will be buying our currency to pay for their purchases here. The two-way nature of these transactions means that as long as relative prices are "right," most of our demands for other countries' currencies will be matched by their demands for our currency, leaving only small differences to be financed by movements of gold or foreign exchange reserves.

Most countries tend to hold as reserves only convertible foreign exchange because it will be readily accepted by almost all countries in payment for goods or services; inconvertible currency may be acceptable only to the country that issued it.

Foreign exchange is required in trade because there is no single currency that is accepted by all countries, although many countries have used sterling and some dollars. [4]

Foreign Exchange Broker. *See* BROKER.

Foreign Exchange Market, (*a*) strictly a financial centre in which foreign exchange (foreign currency) is bought and sold. In Britain the members are the exchange dealers of banks and financial houses, plus several recognized firms of exchange brokers. When governments control the exchanges, business may be done usually only through recognized dealers. (*b*) more generally the complex of dealings in foreign currencies which determine the day-to-day prices of currencies in terms of one another. [4]

Foreign Investment, the acquisition by a government or citizens of a country of assets abroad in the form of bank deposits, foreign government bills, government or industrial securities or titles to land, buildings and capital equipment. Private investment abroad will normally be made in the hope of a higher interest or dividend or other income than can be obtained at home, in expectation of alterations in exchange rates, or in fear of political or taxation changes at home. Government investment is undertaken for political, diplomatic, military or other reasons that may pay little attention to its yield; examples are British loans to Commonwealth and developing countries. The problem is to weigh the political and other advantages, which are difficult to judge, against the additional yield the investment would have earned elsewhere.

The benefit to a country as a whole from investment abroad compared with investment at home may differ from the monetary interest or yield received by the investor because it may affect employment, the productivity of labour, the terms of trade and government revenue. It does not necessarily follow that foreign investment yields a lower "social" return than investment at home. It may be higher, for example, where it cheapens the price of our imports, as it probably did in the nineteenth century. And it does not follow that foreign investment should be performed by governments, which could take the indirect social effects into account, because government investment tends to become political investment, the errors of individual investment tend to cancel out, and if desirable individual investment can be given general guidance. [4]

Foreign Trade. *See* International Trade.

Foreign Trade Multiplier, the net effect on a country's national income of an autonomous increase in its spending at home after taking into account repercussions on consumption caused by the initial increase in spending and income, on imports, on total spending and income in other countries and on their demand for the country's exports. The value of the multiplier will depend on the magnitudes of the marginal propensities to consume and to import in the countries concerned. Its theoretical basis had been questioned. *See* Multiplier. [4]

Forestalling, the medieval practice of buying up supplies before they reached the local market in order to resell at higher prices. These temporary, localized corners were illegal and they became impracticable when improved communications gave access to widespread sources of supply. Also known as "regrating" or "engrossing." [7]

Formalism, a style of economic thought that treats abstract entities as real. It has been argued that the methods of macro-economic thinking (total income, total output, total investment, etc.) used by the Cambridge School of economists and the neo-classical school (largely in Cambridge, Massachusetts), are formalist rather than realist. Their "models" are said to be remote from the everyday processes of the market, and to embody formal rules and laws, generalizations and tendencies applied to large aggregates such as a country, an economy, or society as a whole; but they do not describe how individuals act subjectively in the market as buyers or sellers, lenders or borrowers (or givers and takers). This view is that macro-economic thinking, especially by economists who favour this method of analyzing economic activity, may lose sight of its micro-economic foundations, and therefore reach erroneous conclusions for policy on incomes, growth and technical progress. This criticism was made in the mid-1970's by the Johannesberg economist, L. M. Lachmann. [14]

Forward Exchange Rate, the rate at which domestic currency can be exchanged for foreign currency in the forward market. The current or "spot" exchange rate is determined by the supply of and the demand for currencies in the ordinary market for foreign exchange. In the same way the forward rate is determined by the supply of and demand for currencies in the forward market. For example, a forward rate for sterling against the dollar of $2.30 to £1 is the result of contracts entered into in the forward market. In this case since the forward rate is lower than the "spot" rate, which is "pegged" at $2.40, more pounds must have been sold forward for dollars than at the spot rate. The excess supply of pounds thus forces down the forward rate, so that the dollar gains a premium of 2 cents. This is how the forward market rates are normally quoted in the financial press, i.e. so many cents premium or discount. Usually two rates are quoted: the one-month rate and the three-month rate; they are the result of contracts entered into by dealers to supply dollars, lire, francs, etc., in one month or three months' time against pounds.

A forward market reduces uncertainty to traders, bankers and investors. It enables them to "hedge" against the risk of a change in the "spot" rate by selling (buying) in the forward market a sum equal to the amount they bought (sold) in the spot market. If a man in America with $10,000 to invest for three months finds that short-term interest rates are higher in London than New York, he can convert his dollars into sterling and buy three-month Treasury bills in London, but he faces a risk that sterling may become worth fewer dollars. The interest and even more of the capital may be lost when he re-converts into dollars. To cover this risk he can make a contract in the forward market to sell for dollars the amount of sterling he expects to have when he sells the bills. He thus knows before he enters the deal exactly how many dollars he will finally have. [4]

Forward Integration. *See* INTEGRATION.

Forward Market, a market in "forward" transactions, in which buyers and sellers trade in undertakings to buy or sell commodities (e.g. metal, cotton) or securities or money (e.g. on the foreign exchanges) at a future date for agreed prices. [3] [7]

Franchise, (*a*) in trade, exclusive authority to produce or deal in or retail a product. A franchise to produce may be given to ease surveillance of quality; for example Coca-Cola gave a franchise to produce in England to one firm; motor car companies commonly appoint a main dealer in each region; a government may authorize a person or company to provide a service (education, etc.) subject to conditions as to quality. The calculation is that quality control is more valuable than the stimulation to output and sales that might be produced by competition between all-comers in a free market. [7]

(*b*) a right granted to persons to make use of a property without the grant of exclusive control or possession. For example, department stores grant franchises or licences to traders to sell in their premises in return for a percentage of turnover. "Hyper markets" often use franchising rather than leasing space to traders in the more usual way. [6]

(*c*) in the political process, the electoral mechanism, which ideally decides the legal and institutional framework for the economy, generally determines the magnitude and shape of public goods. But increasingly the mechanism is said by a new economic analysis to be used by political entrepreneurs to maximize/optimize their support/votes/power by offering benefits, privileges or favours to sectional groups, or by manipulating the economy, most characteristically by engineering a boom by inflationary monetary policies in the approach to a General Election, as by both main political parties in Britain since the Second World War. The "economics of politics" has been analysed increasingly by economists in the USA since the 1950's, and more recently in Britain. (*See* Democracy, Economic Theory of.) [13]

Free Coinage, legally unfettered power, in return for a fee, to have bullion made into coin at the government mint. Thus it is not "free" in the economic sense: the fee covers minting ("brassage") and the government charge ("seignorage"). Free coinage in the economic sense is "gratuitous coinage." From 1792 the USA had (legally) free coinage, for silver to 1873 and for gold to 1933. [8]

Free Depreciation, method of writing down capital (for that part of it used to produce the output and profit in the period) at a rate decided by the firm, which is free to write the whole off in the first year or to spread it over a longer period as it wishes. Usually, for tax calculations, stated periods are laid down for varying kinds of capital, ostensibly the number of years it is thought they will last physically. The difficulties of this method are that capital may "wear out" economically (become obsolescent) before it wears out physically; and the timing of economic obsolescence cannot be foreseen. In a system of free depreciation the firm is free to decide the period according to its judgement of the period of likely obsolescence, the value of the physical asset as scrap, the trend in costs of replacement, probable developments in taxes on profits, and other relevant considerations. [3]

Free Economy, one in which the main economic operations and processes are conducted by private enterprise free of direct governmental control and activity. It applies in varying degree to many industrial countries in the mid-twentieth century. It is also of basic analytical importance for economic theory.

In most western industrial countries there has been a trend in recent centuries towards diminished governmental control of economic activity. Gradually feudal and pre-industrial conditions were largely replaced by freely competitive capitalism. In more recent times there has been a general increase in the economic functions of government. Most western countries have a "mixed" free enterprise economic system comprising both public and private institutions. In the UK there are nationalized industries as well as private enterprise; and there are tariffs and controls on imports but no restraints on internal trade. In the USA, UK, Germany and other countries the economy is basically free, the private ownership of capital, competition and free consumer choice working in a framework of laws and institutions relating to property, contract, company organization and monopoly that operate broadly to maintain freedom for producers, consumers, workers, investors and others to exchange goods and services in markets without detailed supervision or direction by governments.

In economic theory Adam Smith was the first to analyse the working and characteristics of a free economy. In *The Wealth of Nations* he argued that every individual knows best how to employ his capital so as to maximize its earnings. His intention is not generally to promote public interest but his own security and gain; but he is led by an "invisible hand" to promote an end which was no part of his original intention. By pursuing his own interest he promotes that of society more effectively than when he tries consciously to promote it. In modern language Adam Smith thus recognized a distinction between "private" and "social" benefits. The difference between him and modern economists is that he thought that (with several important exceptions) the "invisible hand" of self-interest would reconcile private and social benefits, whereas modern economists have argued that the reconciliation requires constant revision of property rights to "internalize" the external effects of private decisions. (Private in this sense refers to an individual or single unit, a person, firm or government department, not private as opposed to public or governmental.)

The concept of the completely free economy is frequently used as a tool in analytical economics. The theoretical model of a free economy assumes that there is a division of labour and private ownership of the means of production; that there is consequently a market exchange of goods and services not obstructed by arbitrary power or sectional interest. It also assumes that the government tries to preserve the free economy. The economy is then free—there is no interference by external factors with processes of trade and production. Starting from these assumptions, modern economic theory has attempted to analyse the working of a completely free economy. At a later stage it turns to the study of the problems raised in some countries by interference with the free economy on the part of government or other agencies using direction or compulsion. [10]

Free Enterprise, a system in which the non-human factors of production are owned privately and are used to earn profits for their owners by producing goods and services to sell directly or indirectly to consumers. The two distinctive features of free enterprise are the private ownership of property and the bearing of the risks and uncertainties of production by *entrepreneurs*. The system is "free" from detailed state regulation and direction but is subject to a framework of laws on property, contract, sale of goods, companies, restraint of trade, patents, copyright and so on designed to create and maintain the institutions of private property, decentralized initiative, free markets, competition and consumer choice.

Economists who advocate a system of free enterprise take the view that private ownership of property is an essential element in economic progress, contributing to the growth of output and therefore claiming a share of it. It is apparent that investment increases the productivity of the worker; without machinery, for example, the worker's output would be much less. This capital is rarely provided free and ready for use by nature; land, for example, may require improvement before it will yield the fullest results. It is essential to the growth of an economy that its full exploitation by the employment of capital should take place; although some of the extra productivity will accrue to capitalists in the form of profits, the workers will probably still be better off. Countries with the highest amount of capital equipment employed per worker tend to have the highest average standard of living. But the accumulation of capital is not automatic; for it requires action by individuals, the *entrepreneurs* of the free enterprise system.

The role of the individual *entrepreneur* within the operation of the system of free enterprise has been the subject of much debate. A guiding principle of many modern theories has been the rebuttal of the Marxist estimation of the capitalist as an exploiter performing merely an historical, transitional role. The justification of the *entrepreneur* in most of these theories has been based on specific functions he is held to perform—not historical and institutional, but "absolute," since they would have to be performed by someone in any conceivable economic order. The main function thus isolated is that of bearing risks which would have to be borne by the community as a whole in a socialist or public enterprise economy. [10]

Free Entry, the absence of government or private restrictions on new producers, individual or corporate, entering an industry or market. Government restrictions are usually embodied in law, as on copyright or patents; more specific restrictions apply to national or local government-owned or controlled industries or services, such as coal, rail, steel, telephones, refuse collection. Private restrictions may take the form of boycotts of buyers, black-lists of suppliers, or oligopolistic production generally. Entry may also be constricted by economies of scale that require new suppliers to enter the market with large capital outlay and risk, or by difficulty of access to raw materials (some minerals) or customers (beer-drinkers). If entry is relatively free, producers and suppliers cannot raise price very much without attracting new producers or suppliers. Similarly professional associations and trade unions cannot raise salaries, fees or wages very much without attracting new workers: hence the use of long periods of "articles" by solicitors, barristers, accountants, actuaries, doctors, etc., and closed shops, demarcation rules, unnecessarily long apprenticeships, etc. An approximate mathematical measure of free entry is the closeness of pay or profits to the competitive market rate. [7]

Free Exchanges, a condition in which the rate of exchange, the price of one country's currency in terms of another, or the number of units of one currency which exchange for a given number of units of another currency, is allowed to vary continuously with variations in the world demand for the supply of them. For the purpose of international exchange a currency is regarded as a commodity which facilitates the exchange of other commodities, and like other commodities its value in exchange for other currencies is subject to the laws of supply and demand. Under free exchanges, if the supply of a currency, i.e. the amount offered for sale at any given time, exceeds the existing demand for it, its value in exchange will tend to fall and so stimulate the demand and diminish the excess supply.

When the external value of a currency unit is not fixed in terms of a precious metal (such as gold), or is not supported by government action, it is nominally free to fluctuate without limit. Wide and unpredictable fluctuations may be considered harmful to a country's foreign trade, and this has led most countries to establish a range of artificial methods to ensure exchange rate stability. Free exchanges may also be described as floating or flexible. [4]

Free Goods, non-economic goods, i.e. those which are not scarce in relation to the demand for them and which therefore have no price or exchange value even though they may have utility or give satisfaction in use. [7]

Free Market, institution (from a place to a possibly far-flung network of relationships maintained by e.g. letter, cable, teleprinter or telephone) to which access by buyers and sellers is unrestricted by government or by private collusion between existing buyers and sellers. Examples occur in occupations like gardening, retailing (most kinds, except where a licence is required from government), manufacturing industries except where nationalized. [7]

Free on Board. *See* FOB.

Free Reserves, mainly the profits of a company that have not been distributed to shareholders and are available for use as required by the directors. [3]

Free Rider, an individual who can benefit from a commodity or service produced by others without himself paying for it (in money, time or effort). The importance of the concept in economics is that if the production of some commodities or services was left to individual motive and decision they would not be produced. Some form of collective agreement that all shall be required (compelled) to participate in production is therefore required; and since the commodity or service will not be produced at all unless all potential beneficiaries participate, agreement is likely. Taxation is the most common method that has developed to compel participation (indirectly, through money) to which all are held to have consented. The "free rider" explains the "public" characteristic of the "public good" concept developed by Paul Samuelson. An example is health insurance (for some risks) which individuals would not undertake unless compelled by government. The requirement is for insurance, not for a specified source of insurance, private or governmental, and only for risks against which individuals would not insure because they think insurance would be provided by government. In practice there is a "free rider" element in many or most activities; whether it justifies voluntary agreement to compel participation depends on the cost of organization, the degree to which common provision is effectively controlled by the individual participants, and its capacity to respond to changing circumstances, notably to liquidate itself when no longer required. [13]

Free Trade, trade unencumbered by tariffs, quantitative restrictions or other devices obstructing the movement of goods between countries. The free trade doctrine, arising out of the classical theory of international trade, is that the fewer the obstructions to trade between countries the more fully the world's economic resources will be used and the higher living standards will be. This deduction follows because free trade tends to extract the maximum advantage from international specialization, with consequent gains in efficiency and world economic welfare. The special endowments of different areas are made generally available: all countries are enabled to buy freely from abroad whenever imports cost less in terms of exported resources than they would if produced at home, and they are encouraged to use home resources with maximum efficiency by concentrating them on lines of production in which their relative efficiency is largest.

The broad principle is still widely accepted, even among economists who question specific aspects of the classical doctrine as enunciated by Adam Smith, Ricardo, Say, Bastiat, and J. S. Mill. The classical doctrine always admitted exceptions. Adam Smith, in *The Wealth of Nations,* following his dictum that "defence . . . is of much more importance than opulence," was prepared to extend protection to industries "necessary for the defence of the country." On these grounds he considered the Navigation Acts to be "perhaps the wisest of all the commercial regulations of England." He also admitted a case for countervailing import duties on foreign substitutes when similar taxes were levied on home-produced goods. But he gave only qualified approval to retaliatory tariffs as a bargaining counter to secure the removal of other countries' tariffs.

Further qualifications to the free trade doctrine were introduced by Alexander Hamilton (*Report on Manufactures,* 1791) and J. S. Mill (*Principles of Political Economy,* 1848), on the ground that there was a case for the temporary protection of "infant" industries. These arguments were broadened, chiefly by Friedrich List, an admirer of Hamilton and a leader of the German Customs Union movement in the 1830's, into a more general case for protection as a stimulus to national economic development. In his *National System of Political Economy* (1841), List argued that free trade hindered economic development once a country had passed beyond primitive agriculture. But even he was not prepared to see the principle of free trade thrown overboard indiscriminately or permanently.

Other qualifications to the free trade argument have from time to time been advanced: for example, to encourage diversification in order to preserve or promote a more "balanced" industrial structure, to stimulate home employment during depression or to protect home industries against "dumping." Monopolistic practices in world and national markets suggest two further qualifications. First, a country, by tariff manipulation, may attract to itself a larger share of the total gains from trade at the expense of other countries (provided they do not try to follow suit). Secondly, if home monopoly causes economic resources to be allocated between uses inefficiently, free trade could magnify these distortions, although on the other hand the widening of markets through trade tends to limit sellers' monopoly power, and protection promotes the growth of monopoly power—"the tariff is the mother of the trust" (F. W. Taussig).

These qualifications do not amount to a rebuttal of the underlying case for free trade, or form a general case for protectionism. Nevertheless, since the 1870's protectionism has grown throughout the world and free trade has lost ground. The decline of the great liberal era in trade, which had spread out from England after the Napoleonic wars, was largely a reflection of the rise of nationalism during the second half of the nineteenth century; contributory factors were the growth of world competition and the "Great Depression" of the 1870's. Similarly the wars of the twentieth century and the world depression of the inter-war years promoted a further growth in protectionism. Politically the protectionist is in a strong position vis-à-vis the advocate of free trade because the benefits of protection are usually concentrated on particular industries or trades and immediately obvious, while its costs or burdens are normally diffused throughout the whole economy and the final consumer cannot easily recognize them. Hence the formation of strong political pressure groups to seek protection. Conversely, the benefits of free trade are long-term and diffuse, and apparent only to the trained observer. They thus exercise little emotive appeal except when allied to the removal of a real or fancied injustice, as in the Anti-Corn Law movement. Nevertheless, since World War II the re-emergence of internationalism and the growth of supra-national institutions have reflected and encouraged re-examination of the case for free trade. The Common Market is forming a large free trade area in Europe, and some economists (J. E. Meade, Sir Sydney Caine and others) have argued for a North Atlantic community that would free trade not only within itself but also with the developing countries of Africa, Asia and elsewhere. [4]

Free Trade Area, an arrangement between two or more countries to eliminate customs and other trade barriers between them while allowing each to retain its tariff against other countries. It is contrasted with a customs union, which provides similarly for free trade between members but adopts a *common* external tariff. Management of a customs union calls for some degree of integration of the fiscal, monetary and social policies of member countries. A free trade area permits more financial autonomy among members but creates problems in the treatment of re-exports within the free trade area of goods imported from outside. Since traders in high-tariff member countries gain by importing from outside the area through a low-tariff member rather than by importing directly, the effective rate of duty on imports of any commodity from outside tends to be reduced to that of the lowest-tariff member. Hence in practice free trade between members is rarely complete but tends to be confined to commodities produced wholly or mainly in the member countries.

Both free trade areas and customs unions tend to divert trade from countries outside and to promote trade within them. Trade diversion is likely to be more, and trade creation smaller, the less competitive the economies of the member-countries. Both create zones of preferential treatment and in terms of the possible advantages of international division of labour are inferior to more general liberalization of trade. But they may be economically advantageous as politically necessary first steps in this direction. A free trade area may lend itself more to extension in this way than does a customs union, since a common external commercial policy may lead to pressure for increased protection to fence it in to facilitate financial or other forms of autarky. This is a main doubt that some economists have had about the Common Market. [4]

Freehold, a form (alloidal) of tenure of property. Originally a tenure which required a tenant to render only such services and obligations as were worthy of a freeman. In time many of these obligations either wholly disappeared or became unimportant. Today a freeholder is the absolute owner of his property and may do what he likes with it by development, sale, transfer or the creation of lesser interests in it, subject only to the law of the land and to the rights of others. These modifications may be far-reaching in practice.

As investments, freehold interests in real property are like ordinary shares in tending normally to reflect general price movements due to inflation or deflation. Where they are sold subject to unexpired leases at fixed rents which no longer reflect current market rents for similar properties, the price and thus the yield of freehold investments will tend to reflect the fixed rents. Because also of management expenses, the average yield on freehold investments tends to be higher than that on ordinary shares, other things being equal. [6]

Freight, strictly the payment for transporting cargoes at sea; loosely applied to the goods themselves. [4]

Friction, Economic. *See* ECONOMIC FRICTION.

Frictional Unemployment. *See* UNEMPLOYMENT.

Friedman, Milton (1912–), American economist, born in New York City and educated at Rutgers, Chicago and Columbia Universities. From 1935 to 1937 he worked for the US National Resources Committee and from 1941 to 1943 for the US Treasury. In 1946 he was appointed Paul Snowden Russell Distinguished Service Professor at the University of Chicago. He has also taught at other American universities and lectured widely throughout the world. His writings have ranged from original theoretical and historical studies for economists to a popular column in a weekly magazine. His most considerable academic work was the *Monetary History of the United States, 1867–1960* (1963); others were *Essays in Positive Economics* (1952), *A Theory of the Consumption Function* (1957), *The Great Contraction* (1965), *The Optimum Quantity of Money* (1969). His best-known popular book for laymen is *Capitalism and Freedom* (1962). He became academically prominent for his leadership of the Chicago School of Economics, which substituted monetary quantity theory for Keynesian theory and which strongly emphasized that economic hypotheses must be tested empirically to achieve credence. More generally he is widely known as the leading advocate of a negative income tax and education vouchers, and of a free market economy. He has been active in promoting a liberal economic philosophy through the Mont Pelerin Society. [2]

Fringe Benefits, payments and services provided by an employer in addition to normal earnings. The earliest "fringe benefits" were probably the welfare services introduced by paternalistic employers during the nineteenth century, but the number and variety has increased during the past fifty years. Holiday pay has been the largest item measured as a cost to the employer. Sick pay and redundancy payments are among the latest examples. Some benefits provide income for the employee in time of need, e.g. occupational pension plans and insurance schemes of various kinds. Non-monetary benefits in goods or services include canteens, social facilities, housing or travel subsidies, discounts on company products, payments in kind, medical services, educational facilities and so on.

Fringe benefits can be measured either as receipts to the employee or as costs to the employer, although the two need not be equal; e.g. employee benefits from an insurance scheme need not be the same as employer contributions. For convenience they are usually calculated as costs to the employer. The cost of fringe benefits varies with staff and manual workers. The latter usually enjoy holidays with pay and some of the welfare services listed above, but staff fringe benefits are more extensive. Pension and sick-pay schemes are more generous, and the fringe benefits of the top executive grades increasingly include company cars and houses, as well as expense accounts.

The development of fringe benefits, in Britain and elsewhere, has been much affected by government policy, by periodic changes in it, and by the alternation of governments that favour or dislike fringe benefits. In Germany occupational pensions have developed much less than in Britain because of the extensive growth of state pensions since Bismarck's legislation in the 1880's. In Britain governments that believe pensions should be provided by the State to ensure that all employees receive them, and that they do not differ too widely, have alternated with governments that favour occupational pensions (arranged within firms or occupations) to suit the circumstances of employees and to encourage saving.

Fringe benefits are sometimes introduced voluntarily by the employer in order to attract and keep employees when labour is scarce, or because high taxation of incomes makes a rise in pay ineffective. Sometimes they are granted because of trade union pressure, e.g. the third week's holiday with pay in some British industries. A payment which an employer is legally required to make on behalf of his employees, such as the National Insurance contribution, is usually accepted as a fringe benefit cost. In general, when benefits are introduced voluntarily, they have much the same purpose as wage payments. A company hopes thereby to attract labour to itself and to retain the labour it already has. In this sense, fringe benefits have increased considerably in the past fifteen years and in some industries are an important part of labour costs. [5]

Frisch, Ragnar A. K. (1895–1973), Norwegian mathematical economist. He was educated at Oslo University, where he was Assistant Professor in 1925, Associate Professor in 1928 and Professor of Economics and Statistics from 1931. He was the originator of the term "macro-dynamics" (and of "isoquant") and has made considerable contributions to the technique of marginal analysis, particularly to the theory of consumer demand. His major achievement was to develop the mathematical possibilities of J. M. Clark's "acceleration principle" in a paper, "Propagation and Impulse Problems," in a memorial volume to Cassel. Hicks said he showed that the acceleration principle established an analogy between economic fluctuations and the "waves" elaborately studied in physics, so that knowledge and techniques acquired for other purposes by applied mathematicians and physicists became relevant to the economic problem. His main published works were *Statistical Confluence Analysis by Means of Complete Regression Systems* (1943), *Maxima et Minima* (1960), and *The Theory of Production* (1962). [2]

Full-bodied Currency. *See* MANAGED CURRENCY.

Full Employment, in economic analysis the situation in which the demand for labour equals the supply forthcoming at the given level of real wages. In these circumstances there can be some unemployment if it is balanced by unfilled vacancies. A situation with no unemployment at all is both unattainable (except in primitive or static society) and undesirable because it would leave no room for adaptation to changing conditions and because it would be chronically inflationary.

Several kinds of unemployment may exist under full employment: (*a*) *Seasonal:* in some industries, as in agriculture and building, work is dependent on the weather; in others the demand for products (clothing, foods, etc.) varies with it. Firms in these industries may require fewer workers in the slack periods. (*b*) *Frictional:* the structure of the economy is constantly changing and labour must move from declining to prospering and expanding firms and industries. Such workers may be unemployed for a period because the transition may require time and cost in moving home or training for new jobs, there may be opposition from trade unions to entry of new workers, reluctance to move to new areas, hope of inducing the government to establish new industries, etc. If the transition is very long the unemployment can be called *structural:* it results from the inability of the economy to re-employ the displaced labour productively. (*c*) *Voluntary:* more rarely some employees are content to be unemployed rather than work at prevailing rates of pay.

In 1944 a British Government White Paper advising on post-war government policies recommended that, to avoid a repetition of the 1930's when a large proportion of the working population were unemployed, economic policy should aim at securing "a high and stable level of employment." Lord Beveridge's report on the social services (1942) had defined full employment as a situation in which the number of vacancies *exceeded* the number of men unemployed, so that the demand for labour was larger than the supply. Full employment in Beveridge's sense has existed in Britain since the war except for short periods. Beveridge's target figure for unemployment was 3 per cent; in post-war Britain it was seldom above 2 per cent until the 1970's in spite of accelerating inflation.

Some economists distinguish between full employment as defined in the first paragraph and *over-full* employment, when the demand for labour exceeds the supply and the number of vacancies is larger than the number of unemployed. The problem for economic policy is generally held to be to maintain full employment and yet avoid inflation; it is made difficult by the uncertainty on when the point of full employment is reached. In British experience full or overfull employment has been almost inevitably accompanied by inflation.

Inflation is a condition in which the total demand for goods and services in the economy is larger than their supply, and it is characterized (if unchecked) by a constantly rising level of prices. Once an inflation is under way rising industrial costs tend to be followed by rising prices. Wage (and other pay) increases are sought to compensate for the decline in real wages and they are granted because they can be passed on in higher prices to the consumer. This further increases costs, and (in the absence of action by the monetary authorities) the cycle becomes self-perpetuating. A policy of full employment that leads to overfull employment can start off an inflation. Since labour is fully employed the employer must pay higher wages to attract sufficient employees. If prices and wages are rising together, as is usually the case, *real* wages may not rise, and trade unions try to keep ahead of the inflation by demanding increases in money wages. An inflationary spiral can also be initiated by increases in other costs or by autonomous price rises due to changes in the conditions of demand arising from increasing incomes or changing social habits.

Various methods of mastering or controlling the inflation accompanying full employment have been suggested. First, some economists argue that a degree of inflation be accepted as a stimulus to growth. The weaknesses of this policy are that continued inflation tends to distort the structure of production, bear heavily on the fixed-income classes (whose real income is constantly reduced by rising prices), sooner or later bring pressure on the balance of payments (as exports increase in price and become less competitive abroad) and that inflation may not remain moderate for long. Secondly, other economists believe there may be a "wages policy" that prevents wage increases from initiating or feeding an inflation, and that it can be achieved by publishing a figure calculated by the government as the highest *average* increase in earnings and salaries compatible with a stable level of prices and persuading the trade unions not to exceed it. One difficulty is that in a changing economy some industries and firms will have to pay more than this figure, others less. The government may be able to apply the policy to its employees in the public sector, at least for a period until recruitment becomes difficult and employees are lost to private industry, where employers and unions make their own settlements, and if a free market in labour is thought desirable the government can only advise and persuade, not direct. This kind of policy will therefore work only if collective bargaining is abandoned or limited. Thirdly, some economists, such as F. W. Paish, argued there was no other way of avoiding inflation except by revision of the post-war British full employment policy. This view was reinforced by statistical studies showing a close relationship between the level of unemployment and the rate of wage increases. An unemployment rate nearer 3 than 2 per cent would ease the pressure on resources, especially on labour. The difficulty was to know precisely when full employment is reached or when the demand for labour equals the supply. Moreover, in the 1970's accelerating inflation did not seem to reduce unemployment, which rose to around 4 per cent in 1972, although it was argued that official statistics overstated the extent of true unemployment (*see* UNEMPLOYMENT).

The dilemma of full employment is that it is socially and politically desirable but difficult to ensure in a country like Britain that exports a fifth of her output to pay for food, raw materials, etc. and thus has to adapt her industries and services to overseas markets that are beyond her control. If there is resistance to change of jobs or homes to regions in which work is available, full employment can still be maintained, and the personal and cultural disturbances of movement avoided, but at the price of a falling standard of life. [10]

Full Line Forcing, a trading practice that makes it a condition of the sale or lease of one product that others must be bought from the supplier and not from competitors. For example, the United Shoe Machinery Corporation leased a patented lasting machine (without any substitute) to shoe manufacturers only if they leased all their other machinery (for which substitutes were available) from United Shoe. The economic significance of full line forcing is that it may provide a means for building up an extensive monopoly. [7]

Function, a precise mathematical expression of a relationship between dependent and independent variables. Thus a variable q (for quantity demanded of a commodity) is a function of the variable p (for price of the commodity) if q depends on p in the sense that by fixing the value of p, one or more corresponding values of q are determined. The variable p, whose numerical value may be arbitrarily assigned, is called the *independent variable;* the variable q, whose numerical value is determined only after a value has been assigned to p, is called the *dependent* variable. When it is wished to indicate a functional relationship between variables, say x and y, without specifying the precise form of the function, the usual notation is $y = f(x)$, meaning that y depends on x in some (unspecified) way. Thus if total income in a community (Y) is defined as generated by (equal to) total spending which comprises, say, consumption spending (C) and Investment spending (I), the identity $(Y = C + I)$ can be converted into a simple forecasting equation if (I) is determined exogenously, i.e. assigned a particular value and if (C) is functionally related to income, $C = f(Y)$. If, further, this function is specified as $C = 0.8(Y)$, (translate: "consumption spending will be four-fifths of income, whatever the level of income"), this yields the equation: $Y = 0.8(Y) + I$ or $Y = I/(1–0.8)$ whence $Y = 5I$.

Functions may involve several variables. For example, the quantity demanded of a commodity will depend on other things than its price; at the least it will depend on the prices of competing and complementary goods, on the consumer's income and his tastes. If the commodity in question is *x*, competing goods *y* and complementary goods *z*, and income and tastes are expressed as Y and T respectively, the functional relationship between *q* (quantity demanded) and the other variables (with *p* denoting price) can be expressed generally as

$$q_x = f(p_x, p_y, p_z, Y, T).$$

The functional relationships may take a number of mathematical forms—linear, parabolic, exponential, logarithmic or stochastic, the last-named indicating a relationship which involves probabilities rather than certainties. [14]

Funded Debt, perpetual loans; usually refers to government borrowings such as 2½ per cent Consolidated Stock and 3½ per cent War Loan which have no fixed repayment dates. Individuals may encash their holdings by selling their stock on the Stock Exchange to another private buyer. Current prices are based on prevailing long-term rates of interest. For example, in recent years 2½ per cent Consols have been quoted around 30, a price which brought the yield to 8 per cent, which is near the yields on new bonds of comparable security. [8]

Funding, generally the conversion of short-term into longer-term, more permanent, obligations. The receipts from the sale of longer-term securities are used to repay shorter-term liabilities. Companies tend to press ahead with funding in times of economic prosperity when share markets are buoyant with high prices and low yields. Government funding operations (including those of Commonwealth and local governments) are likely to occur in times of low long-term interest rates.

This need not always be true. In recent years the term funding has been widely used with reference to National Debt management as an instrument of monetary policy. Sales of long-dated securities, coupled with purchases of Treasury bills, tend to reduce the availability of the latter and thus the liquidity of the joint-stock banks and the credit base of the private sector of the economy. Monetary policy might thus call for funding operations in times of relatively high interest rates. [8]

Futures, the purchase and sale of commodities for future delivery. Futures provide a convenient mechanism for "hedging" market risks; futures markets form an important part of many organized commodity exchanges or markets. They also facilitate arbitrage, widen the market and promote smooth adjustments of demand and supply.

The essence of futures trading is a contract by which one party agrees to deliver a quantity of the commodity concerned at a future time and a given price ("sells"), and the other agrees to accept ("buys"). Generally, futures contracts differ from cash or forward contracts because their terms other than price are laid down by the market or "exchange" in which they are made: e.g. the grade of the product is usually specified, and other grades may be delivered instead of it only if the price allows for differences. Delivery times are also usually subject to rules.

A person who buys a commodity for cash today in the "spot" market and then holds it over a time is "speculating." If price has risen in the spot market by the time he resells it (or sells the goods manufactured from it), he gains: if it has fallen, he loses. Such windfall gains or losses are disturbing to manufacturers and traders who hold stocks in the normal course of business. Hedging by means of futures contracts is an attempt to reduce such risks. Thus if, at the same time as he made a spot purchase, a trader sold a futures contract for a similar quantity, and if he cancelled ("bought in") his futures contract when he resold, loss or gain on the cash transaction due to price changes will tend to be cancelled by an opposite gain or loss on the futures transaction. Although a perfect hedge may be unattainable in practice (because cash and future prices may be "out of line"), hedging permits some separation of the speculative gains or losses arising from commodity price changes and the profits from the normal business of trading or manufacturing. The risks are in effect shifted on to the speculators (brokers) who are specialists in such contracts. Hedging thus illustrates the way in which risk can be reduced by specialization of the market when normal forms of insurance are not possible.

An example of a futures market in commodities is the Liverpool Cotton Exchange. [7]

G

Galbraith, John Kenneth (1908–), Canadian-born economist who moved to the United States, taught at Harvard, and stimulated academic debate and public interest in economics by several clearly-written, witty and controversial books, mainly on the structure of industry and on economic growth. He attracted attention by coining phrases that crystallized his critiques of American capitalism ("the affluent society"), orthodox economists ("the conventional wisdom"), etc. He argued that free enterprise inevitably tended to monopoly ("the military-industrial complex"), that it had set in train equal but opposite tendencies in buying ("countervailing power"), that economic growth emphasized material goods rather than the quality of life ("private affluence and public squalor"), and that since private production had virtually removed scarcity in material goods the emphasis could be moved to the public provision of amenities for the good life. His work had less influence on professional economists, who tended to regard it as over-simplified, than on the general literate public, but he was among the earliest in the 1950's to arouse disquiet about the side-effects of economic growth that other economists, notably E. D. Mishan in Britain, analysed with more refinement. His main works were *A Theory of Price Control* and *American Capitalism* (1952), *The Affluent Society* (1958), *The New Industrial State* (1967) and *Economics and the Public Purpose* (1974). His Reith Lectures (BBC, 1966) on the structure of private industry, later amplified in *The New Industrial State,* were examined and their conclusions questioned by the British economist, G. C. Allen. [2]

Galiani, Ferdinando. *See* Economic Thought.

Galloping Horse, term coined by the British economist, E. G. West, for the spreading private education in the 19th century; in his view the state jumped on an already galloping horse to accelerate its pace (by government action, at first through Board Schools). The debate between economists and economic historians has been about how far education would have developed without the state. The general view has been that state intervention was imperative. The 1870 Education Act is regarded as the beginning of state education. West argued (*Education and the State,* 1965) that education had been spreading in response to demand, although encouraged by state funds (since 1833), and that it was not necessary to replace state financial subsidy by direct control. He has recently argued that total expenditure on education might have risen faster than it has done if taxes had been lower to enable parents to pay fees. This new view is contested by other economists. [7]

Galloping Inflation, economic parallel with an equestrian situation: inflation that increases pace and passes out of control. This may happen when the annual rate of inflation exceeds 5 to 10 per cent and rises to 15 to 20 per cent, for then the value of money is halved every 4 years or so; hence money is held for no longer than is essential for everyday purchases, and this very anxiety to pass it on increases its velocity of circulation, expands the effective total quantity of money, and raises prices still faster. Once the annual rate rises to 20 per cent or above it may soon escalate to 50 per cent or more. Inflation thus moves from a gentle trot, to a canter, and finally to a gallop, which requires drastic action to stop.

The familiar example is Germany in the 1920's, where paper money lost value from day to day and had to be replaced by a new currency. The most common recent example is Brazil, where galloping inflation of over 100 per cent was reduced to a brisk trot of 20 per cent over several years by linking money payments to indices of prices. This process, guided by economists Roberto Campos and Antonio Delfim Netro, was called indexation or monetary correction. The theory was that by diverting attention away from money values to real values, expectations of continuing inflation would gradually be reduced and inflation itself brought under control. [8]

Gambling, in economic theory, the action of individuals in a market situation in which the outcome depends on the actions of people—demanders and suppliers—with conflicting interests. The "game," the form that gambling normally takes, has become a subject of increasing economic study with the application of new mathematical techniques. [7]

Games, Theory of, an attempt to explain the behaviour of individuals with varying preferences. The theory is used to formulate principles as a guide to intelligent action. Game-theory is one of the first examples of an elaborate mathematical development centred in the social sciences. The concepts are derived from non-physical problems, such as the behaviour of firms and individuals in given market situations. The theory draws on known mathematics and, when they cannot be used, creates new mathematical techniques. [13]

Gazumping, the displacement of a buyer who had agreed to pay a price, but had not yet paid it, by another buyer offering a higher price. This could be done where there was a time-lag between the offer and acceptance of a price and the legal completion of a contract, as in house purchase. The practice is regarded as immoral, but economists explain it as the symptom of a sellers' market, in which demand tends to outpace supply at a given price, so that there is pressure on the price to rise. Gazumping breaks the spirit but not the letter of the agreement between buyer and seller; in the long run sellers might be discouraged from gazumping by (house) agents who may fear losing repute. The practice was not exploited solely by one side of the market, as was seen when in 1973–4 the sellers' market in homes turned into a buyers' market and gazumping was replaced by reverse gazumping: buyers who had offered a price did not complete the contract if they could buy at a lower price elsewhere. Buyers may in fact have less reason to refrain from (reverse) gazumping insofar as agents act for sellers rather than buyers. [7]

Gearing, the proportion of a company's annual income allocated to "prior charges" (interest on debentures and preference dividends), the remainder going to the ordinary shareholders. Where it is high the company is said to be highly geared, and conversely. The higher the gearing the larger the likelihood of large fluctuations in ordinary share dividends. If out of £1 million profits, £990,000 is payable in prior charges, a 1 per cent increase in profits will double the amount available for distribution to ordinary shareholders; a 1 per cent decrease would reduce it to nil. A more general term which embraces the notion of gearing is Leverage. [8]

General Agreement on Tariffs and Trade (GATT), negotiated at Geneva in 1947 and brought into immediate effect. It incorporated the key commercial principles—non-discrimination in trade, negotiated reduction in tariffs, gradual elimination of other barriers to trade—of the (abortive) International Trade Organization then under discussion.

Under GATT periodic negotiations for the reduction of tariffs have followed the pattern, established by earlier Reciprocal Trade Treaties, of ("bilateral") agreements between pairs of countries product by product. The bilateral concessions so achieved are extended to all signatories by use of the Most Favoured Nation Clause and by incorporating all individual agreements into a multilateral document.

The multilateral and non-discriminatory character of GATT can be overstated. Concessions between pairs of countries are arranged on the "main supplier" principle: i.e. the products selected are those for which each country is the other's main supplier. Even when generalized, these concessions exert most effect on the two countries principally concerned, and trade between others may be liberalized much less. But tariff reductions have been significant. Even where the reductions amounted essentially to concessions between two "main suppliers" countries, other nations sometimes derived benefits indirectly through the consequent expansion of world trade. GATT also binds its signatories not to introduce new preferences, or to increase existing preferences. Since many of the tariff rates stabilized are *specific* rates (so much per physical unit) rather than *ad valorem* rates (so much per unit of value), rising world prices have also helped to reduce these impediments to trade.

The GATT includes a code of international commercial conduct relating to non-discrimination, quantitative import restrictions (quotas) and internal taxes and restrictions and similar trade principles. Apart from western Europe where progress in dismantling discriminatory restrictions has been swift since 1958, its success in eliminating quotas and other restrictions has not equaled that in tariff reductions. Since in many countries quotas and exchange controls still form the largest impediment to expansion of world trade, this represents a continuing problem for GATT. The standing arrangements, however, provide a forum in which aggrieved nations can air complaints on the general provisions. Customs procedure and valuation—which can be used as discriminatory practices—has been simplified and standardized.

The US Trade Expansion Act of 1962 offered the prospect that the "Kennedy Round" of GATT negotiations would replace product-by-product bargaining with "across the board" tariff reductions. But the diversity of remaining tariffs, the division of interests raised by the Common Market, and the resistance to a decrease in agricultural protection excluded major changes. The future of GATT probably lies in sponsoring multilateral trade negotiations, formulating broad recommendations on trade policy, and providing a consultative forum for the discussion of trade disputes. [4]

General Equilibrium Analysis. *See* EQUILIBRIUM; PARTICULAR EQUILIBRIUM ANALYSIS.

George, Henry (1839–97), a polemical American writer on economic problems. He had no formal education, believing that thought and experience were the best teachers. His widely varied career as gold prospector, sailor, compositor and lecturer indicate that he lived according to his beliefs. His main work, *Progress and Poverty* (1879), was concerned mainly with the problems of income distribution. Using Ricardian methods he argued that the largest incomes in society were derived not from the provision of services but from the fortunate possession of favourably situated land. The rent problem, he argued, was the basic cause of economic crises, the only remedy being a single tax on land which would absorb all pure rents. His book was a big success in America, and he was only narrowly defeated as a candidate for the "Single Tax" Party in the election for mayor of New York City. Although his work had little direct effect on academic thought, because income was not attributed primarily to land but was regarded as having more varied sources, it probably caused later economists to formulate the theory of rent with more precision.

British economic policy has been concerned with the rising value and taxation of land, but it has not so far been able to devise the requisite principles and machinery. The Betterment Levy under the Land Commission Act of 1967 was a short-lived attempt. Anxiety about rapidly rising land values in the 1970's led to further efforts. A difficulty is to disentangle increases in value due to rising demand (caused by rising income) from increases in value due to inflation. The two may be linked: continuing inflation may cause increasing demand for land as a hedge against falling values of money or financial investments. Farming and other land is also taxed more favourably than other forms of property. [2]

Giffen Paradox, an apparent exception to the general law of demand, i.e. that demand falls as prices rises. It says the demand for bread *rises* as its price rises because the expenditure on bread drains the resources of people with lower incomes, raises the marginal utility of their remaining money, and thus reduces their consumption of meat and other foods that cost more than bread; they therefore demand/consume *more* bread as its price rises because it is still cheaper than meat. The paradox thus suggested that the demand curve could slope positively (upward from left to right) in contrast to its normal negative slope (downward).

The paradox was named after Sir Robert Giffen by Alfred Marshall in 1895 (although there is doubt whether Sir Robert Giffen ever made such a statement). Marshall evidently did not know that the paradox had been observed by Simon Grey some 80 years earlier. The paradox was doubted by Edgeworth, who thought that the evidence did not support it and that common sense opposed it. [7]

Gifts Inter Vivos, gifts made during the life of the owner. A method of reducing estate duty, particularly on large estates. Such gifts are usually made to those to whom it was intended to make a bequest under a will. The Estate Duty laws provide that if the owner dies within a period after the gift, its value must be added back to the remainder of his estate for the purpose of assessing liability to duty. Gifts may be exempt if the owner lives for a time after making the gift. [12]

Gilt-edged Securities, those considered absolutely safe, particularly in the payment of interest and in redemption at par (the original nominal purchase price) when they become mature. The current marketable value of many gilt-edged securities (e.g. British government consols) cannot always be considered more stable, however, than the marketable value of many other securities not classed as gilt-edged. Although a gilt-edged security will be redeemed at par when it matures, its market price may fluctuate considerably before maturity is reached and will depend on the nominal rate of interest carried by the stock, the level of interest rates currently being paid on new borrowings, and the period of time to the date of redemption. Thus if the market rate on "safe" long-term loans is 10 per cent no one is likely to pay more than £25 for £100 of similar stock carrying interest at 2½ per cent. [8]

Gini Co-efficient, a statistical measure used by economists to calculate the relationship between the distribution of income (in a given area at a point in time or during a period) and absolute equality or inequality. If the co-efficient is zero, the distribution of income is at absolute equality; if it is one the distribution of income is at absolute inequality. A common use of the co-efficient is to measure the effect of a change in a tax, or of a new tax, on the distribution of income. If the co-efficient is moved towards zero, the tax is progressive, and vice versa. [14]

Giving. *See* ALTRUISM; CHARITY. [13]

Glut, a large surplus or excess of supply of a commodity, frequently temporary, usually caused by over-production. A glut is most serious in perishable commodities (such as foodstuffs), whose prices usually fall steeply with disastrous effects on the incomes of producers. Commodities that can be stored without marked deterioration in quality can be held back in the hope of a rise in price. National and international schemes have been established to regulate supply of such commodities and to reduce fluctuations (e.g. the International Wheat Agreement and agricultural marketing boards in Britain). Unless their controllers have wide powers they are difficult to operate. If they are given such powers the risk is that they will be used to restrain competition permanently and to benefit producers at the expense of consumers. [8]

Godwin, William. *See* MALTHUS, T. R.

Gold Exchange Standard, the substitution of currencies for gold as an international exchange medium. Assets in the form of foreign balances are permitted to count as reserves of a country's central bank. The practice, followed to a very limited extent before the First World War, became widespread after it as countries gradually returned to the Gold Standard. Many of them held dollars and sterling—more particularly sterling—as reserve assets in addition to gold, so that in effect Britain became a banker to other governments and the stability of the system rested on Britain's ability to prevent a run on her (relatively small) gold reserves. The system collapsed when Britain was compelled to abandon the "new" gold standard in 1931 following heavy conversions of foreign-held sterling balances into gold.

After the Second World War a new Gold Exchange Standard gradually emerged with the US dollar as a key reserve currency. The new system was also based on the stabilized but adjustable exchange rate parities between major world currencies established under the Bretton Woods Agreement (1944)—which also established the International Monetary Fund (IMF). But this system also began to display signs of strain in the 1960's, especially after the devaluation of sterling in 1967 was followed by a speculative run on the dollar in the hope (or fear) that the dollar price of gold would be forced upwards: the US gold parity was widely believed to be unrealistic relative to the prevailing commodity prices. The outcome was that the USA abandoned its fixed dollar price of gold: the revised international monetary system that resulted in the early 1970's has been called a "Limping Dollar Standard" under which the US was not obliged to maintain a fixed parity with gold, and other countries pegged their currencies to the dollar or allowed them to float or used direct controls to regulate international payments. The unsatisfactory nature of these arrangements led to proposals for a move towards a system centred on the use of IMF Special Drawing Rights as the only international reserve asset. [4]

Gold Export Point. *See* GOLD STANDARD.

Gold Import Point. *See* GOLD STANDARD.

Gold Points. *See* GOLD STANDARD.

Gold Reserves, stock of gold (supplemented by foreign currencies) held by a country to meet possible demands for payment arising out of its foreign trade. In Britain gold and convertible currency reserves have been held in the Exchange Equalization Account. The importance of the reserves is that they are necessary to meet demands for foreign currency which may be made on Britain as a result of a temporary balance of payments deficit. In total they have fluctuated with changes in the balance of trade on current account (in commodities, services, interest, etc.) and in the short-term and long-term movements of capital (by overseas holders of balances in sterling). The gold and currency reserves of members of the Sterling Area were also held in Britain.

Pressure on the reserves may be countered by (1) raising Bank rate, which attracts foreign capital holders to invest in Britain for the interest; (2) devaluing or depreciating the exchange rate, which makes imports more expensive and exports cheaper, improves the balance of payments, and so increases the reserves; (3) administrative devices (such as exchange control) which prevent individuals from taking gold and currency out of the country either for current transactions or long-term investment. These measures may not be effective if other countries take counter-measures. [4]

Gold Standard, a monetary system in which the gold value of the currency is fixed by law. The monetary authorities are required on demand to give gold of a defined quality in exchange for currency, and vice versa, at a fixed rate. Before 1914 and from 1925 to 1931, when the United Kingdom was on the gold standard and the Bank of England was required to buy gold at £4.2409 per fine oz.

and sell it at £4.2477, the United States Treasury bought and sold gold at $20.67 per fine oz.

The exchange rates between the currencies of gold standard countries are thus stabilized within limits determined by the cost of transporting gold between them. From 1925 to 1931 the "mint parity" of exchange between the dollar and sterling was $4.87 to £1 (20.67 divided by 4.2477). The market rates of exchange tended to fluctuate narrowly around this figure. They were determined by the supply of and the demand for the two currencies. If the demand for dollars increased relatively to that for sterling the value of sterling in dollars tended to fall, that is, the price of dollars in sterling tended to rise. At some point it would pay British merchants with debts to settle in the United States to buy gold at the Bank of England at the fixed rate and send it to the USA instead of the now more costly dollars. The American creditors would exchange the gold for dollars in the US. The costs of exporting gold (freight, insurance, loss of interest on gold in transit) were borne by the debtor, so that the exchange rate (the sterling price of dollars) in London could not rise above the mint parity exchange rate plus the cost of exporting gold. At this upper rate of exchange further pressure would simply cause more gold to be moved out of the country. The exchange rate at which it became profitable to export gold was thus known as the "gold export point." The corresponding "gold import point" was the exchange rate below the mint parity at which it became profitable to import gold.

The gold standard "system" was considered to work in such a way that a sizable movement of gold would tend automatically to set in train a series of correctives. Thus as a result of a gold outflow from a country its total money supply would fall and interest rates probably rise; conversely in the country to which the gold was sent. Capital funds would tend to flow from the low-interest country to the high-interest country in search of higher returns and thus correct the original disequilibrium that had given rise to the gold flow. If this were insufficient the higher interest rates in the gold-exporting country would, over a longer period, tend to reduce total domestic spending in it; incomes and prices would fall, imports would thereby be discouraged and exports encouraged; and conversely in the gold-importing country. Ideally, if prices and wages were sufficiently flexible, international balance would be restored with a minimum of disturbance to the level of employment and real income.

Great Britain and most trading nations abandoned the gold standard in 1931. The immediate cause was the failure of international capital movements to bring about the required corrective policies. The more fundamental reason was that wages and prices did not fall in response to falling demand, so that the burden of adjustment fell on reductions in employment and income. In these circumstances outright depreciation of the exchange rate to cheapen the price of export goods was considered to be less painful than reducing costs (wages and others) and prices.

The gold standard was an international system requiring co-operation from the countries that adopted it. As long as it worked it prevented countries from pursuing isolationist or nationalistic monetary policies that would have slowed down or prevented the development of a world trading economy in which the nations traded freely with one another. Following its collapse in the 1930's there was a growth of discriminating nationalistic policies which restricted multilateral trade. Since the end of World War II the establishment of new international monetary institutions has tried to restore conscious co-ordination between national monetary policies with the aim of restoring and strengthening the trend towards world economy but without the difficult adjustments required by the gold standard. But repeated efforts were at best only partly and temporarily effective. Despite the drawback of an international standard to which currencies could be linked, so that they were more or less fixed in terms of one another, the continuing confidence in gold as a reliable and stable precious metal revived discussion of a form of gold standard in the 1970's. [4]

Goods, in English the noun "good" is usually abstract, meaning usefulness, benefit or blessing, but the plural (goods) denotes the concrete embodiment of usefulness, in short, "commodities." The singular, in the sense of a commodity, is employed by economists to represent the missing singular of "goods." As economics is much concerned with capital accumulation, and capital is a sum of goods, the classification of goods is of theoretical importance. The simplest definition of a commodity is a material means, limited in supply, of satisfying human wants. But there is general agreement among economists only on the element of limitation, since goods which are in superabundant supply, and of which therefore no "economy" is needed, are goods which cannot be handled by economics. [7]

Goodwill, the amount paid for a business in excess of the value of the net tangible assets; it represents the value of the advantages of acquiring an established business.

The price paid for goodwill is high if there is a large demand for the type of business or a desire to eliminate competition by taking over a rival firm. Conversely, an enforced sale may enable the buyer to get the goodwill at a low price.

The buyer pays a capital sum for the right to receive profits larger than those otherwise obtainable on new capital similarly employed. These are sometimes called super profits in accounting language.

Apart from any special influences, the normal method of valuing goodwill is to multiply the average adjusted profits by a figure which varies from one to five, representing the number of "years' purchase." The profits are adjusted for non-recurring and special items, a "normal" rate of interest on capital is deducted, and the period over which the average is calculated must be long enough to give a "reasonable" estimate for future years.

The number of years' purchase depends on the way in which the goodwill was created. Its value may expire after the sale and be replaced by the new goodwill created by the purchaser. For example, it may have depended on the personal skill of the proprietor (hairdresser, dentist) or a favourable location that may be worth less to the purchaser. [3]

Gosplan, the central planning agency of the USSR. It makes recommendations, in a national economic plan of up to five years with details of targets for each main sector, to the Supreme Soviet. It is usually used to judge the performance of the economic system, or its individual constituents. The economic problem here is that, since the targets are influenced by both foreseen and unforeseen developments, neither the system as a whole nor individual plants are necessarily inefficient if output (or any other measure of performance) falls short of the target—or efficient if they exceed it. Increasingly efforts are made to reflect consumer preferences as well as the judgement of the planners as to the output desirable for the economy as a whole. [10]

Gossen, Herman Heinrich (1810–58), German economist. He studied law in order to enter the government service, but while a student at university became interested in political economy. After 1847 he devoted himself entirely to this subject. His main work, *Entwicklung der Gesetze des menschlichen Verkehrs und der daraus fliessenden Regeln für menschliches Handeln* (1854), contains the well-known "Three laws of Gossen," which predated what was later to be known as the marginal utility theory. His theories, however, remained largely unnoticed until they were mentioned by Jevons in the introduction to his *Theory of Political Economy* in 1879. [2]

Government, as seen by economists, is essentially an institution that sells protection and justice to its members or constituents by monopolizing the grant and enforcement of property rights over goods and services and over their transfer to others. The payment for these services takes the form of taxes. The power of the state to obtain payment for these services is that it can provide protection and justice more cheaply than individuals, or small groups, can do for themselves, i.e. there are economies of scale in government. The taxes can be paid because security and enforcement of property rights enlarge the income of the constituents beyond what it would otherwise be, and it is therefore "profitable" to buy them from government. The *net* gain to society as a whole (government plus constituents) is reduced by the "transaction costs" of negotiating and devising new property rights, measuring the benefits, collecting payment (taxes), enforcing rights, and adjudicating on disputes. [13]

Government Broker. *See* OPEN MARKET OPERATIONS.

Government Push, term used by some economists, in contrast to Cost-Push, for inflation that originates in the pressure on government by monopoly trade unions to expand the money supply in order to avoid the unemployment that could otherwise follow wage-costs pushed beyond the marginal productivity of labour. [9]

Grading, classifying products according to technical standards of quality. It is possible only for goods with uniform characteristics satisfying simple needs; thus, wheat is graded, but tea has to be sampled before a buyer can know what he is buying. Grading corresponds to standardization of manufactured goods. It widens markets by enabling buyers to buy at a distance without seeing the goods, and it makes possible sales for future delivery. [7]

Graduated Social Insurance Contributions. *See* SOCIAL INSURANCE.

Grants, Theory of, a development in economic analysis from the theory of *two*-way exchange, or buying and selling, to *one*-way transfer of purchasing services or resources. An economy in which charitable motivation and activity are significant has been described as a Grants Economy by the American economist, Kenneth Boulding (*Economics as a Science,* 1970). Interest in this extension of economic theory is that it is applying to *giving* the same techniques as those with which it analyses the efficiency of *selling:* the laws of diminishing marginal significance, equimarginal returns, etc. The basic reason why the same laws can be applied to both is that the resources that are given, like those that are sold (exchanged), are scarce and must therefore be "economized"; that is, they may do more good if given to A than to B, or to A at one time rather than another, or in one form rather than another, or with some conditions rather than others. [13]

Gratuitous Coinage. *See* FREE COINAGE.

Gravity Models, attempt to explain and predict the movement of resources—goods, money and people—between urban centres by their relative pulling powers. One of the earliest gravitational models was developed by the American economist W. J. Reilly (University of Texas) in the late 1920's, and adaptations of his *Law of Retail Gravitation* are still used as a basis for assessments of the retail trade potential of urban areas. The law states that two retail centres will tend to attract trade from any unit of purchasing power located between them in direct proportion to their relative size (measured in population or some other index) and in inverse proportion to the square of the distance between them and the unit of purchasing power. Thus if the two towns have populations P_1 and P_2 respectively, with P_2 larger than P_1, there will be an intermediate point between them such that a household situated there would be indifferent whether it shopped in town 1 or town 2. The location of the dividing line, according to Reilly's Law, will be where $P_1/d_1^2 = P_2/d_2^2$, where d_1 and d_2 are the distances to town 1 and 2 respectively. Since d_1 and d_2 add up to D, the distance between the two towns, the expression to locate the "dividing line" between the two can be re-expressed as:

$$d_2 = \frac{D}{1 + \sqrt{P_1}/\sqrt{P_2}}$$

The law in its original form simply summarizes what was already evident from the most casual inspection of relative trade—that big centres have more retail attraction than smaller centres. Like most "laws" of its kind it is really a statistical generalization derived from a large number of empirical observations. As a predictive law it has proved of limited use, despite many attempts at more precise formulation. Similar gravity models of varying sophistication have been developed to examine the volume and direction of interaction between sectors of metropolitan regions. [6]

Great Contraction, the monetarist re-christening of the Great Depression.

Great Depression, the contraction in economic activity in most of the western world between 1929 and 1932–33, characterized by falls in production, increased unemployment, and lower prices. For many years it was generally interpreted by economists as caused by a collapse in investment. It was concluded that monetary policy was ineffective in combating industrial declines and therefore that the Quantity Theory of Money (that trade and output would expand if the quantity of money was enlarged) was invalid. Monetary policy was said to be "a string you can pull but not push," "a horse you can lead to the water but not make drink." The Chicago monetary economists argue the opposite: that the Great Depression demonstrated the effectiveness of monetary authorities.

The monetary authorities at the time said they were conducting "easy money" policies. This claim was widely accepted, not least by Keynes, who concluded that monetary policy had failed and offered a new theory of the cause and cure of the Great Depression. He argued that the velocity of circulation of money was not stable, as the classical theory supposed, but volatile. If the supply of money were enlarged its velocity would slow down, and therefore exert no expansive effect on prices, incomes, trade and production, or employment. And if incomes were raised without an enlarged quantity of money, the velocity of money would rise. Velocity was thus a will-o'-the-wisp: it could move up or down in response to changes in the quantity of money or in incomes. So the important element was not the quantity of money but the part of total expenditure that was independent of current income and therefore "autonomous," i.e. largely business investment and government expenditures. The Great Depression, Keynes concluded, was precipitated by a collapse in the demand for investment which reflected a breakdown in opportunities to use capital profitably. The basic cause of the Great Depression was a collapse of investment, which the "multiplier" transformed into a collapse of income. The main conclusion for policy to cure the Depression was that monetary policy was unimportant and should be used only to depress interest rates and so reduce the government's cost of servicing the National Debt (and perhaps to stimulate investment): hence the era of "cheap money," as practised by Dalton in Britain. A further conclusion was that the emphasis should be on fiscal policy—changes in government taxing and spending.

The most recent explanation of the Great Depression is the monetarist theory: that it was caused in the USA by a contraction (of a third) in the quantity of money from 1929 to 1933, which made it longer and deeper than it would otherwise have been. Moreover, the monetarists argue, it was a result of intentional policies of the monetary authorities (the Federal Reserve system). They failed to provide liquid funds when the public wanted to withdraw their deposits, i.e. convert them into currency or money. Research into the monetary history of the time revealed that the falling quantity of money and bank failures were the result not of a shrinking in willing private borrowing but of a fall in the price of government securities, which were periodically marked down. In contrast, since there was no market for private, bad loans, they remained in the bank's accounts at their nominal value. The Federal Reserve system (the "Fed") could have stopped the fall in the quantity of money at any time during the Great Depression, but did not: hence monetary policy was not used to maintain stability in the American economy (and the outside world) but to enforce deflation on it. The Chicago monetarists claim that if Keynes had known this inside history of the Great Depression, not revealed before post-war historical researches, he could not have interpreted its causes as he did or offered the cures he devised. [9]

Gresham's Law, enunciated by Sir Thomas Gresham (adviser to Queen Elizabeth I) after an inquiry into the debasement of the coinage: his conclusion was: "Bad money drives out good." When a debased and a good currency circulate together, people tend to hoard the good and try to pass on the bad in repayment of debts. In time the least acceptable form tends to set the commercial exchange value of the whole currency and the more acceptable are withdrawn because they are worth more and put to other uses. [8]

Grey Areas. *See* INTERMEDIATE AREAS.

Gross Domestic Product. *See* INVESTMENT; OUTPUT.

Gross Income Multiplier, a technique for valuing real property based on applying a factor or multiplier to the gross income derived from the property in the past. The crucial multiplier to apply is obtained from analysis of recent transactions in similar property. [6]

Gross Margin. *See* NET MARGIN.

Gross National Product (GNP), the total value at current or constant prices of the annual flow of goods and services becoming available to a country for consumption and maintaining or adding to its material wealth. (*See* NATIONAL INCOME.) [9]

Gross Output. *See* OUTPUT.

Gross Product. *See* OUTPUT.

Ground Lease, a lease of land for a relatively long term (traditionally 99 years but other terms are common). If the land is unimproved (not built on) the lease usually takes the form of a building lease—granted in return for an undertaking by the lessee to erect a building or buildings on the site to the lessor's specifications. Since the buildings, when erected, provide the lessor with security for the payment of the ground rent, building leases are often preceded by a *building agreement,* that after the erection of the building(s), the owner will grant a lease of the land. The holder of the leasehold interest does not legally own the land, nor is he the owner of a building erected on it, regardless of who built or paid for them. He merely owns an occupation interest in the parcel of land-and-building which will cease at the end of the lease. In turn the lessor retains only the right to the ground rent reserved for the term of the lease plus the reversion to the whole parcel of land-and-building at the end of the lease term. An important difference between a ground lease and an ordinary occupation lease for a term of years turns on the question of security. With an ordinary occupation lease the credit standing of the tenant is important: with a building lease the lessor relies on the improvement to provide security for the rent reserved. Ground leases are sometimes created *after* development and sold off to provide long-term finance, the developer retaining a leasehold occupation interest in the development. [6]

Ground Rent, the rent reserved under a building lease or ground lease. These are leases for a relatively long term (traditionally 99 years, although this period has no particular economic merit and longer or shorter periods are common). Ground rents may be freehold or leasehold. If freehold the ground landlord owns the right to the rent and the reversion to the full freehold interest at the end of the leasehold term: if leasehold a head lessee holding from the freeholder creates a further interest, due to end before his own leasehold term expires, and receives a leasehold ground rent from that interest. The upper limit of ground or site rent payable under a ground lease is fixed by the value of the site when the lease is granted. If the terms of the lease permit, the ground rent reserved may be varied to keep pace with changes in the value of the site; but the rent is always likely to remain low in relation to the full rental value of the site when improved or built on. Ground rents are considered to be low (income) risk investments because the buildings erected on a site provide the lessor with good security for the ground rent. As the reversionary date approaches when the freeholder can expect to receive the full market rent from the whole parcel of land and building, a freehold ground rent investment will also show capital appreciation (unless leasehold reform legislation restricts the lessor's rights on reversion). [6]

Group of Ten, created in 1962 to assist the International Monetary Fund in lubricating the machinery of inter-country payments. Belgium, Canada, France, Italy, Japan, the Netherlands, Sweden, the United States, the United Kingdom and West Germany signed the General Agreement to Borrow and created a fund of 6,000 million dollars (in American six billion) to supplement the automatic lending/borrowing powers of the IMF Switzerland, not in the IMF, added 200 million dollars. To draw on these reserve monies requires the approval of the Ten. [4]

Growth, Economic. *See* Economic Growth.

Growth Point Theory, a recent development in the economic analysis of the conditions of regional economic growth. It was crystallized in the 1963 report of the National Economic Development Council, *Conditions Favourable to Faster Growth.* It identifies sub-regions with exceptional opportunities for expanding employment and creating external economies ("agglomeration economies"), so that regional aid from central government can be distributed not indiscriminately but selectively to the areas where it can do most good by producing most growth.

The advocates of Growth Point Theory have conceded that it can be pushed too far and, like market forces, produce congestion and other external detriments, described as "diseconomies of agglomeration." In practice the task is to decide when the artificial growth point has reached its ideal size to "take off" into natural growth without further government stimulus, and whether it will be able to dispense with the artificial aid. It is thus analogous to an infant industry nurtured on tariffs, quotas, etc. [10]

Growth Theory, the analysis of the elements that decide the speed with which an economic system grows. Economists have been concerned with the underlying determinants of growth over time in the real income per head of a population. These are the slow-moving, long-term, fundamental factors that have fascinated economic thinkers since the age of Mercantilism, through the period of classical and Marxist economics to the modern Keynesian, neo-classical, neo-Keynesian and neo-Marxist economics. The Mercantilists were concerned primarily with total rather than average income or production. The Physiocrats (Quesnay, Mirabeau, etc.) analysed the regulations and restrictions whose removal, they argued, would release productive forces; and Quesnay's *Tableau Économique* can be regarded as a primitive or embryo input-output table. Adam Smith was concerned primarily with the "wealth" of "nations" and the influences that retarded or expanded it. In spite of the title of his book, he was the first economist to fasten attention on production per head rather than on total production. Adam Smith and David Ricardo were apprehensive about the coming of a stationary state, and Thomas Malthus feared the worst on the grounds that population would outrun production. But the classical economists also examined the economics of labour and capital. Marx was concerned about capitalist accumulation. Joseph Schumpeter wrote *Theorie des Wirtschaftlichen Entwicklung* (*The Theory of Economic Development*), a study of the nature and causes of economic development or growth; he identified the *entrepreneur* as the agent of change in re-assembling the factors of production from older into newer and more efficient combinations. Emulation brings imitators until opportunities are exhausted and a fresh wave of entrepreneurial activity renews the long-term trend in economic growth. This theory of development was thus also a theory of the trade (or rather economic activity) cycle. Alfred Marshall's *Principles of Economics* used the then recent (1870's) discoveries of marginal theory to analyse the dynamics, rather than the statics, of the economic world. The preoccupation of nineteenth century and inter-war economists with theories of the trade cycle was essentially a reflection of interest in economic growth and its interruptions through a wide variety of causes—from sun-spots to over-investment or under-consumption or monetary contraction—that eluded them. Keynes in the 1930's revived the Mercantilists' interest in aggregate rather than individual output, but he was concerned with a particular period. As the trade cycle seemed to become milder after the Second World War, economists turned their attention again to long-term growth and the processes of economic development, and new theories were propounded by R. F. Harrod, E. D. Domar, Nicholas Kaldor and others. [9]

Growthmanship, the name given to the emphasis on economic growth to the exclusion or at the expense of other economic objectives and to the concentration on investment as the only or dominant source of economic growth. The term is thought to have been popularized by Vice-President Richard Nixon as a critical description of the fashionable thinking of Americans who claimed that economic growth in the USA had been sluggish.

The economic criticisms of this doctrine are, first, that economic growth is not an absolute objective: it may be achieved at too large a sacrifice of other ends—economic liberty, equality, stability in the value of money and so on. Secondly, it seems to be established by the experience of several countries—western industrialized such as Norway and under-developed in Africa and Asia—that the main causes of economic growth are not technical, such as capital investment, but human. In Britain Mr Colin Clark of Oxford has argued that immediately after a war or some similar catastrophe economic growth can be rapid as wartime damage is made good but that in more normal times the human factors—enterprise, education, inventiveness, etc.—re-assert themselves and they maintain economic growth at a comparatively slow and steady pace. Efforts to force this pace violently, e.g. by denying consumption goods to employees and diverting resources to capital investment, are, as in Russia and other communist countries, India and elsewhere, likely to waste capital and may slow down the rate of economic growth. And efforts to force the pace of economic growth by monetary expansion, as in the early 1970's in Britain, end in inflation when the unemployed or under-employed resources (land, labour, capital) are absorbed into employment. [10]

H

Haberler, Gottfried (1900–1997), Austrian-born economist. He was educated at the University of Vienna, where he graduated in 1923 and 1925, and as a graduate student at the Universities of London and Harvard from 1927 to 1929. He was a lecturer and later Professor of Economics and Statistics at the University of Vienna from 1928 to 1936. In 1936 he went to teach in the USA, where he was Professor of Economics at Harvard University until 1971, when he joined the American Enterprise Institute as Resident Scholar.

Haberler is an economist in the classical liberal tradition, which is reflected in his work and in his civilized, urbane manner in intellectual debate. He came to prominence in the 1930's as the author of *Prosperity and Depression* (1935), a non-monetary survey of the literature of the trade cycle. Most of Haberler's subsequent work has been on the theory of international trade and of money. He was largely instrumental in freeing the classical theory of comparative cost from its association with the labour theory of value, arguing that the comparative-cost principle merged into a general theory of international value in which the equation of reciprocal demand is the central theorem. He has written extensively on monetary questions and favours maintaining the International Monetary Fund in much its present form. One of his most interesting studies has been index number theory, in which he was critical of the validity of objective index numbers and produced a very elegant subjective one associated with recent developments in value theory. [2]

Haggling. *See* HIGGLING.

Hamilton, Alexander. *See* FREE TRADE.

Harcourt, Sir William. *See* ESTATE DUTIES.

Hard Currency, one with a relatively stable value in international exchange. A currency is normally "hard" because its underlying strength is based on the trading position and internal stability of the country, usually shown by a large and consistent surplus in the balance of current payments.

Between the end of World War II and the late 1950's the main hard currency in international trade was the American dollar, its "hardness" being based on the dominance of the US economy and the large balance of payments surplus earned by the USA throughout most of the period. In the 1960's and 1970's this surplus gave place to a varying payments deficit, a corresponding growth of dollar debts to the rest of the world, and a "softening" in the world demand for dollars as an international currency.

The term "hard" is sometimes used to refer to metallic as distinct from paper currency, but this usage is not common. [4]

Harmonization, in the Common Market countries, the assimilation of social and other policies as envisaged by the Treaty of Rome. It is generally thought to apply to welfare benefits and methods of financing them (taxes, social insurance contributions, etc.). There is some debate on how far harmonization means or requires unification or equalization. Insofar as a major aim of the EEC is to free the movement of and competition for labour, comparable social policies might be mandatory because wide differences might distort demand in the several countries. The Treaty also said that social conditions should be equalized in an upward direction. This trend would accompany (and in the event has accompanied) the rising total and personal incomes in the EEC. How far it requires comparability of state benefits depends on the trend in private provision. Of the nine, the UK spends the most on state medical care, West Germany on state pensions and France on family allowances. These differences reflect differences in private provision, which also tend to rise with total and personal incomes. For economists the interest lies in investigating how far state provision is a consequence or cause of inadequate private provision, and therefore how far harmonization of state provision in the sense of equalization is practicable or superior to divergent private provision in each country according to local circumstances or preferences. [4]

Harmony, the basis of the economic doctrine which said that if individuals are left unfettered and free to pursue their interests a natural harmony would result. The theory was propounded traditionally in America and in France by Carey and Bastiat respectively, and it was not strongly rooted in Britain. It claimed that all factors of production would benefit from increasing prosperity if the productive process were left unregulated and not interfered with. Self-interest, even when pursued regardless of other men's well-being, served to work to the benefit of all, whereas all interference with its action was necessarily harmful. The conclusion of this theory was that the role of the state should be limited to the maintenance of "justice"; laws restricting the exchange of commodities or otherwise interfering with industrial liberty under the pretext of securing a better harmony of interest were not only destructive of that harmony but also a violation of man's natural rights.

This view is not the same as that of the classical economists, who envisaged a system of economic liberty within a framework of laws and institutions designed to secure that individual action was harnessed to and therefore served the general good. There is a wide difference between economists who held that "natural rights" should not be interfered with by law and those who held that since the law created and protected property and other rights the law could also modify them if they were exercised in opposition to the general good. [10]

Harrod, Roy F. (1900–1978), British economist. He was educated at Westminster School and Oxford University. He taught at Christ Church, Oxford, from 1922 to 1940, was in government service from 1940 to 1945, and returned to Oxford, where he was Hon. Student of Christ Church from 1967. His early concern, as that of many economists in the 1930's, was with the trade cycle, on which he wrote an *Essay* in 1936. He soon developed his interest in the theory of dynamic economic systems, and wrote the *Essay in Dynamic Theory* in 1939. His two major works after the war were *Towards Dynamic Economics* in 1948, and the official *Life of John Maynard Keynes* in 1951, a volume of economic discussion as well as biography. His concern with public affairs was reflected in his candidature for Parliament as a Liberal after the Second World War, though he later transferred his allegiance to the Conservative Party. Between 1958 and 1969 he wrote several lesser-known books on money, inflation, and general economic policy.

Few modern economists have contributed to the development of the technique of economic analysis over a wider range of subjects than Harrod. The three most important elements in his work have been, first, the development of trade cycle theory, not only in his own notable work but also in his seminal discussions with Keynes during the writing of the *General Theory;* second, the elucidation and examination of the tacit assumptions underlying the theory of imperfect or monopolistic competition; and, third, *Towards a Dynamic Economics,* which went beyond static equilibrium analysis and the accepted boundaries of trade cycle theory to examine the possibilities of setting up "growth models." Harrod was a "tool-maker" rather than a "tool-user," but there is hardly a subject of economic speculation on which he did not shed a ray of light. [2]

Hawtrey, Ralph G. (1879–1975), British economist. He worked in the Treasury for forty-one years from the age of twenty-five, and thus during the last years of the economic nineteenth century (which ended in 1914), the First World War, the post-war boom, the Great Depression, the recovery, and the Second World War.

Among his eight main written works, *The Gold Standard in Theory and Practice* (1919) and *The Art of Central Banking* (1937) were the most highly regarded by economists, although the others were respected for their authority and integrity; Hawtrey's last book was published in 1967, when he was ninety.

The hope that the economy can be managed effectively solely by the manipulation of the supply of money probably owes more to the influence of Hawtrey (at least in English-speaking countries) than to any other economist. For him the trade cycle was a wholly monetary matter. If an undue increase in the supply of money led to a fall in the rate of interest, traders would attempt to build up their stocks (here he condemned the Radcliffe Committee Report for underestimating the rate of interest). The resulting acceleration in the flow of factor earnings, accompanied by a restricted release of goods to the market, would set off an inflationary boom, which could be terminated and reversed by an appropriate restriction in the supply of money and rise in the rate of interest. Unlike Keynes, Hawtrey did not consider the effect of the interest rate upon fixed investment to be significant. [2]

Hayek, Friedrich August (1899–1992), Austrian-born economist, British by nationality. He was born in Vienna and obtained doctorates in law and economics at the University of Vienna. He visited the USA on a research fellowship in 1924, and then entered the Austrian civil service. In 1927 he was appointed the first director of the Austrian Institute for Economic Research and in 1929 Lecturer in Economics at the University of Vienna. He taught in four countries: in 1931 he became Tooke Professor of Economic Science and Statistics in the University of London; in 1950 Professor of Social and Moral Science at the University of Chicago; in 1962 Professor of Economic Policy at the Albert-Ludwigs University of Freiberg, West Germany; and in 1969 Visiting Professor of Economics at the University of Salzburg, Austria.

Hayek's teachers in economics were Friedrich von Wieser and Ludwig von Mises. In his first works in English, *Prices and Production* (1931) and *Monetary Theory and the Trade Cycle* (1933), Hayek presented in English for the first time the "Austrian" business-cycle theory developed by von Mises from the Austrian theory of capital. Hayek's substantial development of the theory, perhaps his main contribution to positive economics, continued in a series of works culminating in *The Pure Theory of Capital* (1941).

Hayek sees capital as a heterogeneous structure of capital goods, not as a homogeneous stock. The process of production extends in a series of stages through time, viewed from final consumption and going back to "higher" stages further removed. If capital goods are to raise final output, they have to be adapted to one another to form an integrated structure of production; if they do not they are mal-invested.

Hayek's trade cycle theory grows out of this Austrian theory of capital. When monetary expansion increases the supply of credit, firms are misled about the availability of real resources for investment. Monetary expansion does not affect all prices and all parts of the economy simultaneously and equally (as is assumed in Walrasian general equilibrium theory). Business men, misled by the expansion in credit, seek to extend the production structure but there are not enough real resources to produce all the capital goods, including circulating capital, required. Hence the initial "boom" is in real terms a period of mal-investment; and the subsequent "crisis" and "depression" are periods in which mal-investments are discovered and the investment pattern adjusted to the underlying availability of real resources.

Hayek's micro-economic analysis of inter-relationships is in sharp contrast to the Marshallian and Walrasian macro-economic price-"level" approach. This view sees money as affecting only the (average) price-"level"; it does not analyse the effects of changes in the monetary stream on *relative* individual prices and price interrelationships. Consequently many economists new to the Austrian approach found Hayek's theories puzzling and obscure.

Hayek differed fundamentally from Keynes, whom he regarded as preoccupied with monetary (rather than real) phenomena and aggregative (rather than relative) concepts. Hayek argued that Keynes's *Treatise on Money* neglected the real structure of production by supposing that, if there were no entrepreneurial profits or losses in the *aggregate*, output would be constant. Hayek argued that if profits in the "lower" stages of production (nearer the consumption end) were accompanied by losses in the "higher" stages, the capital structure would contract, i.e. become less roundabout, and output and employment would fall. He was thus emphasizing relative, in contrast to average, prices as the fundamental influences on total output and employment.

Hayek maintained that Keynes's system of economics was based on the assumption that scarcity need not exist but was created *artificially* by the refusal of people to produce or work for prices or wages that were below arbitrary levels—which he did not explain but assumed to be unchangeable except in the approaches to a boom when scarcity raised prices and wages. Hayek countered that scarcity necessarily affected prices and wages in various sectors of the economy at all stages of the trade cycle long before the boom was imminent. When Keynes told Hayek he had changed his mind and had abandoned the argument of the *Treatise on Money*, Hayek decided not to criticize the *General Theory* because he thought Keynes would change his mind again and criticism would be a waste of time. Hayek disagreed with Keynes's whole approach because it "furthered the temporary ascendancy of macro-economics and the temporary decline of micro-economic theory." His general judgement of Keynes was that before he started to develop his own theories Keynes was not a highly trained or a very sophisticated economic theorist. "He started from a rather elementary Marshallian economics, and what had been achieved by Walras and Pareto, the Austrians and the Swedes, was very much a closed book to him." Hayek doubted whether Keynes had fully mastered the theory of international trade or had thought systematically on the theory of capital; "and even in the theory of the value of money his starting point—and later the object of his criticism—

appears to have been a very simple, equation-of-exchange-type of the quantity theory rather than the much more sophisticated cash-balances approach of Alfred Marshall." (*A Tiger by the Tail: the Keynesian Legacy of Inflation*, IEA, 1971).

Hayek's second major contribution is in methodology. He argued consistently for methodological individualism in the social sciences, further developing the "Austrian" thesis that economic theorems, being based on the postulate of individual human action, provided a unique view of reality from a perspective opposite to that of the natural sciences. In the social sciences, the individual elements—human action—were known; the problem was to build up a theoretical picture of the social structures formed on this basis that were the results of human *action* but not of human *design*. Economic theorems—if deduced from the postulate of human action—are no more "empirically testable" (the approach of the Chicago School) than are the theorems of logic or mathematics. In the social sciences, reality is historical; the "facts" of the social sciences are complex, unrepeatable "events." The data of the natural sciences do not fall into this category.

Hayek's view of the market as an *inter-individual* process is in sharp contrast to the Walrasian preoccupation with the conditions of general equilibrium. Circumstances change continually in real life, and knowledge of them is first acquired by the individuals most directly concerned. As they adapt their actions to the changed circumstances, they alter the prices and/or other elements in the data to which other individuals adapt their actions, and so on. Prices can serve as indispensable communicators of empirical information not obtainable by other means; the market process can thus use more of the data available to individuals more effectively than can other methods that attempt to co-ordinate individual actions.

Recently some historians of economic thought and some younger economists in America have revived interest in Hayek's economic analyses. Hayek made contributions to thinking on the nature of a market economy and on the institutions required for it. He also shed new light on the development of John Stuart Mill's thought (*John Stuart Mill and Harriet Taylor*, 1951). [2]

Head Lease. *See* LEASEHOLD.

Heckscher, Eli F. (1879–1952), Swedish economist who taught at the University of Stockholm. Author of the comprehensive, authoritative work *Mercantilism*, published in 1931, which is indispensable to students of mercantilist policies. The book is thought by some economists to over-emphasize the institutional and political aspects and to pay insufficient attention to the influence of economic trends, particularly the expansion of trade following the decline of feudalism, but it is outstandingly enlightening on the theorists of mercantilism. [2]

"Hedge." *See* COMMODITY MARKET; FUTURES.

Hedonism, a general term for theories of conduct in which the test is pleasure or pain. They were associated with the early versions of the economic principle of utility, but the utility theory of value is independent of hedonist assumptions since it does not specify the wants which induce people to engage in economic activity. These wants may be selfish (pursuit of profit, power, etc.) or unselfish (desire to help others). Conduct cannot always be judged as selfish or unselfish; profit, power, etc., may be sought for self, family, club, political party or church. [14]

Hegel, Georg Wilhelm Friedrich (1770–1831), a German philosopher and professor at Berlin University who has had considerable influence on some social scientists. He wrote little directly in economics except a commentary on James Steuart's *Inquiry into the Principles of Political Economy.* To Hegel the real world was the external phenomenal form of the thought process of "the Idea." He was a systematizer who developed a dialectical method of analysing society and social change. His idealist philosophy was "stood on its head" by Marx, who used Hegel's categories—thesis, anti-thesis and synthesis—in his dialectical materialism. Hegel's theory accorded much importance to the state, which he called "the reality of the moral idea." The strength of his philosophy in Britain (through Jowett, Green, Bosanquet and others) contributed to the growth of "statism" in economic thought and policy. Hegel is one of the most important philosophical sources of "historicism" or "holism" in the social sciences which has in recent years been attacked by the philosopher Professor Karl Popper in *The Poverty of Historicism* (1957, based on a paper completed in 1935), *The Open Society and its Enemies* (1945) and other writings. [2]

Heterogeneity, in economics the quality of difference between goods or services, even if physically or technically similar, so that they are treated by consumers as imperfect substitutes. Thus a small car may be a closer substitute for a moped (technically different) than for a larger model of the same kind. The economic significance of heterogeneity is that it indicates that there is no interrelationship (or only a very remote one) between the demands, supplies or prices of heterogeneous goods. The more heterogeneous an assembly of commodities, the less the demand for (or supply or price of) any one affects the demand for (or supply or price of) the others. [7]

Heteroskedasticity. *See* SKEDASTICITY.

Hicks, John R. (1904–89), British economist. He was educated at Oxford (Balliol College), and taught at the London School of Economics (1926–35) and at Cambridge (to 1938). From 1938 to 1946 he was Professor of Political Economy at the University of Manchester. In 1946 he returned to Oxford (Nuffield College) where he was Drummond Professor of Political Economy from 1952 to 1965. He married the economist Ursula K. Webb.

Hicks's first major work was *The Theory of Wages* (1932), in which he refined and elaborated the classical theory that wages were determined by the marginal productivity of labour. His other main works were on the economics of capital, the trade cycle, demand and monetary theory.

Economics can be divided crudely into those who seek to come to grips with reality by seeing how much can be left out of an analytical argument in order to simplify it (Ricardo, Marshall, Keynes) and those who seek the same end by ensuring that nothing is omitted while reducing the categories of analysis to a minimum (Walras and others). In this rough division Hicks falls into the second group. His clarification (with R. G. D. Allen) of the theory of consumer demand (*Economica,* 1934), his brilliant critical review of Keynes's *General Theory,* and his work on the trade cycle (*A Contribution to the Theory of the Trade Cycle,* 1950) which developed from it, are examples. *Value and Capital* (1939), which proceeded from the theory of subjective value to the study of general equilibrium (deepened by Hicks's extensive work on the theory of the firm) to examine the foundations of dynamic economics, covered as wide a range as any work of original scholarship on the subject. It was considered to have gone far to bring both Marshall and Walras up to date. [2]

Hicks, Ursula Kathleen (1896–1985), British economist (married to Sir John R. Hicks). She was educated at Roedean, Somerville College, Oxford, and the London School of Economics. She taught at the LSE and Liverpool University. Her main interest has been in the theory and practice of Public Finance. Her works in this subject include *Finance of British Government, 1920–36* (1938), *Public Finance* (1955), *British Public Finances, their Structure and Development, 1880–1952* (1954). With A. Lerner and P. Sweezy she edited *The Review of Economic Studies,* in the days when the group of mainly young economists who published their work in it had considerable influence on the development of the science. [2]

Hidden Hand, the force that Adam Smith thought led individuals following their personal interest to serve the common good even though it was "no part of their intention." Here he was distinguishing between *purpose* and *consequence.* His background as a moral philosopher may explain his approach. It is good for man to be moral—to have good intentions; but whatever his *reasons* for action, good or bad, selfish or unselfish, the results may still be good if, in the *result,* they benefit others. Thus a man may work hardest to benefit himself (or, e.g., for his family, or a charity) but what matters to others is whether he is led by his selfish motives to benefit them and the community in general. Morals (good or bad) are thus analysed separately from economics (efficient or inefficient). They are analytically distinct, not necessarily in conflict, but complementary. An action or activity cannot be judged solely by motives but also by consequences; if it benefits others it is not necessarily to be condemned because it is self-interested. "Economic necessity" is a colloquial phrase sometimes used to describe the motives that have led men to work, effort, invention, discovery, and risk-taking that have benefited mankind decades or centuries after. Human motives are varied—the selfless urge to create, to innovate, to self-expression, to serve others, to solve a problem, to conquer a human weakness or a challenge of nature explain much human achievement; the "hidden hand" of self-interest is often more pervasive in everyday life.

Limitations of knowledge may force man to appear to be self-interested because he can know or understand only his immediate surroundings and not the world at large; or his view of the interests of the world at large may differ from that of other men so that agreement on common action may be difficult or rare or imposed only by force. In these circumstances, self-interest or local "causes" may be a necessary "hidden hand" inducing him to serve wider causes he cannot perceive. [14]

Higgling (or haggling), the process by which a price is arrived at for a transaction when there is keen, direct bargaining between a buyer who begins by offering a price he is prepared to raise and a seller who begins by asking a price he will lower. The final price will be the outcome of the relative bargaining skills of the buyer and seller, that is, the capacity to sense the price to which the other can be raised or lowered. Higgling takes place where there are no developed markets in which buyers and sellers have established widely known prices at which supply and demand are equalized. Examples are the markets in second-hand furniture or new products supplied by a small number of suppliers or wanted by a small number of buyers. [7]

Highest and Best Use, describes the form of development for a given land site which will justify the highest bid price or rent for the land for any given array of building and improvement costs. The competition of land developers, armed with various plans for the use of land in various combinations with other factors of production, tends to ensure that sites in an urban land market will be developed to their highest and best uses (within a given framework of public policy on land use). The resulting pattern of urban land use is not haphazard but related to the accessibility of and transport costs associated with particular sites. [6]

Hildebrand, Bruno. *See* Economic Thought.

Hire Purchase, British name for a method of buying consumer or capital goods (and sometimes services) by instalments; the purchase remains the property of the seller until the last instalment has been paid, and so remains as security for the debt. In North America hire purchase is generally known as Instalment Credit.

Hire purchase first spread rapidly in the USA in the 1920's. It spread in post-war Britain, Canada and Australia, but more slowly in Europe.

Hire purchase was developed as the method of buying that best suited people with little capital and relatively low incomes faced with the relatively high values of the increasing flow of labour-saving or pleasure-giving commodities (such as vacuum-cleaners and motor cars). The three main alternative ways seemed less convenient or satisfying: to wait until the purchase price had been accumulated and then pay cash would risk the money being spent; to take possession, accumulate the purchase price and then pay it as a lump sum would make the accumulating sums seem less fruitful than if they were paid to the seller (or the company that financed the transaction), who could use them more effectively to enlarge sales to other buyers; to hire rather than buy outright gave no sense of ownership and prevented the user from expressing his personality or preferences in his property.

Hence hire purchase. It was further stimulated by the rapid growth in technical invention, the rise in incomes which enabled more people to pay deposits and maintain instalments, and the post-war inflation which encouraged consumption spending—even though on "consumer durables" which are a form of consumer "capital"—because it made saving precarious by endangering its value.

In its early years in Britain hire purchase fell into disrepute because of the excesses of traders who "snatched back" goods for which the instalments had fallen into arrears. There has also been some over-selling and fraudulent persuasion by house-to-house salesmen. Hire Purchase Acts before and after the Second World War strengthened the rights of hire purchasers.

In spite of rapid growth in post-war Britain, hire purchase as a source of credit accounted for much less than building society house mortgages (about £3,000 million) or joint-stock bank advances.

In essence hire purchase is a form of banking. Some of the finance houses that pay retailers the cash price to relieve them of the role of financiers describe themselves as industrial bankers. In the late 1950's the British joint-stocks entered into the financing of hire purchase by buying interests in or control of hire purchase finance companies.

Economists differ over the extent to which hire purchase is inflationary. Government attempts intermittently in the post-war decades to repress it by restricting the capital issues of the finance houses, inhibiting bank credit to them, requiring larger deposits and shorter repayment periods proved largely unavailing because in an otherwise free market the finance companies raised funds direct from the public by deposits on which they paid interest at a higher rate than investors could obtain elsewhere.

These government controls had the further effect of disrupting the development of several British industries that showed most initiative and enterprise. They probably also weakened the incentive effect of hire purchase in encouraging people to work for the goods it could enable them to buy.

Hire purchase often provides manufacturing and agriculture with medium-term finance for equipment and livestock. In Britain more than one quarter of the total has been for such equipment, about three-quarters for consumer goods (including durable "capital").

The development of hire purchase in the USA, Canada, West Germany, France, Holland, Italy, Scandinavia, Eire, Australia, New Zealand, South Africa and other countries suggests that it accompanies economic growth in advanced industrial societies. As incomes rise, it seems likely that the security for the loan may change from the merchandise bought to the personal income, standing and credit-worthiness of the buyer. [7]

Historic Cost. *See* Cost.

Historical Method (historicism), the basis of the method of the historical school in economic thought, broadly the theory that scientific economics should be derived wholly from historical research. The view is that the economist should first master historical techniques and then approach economic history to investigate particular patterns or processes. The only kind of general knowledge that is attainable in the social sciences would then grow slowly out of this work. The views of the historical school in this context may be summed up as holding that the economist, as a research worker, should be primarily an economic historian.

The critics of the historical method hold that while history may be instructive it does not necessarily teach much about the future and that it can lead social scientists into fundamental error because there is no reason to expect the present or the future to resemble the past.

Historicism was developed by Hegel and Marx. It has been challenged by Sir Karl R. Popper, who has argued that there can be no prediction of the course of human history by scientific or any other rational methods. [14]

Historicism. *See* Historical Method.

History, Relation to Economics. *See* Economics, Economic History.

Hiving Off, separating part of a firm from the rest and putting it under independent or outside management or control. The word comes from Lord Hives, of Rolls Royce. [3]

Hoarding, the propensity of the public to hold wealth in the form of cash.

Hoarding is not the actual amount of cash holdings of the public. The total quantity of money is fixed by the banking system, and since it must be held (owned) by someone, the total of money holdings must be equal to the total supply. If one individual increases his cash holding, another (or others) must reduce his (their) cash holdings if there is no change in the total supply of money. As a result of an increased desire to hoard by one individual, the distribution of cash holdings by the public may be changed, but the total cash holdings cannot alter unless there is an increase in the supply of money.

The propensity of the public to hoard has important consequences for the stability and efficiency of the economic system. When the desire to hoard rises assets in the form of securities will be sold for cash. These sales will tend to lower the prices of securities, and therefore raise the general level of interest rates, unless the banking system meets the increased demand for cash by increasing the quantity of money. An increase in the desire to hold cash is thus choked off by paying higher interest rates to potential hoarders; but these higher rates tend to check investment and lead to a decrease in incomes and employment. Thus the notion of hoarding has been regarded as at the heart of theories of unemployment. [8]

Hobart Papers, a series of economic studies conceived and edited by Arthur Seldon and published by the Institute of Economic Affairs as analyses of a subject in microcosm with conclusions for policy. The Hobart Papers soon established themselves as the leading stream of academic economic dissection and commentary in Britain in increasing use in universities. Their methodological characteristic was primarily micro-economic and their conclusions were often radical: they examined the working of markets as methods of registering preferences and allocating resources, often in unusual objects like blood, animal semen, car parking, sport, television and breast-milk; and they investigated the reasons why markets were efficient or inefficient, the framework of institutions required for efficiency (laws, money, etc.), and alternative methods of preference-measurement and resource-allocation. The Hobart Papers were considered to have had increasing influence on economic teaching, thinking and policy. The first fifty were published in the 1960's, the second fifty during the 1970's. Number 1, on resale price maintenance by Professor B. S. Yamey (1960), stimulated the academic and public re-appraisal that led to the abolition of this restrictive practice in 1964. Number 4, by Professor D. S. Lees (later Chairman of the National Insurance Advisory Committee), was the first systematic analysis of the consequences of nil pricing in the National Health Service. Number 25, by Professor A. T. Peacock (later Economic Adviser to the Department of Trade and Industry) and Professor J. Wiseman, analysed the application of the voucher system to British education. In number 46 Professor H. G. Johnson argued strongly for floating exchanges, later adopted by British governments. Number 40, on the Land Commission (later abolished), and the economic analysis of Number 48 on the housing market, were written by Professor F. G. Pennance. [2]

Hobson, John A. (1858–1940), English social reformer, economist and journalist. He was educated at Oxford University and was for some time a schoolteacher at Faversham and Exeter. In 1887 he became a university extension lecturer but soon gave his energies to economics and social studies, publishing some thirty-five works and numerous articles and pamphlets. His major works included *The Industrial System* (1909), *The Economics of Unemployment* (1922) and *Work and Wealth* (1914). He is probably best known for his *Physiology of Industry* (1889), written in collaboration with A. E. Mummery. In it he formulates a theory of under-consumption based on a view that expenditure on capital and consumption goods becomes unbalanced because of excess saving by a wealthy minority. These views were unpopular at the time and may help to explain why he was never offered an academic post, but he lived to receive belated recognition from Keynes in *The General Theory of Employment, Interest and Money* (1936). [2]

Holding Company, one which controls the activities of others by acquiring all or most of their shares. It may form a subsidiary company for the purpose or acquire an existing company by buying the shares for cash or giving its shares in exchange.

Most of the large public companies in the UK are holding companies with many subsidiaries, and there is an increasing tendency for companies to form large groups in many industries. A subsidiary usually deals with one part of the industry or trade in which the group operates. Overseas subsidiaries are formed to look after the group's interests in a single country or continent. Subsidiaries may be given a larger or smaller degree of autonomy. Under the Companies Act, 1948, the holding company must publish consolidated accounts covering the whole group.

A holding company does not always hold the whole of the shares in the subsidiary: there is often a minority interest of outside shareholders. In take-over bids the majority of the shares of a company are acquired by another, which may become the holding company. Shareholders are offered shares in the holding company and/or cash in exchange for their own shares. The companies taken over are considered potentially more profitable either because their properties and other assets are not being fully employed or because economies could be made through amalgamation or competition reduced. [3]

Holism. *See* HEGEL.

"Home Service" Assurance. *See* INDUSTRIAL ASSURANCE.

Homogeneity, such close similarity between goods or services from several sources that they cannot be differentiated and so are treated by buyers and sellers as *economically* a *single* good or service. They are perfect substitutes for one another; and the cross-elasticity between them is infinite. Thus gas, coal, electricity and oil would approach substitutability if sold at the same price. The importance of the concept is that it emphasizes the difference between *technical* (or *physical*) and *economic* properties: objects that are technically dissimilar are economically homogeneous if they are regarded as substitutable; i.e. their *objective* differences are irrelevant if they are treated *subjectively* as identical. [7]

Homoskedasticity. *See* SKEDACTICITY.

Horizontal Integration. *See* INTEGRATION.

"Hot Money," a colourful name for the short-term capital which moves between countries because of uncertainty about the stability of exchange rates or the security of capital. If speculators are pessimistic about the ability of Britain to maintain parity with the dollar at, say, $2.40 to the pound they will sell sterling assets for dollars. (Similarly, if they expect the Deutschmark to be revalued upwards, they will try to shift their funds into Germany.) Such movements of short-term capital though speculative are not necessarily the work of professional speculators. Most of the money involved will in fact be held in sterling or dollar bills for ordinary financial or trading purposes. The choice of the financial centre in which it is held will depend on differences in interest rates in New York and London, and differences between the spot and the forward rates for the pound. Hot money is part of the price Britain has to pay for being a major world financial centre, and part of a world economy that supplies her with food and raw materials for which she pays by exporting about a quarter of her national output of goods and services. The quick and unexpected movement of short-term capital, plus the delays in payments between British and foreign firms, can drain the reserves of gold and foreign exchange.

A flight of short-term capital may be triggered by expectations of a trading imbalance; but expectations of interest rate or exchange rate adjustments for whatever reason are just as likely to start a movement. Increasingly in the late 1960's and 1970's world capital markets were subjected to heavy speculative flows of capital despite severe controls imposed by some countries—particularly Britain and France. In the prevailing international monetary climate, such flows were probably inevitable. Under the Gold Exchange standard that applied, countries tended to hold their reserves in various mixtures—of gold, dollars, marks, sterling, francs etc., as well as in SDR's (Special Drawing Rights) against the IMF (International Monetary Fund): at the same time under the then brand of floating exchange rates the relative prices of these assets tended to move infrequently and abruptly rather than smoothly and continuously. In these circumstances, any form of change in the desired composition of reserves involved the movement of short-term assets. It also promoted (inevitably) speculation against exchange rates. [4]

Householder's Surplus, the amount of money over the market price required to induce an owner to sell his home. It is influenced by sentimental ties to a house in which children were brought up, attachment to the surroundings, links with neighbouring friends and familiarity with local facilities (schools, hospitals, churches, parks, sports clubs, walks, old buildings, etc.). A survey in the mid-1960's found that householders unlikely to be affected by airport noise had a householder's surplus of about 40 per cent over market prices: they were asked for their reactions if offers were made for their homes for a large redevelopment. A difficulty is that they may have supposed they could move a *short* distance and thus lose their site but not their neighbourhood. A new airport would have affected a much larger area and, to escape the noise, vibration, etc., they would have had to move a *long* distance away. If this had been made clear to them, their estimate of householder's surplus might have been larger than 40 per cent. [7]

Human Action, name given by Ludwig von Mises to his last major book, which argued that economics was concerned with, and could shed light on, all human activity, not only that concerned with a part of life, as suggested by definitions of economics as concerned with "earning a living," material goods, choice of means to serve known ends, etc. [14]

Human Capital, the facilities, skills, etc. stored in an individual, or in all individuals, whether inherited or acquired. Thus formal education at school or university or by training at work is investment in human beings, the yield on which economists have tried to calculate by relating the cost of the investment to its yield in the lifetime earnings attributable to it. Some economists, e.g. Professor Gary Becker of Chicago University, have specialized in the economics of human capital. [1] [5]

Hume, David (1711–76), Scottish philosopher, historian and political economist. His father owned a small estate in Berwickshire; there Hume received his early education, eventually going to the University of Edinburgh. After a few months in a Bristol business house he went to France, and thereafter, apart from a period as tutor to the Marquis of Annandale, he spent his life in study, being appointed to the Faculty of Advocates in Edinburgh in 1752. His main works, *Political Discourses* (1752) and *Treatise on Human Nature* (1739–40), place Hume as an eminent "natural law" philosopher. He was a critic of mercantilist doctrines, and exerted a formative influence on Adam Smith. He also made important contributions to the theory of money, property and international trade. [2]

Hutcheson, Francis. *See* SMITH, ADAM.

Hutt, William Harold (1899–1989), British economist who has spent most of his life as a teacher in South Africa (Professor of Commerce 1931–65) and the USA (visiting Professor of Economics at several, mostly private, universities). An independent, original and radical thinker with strong non-conformist inclinations.

His first book-length work, *The Theory of Collective Bargaining* (1930), contested the conventional view that trade unions were the weaker bargaining side for wages because, inter alia, labour was perishable. *Economists and the Public* (1936) argued that economists were losing their standing because they had a propensity to give advice that was politically palatable rather than in the long-run public interest. At a late stage he added to his book a critique of Keynes's most influential work, *The General Theory of Employment, Interest and Money,* which had just been published. In 1939 *The Theory of Idle Resources* presented a more fundamental analysis of unemployment than that offered by Keynes. *Plan for Reconstruction* (1943) outlined proposals for post-war reform based on the effective but humane buying-out of vested interests resistant to change. In 1963 he published *Keynesianism—Retrospect and Prospect,* a root-and-branch critique of Keynes written in 1938–9 but not published because of adverse reaction from readers of the manuscript. His views on some weaknesses of Keynes were vindicated by the Swedish-American economist, Axel Leijonhufvud, in his classic *On Keynesian Economics and the Economics of Keynes* (1968); Leijonhufvud named Hutt's *Theory of Idle Resources* as the *locus classicus* for the analysis of the process by which the individual employee decides on the wage-rate at which he will accept a new job.

In *The Economics of the Colour-Bar* Hutt's unorthodox approach was deployed in a critique of the racial policies of the South African government, based on the argument that "the [labour] market was colour-blind" and would ultimately not be suppressed by apartheid. In 1971, in *Politically Impossible . . . ,* he reviewed his teaching on monetary policy, social welfare, Keynesianism, and the trade unions to assess the damaging consequences to economists of accepting the judgement of politicians on the public acceptability of ideas. In 1973 he returned to the economics of the labour market in *The Strike-Threat System,* which argued that the fear of strikes harmed the economic system more than strikes themselves. And in 1974 his *Rehabilitation of Say's Law* maintained that the equivalence of supply and demand had not been disproved by Keynes or any other critic.

Hutt's work often provoked strong initial hostility because it questioned long-established or widely-accepted economic "truths," or was ignored because he developed new terminology unfamiliar to economists in the mainstream of economic thinking. But his teaching was often vindicated by events and eventually recognized. [2]

Hyperinflation, the state of advanced inflation when it has become beyond control by normal or conventional government policy and drastic measures are required to prevent it from disrupting economic life and destroying the economic system. The state is reached earlier in countries unaccustomed to inflation, as in Europe (except Germany and Hungary) or North America, than in countries accustomed to it, as in South America. Its symptoms are rapidly rising prices, weakening faith in the currency, a flight into goods (or other currencies), a shortening of contracts so that they can be revised frequently (e.g. wage-bargains, leases, etc.), an increased demand for "escalator" clauses so that agreed terms keep pace with rising prices, reductions in savings, an increase in dissaving, consumption of capital, export of capital. In the end views become shorter and shorter, and there is a loss of the "principle of organic unity through time" that Keynes emphasized. Unless hyperinflation can be slowed down by "indexing" or "monetary correction," the only solution is abandonment of the currency and its replacement by a new one. Hyperinflations have taken place in Germany (1922–3), Greece, Hungary and China (late 1940's). [8]

Hypothecated Revenue. *See* EARMARKING.

Hypothesis. *See* ASSOCIATED SCIENCES.

I

Ideas, in economics, their influence on policy. The two apparently extreme views are: J. M. Keynes—"the ideas of economists and political philosophers, both when they are right and when they are wrong, are more powerful than is commonly understood. Indeed the world is ruled by little else. Practical men, who believe themselves to be quite exempt from any intellectual influences, are usually the slaves of some defunct economist. Madmen in authority, who hear voices in the air, are distilling their frenzy from some academic scribbler of a few years back. I am sure that the power of vested interests is vastly exaggerated compared with the gradual encroachment of ideas. Not, indeed, immediately, but after a certain interval; for in economic and political philosophy there are not many who are influenced by new theories after twenty-five or thirty years of age, so that the ideas which civil servants and politicians and even agitators apply to current events are not likely to be the newest. But, soon or late, it is ideas, not vested interests, which are dangerous for good or evil" (the last lines in *The General Theory of Employment, Interest and Money,* Macmillan, 1936). J. S. Mill seemed to say the opposite—"Ideas, unless outward circumstances conspire with them, have in general no very rapid or immediate efficacy in human affairs" (*Edinburgh Review,* 1845) ("outward circumstances" are politically favourable conditions). But both could be understood to be saying that though economic ideas have little effect in the *short* run, they may or do have much effect in the *long* run. J. S. Mill's politically favourable climate does not necessarily conflict with J. M. Keynes's influence of ideas on politicians who await or create the climate. [13]

"Idle" Balances (of money). *See* Dishoarding.

Illth, the opposite of wealth, i.e. commodities (or services) that give negative satisfaction or create dissatisfaction. Many objects or activities can be sources of both wealth and illth according to the amounts consumed or used: eating, drinking, smoking can be sources of satisfaction (to the palate, or by maintaining good health or creating a feeling of well-being) up to a point, and sources of illth beyond it (when they are said to have been taken in excess). Working, sport, etc. give satisfaction, with diminishing marginal utility, until the utility is nil; and they then turn into disutility, dissatisfaction, or illth. [7]

Impact (of a tax). *See* Tax, Direct and Indirect.

Imperfect Competition, market situation which does not fulfil all the conditions necessary for perfect competition and which is characterized by one or more of the following features: ability of sellers to influence demand by such practices as product differentiation, branding, advertising; restraints on the entry of competitors into any line of production either because of the large scale of initial investment required or because of restrictive and collusive practices; the existence of uncertainty and imperfect knowledge about prices and profits elsewhere; the absence of price competition. Such market imperfections are characteristic, to larger or lesser degree, of most markets for both goods and factors of production. [7]

Imperial Preference, the system of preferential tariffs on trade between Commonwealth countries and the UK and to some extent among Commonwealth countries.

Up to the 1930's Great Britain was essentially a free trade country despite agitation, dating back to the 1890's, for protection coupled with Imperial Preference to counter rising world competition and protectionism in other countries. The 1915 McKenna duties on a narrow range of imports and the Key Industry Duties imposed under the 1921 Safeguarding of Industries Act had made only a small breach in the free trade position. The 1919 preferential rates on Commonwealth goods also marked only a small step towards Imperial Preference.

This policy was reversed by the adoption of selective protective duties in 1931 and by the Import Duties Act of 1932, which imposed a general duty of 10 per cent on all imports from non-Commonwealth sources except for goods already dutiable and a "free list" of mainly foodstuffs and industrial raw materials. This Act thus introduced a large degree of Imperial Preference confirmed and made reciprocal by the Ottawa Agreements of the same year. Under these bilateral agreements Commonwealth countries granted tariff preferences on many UK goods. In return Britain imposed new or increased "Ottawa Duties" on non-Commonwealth imports—chiefly food and raw materials—and placed quantitative restrictions on non-Commonwealth meat imports. Similar additional duties were placed on non-Commonwealth beef and veal imports in 1936. During World War II and immediately afterwards, the UK negotiated many bilateral trade deals and long-term bulk purchase contracts to ensure supplies for the UK and to conserve supplies of "hard" currencies. These trade-diverting measures supplemented Imperial Preference through tariffs.

The articles of the post-war General Agreement on Tariffs and Trade (GATT) prohibited further increase in existing preferences. Moreover, in the course of GATT negotiations, Britain and Commonwealth countries agreed to eliminate or reduce some preferences. The importance of Imperial Preference has thus been declining. And since preferences were often specific (rather than *ad valorem*) their real value has been diminished by inflation. Britain's membership of

EFTA and, even more, her entry into the EEC further weakened the system of preferences, although special arrangements (e.g. for sugar) were negotiated to avoid hardship for some Commonwealth countries. [4]

Imperialism (Economic). *See* Economic Imperialism.

Import Broker. *See* Broker.

Imports, goods and services brought into a country by commerce. In economics, the imports of a country represent payments in kind to the importing country, made in exchange for the exportation of goods, for services rendered—such as shipping, banking, insurance—for interest or principal repayments on capital exports made at an earlier time, or for movements of gold and silver. After the First World War another source of imports was German reparations to the Allies; Germany was required to export to the Allies to finance her payments.

The difference between the imports and exports of a country as recorded by its customs department is called the balance of trade. The records made at the customs house refer to material commodities, but a country may be importing services, the value of which cannot be and is not entered in the trade returns. They are usually called "invisible" imports. (The values at which imports are officially recorded at customs houses vary in different countries; UK imports are entered at CIF values, that is, values representing the cost, insurance and freight; exports are valued FOB, i.e. free on board, exclusive of insurance and freight.

Historically, imports have been subject to the imposition of various forms of control. From the middle of the nineteenth century to the 1930's tariffs were the principal regulation on imports; in the 1930's other forms of control came into more general use. The Second World War and the unsettled early post-war years made official licences and other direct governmental decisions the main controls of imports, but it also brought a movement to reduce or abolish import controls in order to increase international trade. [4]

Imports, Invisible. *See* Balance of Payments.

Imports, Visible. *See* Balance of Payments.

Imputation, the process of attributing value to productive resources in accordance with their contribution to the value of their products. It was a logical development following the emergence of the theory of subjective value in the 1870's, and it represented an important step in the development of a unified (marginal productivity) theory of the prices of the factors of production by breaking away from the earlier views of distribution as comprising the allocation of income between social classes. These earlier views regarded the share of landowners (rent) as a surplus determined by demand which did not form part of production costs, the share of labour (wages) as determined by the size of the

"Wages Fund" and tending in the long run to a subsistence level (the "Iron Law"), and the residual share as profits.

The theory of imputation argued that the value of factors ("higher-order" goods) was *in all cases* determined by (imputed from) the value of the final ("lower order") goods to whose production they contributed. The value to be imputed to a factor then followed from the proposition that, since the proportions in which factors could be combined to yield a given product can be varied, their relative marginal contributions could be isolated and assessed. [14]

Inactive Money. *See* DISHOARDING.

Incidence of Taxation, the final resting-place of a tax burden, as distinct from its "impact," i.e. the first place where it is imposed. In time a tax may percolate through many parts of the economy. The burden of a tax will tend to be shifted by those who pay it initially, the extent depending on the elasticities of the demand and supply for goods and services and factors of production, i.e. on the degree of imperfection in these markets. Manufacturers will try to shift it to retailers and consumers, who may give up smoking or strike for more pay and pass it back to other manufacturers. Manufacturers may try to reduce the prices they pay to labour and for other factors and thus pass the tax back. If wages are reduced in this way, wage-earners may spend less, and prices and sales revenues fall; the tax incidence is thus shifted onwards by consumers. Thus in the end the people who contribute to the resources which the government acquires through taxation may be very different from those on whom the taxes were apparently imposed. Studies of the ways in which taxes are shifted help in formulating tax policy. [12]

Income, broadly, the receipts of individuals, companies or governments over a stated period, derived from the earnings of individuals or from the ownership of factors of production. Strictly, income and money receipts are not the same. In economics income is closely tied to production, the creation of wealth in the form of real goods and services. When priced, the value of production measures money income. This is not necessarily identical with money receipts, which represent the exchange of *one* kind of asset, a claim on wealth, for another, money, which is a *general* claim on wealth. A speculative builder creates wealth (income) with every day's work on a house: when he finally sells the house for money he is merely exchanging assets.

These distinctions are fundamental in economics however much they may be blurred in everyday usage. Thus for the purpose of economic measurement it is sometimes necessary to impute a notional income where there is no receipt of money (or goods or services). An example is the value of an owner-occupier's interest in his property, a resource that is currently producing an annual flow of income in the form of house-room. More generally personal incomes take the form of and are measured by wages, salaries, interest, profits, dividends and rent: company income accumulates as retained earnings in the form of reserves and undistributed profits: government income comes from the ownership of property. Tax receipts represent transfers from the private sector and are not regarded as income. [9]

Income Determination, Theory of, the Keynesian theory that in a closed economy with no government activity, employment, output and income will tend towards the level at which the flow of desired savings of the community is just equal to the flow of desired investment expenditure on new capital assets.

In Keynes's analytical scheme the level of employment offered and the income arising from it was determined by the level of total demand in the community. In a modern society that uses capital, total demand can be broken down into (*a*) demand for consumer goods and services and (*b*) demand for investment or capital goods. An essential feature of the theory was that these two demands are determined by entirely different factors. The demand for consumption goods was assumed to depend in the main upon the incomes of consumers; the demand for investment goods is assumed to depend upon the present value put on their earning power, or the direct benefit they are expected to yield over their estimated future life compared with their cost.

Consumption demand was related to income in a systematic way by the propensity to consume: except at low levels some part of income will be saved, and whenever income is increased consumption spending rises too but by a smaller amount; in other words, the marginal propensity to consume is a fraction less than one, i.e. less than 100 per cent. It followed that as the level of output and income in the economy rises, a gap will appear between the total spending necessary to support the level of employment, output and income and the total spending on consumption associated with that level of income. The extent to which the community could maintain a given level of output and income therefore depended on the volume of investment expenditure being planned and undertaken. The original feature of Keynes's theory was that, since the community's desire to save and its desire to carry out investment expenditures are put into effect by completely separate decisions by different people, there could be no guarantee that the level of investment expenditure will always be such as to fill the "gap" between income and consumption spending at the level of income required for full employment. The most that could be said is that, given the level of investment as determined by business men's propensity to invest, income will tend to the level which, given the propensity to consume, would yield desired saving just equal to desired investment. This would represent equilibrium—in the sense that only at that level would there be no tendency for income to change—even though men and productive capacity were involuntarily unemployed. At any other level investment would either fall short of or would exceed the "savings gap," total demand would either fall short of or exceed the level necessary to support current output levels, and the level of output and income would be forced downwards or upwards.

Earlier theory had assumed that the general level of interest rates in the economy would tend to bring saving and investment into equilibrium, saving being encouraged and investment discouraged by high rates, and conversely by low rates. Keynes's refusal to accept the saving-investment theory of interest led him to reformulate the theory in terms of liquidity preference—the community's demand for money. Thus a logically consistent general theory of income determination emerged. Liquidity preference and the supply of money determined the rate of interest (and thus the cost of investment carried out with borrowed funds); given the cost of investment, the propensity to invest determined the amount of investment: given the amount of investment and the community's propensity to consume and save out of income, the level of income was determined at the level at which desired saving equalled desired investment.

The theory was adapted to cope with the introduction of foreign trade, taxation and Government expenditure. The simple equilibrium conditions that saving equals investment was merely widened to embrace all spendings "leakages" and "injections" so that it becomes: saving *plus* taxation *plus* imports equals investment *plus* government expenditure on goods and services *plus* exports.

This theory was widely accepted by economists when it was first offered by Keynes in 1936 in *The General Theory of Employment, Interest and Money.* In recent years it has been re-examined more critically in the works of some economists: Leijonhufvud, Friedman, Hutt, and others. [9]

Income, Earned. *See* Unearned Income.

Income Elasticity of Demand. *See* Demand; Elasticity of Demand.

Income, National. *See* National Income.

Income, Notional. *See* Notional Income.

Income, Real. *See* Real Income.

Income Tax, a tax levied upon the incomes of individuals and corporate bodies. It has the highest yield of any tax in the UK, comprising over two-fifths of total central government tax revenue. The cost of collection is under 2 per cent. Income tax was introduced in 1799 by William Pitt during the war against France. It was repealed in 1816 and reimposed in 1842. It has been renewed annually since 1860 by the Finance Acts. The administration devolves on the Board of Inland Revenue (which is responsible to the Treasury) through General and Special Commissioners of Taxes, Inspectors of Taxes and Collectors of Taxes.

Broadly, income tax is charged on all income arising within the UK and all income whatever its source accruing to a person living in the UK. There are some exceptions, such as interest from some UK government securities paid to non-residents. Double taxation agreements have been made with nearly all the Commonwealth governments and several foreign governments which prevents the taxation of income in both countries. Unilateral relief is given where there is no agreement.

Income tax is imposed for the year ending on 5th April at a standard rate. For individuals the tax is graduated by allowance—single and married personal allowances, wives' earned income relief, child allowances, dependent relative allowance, life assurance relief, super-annuation contributions, age reliefs, etc. "Unearned" income attracts an additional investment income surcharge. Incomes of husband and wife are normally treated as one. (Companies are liable to Corporation Tax on their taxable income.)

The tax is levied under one or more of six Schedules:

(1) *Schedule A.* Income from ownership of land and buildings (other than owner-occupation of homes).

(2) *Schedule B.* Income from the occupation of land other than buildings or land occupied for a trade or business. This Schedule is now confined to woodlands.

(3) *Schedule C.* Interest from securities of UK and overseas governments if paid in the UK.

(4) *Schedule D.* Profits of trades, businesses and professions and certain other incomes including interest and income from abroad and some short-term capital gains. This Schedule is divided into eight cases, of which Case 1, the most important, includes the profits of trades and businesses. The normal basis of assessment is the profit earned in the accounting year ending in the preceding year of assessment. Capital allowances are given for some types of depreciating wasting assets.

(5) *Schedule E.* Income from all offices, employments or pensions, i.e. wages and salaries. This tax is collected under the PAYE system.

(6) *Schedule F.* Dividends and other distributions made by companies resident in the UK that are not otherwise exempted.

Direct collection of tax is made in Schedules A, B and D. In Schedules C, E and F the tax is deducted at source and collected from the paying agents or employers. It is deducted at source by companies when paying dividends.

Income tax is a direct and progressive tax. The economic issues raised by income tax are chiefly those of incentives and taxable capacity. At some point the yield may fall off because people may prefer leisure to taxed income. At a further point there may be dissaving to maintain personal expenditure. The tax redistributes income because the yield goes to provide services for all; it may therefore raise total national income by equalizing opportunities in education, raising health standards, improving housing conditions, and increasing the resources of people with low incomes by family allowances, money grants and other benefits. [12]

Income, Unearned. *See* Unearned Income.

Income Policy, name given in Britain to Government persuasion of employers and unions to limit the rise in wages, salaries, profits, rents, etc., in order to prevent or reduce inflation. It rests on the view that inflation is caused by incomes rising faster than output and concludes that their growth must be no faster than output.

Economic analysis suggests that if incomes rise because the flow of money causes or allows incomes to rise faster than output, the solution is to reduce the flow of money (by Bank rate, open market policy or other methods). If incomes rise faster than output because income-receivers can compel employers to pay higher wages, salaries or rents, it must be presumed that increases in costs can be passed on to the consumer in higher prices. This can be done only if there is monopoly among the income-receivers and in the markets for the goods or services they help to produce: the solution is then to restore competition among the factors of production and the products. Or it can be done if government expands the quantity of money and makes consumers willing to pay higher prices without reducing demand; the solution is then to reduce the supply of money, or its rate of increase.

A particular difficulty in restraining all incomes is that wages and salaries are arranged by agreement or contract for a period and are a part of the costs of production; profits are a residual, that is, paid if revenue exceeds costs: it is therefore liable to fluctuate and it needs to be high in risky or new industries if capital is to be attracted to them.

Wages and salaries also need to be flexible in the long run if employees are to be attracted to growing firms. To restrict the rise in employees' pay in every firm to the average increase in national output would prevent wages and salaries from helping to redistribute the labour force from less productive to more productive employment.

Whatever the economic weaknesses, an incomes policy may have political advantages as being less unpopular than restricting demand by preventing inflation or directly outlawing monopoly and restrictive practices in the factors of production or their products. [10]

Inconvertible Note Issue, an issue of bank-notes which a holder has no right to convert on demand into gold or silver held as reserve against the issue.

An inconvertible note issue depends for its success on confidence in the monetary system. [8]

Increasing Returns. *See* RETURNS TO SCALE.

Independent Variable. *See* VARIABLE.

Index Lease. *See* LEASEHOLD.

Index Number, a measure showing by its variations the changes over time or space of a quantity that cannot itself be observed or measured directly. Examples are business activity, the physical volume of production, the general level of wholesale prices. The term index number may be applied to any standardized series of comparative values, usually called "relatives," and the index is an average of a number of "relatives."

The important features in constructing an index number are its coverage, base period, weighting system and method of averaging the observations. The coverage denotes the scope of the information (prices, output, etc.) collected from members of a sample survey and the size of the sample. The base period is that in which data used as the base of the index number were collected, frequently a year, but it may be as short as one day or as long as the average of a group of years. The length of the base period depends on the nature of the information being used, the purpose for which the index number is being compiled, and the need to remove abnormal influences or "bias." The components of an index number are frequently "weighted" according to their relative importance: for example, in index numbers of prices the items may be weighted by the quantity of each item consumed; thus bread may have twice or three times the weight of biscuits. If spending habits change the base period is replaced by a more recent one so that the index number of prices reflects up-to-date expenditures.

In practice the calculation of index numbers cannot easily allow for the underlying conditions that determine changes in economic quantities. Briefly, index numbers could measure the change in price (or some other attribute) over time with weights reflecting *original* (or other *past* values) or *current* values to reflect changing conditions, habits or preferences. In measuring changes in the cost of living, a Laspeyres index of prices uses the unchanging weights in the base year, and a Paasche index uses changing weights in the current year and calculates the cost over the period beginning with the base year. The difficulty is that, if conditions and preferences change, the collection of goods whose prices are being measured also changes, so that some are not supplied and demanded at all in some years, and the change in prices of goods entering into the cost of living cannot be followed through at all. [14]

Indexing, History of Economic Debate, the earliest reference in modern times seems to have been in the period of inflation and deflation during and after the Napoleonic Wars. Between 1792 and 1814 prices rose by about 60 per cent; between 1814 and 1822 they fell by 40 per cent. In the 1820's and 1830's Joseph Lowe, G. Poulett Scrope and G. R. Porter proposed methods of correcting (the modern term is "monetary correction") the monetary standard of value for changes in the cost of living by constructing an index number of consumer good prices. Lowe was the earliest in *The Present State of England in regard to Agriculture, Trade and Finance with a comparison of the prospects of England and France* (1822). Poulett wrote *An Examination of the Bank Charter Question with an Inquiry into the nature of a Just Standard of Value* (1833), and Porter *Principles of Political Economy* (1837), *Political Economy for Plain People* (1833) and *The Progress of the Nation* (1838). Porter calculated the average monthly fluctuations of fifty leading commodities from 1833 to 1837, but neither he nor the other two attempted the calculation of an index. The closest to the idea was Lowe, who proposed a table showing the changes from year to year of "the power of money in purchase" to give annuitants and others the basis for maintaining an agreement "not in its letter only, but in its spirit" by conferring on a specified sum of money "a uniformity and permanency of value, by changing the numerical value in proportion of the change in its power of purchase" every three, five or seven years. Lowe argued that uncertainty about the value of money made landlords reluctant to agree to long leases during inflation and tenants reluctant during deflation. As a result rents fluctuated with the price of corn or land was not leased at all. Agriculture would therefore be more prosperous if the money value of rent were corrected for inflation. In the labour market he remarked that wages in London were "sticky" downwards and so too high during deflation: "nothing will induce them [wage-earners] to assent to a reduction except a guarantee against a recurrence of the grand evil—a rise in prices." The solution was not to interfere in wage bargaining but to enable payer and receiver to give their "money stipulation . . . a permanent value." Lowe also envisaged that the price of and income from government stock would rise with the index of inflation. As a precedent Lowe pointed to the Court of Teinds which had wanted clerical income in the tithes of Scotland to vary with the price of corn but it had not been done because of "the unfortunate neglect of political economy in the education of our public men; and the interest of government, the greatest of all debtors, to allow money to undergo a gradual depreciation"; the second, and possibly the first, reason has a modern application.

Fifty years later, in 1875, Jevons argued in *Money and the Mechanism of Exchange* for a monetary standard of value that would exchange for a constant amount of corn, beef, coal, tea, coffee, etc., so that the legal tender note would be even more stable in value than gold or silver. He therefore proposed a "tabular standard of value," changes in which would be used to adjust contracts fixed in notes. A permanent commission would collect commodity prices and compute average variations in the purchasing power of gold. The scheme would stabilize social relations, guarantee fixed incomes, discourage speculation, avoid frustration in merchants' calculations, reduce bankruptcies.

In the same year Walter Bagehot took a different line in *The Economist.* He objected that Jevons's scheme was unfit for Britain because the increased uncertainty in exchanging notes for gold would discourage her foreign trade; it would disrupt banking because bankers would not know what they owed; it would be difficult to calculate the index, especially in allowing for changes in the quality of the commodities in the "basket"; lastly the paying medium should be identical or interchangeable with a definite quantity of the standard of value but it was itself fluctuating while the standard was fixed. Bagehot therefore argued that the standard of value should remain a precious metal.

In the *Economic Journal* for 1892 Robert Giffen added further objections. Governments were apt to make big blunders in money. Indexing was feasible only with an inconvertible and managed paper currency (gold coins were then currency and notes were convertible into gold and/or silver). The index presented difficulties in construction. Adjusting wages to short-period changes in the index would create difficulties in the labour market (as has happened in the mid-1970's with threshold agreements).

In 1885 and again in 1887 Alfred Marshall proposed a unit of constant general purchasing power. His scheme differed from the multiple legal currency of Jevons in providing for adjustment of the value of contracts fixed in money terms according to changes in the average price level. (He also suggested separately a bimetallic standard but warned against changing the base of the currency.) A quarter of a century later he re-emphasized in an exchange of letters with Irving Fisher in 1911–12, that "every country should have an official 'unit' of general purchasing power, made up from tables of price percentages" so that contracts could be made either in money or in the general "unit."

In 1927 J. M. Keynes proposed that the government should issue an index-linked bond. The capital and interest would be paid not in a fixed *amount* of sterling, but in an amount that had a fixed *value* in commodities as indicated by an index number, so that investors (who had been suffering large losses) would continue to save. The scheme was opposed by Sir Otto Niemeyer of the Treasury on the ground that while informed investors might take such a very long view it would be "too clever" for ordinary people; it was, he argued, more appropriate for countries like Germany, with its large fluctuations in the value of money, than for Britain. He would therefore prefer to see it tried by a private organization like an insurance company before the state issued an index-linked bond. [2]

Indicative Planning. *See* NATIONAL PLAN.

Indifference Analysis, a technique originated by F. Y. Edgeworth but developed in recent decades by economists in order to construct a more satisfactory theory of consumer demand. Before the 1930's many economists held that a consumer derived a given amount of "utility" from the goods or services he bought, that its amount was related to the quantities of commodities he already possessed, and that changes in utility arising from changes in the amount he possessed could be *measured.* During the inter-war years J. R. Hicks and other economists began to shift attention from this "cardinal" aspect of utility to its "ordinal" aspect, i.e. to the view that it was unnecessary to assume that utility was measurable and that a more satisfactory theory of consumer behaviour could be constructed merely on the assumption that the utility from different combinations of commodities could be *ranked* in order of preference by consumers.

Indifference analysis is one aspect of this approach. It assumes that among various combinations of any two commodities, say bread and cheese, a consumer can distinguish combinations which are of equal utility to him and between which he is indifferent, so that he can rank different combinations in order of preference. A hypothetical "map" of a consumer's preferences can then be constructed. A simple analogy is a map of a hill. Imagine a hill to be bounded by two roads at sea level, running respectively north and east from a point of origin. Any point on the hill may then be located by their distances north and east of the origin: the third dimension of any such point will be height above sea level, and contour lines may be drawn connecting all points of equal height. Similarly, if amounts of bread and cheese are measured off along the east-west and north-south axes respectively of a graph, indifference "contours" or curves can be drawn to show all combinations of bread and cheese yielding equal utility to a consumer. The farther to the north-east of the point of origin such curves lie, the higher the level of utility experienced. Given the money prices of bread and cheese and the amount of money income available to spend on them, the consumer may be presumed to choose the combination of bread and cheese which will place him on the highest indifference curve. This "best" combination can be identified in terms of the *relative* marginal utility to the consumer of bread and cheese without saying anything at all about *absolute* amounts of utility derived from them separately, i.e. attempting to measure utility.

Since it dispenses with the assumption that utility is measurable indifference analysis may be regarded as a "better" approach to the theory of consumer behaviour. Some economists have argued that the assumption of measurability is still implicit in the newer formulation. Indifference analysis has been valuable in clarifying theoretical problems and suggesting solutions where decisions or choices between alternatives have to be made, both in private and in governmental decision-making. [14]

Indirect Production, term applied to production of goods used by consumers indirectly, i.e. capital (investment) goods, rather than directly (i.e. consumer goods), and giving more utility by being used later rather than sooner. The importance of indirect production was emphasized by Böhm-Bawerk in developing his theory of interest: a higher rate of interest occurred because of an increase in the indirectness of the productive process (i.e. when more capital was required). The notion was later used by Hayek in the 1930's in his description of the "roundabout" process of production in his theory of the trade cycle and of the contrasting behaviour of capital and consumption goods in successive phases of boom and slump. [3]

Indirect Tax, a tax on goods and services collected indirectly through traders—importers, manufacturers or wholesalers. Indirect taxes may be divided into (*a*) revenue taxes—excise duties, some customs duties, value added tax, (*b*) protective duties—the remainder of customs duties.

Their ultimate incidence depends upon the degree to which the immediate payers can "shift" the burden of tax by raising prices on products to final consumers or lowering the prices paid for productive services which they hire. Unless the goods taxed are those whose consumption expands in step with income, indirect taxes tend to be regressive, i.e. to fall with most weight on people with the smallest incomes. Selectively imposed indirect taxes and periodic alterations in individual rates also affect the pattern of consumption and production; hence the argument for general, non-selective sales taxes or value-added taxes imposed at a uniform rate. [12]

Individualism, in economic theory a name for the competitive method of industrial organization. Originated by the school of Saint Simon, who founded the opposing method of socialism. Individualism was taught in varying degree by John Locke, Bernard Mandeville, David Hume, Adam Smith, Edmund Burke, Alexis de Tocqueville, Lord Acton and the classical economists in general. Individualism is the theory of society that human institutions can develop without a directing mind or deliberate design. Its opposite is the *dirigiste,* collectivist or rationalist theory that society is best moulded by "social engineering" or central direction, planning or control, because men can discern and organize the "public interest." Economists of the individualist school claim that "social engineering" makes the unrealistic assumption that man is rational, clear-sighted and concerned only for the public good; the individualist or competitive economic order assumes that if power is concentrated man will abuse it and therefore that concentration must be prevented because power cannot easily be disciplined. Power is broken up in a competitive order by dispersing the sources of goods and services among a number of suppliers.

The individualists envisaged that a competitive system would require a framework of law that would lead individual motives to serve the public good. Edmund Burke spoke of the need for "well-constructed institutions [in which the] rules and principles of contending interests" would prevent one from prevailing over the others. Adam Smith, Jeremy Bentham, J. M. Keynes, Lionel Robbins, F. A. Hayek, W. H. Hutt, Milton Friedman and other economists were also concerned with the institutional framework required for, and the role of state action in, a competitive society.

The classical economists argued for an individualist order because they thought that if man were to contribute his best to society he should be free to use his inherited or acquired faculties and to be guided by his concern for that part of it he knew and understood—himself, his family, friends and any persons or purposes for which he cared to exert himself. The task of the classical economists was to devise institutions that would harness these immediate ends to serve human needs beyond individual vision. Their solution was the mechanism of the market, which they said would make the individual contribute "to ends which were no part of his purpose." Edmund Burke said that, if individuals were not allowed to associate spontaneously and without conscious central direction by one or a few human beings, "everything about us will dwindle by degrees, until at length our concerns are shrunk to the dimensions of our minds."

The descendants of the Saint Simonians, the economists who preferred state direction and "social engineering," rejected the individualists and condemned the market as an instrument used by powerful capitalist and employer monopolists to exploit employees and the community at large. In recent years some socialist economists in England, Europe and America have re-examined the working of markets although they believe that the state should own and direct the major means of production. Markets have also been used or tolerated in Russia, Yugoslavia, Hungary, Poland and other communist countries.

The main economic criticism of the individualist theory has been that markets are not always competitive but are often dominated by one supplier (monopoly), two suppliers (duopoly), or a small number of suppliers (oligopoly). This has been true of industries in which economies of large-scale production, management, marketing or financing enable a handful of firms to grow and sell more cheaply than the others—as in some countries in steel, coal, minerals, electricity and gas, transport and others. Some of these industries are regulated (in price or service) or controlled by public authorities. The individualists contend that in many industries markets are not competitive because the state in some countries has tolerated or connived at monopoly by failing to pass laws against it (e.g. resale price maintenance), or has encouraged it by inducing producers to collaborate (as in agricultural marketing boards), or has put under a state monopoly an industry that might otherwise be competitive (e.g. coal, road, rail and air transport).

Essentially the economic debate between individualist and socialist economists turns on the legal, administrative and political practicability of making markets competitive. [10]

Indivisibility, or discontinuity, the technical or physical characteristics of a factor of production or commodity which prevent its being used except in minimum quantities. Most machinery and capital equipment must be used in "lumps" of minimum size. A workman is also an "indivisible" unit in this respect; the hands used for an assembly line cannot be separated from the legs that could be simultaneously used for messenger work.

In many cases these exigencies of construction that compel a factor to be used as a single unit can be overcome in a single firm, by altering the terms on which the use of factors can be hired: machinery may be rented or hired for limited periods; specialized skills may be bought from agencies as and when required. Even here there are indivisibilities (there are minimum charges for secretaries, cleaners, economic consultants). Moreover this kind of refinement is not costless; there are therefore economic advantages to a firm in increasing its scale of operations to the point at which it can make continuous use of indivisible factors. For example, at some scales of production it may pay a firm to have a market research department or a staff training school. Where the size of the indivisible unit is large (in relation to annual output) plants or firms will tend to be large: technical indivisibilities tend to determine the size of plant; others, such as financial, the size of firms.

The economic importance of indivisibilities will vary from industry to industry: in oil refining, for example, they tend to dictate plants and firms of large individual size; in farming and high risk industries such as the fashion trades they are less important and are replaced by other influences. In all cases indivisible factors are fundamental in determining how marginal cost of production changes with output from a given plant. [3]

Induced Investment, is made in response to changes in output following an *external* cause, such as an increase in demand for homes accompanying a rise in incomes or an increase in population. The contrast is with autonomous investment, which is made in response to *internal* changes in technique, etc. Induced investment is thus undertaken to produce more of *existing* products, autonomous investment to produce *new* products. The importance of induced investment is in the acceleration principle which, by postulating a relationship between changes in income and the investment it induces, is thought to explain the wider fluctuations in the demand for capital than for consumption goods. [3]

Induction, a method used in economic analysis to draw general principles or laws from observation of real life. For example, it may be found from a large number of industries or countries that, in periods when wages rise appreciably, employers' expenditure on welfare or fringe benefits rises less markedly or falls off. This series of observations may warrant the conclusion by induction that the market for these products was highly competitive, so that an increase in total costs could not easily be passed on to consumers in higher prices and a rise in one cost had to be offset by reducing or limiting the rise in others. A danger of induction is that it is like the historical method in general, which does not justify the conclusion that one development that follows another is necessarily caused by it: other causes less obvious and beyond the observer's attention may have been at work. An assembly of observations ("facts") that followed each other in time is not necessarily illuminating unless they are related to a "theory" (or hypothesis) of cause and effect. Induction can be misleading without a framework of theory and deduction. [14]

Industrial and Commercial Finance Corporation (ICFC), formed in 1945 to provide long-term finance for small and medium-sized firms unable to raise it from banks or public issues—and thus to help fill the Macmillan "gap" in the capital market originally demonstrated by the 1931 Macmillan Report. It was first financed by the joint-stock banks. ICFC's funds are available in several forms, ranging from secured loans to ordinary shares with a lower limit of £5,000 and a maximum in the region of £200,000.

Small firms often reach a critical stage in their development when the capital needed for expansion is beyond the scope of banks but not large enough for a public issue. Banks are traditionally short-term (commonly six months) lenders of working capital, reluctant to become involved in long-term finance. To make a public issue a firm needs to be sizeable: for the small firm the costs of issue may be high. This problem is intensified because the market has become increasingly dependent on institutional investors such as insurance companies and pension funds, which are usually unwilling to deal with small amounts because of the administrative difficulties, and which also have a marked preference for the marketable securities of established larger firms. Moreover, the issue market is closed to small firms wishing to remain private. In the past such firms had to depend on their own saving from profits and on wealthy private investors, but high taxation has slowed growth from both sources. The ICFC was created to fill this gap between bank and stock exchange finance for the small firm. [8]

Industrial Assurance, life assurance in Britain on which the premiums are usually paid weekly by the policy-holder to collectors in his home, so called because it developed among the employees of the industrial north. It is largely conducted by a small number of life assurance companies and friendly societies. It has tended to be overtaken by "ordinary" life assurance as wages rise and wage-earners become accustomed to paying monthly by postal order or cheque. In recent years it has been renamed "Home Service" Assurance. [8]

Industrial Bankers' Association, British trade association of the smaller finance houses in hire purchase observing a strict code of conduct on liquidity of funds and an excess of assets over liabilities. [8]

Industrial Banks. *See* BANKS, INDUSTRIAL.

Industrial Courts. *See* ARBITRATION.

Industrial Democracy, a philosophy that the worker should share in industrial decisions. There have been various theories of industrial democracy, the most extreme form requiring the overthrow of capitalism and its replacement by the government of industry by the workers, as in syndicalism. A refined theoretical system was the Guild Socialism of the Fabians and others; nationalization with worker representation on the board of management was another form.

Milder modern versions argue that the worker should share in the control of industry as a citizen shares in the control of the state. Collective bargaining goes some way to achieve this aim, with the workers' views on matters affecting them expressed by the trade union. Joint consultative committees at various levels can discuss more widely ranging topics of common interest, but, although their role as an advisory body is important, final decisions are still taken by management. The modern concept of industrial democracy, unlike the earlier forms, tends to accept the capitalist system and the position of management, and recognizes that workers cannot share directly in the management of industry. Some argue that a strong and independent trade union movement that safeguards workers' rights provides a realistic degree of industrial democracy.

A new form of industrial democracy developed in the 1960's in the form of workers' consultation or participation. In Germany *Mitbestimmung* evolved in two-tier company boards of which the upper was concerned with major strategy decided by the directors and the lower included workers' representatives for discussion and consultation. In the mid-1970's the British Labour Party proposed that trade unions (rather than employees' representatives) be given half the seats on the boards of the largest companies.

The various forms of industrial democracy are more feasible in a monopoly or large firm that dominates the market than in a competitive market requiring rapid reaction to unforeseen changes in supply or demand. [3]

Industrial Reorganization Corporation (IRC), created by the British (Labour) Government in 1966 to act as an independent merchant bank in stimulating rationalization and concentration, and thereby efficiency in industry. It was empowered to use up to £150 million of public money to lend, on terms it decided in each case, as loan capital with stated interest or as risk-sharing equity. It arranged several mergers where it thought they promoted efficiency, especially in overseas markets against large foreign competitors. Opinion among economists differed about the success of some mergers (notably Leyland and the British Motor Corporation) and more generally about the ability of a government-created and government-financed body to make better decisions than individuals in industry. Where businesses were run by wealthy families or entrenched managers, mergers to yield economies might be desirable if feasible. A policy of mergers might conflict with the opposite policy of avoiding or discouraging industrial concentration and monopoly. The IRC was disbanded by the (Conservative) Government in 1971. [3] [10]

Industrial Revolution, the period in a country's history when it first widely adopts machine methods of producing goods and a transport system to facilitate the extensive regional division of labour necessary to reap the economies of large-scale production. The term was first applied to the industrialization of Britain over the hundred years beginning about 1750. The first phase, up to 1830, was the period of great invention, and subsequent "industrial revolutions" in other countries have not been as dramatic. The most important technical developments came with the use of coal instead of charcoal in the manufacture of iron, in textile manufacture with the invention of the flying shuttle, the spinning jenny and the mule, and above all in the development of steam power. The second phase, between 1830 and 1850, saw the establishment of the comprehensive railway network.

Since many countries are still under-developed, and many peoples are relatively poor, attention has focused on the causes of rapid industrial progress, the combination of circumstances necessary to achieve a "take-off" into rapid growth. Indigenous industrial invention is thought no longer necessary; advanced technological ideas may be adapted by under-developed countries. Economists have singled out population growth, the growth of markets, the widespread discussion and adoption of scientific method, general thriftiness and the availability of capital, and the development of an entrepreneurial philosophy—the capacity to recognize and run risks—as the desirable conditions for economic growth. Most recently the clue to industrial development is thought to be the refinement of property rights to create and strengthen individual inducement to effort and innovation.

Some economic historians have questioned the appropriateness of the term industrial revolution, both because large-scale industry existed in Britain before

1750 and because the developments thereafter were organically related to economic and social developments in the sixteenth and seventeenth centuries. But the pace and extent of developments in the century 1750 to 1850 justify regarding it as a special epoch during which the earlier economic development reached a climax. Thus the period deserves a distinctive descriptive name which "industrial revolution" provides. [3]

Industrial Union, represents all workers in a plant or industry, as distinct from a craft union, which represents workers with the same kind of skills in all plants or industries. An example of the first is the Municipal and General Workers Union, of the second the National Graphical Association. Where an industry is nationalized and run as an entity the two kinds of union become one, as in the National Union of Mineworkers. Industrial unions of skilled and unskilled workers developed with mass production, which assembled them together in single plants. In practice the boundaries of unions (and industries and crafts) are blurred. [5]

Industry, Structure of, its composition by size and number of firms and the degree of independence or integration between them. An industry may be defined as a group of firms producing identical goods, i.e. which the consumer regards as being perfect substitutes for one another although they may be different physically. It might be extended to relate to firms which make a product by the same process. But there is usually a range of firms within what is termed an "industry" in, for example, the census of production, making similar if not identical products by similar methods. If the goods are in close competition with one another the firms may be said to be part of the same industry, just as they may be in competition for the same kind of labour and materials. In practice the definition turns on the nature of the problem under investigation; sometimes a firm may be regarded as part of the car industry, at other times as part of the engineering industry, and so on.

The structure of industry varies with the nature of the product and of the markets in which it is sold, the materials it uses and the technical conditions in which it is produced. In Britain some industries, such as coal, gas, electricity, railways, are public monopolies established under nationalizing legislation. In others the number of firms is very few, as in industrial gases, where the bulk of the output comes from the British Oxygen Company. In others there are many firms of different sizes, as in paint. The retail trade consists of multiples, department stores, co-operative societies and single-shop traders.

A number of influences determine the structure of an industry and how it will affect the position of the individual firm within it. If there are marked gains from very large-scale operation, if the capital costs of setting up new firms are high, if a specialized "know-how" is required, or if a highly specialized labour is employed, the number of firms will tend to be few or relatively little affected by the possibility of new entrants. In the limiting case of a single-firm monopoly, the firm and the industry coincide. If the industry is competitive the older economists discussed its structure in terms of a "representative" firm typifying all the firms and the industry itself: more recent economists have used the concept of "optimum" firms defined as those with the lowest long-run average costs. In a competitive market the industry will tend to be one of relatively small firms each being pushed to operate as efficiently as possible.

It is helpful to think of an industry as a collection of firms working under the pressure of market forces that drive each towards the "best" (most efficient, lowest cost) size. In some industries, however, economies of scale and the nature of demand tend to limit the number of firms and to modify competition. There may, for instance, be competition among a few firms ("oligopoly"), or other forms of imperfect markets in which competition in service or quality become more important than competition in price. In some industries there is a high degree of vertical integration, as in steel; in others there are still many firms each of which specializes in the manufacture of components, e.g. the motor vehicle industry. The spread of lateral integration means that some firms are in more than one industry; thus ICI make man-made fibres, paints, dyestuffs, etc.

Often the most striking immediate impression received in analysing an industry is of a wide scatter of types and sizes. Within the same industry there are very varied firms. Sometimes they work within particular geographical areas or product groups; others cover a wider area of space and output.

Industry thus comprises firms varying in size, from very small in highly competitive markets such as retailing and agriculture, to very large in oligopolistic markets in which there are a small number of sellers of products such as detergents, motor cars, chocolates. Firms have grown for three reasons: first, by expansion or integration because of the economies of scale in technique, management, finance, marketing, or to cope better with the risks arising from fluctuation in the demand for their products or in the supply of their raw materials or labour; secondly, because of state action in creating a legal framework which increases the advantages of size: for example, the Companies Acts provide for the formation of holding companies which offer large financial advantages in the control of many enterprises, and the Restrictive Trade Practices legislation encouraged mergers by outlawing resale price maintenance if enforced by collective action but permitting it if enforced by an individual firm; thirdly, the state has directly encouraged concentration into larger industrial units, for example by the Industrial Reorganization Corporation. The increasing difficulties of managing very large firms is probably the most important reason why firms do not grow indefinitely. In spite of economies of scale in technique, marketing or other respects, firms may find it advantageous to contract out or buy in processes (e.g. bookbinding), components (e.g. electrical equipment for motor cars) or specialist skills (e.g. legal advice, the services of advertising agents). The location of firms in different industries may be determined primarily by advantages of proximity to raw materials, labour supplies or markets.

The structure of industry tends to become less competitive through the operation of organizational and legal influences, but more competitive by the constant inflow of new firms, based on new techniques and methods arising from invention, and by changing demands. Thus the railways had a virtual monopoly for nearly a century but are having to meet competition from road and air transport. Recent legislation in Britain on monopoly and restrictive practices has had the effect of making it easier for new firms to break into established markets. Older legislation on patents and copyright still has the effect of maintaining monopolies in some industries, as in chemicals, medicine and others. [3]

Inelastic Demand. *See* ELASTICITY OF DEMAND.

Inelastic Supply. *See* ELASTICITY OF SUPPLY.

Infant Industries, term employed in seeking protective measures to advance and expand the industries of newly sovereign states or cushion newly established domestic industries in western countries against foreign competition during their growth to maturity by developing economies of scale. The argument in favour of (temporary) protection for infant industries is that, by encouraging a pattern of specialization different from that which would emerge under free trade, a country may eventually derive benefits that will more than compensate for the economic welfare sacrificed. But it provides no justification for what is in effect a permanent subsidy to individual industries, unless additional external economies or community benefits are expected from growth. The difficulty of assessing these economies accurately, and the probability that such measures, initially described as "temporary" or "emergency," may become part of the permanent fiscal structure, make the argument of doubtful value as a guide to policy. [4]

Inferior Goods, those bought in relatively large quantities out of a small income and replaced, or bought in smaller quantities, as income increases. One of the most usual examples is margarine, which tends to be replaced by butter as income increases. An extreme kind of inferior good is illustrated in the so-called Giffen paradox which states that less of an inferior good is bought when its price falls and more as its price rises. If at all, this could occur only when a large proportion of most individual consumers' incomes are spent on a staple foodstuff. If its price rises consumers reduce their expenditure on other foods in order to maintain their total consumption of food. Similarly if its price falls they would be able to spend more on other things and thus expenditure on it would fall. [7]

Inflation, a fall in the value of money due to a persistent expansion in its quantity. When total monetary demand exceeds the value of the goods and services currently available for sale, the economy is subject to expansionary pressure. Business men find trade good and stocks declining; they are under strong inducements to expand output and increase their demand for factors of production. If the economy has large reserves of unemployed resources the main effect of the expansionary pressure will be to raise the level of employment until the unemployed resources are absorbed. But at high levels of employment, where there is little scope for increasing output, the excess of demand over supply causes prices to rise.

In theory the rise in prices should end the inflation by making demand equal supply at the higher prices. In practice inflation tends to become cumulative, since higher prices mean higher costs and higher costs lead to higher prices. The output of many firms is the "input" of other firms, so that higher prices become higher costs, and because of the general buoyancy of incomes and demand higher costs are likely to be paid for by final buyers rather than out of profits. The price/cost spiral is especially evident in wage costs. Higher prices mean an increased cost of living and give a strong impetus to wage claims. Employers are anxious to avoid disruptions to production, and since they know that higher costs can be passed on in the form of higher prices, they are willing to pay higher wages. Trade unions are thus in strong bargaining positions when the level of employment is very high. But the upward pull on wage rates also comes from employers, who are anxious to increase their output and so compete to secure additional labour by offering higher pay. When there is full or "overfull" employment, employers may find it necessary to raise labour earnings simply to retain their existing labour force, i.e. in order to stop employees leaving to take up higher-paid jobs with competitors.

In this situation total money income rises at a faster rate than real income and the difference is available to finance the excess monetary demand which causes prices to rise. An additional pressure on prices comes from the increased investment which business men undertake in order to increase output. In the long run most investment expenditures will result in a substantial increase in the output of consumer goods, but in the short run money incomes are generated by the additional activity without a corresponding increase in the output of consumer goods.

If an inflationary situation continues long enough, people will learn to anticipate the continuous increase in prices and plan accordingly. If people expect the value of money to fall they will have little desire to hold cash or invested savings, and the demand for goods will increase. If prices are expected to rise, people will buy goods earlier rather than later. They will even buy with borrowed money, since the real cost of loans is reduced (and may even be negative) because the value of money which repays the loan is less than the value of the money that was borrowed, and the price of the goods bought with the loan is higher at the time of repayment. Further, when the value of money is expected to continue to fall, business men are likely to base their prices on *expected* replacement costs rather than current costs, and wage claims are likely to be based on *expected* rises in the cost of living. A modest inflation thus tends to become more rapid and, unless drastic measures are taken, may become uncontrollable.

Economists differ on whether a prolonged high level of economic activity can be maintained without inflation. The sufferers from inflation are people with incomes fixed in money terms, such as pensioners, with incomes derived from state benefits or annuities and fixed interest-bearing securities, and salary-earners whose earnings are not closely tied to general prices. So long as the inflation is moderate, and something is done to offset the disadvantages for those with fixed income, some economists believe that inflation is a small and even inevitable price to pay for maintaining high employment and income. The question is whether the inflation can remain moderate.

Inflation in many countries accelerated in the early and mid-1970's. In Britain, the supply of money was expanded by government from around 10 per cent in 1971 to 23 per cent in 1972, and around 30 per cent in 1973. It was argued by economists in Britain and the USA that the effect upon prices took approximately two years (W. S. Jevons said in 1884, "An expansion in the currency occurs one or two years prior to a rise in prices"). Inflation in the mid-1970's was therefore thought unavoidable. Moreover, to stop it by sharp and sudden restriction of the rate of growth in money supply would risk severe unemployment as unexpected falls in demand would make increasing sectors of industry unprofitable. As part of a persistent but gradual restriction of monetary expansion, new and unconventional measures were advocated to mitigate its consequences, notably escalator clauses in contracts; indexing wages, salaries, etc. to keep pace with prices; adjusting the income tax threshold and allowances (otherwise the tax is raised without real income rising and it becomes a tax on capital); indexing depreciation allowances on buildings and equipment; removing taxes from the fictitious profit arising from the purely monetary rise in the value of stocks; and linking social benefits and other government payments (e.g. interest on National Savings) to general prices. A main argument for indexing was that it would thus reduce the revenue derived by government from inflation without raising tax rates and therefore reduce the inducement to inflate. A counter-argument was that in Britain inflation had been used to stimulate growth and remove unemployment, not to raise revenue without incurring electoral unpopularity. (*See* Monetary Correction.)

A further complication may arise from the monetary situation in other countries with which trade is conducted. If their prices are generally stable, even modest inflation at home may create difficulties in paying for imports. If their prices are generally rising there will be other difficulties (the exchange rates and others) in keeping general prices rigidly stable. [9]

Information Agreement, another name for "open pricing." [7]

Information Costs, the effort, time, etc. required to obtain knowledge about current or potential supply of and demand for goods (or services) and their attributes. This aspect of the working of markets is a relatively recent development in economic theory.

Information takes time and costs money: it is not a "free" good (or service). If it were available immediately and costless, so that prices were altered instantaneously in response to changing conditions, all goods would be sold, there would be no queues, waiting, shortages, surpluses, reserve ("buffer") stocks, capital and labour held in reserve, or unsatisfied demands. All resources would be fully employed. Thus imperfect information creates a large activity or "industry" engaged in perfecting it by intermediaries of many kinds: shopkeepers, wholesalers, agents, brokers, salesmen, advertisers, lawyers, advisers, consultants, consumer information and advice bureaux, etc. Consumers also spend much time "shopping around" to inspect and compare prices, qualities, associated services, terms of sale, etc. Since information enables better purchases to be made (or jobs to be found, etc.) people are prepared to pay for it. And it is often easier and cheaper to choose and buy from unused or reserve "unemployed" stocks, which can be inspected or investigated more readily than if they were in use (e.g. furniture) or fully engaged by other consumers (e.g. labour—doctors, teachers, editors, bricklayers, miners, secretaries). Economists thus analyse information as one important reason (among others) for unused, reserve or "unemployed" resources, which are therefore not necessarily "wasted." Even when resources (capital, land or labour) are unused for more immediately obvious reasons, as in declining industries, or seasonal trades, or because of a more general recession, some unemployment of resources is a reaction to the higher costs of assembling information more rapidly. [7]

Infrastructure, the services regarded as the essential basis for creating a modern economy: transport, power, education, health services, housing. It is also described as "social" or "public" overhead capital where the emphasis is on the capital assets that provide the services: roads, bridges, railways, houses, schools, reservoirs, etc.

The "infrastructure" requires extensive capital for its initial creation, but if it does not attract funds from private enterprise it may need to be financed by the state or other public authority. In the nineteenth century British private investors financed most of the railway development in North and South America: roads have seldom been financed by private capital although they can be paid for by tolls; mass education usually requires state aid in developing countries but can be financed privately as incomes rise. Investment in social capital thus does not always yield a profit though it may benefit the economy as a whole. It may be particularly necessary in starting the development process in developing countries. A road which links the interior of a country to its main ports will open up possibilities for production of specialized crops that can be transported to the coast and sold in exchange for goods manufactured in the towns or imported from overseas. The development of an efficient transport system and means of communication can rapidly extend the potential market for the product and promote further specialization.

For most developing countries the creation of the "infrastructure" is best achieved by borrowing from the richer countries because (*a*) income per head is too low to permit much saving, (*b*) even when domestic saving is possible the transfer of resources is often blocked by primitive commercial and fiscal systems. Where for political reasons the pace of development is forced, or where the political unit is small and its economic future doubtful, or where local laws do not secure security for lenders, private foreign loans may be difficult to arrange. Hence the growth in recent years of alternative sources of loans or direct grants such as the World Bank, the Special United Nations Fund for Economic Development, and the governments of the richer countries.

Some economists have argued that just as the industrialized countries advanced by their own efforts, the under-developed would be more firmly based if they did likewise, developing their human as well as their physical resources by creating a framework of laws and institutions in banking, insurance, property, etc., that encourages effort and enterprise, and learning from the industrialized countries the arts of initiative and the capacity to recognize and provide for risks. This process may take longer, but the developing countries probably cannot achieve in a decade what took a century in the West unless they sacrifice the individual liberty and initiative that is thought to be at the root of long-run economic development. In so far as outside loans are desirable, they need not be channelled through governments but could go to widely dispersed private centres of initiative independent of government patronage and control. [1]

Inheritance, the receipt of property on another's death. Property is inherited either directly through a will or indirectly through the laws of intestacy, which are based on the assumption that the deceased would have preferred nearer to more distant relatives.

Taxation of inheritance in the UK is by estate duty, which varies according to the size of the estate. The case for estate duty is urged partly on the ground that inheritance is a windfall, especially for distant relatives. Estate duty has done much to counter the inequalities of wealth created by inheritance. To stimulate the dispersal of large estates, some economists (Rignano, and more recently Robbins and others) have argued that the duties should vary with the size of the bequest rather than with the size of the testator's estate. At very high rates estate duty may discourage the creation of wealth, break up properties into less efficient units or force efficient private family businesses to sell out prematurely. It has been also argued that the desirable direct provision by fathers for their children should be encouraged by differential taxation. The Legacy and Succession Duties, which were abolished in 1949, differentiated between near relations and others, but since then there has been no differentiation. [12]

Initial Allowances, a form of capital allowance: deductions from business income permitted for calculating income liable for tax. They enable a business installing some types of new equipment or undertaking new building to write off against taxable income a larger percentage capital allowance than would otherwise be possible in the initial year in which it was acquired (hence the name). Although *total* capital allowances over the whole life of the equipment are not increased (the "bunching" in the initial year is offset by lower allowances in later years), the privilege is of value to a firm since the allowances are increased in the year in which outgoings are heaviest. Initial allowances were first introduced in Britain in 1945–6. The permitted rates have been manipulated from time to time to influence the extent, timing and type of investment spending in the economy. In 1954 the system of initial allowances was extended and amplified by investment allowances. [12]

Input-output Analysis, the method used by theoretical and applied economists to take account of factors relating to the general balance of the economic system in a factual analysis of the problems of production. It was devised by the Russian-born economist Wassily Leontief.

There are three central elements in this method. First, it deals exclusively with problems of production; the theory of demand plays no part in the hard core of input-output analysis. The problems analysed are essentially technical. The inquiry seeks to determine what can be produced and the quantity of the "intermediate" product that will be used up in the production process *given* the quantities of available resources and the state of technology. It is therefore not strictly "economic" analysis, which is concerned essentially with *changing* values.

Secondly, the analysis is closely linked with factual inquiry. A consequence of this concern with facts is that compromises have been forced on the investigator; input-output analysis employs a model which is more severely simplified and restricted in its treatment of phenomena than many economic theories. Its restriction lies in the exclusive emphasis on the production side of the economy (the simplifications are outlined below).

The third characteristic is the concentration on an economic state which is in balance or equilibrium. Input-output analysis tries to take account of the links between the production plans and activities of the many industries that make up the economy. Each industry employs the outputs of other industries as its raw materials. Its own output, in turn, is often used by other industries as a productive factor. For example, steel is used to make rail wagons which are in turn used to transport steel and the coal and pig-iron used in its manufacture.

Of the simplifying assumptions forced on input-output analysis which are more extreme than those usually employed in theoretical economic models, the two most important are, first, that each industry produces one single output, i.e. no two goods are produced jointly by one industry, and secondly, that all productive factors are employed in a fixed relation to one another.

The basic problem of input-output analysis is to consider what net outputs can be left over from the process of production for final consumption and how much of each output will be used up in the course of the productive activities undertaken to yield these net outputs.

The hypothetical input-output transactions table (Table 6) illustrates the basic procedures employed. The table can be broken into two parts. The smaller 3 × 3-sector table shows the distribution of inter-industry flows and represents the producing sectors' intermediate uses. The complete 9 × 9 (rows × columns) table shows total gross flows in the economy. Summing column (9) gives the flow of total gross outputs; summing (across) row (9) gives the flow of total outlays. (National accounting identities require that total gross outputs equal total gross outlays.) To derive a measure of gross national product (GNP) from the input-output table, all that is necessary is to subtract all intermediate flows to the processing sectors from the total gross output. Alternatively, GNP can be derived by adding the columns representing final income-generating expenditures—Consumption (column 4), Investment (columns 5 and 6), Government Purchases (column 7) and Exports (column 8). Each method yields the same answer, 89.

Reading across any row indicates the distribution of the output of any processing sector. This distribution includes flows to other producing sectors (columns 1 to 3 inclusive) as well as to the final demand sectors (columns 4 to 8). Reading down the columns shows how each sector distributes its purchases. This has added significance when attention is confined to the 3 × 3 transactions table of inter-industry flows: an inspection of outlays there provides a crude recipe of how to make the output of each processing sector. To make £1 worth of industry A's output requires 36p worth of industry A's own output, 23p worth of

Table 6. Hypothetical Input-output Transactions Table

	Processing sector			*Final Demand Sector*					
Outputs → / Inputs ↓	(1) A	(2) B	(3) C	(4) Household Consumption	(5) Stock Accumulation (Gross)	(6) Private Capital Formation (Gross)	(7) Government Purchases	(8) Exports	(9) Total Gross Output
Processing Sector									
(1) Industry A	8	10	4	13	2	1	1	1	40
(2) Industry B	5	9	8	12	2	2	1	2	41
(3) Industry C	9	3	13	10	1	2	3	2	43
Industry producing payments sector									
(4) Consumption	12	12	13	2	1	2	7	0	49
(5) Stock Depletion (Gross)	1	2	1	0	0	0	0	1	5
(6) Depreciation Allowances	1	1	1	0	0	0	0	0	3
(7) Payments to Government	2	1	2	10	2	3	1	2	23
(8) Imports	2	3	1	3	0	0	0	0	9
(9) Total Gross Outlays	40	41	43	50	8	10	13	8	213

industry B's output and finally 41p worth of industry C's output. (These figures were derived by dividing each of the column entries by the respective column sum in the 3×3 matrix.) Deriving these input figures for each column creates a further 3×3 matrix, called a matrix of technical co-efficients, which, when manipulated ("inverted"), provides consistent estimates of the direct and indirect impacts on the economy from increasing (or decreasing) final demand for any given output of a processing sector. The estimate is termed "consistent" because it shows not only the impact on the sector affected, but also all the induced effects upon it and all the other sectors in the economy. (Because these impacts are estimated from the matrix of technical co-efficients—which change over time with changing technology—impact analyses of this kind are usually projected over fairly short periods during which technology is assumed to remain constant.) [9]

Inspection Supply, the stock of a commodity held to reduce the acquisition costs to buyers of making a purchase. These apply more to shopping goods, where consumers compare prices, qualities, etc. before making a purchase, than to convenience goods. [7]

Instalment Credit. *See* HIRE PURCHASE.

Institute of Economic Affairs (IEA), founded in 1956 as an educational trust to publish works explaining the relevance of economics for public and industrial policy. Its authors are drawn largely from economists in the universities, industry, the professions, public service and journalism. They generally approach their subject by analysing the working of markets and the legal and institutional framework required to make them work to the public advantage. The Institute has become the main source of concise academic studies linking economic theory with its implications for policy in industry and government. It specializes in the economics of market systems as devices for registering preferences and allocating resources, private or governmental; and where markets work inefficiently the causes are analysed. In this sense the Institute's approach is methodologically micro-economic except that it studies the macro-economic institutions or environment of market systems, e.g. the monetary system, the laws on property, contract, sale of goods, industrial organization, and monopolies and other forms of restraint of trade. Its authors are often critical of the operation of market systems in practice, e.g. resale price maintenance, company disclosure, mergers, subsidies, international restrictive commodity agreements, trade organizations for political pressure for tariffs, etc., informal agreements to restrict competition in banking or limit entry to the capital or money markets, complicity in agricultural marketing boards, etc. Its specialization in market systems has misled observers into confusing a technical-economic method with a market philosophy. The Institute was founded by Antony Fisher and is directed by Ralph Harris and (since 1959) Arthur Seldon. It has assembled 250 economists as authors and advisers.

The Institute's best-known series of publications is the Hobart Papers. The Institute is financed wholly from private sources: the sale of Papers and books and contributions from individuals and industry. [14]

Institutional Investor. *See* FIRM.

Institutional Monopoly. *See* TRADE MARK.

Institutionalism, a form of economic analysis which depends upon a study of the structure, rules and behaviour of organizations such as firms, cartels, trade unions, the state. The institutionalist approach may be contrasted with market analysis, which emphasizes supply, demand and "automatic" adjustment to movements in prices and profits. In the study of industrial relations, for example, the institutionalist would examine trade union rules, structure and government. Methodological disputes have continued, particularly in the USA, about the usefulness of institutionalism. Some of its critics have made it appear to exclude the economic aspects of human activity. The modern institutionalists may be seen as trying to correct orthodox economic theorists by allowing for the role of social and political structure and organization in the determination of economic events. As frequently happens in the social (and other) sciences, an attempt to correct one error creates a new and opposite one, and some institutionalists are blamed for the prevalence of over-simplified views of their approach as non-economic or even anti-economic. [14]

Insurance, the means by which risks are shared between many people or institutions who face them, so that in the event of a contingency befalling an individual he is compensated for his loss out of the premiums paid by all insured against it. People who insure against a risk which never befalls them secure peace of mind and sometimes avoid the need to hold liquid assets or stable securities to enable them to meet the cost of the contingency.

The main forms of insurance are marine, life, fire and accident. Marine insurance is the oldest, examples existing in the fourteenth century, if not before. The scope of insurance has been extended to cover sickness, accident, burglary, loss of employment and even loss resulting from inclement weather ("pluvius insurance").

Insurance is sold by commercial firms (and so-called non-profit-making, "mutual" organizations), which charge premiums based on calculations of the risk involved plus administrative costs and a profit margin. If experience shows the risk is underestimated premiums are raised. Premiums for life assurance are calculated from actuarial tables giving expected length of life for men and women at different ages, with possible adjustments for family and medical records, occupation, personal habits and so on. Some life assurance policies operate on what is called a mutual basis, under which a proportion of total profits is allocated to policy-holders who hold "with profit" policies (on which the premium is a little higher than for "without profit" policies) in proportion to the sums assured. Over a period in which general business conditions are buoyant such mutuality allows policy-holders to enjoy a share in the high profits earned on investments made with their premiums and the bonus will help to cushion the effect of inflation on the real value of the sums assured.

In addition to insurance provided commercially there are now in most countries extensive social insurance systems administered by the state to cover such contingencies as unemployment, sickness and old age. Very often these schemes differ from insurance proper because the benefits or sums assured are not met out of past premiums accumulated in a fund but out of current premiums and general taxation. The former schemes are based on various methods of "funding," the latter on "assessmentism" (the current premiums are calculated by "assessing" the current cost of benefits).

Insurance companies operate on the basis of the law of large numbers; they must attract a large enough number of insurers against a risk to bring the law into operation and spread the risk widely. Economic decision-taking is much concerned with risk; when a risk is calculable and therefore can be analysed with the help of the theory of probability it can most likely be insured against. In this way the main economic function of insurance is to narrow the area of risk-taking by enabling an *entrepreneur* or firm to convert part of a risk into a contractual cost, the insurance premium. [7]

Insurance Broker. *See* BROKER.

Insured Mortgage, a mortgage of which a party other than the borrower, in return for a premium, assures payment in the event of default by the mortgagor. Where a secondary mortgage market exists (i.e. where a lively trade in mortgages is necessary for a flexible mortgage loan market) mortgage insurance is important to ensure marketability. Most residential mortgages in North America are insured in this way: the practice is less widespread in Britain where secondary trade in mortgages is small. [8]

Integration, bringing together industrial activities under a unified control. It may take three forms: vertical, horizontal or diagonal.

(1) *Vertical integration* increases the number of processes in which a firm is engaged. Examples of "backward integration" are the entry by a car firm into the making of car bodies, the acquisition by a tyre manufacturer of rubber plantations. "Forward integration" is represented by brewers and petrol companies that own or in other ways (by long-term contracts) control retail outlets. In these examples the manufacturer has moved a stage backward or forward in the chain which leads from material and component to manufacture and sale. Firms move in these directions in order to lower costs, ensure sources of supply, secure more control over quality, or establish a closer connection with the market for their products.

(2) *Horizontal or lateral integration* is expansion in one process. "Horizontal" integration refers to the amalgamation of firms making the same product, e.g. the formation of the Imperial Tobacco Company by a confederation of independent firms. "Lateral" integration may be used to refer to the growth of firms in related or different products as in Imperial Chemical Industries, a firm which makes man-made fibres, dyestuffs, non-ferrous metal products and other products. Firms spread in this way partly because similarities in technique or in raw materials lead them to take up a diversity of products, or as an insurance against fluctuations in the markets for individual products.

(3) *Diagonal integration* connotes the existence of (ancillary) service activi-

ties which fit "slantwise" into the main activity of a firm, e.g. a machine-repairing service or carpenters on the staff may make for convenience and economy.

A firm may integrate in all these ways and bring within its area of co-ordination products and processes which it would otherwise have to buy in the market. The method of integration may be either by setting up factories to manufacture components or by acquiring existing enterprises and obtaining the benefits of their employees and experience. [3]

Integration, Lateral. *See* INDUSTRY, STRUCTURE OF; INTEGRATION.

Interest, the price paid for the use of loanable funds. It is normally expressed as so much per cent per year, although it could be expressed as per cent per month or five years. There are many rates of interest; the differences are due to the differences in the duration and the risks of loans. In general, the shorter the loan term and the fewer the risks (of only partial repayment, or non-repayment, or incurring costs to secure repayment), the lower the rate of interest. Examples of interest payments are those paid (or charged) by banking institutions on time deposits and for "call money" lent to discount houses and for overdrafts to personal or commercial customers; by public authorities on central and local government securities and on other loans made to them, such as post office deposits; by institutions such as building societies and hire purchase finance companies; by companies on "debentures," or in the form of dividend payments on ordinary shares (equities).

The main function of a rate of interest, as that of any other price, is to make the supply of loanable funds (i.e. the demand for securities) equal to their demand (supply of securities), and to "ration" the supply among the demanders prepared to pay the price. Changes in demand or supply will cause changes in the rate of interest. If demand for a particular type of loan increases with no change in supply, or if supply decreases with no change in demand, the rate of interest will rise. But in a free market funds will tend to move from less to more profitable uses, and the original differences between the rates of interest for different types of loans will tend to be preserved. Changes in the rate of interest for one kind of loan will also tend to be reflected in similar changes in the rates for other kinds, so that rates of interest tend to change in the same direction throughout the economy. Some interest rates are not determined immediately by market forces; for instance, the rate for bank overdrafts is always above Base rate, usually with 5 per cent as a minimum. Through "cheap" or "dear" money policies, governments can affect the general level of interest rates.

The supply of loanable funds consists of (1) savings by individuals, businesses and institutions, (2) bank loans and advances and bank purchases of securities, (3) the excess of revenue over expenditure of public authorities. Individuals and businesses deciding to increase the supply of loans require also to decide whether (*a*) to spend less on goods and services, (*b*) to postpone repayment of debts, (*c*) to run down cash holdings. In general, the higher the current rates of interest the more the willingness to abstain from current consumption and to lend the savings rather than hold them as cash.

Individuals, businesses and public authorities create the demand for loanable funds when they want more money to spend than they derive from current income and if borrowed funds can be spent on investments which yield a rate of return higher than the cost of borrowing (the rate of interest). In general, the higher the expected return from new investment the larger the demand for loanable funds and, therefore, the more the willingness to pay a higher rate of interest. In government investment projects, however, there is little opportunity of making precise calculations of the relationship between yield and cost because there is no free market in the goods (or services) produced, or in the factors of production (e.g. almost all miners are employed by the National Coal Board), or both. These projects are usually the result of political decisions connected with the desire to influence general economic activity, the provision of welfare services, the view that the so-called "basic" industries should be owned and/or run by the state, etc.

The economic theory of the *general* level of interest rates uses a convenient abstraction—the "rate of interest"—which usually refers to the yield on riskless, fixed-interest securities, such as irredeemable government bonds. Thus, a bond costing £100 and paying £3 per annum yields 3 per cent interest; if the price of the bond falls to £40, the money yield is still £3 but the rate of interest is 7½ per cent. An explanation of this rate of interest now widely held by many economists is Keynes's liquidity preference theory. In brief, it holds that the rate of interest equates the demand for money to hold as an asset with the supply of money available to be held, so that it is determined by the community's preference for liquid cash and the quantity of money as decided by the monetary authorities. Changes in liquidity preference (the supply of money remaining unchanged) or changes in the quantity of money (liquidity preference remaining unchanged) will therefore change the rate of interest. Suppose the demand for money is equal to the supply and the government, through open market operations, increases the quantity of money. Equilibrium has changed to disequilibrium. At the prevailing rate of interest the community is holding more assets in cash which yield no interest, than it wishes. It increases its demand for income-yielding assets, such as bonds, causing their prices to rise and the rate of interest to fall. At the higher prices some owners become willing to sell bonds and to hold cash instead. In this way the surplus cash is finally absorbed by the sellers of securities, and the system is again in equilibrium, but with a lower rate of interest.

This is a monetary theory of interest. Some economists emphasize the "real" forces governing the payment of interest. In a simple non-monetary economy the production of capital goods (investment) can take place only to the extent that the community is willing to forgo the use of resources employed to produce consumption goods. The interest offered for loans (expressed in terms of real resources) would be governed by the additional productivity of investment in methods of production that use more capital (i.e. are more "roundabout"). The interest demanded by lenders would tend to reflect their rate of "time preference," the premium they place on enjoying consumption goods immediately rather than in the future. Together, time preference and productivity govern the supply and demand for loanable resources and thus the rate of interest.

These underlying "real" forces of productivity and thrift are veiled in a money-using economy. They exert their effects in a monetary system by influencing the production of investment goods (thus adding to the demand for "spending" money) and saving, so reducing the demand for "spending" money. The monetary theory of the rate of interest is thus considered to embrace the effects of these underlying forces. [8]

Interest, Bank. *See* BANK INTEREST.

Intermediate Areas, areas identified in the Report on Intermediate Areas (the Hunt Report, 1969), which proposed an extension of benefits available under the Local Employment Acts to districts outside the Development Areas. In Intermediate Areas employment growth was slow or negative but net outward migration, coupled with low rates of natural increase of population, was sufficient to prevent heavy unemployment (although activity rates were often abnormally low, indicating concealed unemployment). The argument for assistance to such areas was that (*a*) if unassisted they might degenerate further; (*b*) if suitable they should share in employment siphoned off from other areas regarded as undesirably "congested." [10]

Intermediate Goods, are used to produce other goods instead of being consumed or used themselves, e.g. wood, glass, rubber, steel, plastic used to build a motor car. At any given moment most goods produced in a developed economy are intermediate rather than final consumption goods. Intermediate goods enter into calculations of national product when they are embodied in consumption goods. But some goods can be both: for example, fruit can be consumed directly, or indirectly by being embodied in other consumer goods such as cakes and puddings. [3] [9]

Internal Economies, reductions in the unit cost of production resulting from changes in the scale of operation within a given firm or plant; thus contrasted with external economies. Most internal economies arise in the use of "indivisible" fixed factors of production which are most efficiently employed at high levels of output and for which there are no substitutes that can be used to produce smaller outputs (or for which the "small-scale" substitutes are disproportionately inefficient). In a similar way internal economies will be reaped when a large firm is able to raise finance more easily and more cheaply than a small firm, and when a large buyer of (say) a raw material is able to buy more cheaply than a small buyer (except when these advantages arise from the exercise of monopoly power). Some economies of scale may be less obvious and less easily measured, e.g. when a firm employing many workers is able to attract a higher general quality of staff because it is able to offer better promotion prospects than the small employer. If there were no limit to internal economies firms would continue to grow indefinitely and the small firms in an industry would be eliminated. In practice diseconomies of scale may sooner or later counteract economies of scale. The most significant diseconomies probably arise from the incapacity of managers to co-ordinate efficiently the widening range of activities performed on a very large scale in growing firms. [3]

Internal Pricing, attaching prices to goods passed from one part of a firm to another, or to services performed by one department for another: for example, calculating the cost of the transport section of a department store that delivers goods to its customers. Also known as transfer pricing. The purpose is to compare the cost of "internal" production with the cost of the goods or services from an "external" source on the open market. It is thus an effort to re-create the market within the firm (or other organization or government ministry). [3]

Internal Rate of Return. *See* INVESTMENT APPRAISAL.

Internalization, inelegant term for inserting the effects of production on third parties ("external effects") into the costs of production. Thus motor car manufacturers or power station operators may be required to fit filters to exhausts or chimneys to reduce or neutralize noxious fumes that harm pedestrians or buildings, or to pay charges to compensate individuals or owners harmed. The study of third-party effects has been intensified partly because of increasing concern about the environment and its pollution by smoke, noise, etc. Economists use the jargon shorthand "internalizing the externalities." [13]

International Association for Research in Incomes and Wealth, founded in 1947, financially supported by Nuffield and Rockefeller Foundations and later by Yale Economic Growth Center. The Association publishes the quarterly *Review of Income and Wealth* and arranges biennial conferences. It moved from London to Yale in 1962. [14]

International Bank for Reconstruction and Development (World Bank) (IBRD), a Specialized Agency of the United Nations established in Washington

(1945) under the Bretton Woods Agreements (1944). Its functions are to furnish long-term loans for reconstruction, promote and supplement private foreign investment, and encourage the expansion of world resources and productive capacity, especially in the under-developed countries. It has generally worked through the International Development Association and the International Finance Corporation.

The IBRD obtains its funds from sale of stock to member countries and from the issue of bonds in world financial centres. It lends either directly to governments or (more frequently) to private firms or institutions under the guarantee of the borrower's government. It may guarantee loans made by private lenders. Unlike its Bretton Woods "twin," the International Monetary Fund, the IBRD does not make short-term loans. It provides advisory and liaison services on economic development. [4]

International Commodity Agreements, arrangements designed to reduce instability in the prices of primary products.

Fluctuations in these prices may damage developing countries in many ways: producers' incomes swing from one extreme to the other, alternate inflationary and deflationary pressure is produced in their internal economies, fluctuations in their export earnings force them to hold large reserves or to cut their development plans in a slump, and political disturbance may arise from the hardships imposed by alternating boom and slump.

The seriousness of this problem has been recognized by several United Nations Committees' reports, and various kinds of international agreements have been suggested to deal with it. The principle behind all of them is to adjust the total supply of the commodities in world markets to changes in world demand so that fluctuations in prices are moderated. There are three main types—buffer stock schemes, quota agreements and multilateral long-term contracts. The 1953 International Tin Agreement was principally a buffer stock scheme with a stock of tin and of money, both contributed by the member nations. When the world tin price fell below a stated level it bought tin and stocked it. When the price rose above a predetermined level it sold. The scheme provided for the imposition of quotas. The Sugar Agreement was an example of a scheme based entirely on the quota system, in which the exports of the producing countries were limited to quantities varied with the level of sugar price on the free world market. This system penalized or frustrated efficient, low-cost producers by preventing them from expanding and driving out inefficient producers, and it tempted consuming countries to buy outside the agreement from non-members when the free market price of sugar fell low. The International Wheat Agreement illustrated the multilateral contract system. Importers agreed to buy, and exporters to sell, stated quantities of a commodity in each year of the agreement.

A maximum and a minimum price were also agreed for purchases and sales. Each exporter was thus assured of a market for his quota at not less than the minimum price, and each importer was certain of a supply equal to his quota at not more than the maximum price. Further, the scheme required the minimum interference with the working of the price mechanism and the pattern of international trade. It was relatively easy to organize because it could work without covering all exporting and importing countries. But again countries were tempted to leave the scheme when free market prices were more favourable than the controlled prices; e.g. Britain left the Wheat Agreement in 1953 to take advantage of the low "free" wheat prices. Moreover, such agreements require a homogeneous product, an easily determined range of qualities and an efficiently organized market, conditions which are fulfilled in wheat but few other primary products.

These agreements have worked in the post-war period in a small number of commodities with some success in reducing fluctuations without appreciably distorting production or trade. The general economic issues are indicated in Commodity Agreements. [4]

International Company. *See* MULTINATIONAL COMPANY.

International Currency. *See* CURRENCY.

International Development Association, an affiliate of the International Bank for Reconstruction and Development, specializing in long-term loans, usually without interest, to developing countries. [4]

International Finance Corporation, established in 1956 to repair a deficiency in the activities of the International Bank for Reconstruction and Development. The bank's lending was confined to government or government-guaranteed projects, as it was felt private enterprise might shy from such aid as carrying government control or interference. The International Finance Corporation's aims are to invest in private undertakings, mainly in under-developed countries, where sufficient private capital is not forthcoming on acceptable terms. The Corporation cannot hold ordinary or preference shares; it is intended to revolve its funds by selling off its assets to private investors when possible. It began with a capital of $100 million and thirty-one member countries. It can raise further funds in world capital markets. [4]

International Investment, movements of capital between nations and institutions such as the World Bank. They may take place when citizens in one country acquire claims against the citizens or governments of others such as bank deposits, government bills and bonds or ordinary shares, or fixed assets in property or factories.

Short-term and long-term movements of capital differ in purposes and effects. Broadly, short-term capital comprises funds likely to be held in the receiving country for only a brief period; they tend to move quickly and unexpectedly. Normally they will be in fairly liquid form such as bank deposits, government bills, or short-dated securities. Short-term capital moves readily in response to changes in relative interest rates, anticipated changes in exchange rates, fears of exchange control or political instability. Apart from fears of major changes, the main cause of movements of short-term funds between financial centres is the relationship between the interest rates in them and the difference between the spot and forward exchange rates.

Because short-term funds, or "hot money," are mobile they may unexpectedly weaken the balance of payments of countries such as Britain which act as banker nations by holding large quantities of liquid funds liable to be withdrawn at short notice.

Long-term capital movements are to some extent subject to the same influences, but they are less likely to move unexpectedly. The major part of long-term private investment takes the form of new branch plants in foreign countries and of reinvestment of profits in extensions to overseas branches and subsidiaries. The motives for long-term capital movements are normally higher interest or profit rates than can be earned at home; but taxation policies in both the home and the foreign country complicate the decision to move capital abroad.

Economic aid from advanced to under-developed countries forms a large proportion of international investment. Most aid still moves directly from industrial countries to associated territories, e.g. from Britain to the dependent territories and from France to countries in the French franc area. Some goes through contributions to UN institutions such as the International Bank for Reconstruction and Development and the Special United Nations Fund for Economic Development. The Bank's standards for loans are exacting. SUNFED was set up to provide funds for development projects which could not meet the criteria of the World Bank. [4]

International Liquidity, the monetary means of paying for imports. Ultimately imports are paid for by exports. The means of payment for purchases from abroad are, as with any other kind of purchase, liquid cash or its equivalent, i.e. monetary: for centuries gold, in more recent times other currencies held in reserve (sterling, dollars, etc.) or short-term loans, and most recently Special Drawing Rights from the International Monetary Fund. The growth in international exchange has thus required more liquidity. Hence the concern with gold supplies and with the availability of sterling, dollars or other currencies readily acceptable to suppliers in other countries, at times Deutschmarks and, in some parts, yen. Gold supplies from South Africa and Russia, and the price of gold, are therefore important. The use of sterling and dollars has fluctuated with their reliability, with the importance of Britain and the USA in world trade, and with the health of their balances of payments. Devaluations of sterling in the late 1960's and the 1970's have weakened confidence in its use as a means of international payment. In 1967 the International Monetary Fund (IMF) established Special Drawing Rights (SDRs) to supplement international liquidity. In 1968 the attempt by the US Government to maintain a fixed price for gold (35 dollars per ounce) broke down and, apart from gold in international financing, a second free market price emerged, which rose three or four times by the mid-1970's. In 1971 the USA made the dollar inconvertible and the IMF Group of Ten revalued their currencies, which in effect devalued the dollar.

The central economic issue in international liquidity is how far it can be expanded to finance trade without becoming *too* easily available to national currency systems: governments could then become indifferent to the maintenance of equilibrium in their balances of payments and fail to reduce costs and incomes when imports tended to become excessive. The general international effect could then be inflationary.

The apparently obvious solution is to float the exchange rates between currencies, completely or partly, so that deficits in balances of payments can be corrected by lower exchange rates and will not require gold, reserve currencies, international borrowing or special assistance from international organizations. Several currencies, including sterling, were floated in the early 1970s. Although economists were increasingly in favour of floating, it may have contributed to the acceleration in world-wide inflation by removing the discipline on governments that stable exchange rates imposed by requiring them to assemble reserves to meet deficits.

An apparently more natural way to increase international liquidity is to let the price of gold rise to its free market level. This course was long urged by economists in the USA, where most of the world's gold had accumulated, and finally two prices developed after 1968.

The most radical solution is a new international means of payment. The nearest approach is the system of Special Drawing Rights of the IMF.

Basically the growing requirement of liquidity to finance international trade can best be met by refining the mechanism of exchange rates so that creeping international inflation can be avoided without avoidable unemployment: the most hopeful methods seem to be wider margins for exchange rate fluctuations, occasional but infrequent changes in exchange rates when underlying market conditions have changed, and perhaps encouraging countries whose currencies are not used as reserves to make their exchange rates flexible. [4]

International Labour Organization (ILO), sometimes regarded as the most successful agency of the inter-war League of Nations. It was created in 1919 by the

Treaty of Versailles and in 1946 was affiliated to the United Nations as a Special Agency. By 1950 it had a membership of sixty countries. It holds world and regional conventions periodically. Its basic goals are the promotion of social justice and improved conditions for labour. Its main difficulties are that since labour markets in different countries vary widely, it may burden some to bring their labour conditions up to the level in the richer countries because this would raise their costs and weaken their ability to compete in world markets. [5]

International Monetary Fund (IMF), a Special Agency of the United Nations, established in 1945 under the Bretton Woods Agreements (1944) with headquarters in Washington. Its aims are to encourage stability of exchange, maintain orderly exchange procedures among its members, sustain a multilateral system of payments for current transactions between members and help to eliminate unnecessary foreign exchange restrictions that may hamper international commerce. Members have a quota, expressed in US dollars, which determines their voting power and subscriptions (paid partly in gold, partly in the members' currencies) and their drawing or borrowing rights against the Fund. The IMF acts as a banker to its members, lending them the currencies they need. In effect the borrower buys the currency with its own currency. Purchases are subject to two qualifications: (1) the quantity of other currencies a member may buy in one year is limited to one-quarter of its quota (this qualification has been waived in recent years); (2) such purchases may be applied only to finance temporary deficits in their balance of payments, and are expected to be cancelled by counter-purchases within five years.

Until the late 1950's the US dollar was the currency in heaviest demand; but in the 1960's and 1970's pressure of demand was also experienced by European currencies. Attention has also switched from persistent shortages of one currency to the adequacy of international financial liquidity in general. World trade has grown faster than trading countries' reserves of gold and foreign currencies. This has put increased pressure on IMF resources which has been only partly alleviated by increasing members' quotas. In 1962 the IMF Group of Ten created a new credit fund on which members in difficulty could draw; in 1964 and 1970 the British Government used it to offset pressure against sterling. In 1970 the new system of international "currency," Special Drawing Rights, was begun. Quotas have also been raised periodically. In these ways the IMF has tried to encourage the development of international trade and payments. [4]

International Payments, payments for goods or services bought from people in other countries. If a British citizen buys a bicycle from a fellow Briton he pays in cash in the form of pounds sterling. If he wishes to buy a car made in Italy payment to the Italian seller is more complicated. The pounds sterling of the buyer must somehow be converted into the lire required by the seller. This introduces a new element—the foreign exchange rate, or the price of lire in terms of pounds. For some time it stood at 1,000 lire to £1, so if the car cost 1,000,000 lire in Italy (ignoring tariffs, purchase tax and transport costs) the British citizen paid £1,000 to his bank, which bought 1,000,000 lire, and paid them to the seller. The price of lire in terms of pounds, like any other price, varies in response to supply and demand, which in turn vary according to the balance of payments between Italy and Britain. If the balance goes against Britain the demand for sterling and its price will tend to fall. If Britain has a balance of payments surplus the demand for sterling and its price rise. Demand for a currency and the supply of it are equated by the exchange rate, so that at the ruling price banks and brokers can buy foreign currencies to settle international transactions. [4]

International Trade, exchange (by selling and buying) of goods and services between people in different countries. It is the method of reaping the advantages of division of labour and specialization. Just as it pays the individual members of a community to specialize in the activities in which they have a comparative advantage over others and to use their earnings to buy their services, it also pays nations to specialize. A dentist may also be a first-class dental mechanic but it pays him to specialize in dentistry and to employ a mechanic. Even if the dentist can make dentures better than the mechanic, it pays him to concentrate on dentistry, where his comparative advantage is larger. The mechanic also benefits by concentrating on the task in which his disadvantage is less.

The advantages of international trade are most obvious in trade between countries in tropical and temperate climates. Even though oranges or bananas can be grown in Britain in hothouses, the cost is such that it is more productive to import them from countries with warmer climates and pay for the imports with exports of textiles and bicycles which Britain can produce more cheaply than they can. The advantages are less obvious, but still real, in trade between countries where natural or geographical conditions are more similar. A simple arithmetic example will show that the gains are real. To use real costs rather than simply money prices it is easiest to follow the classical method of assuming that all goods are produced by labour. Suppose that in Britain 10 days' labour will produce 50 blankets and 10 days' labour will produce 100 bushels of wheat, and in France 10 days' labour will produce 40 blankets and 10 days' labour will produce 60 bushels of wheat. Britain is thus more efficient than France in producing each commodity. Fifty blankets will exchange for 100 bushels of wheat in Britain and 40 blankets for 60 bushels of wheat in France before trade begins. Blankets will be twice as dear as bushels of wheat in Britain, but only 1½ times as dear in France. There will be gain to both countries if Britain exports wheat to France, where it can be exchanged for more blankets than it would buy in

Britain. France gains if it exports blankets to Britain, where they exchange for a larger quantity of wheat than they would buy in France. As long as the exchange rate of blankets against wheat is between one-half and two-thirds trade will be profitable to both.

The explanation of the gains from trade lies in differences in comparative advantage translated into differences in comparative costs and differences in money prices once the monetary exchange rate between the nations is known. A more fundamental explanation is in terms of what causes the differences in comparative costs. The explanation is that countries differ in their endowments of both natural and acquired resources (e.g. climate and human skills), and they will tend to have a comparative advantage in the production of goods which require mostly resources of which they have a relatively plentiful supply. They will tend to export these goods in return for goods whose production requires resources which are relatively scarce and therefore expensive in their countries. [4]

International Trade Organization (ITO), intended as a Special Agency affiliate of the United Nations Organization with the task of devising principles of commercial policy designed to expand multilateral, non-discriminatory world trade. Its charter (the Havana Charter), devised by the fifty-seven nations at the United Nations Conference on Trade and Employment, 1947–8, was to come into effect after twenty or more of the signatory nations had ratified it.

The charter embraced tariffs, quantitative import and export restrictions, subsidies, internal taxes and policy affecting the competitive position of imports, commodity agreements, and restrictive practices affecting international trade. The basic principles were: equal treatment for all (i.e. no discrimination), tariff reduction through negotiation and the eventual elimination of quantitative trade restrictions. But the specific provisions were hedged with exceptions and "escape" clauses that to some extent contradicted the main aims.

Although the charter as a whole has never been implemented, its main commercial provisions on tariffs and other trade restrictions were incorporated into the General Agreement on Tariffs and Trade negotiated at Geneva in 1947. [4]

Interpolation. *See* REGRESSION ANALYSIS.

Intervention, State, the positive action of governments to affect economic activity. State intervention can take the form of regulation, participation, control and direct operation and ownership. Governments have always shown some interest in production because of its political and military consequences (as with bad harvests), their responsibility for the legal framework of property rights, and their need to levy taxation on the incomes derived from production. But state intervention in the modern sense has arisen partly because of the impact upon society of industrialization and large-scale methods of production, and partly as a direct result of the extension of the franchise and the development of democracy, as well as being a by-product of two great wars. The growth of state intervention is a complex process, because once a state decides that some economic achievement or change is desirable it has to examine the secondary consequences of the means chosen to achieve the desired policy; if the secondary consequences are considered to be undesirable further policies will be necessary to cancel them out, and so on. Thus very extensive state intervention can arise out of a modest initial intervention.

State intervention in the modern sense dates from the early nineteenth century when the most important area of industrial activity with which British governments were concerned was that of employment conditions. Legislation was introduced limiting the employment of children and the hours per day they could work; factory inspectors were appointed; female employment was regulated. Towards the end of the nineteenth century legislation providing for state conciliation in industrial disputes was introduced, and later came "fair wages" legislation and the establishment of trade boards (now called Wages Councils) and the Ministry of Labour. Control over economic activity by the state was a feature of both world wars, and legislation governing the distribution of industry is an example of peacetime control. Probably the most important landmark in the development of state intervention in Britain came with the 1944 White Paper on High and Stable Employment (Cmd. 6527), the commitments of which have involved subsequent governments in extending the area of state participation and control. The nationalization of several important industries and the development of national insurance and welfare services have also considerably extended the area of state intervention. Intensification of inflation in the early 1970's also promoted further intervention aimed at control of prices and incomes. [10]

Inventory, a detailed list of a trader's stock which is periodically valued to enable a balance sheet to be prepared. The goods are normally counted, measured or weighed and an assessment or valuation of the inventory made. The generally accepted basis for the valuation of the stock-in-trade or inventory, if the goods are in a readily saleable condition, is either the original cost or the price at which they could be bought in the open market, whichever is the lower.

The inventory of a business at a given time is difficult to estimate because calculation has to be made while trading is taking place, and goods are accordingly constantly coming in and going out. It is necessary to take precautions to ensure that errors do not arise from this cause, and many businesses prefer to close their premises when they are compiling their inventory, despite the corresponding loss of trade.

Inventory "investment" is the increase in the (real) value of business stocks and work in progress in a given period. If the value has fallen there has been inventory disinvestment. [9]

Inventory Disinvestment. *See* INVENTORY.

Inventory Investment. *See* INVENTORY.

Inventory Investment Cycles, periodic fluctuations in inventory investment, that is, the increase (or decrease) in business stocks and work in progress in a period. Although inventory investment is a relatively small part of total demand in the economy it is extremely unstable for two reasons. First, the demand for stocks tends to change in response to alterations in the *rate* of increase or decrease in the demand for goods and services. Secondly, changes in the demand for output initially cause stocks to be either piled up or run down. If the changes in demand persist, the changes in production tend to be magnified by the need to adjust stocks to a more normal level: there is then a tendency to under-adjustment because the changes in output themselves tend to produce further changes in demand in the same direction, and so on. Ultimately there is over-adjustment (like overheating a too cold room by switching on too much space heating) followed by a similar sequence in reverse (like switching off too much heating and cooling the room more rapidly than is desired).

Although fluctuations in inventory investment may not be large enough to cause major fluctuations in national output, they tend to intensify fluctuations arising from other causes. [9]

Investible Funds. *See* CAPITAL.

Investment, (*a*) man-made assets which are used in the production of consumption or of further investment goods. Economic analysis is facilitated by dividing the annual output of goods and services into consumption goods and investment goods (also called capital or producer goods). Consumption goods and services satisfy consumers' wants *directly;* such satisfaction is the object of economic activity. Investment is the use of factors of production to produce capital goods to satisfy consumer wants *indirectly* but more fully in the future.

Factors of production are used to produce a gross output ("gross domestic product"). The capital assets employed are subject to wear and tear and must be maintained or replaced; and some equipment becomes obsolete because of changes in production methods. The deterioration in the income-producing capacity of capital is called "capital consumption," i.e. it is the amount of capital "eaten up" in the course of producing goods or services. If the value of the stock of capital is to be the same at the end of the production period as at the beginning, factors of production must be employed to make good the capital consumed. This process is called "maintaining capital intact." To ensure economic progress, most countries invest more resources in capital goods than are required to replace capital consumption. The deduction of capital consumption from total or "gross" investment gives "net" investment—the net addition to the stock of capital during the period. (Making the same deduction from *gross* domestic product yields the *net* domestic product.)

Investment may be divided into (1) fixed capital, (2) work in progress, (3) stocks.

(1) *Fixed capital* consists of producer goods such as factories, plant and equipment, buildings, commercial transport and rolling stock, roads, canals, railways and docks, and all forms of capital available for the production of consumer or producer goods. (2) *Work in progress* refers to factors of production tied up in the productive process and not completely converted into finished commodities, such as uncompleted buildings or partly constructed cars passing through the assembly shop. (3) *Stocks* refer to finished goods, consumer or producer, not yet sold to a final buyer, such as producers' stocks awaiting collection or in transit.

Investment may also be divided into (domestic) private and public and foreign. *Private* investment consists of all the purchases of capital goods by persons, businesses and institutions. Investment goods are durable and yield services for a number of years. Some consumer durable goods (e.g. cars) have these qualities, but, mainly because of difficulties of measurement, are treated in social accounting not as investment goods but as consumption goods, and the current benefits they yield are not counted into the national product. The main exception is expenditure on house construction. *Public* investment expenditures are defined in several ways. Public utilities and municipal housing are clearly investment expenditures. The social services may be regarded as investment or consumption. Health and education services yield current consumption but can also be regarded as investment in human beings and therefore as much investment as expenditures on hospitals, school buildings or factories.

Foreign or overseas investment consists of the claims owned by people or governments on real wealth in other countries. A country can thus invest overseas only to the extent that it is exporting more goods and services than it is importing; i.e. overseas investment requires productive effort in the same way as the home production of capital goods. Such overseas investment may take the form of loans or credits to people in other countries, the purchase of real assets overseas, or an increase in the country's reserves of gold and foreign currencies.

(*b*) investment has a more specific meaning. The formation of real capital gives rise to paper or financial *claims* on wealth (bonds, shares, mortgages, etc.). There is an active market in such claims, the purchase of which by people or institutions is also described as "investment." This "financial" (or personal) investment should be distinguished from "real" (or community) investment. "Financial" investment refers only to the transfer of the ownership of claims between persons. [9]

Investment Allowances, tax allowances against income for investment in new industrial building or plant and equipment. The effect of investment allowances is to permit a sum larger than the initial cost of new equipment to be written off against taxable income over its life.

The investment allowances are designed to encourage managements to expand production and increase productivity by industrial investment. They form a general subsidy on investment expenditures: as such they have been criticized by some economists as insufficiently discriminating in their effect, especially in periods of high employment when calls on the community's saving are already heavy. In Britain investment allowances (tax reductions) have alternated with investment grants (in cash) as Labour and Conservative governments replaced each other in the 1960's and 1970's. [12]

Investment Appraisal, a technique for assessing the worthwhileness of investment projects; a body of decision rules to guide choice among alternative investments. The major problems to be overcome relate to: the treatment of uncertainty (since the benefits from, and to some extent the costs of, capital projects stretch into the future which can never be known with certainty); the measurement of benefits and costs—even when known with certainty their precise measurement often raises difficulties, particularly where the decisions are made by persons (households) and government (although business enterprises may also have difficulty on this score); and finally the reduction of benefits and costs received and incurred at different dates to a common measure (since a pound received now is not the same as a pound received next month or next year and the two cannot be directly compared without making an adjustment for futurity). Economists have had more success in dealing with the last problem than with the first two, although none can be regarded as completely solved—except perhaps in very simple examples.

To deal with the third problem requires the use of discounting (or compounding) techniques to translate future flows of costs and benefits into equivalent dated sums of money. Where the flows take the form of level payments (or receipts) per period, the rules and tables for finding the present value of an *annuity* can be applied. Where future receipt and payment flows vary from period to period (but are certain), the problem of reducing them to, say, a *present value* requires each individual item to be discounted separately and a sum of all the resultant individual present value estimates found. If V represents present value, $Q_1, Q_2, Q_3 \ldots Q_n$ represent receipts or benefits net of periodic costs in periods $1, 2, 3 \ldots n$, t represents a particular period and i represents the rate of interest per period, the present value of a variable flow of future amounts is given by the following expression:

$$V = \sum_{t=1}^{n} Q_t/(1 + i)^t \qquad (1)$$

The Sigma sign Σ is shorthand for "the sum of": the subscript $t = 1$ and the superscript n indicate the items that are to be summed, so that the whole expression is translated into: "to find the present value, find the discounted value of Q for every period t between $t = 1$ and $t = n$, and add." If the resultant V is larger than C, the initial cost of the investment, the investment is worthwhile. With an unlimited budget at his disposal, the agency considering the investment would accept every proposal that showed $(V - C)$ as a positive value. With a limited budget, it would rank all proposals in descending order of values obtained for $(V - C)$ and choose the highest valued projects until its capital budget was exhausted.

An alternative approach to the problem is to calculate the *internal rate of return* generated by each investment project. This is equivalent to finding a rate of interest to apply to every Q_t in expression (1) above that would reduce V to equality with C so that $(V - C) = 0$. If r is the rate to be found, then to find the internal rate of return of an investment it is necessary to solve the following expression for r:

$$C = \sum_{t=1}^{n} Q_t/(1 + r)^t \qquad (2)$$

Except where Q_t is an annuity, solving this expression for r requires a lengthy trial-and-error process. When r has been obtained for a project, the decision rule then becomes "the project is acceptable if its internal rate of return is higher than the rate of interest the agency would have to pay to obtain the necessary finance for the project, or which it would have to forego if it financed the project from its own resources; i.e. if $(r - i)$ is positive." Again, if the investment agency had an unlimited capital budget it would accept every project with a positive $(r - i)$; if its budget was limited it would rank all possible projects in descending order of values obtained for $(r - i)$ and select the highest values until the budget was exhausted.

The difference between these two methods—comparing investments by *net present values* or by their *internal rates of return*—should not be exaggerated. Economists divide on their relative merits, which often depend on the circumstances of individual decisions; but essentially they amount to the same thing. The important problems in investment appraisal are not those of valuation technique: they are rather how to deal with uncertainty and how to identify and measure accurately the flows of benefits and costs. [1]

Investment Function. *See* PROPENSITY TO INVEST.

Investment Grants. *See* INVESTMENT ALLOWANCES.

Investment Trust, a company which invests its capital in a large number of firms in a variety of industries. The investments are usually in good-class ordinary shares. An investment trust is attractive to investors because it offers a widely spread portfolio plus a cushion of undistributed profits and reserves. Further, the "gearing" provided by fixed interest capital such as debentures and preference shares increases the gain to ordinary shareholders when economic conditions are favourable to high profits. The share price is based upon the market value of the securities held by the trust.

An investment trust shares with the unit trust a wide spread of risk, but has other advantages: (*a*) the gearing, (*b*) the management retains a proportion of the profits for re-investment, (*c*) management expenses are charged against untaxed income (unit trusts must meet these expenses out of taxed income). [8]

Invisible Exports, so called because, like exports, they give rise to payments from people in other countries to residents but without movement of goods between their countries. These payments are generally for shipping, banking, interest on loans, dividends, insurance, migrants' funds, legacies, gifts and, of growing importance, tourism. They can be regarded as the "export" of services. Conversely residents' purchases from people in other countries include these items and are called "invisible imports."

For many years Britain's "invisible exports" have far exceeded her "invisible imports" and this surplus too has assisted the balance of payments. For some years it was argued that the invisible exports were of relatively minor importance. An opposite view is that Britain for a century or more has rarely paid for her imports by exports of goods, and that the invisibles are a fundamental element in the economy. [4]

"Invisible Hand." *See* ECONOMIC THOUGHT; SMITH, ADAM.

Invisible Imports. *See* INVISIBLE EXPORTS.

Involuntary Saving. *See* FORCED SAVING.

Involuntary Unemployment, abstention from work despite readiness to accept it at any (net) price (i.e. wages or salaries above the costs of doing it—fares, working clothes, etc.). The contrast is with voluntary unemployment, which reflects a decision not to accept work at the going rate because looking for a better-paid job or leisure is preferred. Involuntary unemployment is most common in a world general recession, when (at the going rate) there are fewer jobs than job-hunters. In a recession confined to one country, region or town, work may be available at an acceptable rate in other countries, regions or towns. The going rate may be set either by the market or by collective bargaining. [5]

Irredeemable Securities, "undated" securities; those with no stated date for the cash repayment (redemption) of invested capital. Possession gives the holder the right to the income attaching to it but no right to repayment at its nominal par (or "face") value. It can only be converted into cash by selling it for what it will bring in the securities market. Some British government securities are irredeemable. [8]

Isoquant, or Equal-Product curve, geometrical curve showing the (technical) combination of two factors of production ("inputs") required to produce a stated quantity of output. The term was originated by Ragnar Frisch. The isoquant shows that if less of one factor (e.g. labour) is used (perhaps because its price has risen) more of another (e.g. land) must be used to maintain the output. (The rate at which one must be replaced by the other is the rate of technical substitution.) In this technical sense a producer is "indifferent" between the two factors: e.g. a farmer is able to produce the same crop of wheat by using land "extensively" (i.e. employing more land with less labour) or more "intensively" (i.e. employing less land with more labour). One set of combinations of two factors to produce a stated quantity of output traces out one isoquant. A larger quantity of output requires another, similar, set of factor combinations and traces out another isoquant, and so on. Just as a hill can be mapped in height contours that trace out all locations of equal height, a map or family of isoquants will show the factor combinations that yield various quantities of output, with one isoquant for each. A producer faced with stated prices of the two factors and a given budget to spend on them will sensibly aim to buy them in quantities such that if he bought any other combination, his budget would produce less output, i.e. he would finish up on an isoquant "lower down the hill" of output. He thus maximizes the output to be obtained from a given scale of outlay on factors of production, or (saying the same thing the other way round) he minimizes the cost of producing a given output. This is the first stage in a profit-maximizing process that next requires him to find the output (or scale of factor input) that will yield him the largest difference between the outlay on factors and revenue from sale of the output. [7]

Issue Broker. *See* BROKER.

Issuing House, a merchant bank, such as Rothschilds or Lazards, or a house formed to negotiate capital issues, such as the Charterhouse Investment Trust, which advises companies, local authorities, overseas governments and government agencies wanting long-term finance on the kind, terms and timing of issues, arranges guarantees that issues will be fully subscribed (underwriting), sponsors issues with its name and reputation and allots shares. Issuing houses may also act as accepting houses, investment banks or managers of investment trusts. [8]

J

Jawboning, American colloquialism applied to sermons by politicians (or clerics and others) on the economic state of the nation, with exhortation to industrialists to invest more, workers to work harder or more conscientiously, consumers to shop more wisely, and all and sundry to watch the economic indicators and act with foresight. Jawboners usually admonish people to act in conflict with their immediate preferences; they usually offer over-simplified diagnoses and urge ineffective solutions incorporating *simpliste* fallacies. A common source of error is to confuse symptoms with causes, e.g. advocating the prohibition of well-motivated behaviour that would certainly reappear in some other form. [13]

Jevons, William Stanley (1835–82), English economist. He was educated at London University and after a period in Australia he became Professor of Political Economy, first at Manchester and then at London. Jevons was interested in many aspects of economics. Besides being a critic of the classical economists he was also an applied economist, as shown by his *Investigations in Currency and Finance* (1884), which contained several papers all linking statistical investigation and theoretical analysis. But his importance lies mainly in his work in pure theory. His *Theory of Political Economy* (1871) brought together scattered fragments of earlier utility analysis into a comprehensive theory of value, exchange and distribution. He aimed at providing a mathematical exposition of the laws of the market and the theory of value. It was in this work that he formulated and developed the concept of "marginal utility." A twentieth-century echo is that among his other work he argued that the "alarmists" of his day who prophesied the exhaustion of coal supplies overlooked the function of price in regulating demand and economizing use. [2]

Job Analysis (or Evaluation), identifying the elements required in or for an occupation or profession: muscular strength, clear sight, responsibility for failure, leadership qualities, phlegmatic temperament. Each is assigned a weight (or "points"), and the total of points decides the rate of payment per hour, week, month. The system can produce contentment among employees because they are confident that pay is objective ("fair," i.e. without favouritism). But it may weaken the authority of trade unions, which may want prior consultation so that they can be seen to have objected to or approved of evaluation proposals. The method is practicable in the short run but may break down when methods of production change or labour is attracted elsewhere and the economic value of personal qualities changes. [5]

Jobber, a member of the London Stock Exchange. The Exchange has a unique system in which brokers do not deal direct with one another but buy and sell securities through jobbers. A jobber usually specializes in classes of shares, and is not allowed to deal direct with the public.

A Stock Exchange bargain is carried out as follows: an investor asks his broker to buy securities; the broker asks the jobber for a quotation, without disclosing whether he is a buyer or seller; the jobber quotes two prices, the lower of which is the price at which he will buy, the higher the price at which he will sell. The broker usually repeats the process with other jobbers. If called upon to deliver the securities, the jobber must do so.

Jobbers do not charge commission, but make their profit by buying more cheaply than they sell. The margin between the upper and lower quotations is known as the jobber's turn.

Without the jobbing system transactions could take place only wherever selling brokers could find buying brokers with opposite orders, i.e. it would require a form of barter. The existence of jobbers prepared to buy or sell at any time enlarges the freedom with which dealings can take place. [8]

Jobber's Turn. *See* JOBBER.

Johnson, Harry Gordon (1923–79), Canadian economist. He was educated at the University of Toronto School and at the Universities of Toronto, Cambridge and Harvard. From 1966 to 1974 he was Professor of Economics at two Universities: London and Chicago (Chicago since 1959). In 1974 he resigned from London.

Johnson is among the world's leading economic theorists in international trade, money and economic growth. In the Preface to *International Trade and Economic Growth* (1958), a series of "studies in pure theory," he explains the purpose of theoretical analysis as first, "to push the application of known and tested techniques into new areas"; and second, "synthesizing the methods and results of previous writers into a simpler, more readily usable analysis." In both these ways of advancing economic theory Johnson has made an outstanding contribution.

His output is large. Among his other main works are *The Overloaded Economy* (1952); *Money, Trade and Economic Growth* (1962); *The World Economy at the Crossroads* (1965); *Economic Policies towards less Developed Countries* (1967); *Essays in Monetary Economics* (1967); *Aspects of the Theory of Tariffs* (1971); *Further Essays in Monetary Economics* (1972). In his work on international trade he has developed the theory of comparative costs and of why countries engage in international trade; the conditions in which a country can improve its position by imposing a tariff even if other countries retaliate; the effects of different kinds of economic growth (e.g. industrial or agricultural, capital-intensive or otherwise) in increasing or reducing international trade; the general theory of factors determining the balance of payments. In monetary theory his work of exposition, refinement and development ranges over the whole field of general monetary theory, including his well-known lecture on the *Keynesian Revolution and the Monetarist Counter-Revolution* (1970) and international monetary theory. He has made substantial excursions into policy issues, where his vivid and original approach has drawn widespread attention to his proposals. Some of them have been directly related to his theoretical writings, such as his advocacy of floating exchange rates and unilateral free trade. Others have ranged more widely into public policy towards advertising, the role of private enterprise and public planning in economic development, and social and regional policies (*Money, Trade and Economic Growth,* Part 3). [2]

Joint Consultation. *See* CONSULTATION.

Joint Costs, incurred in the production of two or more commodities (or services) and not divisible between them. The most common examples are the administrative or other "overhead" costs of a plant or firm with several products, or of a retail store with several departments. Arbitrary separation (or imputation) can be attempted by allocating costs according to space occupied by machinery for each product, number of man-hours of labour on each unit of output, size and location (nearness to the front entrance) of counters in a shop, etc. [3]

Joint Demand, the relationship between two or more commodities or services such that increases in the demand for one result in increases in the demand for the other(s). Examples are bacon and eggs, tea and sugar, records and record players. A fall in the cost of production and the price of one commodity will stimulate the demand for itself and therefore lead to an increased demand for the related goods and tend to drive up their prices if available supplies are unchanged. Thus the market prices of commodities in joint demand tend to move in opposite directions.

The existence of a joint demand for the products of a manufacturer or seller means he is not concerned simply with matching cost of and revenue from additional batches of each product. An additional batch of, say, bacon, may be profitable even if the additional cost exceeds the additional sales revenue, provided additional profit from the sale of eggs (because of increased demand) more than outweighs the loss on additional bacon. Again, razors may be sold at a loss in order to stimulate the sales of razor blades. The economics of joint demand suggest that advertising may be regarded as a joint commodity in which information is supplied free to consumers. The information is sometimes supplied at a small charge, as in an illustrated catalogue. [7]

Joint Products, two or more goods (or services) produced inseparably, e.g. meat and wool from sheep, soup and leather from turtles, petrol and oil from petroleum. Main products and by-products are joint products. The economic significance of this technical circumstance is that a change in the conditions of demand for one joint product will affect its price, its supply and therefore the supply and price of the other(s). [3]

Joint-stock Banks. *See* BANKS, JOINT-STOCK.

Joint Supply, the relationship between two (or more) products such that changes in the supply of one similarly affect the supply of the other(s), e.g. beef and hides, wool and mutton, gas and coke, petrol and oils. Joint supply can produce complex interrelationships between the demands for and the supplies and prices of different commodities. For example, an increase in the demand for carcass meat which raises its price and produces larger output will necessarily increase the supply of hides and other animal by-products; and if the demand for them remains unchanged, the increase in supply will cause their prices to fall. The general tendency is for the prices of products in joint supply to move in opposite directions.

For producers, joint supply raises problems of allocating production costs between the joint products. Where "jointness" is complete, i.e. where increased outputs of one commodity are rigidly geared to increased outputs of the other(s), it is impossible to separate costs. If the two products are sold in separate markets a producer will aim at the output of the two which will yield the largest difference between the total costs of producing them and the sum of the revenues from their sale. Usually, however, the degree of "jointness" is not rigid. It may be possible, while keeping total cost constant, to vary the output of one commodity at the expense of the other and thus to obtain a ratio of the "additional" or "marginal" cost of one in terms of the other. The most profitable combination of the two commodities for a given cost outlay would then be that at which this ratio was equal to the ratio between the selling prices. Thus it is possible to arrive at a combination of outputs at which profits are maximized even though *total* costs of production cannot be divided between two commodities if producing one always involves producing some of the other. [7]

Journals, Economic, the rapid development of economics in the period since the end of the First World War, and its increasing recognition by universities as a subject worthy of study in its own right, have been matched (and probably to some extent fostered) by a remarkable growth in the number of periodicals publishing articles written by professional economists and intended principally for an academic audience. Before 1920 only a handful of these journals was published; there are now several score published in English. (The American Economic Association has produced a comprehensive, cumulative index of journal articles.)

The majority of these journals aim to be general in their coverage of the subject, but the number of specialist periodicals which confine themselves to particular parts of the field is increasing. Of the more general journals, the most influential of those published in Britain are probably *The Economic Journal,* the quarterly journal of the Royal Economic Society, which was first published in 1890 and regularly includes a section listing the contents of the latest issues of a wide range of other economic periodicals which it receives; *Economica,* published quarterly by the London School of Economics and Political Science; *Oxford Economic Papers,* which is published three times a year; *The Bulletin of the Oxford Institute of Statistics,* another quarterly; and *The Review of Economic Studies,* the journal of the (Anglo-American) Economic Study Society, which is also published three times a year; the *Manchester School,* published by the University of Manchester; and the *Scottish Journal of Political Economy,* published by the University of Glasgow. The leading journals published in the United States are probably *The American Economic Review,* the quarterly journal of the American Economic Association, first published in 1911; *The Quarterly Journal of Economics,* which is published by Harvard University and first appeared in 1886; *The Journal of Political Economy,* published bi-monthly by the University of Chicago; *The Review of Economics and Statistics,* another Harvard quarterly; and the *Journal of Law and Economics* of Chicago University.

Examples of the more specialist journals are *Econometrica,* the journal of the Econometric Society, whose aim is to advance economic theory in its relation to statistics and mathematics; *Social and Economic Studies,* published from the University of the West Indies and concentrating mainly on the problems of under-developed countries; *The Journal of Industrial Economics,* an Anglo-American journal on the economic problems of industry and commerce; and *Public Choice,* an American journal specializing in the political and charity markets, and published at the Virginia State University. Articles of interest to the economist are also published from time to time in specialist journals principally concerned with other, closely related, subjects; e.g. *The Journal of the Royal Statistical Society* and *The British Tax Review.* Other journals which aim at a more general readership than the academic journals, are the *London and Cambridge Economic Service Bulletin,* published by the Department of Applied Economics, Cambridge, and *The Economic Review,* published by the National Institute of Economic and Social Research. The main purpose of these periodicals is to provide a commentary on current economic trends, but both frequently publish articles on more general economic issues. (*See also* list of periodicals on page xlix.) [2]

Juglar Cycle, nine to ten-year economic fluctuations explained by Clement Juglar (the first economist to identify industrial cycles) as the result of innovations in capitalism. Juglar's analytical technique was adapted by Joseph Schumpeter in his emphasis on innovation as the source of the trade cycle. Six Juglar cycles are embodied in a Kondratieff cycle. [9]

Junior Mortgage, a mortgage having a claim which ranks below that of another mortgage. A general term for second, third and subsequent mortgages relating to a property. [8]

"Just Price," moral conception of the amount of money that a seller should ask for a commodity (or service) representing the value of the commodity as judged by the community at large. The term is medieval in origin and is associated with St Thomas Aquinas. (Usury, for example, was an unjust or exorbitant interest on a loan; though Aquinas and most medieval thinkers regarded interest as unjustified and unjust unless the principal was at risk.) Its general sense has been revived in recent times and applied to "fair" wages, meaning the amount that the community believes workers, e.g. nurses, coalminers, refuse collectors, etc., are morally worth, whatever their market value. There is no necessary conflict between "just" and market prices; individuals may rationally wish to pay more as citizens judging desert than as consumers in everyday living. But if market price is removed, its function as an indicator of demand and means of rationing supply is also removed; demand must be apportioned or supply restricted or expanded by other means—public opinion or, if that is insufficient, law or discretionary administrators. A "just" price cannot easily be analysed by economic theory. An economy comprising just prices for goods and services should be based on electoral (majority) opinion as a whole; which may be thought more responsible than individual opinion, and directed from the centre by representatives who may be thought better informed than individual consumers in markets. [7]

K

Kahn, Richard F. (Lord Kahn of Hampstead) (1905–89), British economist. He was educated at St Paul's School and King's College, Cambridge. He was a temporary civil servant from 1939 to 1946 and Professor of Economics at Cambridge from 1951 to 1972. His economic writings mostly appeared in specialist and other economic journals. He was raised to the peerage in 1965.

Kahn is an economist whose influence on recent economic thought has been out of proportion to his published work. His "Notes on Ideal output" (1935) have established him as the principal authority on the problems associated with proposals to maximize welfare by taxing decreasing return industries in order to subsidize industries with increasing returns. In addition he contributed extensively to the study of how equilibrating adjustments may themselves influence the pattern of the equilibrium towards which they move. Keynes generously acknowledged Kahn's origination of the multiplier, and Joan Robinson his part in the development of the theory of imperfect competition. Together with Joan Robinson, Nicholas Kaldor and Piero Sraffa, Kahn dominated the economics faculty at Cambridge for many years. [2]

Kaldor, Nicholas (1908–86), economist born in Budapest, Hungary. He was educated at the Model Gymnasium, Budapest, and came to England to study at the London School of Economics, where he graduated in 1930 and taught until 1947. In the next five years he was in national and international public service. He has taught at Cambridge since 1952, as University Reader and later Professor of Economics. Apart from academic teaching he has been in government service as Director of the Research and Planning Division of the Economic Commission for Europe (1947–9), adviser to the British Chancellor of the Exchequer (1964–8), and to the governments of India and other developing countries. He was a member of the Royal Commission on the Taxation of Profits and Incomes from 1951 to 1955.

Among Kaldor's main published works are *An Expenditure Tax* (1955), *Essays on Value and Distribution* (1960), *Capital Accumulation and Economic Growth* (1961), *Essays in Economic Policy* (1964), *Causes of the Slow Rate of Growth of the UK* (1966).

Although educated in the liberal tradition of the LSE, which was reflected in his teaching and writing in the 1930's, Kaldor was influenced by Keynes and tended to become dirigiste in his thinking and advice to governments, as in his advocacy of a tax on advertising, a capital gains tax and the selective employment tax (SET). He contributed to the development of the macro-economic theory of distribution at Cambridge which applied Keynesian thinking to the distribution of national income between the factors of production.

Kaldor's collected works showed he was an economist in the grand manner, ranging over the entire field of economics: welfare, value theory, cycles and growth. He is a theorist who applies theories to the real world. The "Kaldor effect," linking investment, growth and income distribution, has constantly reappeared in economic discussion. His opinion that the results of theoretical analysis can be applied to real problems brought him into conflict with Triffin and others: the question is whether the economist brings to concrete problems theoretical concepts or a mind toughened by analysing them. Kaldor's approach has led him into concern with fiscal questions in various countries. His generally admired advice to the Indian government was misunderstood and misapplied, but that to a British government on the introduction of the SET and to other governments, which met with less approval among economists, was accepted more or less in its entirety. [2]

Kalecki, Michal (1899–1970), Polish economist. He worked at Cambridge in 1937, at the Oxford University Institute of Statistics from 1939 to 1945, and at the UN Economics Department from 1947 to 1955 before becoming adviser to the chairman of the Polish Government Planning Committee in Warsaw from 1957 to 1964. He was Professor at the Main School of Planning and Statistics from 1961 to 1968.

Kalecki's earlier writing was concerned mainly with the theory of imperfect competition, and during this phase he inaugurated a brisk controversy by producing the concept of "the average degree of monopoly" as a major determinant of the distribution of the national income. Economists are widely divided whether this was an analytical concept or a sophisticated reformulation of Marx's formula for exploitation. His later work, particularly after his return to Poland, was concerned with the theory of economic dynamics; his view was that the main interest of economists is with trend rather than cycle, particularly with the determination of investment decisions by the level and rate of change of economic activity.

His published work was extensive (over two hundred items) including *Essays on the Theory of Economic Fluctuations, Studies in Economic Dynamics, The Theory of Economic Dynamics* and *Essay on the Theory of Growth of a Socialist Economy.* [2]

"Kelly's Directory." *See* Sources, Statistical.

Kennedy Round (of tariff negotiations), an American attempt named after

President John F. Kennedy to expedite tariff reductions under the General Agreement on Tariffs and Trade by replacing bargaining over tariffs on individual commodities by general reductions on most or all commodities of up to 50 per cent. The initiative was made possible by the US Trade Expansion Act of 1962.

The main purpose of the Kennedy Round was a bargain between the USA and the Common Market to agree on tariff units and invite other industrial countries to participate. The USA required concessions on agricultural tariffs which the Common Market countries, especially France, were reluctant to reduce, but reductions in industrial tariffs were regulated in the late 1960's and early 1970's with the EEC, EFTA and Japan. [4]

Keynes, John Maynard, Baron Keynes (1883–1946), English economist. The son of John Neville Keynes, Lecturer and Registrar at the University of Cambridge. He was educated at Eton and King's College, Cambridge, where he was mainly interested in mathematics and philosophy. He eventually turned to economics and came to know Alfred Marshall, who was favourably impressed with his abilities. In 1906 he entered the Civil Service, and for the next few years he served at the India Office, spending his spare time writing a fellowship dissertation which he submitted in 1908. It was rejected, but Marshall offered him a lectureship in economics, which he accepted. It began his academic career. He was later elected to a Fellowship at King's College, and his dissertation was published as *A Treatise on Probability* in 1921. In 1912 he became editor of the *Economic Journal,* and in 1913 secretary to the Royal Economic Society and a member of the Royal Commission on Indian Finance and Currency.

During the First World War, Keynes did important work in the Treasury on Allied loans. At the Paris Peace Conference he was the chief representative of the Treasury, and at the Supreme Economic Council in 1919 he deputized for the Chancellor of the Exchequer. His recommendations on the subject of German reparations were rejected. He resigned, recording his views in *Consequences of the Peace* (1919), a work which made him the centre of the controversy on the economic reorganization of Europe.

The depression of the inter-war years aroused Keynes's interest in the works of Sir Dennis Robertson. His own views on the rate of interest were published in the two-volume *Treatise on Money* (1930) and the revolutionary *General Theory of Employment, Interest and Money* (1936). On the outbreak of the Second World War, Keynes again joined the Treasury, and, although a sick man, gave influential advice on war finance. He was raised to the peerage for his public and academic services in 1942. He played a leading part in the Bretton Woods Conference from which emerged the International Monetary Fund and the International Bank.

Keynes's reputation as the most outstanding economist of his generation lay in the break he was thought to have made with classical theory by trying to show economists and the general public that the economic system should be in equilibrium with a large volume of unemployed resources. Previously economists had tended to concentrate on the distribution of the national product rather than on its size, largely because of the implicit assumption that unemployment would create forces that would destroy itself. They had tended to explain unemployment as due to institutional rigidities within the price system, and their policy recommendations were largely concerned with the removal of these rigidities. The result was that studies of business fluctuations tended to be separated from the main stream of economic thought. In the *Treatise on Money* Keynes had argued the importance of the relationship between savings and investment as a cause of the trade cycle, and in the *General Theory* he tried to explain the factors affecting the level of employment. The community's expenditure on consumption and investment goods determined the level of economic activity, but as incomes rose savings tended to increase. The relative fall in expenditure caused the economy to spiral down into depression. His theory of interest, which differed from the classical theories, was widely thought to show that the system was liable to stay in this position unless expenditure was increased in some way. The policy recommendation following from this analysis was that the government was responsible for promoting public works in order to generate the expenditure that would remove unemployment and in general to maintain demand at a level that would create full employment. The theory also argued out that the reverse process would be capable of removing inflationary conditions. Such views created a great deal of opposition, but eventually Keynes won. The Coalition Government's White Paper on Employment Policy (1944) marked the acceptance of the "Keynesian Revolution."

Some economists were thought to take the Keynesian reaction against classical economics too far: Keynes rebuked them for overlooking the merits of classical economic doctrine and policy. In his 1936 classic book he wrote ". . . the result of filling in the gaps in the classical theory is not to dispose of the 'Manchester System,' but to indicate the nature of the environment which the free play of economic forces requires if it is to realise the full potentialities of production." The intriguing unknown for economists is to judge "what Keynes would have said" in the present day. His followers at Cambridge (England) have adopted or adapted his intellectual constructions, especially in the development of macroeconomic models, to emerge with policies that seem to conflict with the liberal "Manchester System." Keynes's prestige remains massive, and all schools of economic thought would like to claim the support of his authority.

More recently Keynes's thinking has been reinterpreted as a special rather than a "general" theory of employment. Attention has also been directed to structural unemployment which is unavoidable as changes in techniques and home or world demand reduce the markets for products of the older industries and which cannot be removed by raising monetary demand in the economy as a whole.

Keynes's theoretical analysis dominated economic thinking for some thirty years. It has been examined increasingly critically, though by individual economists rather than by Keynes's many avowed followers in Britain, the USA and elsewhere. Many of the doubts are crystallized by the Swedish-American economist, Axel Leijonhufvud, in *On Keynesian Economics and the Economics of Keynes;* the title differentiates between the economic thinking of Keynes and that of his followers, based on what they thought he meant or on extensions of his thought. Leijonhufvud also argues that much of Keynes's critique of Say's Law and classical theory is irrelevant to the analysis of *The General Theory of Employment, Interest and Money.* Other critics of Keynes have been F. A. Hayek, W. H. Hutt and Milton Friedman.

Keynes's emphasis on national totals or aggregates stimulated the development of macro-economics, the study of the behaviour of larger groups, which some economists made the basis of social accounting and national planning. Others believe it has limited value as a guide to policy in a democratic society where changes in techniques and tastes are allowed free play and are not foreseeable, so that macro-economics is complementary to or dependent on micro-economics (the study of the behaviour of individuals). [2]

Kind, goods or services, in contrast to money. Social benefits, for example, may be in cash (family allowances, pensions, etc.) or kind (education without direct payment or housing at a lower-than-market price). The economic difference is that cash is untied and leaves the recipient free to use it as he wishes; kind restricts choice but is a more certain method of ensuring that the benefit is used, or at least reaches the recipients, since cash can be spent on anything with a price. A compromise that leaves some discretion and choice, and is almost as certain to reach the intended recipient as kind, is earmarked purchasing power (e.g. a coupon or voucher). [7]

Knight, Frank H. (1885–1973), American economist, and a leader in the development of economic thought for nearly half a century. He studied economics at Cornell and Chicago Universities. After six years teaching at the University of Iowa he was appointed Professor of Economics at the University of Chicago in 1928. He made his name early by his most influential work, *Risk, Uncertainty and Profit* (1921).

Knight was best known for his explanation of profit under competitive conditions by the uncertainty or uninsurable risk associated with innovation, in contrast to insurable risk. Consequently it would not exist in "stationary state" conditions. He also contributed to the definition and interpretation of social cost (*Quarterly Journal of Economics,* 1924). In *The Ethics of Competition* (1935) and later essays he moved to scepticism concerning the automatic functioning of free enterprise: "with 'gross' inequality in the distribution of wealth, all ethical defences of freedom lose their validity." But he distrusted the exercise of state power and ended up with a preference for decentralized institutions. He was concerned with morals from an agnostic viewpoint (*The Ethics of Competition,* 1935). Knight's influence is seen in the work of former students who have taught at the universities of Chicago, Virginia, California and elsewhere. [2]

Knock-out, a payment to exclude a potential bidder from an auction. It is a restrictive practice and is illegal, but it is difficult to prevent. [7]

Kondratieff, N. D. (1892–1931), Russian economist who discovered long-term (50–60-year) fluctuations or waves in economic activity, prices and exchange: hence Kondratieff Cycle. He argued that long-term fluctuations recurred in regular cycles inherent in capital accumulation under the capitalist system. Schumpeter adapted the Kondratieff cycle to his theory of business fluctuations derived from waves of innovation. The 1780–1840 wave was the first Industrial Revolution; the 1840–90 wave was the era of steam and steel; 1890 to 1950 was the wave of chemistry, electricity and the internal combustion engine. [2]

Kropotkin, Prince. *See* ANARCHISM.

L

Labour, in its broadest sense a basic factor of production used in combination with capital and land to produce commodities or render services; more specifically the number of people working or available for work, or the amount of work done.

The conditions of supply of labour are unlike those of a commodity. An increase in the price of a commodity will induce an increase in supply, but the supply of labour is influenced by a wider variety of conditions, especially in the short run. The number in the labour force depends on the population and the proportion of it who work. Some people can choose within wide limits whether or not to work, e.g. married women, and the net effect of higher wages on the number at work is uncertain: it may increase because more money attracts new workers, or diminish because some married women will give up work when the pay of their husbands rises. The amount of work done depends on the number of employees, the length of time worked and the intensity of the effort. The number of hours worked depends on the relative preference of the employee for income and leisure: if he wishes to earn a high income, he will work longer hours and forgo leisure. Many employees do not have much choice about how long they work but must fit into the arrangement made in agreements between employers or trade unions. In the years of full employment, leisure may be preferred to higher pay: if a worker is satisfied with a wage of £50 a week, a rise in pay from, say £8 to £10 per shift will allow him to earn this amount in five shifts instead of six. What is still called "absenteeism," e.g. in mining, is a preference for leisure, and not necessarily objectionable as the term suggests.

It is unlikely that a worker would use the whole of his increased income potential to demand more leisure in this way, unless he placed no value at all on the other things that additional income could buy; but he may combine more leisure with more income, working fewer hours than he did before.

The efficiency with which a given number of employees produce goods and services, the *productivity* of labour, depends largely on the level of skill or training of the labour force and the distribution of labour and co-operating capital equipment among occupations and industries.

If labour were completely mobile between areas and occupations, movement from low productivity occupations paying low wages to high wage and productivity occupations would be induced by (and would tend to eliminate) wage differences. This movement of labour would be reinforced by a drift of new enterprise and capital to areas where the price of labour was relatively low. In practice, mobility of labour between occupations is limited by lack of education, training, experience and ability, and by the cost and difficulty of personal movement (which in turn may be partly due to government policies on, for example, rent restriction). Immobility of both labour and enterprise capital may be aggravated by trade union restrictions, demarcation rules and regional or national wage agreements that reduce or exclude local wage differentials. These practices hinder the linking of unfilled vacancies with pockets of unemployment, reduce the incentive for new business to settle in low-wage areas, and so act as a brake on economic efficiency and growth. Some economists have argued that the power of trade unions must be strong in order to offset the superior bargaining power of employers, others that the trade unions have impeded the working of the market economy, some that they no longer need the legal privileges given by Acts of Parliament when their bargaining power was weaker than in conditions of full employment. [5]

Labour Force, the part of the population that is at work or seeking employment, i.e. involuntarily unemployed. It thus varies with legal limitations (e.g. school-leaving age), institutional conditions (e.g. state pensions that are raised if work is continued after pensionable age), but most generally by the response to the price of labour. If wages, salaries, etc. were to rise owing to an increase in labour-intensive industries, such as retailing, hairdressing, travel agencies, and other personal services in an opulent society, more people would join the labour force; if wages, etc. fell, as in a declining industry or recession, some people would leave it. In Britain the labour force has oscillated around 25 million, or about half of the population. More married women have joined the labour force than before the Second World War because the pay is valued more than leisure (the price effect), but some may leave their jobs if their husbands' pay rises and they consider it sufficient for the family (the income effect). Conversely the non-labour force, i.e. the voluntarily unemployed, is also a function of the price of labour as well as of demographic, political and institutional conditions. [5]

Labour Market, the institution comprising the demand for, the supply of, and the price of labour. It is analysed by economists with the same tools they apply to other markets: competition and monopoly, elasticities, etc. The labour market can be regarded as worldwide or international (if labour is mobile: e.g. doctors, business executives, governmental officials), national, regional or local. The area within which employees readily change jobs, but outside which they are reluctant to change homes, can be regarded as a localized labour market defined by costs of movement, local ties and institutional factors such as policies of "moving work to the workers." Reluctance to move out of a localized labour market may express a preference for stability to avoid disturbance to family life (schooling, etc.) over higher pay. [5]

Labour Mobility. *See* MOBILITY.

Labour Monopoly, strictly in economic analyses the counterpart of industrial monopoly, a situation in which there is a single supplier or seller. Labour monopoly is possible if a trade union can enforce a closed shop so successfully that the price of labour—wages, salaries, etc.—is affected. The main example in Britain is often said to be in printing. More generally, it is the exercise of bargaining power by a strong union to enforce conditions of work on industry or industrial policies on government. Economists differ on the degree of labour monopoly in particular industries or the economy as a whole, on whether it should be subjected to the anti-monopoly laws applied to industry, and on how far other measures, such as countervailing power, or participation in industry or in government, i.e. syndicalism or corporativism, are necessary or desirable. [5]

Labour Standard, the name given by J. R. Hicks in 1955 to the situation in which the current level of wages is *made* the equilibrium level of money wages by adjustment of monetary policy. He argued that before 1931 the situation had been the reverse: to move towards equilibrium the wage structure had adjusted itself to monetary conditions. Thus under the Gold Standard a deficit in the balance of payments was corrected by a loss of gold or other reserves, the general price level was reduced, and wages fell with employment more or less maintained. After 1931 unemployment rose again following the financial crisis, but this time wages did not fall much; instead the adjustment to equilibrium between prices, wages and unemployment was made by the monetary system. The Gold Standard was abandoned and deflation could therefore be replaced by monetary expansion to maintain employment without wage reactions. Hence instead of a *money* (gold) standard, to which wages and unemployment were adjusted, Britain went on a "*Labour* Standard" to which monetary policy was adjusted. Unemployment rose after 1931 to aid the adjustment, but it has never risen much since then, so the adjustment in the monetary system has had to be all the more flexible. In the post-war world a combination of Hicks's Labour Standard and the determination to maintain full employment has thrown all the adjustment on to the monetary system, which reacts to the Labour Standard and maintains full employment by elastic money supply.

Hicks argued that the Labour Standard was "an unquestionable benefit" because it was protection against the unemployment that had been caused by the discrepancy between the current and the equilibrium wage levels. But the benefit was not certain to be preserved because the Labour Standard, as indicated by the period from the 1930's to the 1950's, had defects. It was a national standard but the Gold Standard it replaced was international; it was therefore likely to complicate international monetary relations if the value of British labour, i.e. labour costs, deteriorated relatively to the value of labour and labour costs elsewhere. And under the Labour Standard the value of money was "a mere by-product" of wage bargaining which tended to pull it down; under the Gold Standard it was the responsibility of the state to keep it up. Before the war, when economic pressures on wages were downward (if costs had risen relatively faster than costs abroad, perhaps because other countries had advanced more rapidly, and it was desired to reduce them), "social" pressures held them up; between 1924 and 1928 wage rates were unchanged, and by 1937 they had barely risen. During the war the rise in wage rates was special to wartime inflation, but after 1945 wage rates rose by 4 per cent a year. The question was whether the Labour Standard had "an inherently inflationary bias."

Very rapid wage inflation could endanger the Labour Standard by diverting productive effort into frequent fixing and re-fixing of wages and prices. The question was whether the rate of wage-inflation could be contained so that it was tolerable without accelerating.

Wages were determined by an interplay between economic factors (the supply of and demand for labour, real rather than money wages) and "social" factors (custom—the attitude to differentials as justified by usage, and equity—the egalitarian attitude to profits). Under the Labour Standard the inflationary effect endangered real wages unless prices were controlled and goods rationed, but these methods were not wholly effective. If differentials were "socially" undesirable and should be reduced, as the British economist Barbara Wootton had argued in *The Social Foundations of Wage Policy* (1955), custom often sanctioned them, though egalitarian sentiment had more power when wages were changing and equalization could be approached by some wages rising faster than others. Under the Labour Standard profits were not compressed where wages rose generally (because of the expansion of money supply to resist unemployment), but indefinite wage inflation was unlikely. The variety of trade unions and wage systems made centralized wages bargaining impracticable. And trade unions could not claim that wages must rise when profits were high since they would then have to fall when profits were low, as they could be in some industries even in full employment.

Hicks concluded that the post-war rise in wages was explained by temporary causes (the dismantling of wartime controls, etc.) and wage rates might again become stable, with improvements in basic rates exceptional rather than normal. Here events after the late 1960's falsified his expectations, but his analysis of the Labour Standard enabled him to prognosticate that if the general level of money wages was pushed upwards by "disturbance to our rate of progress," i.e.

a slow rate of economic growth, the additional strain, unless wage rates were basically stable, would be dangerous. This analysis of the Labour Standard by one of Britain's foremost authorities in the labour market is a good example of the insights that can be yielded by economic theory coupled with knowledge of the market institutions, of the scope for and difficulties in attempting forecasts, and of the clarifying consequences of economic thinking resulting from diagnosing causes even where the forecasts are falsified. [5]

Labour Turnover, the movement of labour into or out of a firm, expressed as the percentage of leavers in the average number employed, e.g. in a firm employing 1,000 people on average in a year, a 100 leavers represents a 10 per cent turnover. Labour turnover is influenced by demographic, institutional and market conditions. Labour turnover is higher among married women than married men (demographic), bachelors than husbands (institutional), secretaries than shop-assistants (market conditions), etc. Less commonly, the term is applied to the economy as a whole, i.e. the total labour force. [5]

Lachmann, Ludwig Moritz (1906–90), economist of German origin, born in Berlin. He was educated at the Universities of Berlin and Zurich. In 1933 he came to England, where he worked on economic theory at the London School of Economics. He taught at the University College of Hull from 1943 to 1948 and then went to the University of the Witwatersrand, Johannesburg, as Professor of Economics and Economic History. He retired in 1972.

Lachmann's main contributions to economic theory are essentially in the Austrian tradition: his systematic analysis of capital as an inter-related structure of capital goods (*Capital and Its Structure,* London, 1956) and his emphasis on methodological individualism in the study of equilibrium. He argues that the concept of an individual equilibrium in relation to the data possessed by a single individual is tenable. The concept of even a partial "market" equilibrium becomes more suspect since it presupposes that a number of different minds are possessed of the same data (and are themselves fully adjusted to one another), so that the plans of all these individuals are mutually consistent. But the notion of a general equilibrium in the economy as a whole is wholly lacking in logical coherence, since it supposes that all individuals everywhere are simultaneously possessed of coherent data so that all their individual plans are mutually consistent. Articles in *Economica,* the *South African Journal of Economics* and other learned journals and contributions to several books have developed his main themes, which he discussed historically in *The Legacy of Max Weber* (1970) and applied in criticism of the Cambridge (England) School in *Macro-Economic Thinking and the Market Economy* (1973). [2]

Lag, the delay between cause and effect. The element of time is important in economic analysis. An example is the lag between an expansion in the quantity of money and the consequential rise in prices. The value of studying lags is that, if they can be established from recent history, they may provide or facilitate predictions. Lags in business activity were developed as statistical "indicators" in the US National Bureau of Economic Research by economists Arthur F. Burns, Wesley Mitchell and Warren Persons. Lag "indicators" may not be reliable in forecasting if unexpected and unpredictable developments neutralize the consequence that follows the cause. *See* LEADS AND LAGS. [14]

Laissez-faire, in classical economic theory a doctrine based on the proposition that the economic affairs of society will in the main take care of themselves if neither the state nor any other body armed with authority attempts to interfere with their working as determined by the individual actions of men.

In the works of Adam Smith the source of wealth for the nation is held to lie in the efforts made by individuals in their use of the factors of production—land, labour and capital—under the inducement of the chance of economic reward. Although this pursuit may be unenlightened or based on self-interest, Adam Smith argued that individuals acting independently are likely to be better judges than any collective body of the means or methods of producing the maximum amount of wealth. This will come about because of the natural order in which the interests of the individual are harmonized with the good of society: an individual can serve his own interest best by rendering services that are desired by others. Interference with the free working of this natural order therefore diminishes the total amount of wealth produced, although interference may be justified on non-economic grounds in exceptional cases, e.g. his famous dictum that "defence is of more importance than opulence."

Laissez-faire did not require absence of government, though this has often been stated. The British economist Lionel Robbins argued that it is incorrect to describe the classical economists as advocating an economic system without state action because they envisaged state activity at many points not only to maintain open markets and freedom for newcomers to compete, but also to provide public goods, protection for the weak, etc.

With the new theories of economic value that were formulated in the nineteenth century, the doctrine of laissez-faire acquired new support. Free consumers' demand, regarded as the force governing supply in the absence of restrictions, was considered as the guarantee of maximum production of wealth and satisfaction; state intervention was deplored since it interfered with the free expression of consumers' demand by altering the conditions of supply and price. Emphasis thus shifted away from the self-interest of each producer making for the maximum production of economic values to the assurance given by the free play of consumers' demand that the production of goods and services would be such as to create the maximum total of human satisfaction. Economists who expound laissez-faire doctrines normally state their case on this ground, urging the necessity for allowing free play to consumers' demand as a means to securing maximum utility in preference to attempts by the state to influence the prices or production of goods and services.

In the nineteenth century the influence of laissez-faire doctrines was extensive. In the twentieth century attention changed to ensuring an equitable distribution of income by systems of taxes and benefits, and state intervention in industry and commerce grew as a new set of economic and social opinions developed. Many economists urge the advantages of a planned economy in which the state would direct the use of economic resources in the interest of the community as measured by estimates of desirable trends in investment, export and consumption. Others, regarded as in the laissez-faire tradition, urge the advantages of a market economy within a framework of law and institutions designed to maintain private property, decentralized economic initiative independent of the state and free choice of goods and services, employment and investment. [10]

Land, in economics, an individual factor of production, differing from labour because it is non-human and from capital because no increase in price evokes an increase in total supply. It performs two functions as a factor of production; it furnishes space for economic activities and a site near the market for the product. Part of the explanation of the high rents of urban land is the high demand for space in or near the centre of the town or city, where sites are usually thought most desirable.

In the productive process, different areas of land have different attributes which affect their productivity: e.g. climate, fertility, quality of the subsoil, water resources, location. Some pieces of land also have attributes that are exhaustible, i.e. consumed in the process of production. Mineral deposits and native forest are examples; soil fertility can also be reduced or exhausted by overcropping or the use of primitive farming techniques, as before the enclosure of land in England.

Land in the economic sense need not be "terra firma" in the physical sense; land under water (such as oyster beds) and even large areas of surface water (e.g. if endowed with fishing rights) may be regarded as land with economic significance. It is often convenient for the economist to analyse land as synonymous with all that nature supplies which is of value, durable and capable of being "appropriated" (taken into ownership as property). This definition thus includes, for example, waterfalls and other sources of water power.

The economic definition of land also clearly distinguishes between land (as a "natural" resource) and capital (in the form of man-made *improvements*). The distinction is analytical. Natural resources have no cost of production; their supply-price is zero in the sense that there would be no reduction in their available supply even if they earned nothing. Their earnings thus depend entirely on the extent of the demand for them and their relative scarcity. In practice the distinction is difficult to draw. In a developed country most "land" incorporates, directly or indirectly, some man-made capital improvement, so that it is impossible to separate earnings into the two categories. Once constructed, man-made improvements that are "sunk" into land (such as a building) are like land in the sense that their earnings depend on current demand for them rather than on their cost of production. But in the long run, when the supply of man-made improvements can be varied, so that it is possible to buy land with or without them, the distinction between land and capital is significant.

The value of a piece of land depends solely on the serviceability and scarcity of its attributes. Only in exceptionally favoured areas or pieces does land ownership or an exclusive right constitute a monopoly. An important city trading site for shops and the only important deposit of a rare mineral are possible examples of a monopoly type control of land. That an area of land is of high fertility or has advantages of situation, for example, confers only limited monopoly power on its owner if there are alternative sites, even though inferior. As long as consumers (or the goods whose production land facilitates) are free to move, land resources are better regarded as competing substitutes than as a collection of sites with unique characteristics that confer monopoly power on their owners. [6]

Land Economics, the branch of general economics which deals with the principles and processes by which land is developed and allocated to various activities and the problems and policies associated with land use. From the outset, economists have been interested in land and rent as part of general value and distribution theory, but the separate study of land use is a comparatively recent development. The study embraces a number of overlapping aspects related to the adaptation of general economic theory to take account of *spatial relationships*—location theory, the pattern of land use and land values or rents, the institutional arrangements affecting the use of land and the organization of markets in land, the interrelationships between areas and the factors determining their relative size, form and growth. Micro-economic and macro-economic techniques are used in the construction of both partial and general equilibrium models ranging from, e.g., analytical models of local housing markets to complex models of the economic structure of a whole region. These studies have built on earlier work which tended to concentrate heavily on descriptive studies of the legal, institutional, social and physical aspects of land use and policy—aspects which are still important but which in recent years have tended to be overshadowed by new developments in analytical techniques. Because urban uses constitute by far the most important category of land use as a whole, *urban land economics* is identified as a separate sub-discipline. More recently, there has been a tendency to regard urban land economics as one aspect of the wider discipline of *urban economics,* which attempts to view systematically the whole range of economic problems associated with urban existence—not only those related to land use and policy but also transport, the provision of common-access facilities ("public goods") and the fiscal and other problems of urban government and general welfare. At this level, analysis and policy has tended to lose its pure economic base and to develop into *urban studies* of a more multi-disciplinary character, although economics remains the most powerful instrument for understanding and guiding the urban economy. [6]

Land Tax, an annual tax levied on properties in England, Wales and Scotland (except where it has been redeemed or the properties are exempt). First imposed in 1692 and renewed annually until 1798, when it was made perpetual. In 1896, because of the agricultural depression, it was enacted that the rate should not exceed 1*s.* nor be less than 1*d.* in the £. In 1949 the tax for all future years was stabilized at the 1949–50 level. In 1951 it was made compulsorily redeemable. [12]

Land Value Taxation. *See* SITE VALUE TAXATION.

Lands Tribunal. *See* ARBITRATION.

Lange, Oskar (1904–65), Polish economist and politician. He was born in Tomaszow Mazowiecki and educated at Cracow University. He made a name early for work on mathematical economics. He was Professor of Economics at the Universities of Michigan and Chicago and acquired American citizenship, which he relinquished to act as Polish Ambassador to the USA in 1945.

Lange was a founder of econometrics and an early advocate of Keynesianism in *Price Flexibility and Full Employment* (1944). In the 1930's he participated with A. P. Lerner and others in the discussion of socialist market pricing as the way to reject the view, strongly argued by the Vienna/Austrian School, that centrally planned economies lacked machinery and motive power for the rational allocation of resources. In a celebrated contribution "On the Economic Theory of Socialism" to the *Review of Economic Studies* in 1937, he sought to reconcile or combine the Marxist emphasis on state ownership of the means of production with the use of an instrument—the market—historically associated with the evolution of private ownership in capitalism. His theoretical work reflected his temperamental attachment to Marxist ideology and to liberal culture, and it was reflected in the development of decentralized economic policy in Poland after the Second World War, where he was Chairman of the post-Stalin State Economic Council in 1957.

In the pre-war period Lange was influenced by Walras and subsequently by Keynes. In *Price Flexibility and Full Employment,* which drew on Hicks's *Value and Capital,* he nearly succeeded in establishing Keynes's employment theory as a *special* case within Walras's truly *general* theory. Lange wrote a series of concise and elegant articles on interest, welfare economics and the relationship between Marxist economics and marginal analysis, and shed clear light on all he approached. His later work concentrated upon the extension of cybernetics to the economic system. It consisted of a re-arrangement of elements of information theory, control theory and the theory of decision-making relevant for the study of economic policy and planning. Lange considered economic cybernetics a tool for socialist administration because "In capitalism the organization of economic processes is elemental and cannot be based on rational principles." Other economists think the technique could be applied to any dynamic process.

Lange maintained contact with economists in the West and occasionally lectured at Oxford and Cambridge, in Europe and the USA. He was hoping to write a three-volume treatise on Political Economy but completed only the first (translated into English in 1963). He was an intellectual bridge between liberal and Marxist economics. [2]

Large Numbers, Law of, the tendency for the divergent characteristics of individual people or objects or experiences to cancel out; the larger the number of individuals the more marked the phenomenon. A group of individuals is therefore less exceptional, more stable and more predictable than an individual. Examples are height in humans, the yield of farms, the output of plants, the life expectation of (average) individuals, the earnings of investments. A common application is to life assurance, where individual premiums are based on the average expectation of life of the group. The danger is that the average can apply fairly closely to all the individuals or be very different from most, or even all, i.e. it may be subject to wide dispersion so that a common life assurance premium would be too high for some and too low for others.

Laspeyres. *See* Index Number.

Last In, First Out (LIFO), a method of valuing stocks by firms, based on the assumption that the latest purchases are the first used in production. The purpose is to value the goods used by the (current or very recent) cost of replacing them. This is a convenient method when prices have risen, but misleading when prices are falling. *See* First In, First Out (FIFO). [1]

Lateral Integration. *See* Industry, Structure of.

Lauderdale, James Maitland, Earl of (1759–1839), British politician and political economist. He was educated at the University of Edinburgh and Trinity College, Oxford, and in 1780 was returned as the Member of Parliament for Newport in Cornwall. He became interested in political economy, and his first work on the subject, *An Inquiry into the Nature and Origin of Public Wealth, and* *into the means and causes of its increase* (1804), took issue with the labour theory of value and substituted a utility approach. His *Three Letters to the Duke of Wellington* (1829) are also of interest because of their early expression of a theory of excess saving. [2]

Lausanne School, school of economic thought whose approach was developed from the 1870's chiefly by Walras and Pareto, economists in the classical tradition who applied mathematics and the theory of general equilibrium to the subject. The School has had much influence on the evolution of economic theory. Its best-known contemporary heirs are the neo-classical economists of Harvard, Paul Samuelson, Robert Solow and others, and J. R. Hicks of Oxford. [2]

Law, Economic, a statement of a general uniformity in the relationship between two or more phenomena of economic life, for example the generalization, "other things remaining the same, the marginal utility of a commodity to anyone diminishes with every increase in the amount he already has."

Economic laws of this kind are positive or behaviourist; they describe what happens, not what ought to happen. They are therefore distinct from normative (moral or juristic) laws, which imply a command or a recommendation that stated courses of action should be preferred to others. There are, however, many instances in economic literature of propositions stated as economic "laws" which are normative propositions. This is particularly true of statements about "welfare." The proposition that "the removal of import restrictions increases total economic welfare in a nation," whether it can be given a precise meaning or not, is normative; if it were presented as a "scientific" judgement to a policy-maker it would imply a recommendation to free trade. This is the result of the moral associations of the word "welfare." It is possible to dispute the status of some propositions in economics. Some economists, for example, would say that "the removal of import restrictions will tend to increase total real national output" is a positive statement, others that it is like the previous statement and for a similar reason normative.

Economic laws which have the same scientific status as the "laws of physics" are therefore positive, not normative. But not all valid, positive propositions about the relationships between two or more economic variables can be described as economic laws. A law must be capable of being applied widely; thus the statement that "other things equal, a rise in the price of a commodity will lead to a fall in the quantity demanded" has sufficient generality to be called a law.

Many of the laws of economics may be stated as truisms or elaborations of truisms. As long as they are put in this way they have no empirical content, i.e. tell us nothing about the real world which can be tested. At the other extreme, propositions in economics may be formulated simply as statements of historical fact. Both terms are useful. A generalization about markets which asserts the existence of certain relationships or tendencies in the real world that can be tested by factual observation is useful: in turn the validity of such a generalization rests on accurate assumptions about individual behaviour in practice. [14]

Law, Relation to Economics. *See* ECONOMICS.

"Laws of the Market." *See* TIME.

"Lay" Days. *See* DEMURRAGE.

Layton, Walter Thomas (1884–1961), economist, public servant, business man. Knighted in 1930; raised to the peerage in 1947. Educated at Westminster City School and at the Universities of London and Cambridge. He was a lecturer in economics at the University of London from 1909 to 1912. Later he became prominent in public service and was a member of several committees of inquiry and missions to other countries, including the USA and Russia. He edited *The Economist* from 1922 to 1938 and wrote *An Introduction to the Study of Prices* (with Sir Geoffrey Crowther) and articles in economic reviews and journals. [2]

Leads and Lags, generally, elements that are found to be ahead of or to follow others, and the time relationship between them. History may indicate a consistent or recurring sequence and time interval between the early symptoms and the late or final results. The relationship could then be a tolerable forecasting device, assuming *ceteris paribus.* For example, some economists say monetary history shows that a change in inflation of prices follows twelve to eighteen months after a change in the expansion of the supply of money. [14]

Lease. *See* LEASEHOLD.

Lease-back. *See* SALE AND LEASE-BACK.

Lease Guarantee Insurance, insurance against default in rental payments due under a lease. The practice, which has grown rapidly in the USA in recent years, has its origins in the financing of shopping centre and other commercial and industrial developments. Typically, mortgage lenders who provide most of the finance tended to insist that the bulk of mortgage amortization instalments should be covered by the rents of prime tenants of first-class security. Because developers relied heavily on them, such tenants were able to negotiate favourable rentals. Smaller, local traders were often regarded as unacceptable tenants, despite higher rentals. By insuring the lease, a minor lessee's covenant to pay rent is converted into a first-class security, fully acceptable to any mortgage lender. The lender's constraints on the developer's ability to allocate space so as to maximize his returns, and discrimination against minor traders, were thus removed at a cost (in insurance premiums) that was fractional compared with the gain to the traders and developers concerned. The degree of market imperfection was thus reduced. [8]

Leasehold, an interest in property for a stated number of years, subject to the payment of an annual rent and the observance of conditions ("covenants") contained in the lease. The principal types are three: (1) *Building or ground leases* are long leases of land ripe for building granted (usually for ninety-nine years) subject to an annual ground rent and a covenant to build to the lessor's specification. (2) *Occupational leases* refer to the occupation of property by the lessee for a given number of years. Dwelling houses may be leased for fairly short terms, or for longer terms which may be ended at the lessee's option at seven-yearly intervals. Commercial property is usually let on seven-, fourteen- or twenty-one-year or longer leases, with or without the option of a break, and often subject to rising rents at stated intervals. The increases may be agreed, or may be the subject of periodic review. Leases under which the rental payment varies in accordance with an agreed index of prices or costs are termed *Index Leases.* Rents based on a percentage of business turnover are not uncommon in some countries and for particular types of property (such as retail shops in a shopping mall). Leases with such arrangements are termed *Percentage Leases.* (3) *Subleases* by leaseholders are subject to the terms of their own ("head") leases and are for periods shorter than their own term. Subleases are not the same as *assignments* of leases, i.e. the disposal of the unexpired term of a lease to a third party.

Capital payments (premiums) are often paid for leases, the annual rent payable being reduced accordingly from the full market ("rack") rent. Since leases are wasting assets, business lessees normally provide depreciation for the capital spent on leasehold premises.

In the UK the rights of parties to leasehold agreements have been very much affected by rent control and by landlord and tenant legislation. In recent years the tendency has been to give statutory rights of continued occupation to lessees at the end of their leases, either at controlled or, in commercial property, at "market level" rents. [6]

Legacy, personal property left at death. A legacy can be of various kinds, for instance, a specific item of the testator's estate or a general legacy of a stated amount of money, e.g. £1,000. Before 1949 legacies were the subject of a special tax called legacy duty then abolished and consolidated with estate duty. A gift of real property is called a devise. [12]

Legacy Duty, a tax on property passing at death. First imposed by the Legacy Duty Act of 1796 as a tax on personal property (except freeholds or leaseholds) received from a person who died with or without a will. It varied with the relationship between the beneficiaries and the testator. In 1947 these rates were fixed at 2 per cent for a husband, wife or children, 10 per cent for brothers and sisters, etc., or charities, and 20 per cent for all other persons. No duty was payable on small gifts or on gifts from small estates. In 1949 the legacy duty was consolidated with the estate duty. The principle of discriminating in favour of the immediate family was thus ended. [12]

Legal Tender, money which, according to law, must be accepted in final payment of a debt or discharge of a business obligation. In Britain coin is legal tender only in limited amounts; "copper" to 20*p.*, "silver" to £10; bank-notes are unlimited legal tender. Cheques (bank "money") and promissory notes are not legal tender. [8]

Leijonhufvud, Axel. *See* ECONOMIC THOUGHT.

Lender of Last Resort. *See* BANKING.

Leontief, Wassily (1906–99), economist and econometrician, born in St Petersburg, Russia. His first academic appointment was in 1927 at the University of Kiel in Germany. In 1937 he was offered a teaching post at Harvard, and became Professor of Economics in 1946.

Leontief is best known for his early conception and construction of sophisticated econometric models. In *The Structure of the American Economy, 1919–1929* (1941; extended to 1919–39 in a second edition in 1951) he presented the input-output table. His approach was developed in *Studies in the Structure of the American Economy* (1953) and his seminal papers were assembled in *Input-Output Economics* and *Collected Essays* (1966).

Leontief's input-output model reduces the primary factors to one—labour, apart from which the inputs of each industry are the outputs of other industries. The inter-industrial relations of an economic system thus mutually provide limitations and possibilities, sources and markets, which can provide a basis for computation. Essentially the input-output table is an advanced and refined mathematical construction to show the relationships between the parts of an economic system which have preoccupied economists for over 200 years (François Quesnay's *Tableau Économique* of 1756 was an early if crude embryo model). Leontief's application of the technique to an examination of the economy of the USA produced interesting results, such as his conclusion that America is a "labour-rich" economy. Variations in his methods have been adopted by some communist economists; the technique is one which seems able to over-ride the ideological gap between capitalist and communist economies.

Thirty years after his first formulation in 1941, Leontief, as President of the American Economic Association in 1970, warned over-enthusiastic econometricians against the over-use or mis-use of models. The empirical information fed into them was fragile: "Uncritical enthusiasm for mathematical formulation tends often to conceal the ephemeral substantive content of the argument behind the formidable front of the algebraic signs." The result was that "In no other field of empirical enquiry has so massive and sophisticated a statistical machinery been used with such indifferent results." He likened the free enterprise system to a gigantic computer capable of solving its problems automatically (or rather semi-automatically, because it could break down and it required attention to operate). Economists and economic models could help to reveal the principles on which it worked and the details of its design. Although industry was using the results of mathematical economic modelling in the forms of Operational Research, Systems Analysis, etc., the methods were very imperfect and were still being improved and perfected. In particular, he argued, models required not only constant improvement but also constantly changing information that only private individuals and organizations could provide. Academic economists should therefore take the public into their confidence and explain their hopes and disappointments in developing econometric methodology and models. [2]

Lerner, Abba P. (1903–82), Russian-born American economist. He was trained at the London School of Economics and taught as Professor of Economics at Roosevelt University (1947–59), Michigan State University (1959–65) and the University of California, Berkeley (from 1965). His work falls into three parts. The first consists of a series of early articles, centred on geometrical analysis and, following upon the work of Joan Robinson and Chamberlin, devoted mainly to the definition and measurement of monopoly power. The second is his exposition and defence of the *General Theory of Employment.* The third, and most important, is his development of a "maximization system," in *The Economics of Control* (1944), which combines an attitude to thinking positively about the aggregation of welfare that is in a direct line of descent from Marshall with long sequences of marginal analysis that Keynes, from whom most of the inspiration seems to have come, would have distrusted. It probably influenced Scitovsky, and indicated that it is possible to combine the most rigorous economic analysis with interest in economic reform. [2]

"Les Économistes." *See* Economic Thought.

Letter of Credit. *See* Accepting House.

Letters of Administration. *See* Executor.

Level Tendering. *See* Collusive Tendering; Common Pricing.

Leverage, the use of borrowed funds to complete an investment transaction. The larger the proportion of borrowed funds used to make the investment, and the lower the investor's equity, the larger the leverage. If, for example, a property produces a rate of return on the total sum invested higher than the mortgage interest rate on borrowed funds, that slice of the total investment covered by mortgage loan finance produces a "surplus" which helps to increase the return on the investor's equity funds. Hence the expression "trading on the equity" to denote the use of leverage. [8]

Lewis, W. Arthur (1915–91), West Indian economist. He was educated at St Mary's College, St Lucia, and the London School of Economics, where he taught from 1938 to 1947. He was Stanley Jevons Professor of Economics at the University of Manchester from 1948 to 1958, and has been Professor of Public and International Affairs at Princeton University since 1963. His writings reflect his preoccupation with public policy, including the planning of socialist enterprises and policies for underdeveloped countries, with which he was largely concerned as academic economist and adviser to governments. His work is characterized by wide sweep, crossing over the boundaries of academic disciplines, combined with rigour and depth of analysis. His *Economic Survey, 1918–1939* (1949), although based on LSE lectures in the 1940's intended to give students a review of major economic developments, remains an important source for the analysis of policy. *Overhead Costs* (1949) examines problems of competition, monopoly policy and management of socialist enterprises, allocation of costs and tariff policy for road and rail transport, the economics of electricity pricing, and excess capacity in retailing. In this and the related *Principles of Economic Planning* (1949) his approach combines economic analysis and common sense. He argued that public ownership should comprise separate enterprises supplying parts of an industry and not a monopoly of the whole of it, and advocated adherence by nationalized enterprises to the economic rules of competition and pricing aimed at financial self-sufficiency. His *Theory of Economic Growth* (1955), perhaps his outstanding work, Marshallian in treatment, non-mathematical and almost sociological, is a comprehensive catalogue of the forces operating on the development of economically retarded countries. It draws heavily on the literature of the subject and on his wide experience and constitutes a masterpiece of constructive synthesis. [2]

Liabilities, the debts of an individual, firm or other organization, or government (National Debt). They form one side of the money and capital markets: they are created by the demand for short-term money or long-term capital that can be used to yield more than its price (the rate of interest). Much of the western economy is based on borrowing that creates liabilities. [3]

Liberalism, Economic, the philosophy which advocates the largest possible use of the forces of competition as a means of co-ordinating human efforts and achieving economic ends, and thus rejects most types of coercion and interference in economic life by interest groups or governments. Economic liberalism does not deny that the state has a role to play in economic affairs, but sees it as helping the competitive process to be as effective as possible and supplementing it where collective action can provide services not supplied through the market. Economic liberalism is often confused with the common misunderstanding of laissez-faire as meaning the complete absence of governmental action. Liberalism is dynamic in aim, emphasizes self-interest as the engine of effort in the general interest, the price mechanism and a competitive framework as the means by which rapid economic progress and maximum human satisfaction can be obtained. [10]

Liberman, Yevsei (1912?–), Russian economist. As Professor at the Institute of Engineering and Economics at Kharkov University he wrote an article in *Pravda* (September 1962), "Plan, Profit, Premium," that opened the academic and political debate on the best ways to improve the planning or administration of Russian industry by linking the reward of state enterprises to profits earned on the capital assets they used rather than to the increase in gross output over the previous year. The background was that Nikita Khrushchev had complained for some time that state plants were putting fulfilment of targets before technical improvement and that the resistance to technical change derived from reluctance, especially among engineers, to take on a heavier work-load and to lose wages.

Professor Liberman argued that the concentration on reaching quantitative targets set by the planners was the reason for the attempts by factory and other managers to strive for low or otherwise easy targets ("*blat*"), to hold unnecessarily high stocks of equipment or raw materials and to hoard labour ("*strakhovka*"), and to reach quantitative targets at all costs—penalizing enterprising plants and workers, ignoring technological advance and tampering with the accounts ("*ochkovtiratelsto*"). Liberman proposed that each plant should establish an incentive fund; payments should be made into it according to the proportion of profits earned to capital used, and payments out of it as premiums and bonuses to managers and employees, to pay for machinery, and for improvements and extensions to the plant. The managers would therefore have an inducement to maximize their profits and incentive funds rather than to hold large stocks of equipment or materials or to hoard labour. Liberman argued that paying a rate of interest, or rather its equivalent, for capital (new plants and equipment) instead of receiving them free from the state would induce the managers to economize in its use.

The Liberman proposals brought into more open public discussion practices that had been evolved unofficially towards these objectives. Alternative uses of capital had been compared in Russian industry by calculating the pay-off or recoupment period ("*srok okupayemosti*") in which capital could be recouped, the shortest periods being preferred (other things equal). This method involved applying a rate of interest according to the amount of capital required and the reduction in current cost it made possible. [2]

Licensing, a method of controlling or restricting or recording the number of suppliers of a product or service, the amount produced or sold, etc. Its economic effect depends on how restrictive it is. If it is confined to recording (i.e. for the purpose of taxation, as with dog licences) it has little effect on supply and price (although, for example, if the cost of a dog licence were high it might discourage people from owning dogs). If it is designed to keep down the number of licences, as with public houses, its effect is to raise the value of the properties that are licensed by making them scarcer than they otherwise would be. Restrictive licensing is an effort to replace the market mechanism, which allocates supplies by price, by a method of allocation based on criteria other than market price and consumer choice. Thus if it is considered the consumers should not be allowed to decide the use of building labour and materials, building licensing can substitute other criteria or "priorities." [10]

"Lie" Days. *See* DEMURRAGE.

Lien, a legal power of a creditor over a debtor's property as security, until the debt is repaid. Examples are mortgages, goods in pawn. [8]

Limited Liability, the restriction on the liability of a shareholder to the nominal value of the shares he holds, if the company is put into liquidation because it is unable to pay its debts.

The principle of limited liability was recognized in 1855 and paved the way for a rapid expansion of joint-stock companies. (Previously shareholders were liable for the whole of their personal possessions.) The principle was extended to banking in 1858; it enabled larger banks to be set up with branches in many towns and cities. The larger banks had more resources and enjoyed more public confidence and were hardly affected by the financial crises which caused the fall of smaller banks in earlier days. The financial losses in the development of the railways were a factor in hastening the general acceptance of limited liability in the joint-stock company.

Limited liability opened up the supply of capital needed to exploit the wide opportunities of economic expansion brought by the Industrial Revolution. The power to assemble small capitals made it possible to use many sums which individually were too small for investment by financially large undertakings, and limited liability thus removed the obstacle that had hindered the advance of joint-stock enterprise.

In the twentieth century the limited liability company is the predominant form of business organization. A series of Companies Acts from the 1850's set out the law relating to companies in general and limited liability companies in particular. There are two types of limited liability company. First, the *public* company, which must have at least seven shareholders and whose shares are bought and sold on the Stock Exchange (nearly all the major industrial and commercial concerns fall into this class). Secondly, the *private* company, which need have only two shareholders but may not have more than fifty. It must not invite the public to subscribe capital and must restrict the right to transfer shares. It does not have to file a copy of its accounts with its annual return to the Registrar of Companies.

The private company has enabled the convenience of limited liability to be shared by small one-man businesses that have formed companies with husbands, wives and families as the shareholders. The sole trader and the partnership have given way to the private company. In many private companies the controlling shareholders must often give personal guarantees for a bank overdraft or a lease of business premises; to this extent their liability is not limited. [3]

Limping Dollar Standard. *See* GOLD EXCHANGE STANDARD.

Linear Programming, a statistical technique for helping to decide the optimum (most profitable) combination of products to be produced by given plant and machinery (the economic "short-period" problem) or the optimum combination of factors of production or of plant and equipment to produce a given output (the "long-period" problem). It is one of the techniques that followed the development of operational research during and since World War II. It has been used to calculate, for example, the optimum combination of the products of a refinery, the optimum combination of ingredients for cattle food, and so on. On a larger scale linear programming has been used to develop models of optimal resource use within a region and has been seen by some as a tool of "scientific" planning. But although linear programming techniques are more versatile than many other planning tools, they are subject to serious limitations. In particular they rely on an assumed set of prices to begin with, whereas an economic model should be able to explain how prices are determined and what are the effects of price changes. The mathematical assumption of linear relationships may also fit poorly the often non-linear relationships of the real world, although to some extent this may be overcome by non-linear programming techniques. [13]

Lippincott, B. E. *See* CALCULATION, ECONOMIC.

Liquidation, the process by which a limited liability company ends its legal existence; often called the "winding up."

Insolvency due to changes in market conditions, inefficient management or other reasons is the principal cause of liquidation. It is the procedure by which a firm that has become unprofitable retires from the economic system. [3]

Liquidity (*a*) generally, the ease with which an asset can be turned into money. Assets range from cash, which is perfectly liquid, through short-term claims and longer-term securities to durable consumption and producer goods (and works of art). Each has a measure of liquidity in descending order. Liquidity can also refer to the degree of immediate command over resources. If wealth is wholly invested in illiquid assets, such as property, it gives little immediate command over resources. To part with cash for, say, a government security, is to part with liquidity and to substitute deferred for immediate command over resources. Thus the degree of convertibility from deferred to immediate command measures the liquidity of an asset.

(*b*) in discussion of monetary affairs, the total supply of money and "near-money" assets.

(*c*) in international trade, the total supply of currency and assets internationally acceptable as liquid.

(*d*) in accounting, the difference between current assets and current liabilities, i.e., between assets that are, or are readily made, liquid—cash, stock, debtors and liabilities currently due. [8]

Liquidity Preference, a means of expressing the demand for money. The total of individual liquidity preferences produces the community's liquidity preference, which determines the total demand for money.

The demand for money is related to the two main functions of money: (1) a means of exchange, and (2) a store of value. From these functions Keynes derived three motives for holding money: (1) the transactions motive, (2) the precautionary motive, (3) the speculative motive.

The *transactions* motive governs the demand for money to finance current transactions by consumers and business men. The amount of money required will depend upon the total value of the transactions. If economic activity, and thus the national income, are high, the total value of transactions will be higher than at low levels of economic activity. The demand for money for transactions will depend mainly on the level of the national income.

The *precautionary* motive governs how much money will be held to provide for future requirements, unforeseen contingencies and occasional advantageous purchases. This demand also will depend mainly on the level of national income.

Money required for the *speculative* motive is held if individuals prefer cash to interest-bearing securities. The amount of money so held depends upon the prevailing level of interest rates (as indicated by, for example, the fixed yield on riskless bonds expressed as a percentage of bond prices), and what individuals think the future rate of interest (and, therefore, the price of bonds) is likely to be. The higher the rate of interest and the stronger the expectation that the rate will fall (and bond prices rise), the weaker will be the desire to hold money and the stronger the desire to hold income-earning assets rather than money; and conversely. [8]

Liquidity Ratio (banks). *See* BANKING.

List, Friedrich (1789–1846), German economist. He became a clerk in the public service and rose to ministerial under-secretary. He was appointed professor at Tübingen, but being an advocate of economic rationalism he had to flee to America in 1825, where he engaged in various activities such as mining and railway organization. His experience caused him to modify his views, especially on economic protection in an under-developed economy. *Outlines of American Political Economy* (1827) revealed his views at this stage. On his return to Germany he reformulated his theories, especially to give them an historical foundation. His work is embodied in *Das Nationale System der Politischen Oekonomie* (1841), in which he emphasized the importance of the nation state and developed a theory of national economic development. [2]

Living Debt. *See* DEBT.

Lloyd's, a corporation in the City of London, engaged in marine and other insurance. The insurance is effected by the underwriters who are members of Lloyd's and who are personally liable for claims made against policies they have underwritten. A company wishing to insure a ship secures the services of a broker who negotiates the amount of insurance required from the underwriters at the lowest possible cost. Several underwriters will usually be associated with the insurance of one vessel, thus spreading the risk. Once the required amount of insurance has been underwritten, a policy will be issued by Lloyd's bearing the stamps of the various underwriters.

Lloyd's dates back to 1689 when a coffee-house in Tower Street owned by Edward Lloyd was the meeting place of business men interested in shipping and in "spreading the risk" of marine ventures. In 1871 an Act of Incorporation made Lloyd's a chartered body governed by the "committee."

Although originally famous for its marine insurance, Lloyd's premiums on fire and accident insurance have been half as much as those from marine insurance. Aviation insurance is increasingly important. [7]

Loan, a transfer of purchasing power between economic units to give financial assistance to the borrower in return for interest (and sometimes other advantages) for the lender. Economic units in this sense may be countries or governments, industrial and commercial enterprises, or private individuals. The borrower usually deposits with the lender either security for the loan or a pledge or guarantee of repayment.

In loans between governments the advantage to the lender may be direct, as in financial assistance to an ally in war, or indirect, as when the loan is aimed at preventing the financial and economic collapse of a state which might undermine the stability of neighbouring states. Intergovernmental loans have taken many forms, ranging from direct loans for money by one country to another to government loans floated in a foreign market with the guarantee of the foreign government. Loans between governments have grown in importance in the present century; they played a prominent part in financing the allied efforts in both world wars, and since the Second World War have contributed significantly to the progress of under-developed countries.

Business loans are frequently granted by banks and other financial intermediaries to industrial and commercial firms as short-term finance for stockholding and to alleviate temporary shortages of liquid assets. In recent years banks and other financial institutions have provided loans for the expansion of companies; and the financing of take-overs has been partly based on loans.

Personal loans are usually made for consumption rather than production. Instalment purchases really involve loans with the article as security, from hire purchase of a car to the mortgage on a house. Frequently personal loans are granted to supply necessities in an emergency which makes extraordinary and unexpected demands on resources. A wide range of agencies provide personal loans, ranging from banking institutions at one extreme to pawnshops at the other. [8]

Loanable Funds, the several forms of money that supply the money market (for short-term lending): a reduction in cash balances ("dishoarding"), the savings of individuals or firms, and an increase by government in the supply of money. The demand comes from people who run down their savings ("dissaving"), or increase their idle money stocks ("hoarding"), and from industry for investment. [8]

Loanable Funds Theory, a theory of the rate of interest—that it is determined by the interplay between the demand for and the supply of loanable funds. It is thus an alternative to the liquidity preference theory of interest rates. [8]

Lobby, a group that tries to influence the course of legislation, formally by documented argument, informally by using personal connections. In Britain lobbies have been regarded as vested interests exerting influence improperly; more recently, as government has become more interventionist, they have become increasingly accepted as informed spokesmen consulted by government. But they have not reached the status they have acquired in the USA as interests registered in Congress. [14]

Localization of Industry. *See* DIVISION OF LABOUR.

Localization of Industry, Co-efficient of, a measure of the degree to which an industry is concentrated in a region. It measures the minimum proportion of an industry's employees that would have to be shifted between regions to produce the same interregional distribution as that of the whole national labour force. [3]

Location of Industry, the study of the territorial distribution of resources, i.e. specialization by areas. It is concerned with the influences that determine the geographical pattern of individual firms and their decisions as to where to build factories, shops or offices.

When a firm chooses its location it may be influenced by a wide range of factors from the relative costs of alternative sites to the irrational whims of the business man. Fancy and chance play a part; liking for a particular district, the accident of having been born in it, and so on. But comparative costs are fundamental; they determine how successful a location will be even if they are not alone in deciding its selection. For example, to make a product a manufacturing firm needs labour, fuel and power, and materials; to sell the product it needs access to a market. In choosing a location, in competitive conditions in which costs are important, it has to balance the advantages of proximity to its raw materials, labour and markets so as to maximize the difference between total revenue and total cost.

In some types of industry or trade one factor may dominate in the decision. Mining and quarrying are rooted to the location of the raw material; some kinds of agriculture are so dependent on climatic or soil conditions that they have an overwhelming advantage over less well-endowed regions; even if these regions can reproduce the desirable conditions artificially, it may be only at costs that cannot be covered by the prices obtainable in the market. In other cases raw materials are the main determinants; e.g. an industry using a bulky material (such as coal) that is costly to transport and loses weight in the manufacturing process in which it is used (as in iron and steel). These plants will probably be located on or near the coalfields. The importance of coal as a source of power explains the early development of industry around the coalfields; before that, proximity to water power had been crucial; now the availability in many areas of electricity makes many industries "footloose" that might otherwise have been tied to particular locations.

If the cost of buying or transporting raw material is high in relation to the value of the final product, it exercises a strong pull on location; e.g., water in brewing and soft-drink manufacture. If it is small compared with the costs of distribution of the final product, as with products sold in mass markets, the location of the market is likely to exert a dominating influence. Consumer durable goods such as television sets, vacuum cleaners and washing machines are examples of products that account, in part, for the growth of industry around London and in south-east England. Some areas influence location as a source of supply of crafts, of specialized knowledge, or financial institutions (such as the Liverpool Cotton Exchange). These acquired advantages may lead industries to continue in areas in which the initial impetus has outlived its original importance.

British governments have taken a considerable interest in the location of industry for two basic reasons: concern about local unemployment and about congestion and the encroachment of cities on the countryside.

Governments faced with immobility of labour are tempted to persuade industry to move to areas with higher than average unemployment, but the political attractions of this policy may have an economic cost in higher prices, perhaps lower output, possibly loss of exports and lower material living standards. [3]

Location Quotient, a technique used in *Economic Base* studies to establish the degree to which activity in an area is basic (i.e. oriented towards exports) rather than non-basic (i.e. oriented towards satisfying local needs). If the area's proportion of total employment in an industry is equal to that for the country as a whole, the industry would have an LQ equal to unity. An LQ more than 1 would indicate that the area was an exporter of that good. For all industries in an area with LQ's higher than 1, the number of employees it would be necessary to shift to achieve an LQ = 1 can then be calculated to give a measure of basic employment in the area. The balance of employment in the area is then regarded as non-basic. [6]

Location, Theory of, the body of economic principles which determine the spatial structure of an economy. It seeks answers to the types of question asked by the proverbial visitor from Mars; "why does this activity take place where it does and not somewhere else?"; "why does the intensity with which land is used vary?"; "why are some urban areas larger than others and produce a different mix of outputs?"; "why do they have different growth rates?"; "why do they have similar basic structural characteristics?"; "why do some people tend to live near their place of work, others to commute long distances?" Location theory attempts to explain the ordering of production and consumption activities in space in terms of internal and external economies of scale, the demand for land, and transport costs. Economies of scale tend to encourage spatial concentration of economic activities, but higher land costs in areas of concentration tend to encourage spatial dispersion of some activities: transport costs act as a balancing factor between the forces of concentration and dispersal.

An early model of agricultural location was developed by the German economist and landowner, J. H. von Thünen. His model explained the most profitable use to which a site would be put in terms of its distance from a central market, the prices for produce to be obtained there, the costs of non-land inputs and the transport costs for particular kinds of product. Von Thünen's simple model yielded a solution showing activities ringing a central city in an orderly, concentric manner, with perishable, bulky and costly-to-transport outputs produced closest to the centre. These uses would produce the highest bids and would preempt sites nearer the city, but their bids would fall rapidly with increasing distance from the centre, so that further out they would be displaced by agricultural activities yielding outputs that involved lower transport costs. The model thus explained not only the pattern of agricultural activity around a central market but also the resulting pattern of land rents and values. It postulated that both intensity of land use and land values would decline with increasing distance from the centre.

The von Thünen model has since been refined and applied to determine the locational pattern of land use *within* urban areas and (in part) of industrial as well as agricultural production. The main difference between models of agricultural or urban location (based on von Thünen) and those of industrial location (based on the early work of A. Weber and later developments by E. Hoover and W. Izard and others) is that von Thünen-type models are centre-oriented, take input and output prices as given, and seek to explain the rent and land use pattern emerging, whereas most theories of industrial location take land rents or values as given, along with input origins and output destinations, and seek to explain how the most profitable location will be arrived at.

Both types of simple model afford incomplete explanations of location and require the support of further studies to explain the effects of economies of localization and urbanization (agglomeration) on location and land use patterns, and further refinements of theory have been directed along these lines. They also largely ignore relationships between centres. Models which attempt to explain the hierarchy of different-sized centres and the way in which they tend to specialize are based on the works of W. Christaller and A. Lösch on *Central Place Theory.* [6]

Locke, John. *See* INDIVIDUALISM.

Lockout, an exclusion of workers from their place of work by employers. In labour market tactics, the opposite of a strike. It is ineffective if applied by one or a few employers whose employees can find work with competitors. [5]

Log Rolling, pressure on government by groups of employers or employees for privileges they cannot obtain in the market to alter the rewards it yields them. The most common example has been pressure for tariffs. Usually the pressure has been exerted mostly by producer groups. Recently consumer groups have organized themselves. [14]

Logic, Relation to Economics. *See* ECONOMICS.

Lombard Street. *See* MONEY MARKET.

London and Cambridge Economic Service. *See* SOURCES, STATISTICAL.

London School, the centre of economic teaching, the London School of Economics, that systematized the theory of Opportunity Cost. In origin the theory was Austrian and Swedish (Wicksteed), but its applications to industry (the nature of the firm, and its internal working) were developed by the London School. The main members and contributors in written material were Lionel Robbins, F. A. Hayek, R. H. Coase and G. F. Thirlby, and in verbal form Arnold Plant, R. F. Fowler, R. S. Edwards and others. The London development of the theory is analysed by J. M. Buchanan in *Cost and Choice* (1969). [2]

Long Period, phrase used by economists to distinguish between changes which can be expected to take place quickly (in the "short period") and those which occur more slowly over the "long period." The distinction is important, for example, when the responsiveness of the supply of a commodity to a small change in price is being considered. Although supply may be inelastic and unresponsive in the short period, given time for, say, investment of new capital equipment to take place, supply may be highly responsive over the long period. The phrase is loose in the sense that the length of the (clock-time) period is not specific, so that what can be considered a short period in one line of production (steel production) may be considered long in another (rag and bone collection), depending upon the time taken for adjustments in equipment to be made. The term is frequently used to mean the length of time necessary for all the adjustments caused by an initial event, like a shift in taste or change in relative factor prices, to work themselves out. [7]

"Long Run." *See* TIME.

Longfield, Samuel Mountifort (1802–84), Irish economist and jurist. He became Professor of Political Economy and later Professor of Law at the University of Dublin. His contribution to economics is to be found largely in *Lectures on Political Economy* (1834). In general Longfield adhered to the basic doctrines of classical political economy, but he introduced several important innovations. He rejected the "wages fund" theory and held that wages were determined by the productivity of labour. He maintained that the rate of interest was determined on the supply side by the willingness of savers to sacrifice the present for the future, and on the demand side by the productivity of capital. His work on tariffs and the trade cycle also tended to anticipate later ideas. [2]

Lorenz, Max O. (1880–1962), Italian economist who gave his name to the Lorenz curve, which shows how a characteristic or variable is distributed within a group. It is most commonly used for the distribution of income to show the degree of equality or inequality per head. [2]

Loss Leader, a commodity sold by a retailer at less than its "trade" price in order to attract custom. Shopkeepers who oppose price competition sometimes refer to all low-price offers as loss leaders; but a selling price which might involve them in a loss may nevertheless yield a profit to a competitor who buys at a lower price because he buys in larger quantities or receives discounts given by the manufacturer to introduce new lines.

Loss leaders are a long-standing form of advertising in retailing from which shoppers may benefit directly. It is sometimes suggested that they lead customers up the garden path: having been tempted into the shop by "call birds" they are then mulcted by being charged enhanced prices on the main stock. This suggestion gives little credit to the common sense of shoppers; even if it were true, shoppers would suffer only if their total purchases cost more. Another objection is to "cherry-picking": shoppers will buy only loss leaders. But if this were so, shopkeepers would soon have to stop it or go out of business.

It is sometimes argued that manufacturers may suffer by having their brands sold as loss leaders on the ground that short-lived price-cutting leads to fluctuations in sales and makes production planning more difficult; so that prolonged price-cutting may cause shopkeepers to stop carrying the brand. There are two difficulties about this view. A manufacturer can scarcely be said to suffer if his sales are increased even though they fluctuate. Further, as only well-known brands make suitable loss leaders, shopkeepers cannot easily keep their customers if they stop selling such goods.

After the abolition of resale price maintenance in Britain in 1964, the use of loss leaders became less frequent because they were less dramatic when retail prices were unenforceable at law, although in some commodities prices were shown as "recommended." [7]

M

M.1, not a motorway but the symbol for the "narrow" definition of the supply of money in its most liquid sense: cash (banknotes or fiat paper money and coins of the realm), money in bank current accounts (in the US "demand" deposits) that can be withdrawn without notice and are thus virtually liquid though (normally) they earn no interest, and, strictly, any other assets that are immediately encashable or acceptable in lieu of cash at their market value. [8]

M.2, a wider definition of money supply: M.1 plus deposits at clearing banks and discount houses. This definition went out of use in the early 1970's. [8]

M.3, the "wide" definition of money supply: it comprises M.1 plus assets that are not immediately liquid but take some time to encash ("liquefy"), and thus earn some interest: money in bank deposit accounts (in the US "time" deposits), and in Post Office Savings Banks, Building Societies (deposits withdrawable in seven days, or even shares encashable in a month), and, strictly, any other assets that can be turned into cash in a short time.

The difference between M.1 and M.3 is thus essentially in the *time* taken to turn invested, interest-earning assets into instant, non-interest-earning cash that will be accepted immediately, without question, by everyone, in payment for goods and services or in repaying debts. [8]

McCulloch, John Ramsey (1789–1864), Scottish statistician and economist. He studied for some time at the University of Edinburgh, and soon decided to devote himself to political economy. His work in statistics led him to be appointed Comptroller of the Stationery Office in 1838, a position he held until his death. McCulloch had the misfortune to be overshadowed by his contemporaries. His main work, *Principles of Political Economy* (1825), shows an unquestioning faith in Ricardo's doctrines, but its lucid exposition of these doctrines served as a basic text until displaced by John Stuart Mill's book of the same title. [2]

Machlup, Fritz (1902–83), Austrian-born economist. He was educated at the University of Vienna. From 1935 to 1947 he was Goodyear Professor of Economics at the University of Buffalo, till 1960 Hutzer Professor of Political Economy at Johns Hopkins University, and later Walker Professor of Economics and International Finance at Princeton University.

As the Director of the International Finance Section at Princeton Machlup produced a constant stream of fertilizing publications. Earlier he wrote extensively and with authority on the economics of competition and monopoly (*The Economics of Sellers' Competition*, 1952). Since the publication in 1943 of *International Trade and the National Income Multiplier*, a work which had considerable influence, most of his publications have dealt with international trade and in particular international financial arrangements. He was a lifelong enemy of the imprecise, and once wrote "A term which has so many meanings that we never know what its users are talking about should be either dropped from the vocabulary of the scholar or 'purified' of confusing connotations." He has done much to tidy up the universe of discourse within which economists operate. His hostile attitude towards labour organization probably derives from his work on monopoly, to all forms of which he is opposed. [2]

Macmillan "Gap." *See* INDUSTRIAL AND COMMERCIAL FINANCE CORPORATION.

Macro-economics, the study of human activities in (large) groups as indicated by economic aggregates such as total employment, national income, investment, consumption, prices, wages, costs. Its use increased after Keynes's *General Theory of Employment.* The purpose of macro-economic theory is, generally, to study systematically the influences that determine the levels of national income and other aggregates and the level of employment of resources. Macro-economic theorists usually abstract from the problem of determining individual prices and their relations to one another and deal with aggregate price indices as determined by the level of total spending. In micro-economic analysis it is usually assumed that other things remain equal when an individual situation is being analysed; this kind of assumption is not made in macro-economic analysis. Macro-economics has its own rules because aggregate economic behaviour does not correspond to the total of individual activities. For example, if wages and production costs fall, a single firm may find it profitable to expand output and therefore hire more workers; but it does not follow that a wage cut will lead to a general expansion of employment in the economy as a whole. Similarly thrift may be desirable in an individual but it can in some circumstances harm the community at large.

There is no clear dividing line between macro-economics and micro-economics. Both can yield useful results, singly or together. Although macro-economics has yielded useful generalizations, indiscriminate and uncritical use of them in analysing situations in the real world can be misleading if micro-economic effects—on relative prices, on the allocation of resources between or the degree of under-employment of labour or capital in individual industries—are overlooked. For example, general full employment (macro-economics) and the policies that produce it can be irrelevant to the structural unemployment in particular firms, industries or areas (micro-economics).

Macro-economics is variously treated in economics text-books and treatises. The tendency has been to present it as a more recent, distinct and (in some books) more relevant development of economic thinking than micro-theory. A different approach (Alchian and Allen's *University Economics*) treats it as derived from micro-exchange and price theory. [14]

"Maintaining Capital Intact." *See* INVESTMENT.

Malthus, Thomas Robert (1766–1834), English economist. His father was a well-educated country gentleman acquainted with many of the foremost philosophers of his day. Thomas was the youngest of the family and was intended for the Church. In 1785 he went to St John's College, Cambridge, where he was mainly interested in philosophy and mathematics. He was elected to a fellowship, entered the Church and for a few years was a clergyman in a country parish. Here he worked on his famous *Essay on the Principle of Population as it affects the Future Improvement of Society,* published in 1789. The first edition, with its broad statements and religious undercurrents, attracted a great deal of attention but much adverse criticism, so that Malthus decided to spend the next few years travelling on the continent gathering data in support of his thesis. His researches were included in the revised second edition published in 1803. In 1806 he became Professor of Political Economy at Haileybury College, a new training school for young men intended for the East India Company. He remained there until 1834. His other main works include *An Inquiry into the Nature and Progress of Rent* (1815), *The Poor Law* (1817), *Principles of Political Economy* (1820) and *Definitions of Political Economy* (1827).

The *Essay on Population* earned Malthus wide recognition; he became a close friend of David Ricardo, entering into a long correspondence with him, was a founder member of the Political Economy Club, gave evidence on several parliamentary committees and was elected a Fellow of the Royal Society. The *Essay* might never have been written if his father had not been an admirer of the philosopher Condorcet, whose ideas had been translated and propagated by William Godwin. In 1793 Godwin published his *Enquiry concerning the Principles of Political Justice, and its Influence on General Virtue and Happiness,* which maintained that man could achieve perfection through reason and understanding. Its optimistic predictions convinced the senior Malthus, but Thomas was disturbed by the chapters on population in *The Wealth of Nations* and by the law of diminishing returns stated by Turgot. His misgivings prompted him to write the *Essay,* which argued that while the means of subsistence tended to grow in an arithmetic progression population grew in a geometric progression. In later editions of the *Essay* he modified this rigid theory into the more general one that increases in population would be limited by moral restraint, vice and misery.

The main effect of the *Essay* was to sweep away the optimistic hopes generated by Godwin and Adam Smith, for it seemed that as population increased less-fertile land would have to be brought into cultivation and the increase in food production would not keep pace with demand. Famine could be avoided only if the population engaged in the moral restraints, such as marrying later and having fewer children. Only the optimist thought this possible. Developments in science showed these fears to be largely unfounded, but Malthus's ideas had much influence on the Poor Law system in Great Britain. In the early years of the century "Speenhamland" poor relief was administered by local justices in relation to the price of bread and the size of the pauper's family. In view of Malthusian doctrine, this policy seemed to increase the possibility of over-population, and in 1834 the Poor Law administration was drastically amended. In economic thought Malthus's interpretation of the law of diminishing returns influenced David Ricardo and caused economics to be known as "the dismal science." [2]

Malthusian Theory of Population, the theory adumbrated by Thomas Malthus to explain the relationship between the growth in food and other means of subsistence and in population. Subsistence grew in arithmetical progression (1, 2, 3, 4 . . .), but population in geometrical progression (1, 2, 4, 8 . . .), so that population tended to outrun subsistence. In the absence of "moral restraints," the resulting over-population was held in check by war, famine, vice and misery. If wages rose above the subsistence level, population would increase and force them down: hence the theory that in the long run wages would tend to fall to a minimum subsistence level.

The rapidly rising population and the misery and unemployment of the early nineteenth century seemed to support the Malthusian theory, and the dangers of over-population were widely discussed in the following decades. Events, however, upset the theory. The increase in population was brought about not so much by a rising birth-rate as by a falling death-rate. The social distress was largely the legacy of the long Napoleonic wars. The means of subsistence later increased much faster than in arithmetical progression because of the unprecedented fertility of scientific knowledge and invention. The ultimate effect of increasing wealth was not to increase population even more but to slow down the rate of growth: large families were replaced by smaller families. The problem of over-population now plagues not the industrialized western societies but the agrarian eastern communities. Moreover, increasing population in the eighteenth and nineteenth century in Britain stimulated agricultural and later industrial improvement, and raised productivity by facilitating specialization (Adam Smith's "division of labour").

The fundamental fallacy of the Malthusian Theory was that it applied a static economic "law" to a period of time. At any *one* time, i.e. when no other change is possible, the more labourers are applied to a piece of land the smaller the return per head tends to become. This is essentially the Law of Diminishing Returns. But over a *period* of time, when knowledge, skill, capital equipment and other elements in production can expand and improve, the number of people who can live off a given amount of land can increase without reducing returns per head. In the event, for the last two hundred years Britain has supported more and more people at a gradually rising living standard.

The classical economists did not overlook improvements in science and technique, but they thought that it delayed the operation of the Law of Diminishing Returns. Improvements in technique, knowledge, etc., go further than that: they may make an increase in population *desirable;* and an increase in population may be *necessary* in order to exploit such massive capital investments as the railways. [11]

Man, Economic. *See* ECONOMIC MAN.

Managed Currency, one in which the quantity of money in a country is regulated by the monetary authorities. If a currency is "full-bodied" (wholly metallic—gold or silver) no management is required, because the quantity of money is governed solely by the quantity of the metal available. A shortage of money will tend to depress the general level of prices and decrease costs, increase the profitability of monetary metal production, and thus in time increase supplies.

Economists thought that the time lags in this adjustment process are so slow that a wholly metallic money supply cannot meet the needs of a modern economy without undesirable fluctuations in prices and business activity. Hence the attempts to adapt the quantity of money to business needs rather than vice versa. This involves increasing or replacing the metallic money supply by token and bank deposit money as well as other credit instruments. Monetary management raises the question of "how much," "when" and "how." These aims of management raise difficult problems of the relative desirability of stable, rising or falling price levels, variable or stable foreign exchange rates, the "political" control of money and so on, which are continually debated by economists, who vary from supporters of wholly managed currencies to others who emphasize the advantages of non-political or "automatic" adjustments of currency systems based on gold. Money is "managed" by the central bank control mechanisms of open market operations, Bank rate, etc. Currency management is now universal, but its problems are not solved. In particular managed currencies tend to be inflationary and in this sense are inherently mismanaged because of the political temptations of inflation (easily raised revenue, full employment, a general sense of buoyancy good for production and profits). [8]

Management Accounting, the application of accounting knowledge to the organization, selection and presentation of accounts to give the managers up-to-date and accurate information about the working of industrial and commercial enterprises and thereby assist them in making the best decisions. [3]

Managerial Revolution, first so described in 1941 by James Burnham in his book of that title, but the processes he observed have long been recognized as a prominent feature of the organization of modern society.

The thesis was broadly that the owners of wealth ("capitalists") are being replaced by the *managerial* social group or class in dominating economic and political life, largely because ownership is being divorced from control in the modern industrial corporation. With the continued growth of large firms and massive concentrations of capital, the ownership of businesses is rarely in one set of hands or even a small group. In the Industrial Revolution the owner-manager, i.e. the "capitalist" who also organized production, was the main figure of economic society.

Legally a limited liability company is owned by the ordinary shareholders: with the increasing size of industrial corporations, several of which have share capital of tens of millions of pounds, it is difficult for one small group of shareholders to hold sufficient shares to exercise control. Thus ownership tends to be dispersed, and control is usually exercised by a small group of professional managers or directors, who may own only a small proportion of the voting capital. Although nominally control of 51 per cent of the votes is needed for control, wide dispersion of votes and the practice of "pyramiding" makes it possible to control a firm with a small shareholding. Thus the professional manager is coming to occupy the key positions in industry and commerce. Burnham argued further that control over the "instruments of production" would be augmented by state ownership of the instruments, and that the managers would themselves control the state, thus achieving a "revolution" in which managers become the ruling class.

A weakness of this analysis is that it did not allow for the emergence of the powerful institutional shareholder (unit trust, etc.) who can influence or control the managers.

Although Burnham formulated the thesis in an extreme form that is not universally accepted, there is wide recognition of the tendency for control of industry in some sectors to pass from the capitalist to the manager. The term managerial revolution has now come to be used largely for this milder form of reorganization. [3]

Manchester School, (*a*) a group of men who were active in advocating free trade and resisted encroachments on laissez-faire in economic and social matters. They were most active in England between 1820 and 1850; their work centred largely on the propaganda of the Anti-Corn Law League. The chief immediate influence of this group, headed by Bright and Cobden, came from the economist Ricardo; they stood for a revolt against regulation, arguing that freedom was the natural condition of the individual and protection a harmful restraint on industry. The group generally opposed factory legislation, but did not overlook humanitarian interests; e.g. the leaders favoured regulation to protect children, although they believed that adults should be free to contract for themselves. [2]

(*b*) *see* JOURNALS, ECONOMIC.

Mandeville, Bernard de (1670–1733), Dutch doctor who practised in London and wrote a poem, *The Fable of the Bees,* the theme of which anticipated later economists in its insight into human motivation and its consequences. Its subtitle, *Private Vices, Public Benefits,* anticipates the distinction drawn by Adam Smith between individual intention and its unintended effects on others (the "hidden hand"). It thus in embryo states the distinction between private and social activity analysed by modern economics, and was an early statement of the harmony between self-interest and public benefit. [2]

Marginal Analysis, the core of modern economic theory, based on analysis of the utility of successive units of a commodity (or service) or the cost of successive units of a factor of production. Marginal analysis first emerged in a distinct form in 1871 in W. S. Jevons's *Theory of Political Economy,* Carl Menger's *Principles of Economics* and Léon Walras's *Éléments d'économie politique pure* (1874). Their contribution was mainly in the theory of value where marginal utility explained the consumer's demand for goods. The marginal utility analysis of Jevons and Menger explained for the first time the allocation of expenditure by the consumer, and formulated the "maximization" solution (*see* below). By the 1890's the concept of the margin had been applied to the theory of distribution and the allocation problem of the producer. Today it is a tool of analysis found in all branches of economic theory.

Since successive units of a commodity have differing degrees of significance, interest attaches to the effects of the loss or addition of the "marginal" (or "last") unit. This applies to consumer goods, to factors of production and to the services rendered by them. Marginal analysis thus deals with the logic of choice. It is applied wherever limited resources have to be allocated amongst a variety of ends, and where the object is to maximize satisfaction. The consumer allocates income in order to derive the most satisfaction from the whole of it. The producer allocates expenditure on various factors of production out of limited resources in order to maximize monetary returns, earnings or "profit."

The solution to the allocation problem of the consumer is based on the law of diminishing marginal utility: equilibrium in distributing a given income is reached when total utility or satisfaction is maximized; this requires that the marginal utility per unit of expenditure is the *same* for all goods. Similarly the solution to the allocation problem of the producer is based on the law of variable proportions: equilibrium in the distribution of a given outlay is reached when factors are combined in the proportion which maximizes physical output (or minimizes the cost of producing it); i.e. when marginal physical product per unit of outlay is the same for every factor. Full productive equilibrium, however, requires the output that will maximize profits. Thus a further condition of equilibrium must be added—that the use of all factors will be expanded to the point where the additional (marginal) cost per unit of output is equal to the additional (marginal) revenue per unit obtained from its sale. [14]

Marginal Cost. *See* MARGINAL ANALYSIS.

Marginal Efficiency of Capital. *See* PROPENSITY TO INVEST.

Marginal Private Net Product. *See* PIGOU, A. C.; EXTERNALITIES.

Marginal Product. *See* DISTRIBUTION.

Marginal Propensity to Consume. *See* PROPENSITY TO CONSUME.

Marginal Propensity to Import. *See* PROPENSITY TO IMPORT.

Marginal Propensity to Invest. *See* PROPENSITY TO INVEST.

Marginal Propensity to Save. *See* PROPENSITY TO SAVE.

Marginal Revenue. *See* MARGINAL ANALYSIS.

Marginal Social Net Product. *See* PIGOU, A. C.; EXTERNALITIES.

Marginal Utility. *See* DIMINISHING MARGINAL UTILITY.

Market, in its general economic sense, a group of buyers and sellers who are in sufficiently close contact for the transactions between any pair of them to affect the terms on which the others buy or sell. Ultimately, every transaction in any commodity or service affects and is affected by every other. A market therefore sometimes indicates in a general way large groups of buyers and sellers of wide classes of goods, e.g., the consumer goods market, the factor (of production) market, the capital market. These broad market categories are helpful when considering the working of the economy as a whole. In the consumer goods market, the quantities and prices of final goods may be seen to be determined by the responsiveness of demand to prices and incomes, and of supply to prices via costs of production. Costs of production depend upon the quantities of factors used and their prices, which are in turn determined by supply and demand in the factor (e.g. labour) market. These factor prices (wages, interest, etc.), together with the distribution of ownership of resources, determine incomes. Income which is not spent in the market for consumer goods is available (directly or indirectly) for the capital market, and the terms on which savings can be borrowed in the capital market influence methods of production and costs.

This is the general sense of "market." The market in a single commodity or class of commodity means the group of buyers buying at the ruling price and potential buyers who would buy at lower prices, and of sellers and potential sellers. Here emphasis is usually laid on producers and ultimate consumers rather than on the wholesale and retail channels by which they are linked. As in the general sense of "market," the market of a single commodity does not imply a particular geographical location. Transactions in some goods are centralized, e.g. securities on the Stock Exchange, copper, tin, lead and zinc on the Metal Exchange, tramp shipping on the Baltic Exchange, fruit in Smithfield market, diamonds in Hatton Garden; but their members act for suppliers and buyers who although far from one another physically are part of the market.

General market organizations are of economic interest for three reasons. First, they help to overcome market imperfections. A perfect market is one in which buyers know the prices being offered by all sellers, transport costs do not cause any buyer to deal with one seller rather than another, and buyers have no personal preferences for dealing with one seller rather than another. In practice there is some imperfection in all markets: in none is the cost of obtaining information zero. But the Stock Exchange and central organized commodity markets are very nearly perfect. Secondly, organized markets often provide means for hedging risks of price fluctuations by arranging deals in future contracts. Thirdly, organized markets provide a meeting place for speculators who buy with the intention of selling later at a higher price (bulls) or selling goods they do not own in the hope of being able to buy at lower prices when delivery must be made (bears).

Most markets have no central organization. They are classified by the number and size of sellers, the number and size of buyers, the degree to which buyers regard the supplies of different sellers as similar, and the ease or difficulty with which new sellers may enter the market. For example, seller concentration is very different in motor-cars and melons, buyer concentration in transformers and tea; cement of different sellers is regarded as much more similar than dresses of different sellers; entry into window-cleaning is easy and into water supply impossible. Hence the determination of prices and outputs in the many types of imperfect market have to be studied separately.

The term has become widely known by its use in the Common Market to describe the European Economic Community. This is a market created by agreement between nine countries to reduce barriers to the movement between them of labour and capital. By thus increasing the scope for exchange of goods and services it illustrates Adam Smith's dictum that the extent of division of labour depends on the size of the market. [7]

Market Forces, the conditions of supply and demand that operate in a free market to determine prices through the decisions of buyers and sellers, lenders and borrowers. The conditions of demand are income, preference, taste, the seasons, information, habit, tradition, the relative pull of conservatism and desire for novelty, and other objective and subjective influences. The conditions of supply are economies of scale, degree of competitiveness, governmental or private restrictions on entry to the market, the relative pulls of tradition and innovation, and the relative significance attached to monetary and non-monetary advantages (profit, power, prestige, public repute, political aspects of policy, etc.) in maximizing returns (measured by profits, sales, size of firm, share of market, etc.).

When used by non-economists the term suggests that "market forces" are beyond human influence or control. Individuals are in practice influenced by mixed motives and by conditions that vary from one individual to the next: objective and subjective, technical and psychological, monetary and non-monetary, short-term and long-term, selfish and altruistic. Ultimately the decisions are human, some motives ultimately over-ruling others. Böhm-Bawerk wrote a classic analysis in 1914, *Macht oder Ökonomisches Gesetz* (Power or Economic Law), which broadly distinguished between economic law, which reflected human wishes and decisions in the free market, and power, generally governmental, which sought to divert or frustrate it. He argued that individuals would ultimately find ways round laws that frustrated them and which they did not accept as morally justified. "Power is not asserted apart from, or in contradiction to, but within and in conformity with, economic laws." Black or "grey" markets are an assertion of economic law over the power that abolishes free ("white") market forces. Resistance to or rejection of high taxation regarded as unacceptable ("excessive") takes the form of tax avoidance (legal re-arrangement of activities to minimize tax) or tax evasion (illegal understatement of income or over-statement of expenses incurred in earning it). Hence the division of opinion among economists: some believe that the power of the state should be exerted to achieve results different from those that would emerge from market forces, generated by individuals with narrow or short-sighted interests, e.g. incomes policies to satisfy the sense of "fairness" or "social justice." Others believe such efforts are unavailing in the long run, except in national emergency or catastrophe or unless enforced by stringent penalties; they would argue that, if incomes policies hold wages below the level they would reach if determined by market forces, employers and employees will find ways round them, e.g. by arranging undeclared pay in cash, untaxed pay in kind, reclassification to validate higher pay, fictitious work, unworked hours, etc. Those who argue this way conclude that in general it is better policy to exert power so that it harmonizes with human proclivities (as expressed in market forces), not against them. [7]

Market Research, method used increasingly by industry to investigate consumers' preferences as a preliminary to advertising or to check its effectiveness in launching a product or to test public opinion on it. It is usually conducted by a sample scientifically constructed to represent the total population of consumers likely to be buyers of a product. The crudities of the early methods have gradually been removed by more careful and refined techniques.

One method of discovering consumer preferences is to "test market" a product in a few towns of various kinds, or to offer free samples, or to try out several advertising appeals. Public opinion on a product, or the advertising for it, can be assessed by interviewing a "panel" of consumers and observing their behaviour in retail shops.

Consumers are also asked if they can recall, recognize or reproduce advertisements by methods originated in the USA by Dr George Gallup and others and increasingly used in Britain and Europe. A difficulty with such methods is that people who can recall or reproduce an advertisement do not necessarily buy the product and that users of a product tend to recall its advertising more often than non-users because of the psychological tendency to "selective perception."

Market research began with the intention of finding the numbers and kinds of people (by age, sex, income, area, etc.) who bought a product or were influenced by advertising. It has more recently tried to discover, by "motivational research," the reasons why people buy some commodities, services or brands rather than others.

In so far as market research can anticipate consumer preferences it can make advertising more effective and avoid waste in producing goods that do not meet consumer requirements. An increase in such marketing costs can thus reduce factory costs so that total costs may be lower.

Market research has been used in politics as well as commerce. It is widely and regularly used to give frequent "readings" of public preferences in political policies and politicians. [7]

Market Share, the proportion of total demand that is supplied by a single supplier. The term is much used in marketing, and an increase in this proportion tends to be hailed as a notable achievement. For it to be such it must not have been obtained by expenditure or costs (high distributor margins, advertising, outlays, sales force pay, etc.) that exceed the net income (profit) from the larger sales, unless market share is regarded as an index of achievement in its own right. "Share" is also an economic, not a technical, category: the total market is supplied by goods that may be physically different but are regarded by consumers as serving the same purpose. Thus a firm's larger sales may represent a smaller share if the total market has been enlarged by a "different" product. [7]

Market Socialism, the use of market pricing by collectivist societies. In 1921 the Russian communist government under Lenin tried to encourage agricultural production by urging the peasantry to increase their output and sell food on favourable terms to the state and the towns, thus using the free market in the New Economic Policy (NEP). This policy was ended by Stalin's decision to accelerate industrialization fed by forced agrarian collectivization. For thirty years, from the mid-1920's until Stalin's death in 1953, markets were replaced by five-year plans of centralized direction to accelerate economic growth. During the mid-1950's Russia and other communist countries—Yugoslavia, Poland, Hungary—experimented with decentralized systems by using aspects of market pricing and incentives.

The theoretical principles of market socialism have been discussed and debated since the 1920's in the West by A. P. Lerner, Oskar Lange (later Foreign Minister of Poland), E. F. M. Durbin and others who favoured it, by von Mises, Boris Brutzkus, F. A. Hayek and others who doubted its practicability, and more recently in periodic conferences for economists from the East and the West in the late 1960's and the 1970's at Rapallo, Florence and elsewhere. [10]

Marketable Securities. *See* NATIONAL DEBT.

Marketing, broadly the processes required to move goods in space or time from producer to consumer. In economics there is strictly no distinction between "production" and "marketing"; both are productive if they make goods and services more capable of yielding satisfaction or satisfying wants by being changed in form, or being made more easily available. Goods serve little purpose unless they are made available to the consumer in the form, at the time, and at the place he is prepared to pay for.

In practice marketing is taken to include market research to discover what consumers want, "test marketing" to learn if what has been produced has accurately interpreted their wants, advertising to inform them it is available and to persuade them to try it, the distribution of samples, demonstrations in local centres or the consumer's home, wholesaling to hold supplies in bulk for distribution to retailers, retailing to hold supplies in smaller lots for sale to the final consumer. In different commodities these processes are elaborated or telescoped. Thus in many "producer goods" such as plant and equipment, marketing requires sales direct from producer to consumer. In others, especially in exports, there may be several kinds of intermediaries such as shipping agents, import agents, merchants of various kinds, some holding stock, others not, and so on.

There has been much change in the structure of marketing in Britain since the end of World War II. Some of the changes follow experience in the USA and other countries. There has been a decline in the various forms of wholesaling in favour of more direct selling by producers by direct mail, in which a catalogue replaces wholesaler and retailer, and by advertising goods supplied direct from the factory to the consumer in his home. Small shops have lost ground to self-service stores, supermarkets and discount houses, which offer lower prices to shoppers prepared to do without personal service, delivery and credit. Small shopkeepers have tried to make themselves competitive by associating, with some success, in "voluntary chains" in which they are assisted in display, advertising, accounting, staff training and so on in return for buying goods from a common wholesaler whose assured outlets enable him to reduce costs. Large retailers have developed "house" brands to compete with manufacturers' brands.

The structure of marketing is also being affected by the abolition of resale price maintenance, stamp trading, the efforts of the co-operative movement to modernize its wholesaling and retailing methods, the success of multiple and chain stores in combining low prices with high quality by arranging for manufacturers to make goods to stated standards so that the resulting "long runs" reduce costs. [7]

Marriage, Economics of. Marriage is one of the non-monetary market situations or activities to which economic analysis has been extended in recent years (others are charity, crime, politics, revolution, etc.). The pioneer in the economics of marriage is Professor Gary Becker of the University of Chicago. In 1973 he presented "the skeleton" of a theory of marriage (*Journal of Political Economy*) based on the two assumptions that individuals try to do the best they can and that the "marriage market" is in equilibrium. With the aid of several more simplifying assumptions he derived conclusions about human behaviour in the marriage market. First, the gain from marriage (over remaining single) varies with income, human capital, and relative differences in wage rates. Second, men differing in physical capital, education or intelligence (apart from the effects on wage rates), height, race or other characteristics tend to marry women with similar values in these characteristics. Third, the correlation between marriage mates for wage-rates, or for characteristics that are close substitutes in household production, tends to be negative. Fourth, the division of output between husbands and wives is determined (as in other markets) by marginal productivities, in turn dependent on human and physical capital, the relative numbers of men and women, and other variables.

In 1974 Professor Becker showed the efficacy of this economic approach to marriage by analysing the economic implications of love between husbands and wives, polygamy, genetic selection, separation, divorce, remarriage. The theory explained why persons who care for each other are more likely to marry each other than are otherwise similar persons who do not, and why polygamy (where legal) has been more common among successful men and its incidence influenced by inequality among men and by differences in the number of men and women. It also analysed the relationship between natural selection over time and assortive mating, which helps to explain the long-term persistence of differences in income between families, and the marriages likely to end in separation and divorce and how the assortive mating of people re-marrying differs from that in their first marriages. Fuller studies later amplified these analyses and tested their hypotheses.

Other American economists worked on the American marriage market, the benefits of women's education in marriage, family investment in human capital, including children, and family decision-making. [13]

Marshall, Alfred (1842–1924), English economist. The son of a cashier at the Bank of England. He was educated at Merchant Taylors' School. His father hoped he would train for the ministry, but he declined a theological scholarship to Oxford, preferring to study mathematics at St John's College, Cambridge. After graduating he spent some time as mathematics master at Clifton School, but returned to a Cambridge fellowship. He soon became a member of a philosophical discussion group which caused him to become interested in the possibilities of developing the human mind. On being told that the volume of productive resources in Britain would not allow the mass of the population the leisure and wealth necessary for study, he became interested in political economy.

In 1868 he was made Lecturer in Moral Science at Cambridge, and this appointment gave him the opportunity to make a thorough study of economics. At first his interest lay in applying his mathematical knowledge to existing economic theory, and he put many of Ricardo's arguments into mathematical form. His work in mathematical economics caused him to arrive at the theory of marginal utility before Jevons's *Theory of Political Economy* (1879), which disappointed Marshall, who was reluctant to present economic theory to the lay public in mathematical form.

In 1875 he went to the USA and studied its protective tariff system. On his return he married Mary Paley, a lecturer at Newnham College, and published the results of his American studies in collaboration with her in *Economics of Industry* (1879). His marriage forced him to resign his fellowship at Cambridge and for a time he was Principal of University College, Bristol. The rigours of administration tended to overstrain him, and he resigned and spent a year in Italy recuperating. He returned to Bristol as Professor of Political Economy in 1882;

after a short period at Oxford, he returned to Cambridge as professor in 1885, a position he held until his retirement in 1908.

Marshall's main publications include *Industry and Trade* (1919), *The Pure Theory of Foreign Trade* (1879) and *Money, Credit and Commerce* (1923), but his major contribution to economic thought is contained in *The Principles of Economics* (1890). He maintained that the principal task of the economist was to study the behaviour of men within the framework of the institutions in which they live. Hence facts must be collected, arranged and interpreted; but the danger must be avoided of presenting interpretations as theorems with universal validity. Institutions changed and man's behaviour was largely determined by them.

In an attempt to make economics a scientific subject, Marshall sought to find a common denominator to measure the activities of men. Hence his analysis was confined to aspects of human behaviour that could be measured in terms of money and were reflected in the price mechanism. The *Principles* thus set out to examine the general relationships between supply, demand and value. Man's economic behaviour was based upon a delicate balance between the search for satisfaction and the avoidance of sacrifice; this approach enabled Marshall to treat utility and costs as the joint determinants of value. They were like the blades of a pair of scissors, neither cutting solely by its own action. He applied this general scheme to the whole field of economic activity. The individual consumer obtained income by balancing the disutility of effort with the utility derived from spending the income derived from it. Likewise, the pattern of his expenditure was determined by the utility to be obtained from a commodity at the expense of the utility forgone in not buying others. The same theme underlay the activity of the whole economic community in its production and distribution of wealth.

Marshall was, however, very much aware of the difficulty of analysing these activities under rapidly changing conditions, and he therefore based his theories on a foundation of "static" conditions. In analysing the influences determining value, under different degrees of competition, he distinguished between "market value," determined when supply was fixed, and "normal value," determined in the short period when supply can be increased with unchanged equipment and stocks of labour and in the long period when the amount of plant can be changed. Finally, he said value must be considered in the "non-static" period when all economic data such as tastes, technology, population, etc., are likely to change.

Although Marshall designed his work to be of use to the layman and to the business man, his influence was most felt among his fellow economists, and he was soon the most prominent economist of his day. Apart from the general popularity of his works, his influence was increased by his teaching at Cambridge, where he trained the bulk of the succeeding generation of economists. This influence helps to explain why Marshallian methods of reasoning and concepts such as elasticity of demand and substitution are to be found in the works of present-day economists. [2]

Marshall Plan. *See* DOLLAR GAP; ORGANIZATION FOR EUROPEAN ECONOMIC CO-OPERATION.

Marx, Karl (1818–83), German socialist, economist and sociologist. Born of Jewish parents; converted to Christianity. He decided on an academic career and studied at the Universities of Bonn and Berlin. While a student he came into contact with a group of Hegelian philosophers who represented the foremost intellectuals and social critics in Germany. He soon became dissatisfied with the scope of Hegelian philosophy and sought a more practical form of social criticism. His radical views made a university career impossible, and he was forced to take up journalism. For a while he worked on the newspaper *Rheinische Zeitung,* eventually becoming editor, but the strict censorship which prevailed at that time caused the suppression of the newspaper, and Marx fled to Paris. There he worked for a while as editor of the *Deutschfranzösische Jahrbücher,* and contributed two interesting articles, a critique of Hegelian philosophy and a statement of his view on the class struggle and the nature of the revolution.

His growing interest in political economy was encouraged by his friendship with Friedrich Engels, who came from a wealthy family of Manchester textile manufacturers. Engels had studied the theories of the English classical school, and his critique of their system influenced Marx. They became lifelong friends. In 1845 Marx moved to Brussels, where he made his first contribution to economics, *La Misère de la Philosophie* (1847). *The Communist Manifesto,* written jointly by Marx and Engels, was published in 1848. In that year Marx returned to Germany; after playing an active part in the revolutions he again went into exile, this time to Britain where, apart from a few visits to the continent, he remained for the rest of his life.

Marx had witnessed the social distress that accompanied Germany's transition to industrialism, and his experiences in Britain led him to believe that the optimistic faith in the free enterprise system held by orthodox economists was unfounded. During his years in Britain he made a systematic study of existing literature on political economy in the British Museum. In 1859 he published his *Critique of Political Economy,* which contained the essence of his economic theories developed later in his famous work *Capital.* The first volume appeared in 1867; later volumes were collected and edited by Engels after Marx's death, the second appearing in 1885 and the third in 1894. The tripartite fourth volume was not published until 1904–10.

This long and involved work is mainly an account of Marx's thesis that the free enterprise capitalist system contained the seeds of its destruction. It is based largely on the labour theory of value: that the value of a commodity is determined by the quantity of labour embodied in its production. Marx's observation that only part of the total value accrued to the labour force as wages led to his theory of "surplus value": that part of total value which accrues to the capitalist rather than to the worker. He ascribed to the capitalist an insatiable thirst for surplus value, and built up a theory of "capitalist accumulation" which maintained that the economic system would gradually cause the control of productive resources to fall into fewer and fewer hands and produce an ever-increasing "proletariat." Marx's concept of the revolution was based on the view that with the advent of commercial crises the numerous members of the expropriated class would overthrow the small group owning the means of production and the "dictatorship of the proletariat" would follow.

Later work on the theory of value and subsequent development of the capitalist system seemed to reject much of Marx's thinking. But his theories reinforced the views of the growing school of socialists who, like Marx, based their thought on David Ricardo's labour theory of value. Through their adoption as the basis of the Russian Revolution and revolutionary movements elsewhere Marx has influenced world political history. [2]

Matching Finance, grant varying with the funds provided by the recipient. Thus, the Australian Commonwealth Government provides matching finance to the States for welfare of various kinds according to the amounts they contribute. The purpose is to stimulate expenditure on welfare but also to encourage care in the use of resources, and to avoid over-dependence on federal finances. [12]

Matching Gifts, gifts that vary with the contribution made by the recipient or with the size of gifts from other sources. The purpose is to assist people in need or good causes without stimulating over-dependence on aid, or on a given source of aid. The economics of giving, a recent development in economic theory, are discussed by the British economist A. J. Culyer in *The Economics of Charity* (1974). [13]

Mathematical Methods, used increasingly in economics as a shorthand and a rapid method of stating the relationships between economic data. They can be used effectively because of the striking similarities in theories in production, consumer choice, international trade, public finance and so on. One purpose is to help establish hypotheses about economic data derived by comparable methods in other sciences, the essential feature of such hypotheses being that they can in principle be tested and, possibly, refuted.

The increasing "technicality" of economic science is in the main due to the use of mathematical concepts. Whether this constitutes "improvement" or not is debated among economists. It is likely that the use of mathematical methods calls for more precise formulation of concepts: it is also possible that some theorems in economics would have been very difficult if not impossible to formulate clearly without the use of such methods. But over-emphasis on mathematical methods can overlook practical usefulness. To make conclusions arrived at by mathematical methods intelligible to laymen so that their relevance for policy can be judged, they must be translated into words. This is not always easy, but it provides a useful check against possible misdirection of effort. Compared with the physical sciences, economics is still in a primitive stage in its ability to predict and test. This contrast is likely to last. The application of mathematical methods in economics is likely to continue to grow although their value will remain uncertain. [14]

Mathematics, Relation to Economics. *See* ECONOMICS.

Matrix, mathematical term for an array (assembly) of numbers or quantities arranged in horizontal and vertical order (i.e. in rows and columns) showing two groups of variables related to each other. Examples are shown in Social Accounting and Input Output Analysis, where its application is explained briefly. In economic models, the expression of relationships in matrix terms is advantageous for computer processing. The device is therefore useful in mathematical economics. The plural is matrices. [14]

Matrix Algebra, mathematical rules governing the manipulation of matrices by addition, subtraction, multiplication and the calculation of inverse matrices (the counterpart of arithmetical division). [14]

Mature Economy, a term used by W. W. Rostow as one of the "Stages of Economic Growth." The mature economy is the third of his five stages and describes a situation in which a country's economy has developed to the extent that it can make full use of the current technology. It is capable of producing anything it wishes, and it does not produce a particular product because of choice, not inability. Britain's arrival at this stage was put by Rostow at 1850; he claimed that in 1851 at the Crystal Palace Exhibition Britain demonstrated "a well-rounded mature economy."

An older meaning of mature economy appeared in the writings of Alvin Hansen and other "stagnation theorists" of the late 1930's and early 1940's. There a mature economy means one in which investment opportunities had been used up, there were few discoveries, and population expansion had slowed down. These factors depressed the level of investment, which reduced the level of demand for goods and services and in turn led to unemployment unless offset by government measures. The policy conclusions were that in a mature economy such as the USA the government would have to increase investment and stimulate consumption in order to maintain full employment. These theories were associated with the "New Deal" in the 1930's, though how far they influenced policy is debatable. [11]

Maximand, the quantity that is sought to be maximized. The maximand of the individual is conventionally supposed to be the utility he can derive from his resources. The maximand of the firm is still probably long-run surplus of income over expenditure, although more recently economists have argued that it is sales, or capital assets, or market share. The maximand of the government department is argued to be its budget (W. A. Niskanen, *Bureaucracy and Representative Government,* 1971). The maximand indicates the objective, so that the economic rules (or laws) that govern the effectiveness of the means used to attain it can be analysed. [7] [10]

Maximin. *See* MINIMAX.

Meade, James E. (1907–94), British economist. He was educated at the Universities of Oxford and Cambridge, and taught at Oxford, London and Cambridge. He was Professor of Political Economy at Cambridge from 1957 to 1968, and Nuffield Research Fellow from 1969.

The range of Meade's publications is very wide: welfare economics, international trade policy, population, development economics, the theory of stationary states and of economic growth. In spite of his valuable contributions to international trade theory (*The Theory of International Economic Policy,* 2 vols., 1951 and 1955, etc.), and to geometrical analysis, he was a tool-user rather than a toolmaker. Samuelson dubbed him "the modern Wicksell"; he can deal with specific problems of social policy with extraordinary lucidity, as in *Planning and the Price Mechanism* (1948). He is an egalitarian social hedonist, or liberal socialist, who thinks that the price mechanism, desirable for economic efficiency, should be combined with state action to help the economically weak. He believes that the high level of employment, which he accepts as a natural priority for economic policy, may be difficult to maintain because of expansionary forces which it may generate. He has argued that the inflationary tendencies of a fully-employed economy, reinforced by social policies to cushion the unemployed, tend to concentrate attention on real wages ("take-home pay") rather than money wages, leading to growing demands for wage increases and an inflationary situation. The solution he proposed was twofold: control of total money demand to make it more difficult for producers to pass on higher money costs in higher money prices without loss of sales; and "social control" over wages and salaries and producers' prices. Control of money demand would require government-imposed wage "norms" and wage tribunals to determine pay claims in relation to the norm; workers who went on strike for more would lose social benefits. "Social control" over incomes and prices would require prevention of monopoly restrictions and freeing imports from all foreign sources, coupled with a floating exchange rate. [2]

Median, an average value. If a set of values for a variable (e.g. price per kilo of sugar in a sample of shops) is arranged in an ascending order of values, the median is the value of the variate which divides the distribution into two halves. If the set comprises an odd number of items the median is the value in the middle: if the set comprises an even number of items then conventionally the median is taken to be the average of the middle two values. [14]

Megalopolis, expression used by Jean Gottmann in *Megalopolis: the Urbanized Northeastern Seaboard of the United States* (1961) to describe the ultimate in uncontrolled urban expansion. As the size of cities increases, at some point they may become contiguous, resulting in a chain of interlocking urban complexes. Gottmann considered that megalopolis had arrived in the USA in the form of a "continuous corridor of urbanization on the Atlantic seaboard stretching from southern New Hampshire to Northern Virginia and from the Atlantic to the Appalachian foothills" and containing nearly forty million people in five of the fifteen largest cities in the USA. Constantinos Doxiadis, the Greek city planner, sees the ultimate stage of urbanization in the international megalopolis, which he calls Ecumenopolis—an urban continuum that would cross national boundaries; but projections of this kind have little economic content and must remain conjectural. [6]

Memorandum of Association, in Britain the charter of incorporation of a limited company formed under the Companies Acts. It sets out: (1) the name of the company, (2) whether the registered office is to be in England or Scotland, (3) the objects of the company, (4) that the liability of the members is limited, (5) the amount of share capital with which the company proposes to be registered and its division into shares of a fixed amount.

There must be seven subscribers to the Memorandum of Association (two in a private company). Each subscriber must sign the memorandum and must write opposite his name the number of shares (at least one) he agrees to take. The memorandum must be stamped as a deed and has to be filed with the Registrar of Companies. [3]

Menger, Carl (1840–1921), Austrian economist. After a short career in the Civil Service he became Professor of Political Economy at the University of Vienna in 1873. His work there, which earned him the title of founder of the Austrian school, can be divided into method, money and pure theory. His importance as an economist, however, derives mainly from the subjective theory of value which he formulated in his first book, *Grundsätze der Volkswirtschaftslehre* (1871). In this volume he defines utility as the power to satisfy human wants, and went on to develop a theory of marginal utility. This idea was published in the same year as Jevons's and Walras's, and so places Menger as one of the three economists who developed the marginal utility theory independently in the 1870's. [2]

Mercantilism, the economic philosophy of merchants and statesmen during the sixteenth and seventeenth centuries. Its background was the "commercial revolution" of this period: the transition from local to national economies, feudalism to merchant capitalism, rudimentary foreign trade to extensive international commerce. The overseas discoveries towards the end of the fifteenth century and the opening of silver mines in America during the sixteenth not only stimulated foreign trade but also produced an abundant flow of metal suitable for use as money, which encouraged the development of an economy based on money and prices. The increased use of money, the expansion of commerce, the revolution in agrarian production and the decline of subsistence production hastened the weakening in the authority of the Church and of canon law and accelerated the growth of private enterprise and the emergence of the merchant capitalist as a dominating force in the economy.

These political and economic changes were expressed in mercantilism. The term does not indicate a set of rigid doctrines. Mercantilism developed over a long period of changing conditions and reflected a wide variety of ideas. But the basic similarity in the notions which appeared in several European countries at about the same time, and which underlay official policy for a long period, makes it possible to regard them as a single body of thought.

Mercantilist doctrine centred on the power of the state, which it was designed to strengthen. A strong central authority was regarded as essential for the expansion of markets and the protection of commercial interests. The interests of the individual were regarded as subservient to those of the state. Accordingly the regulation of wages and interest, the ordering of industry by the grant of monopoly privileges, the use of protective devices and general restrictions on the activities of individuals were accepted and encouraged. The desire for a strong nation-state also underlay the emphasis on "treasure," i.e. the accumulation of precious metals (then generally regarded as the most desirable form of wealth). It was thought desirable both as a source of power and as a stimulus to trade. Since non-producers of precious metals could increase their stock only by a continuing surplus of exports over imports, questions of foreign trade and in particular of the balance of trade were prominent in mercantilist writings.

The commercial legislation of the time reflected these ideas. Imports of goods considered unlikely to add to the productive powers of a country were discouraged by duties, or prohibited. Exports were encouraged by bounties and by drawbacks of duty on imports that were re-exported. The export of raw materials considered essential to home manufacturers was prohibited. Commercial treaties with other countries confined trade to the channels thought most likely to yield export surpluses and thus the desired inflow of the precious metals. The trade of the colonies was confined to the mother country and restrictions placed on their production of competing manufactures. The Navigation Acts encouraged the growth of shipping and thus earnings from the carrying trade.

By the second half of the eighteenth century mercantilist policies were being increasingly regarded as a hindrance to economic progress. Adam Smith's denunciation of the system in *The Wealth of Nations* (1776) was the turning point. "It cannot be very difficult to determine who have been the contrivers of this whole mercantile system; not the consumers, we may believe, whose interest has been entirely neglected; but the producers, whose interest has been so carefully attended to . . ." The classical economists rejected the mercantilist view that the purpose of an economic activity was to provide markets for surplus production and acquire metal to use as money. They held that the purpose of economic activity was to satisfy human wants and that the desirability of foreign trade should be judged by this criterion. Exports were desirable only in so far as they enabled wants to be satisfied by imports more fully than was possible from home production alone. Since stocks of monetary metal could not by themselves satisfy wants, there was no lasting benefit in a continuing export surplus financed by imports of precious metal. Indeed, attempts to maintain such a surplus would tend to defeat themselves because movements of the metals between countries would affect relative national price levels. Instead of creating wealth, mercantilist impediments to free trade thus reduced it by impairing the efficiency with which a country's resources were mobilized to satisfy wants.

Although these views were widely accepted, especially during the nineteenth century, the influence of mercantilist doctrines still lingered on among many statesmen and business men. The re-examination, by J. M. Keynes in *The General Theory of Employment, Interest and Money* (1936), of classical economic theory gave renewed (although qualified) support to the mercantilist view that an export surplus could increase domestic employment, output and income; but he agreed that, in practice, trade restrictions were an unreliable and treacherous means of achieving such expansion. In recent years modern versions of mercantilist ideas have conflicted with the attempts to liberalize international trade and replace national by supra-national authorities or organizations such as the European Free Trade Association (EFTA) and the European Economic Community (Common Market). [10]

Merchant Banks, about a dozen private banks in Britain whose primary purpose was to finance international trade between Britain and other countries and between other countries. Their instrument is mostly the bill of exchange, which they "accept," thus indicating they will pay the amount due. The work requires a network of agents in the main world trading centres, knowledge of many industries and commodities, methods of obtaining information of the standing of firms in many countries and on trade conditions. The merchant bank earns its income (about ¼ per cent of the value of the goods) by lending its name (some of which are Barings, Hambros, Kleinwort-Benson, Lazards, Morgan-Grenfell, Rothschilds, Schröders) to the buyer and seller to enable them to conduct their business with confidence and agree on terms. They also deal in foreign exchange.

Merchant banks tend to specialize on trade in different countries, the governments of which have come to ask them to raise loans in London. Hence they became "issuing houses" for large foreign government loans. Since the end of the war they have also "issued" for British firms at home.

In recent years the merchant banks have widened their activities into general banking and financing (from loans to industry to specialized insurance and hire purchase). They came into public prominence during the 1960's when they advised and acted for firms in mergers. Since not all mergers arranged privately or with government stimulus were successful, and merchant bankers were associated with government policy, the activities of the merchant banks came under some criticism; but they remain an important part of the City and its "invisible" earnings for the British balance of payments. [8]

Merchants. *See* DEALER.

Merger. *See* COMBINATION.

Merit Goods, a somewhat pompous name for goods or services in which government believes individuals should not be allowed free choice because of lack of information about their effects—good or bad. The resultant policy can vary from helpful to officious: from informative labelling or warnings (e.g. the British government health warning on cigarette packets or restrictions on the sale of drugs) to paternalist or autocratic intervention in private life.

The concept has three conceptual weaknesses. First, it is not wants (goods) as such that are beneficial or harmful but rather the *quantities* consumed: a small amount of alcohol need not be harmful, and a large amount of "good" food can kill through obesity. Second, people are affected differently: the quantity that harms some may have no effect on others. Third, the optimum amount can be learned only by experience, except where a single dose is fatal; if restrictions prevent experimentation the optimum amounts remain unknown.

The concept conflicts with Pareto's assumption that individuals must be assumed to know their interests better than others do, or at least less imperfectly; but it does serve to indicate that individuals do not always start with as much information as they might be supplied with, in return for payment or by Government, in order to make better choice. [13]

Merit Wants. Another name for Merit Goods. [13]

Metal Exchange, the largest market in the world for copper, tin, lead, zinc. Opened in London in 1881. All business is conducted by or through some forty members of the "Ring" (a circle composed of four curved benches), who make open "bids" or "offers." Deals are settled verbally across the Ring. Dealings are mainly in "futures" because the principal purpose of the Exchange is to enable producers and consumers to protect themselves against price changes by "hedging." The Exchange was closed during the war, but working was fully restored by 1953. [7]

Metals, Precious (gold and silver), have been commonly used in the past as media of exchange. Since they are relatively scarce they are so valuable that small units command large quantities of goods; they are virtually indestructible; their value remains relatively stable; and they are homogeneous in quality and easily identified. Where confidence in monetary authorities is weak, precious metals are useful sources of coinage because they have a value of their own which gives the holder a sense of security. [8]

Methodology, in economics, is the study of the methods used by economists in their academic work. The work of the economist broadly conforms to two methods—the normative and the positive. Normative economics consists of statements on what individual business or public policy ought to be, based on the value-judgements of the individual economist. Positive (or behaviourist) economics is in principle independent of any ethical position or judgement; it deals with what is, not what ought to be. Its task is to provide a system of generalizations that can be used to make objective predictions about the consequences of change in circumstances. In this sense it is a science.

A further distinction in methodology is often thought to be between micro-economic and macro-economic analysis. Some economists seem to distinguish between the two; others argue that the latter is an implication of the former. (*See* MACRO-ECONOMICS.) [14]

Micro-economics, the study of the economic actions of individuals and well-defined (small) groups of individuals. Prices play a major role in micro-economic theories, the purpose of which is usually to analyse price determination and the allocation of resources to particular uses. Income concepts are not ignored in micro-theory; but individuals earn their incomes by selling factors of production the prices of which are determined in the same way as all other prices.

The theories of individual behaviour and price determination in a competitive economy may be developed in three stages. First, the behaviour of individual consumers and producers is the focal point; each individual is assumed to consider the prices of the goods he buys and sells as "given," and the quantities of his purchases and sales are the "variables" determined in these theories. The market for a single commodity is the focal point of the second stage; other things being equal, the price of the commodity, as well as the volume of purchases and sales, is shown to be determined by the independent actions of buyers and sellers. Finally, in the third stage, interrelations between the various markets in the system are taken into account, and all prices are determined simultaneously.

In recent years there has been a tendency to replace micro-economics by macro-economics, which some economists think more helpful. Other economists consider that macro-economics is valid only in so far as it rests on valid micro-economics, because, although the consequences for a large group (a country) may be different from the consequences for individuals, the behaviour of very large groups such as the population of whole countries cannot properly be interpreted unless the motives and reactions of individuals or small groups of them are analysed or understood. [14]

Middleman, a person who intervenes in the process of purchase and sale either between the primary producer and the manufacturer or the manufacturer and the final consumer. In economics the middleman came to be regarded as a crucially important part of the competitive process; for he performed the specialized function of linking the producer with a market demand that was becoming increasingly distant in time and space. By specializing in this task, the middleman could do it more efficiently and cheaply than others. Moreover, in buying from the producer in anticipation of a sale and in carrying stocks of goods from place to place or through time he was taking important marketing risks, thus easing the burden on the manufacturer. In different industries he is a merchant, dealer, agent, broker, wholesaler, retailer.

In the Middle Ages the middleman was traditionally regarded as an interloper and was frequently abused as a parasite who forced his way between producer and buyer to reap an unnecessary profit. The poor transport and communications of western Europe in the fifteenth and sixteenth centuries created conditions that sometimes justified this view, since merchants often exploited their monopolistic position. From this attitude developed the mass of legislation against "engrossing, forestalling and regrating" in fifteenth- and sixteenth-century England.

Especially since the beginning of the twentieth century marketing and distribution as distinct from production itself has become more elaborate in western economics. The improved quality of many goods and the development of advertising and marketing techniques largely explain this development. But the vogue of the proprietary article and branded good has encroached on the role of the old-style middleman. In retailing he has increasingly been supplanted by the chain store. In the wholesale market he has been supplanted either by the manufacturer expanding "vertically" to control directly the purchase of materials and the disposal of his product, or by co-operative organizations selling on behalf of producers. [7]

Migration. *See* Mobility.

"Milk-bar Economy." *See* Overloaded Economy.

Mills, James (1773–1836), British historian and philosopher. He was educated at Montrose Academy and the University of Edinburgh, where he distinguished himself as a Greek scholar. He became a licensed preacher in 1798, but preferred to teach and study philosophy. He moved to London in 1802, became acquainted with Bentham, adopted his views and became a major exponent of them. His first contribution to economics was a pamphlet on the corn trade written in 1804, in which he argued against subsidy on the export of corn. But his major contribution lies in his *Elements of Political Economy* (1821), intended mainly as a textbook on economics. [2]

Mill, John Stuart (1806–73), English philosopher and economist. He received a remarkable education from his father, James Mill, a friend of Ricardo and Bentham, and one of the leading intellectuals of the early nineteenth century. According to his *Autobiography*, the young Mill began to learn Greek before he could remember (he was told it was around the age of three). At eight years he began to study Latin and was entrusted with the task of teaching it to his younger brothers and sisters. Between eight and twelve he mastered geometry, algebra and the differential calculus before going on to logic. At fourteen he was familiar with all that had been written in political economy. The difficulties of contact with normally educated people were alleviated by his friendship with Mrs Harriet Taylor, whom he later married.

Mill served with the East India Company until 1858 when the Company lost its charter. He was a Member of Parliament from 1865 to 1868, but after the death of his wife (who had collaborated with him in several of his works) he retired from active life and spent his remaining years in Avignon.

His first work was published in 1822, and for the rest of his life he was a prolific writer on a wide range of subjects. *System of Logic* appeared in 1843, and immediately established his fame. Mill claimed that in economics he was nothing more than a pure "Ricardian," but his main work, *Principles of Political Economy*

(1848), contains much original thought. It was a comprehensive survey of economic science as it was known in his day, and it soon became the standard work on the subject. His *Essays on Some Unsettled Questions in Political Economy,* written in 1829 (when he was twenty-three) and published in 1844, would seem, however, to contain his major contributions to economic analysis. [2]

Minimand, the quantity it is desired to make as small as possible. The minimand of a firm is its losses, which may be unavoidable in the short run. The opposite of maximand. [7]

Minimax, a term used in games theory which may also accurately describe behaviour in real life. The minimax principle is that the choice between alternative acts should be based on the worst possible consequences of each and then lie with that which minimizes the maximum disadvantage. The approach is the opposite of the usual judgement of the *best* possible outcomes, although the decision is essentially the same: to minimize the worst or maximize the best possible outcome. [14]

Minimum Lending Rate. *See* BANK RATE.

Minimum Wages are laid down by government where labour is considered weak in bargaining power. Wage rates tend to vary in response to changes in the demand for and the supply of labour in different occupations and industries. But the state and trade unions in wage agreements have set and tried to maintain minimum wage rates. Before and during the First World War the state set minimum wages in "sweated" trades. Since then the Wages Council Acts of 1945–8 have established minimum wage rates in occupations where labour was considered insufficiently well organized, as in catering. Trade unions have tried to enforce fixed wage rates for a wide variety of occupations. One of the objectives of the Trades Union Congress is a legal minimum wage for each industry or occupation.

Fixing a minimum wage rate generally implies that wages have to be raised. In the early years of trade union activity this aim was usually achieved by the craft unions restricting their membership. The restriction of membership reduces the supply of labour, and, given the conditions of demand for it, wage rates tend to rise to "ration" the available labour among employers who pay the higher rates. The unions of unskilled workers, whose membership cannot be reduced by enforcement of apprenticeship restrictions, have to rely upon the strength and influence of their organization, which may be inspired by political, social or other non-economic considerations.

The enforcement of a minimum wage rate for an occupation does not necessarily benefit all employees in it: the employer is not compelled to continue employing all his previous labour force at the higher rate. He may find it profitable to substitute machinery for labour and/or to reduce output. The enforcement of a minimum wage rate may thus cause unemployment; or the dismissed worker may be able to find work only at lower rates. On the other hand, the increased costs of higher wages may ultimately be passed on to the consumers in the form of higher prices, with little or no reduction in employment in the trade, but possible unemployment in other trades. Where one firm employs the whole of a local labour force and is acting monopolistically, the enforcement of a minimum wage may also, for a time, result in no unemployment.

To the extent that wage rates tend to be determined "from above" in this way by notions of social justice rather than by economic forces, differences between wage rates are distorted, and the mobility of labour impaired. On this ground it is considered by some economists that it is better to redistribute income by taxation and free or subsidized social benefits. The alternative is generally to enforce minimum wages at the expense of those who become unemployed because their work is worth less than the minimum: the less-skilled, the young, women and (especially in the USA) coloured workers. [5]

Minorities, Economics of, studies the machinery by which minority preferences in goods or services are expressed and made effective. Briefly, the two main vehicles are the political process and the market. In decisions made by the franchise minorities are, by definition, outvoted by majorities and have to accept their decisions, or organize and convert them, or move to other political units—in local government decisions to other areas, in national government decisions to other countries. In market decisions it is easier for minorities to reject majority decisions and persuade some suppliers to meet their requirements or organize production outside the market. The economic theory of politics developed by Anthony Downs, J. M. Buchanan, Gordon Tullock and others, mostly in the USA, has analysed the power and limitations of minorities. Samuel Brittan's *Capitalism and the Permissive Society* (1973) discusses the theory and its applications in the UK. [13]

Mint, the government department responsible for providing coinage (in Britain the Royal Mint). All coins in Britain are produced at the Mint, which buys the metal it requires, makes the coins, and pays them into the Bank of England for the credit of the Exchequer. Before the First World War anyone could take gold to the mint and demand that it be coined into sovereigns, but in practice gold was coined only by the Bank of England. [8]

Mint Parity of Exchange, the exchange rate between two currencies both of which are legally convertible at fixed rates into either gold or a third "key" currency. The mint parity then expresses the ratio between the two legal rates. Thus if pounds sterling were convertible into gold at £12.50 per oz. and US dollars at $35 per oz., the mint parity would be £1 equals $2.8. [4]

Mintage, a charge made by a government for converting bullion into coins. [8]

Mises, Ludwig von (1881–1973), leading member of the Austrian school of economists. Professor of Economics at the University of Vienna from 1931 to 1938 and at the Institute of International Studies at Geneva from 1934 to 1940. In 1946 became a citizen of the United States, teaching at New York University. He was the author of numerous works on economics and government.

Von Mises was one of the most original thinkers of the Austrian School, and an outstanding teacher. Among his numerous treatises, *The Theory of Money and Credit* (1934) extended the subjective value revolution to monetary analysis. In the first German edition of 1912 von Mises predicted the general character of the Great Depression and developed the Austrian theory of the business cycle. *Socialism* (1936) was probably the most comprehensive analysis written by an economist. *Human Action* (1948) was a systematic analysis of the principles of praxeology—economic theorems based on the postulate of human action.

In *Epistemological Problems of Economics* (1960) and *Theory and History* (1957) von Mises systematically developed the Austrian position that economic theory is logically independent of reality in the sense in which logic and mathematics are independent. Reality for the social sciences is always unique and unrepeatable history.

Mishan, E. J. (1917–), British economist with original, independent mind, clear exposition and depth of feeling. He was educated at the Universities of Manchester and Chicago and has been Reader in Economics at the University of London. He came into prominence in the late 1960's through a series of books examining the "external" harm to the environment by congestion, spoliation of the countryside, the destruction of peace and quiet by aircraft, etc. that accompanies economic growth; he concluded that it should be possible to reduce the general rate of growth or escape from its consequences by enclaves that contracted out of it. He attributed the damage to pressure of population and to laissez-faire in town and country planning that neglected amenity. How far the harmful effects could be stopped only by retarding growth itself was the question on which economists differed. [2]

Mitchell, Wesley Clair (1874–1948), American economist. He was educated at the University of Chicago, where he became acquainted with Thorstein Veblen and absorbed some of his "institutional" approach to economics. After study at Halle and Vienna, Mitchell returned to Chicago. He taught for a time at the University of California and later was appointed Professor at Columbia University. As a public servant he sat on numerous governmental boards and committees, and was one of the founders of the American National Bureau of Economic

Research. His work was mainly on the application of statistical techniques in the investigation of economic phenomena. In *Business Cycles* (1913), *Business Cycles, the Problem and its Setting* (1927) and *Measuring Business Cycles* (1946) he combined statistical and theoretical approaches. [2]

Mixed Economy, one in which some means of production are privately and some publicly owned; in which the allocation of resources and level of activity are decided by individuals, firms, co-operatives, public corporations and public authorities reacting to, creating or controlling market opportunities, and in which the distribution of the product depends upon the personal accumulation and inheritance of wealth, earnings of factors of production, taxes and social transfers such as old-age pensions, public assistance and health and educational services paid for out of taxes.

A mixed economy is thus a mixture of early capitalism where individuals manage what they own (usually in farming, small-scale industry and retailing), managerial capitalism where anonymous shareholders own, but boards of directors control, property (usually in large-scale industry), municipal enterprise, co-operation (usually in consumer or farm purchases but with possibly a fringe of producer co-operatives in small-scale manufacturing), nationalized industry and the "welfare state." Activity is organized by free market transactions modified, regulated or replaced by taxes and subsidies, credit controls, licensing arrangements, marketing boards, anti-monopoly arrangements, and administrative controls and directions.

Today most economies are mixed. None is either completely free enterprise or completely centrally directed. The descriptions "free" and "controlled" are thus relative. Germany is a relatively free economy, Russia a relatively (but not entirely) controlled economy; the USA and the UK are less free than Germany, Yugoslavia and Poland less tightly controlled than Russia. [10]

Mobility, the extent to which workers are able and willing to change their occupation, industry or home, and owners of capital and land to change the uses of their resources. Differences in mobility over time have led some economists to distinguish between short-period equilibrium positions to which prices and outputs tend whilst capital remains in its existing uses, and long-period equilibrium positions of price and output when firms can expand or contract their plant and enter or leave an industry. The pure theory of international trade has been developed to explain the interrelationships of prices, outputs and incomes in and between economies which exchange their products but whose factors of production do not move between them. The more labour (or capital) is immobile between countries, the wider the differences in costs are likely to be, and the more the opportunities for advantageous exchange of its products. International trade is thus provoked by, and is a compensation for, international immobility of the factors of production. For example, the more migration is prevented or impeded, the more the impetus to international trade. If labour and capital were freely mobile the scope (and the "need") for international trade would be less.

Mobility is important to economists examining the potentialities for change and growth, explaining local differences in wages or localized unemployment and analysing possible remedies. Social mobility, the extent to which the social status (usually measured by occupation) of sons differs from that of their fathers, is an indication of social change.

Adam Smith wrote: "It appears evidently from experience that man is of all sorts of luggage the most difficult to be transported," and labour is usually thought generally immobile. Mobility has never been high enough to equalize the percentage employed in all regions of the country or to equalize earnings. In Britain, unemployment percentages have invariably been higher and wages lower in parts of Scotland, the North-East of England and South Wales than in the southern counties. (But comparisons of this kind do not tell the whole story: in part at least they reflect cost-of-living and other differences between areas.)

The movement of labour is extensive, especially over long periods. In Britain a million insured workers out of a total of twenty-five million change jobs each year. Furthermore, there have been marked changes in the distribution of workpeople between industries over time. There has been a long-term trend for people to move out of the extractive industries and manufacturing into the distributive, leisure and personal service trades. The mobility of labour between occupations and industries is eased if the working population is young and growing. Labour may be redistributed by youths entering expanding industries whilst old workers retire and are not replaced in declining industries. Much labour has moved from the south of Italy to the north, from Italy to Germany. And in the last century there were massive movements from Europe to North America, Asia to Europe, Africa to America, Asia to South Africa, and so on.

Movement of individuals up the social scale depends upon the increase in the number of positions of middle and upper status, and upon the ways in which they are filled. Changes in technology which increase the proportion of more technical, highly skilled and better paid occupations, expansion of industries demanding more skill than others, and higher incomes which enable people to spend more on professional services all tend to increase the openings for mobility upward. Low fertility of upper and middle status people failing to reproduce their numbers, and recruitment in industry or public services by open competition rather than nepotism increase the upward mobility that takes place. Some years ago in Great Britain 40 per cent of a large sample of men between the ages of thirty and seventy had the same status as their fathers, 27 per cent had a higher status and 33 per cent a lower status. [5]

Mode, an average value. The mode or modal value of a set of values of a particular variable is the value that occurs most frequently; i.e. it is the "most fashionable" value. [14]

Models, Economic, aids to understanding the working of the economy. Irving Fisher made a model of the price system using a large water tank and floats; A. W. Phillips invented a machine which pumps coloured water through a network of transparent pipes and valves to simulate the flow of national income. But economic models are usually theoretical constructions: the bulk of economic theory consists of models which, if well devised, identify the influences to be taken into account in the real world and the kind of results to be expected from changes in them.

Economists have resorted to model-building because they are unable to conduct controlled experiments. They must therefore isolate from real situations the variable influences and relationships which are believed to be the main determinants of particular results. Having chosen the parts, interconnections and prime movers of a model, they analyse the way in which it works and the changes which additional or different parts and interconnections would make. If a model reproduces important features of real life it provides a guide to understanding and a basis for predictions.

Models may incorporate *individual* economic units such as households and firms, often grouped into individual markets and industries, and the relationships between them. These are called micro-economic models. They help to explain such matters as the determination of prices and outputs of particular commodities and payments for individual factors of production. Macro-economic models have been extensively developed from the construction of *total* or national income accounts by the late Sir Arthur Bowley, by Colin Clark and the late Lord Stamp, and from the theoretical work of Keynes and the Swedish economists. These ignore detail and build up systems of broad aggregates, such as total consumption, total investment, national income and changes in the general level of prices. Macro-economic models are used in an effort to explain and predict the performance of the economy as a whole, e.g. changes in the level of national income, the level of employment and inflation. The British Treasury uses a macro-economic model in constructing the annual budget to estimate its likely effects on the performance of the economy. Planning bodies use macro-economic models when working out the implications of alternative rates of growth.

W. Leontief has devised input-output models which have both micro-economic and macro-economic features and show the sources of the inputs of different industries and the destinations of their output. They are intended to help the detailed investigation of the effects of general changes, such as the reduction in total government expenditure following disarmament. They have so far been constructed only for groups of industries, and for inputs and outputs assumed to be related by constant proportions.

Both micro-economic and macro-economic models may be subdivided into "equilibrium" and "process" models. Equilibrium models specify the conditions under which the "variables" they incorporate would have no tendency to change; but they are used to analyse change. First, they sometimes indicate the direction which adjustments will take in disequilibrium conditions. Secondly, comparison of equilibria with initial conditions differing in a single respect may indicate the ultimate effect of the single difference. An important distinction in the case of micro-economic models is between general and partial equilibrium models. General equilibrium models embrace all the variables of the whole economy; their main purpose is to provide a summary chart of the interrelationships between *all* parts of the economic system. Partial equilibrium models select a few closely interrelated "variables" (e.g. the price of a single commodity and the quantity of it demanded), and work out the mutual interdependence of these few against a background of assumed fixed values for all other "variables."

Equilibrium models ignore the difficulty of tracing the way in which movement is made towards the equilibrium position. But the equilibrium itself may be affected by the path followed and the speed with which different variables change. Process models trace out such paths of adjustment, indicating the conditions under which steady movement, oscillation and rebounds from "ceilings" and "floors" are to be expected.

A further distinction may be made between models which incorporate expectations as determinants of behaviour from those which do not. "Deterministic" models work mechanically, expectational models suppose that economic activity takes place in a world of imperfect knowledge. "Stochastic" models incorporate probabilities of events happening. [14]

Monetarist, economist who emphasizes government's monetary policy as more important for the management of the economy and the avoidance of deflation and inflation than fiscal policy (government conduct of the budget by taxation, spending and borrowing). [8]

Monetary Correction, the use in contracts of escalator clauses, or links with general prices, in order to keep pace with inflation, i.e. to correct prices for changes in the value of money. It is also known as indexing (UK) or indexation (USA). In private contracts monetary correction has long been used in wage bargaining in the form of "cost of living bonuses": in the UK about five million employees have been covered by union contracts with such escalator clauses, and over five million in the USA. Probably many non-unionized employees have similar arrangements, formal or tacit, with their employers. Rents for business buildings are sometimes a percentage of receipts (gross or net after costs). All such incomes or payments arranged as a percentage of a larger price are automatically escalated: car insurance policies that pay the cost of repairs, royalties on books, etc. Contracts for delivery of goods often provide for raising the final price in step with particular costs or general prices.

Government contracts have also had automatic escalator clauses for civil service pensions and wages of some employees; more recently social benefits have been related to rising general prices. *Ad valorem* taxes are escalated automatically; specific taxes *fall* in real terms as prices rise.

Monetary correction came increasingly into academic and public debate in the early and middle 1970's as a means of combating and ending inflation. It had seemed to work in Brazil, where inflation fell from over 100 per cent a year to around 20 per cent in a few years. Canada applied monetary correction to income tax exemptions and allowances and to the various income groups. Sweden and Israel also applied escalation in varying degrees. A US Senate bill proposed that government tax and borrowing measures should be indexed. And so on. Monetary correction began therefore to be examined more closely by economists in Britain, the USA, and other countries. Arguments for indexing were that, by adjusting prices, pay, etc. to rising prices, it would return attention from *money* values to *real* values, and that it would reduce the incentive to government to inflate because it reduced the revenue produced by incomes moving into higher tax-bands in inflation. Arguments against indexing were that it could stimulate inflation by inducing government to raise taxes in order to replace the lost revenue and by causing the public to spend faster because of the apparent acceptance by government that inflation could not be defeated but had to be "lived with." A more subtle objection was that it would remove the effect of inflation in fooling people that their higher *money* incomes were higher *real* incomes: by bringing the rate of inflation into the open, escalator clauses, it was argued, would make people reluctant to accept incomes lower in real terms than they believed them to be. Because of the resulting discontents, incomes would then have to be decided in an authoritarian fashion, of which statutory incomes policies enforced by law may prove to have been an early form. [8] [10]

Monetary Policy, control of the banking and monetary system by a government in the pursuit of stability in the value of the currency, to avoid an adverse balance of payments, to attain full employment or other objectives. The immediate objective is control over the supply of money and credit (or, as the Radcliffe Report said, "the state of liquidity of the whole economy"). It is aimed therefore at all of the financial institutions of a country, which may be regarded as forming a single large credit market.

Monetary policy may be applied through (*a*) the structure of interest rates, (*b*) control of international capital movements, (*c*) controls over the terms of hire-purchase credit, (*d*) general or selective controls over the lending activities of banks and other financial institutions (like building societies), over capital issues and so on.

There is much controversy over the efficacy of monetary policy as a means of economic control, and it is usually employed in conjunction with other measures (such as fiscal policy, direct controls, etc.), but in recent years the researches and arguments of the "monetarists" led by the University of Chicago have rehabilitated monetary policy, although more in the USA than in the UK. [10]

Money, any commodity widely accepted as a means of exchange and a measure of value, in payment for goods and services, or in discharge of debts or obligations. At an early stage in the development of society, when wants and resources were few, exchange was normally carried out by the direct barter of one commodity for another. The increasing complexity of wants and the growth of specialization made such a system inconvenient, since it required a "coincidence of wants" (i.e. if A wished to trade with B he had to have something which B wanted, and B had to have something which A wanted, in quantities and at the times that suited both) and because it provided no objective standard of measurement. Thus it was necessary to use an intermediate commodity, easily recognizable and generally accepted; and exchange thus became indirect.

Early forms of money ranged from sea shells to cattle and women, but they were frequently inconvenient and of unstable value. Accordingly coins were made of precious metals which, because they were scarce and could be graded easily and worked into decorative forms, were attractive as ornament and later as standards of value. For centuries it was thought that coins should have a high intrinsic value, but this is not a necessary attribute of money. It was a relatively simple step from precious metals to "promissory notes" and other pieces of paper as substitutes ("paper money"). Although without high intrinsic value, such notes act as money because they are widely accepted as a means of exchange.

Money acts as:

(1) A medium of exchange—fundamentally it must be accepted in exchange for goods and services, and give its owner the power to buy goods and services.

(2) A measure of value—it must be able to be used to compare the values of goods and services with one another by reference to the standard commodity, i.e. it must be able to serve as a unit of account.

(3) A standard of deferred payments—individuals who agree to receive payment at future dates must be assured that the value they will receive will not be less than at the time of the transaction. It is this quality of money which makes credit possible. The purchasing power of money is in practice rarely stable.

(4) A store of value—money must not deteriorate with time, and its holder should be able to retain it indefinitely for use for exchange.

The properties or qualities of money may be deduced from its functions: divisibility—money must be divisible into convenient units of account; indestructibility—it must not deteriorate with time or wear (few currencies meet this requirement); stability of value—its value should not fluctuate widely over time; homogeneity—all units must be of the same quality; recognizability—to discourage counterfeits; portability—it must have a high exchange value relative to its bulk (this attribute is less important the better developed the credit system). All these properties are implied in the central property of acceptability—it must be taken in exchange for goods and services.

Money may take the form of notes and coin of token or intrinsic value; but in the modern economy the total supply of money available exceeds the quantity of notes, etc., in circulation because of credit. Since credit is universally acceptable as a means of exchange and in settlement of debts, it too is money.

The value of money is measured in terms of what it will buy: if its value rises it will buy more; if its value falls it will buy less. Since the values of all commodities are expressed in prices, the value of money may be measured by the level of prices; if the level of prices rises, the value of money falls, if it falls, the value of money rises.

Movements in the general level of prices are indicated by index numbers—of retail prices, commodity prices, capital goods prices, etc. [8]

Money, Active. *See* DISHOARDING.

Money Illusion, the subconscious or unconscious treatment of money values as though they were real values. Habit, conservatism or lack of sophistication may explain why money is valued at its nominal or face value and not as power to pay for goods and services, i.e. the failure to allow for changes in prices. The euphoria created by rising *money* incomes may explain the buoyancy imparted by inflation, at least in its early phases. Keynes argued that workers would resent reductions in money wages more than in *real* wages. If the economy as a whole or a declining region required real wages to be reduced to make goods saleable or exports competitive, it would be better to raise money wages and prices even further, so that real wages were reduced, rather than cut money wages, which would create dissatisfaction. Possibly money incomes and values generally are symbols of personal standing, while prices are thought to be the result of outside forces beyond personal control: a fall in real pay is therefore easier to accept than a fall in money pay. The money illusion may also help to explain why savers continue to save for a money yield of 8 or 10 per cent when the rate of inflation is 12 or 15 per cent, so that the *real* yield in purchasing power is *minus* 4 or 5 per cent, i.e. the savers are receiving no yield and losing part of the real value of their savings. And the money illusion may also help to explain why interest rates lag behind prices so that borrowing is encouraged, spending stimulated and the inflation accelerates. When the money illusion is realized, a fall in saving may raise interest rates, raise capital costs, make industry unprofitable and precipitate the end of the inflation. [8]

Money, Inactive. *See* DISHOARDING.

Money Market, (*a*) in general terms a financial centre where foreign and inland bills of exchange, foreign currency, bullion and so on are bought and sold. (*b*) specifically in Britain the Short Money Market, the group of institutions dealing in short-term lending and borrowing. (Long-term lending and borrowing are arranged in the "capital market.") The money market is often referred to as Lombard Street because most of the institutions are in the neighbourhood of Lombard Street and the Bank of England.

The main institutions in the British money market are the joint-stock banks, the discount market, accepting houses, the bullion market and the foreign exchange market.

Money market assets are short-term assets (mainly Treasury bills and other bills of exchange) bought and sold in the money market. [8]

Money, Neutral. *See* VALUE.

Money Supply. *See* QUANTITY THEORY OF MONEY; MONEY; M.1; M.2; M.3.

Monopolies Commission, established under the Monopolies and Restrictive Practices (Inquiry and Control) Act of 1948 as a permanent body which could be requested by the Board of Trade to investigate monopolies and restrictive practices in industry and trade. Under the Act, the Board could refer a case to the Commission wherever at least one-third of the output was supplied or processed by one firm or group of related firms in the UK, or "a substantial part" of it, or by an association of firms whose conduct prevented or restricted competition. The Commission could be asked to produce either a wholly factual report or one which also commented on the implications for the public interest.

The Commission initially consisted of four to ten members, including the chairman. Although the first cases referred to the Commission were chosen specifically in order to cover a wide range of allegedly restrictive practices, in the hope that a series of precedents might be established, it soon became apparent that unless the Commission was strengthened it would take many years for a large number of cases to be completed, since only five reports had been published in the first few years. The maximum membership of the Commission was therefore increased to twenty-five by an Act of 1953 and the chairman was empowered to appoint groups of not less than five members to deal with individual cases.

Some of the Commission's early reports on individual industries had commented adversely on the effect on the public interest of collective agreements between firms which restricted competition, and in 1955 it produced a report on "Collective Discrimination" that dealt with restrictive agreements generally. As a result the Restrictive Trade Practices Act was passed in 1956 to provide judicial machinery for dealing with these agreements, which were therefore excluded from the scope of the Commission.

Under this Act the Commission was also reduced to its original size and the full Commission was again required to undertake all investigations. The powers of the Commission were extended to bring mergers under the Commission's scrutiny by the Monopolies and Mergers Act, 1965.

The Commission has never had powers to enforce its recommendations. The Board of Trade has been left to take whatever action it has considered desirable in the light of the Commission's reports. It has usually tried to persuade the firms or trade associations involved to desist from the objectionable practices. Following the Commission's early reports Orders were made prohibiting exclusive dealing or collective boycott arrangements in particular industries.

The Board of Trade publishes an annual report summarizing the work done by the Commission. [10]

Monopolistic Competition, one of a number of economic "models" of market forms used in economic analysis which range from pure competition through monopolistic competition and oligopoly to pure monopoly. Monopolistic competition assumes there are many sellers of products that, although close substitutes for one another, are not perfect substitutes because of product differentiation supported by branding, advertising, etc. Individual sellers thus have some degree of control over the price at which they sell, although where there is no collusion between sellers to restrict the entry of new competitors the degree of monopoly power so conferred is unlikely to be significant. [7]

Monopoly, the control by a single seller of a commodity or service. In the real world all commodities and services compete with others, so few sellers are "perfect" monopolists. In practice, therefore, monopoly refers to a seller of a commodity or service with no *near* substitutes. There is never (or rarely) either complete or negligible monopoly because almost every producer or seller has some *degree* of monopoly, but usually only a small one. There are few absolute monopolists but there is much monopolistic or "imperfect" competition.

Monopolies have several origins. First, the law. The Tudors and Stuarts gave monopolies partly to fill the royal purse. In recent times monopolies have been given to sound broadcasting, the railways and the coal-mines. But they are not absolute: private competition has been allowed to the first two (Independent Television, road transport), and nationalized coal faces competition from oil and atomic power. Patents and copyrights also grant a high degree of monopoly; the question for economists is whether the protection they give from competition is necessary to stimulate research and invention. Statutory Marketing Boards, for example, in hops, eggs and milk, established to promote "orderly marketing," also created monopoly. Import tariffs, quotas and other devices protect home producers from overseas competition and help them to build domestic monopolies. Some economists have argued therefore that "the tariff is the mother of the trust." Others have maintained that "the trust is the mother of the tariff," i.e. that highly organized industries have induced governments to shield them by tariffs: this has happened, but in a competitive free economy it cannot for long seriously frustrate consumers' preferences and in a politically free society it cannot for long seriously frustrate the electors' preferences.

The device of the joint-stock company can be used (as in holding companies) to control a large part of an industry. The law has permitted practices which have been used to restrict competition and build up monopolies.

Secondly, natural conditions can produce monopoly. The scarcity of diamonds, potash and nickel gives the firms mining and processing them a natural protection against competition. Industries requiring very large equipment have few firms or units, normally one in each different market. These are called "public utilities" (a misleading name if it suggests that other industries no less basic to human life, such as bread-making, are not public utilities)—water, gas, electricity, transport. If economies of scale are very large, the number of units in an industry is again likely to be small, as in steel, chemicals. Firms producing commodities that are perishable or bulky in relation to their selling price are "protected" from competition in local markets by high transport costs from distant producers, e.g. bread, beer, soft drinks, but modern transport and packaging have enabled large firms to penetrate into local markets.

Thirdly, firms can generate some degree of monopoly by using advertising, branding, packaging and other devices to persuade consumers that their product is different from others of the same kind.

When studying monopoly, or rather near-monopoly or imperfect competition, economists make the simplifying assumption that the monopolist or the producer in an imperfectly competitive market will produce such an output as will maximize his profits. Thus output, other things (e.g. costs) being equal, tends to be smaller than it would be in a more competitive market. The more imperfect markets are, therefore, the smaller the output. Critics of a competitive economy point out that it does not yield the best results in terms of economic welfare because it is *imperfectly* competitive. Some economists reply that an imperfectly competitive system falls short of an imagined ideal—a perfectly competitive economy—which is impossible to achieve in real life under any system. To judge an imperfectly competitive economy, it is necessary first to make allowance for the degree of imperfection that is created artificially by the state to isolate the form monopoly would take if only its *unavoidable* elements, i.e. due to large-scale production, consumers' preferences, etc., remained. This can then be compared with the practicable alternative under some other system (one in which property is not privately owned and in which production is conducted in response not to consumers' preferences in free markets but to orders from "planners" with authority to enforce their plans). The difficulty about such a comparison is that all kinds of other considerations must be taken into account—not least the political one that a "planned" economy cannot allow people as consumers freedom of choice of purchases and as workers freedom of occupation. A comparison in purely economic terms is incomplete.

Further, the simplifying assumption that near-monopolists in an imperfect market maximize their profits is not always true in practice. The larger the degree of monopoly, the higher the price has to be in order to maximize profits, but the high price may attract new competitors, so it may remain below the "optimum" level. To maximize profits, price (or quality) has to be adjusted whenever demand changes, better value having to be given when demand falls away and less when it increases. But constant adjustment in commodities or services may disturb production, so for sudden or frequent changes in demand the price may again remain below the "optimum" level. Near-monopolists are often sensitive to public opinion and publicity, particularly when there is a general sentiment against monopoly and in favour of competition, as in Great Britain since World War II, except for the merger movement of the 1960's which enlarged already large units. The consumer has also developed a new weapon—advisory services—which enable him to compare products with more knowledge and which make it more difficult to ask higher prices unless they are accompanied by better value.

Some economists argue that the extent of monopoly and the abuses of imperfect competition have been over-emphasized by the critics of a competitive economy who have taken too partial and too static a view: too partial because they have not allowed sufficiently for competition between the products of near-monopolists, and too static because they have looked at a "still" of the economy and not a moving picture in which monopolies are sooner or later broken up by new competition.

Monopoly power may be exercised by a single firm, by a group of firms, by a trade union or any other association of firms or people. (The test is whether, and how far, it can affect price by withholding supply.) There is a clear distinction between restrictive practices employed by a group to convert an otherwise competitive situation into a monopoly and an individual monopoly or near-monopoly situation arising from the economies of large-scale production, low costs and therefore low prices that no other producer can outbid. [7]

Monopoly, Bilateral, a market in which a single seller confronts a single buyer. This situation is rare within a single country but is not uncommon in trade between two countries, especially where all imports or exports are under a single control, as in a centrally-directed state, where trade may take the form of barter without the use of currency. (*See* Bilateralism.) [7]

Monopoly, Institutional. *See* Trade Mark.

Monopsony, "monopoly" buying by a sole buyer. Just as a firm may have monopoly power in the supply of a good or service, so there may be a firm on the buyers' side of the market—the only firm which is buying a factor of production. The textbooks generally analyse monopsony buying of factors, but it applies to any situation in which there is a monopoly element in buying, for example, consumers who banded together in a purchasing agency, a large store that is the only buyer of a product it sells under its name, a big factory in a small isolated locality that is the only buyer of some grades of labour.

Monopsony market conditions contrast with those under perfect competition. In conditions of perfect competition, no one firm is large enough for alteration in its output to affect the price of the product; and in the factor market no one firm buys a big enough proportion of the total services of a factor (say labour) for changes in its demand to affect its price (wage). In monopsony the firm's demand does affect the price at which it can buy its factor services. In the limiting case in which there is only one firm on the buying side, it has a unique position in the market. As it increases or decreases its demand for labour (or other factor), so wages (or other price) will rise or fall. Similarly a buying agency which bought a large share of the output of industry would face rising or falling price as its demand rose or fell. A firm employing all the labour of a kind in an area would find, if it wished to attract labour from elsewhere, that it had to pay a higher wage, and not only to the additional labour but also to all that which it was already employing. Thus the additional cost of employing a further unit of labour would have to include the increase due to the rise in the wage of all labour employed.

This analysis has interesting consequences for the determination of factor prices (*see* DISTRIBUTION). In perfect competition, where marginal revenue equals the price of the product, the wage is equal to the value of the marginal (physical) product. If there is monopsony in the factor market the reasoning discussed under Distribution is generally valid but the monopsonist will engage labour until the marginal revenue product is equal to the marginal wage, and this is the addition to the wage bill when the marginal unit of labour is engaged. The outcome will be influenced by whether the monopsonist is also a monopolist in the product market. [7]

"Monthly Digest of Statistics." *See* SOURCES, STATISTICAL.

"Moonlighting." *See* PAY-AS-YOU-EARN.

Moral Hazard, the proclivity of individuals to increase the likelihood or size of a risk against which they have insured. Moral hazard is intensified if the insurance returns the full value of a loss or claim. In health insurance people may take less care of their health (or call on the services of doctors unnecessarily) if they know the cost of restoring it (or paying the doctor) will be met wholly by the insurer. On these grounds some economists argue that they should pay part of the cost on each occasion—by co-insurance, in which they pay a *proportion* of the cost, or by a "deductible," in which they pay a pre-arranged sum on each occasion. In the latter there is a remaining moral hazard that they will seek unnecessarily expensive medical care, because the cost to them (the "deductible") is the same whether the total bill is small or large. In theft insurance moral hazard may induce carelessness in locking doors or windows or neglect in installing simple safety devices (locks, etc.) to reduce the risk of theft or the size of the loss if it occurs. [7]

Moralizing, inducing a sense of guilt by government exhortation or jawboning to induce industry (employers and employees) to make it act in a way that will make it easier to govern without passing unpopular laws. Examples are bank lending "restrictions," dividend "restraint," "voluntary" incomes policy, "fair" rents, etc. Over short periods moralizing may be expedient and effective in meeting a passing crisis: in the long run it tends to break down. [13]

Morphology, Economic. *See* ECONOMIC MORPHOLOGY.

Mortgage (derived from *mort*—dead and *gage*—a pledge), a charge which a borrower (the mortgagor) gives to a lender (the mortgagee) upon a part or the whole of his property. There are two kinds of mortgage: legal and equitable.

With a legal mortgage a lender has control of the property if the borrower fails to repay the loan made to him. With an equitable mortgage—requiring deposit of title-deeds with, generally, a memorandum of deposit—the lender will have to incur much trouble and expense before he can obtain the sanction of a court to dispose of the property unless certain specific conditions are incorporated in the memorandum.

In banking, if a banker takes a mortgage for a fixed amount it ends the relation of banker and customer and the banker's position is akin to that of an ordinary mortgagee. The advance is made on a separate loan account and not on a working account, and the only entries in the account are credits which reduce the loan. As each credit reduces the amount due under the mortgage, any fresh withdrawal is not covered by the mortgage. The form of mortgage often taken by bankers is to secure all moneys owing at a time with a covenant that it shall have the right to sell the property immediately on default, after demand, or in a stated period after demand. In such a mortgage the relation of banker and customer continues.

In the event of a mortgagor's bankruptcy, if the property is not sufficient to cover the debt, the mortgagee normally seeks a valuation of the security and claims upon the bankrupt's estate for the difference. [8]

Most-Favoured-Nation Clause, employed in international commercial agreements or treaties in which tariff privileges accorded by a country to any other are extended to all others with which it has treaties awarding most-favoured-nation (MFN) treatment. For example, a MFN clause in a treaty between countries A and B might state that B's goods entering A would not be subject to duty higher than that levied on similar goods from any other country, and vice versa. The two countries thus receive in principle an assurance of treatment in tariffs at least as good as that enjoyed by any other country and a safeguard against tariff discrimination.

Unconditional MFN clauses automatically extend the benefits of tariff concessions to all countries enjoying MFN status with the tariff-reducing country, whether the concessions are given freely or reciprocally, that is, in return for concessions. Conditional MFN clauses make extension of the privilege dependent upon the grant of similar concessions by the country benefiting from them.

Before 1914 the unconditional MFN clause in bilateral agreements was thought to be influential in promoting freer trade (although in practice the automatic extension of benefits was often nullified by administrative devices such as tariff descriptions designed to confine a concession to one country). Between the wars the power of the clause was weakened by the use of the conditional form and—more important—by the growth of quotas. There were also doubts about the efficiency of isolated bilateral negotiations based on the MFN principle. The unconditional clause could deter tariff reductions wherever a bilateral agreement to reduce tariffs might result in both parties giving other countries more benefits than they received themselves. After World War II the search for a way out of this difficulty, while preserving the benefits of the MFN clause, led to the General Agreement on Tariffs and Trade (GATT). This provided for the simultaneous bilateral tariff agreements between pairs of countries, the concessions being generalized by the use of the MFN clause and incorporated into a single multilateral agreement.

GATT excludes from MFN requirements countries that go even further in removing tariff barriers by arranging customs unions that abolish all tariffs, such as the EEC. [4]

Motivational Research. *See* MARKET RESEARCH.

Multi-national, adjective (mis)used as a noun for a company with producing facilities in two or more countries and an international outlook rather than a national outlook that divides activities into home and "foreign" (or "overseas"). By the 1970's many American and some British and European companies were multi-national in the first (but few in the second) sense. [4]

Multi-part Tariff. *See* TWO-PART TARIFF.

Multi-product Firm, economic jargon for a firm that makes more than one product. Most firms are multi-product. Economic text-books tend to begin with single-product firms in order to exclude complications like joint costs, which can be introduced when the basic analysis-factor combinations, or complementarity, technical co-efficients, equalization of marginal costs and marginal revenue, etc., have been mastered. Many texts however proceed little or no further, drawing conclusions from the analysis of single-product firms that have little relevance for a world of mainly multi-product business. [3]

Multilateral Long-term Contracts. *See* INTERNATIONAL COMMODITY AGREEMENTS; COMMODITY AGREEMENTS.

Multilateral Trade, trade between many countries. It is the means of extracting the maximum gains from international trade and division of labour. The contrast is with bilateral trade, in which one country makes an agreement to trade with one other. Bilateralism places limits upon consumers' freedom to buy goods in the cheapest market and prevents the realization of full international specialization with each country producing for export the products in which it has the largest comparative advantage.

Where trade is multilateral there is no need for a country to balance its payments to and from individual trading partners. It need only maintain balance of payments equilibrium between itself and the rest of the world as a whole.

If a country adopts bilateralism when the rest of the world is trading multilaterally, and there are no serious problems of unemployment at home, it cuts itself off from the advantages of free trade and lowers the standard of living of its inhabitants. But multilateral trading may be difficult to maintain if a major currency becomes scarce; e.g. the dollar was scarce after the war because the rest of the world was anxious to buy from the USA and ran into deficit with her. Some countries discriminated in their trade not only against the "hard currency" (dollar) area, but also against other countries that insisted on trade deficits being settled in gold or dollars. Further, at one point France tried to cut down her imports from Germany in order to keep her gold and dollars to pay for imports from the USA.

Bilateralism is a form of discrimination. It distorts trade patterns, so that goods are bought from high cost sources, reduces competition, so that inefficient firms persist in their inefficiency, introduces more uncertainty into foreign trade, and in the last resort may make matters worse by stimulating retaliation from the countries discriminated against.

Governments and international institutions such as GATT and the IMF have tried to restore free multilateral trade. They have been helped by the gradual disappearance of the "dollar problem," the successful reconstruction of Europe, the relative stability of the US economy, and increases in world liquidity through the media of the IMF, the EPU and the policies of the US Export-Import Bank. [4]

Multiplier, a theorem originated by R. F. Kahn and developed by Keynes to define the ultimate increase in national income resulting from an increase in expenditure. Thus, if an increase in investment expenditure of £100,000 causes an increase in national income of £500,000, the multiplier is five. Since the level of employment in an economy depends on the level of total expenditure, the multiplier has been used to measure the effect on employment of increases in components of the national income or expenditure. The multiplier is normally larger than one; its significance is that, in order to achieve a given increase in employment or income in a given period, the initial increase in expenditure (which may be by government on goods and services; by persons on consumption; by foreigners on exports; or by business men on capital goods), can be smaller than the desired final increase.

Table 7 shows how the multiplier works. Suppose national income is initially running at the rate of £100 million per period, generated by investment spending of £30 million and consumption of £70 million; the marginal propensity to consume (the proportion of the increase in income that is spent on consumption) is 0.8; and there is an increase in (say) investment of £1 million per period, commencing in period 1. In consequence national income in period 1 will rise by the same amount, and consumption remains constant. In period 2, 80 per cent (the marginal propensity to consume) of the initial increase in income is consumed, so that consumption increases by £800,000; national income therefore

Table 7. The Multiplier at Work

Time Period	Investment £	Consumption £	National Income £
0	30,000,000	70,000,000	100,000,000
1	31,000,000	70,000,000	101,000,000
2	31,000,000	70,800,000	101,800,000
3	31,000,000	71,440,000	102,440,000
x	31,000,000	74,000,000	105,000,000

increases by a further £800,000. In period 3, 80 per cent of the increase in national income in period 2 is passed on as consumption, and national income increases by a further £640,000.

This process continues, and in each period 80 per cent of the increase in income of the previous period is passed on by individuals who, we have assumed, spend £0.8 of any additional £1 of income. Eventually (year *x*, when all the effects are finally worked out), the increase in income will approximate to £5 million as a result of the initial increase in investment of £1 million.

Obviously the larger the fraction of each period's increase that is passed on in induced consumption expenditures, the larger the eventual rise in total expenditure.

The theorem has been applied to an increase in government as well as private expenditure, to investment, external trade, the problem of transferring capital or other non-trade items (like reparations), etc. It appeared to help explain the ultimate effects of an increase in expenditure or investment in an underemployed economy with "slack" to take up, and to do so better than earlier theories that depended, explicitly or implicitly, on the assumption of full (or "high") employment of labour and other resources. And it has been used as a central element in the development of macro-economics. In conditions of full (or "high") employment, it is thought by some economists less relevant or possibly misleading. For example, an increase in investment will then not necessarily expand (real) income but may merely raise prices (including interest rates). The change in real income depends on the resulting changes in expenditure and investment that are not predictable by the multiplier.

While useful in explaining processes, the multiplier is also thought of doubtful use in forecasting since its values in any one period may not necessarily throw much light on the relationship between an increase in spending and income in following periods. [9]

Multiplier, Export. *See* EXPORT MULTIPLIER.

Multiplier, Foreign Trade. *See* FOREIGN TRADE MULTIPLIER.

Mun, Thomas (1571–1641), English economist. Son of a London mercer. He became successful in that trade and obtained wide experience in Italy and the Levant. He became associated with the East India Company in 1615 and soon rose to be director, a position he held until his death. In 1622 he became a member of the Standing Commission on Trade. Mun's contribution to economics dates from 1621 with his *Discourse of Trade from England unto the East Indies.* In it he defended the East India Company from the attacks of the Mercantilists, who objected to the company's export of bullion as detrimental to British trade. Mun argued that as long as exports exceeded imports, the drain of bullion from a country had no significance. This idea was developed in *England's Treasure by Forraign Trade* which he wrote in 1630. Mun's importance lies in his explanation of the balance of trade and his early expression of commercial capitalist ideas. [2]

Mutatis mutandis, a Latin phrase sometimes employed in economics, meaning "the necessary changes being made." For example, "A labour-saving invention will reduce the relative share of labour. The same holds, *mutatis mutandis,* of a capital-saving invention." [14]

Mutual Company, one with no share capital or proprietary shareholders but with assets owned by suppliers, customers, etc. Examples in Britain are several life assurance offices (not called "companies") and savings banks. [8]

Mutual Fund, mainly US term for an investment company that is open-ended, i.e. open to receive additional funds and to invest them, or to sell and redeem them. [8]

Myrdal, Karl Gunnar (1898–1987), Swedish economist. He was educated at Stockholm University, where he was Professor of Political Economy and Financial Science from 1935 to 1950, and from 1960 Professor of International Economy. He was also in politics as Minister of Trade and Commerce from 1945 to 1947 and in international civil service as Executive Secretary of the UN Economic Commission for Europe (ECE) from 1947 to 1957.

Myrdal's name is associated with the theory of cumulative causation. He maintained that, particularly in countries where levels of economic development differ in different regions or where poor and backward countries have trading relationships with rich and advanced countries, the assumption of standard economic theory that equilibrating forces will cause the income levels of the poorer to rise is contrary to experience. Disequilibrating forces may become dominant, and he argued it was safer for developing nations to plan their growth independently, even if it meant relying mainly upon their own slender resources. He was deeply involved in the distribution of Marshall Aid in Europe during the period immediately after the war when the network of commercial information upon which the operation of a market economy depends had disintegrated.

Myrdal's most important publications from a long list are *An International Economy: Problems and Prospects* (1956); *Economic Theory and Under-developed Regions* (1957); *Challenge to Affluence* (1963) and *Asian Drama* (2 vols., 1968). His stimulating theoretical work has drawn criticism from Professor P. T. Bauer. [2]

N

Nation State, the economic unit that replaced manors and feudal baronies. As trade extended over larger areas, innovations and economies of scale made the nation state the more efficient organization for devising, enforcing and policing property rights. The innovations were in arms to keep the peace or enforce property rights (the longbow, pike, gunpowder, cannon, musket). Courts of law and other governmental services yielded economies of scale and grew more efficient as they became more specialized. Costs of longer-distance trade and finance were thus internalized.

The parallel is with the replacement of a large number of small competing firms by a smaller number of oligopolies. [13]

National Accounting. *See* SOCIAL ACCOUNTING.

National Board for Prices and Incomes (1965–71), short-lived British government creation designed to restrain increases in prices and incomes that would otherwise have accompanied the rising rate of inflation beginning in the mid-1960s (from 4.5 per cent in 1965 to 9.5 per cent in 1971). It was calculated that it may have restrained inflation by ½ per cent a year, though at the cost of other effects (encouraging means to avoid wage restraint by other forms of payment like artificial promotion or re-description of jobs, weakening trade union officials vis-à-vis shop stewards, etc.) and causing an "explosion" of wage demands when the machinery lost trade union and general public approval.

The economic problems associated with this and similar machinery are many. First, many firms are growing or declining, and if such price-regulation is to take into account the individual circumstances of each industry as a whole, restraint of wages and incomes will impede the growing firms and subsidize the declining ones. Second, profits fluctuate more widely than wages, and if they are prevented from rising the additional capital required for expansion may not be obtained. Third, wages and profits are *prices* that tend to equate supply and demand as well as forms of *income;* if they are prevented from equilibrating supply and demand, some other machinery for adjusting them to each other has to be created. Fourth, if controls over incomes and prices are to be made effective they require controls eventually over output, imports and exports in each industry and in other parts of the economy until it is largely or wholly controlled by government authority or collective bargaining between organized employers and employees. This fundamental reconstruction of the economy was not the initial purpose of an instrument designed to deal with a problem considered temporary, though it may be desirable on its own merits. The economist *qua* economist has no authority to judge; his authority is limited to showing the consequences, good or bad, of preventing the price mechanism from working. [10]

National Bureau of Economic Research, private American research organization in New York City, founded in 1920. It has published celebrated studies by distinguished economists (Simon Kuznets, Solomon Fabricant) and pioneered or developed estimates and indices later adopted by government departments. [14]

National Debt, the debt of the central government accumulated by borrowing, on which interest is paid. Over three-quarters of the UK National Debt has represented borrowing to finance government expenditure in the two world wars. There are no productive assets to show for this "deadweight" debt. Since World War II the Debt has been substantially increased by peacetime borrowing to pay for housing, schools and other forms of social investment, to provide loans for nationalized industries and new towns, and to build up the international reserves. This part of the Debt may be regarded as "productive."

The National Debt consists of (1) funded debt (Consols, War Loans, etc., which have no contractual repayment date) and (2) unfunded debt, which includes (*a*) floating debt—mainly short-term borrowing against Treasury bills; (*b*) other internal debt—"dated" securities, National Savings Certificates, Defence Bonds, Premium Bonds, etc.; (*c*) external debt—mainly the US and Canadian Loans raised after the last war. The funded debt, plus dated securities, contributes towards the increasing volume of "marketable" securities dealt in on the Stock Exchange. Most of the increase in the Debt since 1939 has been in short-term (floating) and medium-term debt, a result of the low interest rate policy pursued by the authorities during the war and until the mid-1950's. Subsequently, high interest rates associated with inflation have caused holdings of Consols and other "gilt-edged," fixed-income securities to lose much of their capital value.

The "liquid" portion of the National Debt is an important component of the financial structure of banking and financial institutions. The management of the "maturity" structure of the National Debt was regarded by the Radcliffe Committee on the Working of the Monetary System as an integral part of monetary policy in the UK. The interest and management charges are met from general taxation, and thus exert general effects on the economy even though much of the interest is paid back to the community. For example, efforts to keep down interest on government stocks may stimulate inflation. Since part of the Debt is held overseas, interest payments also affect the international balance of payments. Although the effects of the National Debt are thus widespread, its growth must be seen in relation to the parallel growth in national income. Since the 1960's this has fluctuated between 10 per cent below and 20 per cent above that of national income. [12]

National Economic Development Council ("Neddy"), created by the British Government in 1962 to "examine the economic performance of the nation with special reference to future plans in the private and public sectors of industry, consider the obstacles to faster growth, methods of improving efficiency in the use of resources and seek agreement on ways of improving performance, competitive power and efficiency."

The Council comprises independent economists, business men and trade union leaders, presided over by the Chancellor of the Exchequer and served by a staff of full-time and part-time economists. It considered its first task should be to study the implications for manpower and the balance of payments of a cross-section of private and public industry. These problems were reviewed in the report *Growth of the United Kingdom Economy to 1966* published in 1963. A further report discussed *Conditions Favourable to Faster Growth.*

The NEDC was widely welcomed by some politicians, business men and economists as a means of stimulating the British economy after several years in which the national output was more or less stationary. In so far as the NEDC encourages firms to prepare their production programmes more carefully and exchange information, as is thought to have been done by its opposite number in France, the Commissariat du Plan, and direct attention to the obstacles to growth, it was hoped that it would stimulate economic expansion. Some economists have doubts on the grounds that the stimuli to growth are most effective when they are direct, personal and immediate (profit and loss) rather than indirect, impersonal and remote (national production targets), that a council comprising business men and trade union leaders would not be able to advocate action on trade practices such as market sharing and demarcation rules, and that collaboration between firms is likely to result not only in exchange of information but in open or tacit agreements to refrain from competition.

By the mid-1970's "Neddy" was thought to be more useful as a neutral, "academic" meeting place for Ministers, leaders of industry and the trade unions than as a device for stimulating efficiency in the British economy. [10]

National Income, the sum of the values of all the goods and services earned (not *received*) in any period for consumption or for adding to wealth. It may be calculated as the sum of incomes or of expenditures, which must be equal to each other since all expenditure in a country must generate incomes in equal amount.

The national income is the total of incomes of all residents, companies and government bodies derived from current economic activity in the production of goods and services. Some incomes are received but not currently earned, e.g. old age pensions, national insurance benefits, family allowances, interest on the National Debt. They are called "transfer payments" or "transfer incomes" because the purchasing power they give the recipients has been obtained at the expense of other income-receivers who are taxed to provide them. Transfer payments are therefore excluded from the national income. All other incomes, such as wages, salaries, interest, profit, dividends, rents, the undistributed profits and surpluses of companies and public corporations, the incomes of government employees and the armed forces, are included. Some incomes arise from dividends and interest from investments abroad, and part of the incomes arising within the country is paid abroad as interest and dividends to nonresidents. To the incomes arising at home (the domestic national product) is added income received from abroad (e.g. dividends on investments), less income paid abroad (dividends on investments at home owned by people in other countries), to obtain the total national income.

National income is also the money value of expenditures on all goods and services which generate incomes within the country. This figure is not obtained by simply adding together expenditures on all goods and services. There are three reasons. First, some expenditures by businesses are on raw materials and components the cost of which will be reflected in the prices of the final goods or services sold. For example, paper used in a book may be bought and paid for by the printer, who passes on the cost to the publisher in his charge for printing, which is passed on by the publisher to the reader in the price for the book. To count the cost of the paper and the printing as well as the cost of the book which includes them would be double counting. Expenditure on "intermediate" goods and services must therefore be excluded and only expenditures on final products or services counted. There are exceptions to this rule: the government buys some goods and services to provide services to the public, e.g. legal and military, without direct charge. These expenditures must be included because there is no final sale price to register the costs. Again, expenditure on new capital assets, such as houses, factory buildings, machines, or on stocks and work in progress, must be counted, for they would not be reflected in the current cost of production or in the prices of their final products (and are therefore not "intermediate" expenditure).

Secondly, not all expenditures by residents create incomes at home. Some will be on goods and services from abroad and will create income overseas. Conversely, non-residents will make purchases in Britain which generate incomes here. Imports must therefore be deducted and exports added to the domestic expenditure figures.

Thirdly, some expenditure on goods or services is taxed or subsidized. Taxes must be subtracted and subsidies added since they have not produced new income and have been counted once.

The income and the expenditure approaches measure the gross national product—"gross" because they include depreciation—the amount of current income or output required to maintain intact the existing stock of capital. In the course of producing current output some capital is used up: machines wear out, stocks are run down, buildings fall into disrepair. If depreciation were not made good the ability to go on producing would be impaired, so some part of current income must be allotted to maintenance of the country's assets and is not part of current income available for consumption or adding to wealth.

The net national income of the United Kingdom in the early 1960's was approximately £23,000 million; in the mid-1970's it was around £75,000 million. But this more than trebling in *money* terms reflected the more than doubling in prices; the increase in *real* terms was barely 25 per cent.

Increases in the money value of individual incomes and the national income cannot therefore always be interpreted to mean that an individual or nation is better off. The increase may be due merely to rising prices, in which case a higher money income will buy the same amount of goods and services as the earlier and lower money income. In order to discount the effects of rising prices and inflation it is customary to think in terms of *real incomes* (or in the volume of goods and services that can be bought by a given income). A convenient approximation of real incomes (or income at *constant prices*) may be obtained by dividing income by an appropriate index of prices. [9]

"National Income and Expenditure." *See* SOURCES, STATISTICAL.

National Institute of Economic and Social Research (NIESR), founded in 1938 to increase knowledge of the social and economic conditions of contemporary society. It publishes studies of book length, pamphlets and in a quarterly *National Institute Economic Review* analyses the economic situations and makes short-term forecasts. It is financed by grants from foundations, governmental agencies and companies. It conducts research by its staff and in co-operation with the universities and other academic bodies. [14]

National Insurance. *See* SOCIAL INSURANCE.

National Plan (1965–6), short-lived device to stimulate the rate of economic growth. *See* ECONOMIC PLANNING. [10]

National Self-sufficiency. *See* ECONOMIC NATIONALISM.

Nationalism, Economic. *See* ECONOMIC NATIONALISM.

Nationalization embraces two distinct ideas in economics: government *own-*

ership and *control.* These two ideas have sometimes been confused because the term is used loosely to cover many variants of ownership and control. Thus before the Second World War minerals were often described as nationalized on the Continent when they were in practice conceded to and worked by private enterprise although owned by the state. Conversely, it has been made to cover management in the national interest of property still in private ownership, as in the governmental direction of several coalfields in France after the last war. Strictly, nationalization entails both ownership and control by the state. Even within these limits the term is vague, covering diverse schemes from the ownership and detailed control by the state through part ownership with independent management to ownership by the state and control by the workers.

The two principal arguments urged in favour of nationalization by some economists may be described as those of economic efficiency and social justice. The former is the case for state aid in development and superiority in management; the latter incorporates socialist ideas on the necessity or desirability of economic power to be in the hands of the community or its workers. Both arguments have been used in justification of particular cases of nationalization, but one has generally predominated and, although an over-simplification, it is useful to distinguish the two main types of nationalization as socialist and non-socialist. A wide variety of non-socialist motives for nationalization can be distinguished; nationalization may take place for fiscal reasons to raise revenue, for strategic reasons to conserve military security, for development reasons to foster progress, and for "social" reasons to stimulate economic activity in a depression. Since the end of the nineteenth century nationalization has consistently appeared in the programmes of socialist parties in many countries, although in practice there were considerable disputes about the speed and completeness of the change, and many socialists have feared that the system would become inefficient and discredit socialism in principle. A further difference between socialists has been whether or how far nationalization could or should use markets, which reflect the divergent producer and consumer interests in the conduct of industry and the opposing paternalist and "grass roots" conceptions of control.

Before 1939 the chief nationalized undertakings in Britain were the Port of London Authority (1908), the Central Electricity Board (1926) and the British Broadcasting Corporation (1927). In Great Britain the first majority Labour Government of 1945–50 put into practice the programme of nationalization of key industries. Between 1945 and 1948 the government nationalized the Bank of England, civil aviation, the coal industry, transport, electricity, gas, iron and steel and the raw cotton market, and other less important national undertakings were established. Acts to restore road transport and iron and steel to private ownership were passed under the Conservative Government in 1953. Alternation of Labour and Conservative governments has been accompanied by increasing and decreasing nationalization; it has been found easier to nationalize than to denationalize, and the general tendency has been for increasing nationalization of British industry.

A wide variety of methods has been devised for running state-owned enterprises, ranging from an autonomous body organized as a private undertaking at one extreme to a collective administration at the other. In Great Britain the system of the public corporation has been used for all the major nationalized undertakings; it is a hybrid designed to ensure the ultimate control of Parliament while retaining efficient business activity.

Independent of the origin of nationalization and its administration, the state is faced by a common problem: how to ensure efficiency and at the same time exercise adequate control. Where an enterprise is competitive, it must adopt the market yardstick of profits if it is to survive in a mixed capitalist economy. Where the enterprise is monopolistic, the necessity for regulation by such expedients as ministerial control, parliamentary inquiries and consumer councils, etc., frequently conflicts with the necessity for efficiency, and it is often difficult to reconcile these requirements. In Britain the most stubborn problems have been those of pricing—whether to sell at subsidized prices to keep the cost of living and industrial costs down, or to sell at "commercial" (market) prices to earn sufficient to replace capital and to discover uneconomic units. [10]

Natural Law, in classical economics the embodiment of the belief that the natural order of economic matters is inherently simple, harmonious and beneficent. A free market, relieved of all monopolistic restraint, was conceived in the long run to serve the interests of all alike and therefore the greatest good of the greatest number. By what Adam Smith called the "simple principle of natural liberty" the operations of the market were thought to produce prices as low as was consistent with maintaining the flow of goods and services and yet yielding enough return for the effort expended to ensure their continued production. [14]

Natural Monopolies. *See* PUBLIC UTILITIES.

Natural Rights, absolute, inalienable rights over property or services that cannot be removed or transferred by outside authority. From Quesnay (who argued that children and parents had natural rights to services from each other) and other eighteenth-century physiocrats to Herbert Spencer and other individualists (who argued for natural rights over property) many economic philosophers have argued in varying ways that some rights derive from the nature of man and not from law or government. Other schools of economists upholding private property have argued that it is held in trust by virtue of the state's power to protect and enforce property rights at law, and is justified only insofar as it is used to serve the public at large. [13]

Navigation Acts. *See* MERCANTILISM.

Near Money, or **Quasi-Money,** assets that are not liquid or readily liquefiable (like bank current accounts) but can be used indirectly to support payment for purchases or repayment of debt, e.g. bank current deposits, gilt-edged or blue-chip securities, bills of exchange. These assets are not full money because they are not used *directly* as means of exchange. The economic questions are at what point in its use "near" money becomes virtual money, and whether it should be regarded as part of the quantity of money. [8]

Negative Income Tax, American equivalent of Reverse Income Tax (RIT) used in Britain. [12]

Negotiable Instruments, documents in which the property passes by delivery and/or endorsement, e.g. bills of exchange, cheques and promissory notes. The holder is not prejudiced if the title of the transferor or any previous holder is defective: he can sue them in his own name. Cheques are often crossed "not negotiable" to protect the owner against loss by theft. [8]

Negotiation Costs. *See* INFORMATION COSTS.

Nemchinov, Vasily S. (1894–1964), Russian statistician and economist. In the 1920's he wrote studies on the economics of Russian peasant agriculture and then turned to more general theories and applications in economics and statistics. In the free academic environment after Stalin's death he developed the application of mathematics to economics by founding the Central Economic Mathematical Institute, and contributed to the evolving view that the simple planning of a primitive economy could not contend with the problems of the increasingly complex Soviet economy and should be replaced by more sophisticated techniques emerging from economic analysis.

Nemchinov came to prominence in the post-1962 debate on industrial efficiency by writings in *Literaturnaya Gazeta* and *Kommunist* shortly before he died. He argued that the distribution of materials had become over-centralized, economically inefficient and inflexible. Its method of indenting for supplies and distribution by a form of ration cards was inefficient: the ration cards were traded for the total amount of materials *assigned* rather than for the amount *required.* The result was simultaneously surpluses and shortages. Nemchinov's solution was a system of distribution based on economic accounting ("*khozvazchetnaya sistema planirovaniya*"). The central planners would draw up general plans but individual enterprises would not be bound by their assignment until they had accepted it, since they knew their resources and capacities better than did the central planners. The whole system would be more efficient because "whatever is useful and profitable for the national economy as a whole must also be profitable for the individual enterprise." Prices would then reflect the value of materials and labour and would ensure a minimum rate of profitability to the enterprise because they would no longer be divorced from the quantitative quotas or targets set by the central planners. The new prices would also measure the profitability of the resources allotted by the state. Here Nemchinov strongly supported Liberman and others who favoured making the enterprise pay for its capital. By his contribution to this debate Nemchinov played a leading part in evolving the new thinking on the use of pricing in the Russian economy and in the revival of Russian economic scholarship after its repression in the Stalin era. [2]

Neo-classical School. *See* Economic Thought.

Net Advantages, the monetary and non-monetary attractions of competing employments, which tend to offset each other. It explains the structure of relative wages, why some jobs carry higher pay than others. If all employees are of equal efficiency and can move freely from job to job, an individual will take the job in which he sees the largest advantages and least disadvantages, where the net advantages are highest. The advantages and disadvantages will tend to cancel one another out. Work in dangerous or unpleasant conditions will be compensated by high pay; an employee may be willing to accept low wages because of the prestige or prospects attached to his job, or the large amount of leisure it offers, or the opportunity of open-air work, and so on. Wages will therefore differ, but the *net* advantages will tend to be equal in different jobs.

In the real world there is not equal efficiency or free movement. Employees do not move freely from job to job because of ignorance of employment opportunities, disinclination to move, trade union restrictions on entry. And there are differences in training, education, aptitude, age and efficiency. All these causes create barriers between jobs, and further reduce mobility of labour, so that differences in net advantages can remain for long periods. The more information about jobs can be spread, and mobility eased by removal of obstacles and encouragement, the more equal net advantages would tend to become. Information and mobility are therefore equalizers in the labour market. [5]

Net Book Agreement, resale price maintenance in books. After being abandoned in 1852 it was revived in 1890. Alfred Marshall's *Principles of Economics* (perhaps surprisingly, since economists have generally condemned the practice as restrictive) was the first book to be sold under the Agreement with no discount to any retailer who sold it at less than the stated "net" price. The Restrictive Trade Practices Court has judged the Agreement to be in the public interest.

Under its present terms, UK publishers and booksellers have agreed that booksellers will not be supplied unless they agree to sell "net" books at the published price (or higher). One of the few rare exceptions (apart from educational books, which are classed as "non-net") was *Advertising in a Free Society* by R. Harris and A. Seldon which was published by the Institute of Economic Affairs in 1959 bearing a "maximum price."

Net Domestic Output. *See* OUTPUT.

Net Domestic Product. *See* INVESTMENT.

Net Margin, the difference between gross margin and the expenses incurred in earning it. For example, a retailer who sells a commodity for £1, 25 per cent of which is the gross margin (the difference between the retail and the wholesale price) and 20 per cent expenses, earns a net margin of 5 per cent. [13]

Net National Product. *See* GROSS NATIONAL PRODUCT.

Net Output. *See* OUTPUT.

Net Product. *See* OUTPUT.

Net Worth. *See* PROPERTY.

Neutral Money. *See* VALUE.

New Deal, the programme introduced in the USA in 1933 to meet the then economic crisis. The two main objectives were immediate relief for the millions of unemployed who could no longer be taken care of by private charity or state and local funds, and long-term plans for the recovery of business and agriculture. Various Acts were passed in 1933 to create jobs for the unemployed at Federal expense, and by the end of 1934 there had been a marked upturn in business activity, although economists differ about how far recovery would have followed in any event in the absence of the New Deal. The operation of the New Deal resulted in a vast increase in the American national debt, so that at the end of 1935–6 it was double that seven years earlier in 1928–9. Some economists regard the New Deal, with its emphasis on public expenditure to make up for inadequate private expenditure, as the earliest example of the action later advocated by Keynes. [10]

New Issue Market, broadly, the market in new long-term capital. The capital is raised by the financial intermediaries—merchant banks, issuing houses, finance companies and stockbrokers—for industry, commerce, public authorities and other institutions at home and abroad, by new issues of bonds, stocks, shares, etc., or other securities that are usually quoted and then dealt in on the Stock Exchanges. The borrowers' needs may be for new capital to finance business expansion or to convert private into public share capital. Issuing institutions use specialized knowledge to advise on, sponsor and underwrite the issues, thus minimizing the borrowers' risk of unsuccessful issues and smoothing the market.

New issues are made to the public either directly by the borrowing company ("public issue by prospectus") or by an "offer for sale" by an issuing house of shares already bought from a borrowing company. (Most of the former are handled by issuing houses.) Both require public advertisement of prospectuses and other information. In both an important function of the issuing house is to arrange to "underwrite," i.e. to guarantee in return for commission the purchase of shares remaining unsold. They may retain some underwriting themselves but usually "contract out" to sub-underwriters (mainly investment trusts and insurance companies). The cost to borrowers of these issues is apt to be high unless the issue is large and the borrower well known.

The cost of smaller issues and first issues by borrowers may be reduced by "private placings" with buyers of shares with or without the benefit of a Stock Exchange quotation. These arrangements minimize advertising and underwriting costs. The "marketability" of these shares (especially "unquoted" ones) is apt to be limited, so that they are likely to be attractive only to investors who intend to hold them for long periods, such as pension funds and insurance companies, and even then only if placed at a sufficiently low price. Established companies often cut the cost of raising new capital by offering "rights issues" of new shares for cash to existing shareholders in proportion to the shares they hold. The terms of rights issues are made sufficiently attractive to guarantee their success.

Until 1959 the extent, and timing, of new issues in the UK were controlled by the Treasury through the Capital Issues Committee. Treasury consent could still be required for market issues by local authorities and overseas companies. [8]

Nil Price, the absence of a consideration asked for a commodity or service. Nil prices operate in private gifts and some government services (education, medical care, etc.). Goods for which the costs of negotiating a price would exceed the price are also charged a nil price. Strictly private gifts may be made in the hope of a *quid pro quo* at a later time, and government services are mostly paid for indirectly by taxes, rates or social insurance contributions. [13]

Nirvana Approach, term used by American economist Reuben Kessel for the logical error, common in everyday economic debate, of comparing an imperfect economic policy in practice with a perfect policy in hypothesis to the detriment of the former, i.e. comparing a known practice with an unknown ideal. In a sense this error is unavoidable, for, when any new policy is proposed in order to cure the faults discovered in an existing economic technique, it cannot be anticipated what faults the alternative policy may in turn develop. But the term serves as a warning not to conclude that a new policy whose faults are not known is necessarily superior to a policy whose faults are known. [14]

No Par Value, no nominal value. Shares of no par value have been issued in the USA, Canada and Belgium for many years, but not in Britain. Gradually over recent years the drawbacks of a par value, that it is meaningless in a period of changing price levels and may bear no relation to the value of the capital employed, have become more obvious, and the Gedge Committee was appointed in 1952 to consider whether the Companies Act should be amended. The Committee recommended in a majority report that shares of no par value be allowed at a company's option, but the recommendation was not extended to preference shares.

No par value shares represent a fractional part of the equity or capital employed. Their use would make the issue of bonus shares unnecessary. [8]

Nominal Wages, money wages as distinct from "real" wages, the amount of goods and services that wages will buy. The distinction is important in periods of changing prices because nominal wages will diverge from real wages. [5]

Nominal Yield. *See* YIELD.

Non-competing Groups, collections of employees not directly competing with each other, who therefore form separate markets. An increase in the remuneration of, say, engineers would be expected to lead to an increase in the number of other workers being trained and offering themselves as engineers. But semi-skilled workers may lack the ability or education to compete with engineers. In time their sons may acquire these advantages. The significance of non-competing groups is that competition between groups of employees may take a long time to develop and an increase in remuneration can remain for many years before evoking an increase in supply. [5]

Non-linear Programming, a statistical device for helping to decide the optimum (most profitable) combination of products or factors of production. It is more common but more difficult to calculate than linear programming (from which it differs only in that one or more of its elements is not linear) and may be replaced by it on the ground that half (or seven-eighths) of a solution is better than none. *See* LINEAR PROGRAMMING. [14]

Non- (money-using) market Economics, the application of economic theory to human action outside the (money-using) market. From the late eighteenth to the mid-twentieth centuries economics was developed largely by analysing human behaviour in exchange and trade in a market setting, with the use of money in buying and selling, lending and borrowing, saving and investing. Economists have analysed non-market institutions such as the internal working of the firm (Coase in 1936), but especially since the 1950's economic theory has been applied more adventurously and confidently to behaviour in antagonism/adversary situations, crime, charity, education, fertility, labour "participation," leisure and its uses, marriage, politics, racial discrimination, revolution, statistical decision-making. Economic theory has been extended (mainly by American economists at the Universities of Virginia and Chicago) to approach a systematic, unified structure of analysis for all human behaviour and decision-making in the use of scarce resources: both outside as well as within markets, with or without the use of money, in giving as well as selling, motivated by self-interest or disinterest, in small internally non-competing groups as well as between competing groups.

Economic analysis thus seems to be developing as indicated by Ludwig von Mises in *Human Action* (1949). In all these activities or situations human beings have to make decisions on the use of scarce resources, yet economics has only recently been extended to analyse them, possibly because the tools of economic analysis were still being refined and developed and because economists were to a large degree pre-occupied with breakdowns in the economic machinery (fluctuations of booms and slumps, inflations and deflations). Some economists working on these activities or situations argue that they can be effectively analysed by the tools of modern economics. This would constitute decisive evidence of the universality of economic analysis. [13]

Non-price Competition, rival offers of differences in quality, quantity, range of choice, after-sales servicing, credit, etc. It develops when price competition is suppressed by law or by the emergence of large-scale economies which reduces the number of firms to a handful that find competition in quality, etc. less disruptive than competition in price. [7]

Non-rivalness, the capacity of a commodity or service to be consumed by additional consumers without loss to the original consumers. This is the property of a "public good" (or "social good") like defence or street lighting, or inoculation against disease, in which the number of people who benefit can be increased without the benefit being reduced to an individual consumer (or number of consumers). [13]

Non-sequitur, Latin for fallacy in reasoning, "it does not follow." One form, *post hoc ergo propter hoc* ("after this, therefore because of this") is frequent in everyday economic debate: it confuses *subsequent* (a relationship in *time,* in which B merely *follows* A) with *consequent* (a relationship in *logic,* in which B is the *result* of A). Thus, to say that an industry is more prosperous after a tariff on imports of its product is not to show that prosperity was caused by the tariff. The tariff might have induced slackness and inefficiency, and prosperity might have grown even more in due course if there had been no tariff. Hence the effects on the industry's prosperity with and without a tariff must be analysed before conclusions can be drawn. The confusion of time-sequence and logic-consequence provokes caution in using the historical method in the social sciences. Some historians have had a weak sense of what constitutes a proof of cause and effect and have seemed to argue that the economic developments recorded by history were the necessary, "inevitable" result of the developments they followed, without analysing other developments that were technically no less possible but were prevented by chance or other avoidable circumstance. [14]

Non-voting Share. *See* EQUITIES.

Normal Profit. *See* UNCERTAINTY.

Normative, the branch of economics that discusses what "should be" rather than what "is." It thus embodies the economist's personal opinion or value-judgements. Some economists believe that opinion should not be imported into economics, so that it should be *wertfrei.* In practice economists find this a counsel of perfection, but they have no authority *qua* economists for their value-judgements. [14]

Note, Promissory. *See* PROMISSORY NOTE.

Notional Income, imputed income, not received in money (or kind). An example is the "income" received by the owner-occupier of a house from himself as occupier. Although strictly a part of a person's real wealth, notional income is rarely assessed for income tax. In the British income tax code the value of an owner-occupier's beneficial interest in his property was an exception to this rule and was taxed (under Schedule A) until 1963. [12]

O

Obsolescence, economic as contrasted with technical deterioration. A building, a piece of machinery, a skill may be technically (physically) unimpaired but of falling *value* because the demand for it, or for the services it can offer, has diminished or ended. For the economist the significant criterion is economic, not technical. Economic obsolescence can overtake physical deterioration, which indicates that lack of foresight or uncertainty has caused natural or human resources to last too long and to outlive their useful life as judged by demand. (Depreciation of capital in accounts is faulty if designed to accumulate a fund to replace it when *physically* worn out, which may be before or after it is obsolescent.) Obsolescence can take place, wastefully, before physical exhaustion if demand is encouraged to turn to new products or services before the old are worn out. The waste in such "planned" obsolescence, stimulated by advertising, etc., is difficult to judge because it is not known when the current products (e.g. clothes, furniture, cars) would have been abandoned spontaneously in favour of new fashions, styles, models. [7]

Occupational Lease. *See* LEASEHOLD.

Offer for Sale. *See* NEW ISSUE MARKET.

Official Receiver, an official appointed by the Board of Trade to control the property of a person declared bankrupt before a trustee is appointed or to wind up a company in liquidation. [3]

Oligopoly, the market situation in which a product is supplied by a small number of firms whose activities and policies are determined by the expected reactions of one another. The essence of oligopoly is thus mutual interdependence between firms. For simplicity it is sometimes analysed as duopoly, the case of two suppliers. If there are two firms making the same (or a similar) product with a significant share of the market, each knows that a decision about its price or output will affect the other. It must therefore judge its policy by the other's likely reaction to it. Mutual interdependence emerges only with small numbers of firms. If the number were large, i.e. the market were highly competitive, each could suppose it had no influence on any other so that no reactions need be considered. At the other extreme a monopolist does not consider reactions since there are no other firms to react.

Oligopoly creates special problems of analysis. Since in oligopoly each firm acts by mutual reaction and interaction, there is uncertainty. The duopoly (or oligopoly) problem is like a game of cards, a diplomatic battle or a contest in strategy.

In perfect competition and monopoly it is possible to say from first principles what price and output will be. In oligopoly each firm can make more than one assumption about the behaviour of the others. Two cases may be considered with two firms A and B. The first is duopoly (or oligopoly) where the product is homogeneous: A and B produce *identical* goods. In the second there is product differentiation: A and B produce goods which are not identical *in the eyes of consumers.* In the first case consumers are as willing to buy from A as from B. Hence there can be only one price for the product; but it is difficult to know what it will be. The firms might, by collusion, or by chance, behave as if they were (jointly) monopolist. If they engage in a price war, each following the other in cutting price, the result will be closer to a perfectly competitive solution. The larger the number of firms, the less the likelihood of collusion and the more the situation will approach that of perfect competition. In the second case, where each firm has a more or less "separate" product, price cutting has not the same effect: each producer may be able to alter his price without (or with less) fear of reaction; but a price-war seems less likely since the effect of a cut, for example, is damped down because the products are not quite the same. A monopoly solution by merger or collusion is also less probable because each firm will want to continue independently to supply the customers who have become attached to it. In the real world the uncertainties of oligopoly probably encourage policies of seeking a quiet life rather than maximizing profit. [7]

Oligopsony, the market situation in which a product is bought by a small number of buyers whose activities are determined by the expected reactions of one another. It entails the alternatives of collusion (explicit or implicit) or price-bidding between them, as in oligopoly. Oligopsonists may be confronted by many competing or a few oligopolistic sellers. Examples of the former are the small number of large bakers and millers who buy wheat or rye grain from a large number of small farmers, or the relatively small number of county education authorities who buy books or stationery from a large number of publishers or suppliers. An example of the latter is the small number of international organizations that buy the services of international experts in law. [7]

Open Economy, one with no barriers to the entry of capital (long-term), money (short-term), entrepreneurial expertise, labour, goods, services, etc., or to international commercial relations between its nationals and those of other countries. No such economy exists at present, but the nearest approximation is Switzerland. [4]

Open-end Mortgage, a form of mortgage which permits the owner of the mortgaged property to secure additional advances from the lender up to but not exceeding repayment of the original mortgage: in other words, after he has repaid part of the original sum borrowed, a house owner, for example, could borrow a further sum to restore the debt outstanding to its original amount. This provides a convenient and relatively cheap way of borrowing to finance major structural replacements and improvements to property and permitting lenders to strengthen their investment portfolios. The practice is common in the USA, less so in Britain. [8]

Open Market Operations, the measures by which the central bank controls the monetary system by buying and selling securities (chiefly government bonds and Treasury bills) to joint-stock banks or the public.

In Britain open market operations in Treasury bills are conducted through a firm of discount brokers (the "Special Buyer") on instructions from the Bank of England; operations in the gilt-edged market are conducted by a firm of stockbrokers (the "Government Broker") on instructions from the Bank.

Such operations are one of the principal functions of the central bank and are undertaken to influence the level and the structure or pattern of interest rates in the financial markets. A corollary is that the supply of "liquid" assets (on which the level of bank deposit money rests) is affected by open market operations (unless the authorities take action to prevent it). Thus sales of gilt-edged bonds by the authorities will depress their prices (and raise the yields of bonds): it will also reduce the cash reserves of the joint-stock banks as cash is exchanged for bonds (payment is usually made by an individual drawing a cheque on his account at a joint-stock bank; when the cheque is settled, deposits in the joint-stock bank and the joint-stock banks' deposits at the central bank are reduced). Secondary effects result from the attempts of the joint-stock banks to restore the ratio of their assets held in liquid form, reduced by the outflow of cash: they may decrease advances to customers, or sell securities, so that the deposits held by the public will decrease and the ratio of liquid assets to deposits increase.

The Bank of England buys or sells gilt-edged securities almost every day in the money market with the general objective of making it work smoothly. Outside influences, such as the movement of "hot money" from or to other countries, may temporarily upset the market. The government itself in its day-to-day business also exerts a disturbing effect. For example, temporary gaps between government spending and current receipts from taxation may give rise to short-term borrowing, and conversely. Continuous "smoothing" purchases and sales are thus necessary to avoid erratic movements in interest rates. [8]

"Open Pricing." *See* Restrictive Practices.

Operational Economics, analyses and draws conclusions for policy that are administratively practicable and politically possible. Economists are broadly of two opinions. One is that to justify itself economic thinking must yield inferences or recommendations that are of practical use in the real world, i.e. economics must be "operational." A. C. Pigou said "it is the promise of fruit and not of light that chiefly merits our regard." The development of operational research has strengthened this view. The other view is that economists are not competent to judge administrative or political practicabilities, and that they should therefore not prejudge which parts of their theorizing will be found "operational" but should make all their thinking available to practical men. The debate was discussed by W. H. Hutt in *Politically Impossible . . . ?* (1971). His solution was that economists should show both the strictly logical conclusion arrived at from their analysis, whether currently considered "operational" or not, and a second-best conclusion with an explanation of the economic-analytical and political-feasibility difference between the two. [13]

Operational Research, the study of the effectiveness of human behaviour designed to make the best use of scarce resources to serve given ends. It combines observation, experiment, deduction and induction. The purpose is to help managers in industry or public services in making the decisions. Operational research developed rapidly in the armed forces during World War II when essentially economic problems were encountered in making the most effective use of relatively scarce manpower and equipment. It has been applied to industry, where it uses combinations of economists, accountants, mathematicians, psychologists, biologists, physicists and other scientists, with a marked emphasis on mathematics and mathematical models. It has been used, for example, to investigate markets and reach decisions about the marketing and advertising techniques most likely to be effective. It has developed (or applied) new statistical techniques refined with the aid of electronic computers: critical path analysis, discounted cash flow (a new name for an established practice), inventory control (ditto), linear programming, plant siting, transport planning, etc. [14]

Opportunity Cost, the sacrifice of the alternatives forgone in producing a commodity or service. For example, the "cost" of building fifty houses is the factory, or school, or ship, or shops, or offices that might have been built in their stead. This is essentially the law of cost outlined by Wieser. It is often a more illuminating way of conceiving of cost than any other.

In a perfectly ordered competitive economic society prices of goods and services would reflect opportunity costs since the owner of economic resources would not accept a lower reward in one use than he could obtain in others, and no employer of resources would pay more than the minimum necessary to attract resources from alternative uses. But in real life money prices of things may not always reflect opportunity costs because of uncertainty, imperfect knowledge, natural and contrived barriers to the movement of resources, discriminating taxes and subsidies and common or community ("social") costs arising from the actions of individuals. It is argued by many economists that economic policy should be based on full opportunity costs. For example, to answer the question, "Should good agricultural land be built over?" requires a comparison of the opportunity costs for society of the various alternatives. Hence the renewed interest in recent years in "social cost-benefit" analysis for transport, education, medical services, etc. [7]

Optimal, adjective used by economists to describe the best possible, in the sense of most preferred, situation, e.g. optimal apportionment of time, effort, capital or other scarce resources between alternative uses. [14]

Optimum, noun commonly used by economists to indicate the best possible result where decisions are made between alternatives. [14]

Optimum Quantity of Money, term coined and popularized by Milton Friedman for the quantity of money that facilitates the most economic growth with the least inflation. [8]

Option Dealing, a speculative operation on a stock exchange. A person who expects that the price of a security will rise may pay option money to a dealer for the right to buy it at a stated date in the future (a "call option"); or, if he expects the price to fall, he may secure an option to sell at a future date (a "put option"). This practice was prohibited in 1939 by the Council of the London Stock Exchange and restored in 1958. [8]

Opulence, classical term for the modern "affluence" popularized by J. K. Galbraith. Economists first learn the word from Adam Smith's "defence is of more importance than opulence." [14]

Ordinal Ranking, an ordering by *relative* values without regard to their *absolute* measurement. *See* CARDINAL. [14]

Ordinary Share, the entitlement to a part of a company that carries both (*a*) the risk of no yield and of a fall in capital value if earnings do not cover costs and the interest on loan capital, and (*b*) the prospect of profit (and a rise in capital value) if they do. Commonly described as the "equity." [3]

Organization for Economic Co-operation and Development (OECD), succeeded the Organization for European Economic Co-operation (OEEC) in 1961, with offices in Paris, to encourage national economic development and international trade among the OEEC countries and others who joined later. It has provided a permanent meeting-place for the advanced countries to discuss their economic situation and associated matters, such as assistance for developing countries. [4]

Organization for European Economic Co-operation (OEEC), established by the participating European countries to work with the US Economic Co-operation Administration (ECA) to implement the post-war Marshall Plan or European Recovery Programme (ERP). The plan evolved from the historic speech of US Secretary of State General George Marshall at Harvard, USA, in 1947. He proposed co-operation on European recovery between the USA and Europe to replace unilateral *ad hoc* aid by the USA. At that time it was clear that the war had had a far more disruptive effect on the economies and trade of many European countries than had been estimated earlier, and that without further assistance orderly recovery would be threatened by internal deflation or exchange restrictions that would cripple trade.

After the end of "Marshall Aid," OEEC continued as a co-ordinating body for economic co-operation in Europe. In 1961 it was replaced by the Organization for European Co-operation and Development. [4]

Ottawa Agreements, made at the 1932 Ottawa Imperial Economic Conference held to consider means of promoting closer economic integration within the British Commonwealth. The purpose was to increase trade between Commonwealth countries at the expense of other countries. The conference followed the adoption by the UK in 1931–2 first of selective duties and then of a general duty on all non-Commonwealth products other than foodstuffs and raw materials. The Ottawa Agreements gave UK exports of manufactured goods similar preferences in Commonwealth markets, mainly by raising Commonwealth duties on competing foreign goods.

Twelve bilateral agreements were made, seven between the UK and individual Dominion governments, five between the Dominions. In return for new or increased tariff preferences in Commonwealth markets, the UK undertook to (*a*) levy duties on non-Commonwealth goods—copper, linseed, wheat, fruit, butter and eggs, hitherto imported duty free; (*b*) increase the existing duties on a further large range of foreign goods—mainly foodstuffs; (*c*) continue the duty-free admission from the Commonwealth of all products dutiable under the Import Duties Act, 1932; (*d*) place imports of meat and later possibly dairy products from foreign sources under quota restriction; (*e*) maintain specified margins of Imperial Preference. The agreements between the Dominions similarly provided for the reciprocal exchange of increased preferences. [4]

Outlay, the way in which the recipients of income in a country as a whole or in a given sector dispose of their (pre-tax) income. It can be shown in an outlay table or account, usually called an "appropriation account" in the case of companies and public enterprises. Outlay or appropriation accounts may thus be drawn up for all the sectors of an economy, and in theory there is an appropriation account for each income-receiving individual. For example, each individual in the course of a year must dispose of his income in four main ways: he can spend part of it on goods and services for current consumption, he can pay part of it to the state as taxation, he can transfer part of it (e.g. in gifts to friends), and he can save the remainder of it, probably for future consumption. Thus there corresponds to the sum total of the incomes of all private individuals before tax (personal income before tax) a total for personal outlay comprising personal consumption, tax payments and saving, but not transfers because in the total account of all personal incomes and outlays transfers between persons would appear equally as payments and receipts and are thus cancelled out.

In the case of companies, the appropriation account shows the outlay as distributed to the shareholders, the debt-holders or, in the form of taxes, to the government. What remains, undistributed profit, is classed as company saving. Similarly an outlay or appropriation account may be constructed for public corporations, where outlay is upon interest payment and additions to interest reserves, taxes on income and additions to tax reserves, and undistributed income. Finally, an outlay account may be constructed for the combined public authorities (central and local government); here the bulk of the outlay consists of current expenditure either on goods and services or on transfer payments, the latter going chiefly to individuals as pensions, family allowances, etc.

For the UK, income and expenditure accounts are presented for all the domestic sectors (public authorities, corporate enterprises and persons) in the annual HMSO Blue Book, *National Income and Expenditure.* For corporate enterprises, specific appropriation accounts are compiled. For the public authority and personal sectors, figures for income and expenditure constitute an account of outlay when allowance is made for the difference between total current income or revenue and total current outgoings. [9]

Outlay Tax, levied on goods or services, "consumption taxes." Outlay taxes are not directly related to income but to consumers' demand for individual goods and services. Thus they include not only the traditional "indirect" taxes such as customs and excise duties and purchase tax, which are paid by producers at some stage of the production process, but also value-added tax (VAT) as well as taxes charged "directly" on consumers of the services of some capital goods, e.g. local rates on real property and motor vehicle licences. A disadvantage of selective outlay taxes is that they disturb production and consumption. On the other hand they probably affect incentive less than income taxation. [12]

Output, comprises all the goods and services resulting from the economic activity of an individual, a firm, an industry or a country. In accordance with statistical practice, they are measured at the points where they emerge from the production process. Problems of definition frequently arise; thus in personal services where the unit of output is not apparent the appropriate measure is usually determined by considering what the producer is under contract to provide, or what the purchaser actually obtains in a given period, say a year. There are also difficulties in estimating the contribution to total output of government services which are not bought or sold in a market but are generally provided free—so that it is not possible to use the criterion of market contract. In these cases the solution is to decide *ad hoc* on the measure most likely to reflect movements in the output of the service, e.g. the number of patients handled by hospitals, the number of children taught in schools, or the number of cases tried in courts of justice.

Output is normally understood to be gross output; but in the course of production the firm or country will have used goods and services produced by other firms or countries. The most useful definition of output therefore relates to gross output less the goods and services used in production; this amount is called net output. Thus machinery and equipment will probably have depreciated through use, and a deduction is therefore normally made from net output as allowance for wear and tear.

Net output has frequently been called gross product; in these terms gross product after provision for depreciation becomes net product. The total of the net outputs (or gross products) of all the units of production in an economy is the net domestic output, more commonly known as the gross domestic product. Statistics of the components of the gross domestic product are published in the UK annually in the HMSO publication *National Income and Expenditure.* The estimates of output are derived for the whole range of industry and trade, and are based on indices of output for the industries and trades. Their accuracy varies from industry to industry because in some the contribution to total output is much more easily identifiable and measurable than in others. [9]

Output Budgeting, the general description of methods devised, especially for private or governmental non-profit-making bureaus, to relate inputs to outputs in the effort to maximize efficiency in the absence of market or profit tests. The most common, devised in the USA and adopted in the UK in the late 1960's, was the Programme Planning Budgeting System (PPBS). It sub-divided total expenditures or main departments into sub-expenditures or sectional departments, evolved methods of measuring output and tried to devise the least expensive method of providing the services, especially in terms of the opportunity costs. It was thus, like internal or transfer pricing in a large private firm, an attempt to find a substitute for the market inside large organizations without internal (or external) pricing. It continued to be used in Britain when more refined techniques were being devised in the USA. [3] [10] [12]

Over-investment. *See* FORCED SAVING.

Over-population. *See* MALTHUS, T. R.

Over-production, a condition in which more is produced than can be sold at prices sellers will accept. The theory of over-production is a criticism of the classical economic doctrine that a capitalist economic system contains self-adjusting forces which preclude continuous general over-production. This was essentially Say's Law, which Keynes questioned. The essence of the over-production theory is that although production under the capitalist system tends to increase the potential output of a country, the more the production potential increases the larger become the frictions between labour and capital and between production and sale. Marx, and in recent years other economists, have argued that the continued rise in production leads to periodic excess of output, since the workers' demand is insufficient to absorb all the products. With the progress of machinery, periodic unemployment is created which still further reduces the workers' purchasing power; neither capital nor labour can be withdrawn easily from the industries in which they are employed, which are therefore faced with a declining demand for their products: fixed capital remains in declining industries, workers are obliged to accept low wages and production will continue in excess.

Various solutions have been suggested to solve the alleged chronic problem of over-production. Malthus, at the beginning of the nineteenth century, defended widespread "unproductive consumption" to ensure that excess production could be absorbed and the risk of unemployment minimized. There is still debate among economists whether Keynes successfully rebutted Say's Law.

"Over-production" theories are linked with theories of "under-consumption." [9]

Over-valued Currency, one whose exchange value in terms of other currencies is kept higher than it would be without government support. An equilibrium rate of exchange between two currencies is that which, taking good and bad years together, would secure a balance of international payments between the two without restrictions on the demand for foreign currency (protective tariffs, import restrictions, exchange control or deflationary measures to reduce domestic employment and output). Such policies can keep the exchange rate higher than the equilibrium level. A country may have an over-valued currency as deliberate policy, as a device to extract (at the expense of other countries) the maximum gain from trade, or inadvertently because of ignorance and uncertainty. For example, the exchange rate may have been fixed at what appeared to be an equilibrium level which was subsequently seen to be an over-valuation; or trading conditions and capital flows may have changed radically since the exchange rate was fixed, without clear indication whether the change was temporary or permanent. [4]

from employers anxious not to lose labour by dismissal during a (supposedly temporary) decline in sales, or in a general inflationary situation when rising demand is expected to take up slack, or from trade unions anxious to prevent loss of employment following merchanization. In the early 1970's overmanning was generally thought to exist in the printing, dock, shipbuilding and other industries. [5]

Overseas Aid. *See* AID, OVERSEAS.

Overseas Investment. *See* INVESTMENT.

Overtrading, the condition in which a firm's production of goods exceeds its means of financing it ("working capital"). It must then borrow either from its suppliers ("trade credit") or the banks, possibly at rates of interest that make the business less profitable than expected, or unprofitable; or if it cannot borrow it may have to cease trading. [3]

Oxford Economic Papers. *See* JOURNALS, ECONOMIC.

P

Paasche. *See* INDEX NUMBER.

Package Mortgage, one which provides finance for equipment under the mortgage set up to finance house purchase. The equipment to be financed is itemized in the mortgage agreement and usually covers most household equipment other than readily movable items. The package mortgage is an aid to housing sales and can often reduce a homeowner's costs. The practice is widespread in the USA; less so in Britain. [8]

Paish, Frank W. (1898–1988), British economist. He was educated at Winchester and Trinity College, Cambridge, and went to work for the Standard Bank in South Africa in 1921. In 1932 he returned to England to teach at the London School of Economics, where he was Reader in 1938 and Professor of Economics with special reference to Business Finance from 1949 to 1965. During the war he was Deputy Director of Programmes at the Ministry of Aircraft Production.

Although Paish was closer to problems of public policy and financial organization than to the development of pure economic analysis, he added appreciably to the armoury of the economist by his emphasis on, and the use in his writing of, such concepts as the marginal propensity to import. He produced a long, steady and consistent stream of comment and criticism on the restraint and control of inflation, the effects (particularly upon incentive) of some types of taxation, and on monetary policy. He attached much importance to a clear distinction between income circulation and capital circulation when discussing the flow of money, maintaining that economists were still far from possessing satisfactory estimates of money holdings and money flows in a shape required for the formulation of effective monetary policy.

Apart from *Insurance Funds and their Investment* (1934), written with an LSE colleague (George Schwartz, later renowned for his incisive, witty newspaper column), Paish's main written works were *The Post-War Financial Problem and Other Essays* (1950), *Business Finance* (1953), *Studies in an Inflationary Economy* (1962), and *How the Economy Works and Other Essays* (1970).

In two Hobart Papers Paish maintained a close analysis from 1964 to 1971, when his influence was at its height, of the rise and fall of income policy. He argued that a margin of unused productive resources, labour as well as plant and equipment, would have to be maintained if inflation was not to accelerate. For long he contended, from close analysis of the evidence on earnings, productivity, unused productive potential, etc., that inflation was "demand-pull" but that near the end of 1969 it changed to "cost-push." Policy should therefore be changed from indirect monetary and fiscal controls to the second-best direct action of incomes policy to ensure that income did not rise faster than output. He argued that direct restraint was ineffective when incomes rose because of excessive demand for labour ("demand-pull" inflation) but might work when its purpose would be to restrain the use of monopoly power by labour unions ("cost-push"). [2]

Palgrave, Sir Robert (1827–1919), English economist, of Jewish origin. He was editor of *The Economist* from 1877 to 1883. Knighted in 1909. His best-known work is the *Dictionary of Political Economy,* which he edited from 1894 to 1906. [2]

Paper Money, bank-notes readily accepted in the settlement of debts. Its issue is controlled by law. Paper money may be either convertible or inconvertible. Convertible paper money is convertible into a precious metal (coin or bullion) of defined value on demand. In Britain paper money has not been convertible by residents into gold, and exchange controls have regulated its exchange for other paper currencies (dollars, Deutschmarks, Swiss francs, etc.) that have been convertible into gold. Some paper money is convertible into other notes (e.g. Scottish bank-notes). Whether people accept paper money depends on public confidence; making it legal tender by law is not enough. [8]

Paper Value, nominal or money value, in contrast to real value in purchasing power over goods and services. The value of a house, a painting, a share, etc. may rise "on paper" in money terms, but its real value will not have changed if inflation has raised other prices proportionately. Hence "paper gains," "paper profit," etc. [8]

Par Value, the nominal value of shares or investments. If an investment is made in a building society or a savings bank, the par value indicates the sum that would remain invested and could be recovered, say £100. Similarly with debentures. But if a person buys 100 £1 ordinary shares in a company he may pay £3 per share: the par value of £1 has no significant meaning: it is only of historic interest. The par value of ordinary shares bears no relationship to their market value because the capital employed in a business is invariably different from its nominal capital. The preference shareholder occupies a position between the debenture holder and the ordinary shareholder; the par value of a preference share is significant because the interest is based on it. [8]

Paradigm, currently fashionable alternative word for example or pattern. The adjective is paradigmatic. [14]

Paradox of Value. *See* VALUE.

Parallel Pricing, the tendency in oligopoly for firms to follow closely behind a price leader, so that all prices seem to move in parallel, as in bread, electric lamps, petrol and tyres in Britain. Strictly the term is inapt, since it implies instantaneous movement; a better term would be price *leadership,* which implies that the leader is followed by the others after a time-lag, however short. A report of the Monopolies Commission in 1973 found that parallel pricing was inevitable in oligopoly, that it was a restrictive practice that could be undesirable, and that the best remedy was government control over prices. Other economists argued that the harmful effects arose not from parallel pricing as such but from the market dominance of the price leader, and that the more fundamental remedy was to undermine its dominance by removing the barriers to competition from new firms. This solution could work where oligopoly arose from law-created causes such as tariffs or patent laws, but might be more difficult where it arose from economies of large-scale production. [3]

Parameter, in economic theory a constant, in contrast to a variable; more generally the fixed or known limits within which a variable is likely to vary. [14]

Pareto, Vilfredo (1843–1923), Italian economist. After twenty years as an engineer, following an intensive training in mathematics and the physical sciences, he became interested in the economic aspects of contemporary political problems. At an early stage in his studies he worked on the application of mathematics to economics. This interest led to his succeeding Léon Walras to the Chair of Economics at the University of Lausanne, where his work continued the general equilibrium method and mathematical tradition of the "Lausanne School." His *Cours d'économie politique* (1896–7) emphasized the concept of general equilibrium; but his main contribution to economic thought was his *Manuale di Economia Politica* (1906), in which his argument that utility was not measurable led him to elaborate the concept of the indifference curve. [2]

Pareto Optimum, the situation in which no individual can move to a more preferred position except by causing another to move to a less preferred position. If one can be made better off without making another worse off by changing the use of resources, the situation is not (yet) Pareto-optimal. The term thus describes the ideal use of resources, and has become the central criterion of efficiency and wealth maximization in welfare economics, which analyses the conditions required for the optimum use of resources. [14]

Pari Passu, Latin term commonly used by economists to indicate a parallel movement in two (or more) variables, e.g. the values of two or more currencies which are linked to gold will move pari passu. [14]

"Paris Club," colloquial name for the IMF Group of Ten. [4]

Parity, term used in economics to indicate equal treatment or parallel movement, as in purchasing power parity theory. [14]

Partial Analysis. *See* PARTICULAR EQUILIBRIUM ANALYSIS.

Partial Correlation, statistical term applied in economic analysis to a limited relationship between two elements. If one is correlated with a second which is also correlated with (affected by movements in) a third, the first and the second are partly (and not exclusively) correlated. [14]

Partial Equilibrium. *See* EQUILIBRIUM.

Participating (Preference) Shares. *See* PREFERENCE SHARES.

Participation Mortgage, one in which two or more (lenders) own shares, not jointly but co-ordinately. The mortgage is often made to a trustee who issues certificates of ownership to each person with an interest in it and shares out payments of interest and principal *pro rata.* [8]

Particular Equilibrium Analysis, sometimes called partial analysis, a method of analysing the interdependence of economic phenomena in a relatively small sector of the economy, everything outside it being assumed unchanged. *General* equilibrium analysis is designed to show the economic system *as a whole* in a complex pattern of inter-relationships.

Particular equilibrium analysis is concerned essentially with the determination of equilibrium in given conditions. It tries to discover the immediate relationships which determine the prices and quantities of goods supplied and demanded. Very few economic phenomena can be explained in a completely scientific manner or can be forecast accurately. The economist, therefore, finds it useful to assume that, at any one moment of time, certain fundamental economic forces do not change. For example, in analysing the demand for a commodity, consumers' preferences, income, the prices of all other goods and other conditions of demand are assumed constant. Only the price of the commodity is assumed to vary. The effects on the quantity demanded and upon the other elements are then traced step by step. In particular equilibrium analysis the economist cannot and does not attempt to explain the "dynamic" or "historical" elements in the problem over a long period. [14]

Partnership, a form of entrepreneurial organization. The law recognizes a partnership if the parties intend to carry on business in common with a view to profit, whether there is a written agreement or not. In Britain the law is set out in the Partnership Act, 1890. If no agreement is made to the contrary, profits must be shared equally, but it is usual to have an agreement dealing with profits, salaries, drawings, goodwill and any other important matters.

The liability of partners is not limited; a partner is liable to an unlimited extent not only for his own share of the debts of the firm but also for the shares of his partner or partners in so far as they are unable to pay their debts. A partner is also liable for all acts of a co-partner within the scope of the business.

The growth of the private limited liability company has reduced the number of partnerships, except in the professions such as medicine, law, accountancy, retailing, estate management, where the firm or partnership is still the recognized common form of business organization. [3]

Passive Balance of Trade. *See* BALANCE OF TRADE.

Patents, (*a*) originally the exclusive right, granted to individuals by Elizabeth I, James I and other sovereigns, to produce, import or deal in a commodity; made illegal by the Statute of Monopolies, 1624, but continued by the Stuart kings until the Bill of Rights, 1689, transferred the power to Parliament. (*b*) in modern times, legal rights to the exclusive use of inventions for a period, normally up to sixteen years. Patents may affect the amount, direction and disclosure of invention, but it is difficult to know to what extent. When an invention requires a large amount of capital for development and for production, a patent monopoly may increase the likelihood of an invention being used by reducing the risks of investment. On the other hand, when the capital required is modest and the invention would be used in any case, it is likely to be exploited on a smaller scale under a patent monopoly than in competitive conditions. The new historical interpretation, which sees the contrasting development in the advanced and the developing countries in terms of the former's earlier refinement of property rights, is also relevant; such an interpretation emphasizes the use of patents in encouraging new processes and inventions. The central economic issue is how to achieve the optimum duration of patent protection so that it encourages innovation without discouraging competition from still newer (but excluded) techniques. [7]

Patinkin, Don (1922–97), Israeli economist born in Chicago. He was educated at the University of Chicago and taught there and at the University of Illinois. In 1949 he went to lecture at the Eliezer Kaplan School of Economics and Social Sciences, Hebrew University of Jerusalem, where he was appointed Professor from 1956. In 1969 he became Director of Research at the Maurice Falk Institute for Economic Research in Israel.

As a specialist in monetary economics, Patinkin made a major contribution to the debate on Keynesian economics in his extension of the Walrasian general-equilibrium apparatus (as re-defined by Hicks) to a monetary economy, thus overturning the Keynesians' view that "money does not matter." This integration of monetary and value theory (in *Money, Interest and Prices,* 1956) treats money as parallel to any other good that is the object of utility-maximizing choice, attributing "utility" to the services provided by real money balances.

Patinkin is one of the most thorough-going critics of Keynes's theory of employment, which he contests as internally inconsistent and superfluous in practice. The first criticism centres upon the absence of a supply function in the equations of Keynes's *General Theory* and upon the definition of "involuntary unemployment." Some economists have difficulty in following Keynes's reasoning because of the ambiguity of a supply function which represents the determination to supply preconceived quantities of output irrespective of demand conditions, except in the very shortest of periods. Other economists who have also questioned the manner in which Keynes defined "involuntary unemployment" nevertheless consider the concept valid in practice. The second criticism depends not on logic but on observation; the question is whether the equilibrating forces invoked by Walras have been dominant during the last century.

After his emigration to Israel, Patinkin specialized in the monetary aspects of the Israeli economy and wrote *The Israeli Economy: the First Decade.* [2]

"Pay-As-You-Earn" (PAYE), the system of collecting income tax from employees, recommended by Keynes, introduced in 1944 and substantially unchanged. Until the outbreak of the Second World War employees paid income tax direct to the tax collector at half-yearly intervals, but the war-time increase in tax rates and in the numbers of taxpayers made it desirable to introduce a system under which tax would be automatically deducted by employers from current earnings. The PAYE system is cumulative, so that the total tax deducted up to a given date in the tax year keeps pace with total pay received. Before the beginning of the tax year each employee is given a code number which depends on the personal allowances due to him and on some income apart from regular earnings. By using this number in conjunction with tax tables issued to him, the employer can calculate at the end of each pay period the employee's taxable pay and tax due at a given date. If the employee's earnings have declined, so that the tax he has already paid exceeds the amount due, he is given a refund.

There has been discussion among economists about the effects on effort and incentives of emphasizing the income tax by deducting it from each week's or month's pay. Some believe it is one reason for "moonlighting," i.e. doubling up a second job in the evenings or at week-ends which is paid in cash and thus escapes the PAYE tax net. The Royal Commission on the Taxation of Profits and Income (1955) attributed the disincentive effects of income tax to high rates of tax rather than to the PAYE system of collection, but its judgement on the disincentive effects of taxation was not accepted universally. Since under PAYE government tax receipts vary closely with income and employment (and government expenditures do not), the system probably helps to stabilize the level of total demand in the economy because the government tends to "run" a budget deficit in times of declining general demand and a surplus in times of booming demand. [12]

Payments, Balance of. *See* BALANCE OF PAYMENTS.

Peace, Industrial. *See* INDUSTRIAL PEACE.

Pegged Rates of Exchange. *See* CURRENCY.

Pension, term used generally to indicate the form in which income is received in retirement. Individuals accumulate a pension by saving. Pensions can be one of the "net advantages" of competing employments: remuneration in pensioned employment tends to be lower than in comparable non-pensioned employment. In many countries the state has also required citizens to contribute to state pensions.

In Britain occupational pension schemes have grown rapidly since the end of World War II. They began in the Civil Service in 1834, and have spread to private employment, where they replaced *ex gratia* payments given at the discretion of the employer to retired employees. Occupational pensions have become a form of deferred pay. Occupational pension schemes are usually funded, that is, contributions from the employer and/or employee are paid into a fund which is invested to yield the eventual pensions. Funded schemes first spread in the 1920's; they began with salaried employees and have been extended to wage-paid employees. By the mid-1970's around twelve million employees were covered by occupational pension schemes, four million in the public service and nationalized undertakings, nearly seven million in private industry. There were four main causes at work: (1) high taxation of profits has increased the value of the tax concession on employers' contributions; (2) an employee with a right to a pension can be retired with less ill-feeling and hardship than one without; (3) when the competition for labour after the war became intense because of full employment, pensions were used to attract and keep employees and competition induced more employers to offer pensions; (4) as incomes rose and became less unequal, wage-paid employees regarded a pension as one of the "fringe benefits" of employment.

A defect of occupational pensions is that they may be lost when an employee changes jobs and they therefore reduce the mobility of labour. This applies to both private and public employment; in the Civil Service and local authorities pensions are preserved when employees change jobs within public employment but not necessarily if they move to private employment. By the mid-1970's the general intention of all government was to encourage preservation of pension rights or to require it by law.

The ultimate incidence of the cost of occupational pensions is not the same as the immediate impact which falls on employers and/or employees. Employers may be able to pass on the cost to the consumer in higher prices (or lower quality or a narrower range) or avoid an increase in total labour costs by reducing other employee benefits. In a competitive market for labour it does not much matter whether employees pay into "contributory" schemes or not ("non-contributory") because if the impact of the whole of the cost of pensions is initially on the employer, there are likely to be offsetting adjustments, perhaps in pay or welfare benefits. On the other hand employees who contribute to a pension scheme may value it more and be prepared to contribute more to it voluntarily.

Occupational pension schemes may be either insured with a life assurance company or self-administered by the employer, who undertakes the risks that pension claims will be higher than anticipated and who invests the fund himself (usually through a pensions committee on which the employees are represented).

People accumulate income for retirement also through personal pensions and by saving in various ways, in savings banks, in ordinary shares, in buying a house, etc., which can be changed into a regular form of income.

Private occupational pension schemes have the advantage that they can be arranged to suit the needs of individual employers and to some extent of employees. The advantages of state pension schemes are that their administrative costs can be lower, they create no barriers to mobility of labour, and they can be used as a form of taxation to redistribute income from the younger to the older people.

The growth of occupational pension schemes has probably been both encouraged and retarded by the development of compulsory state schemes. State pensions have helped to familiarize employees with the advantage of a regular income in retirement; on the other hand, they have required increasing amounts in contributions from employers and employees and have so reduced the financial ability and the wish to accumulate pensions privately.

As occupational pension schemes become more general, and pension rights become more widely transferable when people change employment, the power of pensions to attract and hold employees weakens and they may be supplemented by other forms of employee welfare or fringe benefits.

Most western countries have state pension schemes, which differ in the ages of retirement (of men and women) at which the pension is paid, the proportion of employers' and employees' contribution to employees' earnings, the amount of the pension, the extent to which it is subsidized from general taxation, the extent to which retirement (full or partial) is required to qualify for the pension, and in being paid irrespective of income or subject to a means test. But within each country much the same conditions apply to all individuals. Broadly, the more modest the state pension the larger the development of occupational pensions schemes, and vice versa. [5]

Per Capita, "per head." Economic quantities can be expressed as averages per person, e.g. income, expenditure. [14]

Percentage Lease. *See* LEASEHOLD.

Perfect Competition, an analytical "model" of the pure form that a market would take if (*a*) there were many sellers of absolutely identical products in relation to their total sales so that none could influence market price by varying the quantity he was prepared to market; (*b*) buyers and sellers were aware with complete certainty of prices and opportunities available everywhere in this and other markets; (*c*) significant economies of scale were absent so that no one seller could grow to dominate or influence the market (i.e. producers would remain relatively small-scale), and (*d*) there were no barriers of any kind to the movement of factors of production or of *entrepreneurs* from or to the rest of the economy. Under these circumstances competition among producers would in the long run ensure that every producer was operating with the most efficient size of plant and equipment, producing the most efficient (i.e. lowest cost) output, and was earning only the minimum amount of profit necessary to maintain the minimum necessary number of producers in the industry. Apart from wider considerations (e.g. of dynamic growth, of inter-relationships between industries) the model of perfect competition yields an "ideal" output in the sense that the price consumers would have to pay to obtain additional supplies of a commodity produced under these conditions would, in both the short run and the long run, be just sufficient to bid the necessary productive resources away from alternative uses. If production were everywhere organized in this ideal manner the price system would thus secure an optimum distribution of economic resources to reflect consumers' preferences in the most efficient way. The model thus provides a norm or yard-stick of economic efficiency in the allocation of resources. [7]

Permanent Consumption Hypothesis. *See* PERMANENT INCOME.

Permanent Income, a notion introduced by Friedman in the analysis of the relationship between consumption and income. Permanent income is the income *expected* in the *long* run; and it is permanent rather than current income to which general consumption behaviour relatively to saving is adapted. It is contrasted with short-period ("temporary") income. When permanent income exceeds short-period income the difference is saved (and dissaved if vice versa). Thus in the short run saving rises as a proportion of income but in the long run tends to be stable. [9]

Perpetuity, an annuity whose payments continue indefinitely, for example the rent from leased freehold premises, or the annual amount payable on an irredeemable Government Bond. Because the payments continue indefinitely, the *compound amount* of a perpetuity is meaningless. The *Present Value* of a perpetuity is given by the expression $V = A/i$, where V is the present value, A is the perpetuity payment and i is the rate of interest at which V can be invested. [8]

Personal Investment. *See* INVESTMENT.

Personal Loan. *See* ADVANCE.

Petty, Sir William (1623–87), an English statistician and economist who linked these two subjects and so became a pioneer in both. He has been called "the founder of political economy" and also a pioneer of comparative statistics. His best work was *Political Arithmetik,* probably written in 1672 but not published until 1691 because it contained opinions thought likely to offend France. Petty outlined his approach in this way: "Instead of using only comparative and superlative Words, and intellectual Arguments, I express myself in terms of Number, Weight or Measure; use only Arguments of Sense, and consider only such Causes as have visible foundations in Nature." Petty's outstanding contributions to economic methodology were contained in this book and in surveys of Ireland which he conducted when he was a commissioner of land distribution there under Cromwell. *The Political Anatomy of Ireland* was published in 1672. In it, and in the *Treatise on Taxes and Contribution* (1662) and *The Quantulamcunque, A Tract Concerning Money* (1682), he made interesting contributions to the theory of value, fiscal policy and the theory of foreign exchange. His importance in the history of economic thought is that he was among the first to break away from the earlier realist tradition and prepared the way to classical economics.

Petty drew attention to the tendency of the structure of employment to shift in the direction of services with economic development: this process has been called "Petty's Law." He was a friend of Samuel Pepys and one of the founder members of the Royal Society. [2]

Petty's Law. *See* PETTY, SIR WILLIAM.

Phelps Brown, Ernest Henry (1906–94), British economist. He was educated at Taunton School and Wadham College, Oxford, and taught economics as Fellow of New College, Oxford, from 1930 to 1947 and as Professor of the Economics of Labour at the University of London from 1947 to 1968. He was appointed a member of the Council on Prices, Productivity and Incomes in 1959 and of the National Economic Development Council, 1962.

Apart from a stimulatingly original text-book on economic theory (*The Framework of the Pricing System,* 1936), most of Phelps Brown's work has been in line with his 1972 presidential address to the Royal Economic Society: an attempt to use the discipline of economics to produce useful advice to those who frame and execute public policy (he warned economists against over-use of mathematics). His main subject is industrial relations. The research he has undertaken, or organized and controlled, has produced much of what is known about the structure of trade unions (*The Growth of British Industrial Relations,* 1959), the pattern of earnings throughout the United Kingdom, and the reactions of the supply of labour to absolute and relative changes in wages (*A Century of Pay,* 1968; *The Economics of Labour,* 1963). He has clearly analysed and demonstrated the possibilities, but also the limitations, of constraint and persuasion in wage bargaining. [2]

Philanthropy, Economics of. *See* GIVING.

Phillips, Alban William H. (1914–75), New Zealand economist. He was trained in electrical engineering, which he put to imaginative use in economic models. He was educated at New Zealand State School and the LSE. He taught economics at the LSE from 1950 and was appointed Tooke Professor of Economic Science and Statistics in 1958. From 1967 to 1970 he was Professor of Economics at the Australian National University in Canberra (Professor Emeritus since 1970).

He is best known for the "Phillips Curve," which identified a relationship between the change in money wages and in unemployment; the evidence to test the hypothesis was presented in *Economica,* 1958. For many years thereafter it was widely held that the lower the amount of unemployment, the larger the rate of change in wages. The main implication for economic policy seemed to be that there was a choice between low unemployment and price stability (or slow inflation). There was a given amount of unemployment that was compatible with stable prices. If unemployment was reduced below this figure, inflation would take place. Towards the end of the 1960's faith in the "Phillips Curve" weakened when rising prices were accompanied by rising unemployment. This coexistence—stagnation—could be explained partly by increasing trade union pressure for more pay, granted by employers at the expense of employment, by increasing pressure for support of unemployed people by social benefits, so that the incentive to move to a new job was weakened, and by similar changes which "shifted" the "Phillips Curve" to the left, so that for a given rate of increase in wages there was less unemployment. Later criticism by Friedman, Phelps and other economists held that the curve was vertical, since beyond a point further inflation would not increase employment.

In *Economica* (1956), Phillips made a contribution to the theory of economic dynamics by examining the movement in an economic system when the data change. [2]

Physical Controls, direct quantitative limitations on consumption or production, in contrast to indirect monetary or fiscal (tax) controls; examples are rationing by coupon (rather than by price), licensing by official decision and document, quotas on imports, controls on hire purchase down-payments and period of repayment, etc. [10]

Physiocrats, a group of eighteenth-century French writers. The name (from "physiocracy," meaning the rule of nature, or natural law), coined by one of them, has passed into the history of economic thought, but they were known to their contemporaries as "les économistes." The founder of the group was Quesnay (1694–1774), the physician of Louis XV and Madame de Pompadour. The *Tableau économique* of 1756 contained his main ideas, which were widely disseminated by his followers, Mirabeau (1715–89), Mercier de la Rivière (1720–93), Le Trosne (1728–80), Dupont de Nemours (1739–1817) and others. Their views differed slightly, but they were united by the philosophy of common "natural law" and a belief that true wealth derived only from the soil. Industry was unproductive because it combined things already produced, and commerce merely moved them around. Agriculture alone yielded a "produit net" because it was a free gift of nature worth more than the expenses of production. Physiocratic policy was confined mainly to measures designed to increase the productivity of land, such as improved systems of tenure and more efficient forms of marketing. Their view that internal and foreign trade should be free from restriction led them to attack the prevailing mercantilist regulations and to invoke the principle of laissez-faire, by which they meant the removal of obstacles. [2]

Pierson, N. G. *See* CALCULATION, ECONOMIC.

Pigou, Arthur Cecil (1877–1959), English economist, educated at Harrow and King's College, Cambridge, where he was elected Fellow in 1902. In 1908 he succeeded Alfred Marshall to the Chair in Political Economy at the university, which he held until his retirement.

Pigou's main aim was to extend and clarify the theoretical apparatus of Alfred Marshall. At one time this approach caused a lengthy debate with Lord Keynes. His work came under heavy criticism in the numerous footnotes of Keynes's *General Theory.*

He was a prolific writer, perhaps best known for his earlier work such as *Wealth and Welfare* (1912), later expanded into his famous *Economics of Welfare* (1920). This pioneering work examined particular policies in relation to their effects on the distribution and size of the national output, and on the divergence in the effects of economic activity on those who conduct it (marginal private net product) and on society as a whole (marginal social net product). This distinction has in recent years been applied to national policy on transport, social welfare, land planning, etc.

His emphasis on the size, distribution and stability of the national income also underlies his other major works, which include *Theory of Employment* (1933), *Economics of Stationary States* (1935), *Employment and Equilibrium* (1940) and *Lapses from Full Employment* (1945).

Pigou's wide interpretation of the conditions of his professorial chair led him to play an active part in public life which earned him a wide reputation outside academic circles. He was a member of the Committee on Currency and Foreign Exchanges (1918–19), of the Royal Commission on Income Tax (1919–20), and of the Committee on Currency and Bank of England Note Issues (1924–5), which recommended the restoration of the gold standard at the pre-war parity. [2]

Planned Obsolescence. *See* OBSOLESCENCE.

Planning, organizing the use of the factors of production by central direction, instead of by the profit motive in a market economy. The conclusion of "classical" economic theory, that in free competition the working of the profit motive will result in the best possible allocation of resources, is challenged by the advocates of economic planning. They claim that in existing capitalist countries many usable factors of production are left unemployed, those employed are used with widely varying efficiency by different *entrepreneurs,* free competition does not exist, and unplanned economies produce large-scale monopolies and restrictive devices designed to maintain profits by limiting production or maintaining prices.

Economic planning has been advocated as a means of promoting national strength and self-sufficiency, but it is usually understood to mean planning in time of peace rather than war. In this sense, planning is designed to serve a philosophy of social welfare.

Widespread unemployment in most capitalist countries between the First and Second World Wars led to the advocacy of planning to achieve full employment and avoid fluctuations. On the other hand, in the Soviet Union the main difficulty in this period was the shortage of goods to meet demands of all kinds, and the emphasis of planning was put on maximum production and the best allocation of factors rather than on full employment. Advocates of planning in capitalist countries like Britain and France emphasized the need to maintain total demand continuously at a level adequate to absorb all current output at economic prices. It was held that capitalism could not maintain full employment unless the state intervened to restore the level of demand whenever a contraction appeared imminent. Economic planning in these circumstances can take several forms: it can influence the amount and character of production through direct public orders for goods and services; it can influence private demands for goods and services by tax remissions or subsidies to investment; it may regulate incomes so as to affect the level and nature of demand; or it may involve the nationalization of privately owned industries which occupy key positions in the economy.

Under fully socialist conditions, as in the Soviet Union, economic planning covers a wider range and becomes a direct public planning of the distribution of productive resources in relation to the planned distribution of the national income, between public and private uses, between investment and consumption, and between groups of consumers. [10]

Planning, Economic. *See* ECONOMIC PLANNING.

Planning, Programming and Budgetary System (PPBS). *See* OUTPUT BUDGETING.

Plant, Arnold (1898–1978), British economist and public servant. He was educated at Strand School and the London School of Economics. His first academic appointment was as Professor of Commerce at the University of Cape Town in 1924. He returned to the London School of Economics in 1930 as Sir Ernest Cassel Professor of Commerce in the University of London where he taught (except during the war) until he retired in 1965 as Professor Emeritus. His study of David Hume's philosophic writings led to his analytical interest in the economics of property, which he developed in essays or addresses on patents and on copyright (1934), and on intellectual property in literary, dramatic, musical and artistic works (1952) and numerous other aspects. Organizing and administrative university work, wartime and post-war public service and ill-health prevented completion of a treatise on property. He also studied and wrote on the economics of colour and immigration and on economic processes in industry. He served on the newly-created Cinematograph Films Council from 1938 to 1969, on the Monopolies and Restrictive Practices Commission from 1953 to 1956, and on other government committees. He was a temporary civil servant in the Second World War and was frequently consulted by Government when he returned to the LSE in 1946. He was knighted in 1947. His influence on economic thought and policy was exercised in the main verbally through his university teaching (and is seen in the works of his colleagues and students), through public lectures to business men, scientists, engineers and others in many countries, and through work in the civil service and as a government adviser. Some of his scattered writings are assembled in *Selected Economic Essays and Addresses* (1974). [2]

Plato. *See* SOCIALISM.

Playing at Competition, the term used by the critics of market socialism to emphasize that the competition between state enterprises envisaged by it would not reproduce the advantages of competition under capitalism. Since the means of production would not be owned by the state employees who manage state enterprises, they would not have the inducements of personal profit and the sanction of losses or the pressure from shareholders that impel competitive capitalists to maximize profit. In capitalist industry salaried managers may also lack the incentive of personal gain; but there is still personal advantage to be derived from maximizing profit in the long run rather than size or output or prestige achieved by ignoring profit. Furthermore, control by owners remains over much of private industry and they can influence the attitude to profit of salaried managers; passive investors such as pension funds can become active if profitability is persistently ignored; and in a free market for capital private companies must earn profits to pay the market price for funds to invest in capital. These pressures and inducements were absent from state-owned plants in communist countries, which for long were ordered to maximize *physical* output, not value of output. Some concession to this view was made by the devices for profit bonuses for plant managers devised by Liberman and other Russian economists in the 1950's and 1960's and by economists in Yugoslavia, Hungary and Czechoslovakia in the 1960's and 1970's (*See also* Czikos-Nagy, Bela; Sik, Ota.). [10]

Ploughing Back, the practice of retaining undistributed profits in the business. They represent its saving out of income. Also known as "self-financing."

Most businesses find they need more capital as they develop and expand, and much of it is provided by ploughing back profits. Most companies carry forward part of their profits, or put it into reserves.

The capital employed in the business includes the undistributed profits carried forward, thus:

A. B. C. Limited

Issued Share Capital	£500,000
General Reserve	100,000
Undistributed Profits	175,000
	£775,000

Both the general reserve and the undistributed profits represent past profits ploughed back or saved.

The equity of the business (the break-up value of the ordinary shares if the assets were sold) increases as the undistributed profits increase. If a new issue of shares is made, the price would have to take into account the amount of profits ploughed back.

Many companies with large undistributed profits convert part of them into permanent capital by issuing bonus shares to existing shareholders. Between 1947 and 1958 the former British profits tax fell more heavily on distributed than on undistributed profits, thus giving a tax incentive to companies to retain profits rather than distribute them as dividends, whereas in Germany retained profits were then taxed at a higher rate than distributed profits, thus encouraging the payment of profits to shareholders.

Ploughing back is criticized by some economists because it inhibits shareholders' power to say whether they want the profit earned by their capital to be put back into the same company or whether they would prefer to invest it elsewhere. It removes the "market test" of investment: directors may use profits in their business to build up their "empires" even though it could earn more (for their owners and for the community at large) in other firms, or other industries, or other countries.

The English economist R. F. Fowler argued that all profits should be paid out to shareholders, who could then decide whether they wished to reinvest any of it in the same company (and the capital itself be redistributed in this way with the same purpose). [3]

Polanyi, Michael (1891–1976), Hungarian scientist by training and economist by intuition. He was educated at Budapest and Karlsruhe Universities and then became Privatdozent at the Technische Hochschule, Berlin (1923). He was Professor Emeritus, University of Manchester from 1958, having previously been Professor of Physical Chemistry there (1933–48) and Professor of Social Studies (1948–58).

Polanyi was a distinguished scientist (FRS 1944) who turned to economics and later to philosophy: *The Contempt of Freedom* (1940); *The Logic of Liberty* (1951); *Beyond Nihilism* (1960). In *Full Employment and Free Trade* (1945) he argued that the essential message of Keynes's *General Theory* was that the state should control the money supply through appropriate budgetary policies, not by state-planned investments. His analysis of the *General Theory* in monetarist terms seemed to indicate a synthesis between opposing doctrines in the theory and practice of demand management. Polanyi's view of the Russian economy (*USSR Economics*, 1935) was that the achievement of full employment had been due not to state planning but to the maintenance of a high level of monetary demand. The role of state planning was largely to attempt to control the resulting permanent state of inflation, and as such it modified but did not replace the market economy introduced in 1921, after the collapse of the attempt to replace it by central allocation of resources. [2]

Policing Costs, the resources required for the supervision and enforcement of rights to use or transfer or hire goods or services ("property"). If policing (negotiation or property enforcement) costs exceed the price that could be obtained for a commodity, or service or amenity (say, fishing rights), it is not worth charging for it. But if the service is made available without payment, it will have to be rationed by other devices—waiting lists, queuing, etc. When devices are developed that reduce policing costs, e.g. parking meters that are cheaper than a large force of attendants or wardens, more precise pricing becomes feasible. Where policing costs are relatively low because labour is cheaper, e.g. theatre-staffs in Austria contrasted with Australia, pricing can be more refined, e.g. gallery seats can be made cheaper than stalls. If water can be metered, prices for various uses (domestic, garden, entertainment, industrial, etc.) can be adjusted to equate supply and demand for each use. Devices are available (meters to take coins) that reduce the policing costs of television programmes so that viewers can buy the ones they want and not the whole channel (the British government has not encouraged their use; in the USA restrictions were relaxed in 1970). Vending machines which accept coins are also a method of reducing policing costs and making finer adjustments possible by pricing without rationing by time (waiting, queuing, etc.). Technical development will reduce policing costs, extend claims to property rights (e.g. Iceland fishing limits) and improve conservation of natural resources. [13]

Political and Economic Planning (PEP), a research organization founded in 1931 as a charitable trust for educational purposes to study and publish works on economic problems for the guidance of policy makers. Its work is conducted mostly by its staff, occasionally supplemented by outside workers. Its method of work is to assemble, for each project, a group comprising people concerned professionally with aspects of it, together with non-specialists. The full-time staff prepare working papers and reports and direct and carry out field-work and analyses. Its publications comprise mainly two forms, major reports and *Planning* broadsheets. It is financed by grants from foundations, contributions from individuals, firms and institutes, and the sale of publications. [14]

Political Arithmetic, an early name in England for the body of study and knowledge later known as "political economy" and in modern times "economics." The term was used in 1690 in a book by Sir William Petty. [14]

Political Economy, the common name for economics until recent times. The dictionary edited by Sir Robert Palgrave from 1894 to 1906 was called the *Dictionary of Political Economy.* [14]

Political Market, the institutional situation through which public goods are provided. The private market cannot provide them because individuals cannot be excluded from their benefits and cannot therefore be required to pay by being charged a price. And the charity market cannot provide them because voluntary or charitable contributions by individuals would have no perceptible effect on supply, which might therefore fall short of the amount that all individuals together would want. Men can therefore indicate such wants only collectively, through the political process of elections, majority decisions, party organizations and representative institutions, etc. Therefore the political market decides the quantity and quality of defence, external and internal, law and justice, street lighting, etc.; and the penalties on "free rider" individuals who try to evade payment. The political market is the subject of the theory of public choice, developed mostly in the USA, and there mainly by the Virginia School, since the late 1950's. [13]

Politician Push, name given to the form of inflation induced by pressure on politicians to expand the supply of money and so avoid the unemployment that would otherwise follow wage-costs pushed up beyond the marginal productivity of labour. It was adapted by economists who emphasized the role of the *institutional* factor of monopoly trade unions to distinguish politician push from "cost push" inflation; while the *instrument* of inflation was the same in both (the money supply), the failure of politicians to control it was explained by political pressure from the unions to expand it. These economists therefore agreed with the monetary economists on the mechanism of inflation but differed from them on its chief cause, which they maintained was political rather than financial, i.e. it was a defect of legal institutions rather than the monetary mechanism *per se.* [9]

Politics, Economics of, the analysis of political entrepreneurship in the provision of public goods. The economic analysis is conceptually symmetrical with the analysis of industrial entrepreneurship in the supply of private goods, but with variations arising mainly from the difference in the method of payment (taxes instead of prices) and the absence of machinery for individual evaluation of the product. [13]

Politics, Relation to Economics. *See* ECONOMICS.

Poll Tax, a tax levied equally on each person or head. When incomes are unequal a poll tax is regressive. One of the earliest provoked Wat Tyler's Peasants' Revolt of 1381. A recent one is the social insurance contribution which in some countries is the same for everyone irrespective of earnings. [12]

Pollution, Economics of, is concerned with the supply of and the demand for pollution (because alternatives are preferred to preventing it). The supply of pollution comes from over-use of the environment (over-fishing etc.), neglect (lack of exclusive property rights or difficulty of enforcing communal property rights), or despoliation (by fumes, noise, etc.). The "demand" comes from the refusal to abandon the activities that produce it—rapid technical change and growth in industrial activity generally. The difference between the economic and the technical or lay view is that laymen tend to regard the avoidance of pollution as desirable at *any* cost; economists point to the cost (in slowing down industry or mining, growth generally, living standards, the means to assist developing countries, etc.). Both views have been analysed by economists: E. J. Mishan (*The Costs of Growth*, etc.) and Wilfred Beckerman (*In Defence of Economic Growth*, 1974). [6]

Popper, K. R. *See* Historical Method; Positivism; Social Engineering.

Population, the number and characteristics of the inhabitants of an area. The scientific study of population and its movements could not begin until reliable statistical data became available. The provision of such figures requires an efficient governmental machine capable of organizing their collection. Few reliable population figures exist for any period before the eighteenth century. Statistical information is of two kinds; first, censuses attempt to enumerate every member of the population alive at a given point of time and collect information about sex, age, occupation, etc. In English-speaking countries censuses take place generally every ten years. Census statistics are not alone sufficient for a detailed study of population movement; in the absence of migration, population increases by births and decreases by deaths, and in many parts of the world births are closely associated with the number of marriages. Continuous figures of births and deaths need to be available if changes in numbers are to be studied in detail. It is also desirable to have figures of migration. In many countries births, marriages and deaths have to be registered for administrative and legal purposes, and the "vital statistics" are derived from them; in other countries registration is less systematic and definitions of births (e.g. as "live" births or otherwise) differ so that international comparisons of infant mortality (and other indicators of health or welfare services) are unreliable or misleading or meaningless.

Large areas of the world have no census and few vital statistics. China constitutes the biggest gap in modern knowledge, since it has been estimated to contain one-sixth of total world population. For many other areas data are scanty and unreliable; and official estimates must be treated with caution. Knowledge of the present population of the world is precarious, but what is known of the history of population is even more so. In general there are no trustworthy figures for any part of the world before 1750 and recourse must be had to partial figures or indirect evidence. The figures that exist show that world population has been growing at an accelerating rate since 1650.

The economic problems of the population of individual countries are broadly related to its size and structure. In the economic sense a country's population may be too large or too small. A small population in a country may inhibit development through the simple and crude lack of manpower, as in the early days in North America and Australia. More significant is the limited scope for specialization and the division of labour, for as a society becomes larger the possibilities and advantages of specialization usually grow simultaneously. Conversely, an excessively large population may produce poverty and slow development because of the relative inadequacy of the physical resources of production, as in India, China and parts of Africa and South America. Larger populations can secure more output and food supplies, other things equal, only by cultivating less fertile land and employing existing land and capital more intensively. There are also economic problems in the age structure of the population relating to the ratio of young to old members of the population. Normally there are minimum and maximum age limits below which children and above which old people must be regarded as dependants; the range between these two limits contains the producers of a country. The ratio of producers to dependants is thus relevant to the well-being of a country; other things equal, the country with the higher producer-dependent ratio is better off.

Further economic problems are connected with the growth of population. It has been argued that a growing population will tend to be young and enterprising and economic progress will be correspondingly more rapid, as in nineteenth-century Britain and America. But the more serious problem at the present time is the consequence of population in parts of the world growing at an excessive rate. This problem is especially serious in parts of Asia, and India and Japan have attempted to spread knowledge of methods of birth control to check population growth.

The most famous theory of population is that of the English economist Malthus. He maintained there is a tendency for population to grow in a geometric progression and to outstrip the growth in the means of subsistence: in his view the only limit was provided by the pressure of population on subsistence. A rise in living standards would merely raise the birth rate until any gain was wiped out by an increase in human numbers. Malthus's gloomy conclusions, although influential on policy, were not supported by events. Attempts have been made since to find other mathematical "laws" of population change; but there is now general agreement that any attempt to discover a "law" of human population will fail unless it takes account of institutional and social conditions. [11]

Pork Barrel, American term for appropriation of revenue for local projects, arranged under pressure from local legislators primarily for political (electoral) purposes. The process is politically an easy option because the projects (roads, harbour improvements, etc.) create evident improvements; the beneficiaries are identifiable and organized, the opportunity costs (from hospitals to holidays) are difficult to calculate, the sources of finance (taxpayers) are dispersed, and legislative "deals" with opponents can be arranged. The economic justification is difficult to refute because a comparison between the benefits and the costs is not easily made. (*See* Cost-Benefit Analysis.) [13]

Portfolio, in financial economics the shares, deposits, unit trust holdings and other securities owned by an investor. If it is vigorously managed to maximize yield and capital growth, it is "active"; otherwise it is said to be "passive." [8]

Positive Economic Laws. *See* LAW, ECONOMIC.

Positive Economics, a fashionable term for that part of theory and its application that analyses causes and consequences without ethical judgement—"what is" rather than "what should be" (normative economics). In modern economic language it develops hypotheses that can be tested (and therefore refuted) by empirical evidence. The older term "behaviourist" was more explanatory in indicating that this branch of economics is concerned with how human beings "behave." [14]

Positivism, the doctrine that all knowledge relates to observable facts and relationships about phenomena whose nature or origin can be accepted without questioning. The doctrine was first expressed by the French philosopher Comte in the nineteenth century; his aim was to observe historical phenomena and to infer from them scientific "laws of motion" of society corresponding to those of the natural sciences. This notion, and its corollary—that from such "laws" it is possible to predict the "path" of social change—have been extensively criticized in recent years, notably in the works of Professor Karl Popper. [14]

Post hoc ergo propter hoc, a Latin phrase meaning "after it, therefore because of it." Used by logicians and economists to draw attention to the fallacy of supposing that because B follows A, A is the cause of B. For example, if a fall in the price of a commodity follows the levy of a tariff on imports, it does not follow that the tariff caused the fall in price. The tendency is for a tariff to *raise* prices. If after a tariff the price fell, it would probably have fallen even more if the tariff had not been applied. The fallacy is a logical trap which non-economists discussing economic aspects of social or industrial activity are apt to fall into. [14]

Post-war Credits, a form of forced saving used to reduce government borrowing in 1941 when taxation was insufficient to meet war-time government expenditure. Some income tax allowances were reduced and the additional tax credited to the taxpayer for repayment after the war. The total amount of post-war credits created was about £800 million. As the repayment of such a large sum in a short period would have had a strong inflationary effect, a scheme of gradual repayment was introduced in 1947. In the early 1960's a large part of post-war credits were still outstanding. Repayments could be claimed by a man of sixty-three or a woman of fifty-eight and in hardship and ill health. Compound interest of 2½ per cent tax free was paid on outstanding post-war credits from 1959. The credits were repaid in 1973. [12]

Praxeology, the general theory of human action "material and ideal, sublime and base, noble and ignoble," (Ludwig von Mises). Economists of several "schools" (Austrian, Chicago, London and others) have argued that the transition from the classical labour theory of David Ricardo to the subjective choice and preference theory of value of the Austrians was from a theory concerned with *material* goods to a science concerned with *every* side of human activity. Economics is the study of choice, and *all* human behaviour entails choice; so economics has been said to have passed from political economy to praxeology. [14]

Prebisch, Raúl (1901–86), Argentinian economist. He was educated at Buenos Aires University, where he was Professor of Political Economy from 1925 until he retired in 1948. After public and government appointments in Argentina, he became Secretary-General of the UN Economic Commission for Latin America from 1948 to 1962, and Secretary-General, United Nations Conference on Trade and Development (UNCTAD) from 1964 to 1969. Since 1962 he has also been Director-General of the Latin American Institute for Economic and Social Planning at Santiago de Chile.

Prebisch supports the thesis that the poverty of many of the poorer countries is due, for the most part, to the bad and worsening terms of trade at which primary products exchange with manufactures. The remedy he advocates is the development of manufacturing industries behind protective tariffs. It is difficult to find theoretical support for this view, which assumes that the products of industries with increasing returns will continue in the long run to rise in price relative to the products of industries with decreasing returns, except by showing not only in exceptional cases but also in general that equilibrating forces fail to operate in the world market. Prebisch's views were first presented in a 1949 article in *El Trimestre económico* and developed and refined in *The Economic Development of Latin America and its Principal Problems* (an official report of the UN Economic Commission for Latin America, New York) in 1950. [2]

Preference Shares, securities that give their holders a prior claim over holders of ordinary shares, both to payment of dividends and to the return of their capital if the company goes into liquidation. Holders of preference shares are usually entitled to receive dividends only at a fixed rate (e.g. 5 per cent on the par value of the share) but "participating preference shares" also entitle their holders to a limited share in residual profits, if any. If no dividend is paid to holders of "cumulative preference shares" in a given year, their entitlement is carried forward and must be met in a following year together with the dividend due for that year, before payment may be made to ordinary shareholders. Holders of preference shares usually have more restricted voting rights than ordinary shareholders.

To a company wishing to raise new funds, an issue of preference shares has the advantage over an issue of loan stock that in a bad year there could be no legal obligation to pay dividends on preference shares, whereas interest payments on loan capital would have to be met. For investors, preference shares have the advantage that income from them is likely to be more secure than it would be from ordinary shares. There have been relatively few issues of preference shares in the post-war period because inflation has turned the attention of investors to ordinary shares which tend to yield higher dividends as prices rise, output expands and profits increase. [8]

Preobrazhensky, E. (1886–1937), Russian economist. He was the theorist of Trotskyist opposition to Lenin's New Economic Policy (NEP) of attracting the peasants into the Soviet system by encouraging private accumulation instead of by coercion. Lenin argued the peasantry should be told "get rich . . . accumulate, develop your economy." Industrial capital after the war was not being fully used and it was argued that investment in labour-intensive light industry and agriculture could yield quick returns. Preobrazhensky countered by arguing that continuing shortages of goods could be prevented only by large increases in industrial investment, for which labour could be obtained only from agriculture; and he attacked Lenin's view about encouraging peasant accumulation by observing that it resembled the "primitive capitalistic accumulation" condemned by Marx. Preobrazhensky argued that the state should use its power as a buyer (monopsony) to turn the terms of trade against the peasants by suspending the law that value was determined by the free market of the NEP and requiring them to sell their produce cheaply. Later, after the expulsion of Trotsky and other critics from the USSR, Stalin changed his view from support of Lenin's NEP to rapid industrialization based on forced collectivization in agriculture. [2]

Present Value. *See* Discounting.

Present Worth. *See* Discounting.

Prestige Goods, those that provide an exception to the general law of demand that demand falls when price rises. The demand for goods bought for prestige *rises* when their price rises. Prestige goods are "worth" more when their price rises because others regard their price as an indication of capacity to pay, or wealth, or social status, or because they have become more rare and exclusive, thus appealing to snobbery. [7]

Price, the amount of money given in exchange for a commodity or service; in other words, the value of a commodity or service in terms of money. In buying goods and some services it is called "price"; in hiring labour services "wages," "salary," "fee," etc.; in borrowing money or capital "interest"; in hiring land or building "rent."

Price is determined by the interaction of supply and demand. If demand increases the price tends to rise and vice versa; if supply increases the price tends to fall and vice versa. The extent of the change in price is determined in the first case by the elasticity of supply and in the second by the elasticity of demand.

In a free market prices perform two main functions: (*a*) they provide information (*see* INFORMATION COSTS) that guides consumers in shopping and indicate to producers whether supply needs to be adjusted to changing demands, (*b*) they ration available supplies among consumers. If prices are prevented from reaching the "equilibrium" level at which the total demand and supply tend to be equal, it is difficult to know how much of each commodity or service the public demands, that is, how it wishes to allocate its purchasing power between all the commodities or services available. For example, if rents are pushed below the free market level a housing shortage is created which it may be impossible to remove except by subsidizing house-building.

More generally in the community at large prices are not only indicators of changing supply and demand but also forms of income. Wages and salaries are not only the price of labour but also its income. There may therefore be social and political resistances to allowing wages or salaries to vary freely in order to adjust supply to demand. For example, the prices of the primary products of the underdeveloped countries, such as cocoa, coffee, rubber, sugar, tea, tin, wheat and others, would tend to fluctuate with changing harvests and world demand. Such fluctuations would be desirable to stimulate the required adaptation of supply to changing demand. But some of these countries, such as Barbados, Bolivia, Mauritius, Burma, Brazil, depend on one or two main products, and changing prices mean changing standards of living for many of their inhabitants. Hence the attempts to stabilize prices by output regulation schemes, buffer-stock schemes, bulk sale contracts, marketing boards, etc. Such methods often have some success in the short run but tend to weaken in the long run as populations grow, new supplies are opened up, old sources dry up and industrial techniques change.

If price cannot be used to indicate changes in supply and demand and to "ration" available supply among the "demanders," a substitute method must be used. Supplies of productive equipment such as building materials can be allocated by licensing, and consumer goods can be rationed by coupons (which thus replace money). If such substitutes for prices are by-passed by "black markets," "illegitimate trading," etc., they may require strict legal penalties. [14]

Price Control. *See* PRICE FIXING.

Price Discrimination, varying the prices of a commodity or service in different markets according to the elasticity of demand in each. For example, a barrister or doctor may charge according to "what the traffic will bear": more wealthy clients and customers are charged more than the less wealthy. Price discrimination is possible when the *entrepreneur* is a monopolist (or when there is collusion among sellers to discriminate in price) and when consumers cannot move from one market to another or buy in one market and resell in another. When there are many sellers consumers will tend to transfer from one to another if they can buy more cheaply. The same commodity may be sold at different prices because consumers do not know that others are getting it more cheaply. Discrimination may occur in the sale of direct personal services, e.g. medical or legal, because they cannot be resold. Distance (because of costs of transport) and frontier barriers (e.g. tariffs) are other reasons for the existence of separate markets for the same commodity. The monopolist may take advantage of the protection offered by a tariff and sell at a higher price in the home market. In the world market his price will be lower because he is faced with competition from other sellers.

Price discrimination is profitable only when the conditions of demand in the markets are different. If the elasticity of demand in two markets is identical, the monopolist will not find it profitable to charge different prices. A unit of output produced at a given cost transferred from one market to the other will result in a loss of revenue in the first market equal to the increase in revenue in the second; so there is no advantage. If the elasticities of demand differ, the monopolist will charge more where the demand is less elastic, and less where demand is more elastic, until the changes in revenues in both markets are equal to each other and to the marginal cost of producing the commodity or service. [7]

Price-earnings Ratio (P/E), the relationship between the market price of an ordinary share and its current (or latest) earnings, i.e. the reciprocal of the earnings yield. P/E indicates the price (capital outlay) required to buy the equity income. A sizeable firm of good repute would attract a higher P for each unit of E than would a new, small or less stable company. P/E is thus a measure of a firm's success. A high P/E indicates a growth stock, although investors who want a steady if unspectacular yield may prefer a low P/E. [8]

Price Effect, in the analysis of demand and supply, the effect of a change in price is a combination of its *substitution effect* and its *income effect.* The substitution effect always operates in the expected direction, e.g. a fall in the price of beef (relative to other meats) will always encourage consumers to switch purchases from other meats to beef; a rise in the price of beef will encourage a switch from beef to other meats. The income effect is the effect on consumers who are made poorer by a price rise, richer by a price fall (their income buys less—or more—than it did before). The income effect on the quantity demanded is uncertain. Normally, the income effect may be expected to reinforce the substitution effect of a price change; when the price of beef falls, buyers substitute beef for other meats *and* buy more because their income goes further. But sometimes the income effect may work against the substitution effect. Thus a rise in income tax that reduces a man's take-home pay for working is equivalent to a fall in the income price of leisure (if he works less hard and takes time off he sacrifices less net take-home pay than he would have done before the income tax went up). The fall in the price of leisure relative to other things will encourage a substitution of leisure for other things: he will tend to work less. But the reduction in his net take-home pay also makes him poorer and this income effect may stimulate him to work harder to restore his net purchasing power. The combined price effect may thus either encourage or discourage work (for taxed income, at least). Economists differ in their view of the real-life importance of such cases of potential conflict between income and substitution effects. [7]

Price Fixing, a term used to mean "deliberate" price fixing in contrast to the idealized situation of perfect competition in which price is the automatic outcome of an impersonal process. There are several common cases. First, prices may be fixed by a monopoly in the sense that it can make a calculated assessment of them. An example is the nationalized electricity supply industry. In competition, the ability to make profits is an indicator of efficiency; in monopoly high profits might reflect merely the exercise of monopoly power and low profits might reflect inertia as costs floated up to prices.

Secondly, prices may be fixed by trade associations or monopolistic agreements. Resale price maintenance (before legislation outlawing it in Britain, the USA, Canada and other countries) set the price which distributors (wholesalers or retailers) were required to charge for a product and did not allow the individual distributor to compete directly on price.

Thirdly, a government may fix prices at which products or services may be sold. In Britain and other countries there was much price-control during the First and Second World Wars, and some of it was continued after the war. For example, rent control was begun as an emergency measure in Britain in 1915 and remained for over half a century.

Fourthly, collective bargains between trade unions and employers set rates of wages and wage-differentials which form a national basis for the payment of employees in individual occupations and particular grades of labour.

Price-fixing policies and agreements are usually defended on the grounds that they reduce uncertainty and encourage stability in production. In some cases it is argued that they ensure standards by protecting the consumer against cut-price sellers who would debase quality. They are criticized on the grounds that they lead to price rigidity, shelter inefficient producers and distributors, and hold back innovation. Government regulation of prices has also been criticized for preventing price from equating supply and demand. In rent control, for example, it is argued that setting a maximum price (without rationing) below the market equilibrium level led to shortage (excess of demand over supply at the fixed price) and attendant difficulties. In international commodity agreements for several of the products of mainly agricultural countries, price fixing has brought only temporary aid but increased the fundamental problems by stimulating production by high-cost producers and encouraging new producers into the market. Furthermore, fixing a price does not prevent fluctuations but transmits them to supply and/or demand and may therefore intensify the disturbances. [7]

Price Leadership, a situation in which the price of a product is set by a major firm in an industry and followed by the others in it. Price leadership is most likely in oligopoly, when the number of firms is few, and characteristically when the product is more or less homogeneous. A good example is steel; the United States Steel Corporation is often cited as a typical case. It has the largest capacity in a well-defined industry; it sets the price and the small number of other firms in the industry follow it. As a solution of the oligopoly problem price leadership has the virtue of removing the uncertainty about the reactions of rivals. Everybody knows what the price is and when to change; the behaviour of the price leader gives the signal.

The biggest firm need not be the price leader. Suppose that the firms have similar but not identical shares of the market but that the smaller firms have reduced price and the bigger ones have followed them. The larger units might wish to raise price because at the lower price they are not maximizing profits, but since the smaller units fear the disproportionate effect on them of falling total sales if prices are raised, they will not increase price and cannot be made to do so. The firms with the smaller shares of the market thus set the price. This cannot happen where market shares are unequal and there is a dominant firm. [7]

Price Maker. *See* PRICE TAKER.

Price Mechanism, a device for limiting to particular uses the use of resources and the consumption of goods with alternative applications. It is thus a means of guiding, controlling and "rationing" production and consumption.

Prices are the money values of goods and services. In particular cases and at a particular time they may be determined by custom, by an arbitrary authority, by higgling in separate transactions, by a privileged monopolist or by competition in a free market. But in general the price mechanism under a system of broadly free competition serves as a co-ordinating device for goods produced for sale in markets to consumers who buy with the money they have received from payments for their own productive activity.

The price mechanism is a characteristic of the complex modern economy; it operates in different forms and to differing extents in various countries. In earlier societies it did not exist. The adoption of the price mechanism as the co-ordinating force in economic development indicates, historically, its superiority over other possible mechanisms, such as political authority, to carry out a deliberately conceived policy. This superiority rests on two considerations. First, the employment of money as a conventional unit of reckoning values eases comparison and makes choice between goods more informed and accurate. The use of prices as guides to the selection of occupations, the purchase of goods and generally in the organization of economic activities has tended thus to sharpen economic judgement and to make choice more fruitful. Secondly, the price mechanism provides a convenient means of enforcing checks on the use of resources which are inescapable but which are more accepted in so far as they appear to be the work of fate. The application of scarce means to specific ends unavoidably excludes their use for others; the necessary frustrations and deprivations of the economic process inevitably appear less onerous when they are not enforced by the arbitrary will of human authority.

The criticisms levied against the price mechanism normally derive from practical disillusionment rather than from theoretical inquiry. When working men found that the price mechanism in a free market worked unfavourably to their interests they determined to bargain collectively and to sell their labour not at free market prices but at "fair" prices. Businessmen saw that free market prices for their goods were not always profitable, and collusion and other forms of restriction openly became more widespread. Consumers became aware that prices were no longer the outcome of a multitude of spontaneous forces represented by the bids and offers of innumerable individuals in pursuit of private interests. The result was that in various directions practical expediency brought about a considerable departure from the rules of market conduct prescribed by the price mechanism. Resources were not allowed to flow without help or hindrance where prices dictated; they were diverted (e.g. by subsidies, tariffs and trusts); methods of production were no longer based solely on cost-price considerations; there were others (e.g. factory legislation, health regulations); the distribution of income by the processes of the market was interfered with (by collective bargaining, rate regulation, etc.). In these and other ways the working of the price mechanism has in the twentieth century been amended, restricted and in some cases destroyed at least for a time. On the other hand recent developments in the communist countries, Russia, Yugoslavia, Poland, Hungary and others, suggest that prices and markets cannot be suppressed easily, generally or permanently, but tend to form spontaneously where individuals or groups find they can benefit from exchange of goods or services. [7]

Price Support, American term for government maintenance of (agricultural) prices above the market level. The argument for it has been that farmers are faced by climatic and other conditions they cannot control and should therefore be given some stability by the consumer through the tax system if not through the market; otherwise they will not produce food. This economic argument is questionable: if the fluctuations in conditions are more or less regular they can be allowed for; and, if irregular, resources left over from good times can be conserved for bad times. The reasons for price support are probably more political (large numbers of small farmers) than economic. British and European agriculture is given price support in the EEC. [6]

Price Taker, a supplier who sells such a small proportion of the total supply that he cannot affect the price by altering his output; he therefore must "take" the market price as an unalterable datum and determinant of his production or selling policy. He may also be a price taker in buying factors of production (e.g. labour) if he buys in such small quantities that an expansion in his demand will have no effect on price (e.g. the wage rate). A *Price Maker* is so dominant in the market that any significant change in the quantities of output he sells or inputs he buys will cause their market price to change. [7]

Price "War." *See* COMMON PRICING.

Prima Facie, "at first sight," Latin term frequently used by economists in discussing the apparent rather than the real causes or consequences in an analytical or applied problem. [14]

Prime Cost. *See* COST.

Prior Charges. *See* GEARING.

Prisoners' Dilemma, a situation in the economic theory of games, discovered in the early 1950's. The dilemma occurs when individuals, or firms, or political parties, cannot arrange a binding agreement among themselves because they cannot control the others' decisions. The analogy is with prisoners interrogated separately, each of whom knows that if none confess all will receive a light sentence for want of hard evidence: if one confesses (and the others do not) he will go free and the others will receive harsh sentences: if all confess each will receive a sentence less severe than if all but one remained silent, but more severe than if none confessed. If each acts to protect himself he will confess whatever the others do. But what is rational for each one in the absence of agreement nevertheless leads to a situation in which all are worse off than they might have been with agreement.

This dilemma is common in politics and decisions on public goods. Each individual has therefore to choose the "optimum" that is the best available but is not as satisfactory as it would have been with a binding contract. For example, in considering how to help the poor, a man may contribute £10 to a charity or vote for a tax of £10 per head to be spent by a local, regional or national government. In none of these situations is it possible to make an agreement with others. The cost would decrease from the first to the fourth of these alternatives because the larger the unit of government the less the influence of the individual's vote on the final decision. He can therefore indulge his charitable impulse, or derive pleasure from being thought by others to be charitable, most cheaply by voting for the national tax, next for the regional tax, next for the local tax, and finally by donating the £10 to a private charity. The tendency would therefore be to vote for the national tax in which every individual would feel his vote earned least weight. But the effect would be that, since every individual voted for it, it would become law and enforced on every individual though each did not want to be charitable sufficiently to donate privately yet wished to feel charitable, or to be thought charitable by others. Because of the difficulty of arranging a binding contract with other individuals on how much to donate to charity, he (and they) end up paying more than they really wish. [13]

Private Company. *See* LIMITED LIABILITY.

Private Enterprise, the economic activities of a community which are independent of government control and directed to satisfy private wants. In spite of the recent growth of public ownership, productive activity in most western countries is still predominantly in the hands of private enterprise, based on the institution of private property, the principal distinguishing feature of a capitalist society. The essence of private enterprise is freedom of economic activity: subject to certain restrictions, people are free to use their property, income and skills in the ways they please.

In attempting to produce efficiently and avoid waste, every society faces the same economic problems: the quantity and type of goods it should produce, the best techniques and locations of production, the appropriate channels of distribution, etc. The significant feature of a private enterprise system is that individuals acting independently and without government control or direction manage to solve the problems more or less to their satisfaction. The overriding desire of business men is to make their enterprises as profitable as possible. In general, it is profitable to produce only what people are prepared to pay for, and if markets are competitive the interests of the manufacturers and the community tend to coincide. Every penny a consumer spends on a commodity is in a sense a "vote" in favour of its continued production. The changing flow of consumers' expenditure provides a continuous "referendum" as a guide to production. Rising prices and profits, usually a sign of strong demand for a commodity, act as a stimulus to production; and falling prices and losses, which indicate that resources could be better employed elsewhere, tend to discourage production. Since it also pays to produce as efficiently as possible, the aim of higher profits tends to lead to an economic use of resources.

The private enterprise system in practice is often far from perfect. The interest of the public and of private business are not always identical. The working of the system may be marred by the activity of groups trying to obtain for themselves (at the expense of the rest of the community) positions of greater advantage than could be enjoyed under free competition. The sluggishness of some prices, or of responses to price changes, may lead to long periods of maladjustment. To promote and sustain smoother working of a system a framework of law and institutions is necessary. Some economists suggest that these problems can be solved only by abandoning private enterprise and substituting a government controlled economy. Others contend that private enterprise offers considerable advantages, such as a flexible system of meeting the community's needs without elaborate administrative machinery or restriction of individual freedom. [10]

Private Investment. *See* INVESTMENT.

Private Placings. *See* NEW ISSUE MARKET.

Private Sector, that part of an economic system which is independent of government control. Broadly the private sector coincides with the productive activities operated by private enterprise. They include a wide range of organizations from the one-man firm to the giant corporation, all controlled and managed by private individuals guided by their desire to maintain or increase earnings and profits by selling the goods and services the public demand. [10]

Probate. *See* EXECUTOR.

Producers' Goods. *See* DURABLE GOODS.

Product Differentiation. *See* TRADE MARK.

Production, any activity which serves to satisfy human wants. In its widest sense production includes the efforts of all the service and professional occupations—actors and accountants, ballet-dancers and butchers, dentists and dustmen, and so on. On the manufacturing side it embraces not only the process of manufacture but also the work of people engaged in moving goods from factories and farms where they are useless, to the households of the consumers where they are useful—the activities of transport, warehousing, wholesaling and shopkeeping.

The general standard of living of a community rests essentially on the quantity of goods and services available per head of the population, and this in turn depends on the volume of production. Redistributing income from rich to poor will have little effect if the rich are in a small minority. It is only by raising production that substantial improvements can be made.

The volume of production depends mainly on the quality and quantity of raw materials, labour and equipment; the extent of technical knowledge; the quality of political and business organization. Significant changes in the level of production can be achieved only by altering one or more of these elements. If a community refrains from using all of its output for current consumption it can raise future production by using its resources to improve the land and to increase the quality and quantity of its equipment, technical knowledge and labour force.

Every producer faces two basic problems: what combination of resources to use in order to produce efficiently, and how much of a commodity to produce. Failure to solve these problems will result in wasteful production techniques, as well as unwanted surpluses of some goods and shortages of others.

Economists have shown in the theory of production that producers tend to solve the two problems by expanding their hire of factors of production to the point at which the revenue gained from selling the output of an additional or "marginal" factor (its "marginal revenue product") is just equal to the additional or "marginal" cost of hiring it: this is the output at which the marginal cost of output is equal to its marginal revenue. A clothing manufacturer, for example, will tend to increase output by using machines and labour so long as the revenue from the output of an additional machine or worker is larger than the extra cost, but will stop using more machines at the point where an additional machine costing £1,000 a year to run produces only £1,000 worth of clothing, and similarly will stop hiring more labour when an additional man at £2,500 a year adds only £2,500 to the value of output. A stage will be reached in every organization when further additions of equipment and labour will make successively smaller contributions to total output, as the factory approaches the physical limit of its capacity set by the size of its management, administration and its factory space (diminishing returns). A loss will be made on marginal output (and total profits thus decreased) if output is pushed to the point at which the additional cost of production is higher than the value of the additional output. The marginal loss indicates that output has been carried too far, and that the marginal equipment and labour could be used more profitably elsewhere to the benefit of the community. On the other hand, any level of output short of the point at which marginal revenue equals marginal cost will not be in the public interest either, since it means that the value placed by consumers on the additional output is higher than the cost of making it. When consumers are prepared to pay more for something than its full cost of production, there is a strong indication that output should be increased. Only when output has reached the point when the revenue from each additional factor of production is equal to the additional cost will production have reached the point which best satisfies the interests of consumers.

At this stage the producer will also have solved the problem of combining the factors of production to produce the output as cheaply as possible. In deciding how to produce, each manufacturer usually has some choice between different amounts of machinery and manual labour, between automatic and semi-automatic machinery, and so on. The rule for selecting the least expensive combination is to continue to substitute a cheaper for a more expensive factor of production until no more cost reductions can be made by further substitution. If, for example, a fully automatic machine costing £500 a year to run can produce £1,500 worth of goods and a man at £2,500 a year can produce £5,000 worth of identical goods, it will be cheaper to substitute machines for labour since every £1 invested on machines will yield £3 (£1,500 divided by 500), whereas every £1 spent on hiring labour yields only £2 (5,000 divided by 2,500). Substitution will continue to lower costs until the yield of a pound spent on machines is no larger than that spent on labour. Further, to maximize profits, the hire of both men and machines will be increased as long as extensions of output increase profits. Both the cost-minimizing and the profit-maximizing conditions will be satisfied when the value of output of each marginal factor is equal to its marginal cost. If at the margin an additional machine costing £1,000 adds £1,000 to output and a man at £2,500 produces just £2,500 worth of goods, the value of output per pound invested in both is the same. [3]

Production, Marginal. *See* DISTRIBUTION.

Production Function, the relationship between inputs (of land, labour, capital) and outputs (of products) in a given state of technology. It may refer to a single firm or the economy as a whole. The function is capable of being manipulated in mathematical form. The general principles of the relationships between inputs and outputs are discussed in Production. [3]

Productivity, the output of a unit of a factor of production in a stated period. For example, the productivity of labour is usually measured as output per man per year (or other calendar period), or output per man per shift or per hour. Strictly, the term is best related to a single factor; when a group of factors, as in a firm, is being analysed, it is more common to use the term "efficiency."

When a factor of production becomes more productive, output rises per unit of input; in other words, a smaller input is required to obtain a given output. If other things, including the prices of all inputs, remain the same, the cost per unit of output will fall. The share of the factor in unit cost will diminish even if cost does not fall for the enterprise as a whole. The productivity of a country's resources thus governs the level of its real costs and determines how much of particular resources have to be used to achieve a given result. Hence if labour in one country (or firm) has a higher productivity than that in another country (or firm), it can "afford" to earn more in terms of money without having higher costs. The history of the rising standard of living in western Europe and the North American continent has been the history of a steep rise in productivity.

The measurement of productivity raises problems of valuation and "imputation" (attributing yields to each factor within the group). The difficulties of valuation are those of trying to add together "apples and pears." Outputs and inputs are rarely homogeneous and cannot easily be compared through time, between countries or between industries. The "same" product may differ in quality, the "same" labour in "skill." In principle these difficulties can be overcome by valuing the physical outputs and factors in terms of money, but it is not easy to rely on the prices available for measurement. For example, the price of a product in one country may be higher than in another because there is a larger degree of monopoly. A similar problem exists in international comparisons where the exchange rates between currencies are officially maintained at levels that do not reflect the real relationship between prices in the countries. The problems of imputation arise from the use of factors in combination. If changes in output require changes in the amounts of more than one type of factor, it is hard to ascribe a change in productivity to one factor rather than another.

These difficulties and others (such as measurement of the output of office staff or teachers) are formidable. Nevertheless broad, serviceable computations can be made, changes indicated and differences between countries, regions, industries or firms established. Where, for example, differences are large even after allowing for the oversimplifications and exaggerations of the statistics, productivity measures provide a guideline and serve to direct attention to the relevant factors of technology, capital equipment, market forms and organization. [11]

"Produit Net." *See* CANTILLON; PHYSIOCRATS.

Profit, in everyday language, a surplus of income over outgo ("expenses"); more generally, "profitable" means "worth doing" or "paying"; in economics, profit is given a more precise meaning.

Profit was regarded by some nineteenth-century economists as the wages paid to the *entrepreneur* for his work; by others as the rent paid to him for his special knowledge; by yet others as the interest on his capital. In accounting the profit shown in, say, a shopkeeper's or farmer's profit and loss account may include elements of all three kinds of payment or price.

The early classical economists tended to explain profit as the recompense for risk-taking. This is still an illuminating theory (*see* below); the difficulty is that ownership is often divorced from control, and it is not easy to say how the risk is divided between the shareholders, who receive what is left after paying all costs, and the *entrepreneurs,* who traditionally are the risk-takers but who even as directors are essentially salaried servants of the enterprise. A second difficulty with this theory is that many risks can be foreseen and therefore discounted, and large numbers of similar risks can be grouped together and each one converted into a known cost by insurance.

Alfred Marshall regarded profit as the reward of enterprise or "the earnings of management." But in this sense profit is a form of wages paid for a special kind of labour.

The American economist J. B. Clark came nearer to the true nature of profit when he explained it as the result of *change.* He argued that in a static and perfectly competitive economy the prices of commodities or services would cover their costs (including management) and no more. But change would upset this equality because the effects of, say, increasing population or income would take time to spread throughout the economy. In the meantime prices in some sectors would exceed costs as defined, giving rise to "true" profits (or costs would exceed prices, giving rise to the opposite, losses).

Another American economist, Frank H. Knight, took up the theory from this point and argued that change as such could not explain profit because some changes could be anticipated and so could be allowed for before they happened. If there were perfect foresight, all changes would be foreseeable, and change could then not bring about profit at all. The cause of profit was therefore *uncertainty:* profit arose not from change itself but from the *unpredictability* of change.

In this sense profit is present in all kinds of economic activity, not only entrepreneurial activity. It is not a separate category of income so much as an element that enters into the rewards of all factors of production to some extent, although it is most easily illustrated in the earnings of enterprise. In an economy in which there was no risk, every factor of production would have some minimum price at which it would be attracted to each occupation: if its reward fell below this "supply price" it would not be supplied. The presence of uncertainty in real life increases these minimum supply prices by a "risk premium" the size of which will depend on the individual attitudes of the owners of factors to the risks of various occupations, and the *expectation* of which must be forthcoming before the factors will be made available to any use. In businesses the complex of such expectations constitutes the "normal" level of profits to which competition will in the long run be edging the earnings of enterprise. But innovation and change are constantly causing revision of expectations, short-run profits may surpass or fall short of expectations, and monopolistic practices try to perpetuate positions of economic advantage, so that profits at any one time in real life are likely to comprise a number of elements of which "pure" profit is only one.

This view of profit as a risk premium is illuminating for two reasons. First, it suggests that in the absence of monopolistic practices the cost to society of risk-bearing is unlikely to be large. Secondly, it indicates that profit in the sense of a risk premium is likely to be present in any kind of economic system, whether based on private enterprise or on state ownership and planning. As long as there is uncertainty about output or the performance of labour, management of any other factor of production, state planning has to take it into account in its decision-making. The only way in which it can abolish profit is by preventing change so that wants can be foreseen without uncertainty. [3]

Profit, Normal. *See* UNCERTAINTY.

Profit, Pure. *See* UNCERTAINTY.

Profit-sharing, a system by which a company regularly distributes a proportion of the profits to its employees. Profit-sharing payments are in addition to wages and salaries; unlike production bonuses, they do not depend on increases in productivity; they are not *ex gratia* payments made at the discretion of the firm but are part of the terms of remuneration. They may act as an incentive to enlarge output since employees benefit directly and proportionately to an increase in profits. They may also have an educational value in acquainting workers with the fluctuations in profit as a residue left after costs known in advance are paid. But they are of limited use as a means of sharing the risks of enterprise between shareholders and employees because the latter cannot easily share losses.

Many profit-sharing schemes were introduced in Britain during the early years of this century, but many of them were abandoned in the inter-war period, often because there were no profits to share. Several large companies have operated profit-sharing schemes. In one type of profit-sharing an employee buys shares in the company and is entitled to share in the profits as a shareholder.

Profit-sharing is intended to improve labour relations and give the worker a sense of participation and loyalty. The part which profit-sharing can play depends on the general "climate" of industrial relations. Profit-sharing may make good relations better, but it may not easily make bad relations good. [3]

Profit Tax, a tax levied on profits earned in production, commerce or finance. In Britain it was first levied as such in 1947. It was intended to secure moderation in wage demands, and to stimulate the ploughing back of profits by taxing dividends distributed to shareholders much more highly than money left in the business. The different rates charged on distributed and undistributed profits were merged into a single rate in 1958. The anti-inflation case for taxing distributed profits at a higher rate was never clearly established. The differential rate encouraged the retention of profits and made established companies less dependent on the capital market for finance for expansion; but it thus discouraged competition and encouraged monopoly and did not encourage efficiency or ensure that the community's savings were being used in the most efficient manner (as they would tend to be if companies had to bid for them competitively).

Other things equal, a profits tax, taken with income tax, reduces the range of profitable projects and discriminates against riskier ones (since high profit prospects which compensate for high risk are taxed but there is no corresponding reduction in the risk of loss). When the government spends the proceeds of tax it can offset some of these effects (e.g. by maintaining high employment, giving subsidies and tax reliefs to encourage investment). The net effect is uncertain, except that the responsibility for business decisions thereby tends to move to or to be qualified by the actions of, the Government.

In 1965 the Corporations Tax replaced the profits and income taxes on company profits. [9]

Programming, Linear. *See* LINEAR PROGRAMMING.

Progressive Tax. *See* TAXATION.

Proletariat, a term borrowed from the French, used to describe people who own no property and therefore depend for their livelihood on their ability to earn wages in return for work. The Latin *proletarius* was applied to citizens who had no property and who met their obligations to the state with their children, *proles.* In Marxist theory it is the members of the proletariat, having "nothing to lose but their chains," who will carry through the anti-capitalist revolution. In the western democracies the proletariat have gradually acquired property through buying houses and other assets and saving through life assurance and pension schemes, although its distribution remains very unequal. [5]

Promissory Note, defined by the Bills of Exchange Act, 1882, as an unconditional promise in writing made by one person to another signed by the maker engaging to pay on demand or at a fixed or determinable future time a stated sum of money to or to the order of a specified person or to the bearer. It differs from a bill of exchange or cheque since there are only two parties instead of three. The maker of the note is primarily liable; the drawer of a bill is liable only if it has been negotiated and if the person or institution on whom it is drawn does not accept or pay the bill. [8]

Propensity to Consume, the relationship between consumption spending and the income that gives rise to it. The concept was evolved by Keynes in his *General Theory of Employment, Interest and Money* in 1936. Assuming that no changes take place in a family's capital wealth that might affect its consumption spending, and that other "outside" influences such as the level and distribution of taxation and government controls remain unchanged, the level of consumption spending is taken to depend on the level of income (both being measured in real terms). This relationship is called "the consumption function" or "the propensity to consume." For the community as a whole it is thought to depend upon "subjective" or psychological attitudes towards thrift, business attitudes towards dividend distribution and the accumulation of reserves, and the way in which income is distributed in the community. Keynes's central proposition is that whenever income increases (or decreases), consumption spending will also increase (or decrease) *but not by as much as the change in income.* In other words the *marginal* propensity to consume (the proportion of an increment of income spent on consumption) is considered to be a proportion less than one or less than 100 per cent.

The importance of this concept for Keynes's theory of total employment and output in the community is that if for any reason economic activity (and thus employment and income) increases, the additional consumption spending generated would be insufficient to sustain employment and income at the new level unless non-consumption spending was simultaneously increased to fill the "gap" caused by part of the increased income being saved and not spent on consumption. This gap demonstrates the importance of investment (non-consumption) spending in determining the level of output, employment and income. By the same token, an autonomous increase in investment spending by businesses will raise employment and income which will (through the marginal propensity to consume) raise consumption spending and thus employment and income again, and so on in a chain or multiple fashion. The extent of these induced changes in spending will depend on the size of the marginal propensity to consume, which thus forms the basis of Keynesian "multiplier" theory.

The later Friedman hypothesis of "permanent income" was a contrasting approach to the consumption function. [9]

Propensity to Import, the relationship between national income and expenditure and spending on imports. It is analogous to the Keynesian propensity to consume.

This relationship was developed to assess the total effect of a change in total spending (and thus employment and income). Economic activity is generated by the sum of all domestic expenditures in a country plus spending by other countries on its exports. Domestic spending, however, does not all generate employment and income in the home country; some of it is siphoned off into a demand for imports which generates employment and income in other countries. The extent of this "leakage" of spending power depends on the propensity to import. The *marginal propensity to import* is the part of an increase in national income that will be spent on imports.

Anything which causes the level of income to change will also cause imports to change in the same direction. Since an increase in exports increases activity and income in the export trades, this increase in total income will lead in turn to increased imports. The ability of an increase or decrease in exports to generate an increase or decrease in imports in this way is one element in the attempt to explain how trade between nations tends to be brought into balance and how booms and slumps in economic activity tend to spread from one country to another.

Whether imports will fluctuate more than or less than proportionately for a given change in income will depend not only on the marginal propensity to import but also on the dependence on external trade. In the USA, although the marginal propensity to import may be small, the average ratio of imports to total income is probably even smaller, so that fluctuations in income may produce more than proportionate fluctuations in imports. In the UK the marginal propensity to import is high but the average ratio of imports to income is even higher, so that fluctuations in income tend to produce less than proportionate fluctuations in imports. [9]

Propensity to Invest, term used by Keynes to describe the willingness of private *entrepreneurs* to spend on capital goods. (Investment by public authorities is determined by political as well as economic influences.)

In Keynesian economic analysis the level of investment depends on profitability, an assessment of which requires a comparison of the outlay required to produce it and the (present) value of the stream of expected future receipts, discounted at an appropriate rate of interest. For example, the present value of £1 per annum receivable for twenty years is £12.46 at 5 per cent, £11.47 at 6 per cent, and so on. The rate of interest chosen for the calculation will reflect the rate at which an *entrepreneur* can borrow in the market, but will normally be higher than this rate to allow for the riskiness and uncertainty of the venture. If the value of the discounted stream of expected receipts is larger than the outlay, the investment is profitable and, other things being equal, will be undertaken.

Profitability may also be assessed by comparing the rate of return on the outlay (expressed as a rate per cent) yielded by the expected flow of receipts with the minimum expected rate of interest. If the rate of return over cost is larger, the investment is profitable.

This second measure is more useful in discussing the influences determining the level of investment. The rate of return over cost to be obtained from additional expenditure on investment of the most profitable type (which Keynes called the "marginal efficiency of capital") will affect the level of investment. At any time, with a given level of interest rates for borrowed funds, expenditure on investment will tend to be carried to the point at which the marginal efficiency of capital equals the general rate of interest adjusted for risks and uncertainties. As the supply of capital goods increases, higher costs of production and/or lower expected receipts from further output will reduce the marginal efficiency of capital until this equilibrium is reached. The level of investment as a whole, therefore, is determined by (*a*) the state of expectations, and (*b*) current interest rates.

Given the former, the lower the interest rates the larger the amount of investment. The stimulus of investment from lower interest rates will also depend on the durability of capital goods and the degree of risk. Broadly, the greater the durability and the smaller the risk the stronger the stimulating effect of a downward shift in interest rates; and conversely. Thus, other things being equal, plans for new building are more likely to be affected by changes in interest rates than, say, investment in industrial machinery and equipment. [9]

Propensity to Save, the obverse of the propensity to consume. Saving is defined as that part of income which is not consumed, and the marginal propensity to consume is defined as the increase (or decrease) in consumption spending resulting from a given increase (or decrease) in income. [9]

Property, the legal right to exclusive use of resources and to exclude other people from their possession, use or control. The resources are usually tangible, such as personal possessions and physical means of production, but they may also be intangible, such as patented ideas. Property rights may vest in private persons, groups or public authorities.

Property is one of the fundamental social institutions. Its economic rationale is that ownership encourages the careful husbanding of scarce resources. An example is the wasteful exploitation of resources in which there are no property rights, such as the overfishing of deep-sea fishing grounds. Economic arguments have been used to support private property at least since Aristotle, the main ones being that widespread ownership means dispersed powers of initiative, and that the accumulation of property provides a powerful stimulus to work and thrift.

In present-day economic analysis and policy, property features prominently. It is a determinant of the distribution of income. Inheritance, gift, capital gains and other taxes on property are analysed in public finance. The use of property by its owners may confer or impose (indiscriminate) gains or costs on other members of the community. To this extent the pattern of market costs and rewards that influence the extent and rejection of the use of resources may only partially reflect costs and benefits to the community as a whole. This is seen as a defect of the operation of markets and a case for government intervention. The concentration of control of property in joint-stock companies is investigated as a basis of monopoly power. The divorce of ownership from control in joint-stock companies is of central economic importance as a characteristic of modern industrial organization. [10]

Property Rights, the expectation of an individual, or group of individuals, that his/their exclusive use of resources will be assured. The more surely his entitlement is respected by law or usage, the more he is likely to pay for them. The rights attach to the owner, not to the property, and trade consists of an exchange of rights over property rather than of property itself, which would be useless if there was no power to use (or transfer, or hire, or sell) it. Hence nominal ownership of property without rights over it is valueless. And hence the importance of effective methods of asserting or enforcing rights over property owned in common, as by shareholders in corporate property or citizens in socialized property. Physical transfer and possession may be necessary to the use of property rights, e.g. clothes or furniture, but physical transfer may not be necessary, e.g. fishing rights.

Property rights are the creation of law or usage. They may be altered by change in both. [13]

Property Tax. *See* RATES.

Proportional Tax. *See* TAXATION.

Protected Bear. *See* BEAR.

Proudhon, Pierre. *See* ANARCHISM.

Psychology, Relation to Economics. *See* ECONOMICS.

Public Choice, a comparatively recent development in the application of economic theory and analysis to political decision-making. Specifically it jettisons the conventional assumption of traditional economic theory that there is a contrast between market behaviour as motivated by self-interest and political behaviour as motivated by the public good. It sets out to evolve a positive (behaviourist, ethically neutral) theory of the incentives and deterrents in making political decisions on the use of resources, as a necessary preliminary to the development of normative analysis of proposals for policy to improve the use of resources.

The theory of public choice has been developed in the USA mostly by Professor J. M. Buchanan and Professor Gordon Tullock of the Virginia School, and by others associated with them. It is related to the relatively new "economics of property" and the "economics of law," the three together becoming known as "the new institutional economics." The foci of analysis are the limits ("constraints") on political decision-making imposed by the structure of law, the distribution of property rights, and the legislative and administrative aspects of the political/governmental process. Public choice theory studies the effects of bureaucratic behaviour on the size and growth of government; the comparative bureaucracies of government, public corporations, non-profit organizations and commercial profit-making companies; the adversary system in judicial proceedings; the economic implication of John Rawls' *A Theory of Justice;* the economics of metropolitan consolidation; the desiderata of university teachers, students and administrators; and the political pressures in the fuel situation and other situations of political decision-making in the use of scarce resources. Formal mathematical models are being developed for public choice decisions. The headquarters of public choice theory is the Center for the Study of Public Choice at the Virginia Polytechnic Institute and State University; it publishes the journal *Public Choice.* [13]

Public Company. *See* LIMITED LIABILITY.

Public Deposits. *See* BANK OF ENGLAND.

Public Finance, the study of the nature and effects of the government's use of fiscal instruments—taxing and spending, borrowing and lending, buying and selling. It includes the interrelationships between government agencies, as between the central government and local authorities of a single country. It is sometimes considered to include the study of public utilities and nationalized industries, which may be self-financing like any other business and thus lie outside public finance "proper," but their relationship with government often brings them into the discussion of public finance.

The essential subject-matter of public finance is the provision by public authorities of "public" or "collective" goods or services from which it is impossible to exclude individuals, such as defence and public health, and the way in which they are financed. When the government spends money on, for example, the armed forces or education, it affects the pattern of production and consumption. Levying taxes to pay for government spending (and the way in which it benefits particular groups) affects the distribution of income and wealth. The magnitude and distribution of taxation affects the type and level of total output; so will government decisions to finance part of its expenditure by borrowing rather than taxing, or to levy taxes in excess of budgeted expenditures. The management of the National Debt (the accumulation of earlier borrowing) raises problems for monetary policy. Taxing and spending affects the nature and amplitude of cyclical business fluctuations and, in the longer run, the rate of economic progress.

The central government is thus not a separate sector of the economy, concerned only to supply community needs that the market cannot supply adequately or at all. It also "holds the ring" in its ability to influence economic activity as a whole. Discussion of public finance must therefore either assume or analyse the aims of fiscal policy. Possible policy aims include a high and stable level of employment without inflation, a high rate of economic growth, a strong currency, a more equal distribution of income, a high degree of freedom of choice for consumers, employees, traders, investors, business men and others. One aspect of public finance is to examine such aims, whether explicitly stated or not, to consider how far practice diverges from them, how far they are compatible with one another, and to show the nature of possible conflict.

"Principles" of taxation are commonly analysed in the literature on public finance. Taxation, it is variously argued, should be "just," "equitable," "economic," etc. These terms are rarely defined rigorously and can be interpreted in various senses, so that writers have used them to support recommendations for proportional, progressive or even regressive tax systems. No principles of taxation can be inferred from economic analysis alone, without assumptions based on political and ethical judgements. Nevertheless economics can help in examining the general effects of alternative fiscal proposals on prices, interest rates, saving, investment, incentives, profits, business location and organization, production, employment, incomes, wages and so on. [12]

Public Goods, commodities or services with three properties: they are non-rival, i.e. they can be used or consumed or enjoyed by an increasing number of people without the amount available to others being diminished, e.g. defence, preventative medicine (anti-malarial treatment of still water, etc.), street lighting; they are available to everyone in the catchment area independently of the size or existence of payment; and they cannot be withheld from non-payers and must therefore necessarily be financed by collective agreement enforced by law. Many goods and services embody a degree of "publicness" (i.e. cannot be confined to people who pay the market price): few are completely "public." Goods or services provided for payment in the market often confer gratuitous benefits on third parties; conversely goods or services customarily provided collectively often have non-public private properties, e.g. in education, housing, medical care, refuse collection, fire fighting, police.

For example, outsiders are not affected if a Council tenant has pink spots or green stripes on his bathroom wallpaper. Indirectly, by making him feel better (or worse), it may make him more (or less) efficient at work; but in this indirect ultimate sense every private act or decision is likely to have an influence on third parties and there are no purely private acts or decisions at all. And in that sense the word private has no meaning. Again, in education, the benefit may be private if it increases the individual's appreciation of the arts, love of nature, etc. And in medical care the benefit is private if the individual who has varicose veins treated is enabled to avoid discomfort or enjoy his garden with less effort. [13]

Public Interest (National Interest, General Interest), terms commonly used in political debate on economic policy to denote the benefit or advantage of the community as a whole in contrast with private or personal interest. An example is the proposition "Shipbuilding (or the docks, the railways, insurance companies, the pharmaceutical industry, banking, etc.) should be run in the public/national/general interest, not for the private owners/directors/shareholders." Sometimes the public/national interest is identified with, or replaced by, the interest of the employees, for whose benefit it is argued an organization or industry should be run, whether or not it can cover its costs in the open market.

The term has strong political, moral and emotional connotations but economists can also examine its economic implications in a positive (i.e. behaviourist, non-normative) sense. As a general proposition the argument is self-evident: no economist would argue that resources should be used to benefit private interests if they conflicted with the general interest of the community at large: the question is whether private interests necessarily conflict with the general interest and the circumstances in which they conflict, or are neutral, or further it. This approach leads to analysis of the institutions of property and the laws on contract, sale of goods, etc. Here conclusions or doctrines run from Adam Smith (public interest is generally best served by allowing people to pursue the private interests they can perceive) to Karl Marx (private property is theft). The proposition is not universal and therefore not absolute: the case is rarely made for producing elemental "basic" commodities like food or clothing to serve the public rather than the private interests of bakers or tailors, so that private interests do not *necessarily* conflict with the national interest. The case is usually argued for each service or industry on grounds special to it, e.g. that control by directors or private owners would lead to monopoly, or that industry should be organized according to "social" rather than merely commercial criteria (as in rail transport), or that the private owners are inefficient (shipbuilding etc.), etc.

The proposition also implies that services or industries run to serve private interests are not accountable to the public and that services run to serve the public interest (like nationalized industries, public corporations, and government-run services) are accountable to the public. Here economic analysis turns on the effectiveness of competition in compelling industries run by private controllers to serve the public or make losses and go out of business, and on the motivations and accountability to the electors of political or official controllers of public services.

The term "Public Interest" indicates an intention without necessarily ensuring performance. There is a distinction between purpose and result. Economists debate the technical efficiency or effectiveness in a wider sense of services or industries, in Britain and other countries, designed to be controlled in the public interest, and their conclusions or judgements vary from success to failure. [10]

Public Investment. *See* INVESTMENT.

Public Ownership. *See* INVESTMENT.

Public Sector, that part of a nation's economic activities which comes within the scope of the central government, including social insurance, the local authorities, nationalized industries and other public corporations. In the last fifty years there has been a rapid growth in the public sector in many countries. Since 1914 total expenditure by UK government authorities on goods, services and income transfers has risen from less than a fifth to two-fifths of total national income (gross national product). About half is spent on social services, principally education, health, housing, pensions, other welfare services or benefits and money grants. Local trading services and nationalized industries generally aim to be self-financing from the sale of their goods and services. The remainder of the public sector is usually financed by taxation or borrowing from the public, but local authorities and public corporations frequently borrow direct from the public, the former mainly for housing, the latter for industrial capital. Charges for public sector services are occasionally resorted to when tax finance runs short. Museum charges were tried for a brief period, and nursery school charges have been proposed. Hospital "boarding" fees have been considered by governments of the two main British parties. [10]

Public Utilities, group of industries in a monopoly position supplying "essential" goods and services, subject to public regulation designed to ensure that they operate "in the public interest." It is difficult to say which industries fall within this definition since what constitutes "the public interest" or "essential goods" is a matter of personal and political opinion. Consequently the sort of industries subject to government regulation varies over time and between countries according to public opinion and the aims of the ruling political party. Public transport, for example, is run by the state in some countries and left to private enterprise in others.

Broadly, the industries most commonly regarded as public utilities are those providing services by means of wires, cables, pipes and rails: namely, gas, water, electricity, telecommunications, sanitation, railways. They have one common requirement—large quantities of expensive, specialized equipment. To keep prices low, and at the same time earn sufficient revenue to pay for substantial interest and depreciation charges on their capital, individual producing units in these industries—waterworks, power stations, bus or train services, etc.—must serve as many customers as possible. For this reason it is usually uneconomic to have more than one type of each undertaking—one gas works, one generating station, etc.—serving a given area. In such industries competition tends to be ruinous to all but consumers, and short-lived since the large investment necessary limits the number of producers and collusion inevitably follows intense competition. Hence the term "natural" monopolies.

Whenever production takes place under these conditions it generally leads to a case for some form of public regulation, ranging from price control or limitation of the rate of profit earned on invested capital to outright public ownership and operation. Public regulation however poses many problems of principle:

what is a "fair" price, or a "fair" rate of return on capital, what is meant by "capital" in this context; if the industry is nationalized what should be the policy on output, prices and organization; and so on. Again, when technological and other change throws up competing substitute services (roads for railways, fuel oil for coal and other energy sources) it is necessary to decide whether the public interest is better served by suppressing the substitute and bringing it within public regulation or by relaxing the pricing and operating constraints on the regulated industry and allowing the new product or service to compete freely. It is a set of broadly common economic problems such as these, rather than technological characteristics, that defines the "public utility." [10]

Public Works Loan Board, considers applications for loans by local authorities and other prescribed bodies and collects the repayments. Most of the loans have been made to local authorities for capital projects sanctioned by government departments. The security consists of the local revenues of the authorities.

The funds provided by Parliament are drawn from the Local Loans Fund through the National Debt Commissioners. Rates of interest are fixed by the Treasury, and tend to reflect its borrowing rates. The Public Works Loan Board has continued to be the main resource of capital funds for the smaller local authorities. [12]

Pump Priming, the attempt to revive a depressed economy by government spending financed by budget deficits. In theory it is tapered off when private spending has been stimulated sufficiently. The implication is that such expenditure is like priming a pump (the economy) which will then continue to operate without further help. In the early stages of the USA "New Deal" administration in the early 1930's pump priming expenditures were thought to be sufficient to lift the economy out of depression. Subsequent refinements of multiplier and accelerator theory were thought to reveal weaknesses in the pump priming doctrine. Deficit spending, if continued too long, may cause a more than proportionate increase in total spending; but the level of spending will gradually drop back again once the government spending is discontinued, unless in the meantime private spending financed by loans has been stimulated sufficiently. This last condition is more difficult to predict with certainty; and even so it is not likely to survive the reduction in total spending when government spending is withdrawn. The inference is that to stimulate recovery from a major depression the "priming" would need to be substantial and contained for a long period. [9]

Purchase and Lease-back. *See* SALE AND LEASE-BACK.

Purchase Tax, a tax levied at various rates on the wholesale gross value of selected commodities. It formed part of British Customs and Excise duties (accounting for about one-fifth of revenue from duties in the early 1970's). It altered the relative prices of goods and thus distorted the pattern of consumption and production. Periodic alteration of rates of purchase tax also disrupted production planning and, since the tax was levied on wholesale values, produced chance gains or losses on retailer's stocks. Variation of purchase tax rates and goods taxed was used as a fiscal weapon to restrain and guide consumer spending. In 1973 purchase tax was replaced by a uniform Value-Added Tax. [12]

Purchasing Power Parity, a theory propounded by the Swedish economist Gustav Cassel in 1916 that claimed to explain international exchange rates between currencies in terms of the purchasing power of their home countries. But when the exchange rate was £1 = $2.4 it did not always necessarily indicate the relative purchasing power of the two currencies at home. The theory has a more valid form in which it tries to explain *changes* in the foreign exchange rate by *changes* in the relative purchasing power of the two currencies. If inflation takes place in one of the countries the domestic purchasing power of its currency will fall as prices rise, but as prices rise its products will become more expensive to foreigners while its own citizens will tend to buy relatively cheaper imports rather than home-produced goods: thus, if capital flows do not alter, the reduced foreign demand for its currency and its own increased demand for foreign currencies will cause its exchange rate to depreciate. This is the best case that can be made for the theory. Even so, it is open to criticism: e.g. the wartime sale of foreign assets by Britain, which reduced her foreign investment income and necessitated increased sales of export goods, required a larger post-war change in the exchange rate than would have been necessary merely to preserve parity of relative internal purchasing powers of dollars and pounds. The basic explanation of the foreign exchange rate is that it depends on supply and demand, and purchasing power is only one influence among many that determine supply and demand. Others are changes in national income, in productivity (e.g. in export industries) and in the flow of capital. If British investors wish to buy assets and make loans abroad without any matching desire by foreigners to lend to Britain, the exchange rate will tend to depreciate. Purchasing power parity is thus only a partial explanation of exchange rates, although when other circumstances are generally stable it can give a rough guide to them. [4]

Pure Competition, one of a number of economic "models" of market forms used in economic analysis which range from pure competition through monopolistic competition and oligopoly to pure monopoly. The model of pure competition assumes many sellers (in relation to total output) of identical products none of whom can influence the market price by varying the amount he sells. Under these assumptions every firm would be maximizing profits when it had expanded output to the level at which the additional (marginal) cost of producing additional units of output was just equal to the market price of additional units. Expressed another way, it would expand its hire of factors to the point at which additional input factors of production made an output contribution just equal in value to their cost. [7]

Pure Profit. *See* UNCERTAINTY.

"Put Option." *See* OPTION DEALING.

Pyramid Selling, a complicated sales promotion technique of direct sales to the public by selling teams arranged hierarchically, the members of which are persuaded to buy their way into the organization and in turn receive rewards for recruitment of further sales members as much as for the sales they achieve. Pyramid selling and similar schemes have been declared illegal in several countries: in Britain they were controlled by the Fair Trading Act, 1973, and those aspects of schemes which impose hardship on their gullible members were made illegal. [7]

Pyramiding, concentrating control over joint-stock companies by a series of controlling interests in holding companies and their subsidiaries. For example, a company with a capital of £200,000, half in ordinary shares and half in fixed-interest shares, may be controlled by the ownership of £50,001 ordinary shares. An even smaller number of shares will suffice for effective control if the rest of the shares are widely held. The £200,000 capital might be employed to buy 50 per cent of the ordinary shares in a company with £800,000 capital, half in ordinary and half in fixed-interest shares. The £800,000 might be used to buy 50 per cent of the ordinary shares in operating companies with capital of £3,200,000, again half in ordinary and half in fixed interest shares. In this way the Van Sweringen brothers in the USA acquired control of railway assets exceeding $2,000 million with an investment of less than $20 million. [3]

Q

Quantitative Control, another name for physical, in contrast to economic or financial, control of the economy by government. Thus rationing or licensing regulates demand or supply by specifying quantities of goods or services that may be bought or sold, lent or borrowed. In contrast economic or monetary controls regulate the economy indirectly by expanding or reducing the supply of money or purchasing power by rules on bank lending, hire purchase restrictions, changes in taxes, etc. [8]

Quantitative Economics, that part of economics concerned with the collection and analysis of statistical information. It involves the examination of economic quantities, e.g. the level of output, employment, prices and interest. By using economic principles to interpret measurements of this kind, the economist can build up a picture of the working of an economy, assess the economic impact of changes in its structure and assist in forecasting probable developments. But the economist must also take account of the less measurable social and psychological forces. An assessment of the probable effects of a radical change in income tax, for example, would be incomplete without a study of its impact on incentives to work and invest, and hence on output. The development of national income statistics has run parallel with an increased emphasis on the quantitative analysis of economic aggregates or macro-economics. Some economists argue that this tendency has gone too far, and that micro-economics, the analysis of *individual* responses to economic stimuli on the side of demand or of supply, remain fundamental because statistics cannot measure individual responses accurately and because some responses may take forms which, although important, are not measurable. [14]

Quantity Equation. *See* QUANTITY THEORY OF MONEY.

Quantity Theory of Money, asserts that the general price level depends on the amount of money in circulation. It is usually formulated in terms of the "quantity equation": MV = PT, where M is the quantity of money (including bank deposits) and V is the velocity of circulation of money, i.e. the average number of times which a unit of money is spent during a defined period for a quantity of goods and services T whose average price is P.

The equation states that the total quantity of money spent in a period (MV) is equal to the volume of transactions multiplied by the price of each transaction. It is therefore essentially a truism, and does not show a *causal* connection between the components ("variables") in the equation. For the quantity theory to hold good further assumptions about the behaviour of V and T must be true. It does, however, serve as a rudimentary outline of the problems involved; it emphasizes the truth that the supply of money influences the price level and may be a cause of inflation.

This is the "transactions" form of the quantity equation, originally outlined by Irving Fisher. The value of money can also be considered as determined, like the price of other commodities, by the demand for and the supply of it. The basic equation is then $M = kPT$, where M, P and T have the same meaning as before and k is the proportion of the community's expenditure on goods and services which on the average is held as cash during the period. This is called the "cash balance" form of the quantity equation, developed by the Cambridge school of economists. Since k is the reciprocal of V (e.g. if V is six times per period, then k is one-sixth of expenditure), the differences between the two forms of the equation are not fundamental. But the cash balance approach emphasizes that changes in the demand for money (k) may be as important as the quantity of money (M) in determining P and opens the way for a closer examination of the influences governing k.

Keynes analysed these influences as of three kinds. He argued that money was demanded broadly to satisfy three motives—the transactions, precautionary and speculative motives. The first refers to money required to pay for current transactions—i.e. everyday purchases. The second refers to money demanded as inactive balances held to provide against unforeseen contingencies. The third refers to money held as a pool available to take advantage of movements in the market prices of other forms of wealth (e.g. securities). The simple form of the quantity theory considered only the transactions demand for money. If money were demanded only because of its command over other goods, which remained unchanged in total, P would vary as M. But this simple relationship breaks down if a part or the whole of an increase in M flows into inactive balances (for the precautionary and speculative motives), thus having little or no effect on commodity prices. The simple quantity theory relationship is also weakened by possible variations in T, i.e. in the total output of goods and services. The followers of Keynes maintained that the influences determining the general level of prices are more complex than the quantity theory in both forms envisaged. Friedman and his followers claim that, with refinement, the quantity theory has been vindicated by monetary history. [8]

Quasi-money, "half," "part," or "near" money: an asset—physical or financial—which can be offered instead of money and will be accepted by some people in some circumstances. Money (coins or notes) is universally accepted in all circumstances. Quasi-money could range from an IOU or a bill of exchange to an object of known value. [8]

Quasi-monopoly, a degree of monopoly somewhere between nil (in perfect competition) and total (perfect monopoly). A duopoly consists of two firms with quasi-monopoly. More loosely, industries with substantial economies of scale will comprise a few large firms, each with quasi-monopoly. [3]

Quasi-rent, the earnings of a specialized and durable factor of production in a (short-run) period during which its supply cannot be enlarged or reduced.

Originally the concept of *economic rent* was developed by David Ricardo to explain the payment for land as a factor contributing to production. Unlike man-made factors of production and labour itself, unimproved land could not be said to have a cost of production which had to be covered to ensure that it would be made available for production. The size of its remuneration would depend entirely on the demand for the fixed supply: even if the remuneration fell to nothing the land would still be there. It followed that the remuneration of land, called rent, could not be considered as part of the cost of production of commodities. It was essentially a *surplus,* the extent of which would be determined by the demand for the commodities whose production it facilitated: when this demand was high or low, the rent of land would correspondingly be high or low.

The concept was applied by Alfred Marshall to the determination of the price or payment of all specialized factors of production in the short run when their supply could not be changed. In a short-run period defined in this way, such a factor is like land in its economic characteristics, and its earnings can equally be regarded as a form of rent. But in the longer run its earnings cannot be regarded as determined entirely by demand in this way because unlike land its supply will be increased or reduced according to whether resources invested in it yield a return larger or smaller than what could be earned from alternative investments of comparable risk. In the long run therefore its remuneration is determined by its supply as well as by the demand for it.

To emphasize this short-run nature of the economic rents earned by specialized factors of production, Marshall called them "quasi-rents." The short-run earnings of a firm in excess of its expenditure or outlays on wages, materials and other variable "inputs" of factors are quasi-rents in this sense. They represent the returns attributable to the specialized "fixed" factors employed. In the short run they may be less or more than the minimum necessary to secure that they are eventually replaced; but in the longer period competition will tend to ensure that the earnings approximate to a "normal" rate of return on the cost of replacing them. The essence of the distinction is still that of the original concept of rent; i.e. quasi-rents form no part of the costs that must be covered in the short run to secure the production of commodities; they form an economic "surplus." [6]

Quesnay, François. *See* ECONOMIC THOUGHT; "TABLEAU ÉCONOMIQUE."

Queueing Theory, (*a*) attempts to explain the rates at which or the proportions in which productive facilities or services should be provided in order to maximize efficiency and minimize cost. Queues are created by the uncertainty about the rate at which the facilities or services are required. For example, taxi drivers cannot be sure when passengers will want their services and so do not arrive at taxi ranks at the precise time when they are wanted. Delivery vans may not be able to arrive at a factory at the precise time when goods are ready for collection. Queues of people and goods therefore form. The resulting pool of unused (waiting to be used) resources is thus the outcome of imperfect information and the costs of making it more perfect (or less imperfect).

If prices were infinitely flexible raising them might reduce some queues so that those who do not wish to pay higher prices fall out. But it is impracticable to alter prices with this degree of refinement, and imperfect knowledge about the demand for the facilities or services makes queues inevitable. Queueing theory attempts to indicate how queues can be reduced by observing the rates of arrival of goods or people, the average period of waiting, the frequency with which facilities or services arrive. It may then be possible by improving the flow of information to reduce the queues or to time the arrival of facilities or services so that they synchronize more nearly with the demand for them. Where such methods cannot be tried as practical experiments, because it may be too costly to change established procedure unless it is sure that the new methods will be better, it may be possible to construct mathematical models to see how the new methods might work by calculating or estimating the average length of queues and the chance that, for example, a taxi passenger or a consignment of goods will have to wait. Where such mathematical solutions are difficult, a paper experiment, known as simulation, may help by assuming that persons or goods that need the services arrive at stated intervals and that the service for each person or consignment takes a given time. Where queueing is found in more complex situations, it may be possible to use electronic computers to "simulate" or reproduce the processes.

(*b*) more generally queueing is caused by a gap between the equilibrium price that tends to emerge in the market and the price charged (because fixed by government, private whim, etc.). When the price is below the market level the available supply is rationed by queueing (or waiting), e.g. Council housing (rents below market level), hospitals (nil price).

(*c*) crude pricing may also create queues, e.g. charging the same price for cinema seats which vary in comfort. [7]

Quotas, (*a*) in the economics of international trade, a method of protecting home industries from foreign competition or of reducing pressure on the balance of payments by limiting imports. For protection the quota is more certain than a tariff in its effects on the quantity of imports. Both will generally cause a rise in price in the home market for the imported goods. The object of the tariff is to raise the price of the import and reduce the demand for it; the object of the quota is to reduce the supply of the imported good in the home market, so that its price will tend to rise. In both cases demand will be diverted towards the products of the home industry that competes with the import. When a tariff is used the government gains revenue from the imported good: an increase in price due to a quota is likely to benefit either the foreign producer or the domestic importer by raising revenue per unit sold. A government which imposes quotas may be able to obtain a share in the gains by marketing the commodity itself. Alternatively, having imposed a limit on the quantity that may be imported, it may auction to the highest bidder the right to import the commodity.

(*b*) in cartels and in international commodity control agreements, a quota is a stated amount of output allocated to member firms or nations up to which they are allowed to produce and sell. The purpose is usually to increase prices and profits or reduce fluctuations in them. [4]

R

Rack Rent, the full (market) rental value of land and buildings as determined by the demand for them and their supply. The rent paid under a lease may often be less than the full rack or market rental value of the premises, e.g. if a capital sum ("premium") has been paid, or if rental values of comparable property have risen during the lease. Conversely, the term is used as a criticism to mean "exorbitant" rentals such as might emerge during a period of exceptionally high demand for houses, flats or land. At such times competition among, say, tenant farmers may lead them to offer or accept higher rentals than they would need to pay if the pressure of demand were less or when the supply were increased. [6]

Radcliffe Committee (on the Working of the Monetary System), appointed by the British Chancellor of the Exchequer in 1957. It reported unanimously in 1959 that the monetary mechanism could not, as operated through changes in Bank rate, be relied on to control the economy but should be supplemented by increasing use of physical and other controls (on consumer credit, capital issues, insurance companies, and other institutions that compete with the banks as lenders), particularly in "emergencies," and that there should be more political control over the banking system. The report was criticized by some economists as underestimating the potential power of monetary policy by failing to allow for the reason for its inability to prevent inflation in the 1950's: the rise in prices reduced the "real" rate of interest, high income and profits taxes reduced the net cost of borrowing, higher interest costs could in part be passed on in higher prices, self-financing made firms partly indifferent to the higher cost of capital. Other economists thought the Committee did not go far enough in advocating physical controls in place of interest rates and controls over the supply of money. [8]

Random Walk, a term used in the theory of stock market prices. It postulates that security prices on successive days are independent of one another, and that the best estimate of tomorrow's prices is that they will be the same as today's. If the prices were inter-dependent the relationships between them could in time be learned and used by investors who would find it profitable to buy and sell securities in the light of experience and so eliminate the relationships. A study of past prices is therefore not a good basis for advice on investment. [7]

Rank-size Rule, generalization which attempts to express in precise terms the hierarchical structure of cities. In its simplest form it says that if cities are ranked by population size, the size of the city in the *r*th rank will be 1/*r* the size of the largest city. It is generally expressed in the form $r.P_r^a = A$ where *r* stands for rank (e.g., first, second, third, etc.), P_r stands for the size in population of a town of rank *r*, *A* is a constant, approximately equal to the population of the largest city, and *a* is an exponent (power), approximately equal to 1. The rank-size rule, which is chiefly associated with the work of the German economist G. K. Zipf, is an example of a "statistical" law: i.e. it is an approximation to the kind of regularity that statistical investigations of the size and rank of urban areas suggest. It is not an inevitability but is best regarded as an expression of a regularity that tends to emerge in many countries from the countless location decisions of individuals. The data for England and Wales do not conform very well to the rank-size rule, possibly because of the excessive dominance of London in the urban hierarchy and of the proximity and influence of European centres. [6]

Rate Deficiency Payment, grant made from the central government to local authorities whose rate resources per head of population (adjusted for age, sparsity, etc.) fell below the national average. The grant was paid direct to all rating authorities entitled to it. It was introduced in 1958 to replace the former Exchequer Equalization Grant, which had a similar purpose but which had been criticized because the central government had insufficient control over its amount in any one year and because its method of distribution produced anomalies between different local authorities. The Exchequer Equalization Grant in effect had made the central government an additional ratepayer on the amount by which the rateable value of an area fell short of the national average: the amount payable thus depended on the amount of local expenditure and was an uncertain or "open-ended" commitment for the central government. The Rate Deficiency Payment attempted to remove this risk to some extent by relating the amount of grant payable not to an authority's expenditure in any year but to the three-yearly average expenditure of all authorities of a similar class: it was also distributed direct, whereas the Exchequer Equalization Grant was distributed only to county boroughs and county councils and filtered downwards from them through a complicated system of adjustments to rate precepts and "capitation" payments. The Rate Deficiency Payment was replaced in 1966 by the Rate Support Grant. [12]

Rate of Exchange. *See* FOREIGN EXCHANGE.

Rate of Interest. *See* INTEREST.

Rate Rebates, a form of additional relief from the payment of rates, granted since 1966 to ratepayers whose income and needs satisfy prescribed rules. The rebates extended the reliefs given to all domestic ratepayers which had reduced their rate poundages relative to other ratepayers. [12]

Rate Support Grant, Exchequer grant to local authorities introduced by the Local Government Act, 1966, which replaced the former General Grant and Rate Deficiency Payment. The RSG consisted of three elements. The *needs element* was broadly similar to the former General Grant and was based mainly on the total population and number of dependants in an area. The *domestic element* was payable to all authorities as compensation for loss of rate income resulting from government measures to reduce the burden of rates falling on householders. The *resources element* replaced the former Rate Deficiency Payment and was paid to any local authority with rate resources per head of population below the national average. The calculation of the RSG was based on: (*a*) local authorities' allowable expenditures for the year less direct subsidies and any specific (allocated) grants received; (*b*) current and expected levels of costs; (*c*) variations in forecast demand for local services beyond the control of individual authorities; and (*d*) the planned expansion of particular services. [12]

Rates, taxes on property levied by local authorities in order to finance local public services and amenities. The principle underlying the assessment of rates is that occupiers of land and buildings should contribute to the finance of local services in proportion to the value of the property they occupy. The property value on which rates are based is equal to the annual value of the rent which it is calculated the property earns, or could earn if it were let, less the cost of repairs and insurance. The amount an occupier may be called upon to pay is determined by the rateable value of the property and the rate in the pound charged by the local authority. If the rateable value of a house is assessed at £200 and the rate poundage decided by the authority is 50*p*., £100 is charged in rates each year. Property is valued for rate assessment by the Inland Revenue but rates are fixed and collected by the local rating authorities (in England and Wales the county and non-county boroughs, urban and rural districts).

As a tax, rates are uncertain in their incidence since producers of goods and services who pay them may be able to shift the burden by raising prices asked (for goods) or lowering prices offered (for the factors of production) wherever possible: rates on occupiers of houses or flats may be in no way related to income or to the usual measures of individual capacity to pay tax. Rates are commonly regarded as a "stable" form of revenue: the meaning of this term is uncertain so long as the rate poundage or rateable values can be changed. They are also regarded as a tax on housing standards; but its practical importance in this sense is doubtful if the government and local authorities can maintain standards in other ways. A more serious criticism is that the widespread use of rateable value per head of population as an index of the relative wealth or poverty of an area, for the purpose of calculating grants payable from the central government to local authorities, produces many anomalies in practice. Against these criticisms it is argued that rates are relatively cheap and easy to collect and are a familiar tax which it would be a mistake to dismantle in favour of an untried form of local taxation such as a local income or sales tax. But this is an objection that can be made against many reforms or against reform in general.

Rate income forms a falling proportion of total local authority income in England and Wales. During the twentieth century grants from the central government have been growing and now exceed rate income, reflecting the growth of "social service" expenditure in local authority outlays. This tendency towards a larger degree of central control of types and standards of service, coupled with increased central government responsibility for finance, is thought likely to continue. Some economists argue that the central government should assume total responsibility for the finance of major social service expenditure such as education, others that in a society with rising standards of living and increasingly equal incomes such services could be paid for directly by individuals or families. Either of these alternatives would reduce rates to the point at which reform of local taxation and grant distribution was possible. [12]

Rationalization, the concentration of an economic activity into fewer units. In principle, the purpose is to increase efficiency and lower costs by economy in the use of resources through eliminating duplication of effort and encouraging standardization in method and output.

Within an individual business unit rationalization might mean the concentration of activities formerly dispersed; within a firm as a whole it might mean the organization of production by "divisions." For example, instead of making a component in scattered factories, it might be made in a single plant or in a few plants. Instead of an organization in which people had been responsible for very dissimilar activities, there might be a "divisional" structure in which each unit would be more or less similar, although co-ordinated.

Rationalization thus exploits the principle of specialization by internal reorganization within a single enterprise or by association or merger of firms. The latter is linked with the idea of rationalization within an industry as a whole, the gains of which are, in principle, the elimination of inefficient firms and of uneconomic overlapping of activities between firms. Since large-scale mergers may require transfer in employment and redundancy, rationalization sometimes provokes hostility and in the recent years of full employment it is often accompanied by claims for compensation for loss of employment. [3]

Rationing, allocation of supplies of goods and services among consumers by means of coupons to replace or supplement the rationing function of money prices in a free exchange economy.

In exceptional circumstances, such as war, when there are sudden, severe or prolonged shortages of commodities regarded as essential, prices may rise beyond the means of people with lower incomes. Government enforcement of low prices would not ensure minimum supplies for all, because those "first in the queue" would get as much as they could pay for and those at the end might get little or nothing. Rationing goes to the root of the problem by removing money as the source and measure of demand and ensuring supplies for all.

In a system of rationing based on coupons, everyone receives coupons entitling them to buy a limited amount of a commodity, usually at a fixed price. As the total "purchasing power" of the coupons issued is made equal to the available supply, no one goes without (if the price is fixed sufficiently low), although many or most people have less than they would normally buy.

This system can be made more flexible by issuing coupons for a range of goods, such as all clothing or household equipment, rather than for a single commodity, thus giving the purchaser more freedom in deciding how to spend his coupons. Prices of rationed goods are fixed in terms of coupons as well as money and are occasionally adjusted to accord with the prevailing state of supply and demand. Ration coupons are, in a sense, a second form of money, with a specialized and limited circulation. They were used in many countries in and after World War II, and are used in some communist countries in peacetime. [10]

Real Balance, the real value (i.e. purchasing power over goods and services) of money held in cash or liquid assets. The conventional or customary "balance" between the assets people *hold* in money and their *expenditure* of it is disturbed if the prices of goods and services fall. Their real balances will then increase. They will therefore spend more and save more by increasing their supply of funds in the money market for loans, which will tend to reduce interest rates and thus in turn stimulate investment. The theory is thus that the real-balance effect is to increase both consumption and investment. [8]

Real Income, money income adjusted for changes in the level of prices. Comparisons of national income totals over a number of years require adjustment in this way to show changes in real income. The "general level" of prices is an abstraction, and adjustment in practice means using a series of indexes reflecting price changes in broad categories of expenditure on consumption, capital, exports, etc. Even so the resultant figures of real income reflect real economic welfare only imperfectly. They do not, for example, wholly reflect changes in quality or range of choice of goods and services.

Most theoretical economic relationships between income and other "variables" (such as demand, consumption, expenditure, saving) are expressed in real terms. [9]

Real Investment. *See* INVESTMENT.

Real Wages, an index of wages expressed in terms of money's worth; i.e. they are money wages adjusted for the value of money to reveal the change in the amount of goods and services they will buy. If both money wages and prices generally rise by, say, 5 per cent in a year, real wages have not changed.

Wage comparisons are also made between places. Wages in Region A may be twice as high as wages in Region B, but if prices in Region A are also twice as high, real wages are equal. It can therefore be misleading to study only money wages in deciding how well or badly a group of employees is paid. Expressed in the form of an index, real wages are calculated by dividing an index of money wages by an index of prices to give an index of wages at constant prices.

The debate between Keynesian and other ("Classical") economists largely centres on how workers will react to (or even recognize) a reduction in their real wages caused by (i) a *reduction* in money wages and (ii) an *increase* in money wages more than offset by a rise in prices. [5]

Rebates, Aggregated. *See* AGGREGATED REBATES.

Recession, a modern name for slump; a modest reduction in economic activity. [9]

Reciprocal Externalities. *See* EXTERNALITIES.

Reciprocity, the practice of according another country trade concessions identical with those granted by it. Often confused with free trade; it is more accurately interpreted as what used to be called "fair trade," i.e. the doctrine of *quid pro quo* in overseas commerce, offering free trade to free trade states, and repaying protection by protection.

Reciprocity has been employed by the USA since 1934 under the Reciprocal Trade Agreements Act, which sought to alleviate depression in the USA by expanding exports through bilateral negotiations. Tariff reductions conceded under the Acts are extended to all favoured nations under the most-favoured-nation clause. [4]

Reconciliation of Optima, the process of maximizing the utility from a combination of objectives. Because of the underlying scarcity of resources, no single objective can be achieved perfectly or in full: to do so would entail too large a sacrifice of other desired objectives. It would be possible, technically, to avoid any loss of life from industrial accidents by banning or fencing some kinds of machinery, or from road accidents by enforcing walking-pace speed limits for vehicles; but these measures would slow industry down and even reduce living standards, a price many would think too high to pay. Life could also be lengthened by transferring enough resources from education, housing, ship-building, defence, etc. to medical care, but some people would prefer more education, etc. to prolonging life (especially beyond mental vigour). Life itself is therefore not absolute if the purpose is to make the most of scarce resources. The general rule applies that the productivity of resources is maximized when the marginal yield (i.e. from the "last" £1 or £1 million) is equalized in all uses.

Risks are entailed in reconciling optima and maximizing their combined utility. Ill-health or even death from alcoholism or obesity can be avoided by under-eating or not drinking at all, but some people prefer not to make such sacrifices and are prepared to run these risks.

These decisions in reconciling optima, and the sacrifices and risks entailed, are relatively simple because they are made by individuals who know the alternative and can decide between them. Reconciling optima is more difficult when there is a mixture of private and public decisions, between services that are partly private and partly public in economic nature. This has been the situation in post-war British economic policy. The objectives, and the prices to be paid for them, were indicated in the celebrated wartime Coalition Government White Paper on Employment Policy (1944), which laid down that if "a high and stable level of employment" was a central objective of post-war policy, it would result in uncontrollable inflation unless there was "restraint" in wage payments. Full employment did not exonerate the citizen from "the duty of fending for himself"; it should not result "in weakening personal enterprise"; and it must not lead to "failure of workers to move to places and occupations where they are needed."

In the following decades full employment was made sacrosanct; the White Paper caveats were minimized, but its apprehensions were fulfilled. Economists such as Peacock, Seldon, Wiseman and others associated with the Institute of Economic Affairs advocated reform of indiscriminate Welfare State benefits because of their effect on individual responsibility, Pennance investigated the effects of subsidized housing on geographical mobility, and Lincoln, Hutton and others emphasized the effects of trade union power on occupational mobility. But general recognition that the optima—indiscriminate benefits and personal independence, low-cost housing and geographical mobility, trade unions and occupational mobility—were irreconcilable, was slow.

The attempt to reconcile full employment and stable prices produced varied government devices which usually overshot the target and produced a succession of "stop-go's." Various forms of controls over wages and incomes, generically described as "incomes policies," were tried but were rarely effective for more than nine or twelve months: they mainly held back increases that were made up in arrears when the controls were finally resisted as too rigid. The efforts to repress inflation by suppressing its symptoms created a new short form of economic cycle as the action taken to deal with one symptom—rising, unemployment or accelerating inflation—sooner or later aggravated the other. Despite repeated evidence the continued expectation, or hope, in the post-war years was that all the objectives could be reached together, that the optima were, in some way not yet discovered, reconcilable.

Hence a new form of four, five, or six year cycles of alternating "reflation" and "disflation" ending in balance of payments crises requiring sudden reversals of policy. Between 1952 and 1973 five such cycles could be traced: 1952–57, 1958–61, 1962–65, 1966–70, and 1971–73. The rate of inflation grew from cycle to cycle, especially from the early 1960's, and the deficit in the balance of payments rose as a proportion of the national product. The British economist Peter Jay (son of economist and Labour Minister Douglas Jay and son-in-law of Labour Chancellor of the Exchequer James Callaghan) argued that the deterioration could not continue indefinitely, and that the strain would be thrown on two other optima objectives: free collective bargaining and representative democratic institutions. The gradual degeneration of the economy had been masked by the upward spasms in the new cycles, which had encouraged wishful thinking that they could be extrapolated indefinitely by the discovery of an "economist's stone" that would achieve all the optima simultaneously. This ungrounded optimism had been encouraged by the view, taught by some British economists in the 1960's and applied by the 1970–74 Conservative Government, that the British growth rate was too low and that "stop-go" could be replaced by a policy of "going for growth," which meant by fuelling it by monetary expansion. They had not observed the tendency during the whole period for the price of full employment to be not merely inflation, as the White Paper had warned, but accelerating inflation and, moreover, for the intervals of "incomes policies" (and the governments that tried them) to shorten.

This process of shortening could not last much longer. Prices and unemployment from the late 1960's rose together ("stagflation"), but governments could use "incomes policies" only for shrinking periods. The remaining untried solution was disinflation by reducing the expansion in the money supply. But the result would be unemployment as the sectors of industry artificially sustained by monetary inflation became uneconomic. Since public opinion had been led to expect that all the optima were attainable together, they would vote out of office a government that attempted a solution which at last recognized that some optima could not be attained. Continued inflation had made democracy ungovernable except by more *dirigiste* controls that removed private freedoms in everyday economic life. Inflation as a method of maintaining full employment had thus won a Pyrrhic victory; it had passed out of the control of free institutions and had sounded the death-knell of political democracy.

In the mid-1970's the USA seemed able to avoid this outcome because her trade unions did not wish to bring the market system down by increasing wage inflation on top of monetary inflation, Germany because of her historic anxiety about inflation, and Switzerland because of her strong attachment to democracy. But Britain, France, Japan and other countries seemed likely to succumb, short of accepting the warnings of the 1944 White Paper that full employment required a willingness of workers "to move to places and occupations where they are needed."

Economic analysis can thus show that some optima/objectives are unattainable as absolutes, and that the consequences of effort to achieve conflicting objectives simultaneously leads to collapse in the weakest. [13]

Recoupment. *See* BETTERMENT.

Re-cycling, a term of recent origin, used to mean (*a*) the reprocessing and reuse of raw materials like paper and glass to reduce their disposal as refuse polluting or degrading the natural environment, and (*b*), even more recent, the return of the large earnings of the Arab oil producers to the industrial countries for profitable investment to the advantage of both. The question for economists is how far re-cycling will take place by spontaneous reaction in the market and how far it requires encouragement by government (raw materials) or international agreement (oil finance). [7]

Redemption, liquidation of a debt or bond by repayment in cash at maturity by companies or government. [8]

Redeployment, polite word for changing or shifting resources from declining (less profitable) to growing (more profitable) use. It is more delicate than talk of moving workers in an economy where labour is reluctant to move (possibly for good reasons), and gives a favourable impression of being more concerned instead with more effective application of resources. [5]

Redundancy, the condition in which an object no longer serves its purposes or is superfluous to requirements. The term could apply to capital but is mostly used about labour. Constant changes in technical conditions of supply, and social, psychological or other conditions of demand, make workers redundant. In the last century, textile weavers were made redundant by machine-looms, canal bargemen by the railways, hansom cabbies by taxis, straw-hat makers by the barehead "cult," and railwaymen by the motor car and the aeroplane. Probably the most difficult problem in economic policy is to help redundant workers to move to new jobs, which may mean (unwanted or unavailable) new homes.

In Britain redundancy has intensified the human problems of adaptation to change. British governments have introduced re-settlement grants, re-training grants, transport grants and redundancy payments. But mobility has been hampered by subsidized Council housing which penalizes the family that moves by increasing the cost of moving (loss of subsidy) and by trade union obstruction to technical change and closed shops to new members. For economists, the question is how far the costs of redundancy are borne (behaviourist economics) or should be borne (normative economics) by the individual employee, the employer, and/or the government. Insofar as redundancy is a foreseeable risk, insurance through government, or by saving for the "rainy" day, can reduce the costs, but not entirely. Change disturbs personal, family and social life, and effective means of easing it have to be found. Direction of labour is used by western countries in war, and East European countries in peace. [5]

Reflation, the first phase in the recovery of an economy from a slump before the stage of full employment and inflation with rising prices is reached. A slump is characterized by a widespread surplus of unused resources—idle machines, large stocks of unsold goods and high unemployment. Recovery from this situation usually requires an increase in total expenditure on goods and services. Once started, it tends to grow, extra spending creating extra employment and incomes, which in turn lead to more spending. Previously unemployed resources are drawn into production to meet the rising demand. At first, because each round of extra spending is matched by an increased supply of goods and services, there is little rise in prices. Eventually, when all resources are fully employed, no further increases in output will be possible. If demand continues to increase, prices will rise, thus marking the end of the reflation phase and the beginning of inflation. [9]

Refunding, extinguishing a debt or bond by a new debt or bond, at a lower or higher rate of interest. [8]

Regional Policy. *See* DEVELOPMENT AREAS.

Regrating. *See* FORESTALLING.

Regression Analysis, a statistical technique used by economists to deduce a general tendency or "pattern" from a number of individual observations of economic behaviour or relationships. An example is the increase in family or national expenditure on food as personal or national income rises from year to year. This relationship can be shown as a series of points on a "scatter" diagram. Income is the major or "explanatory variable" and expenditure on food the "dependent variable." The clustering of the points will indicate whether they seem to form a straight line or a curve. The "best fit" is the line or curve which takes in the most points on or near it and leaves the least far from it. The line or curve then indicates the general or average relationship between expenditure on food and incomes. Readings can be "interpolated" between any two points or "extrapolated" if the line or curve is extended at both ends; if the line or curve is carried forward in time it enables predictions to be made about the probable expenditure on food in a given year as income rises in the future. If the observed points are scattered widely around the line or curve the predictions can be made with less certainty and within wider margins of errors (which can be calculated) than if they "fit" more closely. Regression analyses can also be used for more than two quantities ("variables") that seem to be related to one another.

Regression analysis can at best yield only approximate general relationships because the observed readings may not be sufficiently numerous, they may be affected by other influences than the ones being studied, the explanatory variable must not be affected by the dependent variable, the data arising from the observations may have been measured imperfectly, and so on. The economist must use judgement based on experience (which may itself not be an infallible guide) in deciding on the methods that best avoid these possible sources of error. He may have to choose a method that is at best a compromise. Like other techniques in the social (or natural) sciences, regression analysis requires subjective judgement as well as objective knowledge. [14]

Regressive Tax. *See* TAXATION.

Regulator, term first applied in the 1960's to changes in customs or excise tax rates made with little notice to supplement the main tax changes in the annual budget (or autumn secondary budget). The purpose was to make fiscal policy more effective in preventing inflation or deflation by making tax changes more frequent and more gradual—a broad parallel with "fine tuning" in monetary policy by more gradual but more frequent changes in interest rates. Economists differed about the regulator's *rationale* and effectiveness. [8]

Relativities, term evolved in the 1970's to describe differences in employees' pay that would be sanctioned by "public opinion" as "fair" or "just," in contrast to pay differences determined by "market forces" or sanctioned by industrial tradition or craft custom. The term evolved in a situation in which "market forces" were not allowed to work because of trade union opposition. The two terms, "differentials" and "relativities" thus refer to the differences seen by people as individual consumers in the market and as citizens forming general or collective moral judgements. Insofar as they arise from the incompatible viewpoints or decisions of individuals in their everyday lives and their philosophic preferences, they indicate ambivalence and conflict that requires to be resolved. The gap has appeared most with government-employed workers: coalminers, teachers, nurses, etc. have been thought to be morally "worth" more than they were paid by government because of the "importance" of their work. In the short run the government has been a monopsonistic buyer of their services; they may not have been able to move to other employment easily; they may have preferred "public service" to higher pay in private industry or commercial work. The Relativities Board was created in 1973 to reflect the general or collective moral judgements about "fair" differences in pay but could not do much in government employment because of government attempts to restrain rises in incomes and, more fundamentally, the deficiency in government revenue for higher pay in education, the National Health Service, etc. [5]

Rent. *See* Economic Rent.

Rent Officer. *See* Rent Restriction.

Rent Restriction, government control of the level of house rents below that which would prevail in a free market. Rent restriction was introduced in the UK in the First World War to protect tenants from the hardships of high rents when there was a national housing shortage. Government rent controls were gradually although not completely relaxed during the inter-war years but were reintroduced to embrace most residential property in 1939 as one of a wide range of other controls aimed at checking the inflationary effects of excess demand and wartime shortages. Rent restriction remained virtually unchanged until the Rent Act in 1957, which freed the more expensive properties from control and was intended to be the beginning of relaxation. The Rent Act of 1965 reversed this process, extended security of tenure to most tenants, and introduced the regulation of rents for practically all dwellings. The basis of regulation was the determination of a "fair rent" by local Rent Officers or Rent Assessment Committees. In 1974 this system was extended to furnished as well as unfurnished homes, which then also began to diminish in supply.

Rent is a price paid for the hire of living accommodation and in a free market it is determined, like all other prices, by the interplay of supply and demand. Freely determined market prices play an important role in securing the efficient allocation of scarce resources. A strong demand which has outstripped the supply of a commodity will be reflected in a high or rising price. This will tend to stimulate its production and discourage consumption, so narrowing the gap between supply and demand. Government control of market prices, such as rents, may hinder them in their function of equating supply and demand.

Wasteful anomalies are created by rents that are fixed administratively rather than by market forces. Over-consumption of housing is encouraged while supply of privately supplied rented homes is discouraged. Upkeep of existing stocks is discouraged and new building for private renting becomes exceptional, so that tenure tends to become polarized between owner-occupation and rented

(Council) housing which has to expand to fill the gap. The aim of restriction—to help poorer families—is achieved only crudely: since restriction of rent is not related to the income and needs of renters, some who need no help are aided at the expense of others in more need. [10]

Rentier, in the strictest sense, a person living on interest payments from government securities. It was applied originally only to the holders of *rente*—a type of French government security, but is now more loosely used to describe any person whose income is "unearned" and derived solely from the ownership of capital—interest, rents or dividends, rather than "earned" income in the form of salaries and wages. [8]

Repressed Inflation. *See* OVERLOADED ECONOMY.

Reputation Monopoly. *See* ADVERTISING.

Resale Price Maintenance (RPM), the stipulation by a manufacturer of the price at which distributors may resell his product. The manufacturer sets the "trade" price to retailers and in addition fixes their additional gross "profit" or margin. In Britain, the USA and other countries this practice has normally but not exclusively been confined to branded goods, such as books, chocolate and sugar, confectionery, cosmetics, electrical goods, motor cars and accessories, proprietary medicines, radios and television receivers. A manufacturer makes his prices known by price-lists, price-tags, display cards and advertising.

Collective RPM was outlawed in Britain in 1956 and individual RPM in 1964. Before 1956 associations of manufacturers, wholesalers and retailers had enforced RPM throughout entire trades. These associations were generally formed on the initiative of distributors, who could threaten to boycott a manufacturer who did not maintain his prices. The associations possessed the powerful sanction of being able collectively to cut off an individual retailer's entire supplies, and they sometimes set up private courts to prescribe this or lesser penalties of fines or warnings. In public discussion the main objection to collective RPM was against these private courts; but on economic grounds RPM was undesirable more fundamentally because it tended to ossify existing, and impede the emergence of new, channels of distribution.

RPM limits price competition between retailers. A retailer providing the same services as competitors cannot undercut them in order to expand, even though his costs may be lower. A retailer providing fewer services than competitors cannot charge correspondingly lower prices. And a retailer who is newly established or poorly located cannot give consumers the inducement of a lower price to patronize him. The result is that competition is concentrated on services or other attractions: credit, delivery, wide assortment of stock, more staff, better premises, advertising, perhaps trading stamps, etc. Price competition is therefore confined to non-maintained goods, but they are few among the products sold by such retailers as chemists, booksellers and tobacconists.

Price maintenance normally raises distributor's gross profit margins and, as this is seldom offset by a proportionate fall in the volume of sales, makes the total of gross profits in distribution larger than it would be if there were competition in price. This does not mean that the rate of return on capital invested or managerial earnings are higher. More shops tend to be opened and they offer more services, so that the net return on capital is no higher than elsewhere; but the volume of resources engaged in retailing is larger than it otherwise would be.

In 1964 the power of an individual firm to enforce RPM was curtailed in Britain. In Canada and some USA states price maintenance, individual as well as collective, is illegal. [7]

Research, Market. *See* MARKET RESEARCH.

Research, Motivational. *See* MARKET RESEARCH.

Research, Operational. *See* OPERATIONAL RESEARCH.

Reserve Currency, foreign currencies held with gold as means of paying for imports if the proceeds received for exports fall short. Strong, stable or "hard" currencies are preferred: dollars have been occasionally replaced by Deutschmarks or Swiss francs. [4]

Reserves, earnings earmarked by a company or country for specified or general purposes. Most firms set aside in this way part of their profits each year before paying a dividend. Reserves may be formed for defined purposes such as extending productive capacity and research programmes, or simply as a general protection against the effects of unexpected losses. Company reserves are rarely kept in the form of cash but are invested either in the business itself or outside the firm, usually in interest-bearing securities. Finance houses, insurance companies and particularly banks, however, have to keep a part of their reserves in cash to meet the day-to-day requirements of their clients.

A country's reserves consist of a balance of gold and foreign currencies used for international trade. If the amount of foreign currency earned by a country's voluntary sales of merchandise, services or capital assets abroad is temporarily less than its currency liabilities for merchandise, services and capital assets bought from other countries, the deficit can be met by running down its reserves, which thus act as a buffer stock in preventing undesirable temporary fluctuations in either trade or foreign exchange rates.

The "crises" in Britain's balance of payments since World War II have been intensified by her meagre reserves. Before the war she held reserves sufficient to pay for eight or nine months' imports; since World War II her reserves have been less than three or four months' value of imports. The USA, Germany and other countries have held much larger reserves in proportion to their external trade. [3]

Resources, human capacities, animal properties and material objects (land, its flora and fauna, water and other substances) that are scarce relatively to the demand for them and are used, often jointly, to produce goods and services. Thus land, grass, a cow, a farmer and his equipment together produce milk. All resources are scarce in the sense that there is not enough of them to produce all the goods and services required to satisfy every human want (even fresh air is scarce in deep mines). The limits to resources are set by nature and knowledge. Resources can be used in varying combinations to yield varying combinations of goods and services. The principles or "laws" that govern the ways in which man chooses between alternatives form the essential subject-matter of economics. [14]

Restraint of Trade, restriction of competition by contracts between sellers and buyers of businesses, between employers and employees or between two or more businesses. For example, the seller of a business may agree not to set up a competing firm within a stated period. The Elizabethan view that all contracts in restraint of trade were void as tending to create monopolies has been modified. Such contracts are now *prima facie* void, but not if they are "reasonable" in the interests both of the contracting parties and the public. The attitude of the court differs towards agreements between seller and buyer who are likely to be on equal terms and agreements between employers and employees. W. H. Hutt has questioned the prevailing view that "no more perishable commodity is brought to market than a man's labour." Restraints which would narrow the choice of new employment have been regarded as void if they did not protect the employer's trade connection and/or secrets. Judges have insisted that there must be a proprietary interest to be protected: a covenant not to compete is not enforceable, including an agreement between employers not to compete for labour.

In Britain many agreements between businesses for regulating their trade, even if not contractual in the strictly legal sense, are now within the ambit of the Restrictive Trade Practices laws, or are subject to possible scrutiny by the Monopolies Commission. [7]

Restrictive Practices, contrivances of business men, professional workers or wage-earners which limit output and protect or make profits, fees or wages larger than they otherwise would be. Some practices—such as price agreements between firms, scales of fees agreed by professions, high wages negotiated by strong trade unions—are aimed directly at increasing or maintaining remuneration, but as the higher price reduces the amount likely to be sold the effect is the same as a restriction of output.

Restrictive practices of businesses may consist of associations fixing prices, terms or conditions of purchase, sale or lease of a product, excluding enterprises from (or allocating or dividing) a market or field of business activity, allocating customers, fixing sales quotas or purchase quotas, discriminating against particular enterprises, limiting production or fixing production quotas, controlling the rate at which new techniques are introduced and using patents to foster monopoly power.

These practices are objected to because they divert resources away from employments that consumers would prefer, raise prices, inflate profits and protect inefficient high-cost firms. They are sometimes defended as means of preventing "cut-throat" competition during slumps, maintaining standards of quality, facilitating technical co-operation between competitors, providing an offset to the power of large customers or suppliers and raising earnings from exports. It is also argued that agreements between firms do not destroy competition but transfer it to the conference table and into efforts to reduce costs, improve quality or service, increase research, and stimulate innovation or facilitate co-operative advertising.

Under the Restrictive Trade Practices Act, 1956, agreements between firms in Britain have to be registered and examined by the Restrictive Practices Court. Some 2,000 agreements were registered and more than 1,000 abandoned following the early judgements. The long-run effects are difficult to judge. Former restrictive practices between independent firms have become the internal policy of mergers, price leadership may replace price fixing, implicit agreements may be reached by the exchange of price-lists ("open pricing").

Restrictive practices of labour attempt to protect workers from losing their jobs as a result of technical change and to build and exploit monopoly positions. The demarcation rules in shipbuilding, many of which originate in the efforts of shipwrights to protect their employment as steel and other materials replaced the traditional timber, provide examples of the first type. Attempts to build up and make the most of monopoly positions are found when work is localized or special skills are required. In newspaper printing the work is localized and skilled, and limitations on numbers of apprentices, manning rules, etc., are common in the printing unions. The localization of fruit and vegetable wholesaling at Covent Garden has enabled the workpeople to dictate who shall do what and to limit recruitment. The special skills required by barristers have enabled them to lay down conditions of employment; thus a QC may be engaged only with a junior barrister at two-thirds of his fee. Some economists suggest that professional qualifications are often set at unnecessarily high levels in order to limit entry and maintain existing members' incomes.

It has been argued that many of these labour practices are not restrictive but serve to maintain standards of good work, of safety and of health, or prevent exploitation of workers by excessive speed-up, overtime or undermanning of machines. In Britain the National Joint Advisory Council some years ago asked for joint reports of trade unions and employers on restrictive labour practices in 190 industries. When it reported in 1959 it had received replies from 112 industries; 64 claimed they had no difficulties, 42 that they had or were setting up machinery to deal with restrictive practices, 6 required more time or were unable to submit a joint report. This response was interpreted as suggesting that restrictive practices were not a widespread problem; on the other hand employers and unionists may have wished to let sleeping dogs lie, perhaps because restrictive labour practices affect competing employers equally, and because they may slow down or prevent the emergence of aggressive new competitors. It is not easy to discover the extent of restrictive practices in any economy except by making it as competitive as possible by changing the laws that permit or encourage them. [7]

Retail Sales Tax. *See* SALES TAX.

Retailing, selling goods in a state ready for final consumption or use to private consumers, usually in shops or stores but also from kiosks, market stalls and by door-to-door trading. Trades involving more than distribution, such as catering in cafés and restaurants, hairdressing, shoe repairing and car repairing, are often considered to be separate from retailing. The proportion engaged in retailing in most western countries in Europe, America and Australasia has increased throughout this century as growth in output per head in production has outstripped that in retailing, new goods have been introduced and advanced stages of urbanization have been reached.

In Britain about half of all retail sales are made by large-scale retailers. In the mid-1970's multiple traders owning ten or more shops accounted for more than a quarter of total turnover: one-half these sales were of food. Multiples were also important in footwear, men's and boys' clothing, pharmaceuticals, furniture, radio and television, and household appliances. They first grew to importance at the end of the nineteenth century, but they have been expanding more rapidly than other types of retailer since the Second World War. They gain economies of scale in purchasing, stock-turnover and skilled merchandising, and they have been quick to exploit new methods such as hire-purchase, self-service and mixed merchandising in supermarkets. Retail co-operative societies accounted for over one-tenth of total sales. Department stores held about 5 per cent of the total trade, but faced difficulties with the increasing congestion of large cities. Variety chain stores also accounted for 5 per cent of total turnover. Since the Second World War they have increased the sales area of their stores, abandoned their concentration on low-priced lines, bought from independent producers to their own specification and adopted "house" brands. A recent development has been the expansion of mail order houses offering the convenience of shopping at home, including a widening range of goods in their catalogues, organizing credit clubs, and building up sales as a proportion of the total. In these ways retailers have reduced the dominance by manufacturers of consumer goods markets.

Despite the important part played by large organizations, retailing is not highly concentrated. Retailing is a way of life as well as an occupation, and more than half a million of those engaged in it are working proprietors or unpaid family helpers. Small retailers are attempting to gain economies of scale by forming buying groups and joining "voluntary chains" organized by wholesalers with whom they contract to buy specified goods for stated periods and therefore pay lower prices than if they continued to buy independently. Although many small retailers are likely to be eliminated as multiples continue to expand, they have proved to be resilient in the face of change. [7]

Returns to Scale (Increasing and Decreasing), an economic law used to describe the relationship between the output of commodities and the scale of input of factors of production in the *long* run when the quantities of all the factors, used in unchanged proportions, are increased or reduced. This law is distinguished from the law of variable proportions or diminishing returns, which refers to the effect on output in the *short* run when the proportions of *one* factor relative to other (fixed) factors is changed but otherwise the quantity of the factors is not changed.

At small scales of production, the efficiency of a productive enterprise, measured as the output obtained per unit of factor employed, can often be increased by increasing its size. Conversely, increases in scale beyond a point may decrease productive efficiency. Increased efficiency, measured as increasing returns, may follow increases in scale because of the wider scope for specialization of labour and equipment. Workers can be concentrated on a narrower range of tasks or processes. Specialized equipment can be installed. Large-scale equipment, such as a canal or railway track, requires large scales of output if it is to be used efficiently.

These "economies of scale" arise from the *indivisibility* of the factors of production. Specialized equipment either cannot be reproduced at all in smaller sizes or can be reproduced only at higher cost per unit of output. Similarly the higher proficiency of workers specializing on a narrower range of processes cannot be reproduced if the degree of specialization is less. Management, marketing and finance are also subject to indivisibility: at a given point either they may be more efficiently employed at larger scales of output, or more specialized division of labour becomes possible.

These tendencies operate within limits. Beyond a point in the scale of output, indivisible equipment, earlier underemployed as measured by its optimum efficiency, may become overemployed. Continued specialization of labour and equipment may produce problems of supervision and co-ordination. Increasing scale of management creates difficulties of control and rigidities. The scale of production at which "diseconomies of scale" appear will vary from industry to industry and often depends on the calibre of management. Eventually in all industries they will tend to outweigh the advantages of further specialization, and decreasing returns, that is, decreasing output per unit of input of the factors of production will result.

The distinction between returns to scale and diminishing returns was not always made clear in the nineteenth-century economic literature. Increasing returns were thought to apply to manufacturing industry and diminishing returns to agricultural industry. It was seen later that both apply to all industries at different scales of operation. Another common error was the failure to distinguish between the increasing returns achieved by varying the amounts of the factors in a given state of technological knowledge and the "historical" increasing returns produced during the nineteenth and twentieth centuries by invention and progress in technology, to which there would seem to be no limit. [3]

Revaluation, (*a*) a devaluation or up-valuation of a currency. [4]

(*b*) an updating (usually an increase) in business assets (mainly shops and other property) in the light of changing market conditions and (in recent years) of inflation. [3]

Reverse Income Tax, a device for abolishing poverty by "topping up" low incomes to enable relatively poor individuals or families to pay for purchases. The idea is said to have originated with the "negative income tax" of the American economist Milton Friedman. In principle it goes back to the Speenhamland System of 1795 in which wages were made up by grants from the rates according to fluctuations in the price of bread. The objection to the principle goes back to the early nineteenth century in which Speenhamland is said to have led to widespread misery by destroying men's incentive to look after their families by working. Experiments in 1968–73 of a form of reverse income tax in the USA did not reveal a damaging weakening of incentives.

The advantage of the device over conventional social benefits in general is that the "topping up" is based on written returns of income and family tax allowances for specified purposes and thus dispenses with means tests. [10]

Reverse Yield Gap, the amount by which the yield on gilt-edged securities (irredeemable consols) exceeds the yield on ordinary equity shares. Normally the gap could be expected to lie in the opposite direction, i.e. the yield on ordinary shares, which are the most risky investments, exceeds the yield on gilt-edged securities, which are the least risky. This was the situation in Britain until 1959, when the gap went into reverse. The main reason was that ordinary shares offered the prospect of a growth in value of the principal invested, which remain unchanged in money terms in gilt-edged securities and therefore fell in real value as the general price level rose. Investors thus tended to move from gilt-edged into equities, depressing the price of the former and raising their yield, while at the same time raising the price of the latter and lowering *their* yield. [8]

Reversion, term used in ground or building leases by which the freeholder grants a long lease subject to a ground rent and a lessee's covenant to erect a building to the freeholder/lessor's specification. The freeholder/lessor is left with the right to receive the ground rent for the specified term plus the *right to the reversion,* i.e. the full freehold rights over the parcel of land-and-building at the end of the lease term. Another term for the right to the reversion is *reversionary interest.* At the outset of a long lease, the initial value of the (distant) reversion is insignificant: it increases in significance as the unexpired portion of the lease term gets shorter, the rate of increase depending on the rate of interest at which futurity is discounted and the difference between the ground rent reserved under the lease and the full letting value of the parcel of land-and-building. [6]

Review of Economic Studies. *See* Journals, Economic.

Review of Economics and Statistics. *See* Journals, Economic.

Revolving Credit, a form of loan in which repayments by instalment are matched by new debts (purchases) so that the total remains unchanged. This method of extending credit has been increasing because administrative costs are lower than in older forms (instalment credit, etc.) in which old debts are extinguished and replaced by new ones; and lower costs mean that credit can be extended to more risky customers. [8]

Ricardo, David (1772–1823), English economist of Jewish descent; a leading member of the classical school of political economy. He completed his formal education at the age of fourteen but his business ability led him to become a wealthy stockbroker and he retired from business at the age of forty-two. The bulk of his economic publications appeared during the remaining nine years. They reveal deep analytical insight, and quickly established his reputation as a leader among economists. He became influential in public life and was elected to Parliament in 1819.

Ricardo became interested in political economy in his late twenties after an earlier flirtation with the physical sciences (during which he became a founder member of the Geological Society). His early interest lay in the monetary problems arising out of the Napoleonic wars and led to his important and best known essay, *The High Price of Bullion* (1810). It was followed in 1815 by his essay *On the*

Influence of a Low Price of Corn on the Profits of Stock and in 1816 by *Proposals for an Economical and Secure Currency.* His most important work, *The Principles of Political Economy and Taxation,* first appeared in 1817. The third edition (1821) is the final version to which reference is usually made.

The *Principles* embodied Ricardo's main achievements in the theory of value and distribution. The importance of the latter to him is shown by his statement in the preface to the first edition that "to determine the laws which regulate this distribution [of economic produce] is the principal problem in Political Economy." His theory of value was a quantity-of-labour theory. He dismissed "scarce" (i.e. irreproducible) commodities; he concentrated on the mass of goods that may be "increased by human industry" and tried to demonstrate that the exchange values of commodities will be proportional to the quantities of labour embodied in them (including "stored-up" labour in the form of machines, etc.). The simplicity of this proposition was stretched in later passages on production requiring the use of proportions of capital and labour of varying qualities, but Ricardo retained it as a fundamental element in his theory.

The explanation of the distributive shares of the three factors of production, land, labour and capital, was implicit in Ricardo's theory of value once the rent of land had been eliminated. The rent of land was regarded as a surplus over cost of production, the extent of which was determined by the differing fertility and situation of land. Price that would warrant production on the poorest or worst-situated land would yield a surplus over production costs on more favoured plots, which would be appropriated in rent by landowners. Thus rent could be ignored as an element in cost of production: "corn is not high [in price] because a rent is paid, but a rent is paid because corn is high." This explained the distributive "share" of land. That of labour was determined by the amount of capital available for the payment of wages and by the size of the labour force; and profit was the residual: "there can be no rise in the value of labour without a fall of profits." This theory of distribution had much influence on other economists. It suggested that, as population grew, the increased demand for food would tend to raise rents and the price of food: hence wages would rise and profits would fall. The community of interest expounded by Adam Smith no longer seemed to be valid, a view later elaborated by Karl Marx and the "Ricardian" Socialists, and in recent years by Cambridge neo-Ricardians. [2]

Rigging, fixing a price higher than it would otherwise reach, either by collusion among some suppliers to keep other suppliers out of the market, or by some other means. [7]

Rights Issue, an offer of new shares to shareholders in proportion to shareholdings (e.g. one to every five held), usually below the market price. The object is to reduce the cost of raising new capital. [8]

Rigidity, the failure of an economic system to respond promptly to changes in demand and technology. In order to produce efficiently the goods and services that consumers demand, an economy must be sufficiently flexible to vary and match its output to changing tastes by adopting the best methods of production. The working of the price system in a competitive enterprise economy offers powerful inducements to ensure that this happens by making rapid adaptation profitable. Thriving industries can usually offer sufficiently high earnings to attract the labour, capital and business skills they need for expansion, drawing resources away from the less remunerative, declining industries whose products are in falling demand. But social and institutional factors may hamper the effectiveness of the price system's incentives.

Experience in the 1930's and in recent years shows that labour may not move easily from areas with declining industries such as cotton and coal mining to regions where industries are expanding. There are many reasons: the reluctance to pull up roots and start life in a new community, the cost of moving, a shortage of suitable accommodation and so on. Moreover, both labour and business may distort the proper flow of resources by restrictive practices. Some trade unions and professional organizations, by insisting on unnecessarily protracted training and apprenticeship schemes, deter new entrants; and powerful firms with a high degree of monopoly may restrict the expansion of output in order to maintain high prices and profits. [7]

Risk, a possible occurrence, the probability of which may or may not be measurable.

All forms of business activity involve risk: first, because market conditions of demand and supply at the end of a business operation may differ from those anticipated when it was arranged; secondly, because of "natural" hazards—such as weather and disease, and those with a human element—fire, accident, mechanical breakdown, dishonesty, bad debts, incompetence, strikes and so on.

Business organization requires a continuous effort to eliminate or minimize risk, either by dividing and shifting it (at a cost) on to others better qualified by aptitude, experience or specialization to bear particular forms of risk through insurance, futures trading, sub-contracting, or by practices aimed at stabilizing markets and reducing competitive risk, such as branding, advertising, association or combination with other firms, promotion of favourable legislation and governmental control.

Risks which cannot be removed or profitably shifted must be borne by the *entrepreneur.* He will generally do so only as long as his expectation of profit outweighs the chance of loss. In economic theory uninsurable risk, or uncertainty, thus plays an important part in the theory of profit. [7]

Road Fund, created in Britain by the 1909 Development and Road Improvements Fund Act, financed solely by taxes on motorists (a tax on petrol and a vehicle tax) and intended to be spent entirely on road improvements and new roads. As an emergency measure in 1915 part of the Fund was diverted to the National Exchequer. This practice was continued after the war when it became clear that post-war chancellors did not accept the original purpose of the Fund. In what became popularly known as "raids on the Road Fund," an increasing amount of its capital and revenue were taken for other government expenditure. The Finance Act of 1936 ended it as a separate Fund financed by special taxes, and treated it as part of the Civil Estimates like any other government department. It was formally abolished in 1955. [12]

Robbins, Lionel Charles (1898–1984), British economist and public servant. He was born in Sipson in Middlesex and educated at Southall County School, University College, London, and the London School of Economics. After lecturing at the LSE and at New College, Oxford, he became Professor of Economics at the LSE in 1929 for thirty-two years until 1961, with an interval during the war in the economic section of the War Cabinet Office. He continued to combine teaching at the LSE (until 1966) with chairmanship of the *Financial Times.* A book he began on the principles of economics remained unfinished when he became Chairman of the Committee on Higher Education. Robbins was deeply interested in the arts (like other economists—Keynes, Peacock, Yamey, Baumol) and was active as a trustee and chairman of the National Gallery and on the Board of the Royal Opera House.

Robbins disclaimed "outstanding intellectual discoveries" but apart from clarifying the definition of economics in his first major book he had far-reaching influence on economic thinking, teaching and, intermittently, on policy over forty years. His career and life also show the influence of economic thinking (right or wrong) on policy.

After early attraction to socialism Robbins became a leader of neo-liberal economic thought. But he scrupulously separated his value-judgements from his analysis: he argued forcefully that behaviourist (positive) economics should be rigorously separated from normative economics and that economists had no authority, *qua* economists, to offer judgements. (He criticized his teacher, Hugh Dalton, and others, for arguing that the economic theory of diminishing marginal utility of income validated a redistribution of income in the direction of equality; he insisted that the case must rest on non-economic grounds). In turn he was criticized by other economists for too severely segregating the two branches of economics and for draining economics of utility and even humanity. His reply was that the distinction between analysis of what is and prescribing what should be went back to David Hume. It did not mean that economists should have no views on ethics and policy; on the contrary "it is only if one knows how the [economic] machine runs or can run that one is entitled to say how it ought to run. That indeed was my claim for the ultimate significance of economics."

Robbins's first book was his most austere. *An Essay on the Nature and Significance of Economic Science* rejected the older definitions of economics as the study of man in relation to material welfare in favour of a definition in terms of the *scarcity* aspect of all purposes, material or not. He coined the celebrated definition used by economists for forty years: "The science which studies human behaviour as a relationship between ends and scarce means which have alternative uses." The origin of this approach indicates its significance. Robbins had been asked to lecture on the Economics of War, yet a widely-used textbook at the time, Edwin Cannan's *Wealth,* specifically excluded war and its accompaniments from the scope of economics. Robbins was interested in the arts—concerts, the theatre, decorative architecture (see below)—which were not "material" but had clear economic aspects. He concluded that the idea of material welfare was a will-o'-the-wisp and that the characteristic quality that lent itself to economic analysis was scarcity of the means, not materiality of the ends. The notion of scarcity was implied in the thinking of the Austrians and Wicksteed and others who developed the marginal utility theory of value, which derived from the disposal of goods or services that were ultimately limited in supply and not available freely. The scarcity approach, said Robbins, disposed of the notion of economic ends and revealed that it was the *means* to achieve them that were economic; it clarified the distinction between the *technical* as a problem of achieving one given objective and the *economic* with more than one objective (hence the unavoidable task of making a choice); it showed that economic "quantities" were essentially *relative* concepts not *absolute* entities ("nothing is valuable but thinking makes it so"); and so on.

Robbins combined austere rejection of the claims made for *economic* authority for *moral* value-judgements with an intense interest in economic policy. He distinguished between "economics" (what other economists call positive economics) and "political economy" (what they call normative economics). In political economy he evolved a distinctive approach which provoked a sharp difference with Keynes, who had been invited by the Prime Minister, Ramsay Macdonald, to chair a secret committee of the Economic Advisory Council in 1930–1 on the gathering world depression. The clash of ideas and Robbins's retraction was recounted in his *Autobiography of an Economist* (1971), and became of renewed interest shortly after its publication, when, for the first time since 1930–1, there was talk of wide-ranging economic depression in the mid-1970's after the monetary inflation under the 1970–4 Government.

Keynes had asked Robbins to serve on the Committee, but Robbins differed from Keynes, and the other members (A. C. Pigou, H. D. Henderson and Josiah Stamp), on increased public expenditure, which he opposed, and on free imports, which he supported. He wrote *The Great Depression* (1934) to support the former view, but later said it arose from "a fundamental error of perspective." He said he had been influenced by the classical view that economic crises were caused by excessive conversion of circulating capital into fixed capital, reformulated by Gustav Cassel as an inadequacy of saving to absorb current output of real capital at remunerative prices, and by the Austrian School (mostly von Mises and Hayek) as the failure of money rates of interest to reflect the relationship between the dispositions to save and to invest. He later thought this theory could explain earlier economic crises but not that of 1930–1 because, whatever the causes of the boom up to 1929, in the form of inappropriate investments encouraged by expectations in turn stimulated by too easy monetary conditions, they were "swamped" by the spreading deflationary forces. It was therefore inappropriate to advocate writing down mistaken investments and easing capital markets by encouraging saving and reducing consumption. This was "as unsuitable as denying blankets and stimulants to a drunk who has fallen into an icy pond on the ground that his original trouble was over-heating." Robbins therefore regretted his opposition to increased public expenditure and monetary expansion to stimulate demand and employment. He did not retract his opposition to Keynes's proposals for tariffs on imports and subsidies on exports because he judged tariffs would not be politically easy to remove after the immediate crisis and that they would more probably spread. Robbins was proved right as tariffs and economic nationalism spread in the 1930's. The general inflationary influence of government expenditure and monetary policy designed to maintain full employment also spread after the Second World War, and has been politically difficult to remove (*see* LABOUR STANDARD).

Robbins's concern with economic policy was shown in a series of books, some incorporating lectures and essays addressed to audiences round the world. *Economic Planning and International Order* (1937) examined the nature of national planning and its consequences for international relations. *The Economic Basis of Class Conflict and Other Essays in Political Economy* (1939) dealt with the market and Marxist theories of class conflict, with restrictionism, monopoly, territorial sovereignty, protection, agriculture and government expenditure. *The Economic Causes of War* (1939) questioned the Marxist theory of imperialism and offered other theories of the causes of war. *The Economic Problem in Peace and War* (1947) discussed the lessons of war for the scope and limitations of collectivist and competitive methods of economic control. In *The Theory of Economic Policy in English Classical Political Economy* (1952) he substantially vindicated David Hume, Adam Smith, David Ricardo, T. R. Malthus, Robert Torrens, Nassau

Senior, J. R. McCulloch, James Mill, John Stuart Mill, Jeremy Bentham and J. E. Cairnes of the charge of inhumane *laissez-faire*. *Robert Torrens and the Evolution of Classical Economics* (1958) was Robbins's longest and perhaps most "academic" book. *The Theory of Economic Development in the History of Economic Thought* (1968) and *The Evolution of Modern Economic Theory* (1970) assembled essays on aspects of their titles.

Lionel Robbins was one of the outstanding liberal economic thinkers of recent times. Through the effect of his teaching and writing on colleagues and students, and his war and post-war government work (he helped Keynes negotiate the American loan in 1945), he was, next to Keynes, probably the most influential British economist of his day. [2]

Robertson, Sir Dennis Holme (1890–1963), English economist. He was educated at Cambridge and became Reader in Economics at Cambridge in 1930. In 1938 he was appointed Sir Ernest Cassel Professor at the University of London (London School of Economics). He returned to Cambridge in 1944 as Professor of Political Economy. During World War II he was adviser to the Treasury, 1939–44. Apart from his teaching career his main interest was in monetary theory and practice and in trade cycle analysis.

His main works were: *A Study of Industrial Fluctuations* (1915), *Banking Policy and the Price Level* (1926), *Essays in Monetary Theory* (1940) and *Britain in the World Economy* (1954).

His writings, which were graceful, suave, persuasive and laced with wit, had much influence on J. M. Keynes, whose strictures on classical economics he could not accept fully.

In 1957 he was appointed to the Council on Prices, Productivity and Incomes and took a major part in writing its early reports. [2]

Robinson, Edward Austin Gossage (1897–1993), English economist. Austin Robinson was educated at Marlborough College and Christ's College, Cambridge, and was Emeritus Professor of Economics at Cambridge University from 1966 (Professor, 1950–65). He was one of the most eminent of the rare British economists who combine a wide knowledge of the workings of industry with command of economic theory. His *The Structure of Competitive Industry* (1931) remains outstanding after nearly half a century for its clear exposition and highly readable style. It examined the forces which determine the size and structure of firms and the minimum efficient scale of an industry. It showed how technical, managerial, financial, marketing and risk factors conditioned their optimum size and organization, and to what extent the optima could be reconciled. Robinson's *Monopoly* (1941) was a sequel which analysed the meaning of monopoly conditions, the forms they take, their virtues and vices and the attitude to them of the law and public opinion. Although some of his conclusions (notably on the "optimum firm") have been disputed, Robinson's writings continue to be recognized as outstanding in their application of realistic analysis to industrial structure and conduct and its economic effects. Professor Robinson has been Secretary of the Royal Economic Society (1945–70) and joint Editor of the *Economic Journal* (1944–70). His other books include *Economic Consequences of the Size of Nations* (1960) and *Problems in Economic Development* (1965). [2]

Robinson, Joan V. (1903–83), British economist. The leading female economist and one of the most influential of her day on economic teaching and thinking, though not on policy. She was educated at St Paul's Girls' School and Girton College. She taught at Cambridge University from 1931 to 1971.

Her first major work was *The Economics of Imperfect Competition* (1933), in which she broke away from the traditional analysis of competition between homogeneous commodities to develop, by geometrical analysis and illustration, analysis of imperfect competition between commodities each with an element of institutional monopoly created by product differentiation by advertising and other marketing devices. As with the formulation of marginal utility in the early 1870's, the theoretical development was evolved independently at much the same time by E. H. Chamberlin

Joan Robinson's later and post-war works followed different, Keynesian and Marxian, lines: *An Essay on Marxian Economics* (1942), *The Accumulation of Capital* (1956), *The Marxian Theory of Economic Growth* (1963). Her forthright judgements and vigorous criticisms of other schools of thought were reflected in her oral teaching and some written work, and her influence increased over the economics faculty at Cambridge. In *Economics: An Awkward Corner* (1966) she argued forcefully that there was conflict between macro-economic management by government and micro-economic allocations of resources in the market because competition did not allocate the individual use of resources in the light of collective objectives any better than it did total demand in the economy as a whole. Hence the market economy in a regime of partial laissez-faire was inefficient. Among her later works were *Freedom and Necessity* (1970) and *Economic Heresies* (1971).

As her work developed, Joan Robinson moved from providing one of the most distinguished examples of what can be achieved by the technique of partial analysis, in *The Economics of Imperfect Competition*, to a position critical of both partial analysis and of the preconceptions upon which she considered it to rest, as appears from *The Accumulation of Capital*. The former, following Sraffa's seminal article, examined the conditions in which competition could serve the sovereignty of the consumer and suggested that they might be rarely encountered. As early as 1933, involved in the stream of discussion which preceded the

1936 publication of the *General Theory,* she wrote a review, "The Theory of Money and the Analysis of Output," in which she argued that monetary analysis was identical with the theory of social aggregates. This approach dominated her later work. *The Accumulation of Capital* was a macro-economic work that tried to define the conditions of development. It was non-mathematical in presentation and a development of Keynes, and was held by Tibor Barna in his *Economic Journal* review to fulfill Harrod's requirements for the economics of the future, that it should be "dynamic and not static, general and not partial, and . . . evolve principles that would lend themselves to empirical verification." [2]

Rogers, James Edwin Thorold (1823–90), English economic historian. Educated at King's College, London, and Magdalen College, Oxford. He became an ordained member of the Church of England and was for some time a curate near Oxford; but in 1870 he left the ministry. Although his education was mainly confined to the classics he became interested in political economy through the free trade and co-operative movements. He eventually became Professor of Economics and Statistics, first at London and then at Oxford. His main work is the seven-volume *History of Agricultural Prices in England, 1259–1793* (published between 1866 and 1902). This was a detailed collection of data based on original sources. The figures are interpreted in *Six Centuries of Work and Wages* (1884) and *The Economic Interpretation of History* (1888). [2]

Roscher, Wilhelm (1817–94), German economist. He studied economics and political science at the University of Göttingen and eventually became professor at the University of Leipzig, where he taught for forty-six years. He tried to illustrate the theories of the classical economists in historical terms. Although he published many works, the five volumes of his *System der Volkswirtschaft* (1854) were the most influential. [2]

Rostow, Walt W. (1916–), American economist and historian. He was educated at Yale and Oxford. After a year as Professor of American History at Cambridge he became Professor of Economic History at the Massachusetts Institute of Technology (MIT) from 1950 to 1965. In 1966 he was appointed special assistant to President Johnson.

Rostow's *The Process of Economic Growth* (1952), following his study of the development of the British economy in the nineteenth century, set out to present a theoretical framework within which research should be organized. He was highly critical of the view that economic motivation and opportunity play a dominant part in growth: he considered that the task of economic theory was to provide a framework within which the behavioural sciences, such as psychology and sociology, could make their contribution. The five-stage growth model he offered (traditional society, preparations for take-off, take-off, drive to maturity, finally maturity) utilized "propensities" to develop science, to apply science, to accept innovation, to seek material advancement, and to breed. Propensity was defined as expressing the response of a society to variations in income and profit possibilities. Economics measures changes in these variables; the other sciences explain the changes. Rostow said it was an historian's book about economics. It aroused much controversy among economists. [2]

Roundabout Process, the colloquial name for a process associated with the theory of capital analysed by Böhm-Bawerk and the Austrian School. It describes the use of indirect or "roundabout" methods of production to increase output. The more "roundabout" the methods, i.e. the more time was put into devising more efficient tools and equipment, the more efficient they would be, and the larger the output they would produce. A man may catch one fish by hand and eat it sooner than if he postpones consumption for a day and catches four fish indirectly by making a net that reaches further than his hand; if he spends a week making a boat he might catch ten fish. The more roundabout the capital used, the more resources will be borrowed and the higher will be the rate of interest. This theory of capital and its price, interest, was developed and applied to trade cycle theory and general economic policy most notably by F. A. Hayek in Britain and by von Mises in the USA. [1]

Royal Economic Society, the senior British association of economists, mostly comprising economics graduates of British universities. Its members are Fellows and its publication is the quarterly *Economic Journal.* J. M. Keynes was Editor from 1912 until 1944. The "*EJ*" is for this reason primarily associated with the University of Cambridge and the Keynesian approach to economics. [2]

Royalty, payment by a person or company to the owner of property or to the creator of original work for the privilege of using it commercially. It is essentially a method of sharing the revenue from the sales of a product between the company supplying the finance and marketing skill and the persons contributing property in the form of original work.

The royalty system is commonly used, for example, where an author is paid by a publisher a percentage of the selling price of a book; a landowner is paid by a mining company for the privilege of exploiting his land; a patentee is paid by a manufacturer for the right to reproduce his invention. [7]

Rubber Exchange, in Britain the room where trading in rubber takes place, situated in the London Commodity Exchange in Plantation House in the City of London. Business is transacted between importers, brokers and dealers and is regulated by the Rubber Trade Association. Facilities are provided for trading in "spot" supplies and supplies for forward delivery in a variety of grades. The Settlement House of the RTA also provides clearinghouse facilities to assist trading in standardized "futures" contracts (not normally completed by actual delivering of rubber), by means of which producers, merchants and manufacturers are able to reduce the risks arising from price fluctuations. [7]

"Rule of Reason." *See* TRUST BUSTING.

Run, a process of widening, cumulative demands on a bank, or other financial institution, to return money deposited with it. In the nature of its business it cannot return all money deposited, since it will have lent most of the deposits to other customers. The result may be a bank failure. The Great Depression is said to have begun, or to have been sparked off, by a run on the Kreditanstalt (Credit Institution) of Vienna. [8]

Runaway Inflation, inflation that has proceeded so long or so fast that confidence in the currency has expired and it is not held as a store of value but spent on goods or foreign currencies or precious metals as soon as it is received (or even before, in anticipation). It may then be difficult to slow down the rate of inflation because reduction in the quantity of money is offset by continued increase in its velocity of circulation. In such circumstances the only solution may be replacement of the currency by a new one, as in pre-war Germany and post-war France. [8]

S

Saint-Simon, Comte de. *See* SOCIALISM.

Sale and Lease-back, or Purchase and Lease-back, a method of business or (less commonly) personal financing. As the expression implies, the underlying transaction has two aspects: real property owned and used by a business is (*a*) sold, subject to (*b*) a lease-back of the property (or part of it) for a long term to the seller. The purpose is to obtain business financing in larger amounts or on more favourable terms or carrying more tax advantages than would be possible with alternatives open to the business (such as mortgaging the property, issuing shares or loan stock, or bank borrowing). The property need not necessarily be in existence at the time the lease-back transaction is arranged: for example, some developers have concluded arrangements with investing institutions such as Insurance Companies or Pension Funds whereby the institution purchases a site selected by the developer, finances the construction of a building to the developer's specification and leases the completed property to the developer. The attractiveness of lease-back transactions to both parties obviously depends on the terms of the transaction. The purchaser of a property looks to the stability and security of the lessee and to the prospect of long-term increases in capital value over and above those associated with rental increases negotiated in the lease: the lessee/seller of property is probably concerned more with immediate and cheaper financing rather than with the prospect of capital appreciation he might enjoy by retaining the freehold and borrowing by other means. The growth of the practice in Britain after the Second World War initially reflected exigency in alternative sources of finance and stringency among mortgage lenders; later it reflected the investment preferences of Insurance Companies and Pension Funds seeking profitable outlets for their massive funds. [8]

Sales Tax, a tax levied at a uniform rate on all products and collected at the point of retail sale. It is contrasted with the British purchase tax, which was levied only on some goods at varying rates and was collected at the wholesale stage, and with the Value-Added Tax (VAT), collected at the point where goods passed from one stage to another. The purchase tax was administratively convenient; the number of tax collection points was minimized, and variation in rates and the goods chosen for tax could be used to encourage or discourage consumption of particular goods. On the other hand a selective tax of this kind distorted consumers' preferred patterns of expenditure and could make some lines of production less competitive than they otherwise would be. Changes in the rates of tax could also disrupt production planning and produce arbitrary gains or losses on retailers' stocks. A general retail sales tax would not suffer these defects to the same degree. It would also permit the taxation of services. For these reasons it has often been advocated. The main argument that has been used against its adoption is that retail sales tax would increase the costs and administrative difficulties of collection. [12]

Samuelson, Paul A. (1915–), American economist. He has been Professor of Economics at the Massachusetts Institute of Technology since the age of twenty-five. His varied talents have been seen in the higher criticism and developments in mathematical economics, a widely-used textbook (*Economics*) and a column in *Newsweek.* He has made substantial contributions to economic science as an ideological originator, a teacher and an adviser. In *The Foundations of Economic Analysis* (1947) he demonstrated the identity and interdependence of static and dynamic analysis. Schumpeter said "the theory of maximizing behaviour . . . had never been made to stand out . . . reduced to its logical fundamentals before." Samuelson has taken part in the development and explanation of linear theory (*Linear Programming and Economic Analysis,* 1958), and written on welfare economics and international trade. His most controversial proposition, the "factor price equalization theorem," is that free trade will tend to bring about absolute equality of wages throughout the inter-trading area, irrespective of original differences in factor endowment. He is generally regarded as a Keynesian. [2]

Satisficing, term coined by the American economist H. A. Simon to characterize a goal of business behaviour. He argued that business behaviour was likely to be influenced by psychological drives and that action promoted by such drives tended to terminate when the drive was satisfied. Accordingly he argued that a firm's goals were likely to be not the maximization of profit (as he considered economic theory typically assumed) but the attainment of a desired rate of profit, share of the market or volume of sales. In other words, firms would try to "satisfice" rather than maximize. Another American, G. Katona, independently made similar comparisons of economic and psychological theories of business behaviour. [3]

Saturation, the economic, as opposed to the technical, satiation of a market. The common examples are durable consumer goods (e.g. motor cars) per household. Economic saturation generally restricts consumption severely, despite the fact that there is no fixed *technical* "coefficient" between the two. Saturation is influenced by price, within technical limits which may be wide or narrow. The lower the price the more units a household will absorb, if not in *quantity* (because no person can look at more than one television receiver at one time: the technical co-efficient is one to one) then in *quality*. Demand is therefore not rigid or inelastic. Fashion, income and technical innovation also influence saturation: changing fashion, rising incomes and innovation can enlarge absorption and postpone saturation, possibly permanently, by shortening the life-span of each purchase and increasing the rate of replacement. For example, in the USA a wide range of objects, from factories and office buildings to private furniture and motor cars, are scrapped and renewed more frequently than in Britain or Europe. [7]

Saving, the excess of the (current) income of persons and companies over their (current) expenditures: that part of income after tax which is not consumed (by persons) or distributed (by companies).

In a given period the total of personal and company saving, sometimes called "private" or "private sector" saving, is available to meet the spending in the private sector on real capital assets ("capital formation" or "investment"). Any balance is "lent" to, that is used to acquire financial claims against, the banking sector of the economy (bank deposits), and/or the public authorities (currency notes, national savings, gilt-edged securities and other public liabilities).

Thus, in the private sector of the economy, saving in a period equals capital formation plus any increase in financial claims on (or reduction in liabilities to) the banking and public sectors and the rest of the world. In the same period, to the extent that it is financing it by the issue of new financial claims (borrowing), the public sector's spending on current and capital account will be larger than its current income from taxation, trading and property, and conversely. Thus, for the economy as a whole, the financial claims in the period cancel out, since they are assets of the private sector and liabilities of the public sector. This leaves total national saving equal to domestic investment in real capital assets plus any overseas investment (in the form of financial net claims acquired against foreigners). This equality, or rather identity, between saving and investment is basic to national income and social accounting techniques. [8]

"Savings Gap." *See* Income Determination, Theory of.

Say, Jean Baptiste (1767–1832), French economist. Originally he intended to follow a career in business, but became interested in political economy after reading Adam Smith's *Wealth of Nations*. In 1814 he was sent by the French Government to study economic conditions in Britain, the results of his studies appearing in *De l'Angleterre et des Anglais*. He began teaching economics in 1816, and a Chair of Industrial Economy was founded for him at the Conservatoire des Arts et Métiers in 1819. In 1831 he was appointed Professor of Political Economy at the Collège de France. His main works, *Traité d'économique politique* (1803) and *Cours complet d'economie politique practique*, follow the tradition of

Cantillon and Turgot. His conception of economic equilibrium (Say's Law) that supply created equivalent demand had much influence on economic thought. It was radically criticized by Keynes but has been defended by Hutt and other economists of the classical tradition (W. H. Hutt, *A Rehabilitation of Say's Law,* 1975). [2]

Scale, (*a*) in preferences, an order in which some objects are preferred to others. The device is applied in the theoretical analysis of indifference between combinations of two or more objects. [7]

(*b*) in production, the conditions in which factors are combined or recombined in the long run when there is time to adjust them to changed market conditions. [3]

Scarcity, in economics the lack of a commodity in relation to the demand for it. It does not apply simply to goods which are few in number. A unique but obsolete machine tool which is not required even by museums or scrap merchants is not a scarce good in the economic sense. Economists distinguish between "free goods" such as sunshine, air and water, which are normally available in such abundance that they have no price, and "economic goods," which are scarce in relation to demand and so bear a price.

Most goods and services are scarce because, at any given time, the supplies of raw materials, machinery, land and labour needed to create them are also scarce. Thus, whatever its political or social forms, every society must decide how best to allocate its productive resources and how the resulting limited supply of goods and services is to be shared out among the community. If all productive resources are fully employed, an increase in the output of one commodity or service can be produced only by having less of another—more refrigerators means less steel for cars; more land for factories and roads means less for agriculture; more teachers may mean fewer nurses or social workers; and so on.

In time, by adding to its stock of productive resources, a community can increase its total output of goods and services, but even here the rules of scarcity apply. The limited amount of building materials, land and labour must be allocated between, for example, factories to increase the supply of manufactured goods and universities to increase the supply of scientists and engineers.

These problems are fundamental to rich and poor societies alike, and to every political system from capitalism to communism. Economics is essentially a study of the problems arising from scarcity. If all goods were so abundant that they were free, there would be no economic problem, because the need to decide how best to allocate resources would not arise. [14]

Schmoller, Gustav. *See* Economic Thought.

Scholasticism, a name applied to the most typical ideas of the medieval schoolmen, who wrote from the ninth to the early fifteenth centuries. In economics the most important thinkers were Saint Thomas Aquinas and Duns Scotus. The schoolmen tried to rationalize the doctrines of the Church, e.g. to relate the doctrines on trade and usury to economic developments in the Middle Ages. The concept of the "just price" had to be successively adapted to extensions of trading and developing commercial practices. In a sense the decline of scholasticism may be seen as the acceptance by the Church of the workings of the law of supply and demand. [2]

Schuman Plan. *See* EUROPEAN COAL AND STEEL COMMUNITY.

Schumpeter, Joseph Alois (1883–1950), Austrian economist. Born in Moravia, then part of the Austro-Hungarian Empire, and educated at Vienna. After a brief period in Egypt he became Professor of Economics at Czernowitz and later at Graz. After the First World War he was a finance minister in the Austrian Republic but soon gave up this occupation to become professor at Bonn. He stayed at Bonn until 1932, when he moved to Harvard.

Schumpeter's work was taken seriously at an early stage in his career, Böhm-Bawerk especially devoting lengthy discussions to his views. He was a fertile writer; his works cover all branches of economics. *Capitalism, Socialism and Democracy* (1942) and *History of Economic Analysis* (published posthumously in 1954) give only a small indication of it. In his *Theory of Economic Development* (1912) and *Business Cycles* (1939) he analysed the capitalist system and put forward the theory that innovations made by *entrepreneurs* are the strategic factor in economic development and occupy a central position in the process of the trade cycle. [2]

"Scissors" Simile. *See* MARSHALL; VALUE.

Scitovsky, Tibor (1910–2002), Hungarian-born economist. He was educated at the University of Budapest and at Cambridge (Trinity), Paris (École des Sciences Politiques) and the LSE. He was Associate Professor of Economics at Stanford from 1946 to 1957, Professor of Economics at the University of California at Berkeley from 1957 to 1968, and since then has taught at Yale. For two years, 1966 to 1968, he was a Fellow at the Development Centre of the Organization for Economic Co-operation and Development.

Scitovsky's best known work is a text book, *Welfare and Competition* (1950), in which he brought together the then latest developments in price theory and welfare economics, to both of which he had himself contributed, in order to explain the working of the pricing system in perfect and imperfect markets under conditions of full employment, and to consider its ability to allocate resources and products efficiently in the sense of maximizing "economic welfare," in so far as that term could be defined. Apart from sharing the failure of all economic theorizing so far to decide whether or not interest constituted a compensation for a recognizable cost, *Welfare and Competition* was at least as good as any other work on the subject, and its geometrical exposition was unsurpassed. Scitovsky has also contributed to the discussion of welfare economics in relation to international trade (*Economic Theory and Western European Integration*, 1958) and played a prominent part in the long debate on the possible use of the compensation principle to maximize economic satisfaction. [2]

Scottish Journal of Political Economy. *See* Journals, Economic.

Scrip, a "bonus" of new shares issued without charge to shareholders in proportion to shareholdings, e.g. one to six, by subscription certificate. The contrast is with a rights "issue," which is an *offer* of shares at a price designed to raise additional capital. A scrip usually embodies in a firm's capital the profits held in reserve. [1]

Search Costs, the time and effort (etc.) spent in discovering the terms on which goods or services are available in the market. If prices, qualities, etc. are stable or predictable, search costs are low; if unstable or unpredictable, they are high. But, beyond a point, further search will be abandoned in favour of waiting or queuing for a commodity or service whose price, quality, etc. are known, even if it is slightly more expensive than buyers might find if they sought further. In these circumstances some suppliers might carry stocks to reduce buyers' search costs and reduce queuing or waiting. Conversely, where search costs are very low, because the market is more or less perfect, as in a stock exchange, no stocks are kept, there is no waiting or queuing, but prices change frequently to adjust changes in demand and supply. [13]

Second Best, Theory of, a recent addition to theories analysing ends and the best means of achieving them. If the first-best situation, like the Pareto optimum, cannot be reached because one condition of optimality may not be attainable, achieving the others may not yield the best possible solution for the system as a whole. The common example is that of tariff reduction to yield gains from international division of labour. The theory/hypothesis is that, although reduction of *all* tariffs is desirable, a reduction of tariffs among a small number of countries with tariffs will not necessarily make the situation better for the group as a whole. A removal of resale price maintenance from one commodity will not necessarily improve the distribution of others. Short of removal of *all* tariffs, or RPM in *all* commodities, a second-best solution that seems to conflict with the general principle may be better.

Second-best solutions have yet to be worked out fully in economic theory, and even more so in practice. One interim solution, proposed by the British economist Ralph Turvey, is to go for a third-best solution, in which effort is concentrated on reaching the optimum solution in one sector of the system.

A more pragmatic approach argues that no policy can take all remote effects into account, so that concentrating on the first-best and trying to approach it may give as good results in an imperfect world as striving for a conceptually clearer but practically unattainable second best. [14]

Secondary Banks, institutions that developed outside the established clearing banks in a period of rapid change and/or inflation. Secondary banks were prepared to lend on riskier undertakings, though at higher rates of interest. They may thus have fertilized ventures that might not otherwise have made headway, but they were more vulnerable to adverse change. [8]

Secondary Boycott, measures undertaken to influence an employer not directly engaged in a trade dispute in order to bring pressure on employers who are directly involved. Examples are denial of supplies and prevention of sales, e.g. barring fishmongers from access to a quayside market. British and American law has distinguished between lawful primary boycotts and unlawful secondary boycotts. British labour disputes in the 1970's polarized opinion between making secondary boycotts legal in order to strengthen the unions, and penalizing them to prevent disruption of industry as a whole beyond firms directly involved in disputes. [5]

Secondary Market, the sale and purchase of securities or commodities outside the established markets or exchanges. Unquoted securities may be privately placed with brokers or other institutions. [7]

Secular, long-term rather than short-term (not lay rather than clerical). Economic change is usually made up of several elements: short-term (e.g. seasonal), medium-term and long-term. These are relative terms. The secular movement in the standard of living in the West has been upward for two centuries (after a thousand years of little change), but the rate of increase fluctuated with roughly ten-year trade cycles before the war and with milder, less regular fluctuations after 1945. [14]

Securities, written or printed documents of title giving the holder a right to property not in his possession. The term is normally used to denote investments generally and in particular refers to income-yielding marketable claims such as stocks and shares.

Classes of securities vary with the risk element. (*a*) Debentures are loans in joint-stock companies paying fixed rates of interest. (*b*) Preference shares also yield a fixed rate of interest; they have a prior claim to dividends over ordinary shares, and sometimes to repayment of capital on a winding-up. The dividend on cumulative preference shares "accumulates" if it is not paid because profits are inadequate. (*c*) Ordinary shares, or "equities" as they are commonly called, have no special rights to dividends; but they usually control the company as they have the voting rights at annual general meetings; if they carry no votes they are sometimes described as "A" shares. Their value is represented by the net assets of the company (after deducting preference share capital). (*d*) Government stocks and local government stocks are often referred to as "gilt-edged securities" because they have been regarded as absolutely safe, although the medium-term and long-term loans suffer from the effects of inflation much more than equity shares. Gilt-edged securities can be split into (1) short-term loans such as Treasury bills; (2) medium-term and long-term loans, including the permanent loans such as Consols and the various dated stocks; and (3) National Savings Certificates, Tax Reserve Certificates, Defence Bonds and Post Office Savings Bank deposits, which can be encashed at any time but which cannot be sold. (*e*) Other types of securities are bills, mortgages, assurance policies, shares and deposits in building societies, etc. [8]

Securities, Dated. *See* YIELD.

Securities, Irredeemable. *See* YIELD.

Seignorage. *See* FREE COINAGE.

Selective Employment Tax, tax levied on firms according to the number of people employed: introduced in Britain in 1966, at a higher rate in services in order to move labour into manufacturing. It was said to have been advised by the Cambridge economist Nicholas Kaldor. It was levied on all firms but was returned to some (e.g. in agriculture) and with a premium to manufacturing firms. It provoked much controversy and was ended in 1973. [12]

Self-financing. *See* PLOUGHING BACK.

"Self-service" Store. *See* MARKETING.

Sellers' Market, one in which sellers hold the stronger strategic position of bargaining advantage because buyers are prepared to buy, at existing prices, larger amounts of goods than sellers are currently able to produce or prepared to market. Sellers' markets may be caused by increases in demand for durable commodities whose existing supplies can increase only very slowly (e.g. houses), or for commodities which are themselves produced with specialized equipment that takes time to produce, or because of misplanned production or output deficiencies (e.g. crop failures). Manufacturers' stocks are then run down, prices forced up and abnormal profits earned until output is increased or demand falls away. When demand grows continuously, capacity may lag for many years; but the duration of a sellers' market usually depends upon the mobility of factors of production, their degree of specialization, and the time needed to bring new plant into use. A sellers' market in hula hoops would be dissipated quickly by an influx of plastic extruders; a sellers' market in oil products might persist for ten years whilst additional production, transportation and refinery facilities were built.

All markets may be converted into sellers' markets by a general excess demand caused by monetary inflation. At such times men and resources are fully employed and output can be increased only with additional capacity created by investment and improved methods. Whilst it is taking place investment diverts resources from current production, and when completed it only partly offsets excess demand because the resulting increase in real income reinforces demand further. During a continuing inflation stocks of goods may be accumulated beyond current requirements as a hedge against rising prices and so the sellers' markets may be strengthened further. [7]

Senior, Nassau William (1790–1864), English economist. Educated at Eton and Oxford University; he was called to the bar in 1819 and appointed a Master in Chancery in 1836. In 1825 he was appointed Drummond Professor of Political Economy at Oxford.

Senior was active in both the academic world and in the affairs of government, serving on several royal commissions. In his main works, *Introductory Lectures on Political Economy* and *An Outline of the Science of Political Economy* (1836), he stated his views on the scope and method of political economy, which he regarded as a purely deductive science. His work places him as one of the founders of pure economics. [2]

"Set-off." *See* BETTERMENT.

Settling-day, the day on which payment has to be made for dealings in Stock Exchange securities which have taken place since the previous settling-day or account day. Settling-days fall on Tuesdays and there are twenty-four in a year, so that there are twenty accounts of a fortnight in duration and four of three weeks. [8]

Shackle, George L. S. (1903–92), British economist. He was educated at Perse School, Cambridge, the London School of Economics, and New College, Oxford, and taught at the University of Liverpool (Brunner Professor of Economic Science from 1951 to 1969).

The central theme of Shackle's economics is uncertainty—the role of the unpredictable in economic decision-making (*Uncertainty in Economics and Other Reflections,* 1955; *Expectation, Enterprise and Profit,* 1970, etc.). This is the foundation of his work on the rate of interest and of his criticism of economists who apply frequency-ratio probability to unique situations. His view of the uncertainty of economic prediction is based on kaleidostatics: "The economy is in the particular posture which prevails, because particular expectations, or rather, particular agreed formulas about the future, are for the moment widely accepted. These can change as swiftly, as completely, and on as slight a provocation as the loose, ephemeral mosaic of the kaleidoscope. A twist of the hand, a piece of 'news,' can shatter one picture and replace it with a different one" (*A Scheme of Economic Theory*, CUP, 1965). Some critics held that Shackle did not deal adequately with the notion of statistical dynamics, based on a (concealed) "orderliness" in the varied personal anticipations and reactions of individuals. The abstractness of Shackle's subject-matter is saved from aridity by the quality of his writing. [2]

Shading, lowering prices by degrees: in response to falling demand, intensifying competition, adverse publicity, etc. A useful term, common in the USA and being used more widely in Britain. [7]

Shadow Pricing, the calculation of notional or imputed prices where they are not obtained from markets. The intention is to provide approximations to relative values or the costs of factors of production used for commodities or services. Where markets are not available, as inside a firm, or are considered undesirable, as in a centrally planned economy, shadow prices may be calculable. A firm may calculate internal or transfer prices by accounting estimates. A planning board may be able to use linear programming to calculate shadow prices. If the costs of collecting the information needed to use this technique are high, and the weights (valuations) initially assigned by the planners to commodities are unrealistic, the planners could begin with arbitrary shadow prices, assemble "bids" for resources from plant managers, adjust the initial prices until demand and supply are equated, and allocate the resources accordingly. In practice the experience of bidding for resources within the Russian economy indicates a tendency to overbid to secure the amount of resources desired. Some economists claim that refinement in techniques will perfect the methods and improve the results. [3]

Share Certificate, document supplied by a company to each shareholder showing the number and value of the shares he holds. [8]

Shares, documents indicating that the holder participates in the ownership of a company and has a claim to part of its profits. The type and number of shares held define the rights of the holder and the extent of his ownership.

Although there are many types of shares they are all variants of two main classes—preference and ordinary shares, sometimes known as prior and equity capital.

Most types of preference share entitle the holders to a stated amount of the company's profits, which must be paid before dividends are distributed to ordinary shareholders. A 4 per cent preference shareholder, for example, would be entitled to draw from the company's profits, before ordinary shareholders, £4 for every £100 invested. Although preference shareholders have first claim on profits when they are earned, they have no claim on the company in bad years when it fails to make profits. Most preference shares are issued with "cumulative rights" entitling the holder not only to dividends for the current year but also for previous years if they were not paid. Normally preference shareholders have no voting powers in the election of company directors.

The ordinary shareholder receives not a fixed amount of profit but whatever is left after preference shareholders have been paid. In good years this may be a lot, in lean years little or nothing. If the company is brought to an end, the ordinary shareholder usually ranks behind the preference shareholder in the repayment of capital. Since ordinary shareholders bear more risk than other owners of the company they have the right to elect the directors to manage it. [8]

Shenoy, B. R. (1905–78), Indian economist. He graduated from Banaras Hindu University and the London School of Economics and joined the then University College, Colombo, as Lecturer in Economics in 1936. After service with Indian and international organizations (the International Monetary Fund and the International Bank for Reconstruction and Development) he returned to university teaching from 1954 to 1968 as Director and Professor of Economics at the University School of Social Sciences, Gujarat University. He retired in 1968 to become Director of the Economic Research Centre, New Delhi.

As a member of the Panel of Economists of the Indian Planning Commission in 1955, Shenoy appended a lone minute of dissent to the draft of the second five-year plan, emphasizing the dangers of the scale of inflation envisaged in the plan. Since then he has been the foremost academic critic of the investment and economic policies of the Indian Government. He argues that investment in heavy industries denies agriculture the resources necessary for development, although agriculture employs three quarters of the population and generates half the national income (the industrial sector, both public and private, has received the largest investments). Shenoy is critical of India's exchange control policy for subsidizing imports and penalizing exports, thus exacerbating India's exchange difficulties and stimulating illegal markets in foreign exchange. Shenoy has also argued that foreign aid has supported mal-investment by supplying the foreign exchange when domestic resources proved inadequate. His views and analysis are diametrically opposed to those of virtually every other economist writing on India. [2]

Sherman Act. *See* Trust Busting.

Shift-share Analysis, a framework of empirical analysis used in studies of regional growth. Earlier studies had tended to analyse regional growth in terms of a region's relative *share* of rapidly growing and of stagnant industries. Further studies revealed that a region might grow not only because it contained an above-average proportion of rapidly growing industries, but also because it might be gaining an increasing proportion of an industry or industries, whether or not they were growing rapidly, because of *shifts* in the locational pattern of industry. The study of such shifts tries to measure the total relative shift in regional indicators of economic activity in terms of the difference between the regional change occurring and the change that would have occurred had the region grown at national average rates. The total shift comprises a *proportional* and a *differential* element. If a region specializes in activities that have a slow growth rate nationally it will tend to show a downward proportionality shift over time: if industry is tending to grow at a faster rate than in other regions it will tend to show an upward differential shift. The sum of the proportional and differential shifts is the total shift. [6]

Shifting, Tax. *See* TAX, SHIFTING AND INCIDENCE.

Shifting Value, contention, first advanced in the Final Report of the Expert Committee on Compensation and Betterment (Uthwatt Report), 1942, that although the public control of land use necessarily shifts land values (increases some, decreases others) it does not destroy them since neither the total demand for development nor its average annual rate is materially affected by land planning controls. If control prohibits development on one site, demand simply shifts to some other site and total land values are unaffected. The Report offered no economic analysis to support this contention, which received considerable criticism from economists and land practitioners. [6]

Shopping Goods, those usually chosen after "shopping around" between competing shops: e.g. furniture and other goods that are either not easily standardized or sold in different places on different terms, so that information about better value can be obtained by comparing prices, quality, service, etc. The contrast is with "convenience" goods, which are standardized or sold in readily recognizable and comparable form, and with "specialty" goods, in which each shop has a "unique" product, such as clothes cut by personal tailors. [7]

Short Money Market. *See* MONEY MARKET.

Short Period, phrase used by economists to distinguish between changes that can be expected to take place quickly and those that occur more slowly over the "long period." The "long period" is one long enough to permit full adjustment to a change in the underlying conditions, e.g. a period in which the number of firms in an industry, or the scale of equipment used by any one firm, is able to change. Conversely the short period is one which permits only partial adjustment, e.g. a situation in which a firm can respond to variations in demand only by using its existing plant and equipment either more or less intensively.

The distinction is analytical. In practice the actual clock-time or calendar-time necessary for adjustment differs from industry to industry; e.g. the "short period" in arable farming is probably longer than the "long period" in services such as domestic window cleaning, which requires little specialized capital equipment. Because only partial adjustment is possible the elasticity of supply of a commodity in response to changes in its price is likely to be less in the "short period" than in the "long period" after time has elapsed sufficient for the factors of production to be fully adjusted to the changes. [7]

"Short Run." *See* Short Period; Time.

Shove, Gerald Frank (1887–1947), British theoretical economist of socialist and pacifist views. He was educated at Uppingham and King's College, Cambridge, of which he was a Fellow and Lecturer. He was later Reader in Economics at Cambridge University.

Shove was an eminent member of the group of Cambridge economists of whom Schumpeter said, "By critical and positive suggestion they help other people's ideas into definite existence. And they exert anonymous influence—influence as leaders—far beyond anything that can be definitely credited to them from their publications." Shove was a pupil of Marshall, whose general system of thought he adopted and developed. His most important work was "The Place of Marshall's Principles in the Development of Economic Theory" in the *Economic Journal* in 1942, a scholarly and authoritative assessment, written with an assured knowledge of Marshall's predecessors and successors. He also made valuable contributions to the theory of the firm. [2]

Sidgwick, Henry (1838–1900), English philosopher and economist. He was educated at Rugby and Cambridge, and although trained as a classical and mathematical scholar he soon turned to the study of practical philosophy. In 1859 he was elected to a fellowship at Trinity College, Cambridge, and became Lecturer in Moral Philosophy in 1869. Sidgwick played a large part in the development of the university, being mainly instrumental in the introduction of the moral sciences tripos. He was appointed Knightsbridge Professor of Moral Philosophy in 1883. His main contribution to economics is to be found in *Principles of Political Economy* (1883), in which he showed a profound interest in the social questions raised by the classical political economists. [2]

Sik, Ota (1910–), Czechoslovak economist. In the 1960's he was a little-known economist in a communist country who wrote on the forms of market that could advantageously be incorporated into the macro-economic framework of a centrally planned society. He was head of the Economic Institute of the Czechoslovak Academy of Sciences at the time of the 1963 economic crisis, when he advocated reforms in economic administration in line with the views put forward in Russia by Liberman and Nemchinov. He argued the case for developing a system of prices which represented the value of the resources employed and encouraged their economic use by reflecting in the rewards of factors their effectiveness in adapting output to the expressed demand of consumers. In *Plan and Market under Socialism* he developed these and similar concepts further and, in what was probably the most fruitful work to emerge from a communist source, argued forcefully that an efficient pricing system is not contradictory to effective planning but is essential to its success. The effective pricing of productive resources was thus only historically associated with exploitation and was not an integral part of the process.

Sik came into prominence in 1968 as a Deputy Finance Minister in the Dubcek government, after which he taught economics at the University of Basle, Switzerland, and wrote *Der Dritte Weg* (*The Third Way*), published in Hamburg in 1972.

In his writings Sik has been concerned to elaborate the economic theory underlying the integration of a market system into macro-economic planning. He judged that, in spite of its inadequacies, the market was "an irreplaceable criterion for socially useful and necessary activity in individual enterprises" and that its disappearance in communist countries had caused a conflict between individual activity in production and social needs. But it could not ensure humane conditions in production and in the distribution of income. It must, therefore, be put into a macro-economic framework that set broad aims, and be accompanied by a planned economic policy. The combination of collectivized ownership of capital and a market system could avoid the alienation of the workers and their concentration on wages, which was inflationary, by making them owners with a direct and immediate interest in the growth of capital, the use of profits, and decisions on investment. It would thus be the "third way" better than both capitalism, in which capital was owned by relatively few, and nationalization, in which alienation was not removed but deepened by the bureaucratization of management.

Der Dritte Weg discussed the mechanics of capital accumulation, provision for ensuring initiative and founding new enterprises, and the organization of a system of collectivized ownership of capital using the market mechanism. [2]

Simple Interest, the interest on a principal sum invested or borrowed, calculated on the original sum invested or borrowed. (Compound interest is calculated on the sum of principal and accumulating interest.) If P is the principal sum, r the rate of interest for one year and t the time period in years, simple interest (I) is calculated by the formula

$$I = Prt$$

and the amount (of principal plus interest) at the end of the period is

$$S = P + I$$

These two equations are called the fundamental equations of simple interest, and all computational problems involving simple interest can be solved with their aid. [8]

Simulation Models, abstract representations of systems and their components. Early simulation models tended to employ simple physical analogues, such as hydraulic models to illustrate electricity flows or the flows of spending and income in an economy. With the advent and development of modern computing technology, the degree of abstraction possible increased significantly. Nowadays, simulated systems are usually represented by mathematical expressions that depict the behaviour of their principal components and the interactions among them. Simulation modeling is applied to a wide range of subjects, e.g. insect behaviour, production systems in large factories, the structure of urban regions, national and regional economic systems. Environmental impacts of various kinds of activity are increasingly tested in simulated environments and economic policy is similarly tested in a simulated economic environment, usually based on large-scale econometric models. Simulation models thus try to overcome some of the difficulties of experimentation in the social sciences: where large-scale public investment is involved it is sometimes possible to avoid extremely costly errors by discovering errors in solutions at the model stage.

Some critics of the method suggest the opposite, that their use encourages inflation in the scale of decision-taking that can produce colossal failures and waste of resources, and that since the knowledge gained from the use of simulation models is directly proportional to the knowledge fed into the model in the form of assumptions, they add nothing to knowledge of cause and effect. [14]

Sinking Fund, (*a*) a charge against profits to provide for the maintenance of capital intact at the end of the life of a "wasting asset" (such as a lease), or (*b*) an appropriation of profits to provide for a known future liability such as the repayment of a loan: the sum is that which must be deposited annually at compound interest to produce the required amount in the given time. The higher the rate of interest and the longer the term of years, the smaller the annual deposit need be. [1]

Sismondi, Jean (1773–1842), Swiss economist and historian. He was born into an old French family which took refuge in England during the revolutionary disturbances of 1793–4, but in 1800 he returned to his native city of Geneva and from 1809 began lecturing at the Academy on ancient history and economics. His early contributions to economics, *Tableau de l'Agriculture Toscane* (1801) and *Traité Commerciale* (1803), show him as a disciple of Adam Smith, but his later work, *Nouveaux principes d'économie politique* (1819), represents a protest against the orthodoxy of his time. He challenged the doctrine that competition established an equilibrium between production and consumption, and argued that over-production and crises were an inevitable part of the economic system. [2]

Site Value Tax. *See* TAX, SHIFTING AND INCIDENCE.

Skedasticity, fancy Greek term for variance, a statistical measure of the dispersion of a group of individual items around their arithmetical average. If an individual variable varies with another variable or changes over time it is called heteroskedastic; if constant, homoskedastic. [14]

Sliding Peg. *See* CRAWLING PEG.

Slump, decline in economic activity marked by widespread unemployment and a fall in production, profits and prices. It is sometimes called a depression or, in mild cases, a recession. A slump usually follows a boom—a period of full employment, high production and rising prices.

The reversal of boom conditions and the decline into a slump is caused by a fall in total spending which, if unchecked, tends to develop into a cumulative movement spreading throughout the economy. A fall in sales will force some firms to reduce production by dismissing employees or hiring them only part time. This falling demand for labour means reduced incomes and spending, which in turn create a further decline in output and employment elsewhere. Prices and profits will tend to be cut in an effort to clear swollen stocks of unsold goods in shops and warehouses. Consequently business men will tend to take a pessimistic view of the future, reduce expenditure on new buildings and equipment and so unwittingly give an extra push to the downward movement of the slump.

A sharp decline in demand sufficient to generate a slump usually occurs in the durable or capital goods section of the market because a householder's decision to buy a new refrigerator or a business man's plan to build a new factory can be postponed indefinitely or advanced suddenly, so creating the possibility of wide fluctuations in total spending. By contrast, the total demand for non-durable goods such as food and transport is less easily deferred and much more stable. [9]

Slutsky, Eugen (1880–1948), Russian economist and econometrician. After the Revolution he was appointed Professor at Kiev University and stayed for eight years (1918–26). From 1934–48 he was at the Mathematics Institute of the USSR Academy of Sciences.

Slutsky is best known in the West for early work on the economics of demand. He argued (in 1915) that a theory of demand need not be based on measurable utility. This approach anticipated that of Hicks and Allen in 1934. He analysed the income effect separately from the price effect. In econometrics he identified regularities or oscillations in moving averages of series, whether or not they were random. [2]

Small-scale Production, production in small factories or workshops (which may be part of a large firm) or production by small firms (which implies small factories). The meaning of "small" is partly a matter of definition. The British Census of Production distinguishes size according to the number of persons employed. Another distinction could be made in terms of capital employed. The important point is the way in which total output is divided between firms in an industry. Small-scale production in this sense may refer: (1) to a situation in which the total output of a product or group of products is made by a large number of firms none of which contribute a significantly large part of it; (2) output comes from a few firms each of which is small; (3) small units exist together with bigger firms producing the same or similar commodities.

Small-scale business is likely to persist to some extent because of conditions in the market, e.g. imperfect communications; habit and convenience may enable the small shop to survive despite the economic advantages of larger enterprises; the same may apply to craft production. In both there may be the attraction of real or imagined specialist qualities of product or service. The absence of considerable economies of scale and the existence of diseconomies at relatively small size of unit are also important. Hence agriculture has lent itself to small-scale production because of the importance of personal management, supervision and judgement and the consequent limitations on the use of large-scale management. The framework of law and custom in the inheritance of land may reinforce this influence. Similarly, small units often persist where personal service and immediate after-sales service are important: hairdressing is an example of the first; small paint firms of the second. Even within big firms small-scale production of particular lines may take place.

It is typical of the variety of economic life as a whole that small-scale production persists and is renewed alongside large-scale enterprise in the same or similar industries and markets. This independent vitality reflects the capacity of the small unit to satisfy individual requirements and to benefit from particular or local conditions; it depends also on the continuing inventiveness and optimism of new entrants. [3]

Smith, Adam (1723–90), Scottish economist. His father, a judge advocate and comptroller of customs, died just before he was born and he was brought up by his mother in Kircaldy. At the age of fourteen he became a student at the University of Glasgow, where he came into contact with Francis Hutcheson, who had also been the teacher of David Hume. Hutcheson had much influence on Smith, and was largely responsible for his ideas on political liberty. In 1740 Smith won a scholarship to Oxford and spent the next few years at Balliol College. Oxford was in a decline, but though he received little formal education he made good use of his time and read widely.

In 1747 he returned to Kircaldy and soon afterwards began to lecture at the University of Edinburgh. A few years later he was appointed to the Chair of Logic at the University of Glasgow, moving to the Chair of Moral Philosophy when it became vacant in 1752. His lectures at Glasgow gave rise to his first major work *The Theory of Moral Sentiments,* which appeared in 1759. The book was highly successful and came into the hands of Charles Townshend, the statesman, who was so impressed with it that he offered Smith the position of tutor to the young Duke of Buccleuch. Smith accepted the offer, resigned his chair and in 1764 began the Grand Tour of Europe with the duke. At Toulouse he expanded part of his lecture course at Glasgow; this was the beginning of his great work *An Inquiry into the Nature and Causes of the Wealth of Nations.*

He returned to Britain in 1766, retired to Kircaldy and set about revising and finishing his work. It was finally published in 1776, and brought him considerable fame. The book was essentially a study of the creation of wealth. In itself this was not new, for it had been the concern of the Mercantilists and the Physiocrats, but whereas the former believed that wealth derived from a favourable balance of trade, and the latter from land, Smith argued that wealth arose out of labour. He began with the celebrated description of the division of labour which increases wealth because it increases the dexterity of the labour force, saves time and permits the use of mechanical devices. The limits to the division of labour are set by the size of the market and the "stock of capital."

The question of economic growth led on to the famous Book IV, in which Smith put forward his thesis that freedom within an economic society would lead to the greatest possible wealth. In many respects the argument is based upon *The Theory of Moral Sentiments* because the social harmony he described was dependent upon the delicate balance of man's conflicting motives. The search to satisfy individual self-interest would benefit society and would be limited by the self-interest of others. Producers sought to earn the largest possible profit, but in order to do so they had to produce goods desired by the community. Further, they must produce them in the right quantities, otherwise too much would cause a low price and a low profit, while too small a supply would cause an increase in price and eventually an increase in supply. The delicate mechanism of the "invisible hand" was also at work in the markets for the factors of production, providing harmony as long as factors sought the largest possible earnings. The right goods would be produced at the right prices, and the whole community would achieve the largest possible wealth as long as free competition held sway; but if competition were restricted, the work of the "invisible hand" would be impaired and society would suffer.

The immediate success of the book was due to its brilliant systemization of economic thinking round the central concept of markets and to the intellectual justification it provided for the newly emerging industrialists who were interested in ridding Britain of mercantilist controls. In a short time *The Wealth of Nations* was on the bookshelves of economists and politicians and provided the code of economic behaviour that served Britain for most of the following century, its bright prospects only slightly dimmed by the gloomy predictions of the Rev. Thomas Malthus and David Ricardo. Adam Smith "persuaded his own generation and governed the next." [2]

Smith, Henry (1905–88), British economist. He started life as an errand-boy at thirteen and a half. He went to Christ Church, Oxford, with an extramural scholarship at twenty-five, graduated in Politics, Philosophy and Economics with First Class Honours, and was awarded a three-year post-graduate scholarship. He was appointed Lecturer in Business Finance at the University of Liverpool in 1935 and resident economics tutor at Ruskin College, Oxford, in 1937. After wartime service at the Ministry of Food he returned to Ruskin College as Vice-Principal (1947–70). He served on the Civil Service Arbitration Tribunal from 1948 until 1964. In 1962 he absolved wage arbitration from the charge of spreading inflation, which he argued was the responsibility of government in fiscal policy. He criticized the Conservative Government for trying to confine wage arbitration within the narrow limits of wage "pauses" and "guiding lights" and advised that arbitrators would not serve if they were made "slightly dirty rubber stamps." In his Hobart Paper *The Wage Fixers* (1962) he set wage arbitration in the context of fundamental economic principles: the marginal productivity theory, the extent to which wages determine or are determined by product prices, etc.

Henry Smith taught and wrote on economics with a rare familiarity with and understanding of both liberal and Marxist economics. He wrote on the theory of imperfect competition and attempted to apply it to the problems of the retail market (*Retail Distribution, A Critical Survey,* 1937). His main work consists of an attempt to put the valid concepts in Marx into current economic terminology, to define in economic terms what constitutes a socialist society (*The Economics of Socialism Reconsidered,* 1962), and to estimate the chances of anything like it emerging from the political processes of the existing world. He assembled his general approach to economics in *A Prospect of Political Economy* (1968), in which he gave more space to the thinking of Marx than do most economic texts on political economy. Keynes referred to Henry Smith for advice on books about Marxist economics when considering them for reviews in the *Economic Journal.* [2]

Smithsonian Agreement, arranged by the IMF Group of Ten at the Smithsonian Institute, Washington, in 1971, to raise the US gold price (from 35 to 38 dollars an ounce), to re-align currency values (which effectively up-valued other currencies), and to widen the permitted fluctuations around the new par values. [4]

Social, adjective, commonly used in popular economic writing, to which economics cannot attach a clear meaning, except that used by Pigou: external economic effects. Private economic effects plus social economic effects equals total economic effects. The debate between economists is about how far external effects are being internalized, or, as Coase argued in 1962, could be internalized by more precise definition and delimitation of property rights. In literary writing or pseudo-professional journalism "social" is often used as distinct from, or in conflict with, "economic."

The word could be used in a significant sense to refer to public goods, which cannot be provided in the market and must therefore be supplied "socially," i.e. by collective decision and financing. This meaning could take in the "social" services insofar as they are public and not private.

In its wider sense social means or implies that decisions through the political process are necessarily superior to private decisions in the market. This is the focus of the debate among normative economists. [14]

Social Accounting, the system of accounts which provide the framework for describing the market relationships within (and between) national economies in quantitative terms. Subject to the limitations of the system and the reliability of the data, the accounts enable the present to be compared with the recent past; they can yield useful statistical information to individuals and institutions; and they help governments to assess the effectiveness of economic policy and to derive some guidance to future policy.

All forms of economic activity can be reduced to three basic categories: production, consumption and accumulation (adding to capital wealth). If every buyer and seller in the economy were provided with three accounts corresponding to this basic division, all transactions could be recorded in them. *One* would record income and outgo relating to productive activity, and show net income as the balance between the two. A *second* would record the way in which the net income (plus any other income received) was divided ("appropriated") between outlay and saving. The *third* would show how saving (plus any other capital funds received) was used to finance investment or to make loans to other transactors.

If these accounts were consolidated into three "national" accounts, transactions between individual transactors within and between the "national" accounts would cancel out, leaving only the "net" position of the economy as a whole in relation to production, consumption and accumulation. This system of accounts would still be incomplete since it ignores transactions between the economy and the rest of the world. But it could be completed by including a fourth account recording such transactions between people in different national economies.

The four consolidated accounts reflect the fundamental Keynesian "identity equations" on which the system is based, that in a "closed" economy:

Income = Consumption plus Investment;

Saving = Income minus Consumption;

Saving = Investment,

(= is the sign for "is identical with.")

These relationships may be presented in the form of a table called a "matrix," of which Table 8 is an example.

Each internal economic activity and transaction with the rest of the world has a receipts row and a payments column. For instance, the receipts in the production row consist of consumption plus investment plus exports, and the total receipts finance the total payments to the factors of production and for imports

Table 8. Social Accounting

	Receipts				
Payments	Production	Consumption	Accumulation	Rest of the World	Total Receipts
Production	—	C Consumption expenditure	I Investment	X Exports	$C+I+X$
Consumption	Y Income paid to factors of production	—	—	—	Y
Accumulation	—	S Saving	—	—	S
Rest of the World	M Imports	—	$I(f)$ Overseas investment (+) or disinvestment (−)	—	$M \pm I(f)$
Total Payments	$Y+M$	$C+S$	$I \pm I(f)$	X	—

in the production column. "Exports" means all payments due from abroad and "imports" all payments due to other countries. When "exports" exceeds "imports" the country is investing (accumulating) the difference abroad, and when "imports" exceed "exports" the country is "disinvesting" the balance abroad, i.e. selling investments. Since gross saving must equal gross investment expenditures, when "exports" are greater than "imports" saving is equal to home investment plus investment abroad, and when "imports" exceed "exports" saving is equal to investment less disinvestment abroad.

In practice it is impossible to collect this information for each transactor in the economy; to compile the accounts transactors are grouped into "sectors": persons, companies, public corporations, central government and local authorities. Normally only consumption ("appropriation") and accumulation ("capital") accounts are prepared for these sectors. The sector accounts form the units that are then consolidated into single accounts for the whole economy. The production ("operating") account is invariably a national account.

All this implies that the sector account for each economic activity is drawn up on the "double entry" principle and records all the receipts from and to each sector's other accounts and from and to other sectors. In each account receipts and payments must balance. In what is called a completely integrated or "articulated" system, both ends of each monetary flow can thus be seen—a payment in one account becomes a receipt in another. In a detailed system with numerous accounts, complete articulation is rarely achieved because the statistical data is incomplete, but reducing the number of accounts by grouping makes it possible to reach complete articulation.

Social accounting has been developed in recent years with the increasing use of macro-economics. Some economists are sceptical of its uses on the ground that it treats the economic process as "purely objective and mechanical . . . a sort of huge waterworks" (Wilhelm Röpke), and that summarizing concepts like averages and totals "substitute constants for preferences, judgements and decisions and can be misleading unless accompanied by independent consideration of the problem of individual choice and pricing involved in adapting scarce means to alternative ends" (W. H. Hutt). [9]

Social Accounting Matrix ("SAM"), a model demonstrating the processes of economic growth, based on input-output and regression analysis, constructed by economists at Cambridge. The 1965–6 National Plan used it to assess the ability of the economy to reach stated "targets" (e.g. 4 per cent annual rate of economic growth), assuming a given rate of expansion in the labour force, personal and business expenditure habits, etc., and to foresee where shortages and "bottlenecks" were likely to occur.

If the calculations of such growth models suggest that the "bottlenecks" will be numerous or severe or that the targets cannot be reached, the conclusion is either that the original targets were unattainable or that the model is defective. They also require subjective judgement or intuition in selecting the information to be used, and the results are therefore to some extent not wholly objective or "scientific."

A general limitation or weakness of growth models, which are being used in Britain and America, is that the accuracy of the solutions they indicate depends on the quality of the information fed into them. More generally, although they are being refined, they have yet to warrant the belief that they can allow for rapid and unforeseen changes in demand (tastes, etc.) and supply (technology) and the resulting alterations in prices, costs and values. [11]

Social and Economic Studies. *See* JOURNALS, ECONOMIC.

Social Benefits, goods or services provided by government, in the wider sense (all such benefits) or in the narrower sense of welfare or social services. Social benefits have also been described as the "social wage," the obverse of taxes, as distinct from private wages (gross pay less taxes of all kinds, leaving take-home pay). In the wider sense social benefits comprise about half the national income, in the narrower sense about a quarter. The economic questions are how far social benefits are public goods as defined in economic theory, whether social benefits are provided efficiently, i.e. at least cost, whether taxes are the optimal way of financing them, whether the quantity of individual social benefits, from defence to libraries, are those most preferred, and whether they would be smaller or larger if organized and financed in other ways. These are questions on which behaviourial (positive) economic analysis can shed some light, though they are also matters of normative economics, the study of political institutions and social philosophy. [13]

Social Choice, another name for a relatively new study, the economics of public choice. [13]

Social Cost, the total cost to society of any form of economic activity. In a free enterprise economy the fact that consumers are willing to buy a commodity or service indicates that society wishes its scarce resources to be used to produce it rather than other goods or services that consumers refrain from buying at existing prices. In this sense consumers' choice exercised through the price mechanism puts society's scarce resources to their most valued uses. One reason why it may not do so in practice is that the money price of a commodity may not reflect the full "social" cost of production, so that consumers demand more of it than they otherwise would. For example, smoke pollution and traffic congestion impose indiscriminate costs on the community which are not reflected in the prices of goods produced by the factories giving rise to them. These indiscriminate costs, in the form of decreased efficiency of other factors, or decreased enjoyment of consumers of other goods, when added to private costs, make up the social cost of production of any commodity.

Divergence between social and private cost leads to the case in principle for restraining free exercise of choice by individuals, either by prohibiting or limiting certain forms of production or by imposing conditions to be satisfied before production is permitted, such as smoke control, building regulations, traffic control. The difficulty lies in practice, since the definition of indiscriminate costs to be included can often be widened to justify any degree of restriction of free consumers' choice considered desirable on political grounds. It has also been argued that to some or a large extent social costs are taken into account in market decisions, or could be if property rights were defined appropriately to "internalize" the social costs (R. H. Coase and others). [13]

Social Engineering, a term apparently first used by Roscoe Pound, the American philosopher, for the manipulation of a social and economic community, or parts of it, by central or co-ordinated action for a specific purpose. A more refined definition distinguishes between what Professor Karl Popper calls "piecemeal" social engineering and comprehensive, "holistic" or Utopian social engineering.

Comprehensive social engineering conceives of society as a piece of machinery that can be created, guided or directed. For example, it may envisage town planning as a whole, based on social surveys of urban slums, suburban "sprawl," traffic flows, siting of factories in relation to residential areas, shopping centres, recreational facilities and so on. It is an attempt to apply the principles of technical or mechanical engineering to human beings and their social and economic inter-relationships. The aim is to anticipate needs, avoid waste and achieve desired communal aims.

The concept has critics among economists, who doubt whether economic society can be created or redesigned as an entity to satisfy the needs and preferences of the individuals who comprise it. They hold that human institutions have not been the result of conscious decision but have grown as the undesigned results of spontaneous human action co-ordinated by impersonal market relationships. Their reason is that man has only limited knowledge of social processes and makes the best decision when confined to piecemeal alterations of the social and economic structure based on the knowledge within his personal grasp and understanding.

A subsidiary form of (comprehensive) social engineering is based on the view that the market prices on which individuals decide their economic choices yield incomplete guides to the most effective use of resources from the point of view of the community as a whole, and that therefore man must take into account *social* costs and benefits as well as *private* costs and benefits. This view derives from A. C. Pigou, who distinguished between the marginal social and the marginal private net product of economic activity. In recent years it has taken the form of social cost/benefit theory and has been applied to education, health services, transport and defence. It has been argued by several economists that these costs can be taken into account in the working of the market. There is therefore debate between economists on whether the distinction between private and social costs or benefits constitutes a theoretical case for social engineering. [10]

Social Goods, another name for public goods. [13]

Social Insurance (also called national insurance), sharing risks through the state. The main risks commonly covered in western countries are ill health and unemployment; old age or retirement, which are certainties rather than risks, are usually included. Lesser risks are covered by widows' and orphans' benefits, maternity benefit, death benefit. In Britain almost everyone is required to contribute towards social insurance on the ground that it is good for the individual and for the community as a whole, and that if individuals are not compelled to insure through the state they would not insure at all or sufficiently.

Social insurance is said to ensure "social security" and if comprehensive is said to be the foundation of the "welfare state." Social insurance is more comprehensive in Britain than in most other western countries, although some countries in Europe have larger insurance schemes for some risks.

Social insurance is usually paid for in the first instance by employers, employees and the state out of general taxation. This is the immediate impact of the cost; the ultimate incidence is more difficult to trace, since all three sources may pass on the cost to others. Employers in a strong bargaining position with their customers or employees may pass part of it on in higher prices (or lower quality) or lower staff welfare benefits. Employees in a strong bargaining position, as in full employment, may pass it on in higher wages to employers, who may have to absorb it in lower profits or be able to pass it on in turn in higher prices or other ways. The state may finance its part of social insurance by lessening its expenditure on defence or aid to underdeveloped countries or other expenditure or by raising more revenue from taxes.

Social insurance has three main general economic advantages over private insurance. First the underwriting costs may be lower because larger numbers share the risks. Secondly, the administrative costs of collecting premiums, paying benefits, keeping records, etc., may be lower because of the larger scope for standardization of forms, rules, etc. Thirdly, in pension benefits there is no difficulty in tracing employees who change jobs in their working lives so that there is no discouragement to mobility of labour; this is more difficult to arrange in private pension schemes because employers usually install them to discourage employees from moving though pension rights can be made transferable by law.

There are several main economic disadvantages of social insurance compared with private insurance. First, standardization prevents social insurances from being adapted to the circumstances or preferences of firms or individuals. For example, "flat rate" contributions for ill health and unemployment insurance do not vary with the risk of accident or unemployment in different jobs, firms or industries; contributions for pension benefits do not allow for the different ages of retirement that might be desirable in, say, mining and accounting. Secondly, compulsory contributions probably reduce private saving (for pension benefits) that tends to be invested in the more progressive and profitable firms. Thirdly, in Britain and some other countries, social insurance is no longer based on a fund accumulated out of contributions but on the taxing power of the state; it is therefore subject to the risk of arbitrary political decision. Fourthly, social insurance requires high taxation which may discourage incentive and reduce the incomes out of which the contributions for it are paid. Fifthly, it employs scarce political and administrative resources that might be put to other uses.

A further economic effect is that since social insurance contributions are (with one exception) a form of poll tax that does not vary with income within each sex or age group, they are regressive. Some economists believe this has economic drawbacks since it intensifies inequalities in income and therefore in opportunities generally. Others believe it has advantages in emphasizing the costs of state welfare. Recent statistics for Britain suggested that households with middling incomes are paying about as much in taxes (including local rates) and social insurance contributions as they receive in social benefits as a whole.

The exception to the flat-rate contributions is the contribution (to a pension benefit) graduated according to earnings (within a defined range) in Britain and some other countries. The proposal has been made that the sickness and unemployment contributions and benefits should also be graduated so that they become (within the earnings range) more nearly proportioned or progressive. This raises the question whether social insurance is intended to ensure minimum standards in sickness, unemployment or retirement so that individuals need not become dependent on others, or the maintenance during such periods of customary or habitual modes of living, and if the latter whether the additional insurance of people with higher income must be made through the state or could be made through competitive insurance organizations. These issues are partly social and political as well as economic. [10]

Social Ownership (Public Ownership), ownership of industry by individuals collectively as members of the community or society. The contrast is with private ownership of industry by individuals as sole traders (shopkeepers, doctors, etc.), partnerships (solicitors, estate agents, actuaries, accountants, etc.), or shareholders in companies. The term is commonly used in political debate but has economic implications. In principle the case argued for social (public) ownership is that the resources would be used for the community or society as a whole rather than for the private interests of the individuals who own private industry.

The economic grounds on which social/public ownership has been urged are that in industries with very large-scale economies there is "natural" monopoly which makes output less and prices higher than the optimum, that externalities make output larger or smaller than the optimum, that social ownership can redistribute income by providing services below cost, and that it can facilitate participation by employees.

In Britain these arguments have been used in favour of the nationalization of coal, steel, gas and electricity. In transport the argument was for protecting the railways against road competition. In water, road and air services the argument for public ownership has turned on the maintenance of safety standards.

In practice the efficient use of resources depends on control as well as, or rather than, ownership. Here there is a distinction that parallels the divorce between ownership and control in privately owned industry. This divorce was analysed and documented by Berle and Means in *The Modern Corporation and Private Property* (1932). They argued that the owners of private industry (the shareholders) increasingly did not control it, and that its controllers (the directors and senior executives) did not own it. Hence the important consideration was not ownership but control; and this central thesis remains even though the Berle/Means analysis was over-drawn.

In social/public ownership the theory is that the use of resources is controlled by politicians, civil servants, public officials, etc. in the interests of the owners, and the question is again how far the owners can effectively control the controllers. In practice dissatisfied owners can dismiss incompetent or corrupt politicians by electing opposition parties, and the activities of government departments, nationalized industries (e.g. railways and coal mines) and public corporations can be investigated by Parliament, questioned by electors, etc.

The advantage of social/public ownership is that in principle it can take a wide and long view of the benefits and costs. Its weakness is that the owners have fewer means than in private ownership of influencing the controllers because the lack of competition excludes independent tests of efficiency or competence, which must therefore be examined or checked by investigation. Various methods have been attempted to replace competition in Britain: in the 1960's the nationalized industries were required to cover their costs and earn a specified yield on their capital (provided by the owners through taxation); in the USA public utilities have been regulated so that their rates and charges are not used to reflect their monopoly power (Stigler and others have argued that the regulations have largely failed); in the East European countries the managers of socially/publicly owned plants have been required to cover their costs, earn a return on their capital, compete for materials, etc. A difficulty with subjecting socially/publicly owned industries to such market tests is that it may be considered desirable for them to continue in production if they cannot cover their costs and make a loss on the grounds that they provide a "social" rather than a "commercial" service, e.g. British Rail branch lines may be kept running if local authorities finance their losses.

The problem of pricing in socially owned industries has preoccupied welfare economists: whether prices reflect the real (including social) costs of production. Fundamentally, the argument can be boiled down to differences between average and marginal cost pricing and between marginal private and marginal social cost pricing. It is first necessary to define what is being measured, i.e. what is the unit of output (e.g. in transport the additional cost of one more passenger, or ton of goods, or the extra cost of adding one coach or wagon to a train, or of adding to a line's capacity to provide one extra train per unit of time). Second, it is necessary to know whether the cost of adding one unit is more or less than the average cost of producing all the units, i.e. whether average costs are rising (when marginal cost will be above average cost), or falling (when marginal cost will be below average cost) with output. Optimal allocation of resources requires price to be set equal to marginal cost, so that marginal consumers pay the cost of the additional resources detained to satisfy their demands. But this method of charging will not cover the full costs of operation if marginal costs lie below average cost, unless some other system than charging a uniform price to all users is adopted. Third, the example of congestion, in which one additional unit (e.g. a vehicle) can substantially increase the congestion costs (of time, fuel, wear-and-tear, etc.) falling on other road users, even though it may pay for all private costs it incurs, indicates the strength of the case for imposing prices that reflect the real cost of using the road (railway, electricity supply, etc.) to all users or consumers. Fourth, to use the same example, it is necessary to know whether prices charged to individual road users should not only cover all costs incurred by all road users but also any "external" costs which road users impose on other members of the community. Faced with mounting losses, governments have attempted to set financial criteria which imply long-run average cost pricing in these cases; but short-run electoral considerations and the pressures of inflation have led them to hold down nationalized industries' prices well below average costs and even below marginal costs, and to pay lump-sum "compensation" partly to offset past losses (introduced under the Statutory Corporations (Financial Provisions) Act, 1974).

The machinery of enforcement of the owners' interest is that of representation of the owners in Parliament. Apart from the constitutional position that a Member of Parliament is not a delegate who, like a barrister, acts for his clients, but a legislator elected for his personal qualities and philosophical position, he may be able to represent only a majority, which may be as low as 51 per cent, even where he wishes to reflect his constituents' opinions. He can represent majority opinion effectively in decisions on a communal, collective, or "public" good, such as national defence or local street lighting, but this machinery of representation is not effective in private goods such as a family's preference for a single-sex or Catholic school, or for an individual's preference for privacy in sickness, where the majority decision in "social" ownership can deprive up to 49 per cent of their preference or sense of ownership.

The new economic theory of politics is also relevant. If, as Schumpeter and others have argued, politicians' behaviour can be analysed as maximizing their short-term electoral returns, they cannot be assumed to be concerned solely or primarily with the long-run public interest. The term "public" (or "social") ownership may therefore express intention rather than performance: resources may be nominally owned by the public in common but in effect controlled in the interest of the controllers.

Social (public) ownership raises issues that are political as well as economic. The economist's competence does not authorize him to condemn (or support) it on the grounds that it is uneconomic but to demonstrate that, if it is desired on political or other non-economic grounds, its losses have to be made good by resources that have an opportunity cost, e.g. uneconomic railway branch lines or coal pits entail a sacrifice of schools or hospitals or other desired forms of activity. [13]

Social Security. *See* Social Insurance.

Social Services, a general name for state welfare. [13]

Social Wage. *See* Social Benefits.

Social Welfare, a general descriptive term for the well-being of society as a whole. The concept seems clear, but its measurement, or a comparison between the social welfare of two societies (the UK and the USA, or Scotland and Sweden, or W. Germany and E. Germany) is difficult. In economic theory satisfaction is represented by the values attributed by people, individually or collectively, to goods and services, tangible or intangible, appropriated or unappropriated. A. C. Pigou said economic welfare was "that part of social welfare that can be brought directly or indirectly into relation with the measuring rod of money." This is a relatively narrow definition. Money can measure the Gross National Product, which has weaknesses as an indicator of social welfare. (*See* GNP.)

The social welfare "function" is a ranking of preferences by society as a whole between alternative possibilities, e.g. between a situation in which wealth or income are distributed more equally or less equally by inheritance, effort, chance, monopoly, taxation. "Society" is assumed to have a corporate personality. In practice, the ranking is made partly in the market, where preferences may be distorted by monopoly, and partly by elected representatives, who do not know individual preferences between specific personal government services. If the social welfare "function" is to represent human preferences, market imperfections and government imperfections must be removed. If they cannot be removed the "function" is a questionable concept. [13]

Social Welfare Function. *See* SOCIAL WELFARE.

Socialism, (*a*) a collection of philosophical theories, (*b*) the practical programmes of many left-wing political parties. Broadly, socialism aims, in varying degrees, at a form of classless society, to be achieved principally by transferring private property to state ownership and replacing the profit-motivated free-enterprise system of free markets by central state planning. Although socialist programmes usually entail redistribution of income from rich to poor, they also emphasize equality of opportunity.

It is claimed that socialist theory can be found, in embryonic form, in the writings of Plato, and that the early Christian communities anticipated collective ownership. Most historians agree that the first ideas of modern socialism originated towards the end of the eighteenth century in such writers as Babeuf (1760–97), who demanded public ownership of land and industry, and the Comte de Saint-Simon (1760–1825), who called for central planning that would benefit the public. Socialism developed essentially as a response to the problems posed by modern industrialization and drew its strength largely from the industrial working class although its leadership was often middle class in origin.

Socialists are sharply divided on both the method and the degree of socialization. The extreme socialist view was rigorously argued by Karl Marx in a series of books and pamphlets published between 1848 and 1882. He claimed that a socialist state could be achieved only by completely overthrowing all capitalist institutions and replacing them by state ownership and control with a one-party dictatorship of the proletariat. These ideas inspired the Bolshevik Revolution in 1917, subsequently forming the basis of Russian political thinking and action. Most of the left-wing parties of western Europe are far less radical; they accept parliamentary democracy, aim only at state ownership of key or basic industries, combined with government planning and social security schemes.

In recent years left-wing parties in Europe have tended to replace general by selective state control of industry in their political programmes, and some socialists have argued that state ownership is not essential for socialism.

The debate between liberal and socialist economists on the economics of socialism in recent years has largely centred on its ability to arrange the efficient use of resources in the absence of free markets. Some socialist economists have argued that socialism requires and can use markets to indicate consumers' preferences. Yugoslavia has combined state ownership of the major means of production with some freedom for the managers of state enterprises to respond to market prices, and Poland and Hungary to a lesser extent. Russian economists have raised the question whether profit might be a useful guide to state enterprises. [14]

Sociology, Relation to Economics. *See* ECONOMICS.

Soft Currency, one with a relatively unstable value in international exchange or whose external value tends to fall in the long run. Normally a currency is "soft" because of the weakness of its balance of payments, which may be in deficit for long periods. For many years after the Second World War sterling and most continental currencies were "soft," largely because of the need to buy capital and consumer goods from America and because of trading weaknesses resulting from the war. In recent years they have become "harder" and some, such as the German mark, have been exceptionally strong. After many years of being "hard," the dollar became "softer" in the 1960's and 1970's. Usually soft currencies are not readily accepted in payment of international obligations and are therefore not convertible into gold or strong currencies.

The term "soft currency" is sometimes applied to paper as distinct from metallic currency. [4]

Sombart, Werner (1863–1941), German sociologist and economic historian. He was educated at Pisa and Berlin and was for some time the secretary of the Chamber of Commerce in Bremen. He became professor at the University of Breslau in 1890 and at Berlin in 1917. He was a member of the younger German "historical school" and his major works are not primarily on economics, but *Der Moderne Kapitalismus* (1902) discussed the development of capitalism based on the historical approach. [2]

Sources, Statistical (economic), the study of practical economic problems is sometimes enlightened by quantitative measurements such as the level of crude steel output, the number of people unemployed, the size of the national income. The economist is therefore interested in statistical information, the analysis and interpretation of which is sometimes helpful for applied economics. The following summary of the main sources of basic British and international statistics suggests where the reader may look for others.

Official statistics collected by government departments and published by the Stationery Office are an important source of information for almost every aspect of the economic life of the community. Nearly all these figures, along with those of previous years as a basis for comparison, are assembled in the *Annual Abstract of Statistics.* Its *Index of Sources* is particularly helpful to the lay reader: it gives the names of all the departments collecting the figures and the official publications in which the information originally appeared.

A narrower selection of more up-to-date monthly or quarterly figures appears in the *Monthly Digest of Statistics.* A useful guide to this publication is the supplement *Definitions and Explanatory Notes.* The most up-to-date and detailed statistics on the output of some main commodities are published as soon as they are available in the *Business Monitor* series. Another basic reference source is the monthly *Economic Trends,* which shows in tabular and graphic form key figures on employment, output, prices and finance, and contains reviews of current economic developments. Other "official" sources are the monthlies *Financial Statistics* and *Social Statistics.*

One of the most important figures for the economist is that of total national income, which includes all private incomes and government revenue and provides a measure of material living standards. Estimates of national income, divided into component parts, appear in the annual *National Income and Expenditure* "Blue Book," whose detailed tables, covering such important items as personal income and expenditure, capital formation and the division of national income into wages, profits, etc., give a revealing picture of the working of the whole economy. The National Institute of Economic and Social Research publishes in its *Economic Review* a quarterly survey of current developments and forecasts trends in the economy.

Readers studying foreign trade will find a fairly detailed account of all the commodities bought and sold abroad, classified by types and country of origin and destination, in the monthly *Accounts relating to the Trade and Navigation of the United Kingdom.* An even more detailed record is published in the four-volume *Annual Statement of Trade of the United Kingdom.* A broader picture of the general pattern is shown in the monthly *Report on Overseas Trade,* which also has sections dealing with the external trade of other countries.

The *Census of Production* covers all major industries, gives the size and number of firms in an industry, the value of stocks, expenditure on raw materials, labour and equipment, etc. Sample censuses are taken every year and a full census usually every three or four years. The first was taken in 1910. The *Census of Distribution* covers sales, employment, etc., in retail trades. The first was in 1951.

Most of the important international statistics can be found in the *United Nations Statistical Year Book* and the *United Nations Demographic Year Book.*

The Organization for European Co-operation and Development (OECD) publishes a bi-monthly *General Statistical Bulletin* with a survey of current economic developments in western Europe and detailed information on individual countries.

Apart from official statistics a vast amount of information is collected by private organizations. Many trade associations compile figures for the total output of their industry from information supplied by their members. These figures are not issued to the general public but are sometimes made available to outsiders with a special interest in the industry. Most trade associations are listed in *Kelly's Directory.* Many useful statistics are also collected in the course of surveys by market research organizations, independently run or attached to advertising agencies, large firms or financial institutions. Most of these surveys are confidential but some are available to the public. As there is no comprehensive central record of all these reports, each organization must be approached separately.

Research and educational organizations and institutes, such as the Acton Society, the Institute of Economic Affairs, the National Institute of Economic and Social Research and Political and Economic Planning, publish primary statistics and other information derived from original research and secondary or "processed" statistics based on it. Government departments and private trade organizations publish largely primary information.

Numerous trade, economic and financial journals also publish primary and secondary statistical information. Among the best known are *The Economist* and *The Times Review of Industry.* The latter includes figures from the *London and Cambridge Service*—a series of ninety leading statistics going back to 1914, which are particularly useful in the analysis of long-term trends. [14]

Sovereignty, Economic, the degree of authority exercised by a political unit, usually a nation state, over its economic affairs. A difficult concept, partly because although a country may have much legal authority economic circumstances may reduce the extent of its effective control. Its economic sovereignty in a legal sense is limited by, for example, ratification of GATT and International Labour Conventions, or membership of a customs union; but its effective economic sovereignty may be limited further by its market position in external relations, e.g. its foreign indebtedness or a higher elasticity of demand (i.e. a more competitive market) for its exports than for its imports. For Britain, adhesion to the Common Market entailed a loss of legal sovereignty over national affairs (and acquisition of a share in legal sovereignty over European affairs), but the British economy has not had absolute sovereignty since the development of its overseas trade. [10]

Special Area. *See* DEVELOPMENT AREA.

"Special Buyer." *See* OPEN MARKET OPERATIONS.

Special Deposits, a system devised by the British Treasury in July 1958 to reduce the liquidity of the joint-stock banks and induce them to cut down advances and reduce the level of deposits (and hence the supply of money). These deposits were paid into the Bank of England and could not be withdrawn; they were therefore completely illiquid, and to retain their liquidity ratio the banks had to reduce lending or their holdings of securities, or both. Special deposits were first ordered in June 1960 as part of general credit restriction; and all London clearing banks were required to deposit the equivalent of 1 per cent of their gross deposits. The deposit requirement may be varied. [8]

Special Drawing Rights (SDRs). *See* INTERNATIONAL LIQUIDITY.

Special United Nations Fund for Economic Development (SUNFED). *See* INFRASTRUCTURE; INTERNATIONAL INVESTMENT.

Specialization, breaking down economic activity so that each factor of production may be devoted wholly to one part. Specialization of occupation is also referred to as division of labour. It makes possible fuller use of innate abilities, the acquisition of skill by training and practice, time-saving by providing continuity of work and the transfer of mechanical operations and routine controls to machines. Specialization of capital—machinery and plant—makes possible the use of equipment of at least minimum efficient scale. Specialization of land in particular uses enables advantage to be taken of least-cost locations for production.

All kinds of specialization illustrate the working of the principle of comparative advantage. Factors specialize not on the jobs at which they are *absolutely* best but on those for which they are *relatively* most efficient. Thus, a manager may be the best typist in the country, but he will leave his typing to his secretary and specialize on the tasks of co-ordination and control at which he is relatively even more efficient than his secretary. The land of Westminster may be better for wheat-growing than East Anglia but it is specialized in uses for which it has relatively larger advantage, e.g. office sites or government buildings.

Specialization is not all gain. It implies co-operation between work-people and owners of factors of production, none of whom produce more than a tiny fraction of their individual needs; therefore resources are required for tasks of organizing the co-operation. Secondly, the dependence of everyone on everyone else can make people vulnerable if the economic pricing system does not work smoothly. If individuals lack versatility unemployment may result, when prices and wage rates are inflexible, if the demand for their specialty falls. Thirdly, it is argued that specialization stunts the development of character and reduces much work to stultifying monotony.

Specialization has engaged the attention of economists from the beginning of their science, partly because it has been the essential source of the increase in the variety and quantity of goods produced, and partly because specialization necessitates exchange of products between specialists, and exchange has been one of the main subjects of study.

The degree of specialization depends upon the extent of the market; the inhabitants of the Isle of Man could not provide sufficient outlets for even one small works making washing-machines, but the population of Britain provides the opportunity for a number of works to specialize on different types of machine and components for them. Specialization can therefore be more intensive the larger the population, the closer they live together, the better the means of communication, the fewer the restraints on trade and the higher incomes are per head. Some economists see the process of economic growth as increase of specialization leading to higher output, increase of specialists' incomes, increased spending providing opportunities for further specialization and so on. [5]

Specie Point. *See* GOLD STANDARD.

Specific Tax. *See* AD VALOREM.

Speculation, buying at a low price in the hope of selling later at a higher one. Speculation is popularly associated with easy profits made by wealthy men, distinguishable from gamblers by their operation in commodities and securities instead of at the casino tables. In practice intelligent speculation, unlike gambling, can benefit the community as well as the speculator. Speculators may buy wheat cheaply at harvest time when it is abundant, hoping to make a profit by selling it in the spring when they expect prices to be higher. If they are correct the community will also benefit because stocks are carried over from a period of abundance to one of relative scarcity, evening out the supply coming on to the market and helping to stabilize prices. Their August buying swells demand and checks the fall of prices; the spring selling keeps prices lower than they would otherwise be.

Speculators are seldom concerned with production; they confine themselves to buying and selling. In the markets for metals, timber and other commodities they relieve producers of much of the risk of price fluctuations. The specialist risk-taker, who is skilled at interpreting price movements and statistical information, is better placed than the typical producer to forecast prices and avoid severe losses.

Badly judged speculation may magnify price fluctuations to the detriment of the economy but also ruin the speculators. Well-informed speculation on the Stock Exchange, based on underlying market conditions, helps to stabilize the pattern of share values, reflecting fairly accurately the community's demand for different types of physical capital, which encourages the growth of new enterprise where it is most needed. But irrational waves of wild optimism or pessimism tend to cause severe fluctuations in share prices which obscure the probable growth prospects of particular industries and make well-considered investment difficult.

Since the 1930's the growth of government price stabilization schemes for many commodities has reduced the activities of speculators. The function of speculation or the risk of judging future prices has not been eliminated, but transferred from private individuals to the government. This development emphasizes the essential difference between speculation and gambling; the speculator undertakes risks which arise naturally from the inevitable uncertainty in a constantly changing economy; the gambler bears risks created artificially by the game itself. [7]

Speculative Motive. *See* QUANTITY THEORY OF MONEY.

Speculator. *See* ARBITRAGE; SPECULATION.

Spot. *See* ARBITRAGE.

Sraffa, Piero (1898–1983), Italian economist. He was educated at the University of Turin and was a Fellow of Trinity College, Cambridge from 1939, and Emeritus Reader in Economics. Most students of economics associate Sraffa with the article "The Law of Returns Under Competitive Conditions" (*Economic Journal,* 1926), which laid the foundation for the English version of the theory of imperfect competition, and with the definitive edition of the works of Ricardo upon which he was engaged for many years, *The Works and Correspondence of David Ricardo* (1951–5). In *Production of Commodities by Means of Commodities: Prelude to a Critique of Economic Theory* (1960), he attempted a rehabilitation of classical (pre-marginal) economics; he hoped it might serve as the foundation for a critique of marginal analysis. Although he wrote much less than other members of the neo-Keynesian, or more accurately neo-Ricardian, School at Cambridge, he has been described as its most original thinker, and the one who inspired the work of most of the others. [2]

Stabilization, Economic, the use of monetary, fiscal and other techniques to avoid deflation or marked inflation in the industrial nations of the western world. Since the end of the Second World War most of the governments of the western democracies have undertaken to maintain high and stable average levels of employment, and many to stabilize the value of their domestic currencies.

Income and employment in the industrial countries tend to fluctuate. A slight disturbance to the level of income or demand tends to become cumulative and so generates either a large fall in demand for the output of commodities and services and for the labour normally employed in producing them, or a sharp increase in demand which at full employment cannot be matched by an increase in output and therefore bids up prices and wages, causing inflation. The main influence in these processes in either direction is business men's views on the prospects for making profitable investments in machinery, buildings and stocks of goods and raw materials. If the initial change in income is downward they are apt to take a pessimistic view and reduce their purchase of investment goods. Demand for the outputs of the industries which produce machines and construct buildings declines. These industries lay off labour, reduce their demands for raw materials and cut back their purchases of machines. The workers who are now unemployed reduce their purchases and may default on hire-purchase payments, which in turn reduces the incomes of shopkeepers and finance companies. The interactions between falling incomes, investment and employment produce a vicious downward spiral which may generate heavy unemployment unless checked by government action.

If from a position of full employment an initial upward push is given to money incomes, prices start to rise. In anticipation of further price increases, people buy early and increase their stocks so that inflation becomes cumulative unless checked.

Although satisfactory practical solutions to these problems have not yet been found, governments have developed several lines of defence and have acquired a fairly high degree of control. The first line of defence is the so-called "built-in stabilizers." Progressive income tax, unemployment benefit and national assistance form the main ones in Britain. When incomes and employment begin to fall, the government's revenue from taxes is reduced and its expenditure on social security payments rises. Incomes therefore fall much less than in the absence of the stabilizers. Secondly, if more is required to push income back to the full employment level, the government can use a battery of monetary and fiscal weapons. Interest rates can be lowered and credit eased to encourage firms and individuals to borrow and increase their spending on both consumption and investment. Taxes can be lowered to give people more money to spend or to cheapen goods and encourage spending. The government itself can increase its spending either directly or through the nationalized industries. These measures can be put into effect in the opposite direction to check inflation, though raising taxes could be inflationary if it reduces "take-home" pay and stimulates wage demands that government enables employers to accept by expanding the money supply through fear of unemployment.

The problem of economic instability is at least as serious for the under-developed countries of the world as for the industrial nations. For them the main cause of instability is not fluctuations in domestic investment but changes in their earnings from exports. Most of them specialize in a narrow range of primary products such as cocoa, coffee, groundnuts, copper, rubber, oil. Their earnings from the export of such products form a large part of their national incomes, and fluctuations in their export earnings therefore cause marked swings in their national income. It is difficult to damp them by the fiscal and monetary techniques used in more advanced economies that are less dependent on foreign trade. Even if they could keep up incomes by expansionary techniques at home when export earnings fall, so much of the supported incomes would be spent on imports that the foreign exchange reserves would soon be depleted by the resulting deficit in the balance of payments. Economic stabilization in these countries is thus thought to require more direct action to reduce the fluctuations in export incomes, e.g. national or international buffer funds and stocks. More fundamental policies, such as insurance, saving and other methods, have been urged by some economists on the ground that fluctuations in the prices of primary products are unavoidable, and may be desirable to indicate changes in international supply and demand. [9]

Stag, a speculator who hopes to make a profit by securing an allocation of new shares and selling them immediately at a premium. The operation succeeds only if shares are being offered for sale by a company with good prospects so that the demand for its shares exceeds the amount of the new issue and the opening price on the Stock Exchange exceeds the issue price. The difference between the two, less expenses and taxes, is the stag's profit. Unlike the investor, the stag buys only with the intention of selling. Since only a fraction of the issue price has to be paid on allocation (the remainder at a later date), the stag aims to finance the purchase of the shares by the proceeds from their sale. In this way a sizeable turnover in shares can be handled on a small bank balance. The stag takes the risk of a general slump in share prices or a loss of confidence in the company. The new shares may then open at a discount and if the stag sells he may make a large loss or is forced to keep shares he had no intention of buying. [8]

Stagflation, a simultaneous rise in prices (due to a fall in the value of money) and in unemployment (denoting stagnation). For long after (and before) the Second World War it was thought that inflation and stagnation/unemployment were mutually exclusive, i.e. that inflation would absorb all unemployed resources and increase output, at least until all the unemployed were re-absorbed. In the early 1970's unprecedented expansion in the quantity of money and inflation did not seem to remove unemployment, which in official figures in 1972 rose to around a million, or some four per cent of the labour force. It was argued that the official statistics substantially over-stated the number looking for and ready to accept work at prevailing prices for labour. Even so, the true figure of unemployed was probably higher than it would have been if labour had been able to respond to rising monetary demand. Unemployment varied widely by region, with continuing and sometimes severe shortages in some areas and some occupations (building, engineering, printing, public services, etc.). It seemed that inflation was unable to absorb the unemployed because labour did not move to areas where demand was high. [10]

Stagnation, the situation in a sluggish economy, with minimal growth, unresponsive to opportunity to develop. In the 1960's and 1970's some economists described Britain as a stagnant society in contrast with Europe, which had a faster growth rate in income per head and living standards. The reasons were variously said to be complacency, nepotism, a preference for leisure, restrictive practices, excessive taxes on income, government discouragement of industry, moral opposition to profit and high monetary rewards in general, and concern to preserve the environment. [10]

Stamp, Josiah Charles, first Baron Stamp (1880–1941), English statistician, economist and administrator. His formal education ended at the age of fourteen when he entered the Civil Service. Apart from a short period in the Board of Trade he spent the next twenty-three years in the Inland Revenue Department. He prepared at home for an external degree in economics from the University of London, and did so well that he was encouraged to write a thesis, later published as *British Incomes and Property.* In 1919 he left the Civil Service and went into industry, but maintained his public work, achieving an international reputation for his work on German reparations. His writings, which include *Principles of Taxation in the Light of Modern Developments* (1921) and *Wealth and Taxable Capacity* (1922), show an unrivalled knowledge of taxation and its problems. [2]

Stamp Duty, a tax levied by affixing or imprinting stamps to documents, mainly those dealing with financial transactions. If unstamped, these documents are invalid. Great Britain abolished a flat-rate stamp tax on receipts and bank cheques in 1971 but maintains a stamp tax on documents, etc. [12]

Standard Money (coinage). *See* Coin.

Standard of Living, has various meanings ranging from simple assessment of housing and other basic living conditions to sophisticated ideas about the style of living regarded as appropriate to a particular occupation or social background. In economics it usually refers to the amount of goods and services normally consumed by a person with a given income.

Because of the difficulties of an item-by-item comparison of changes in living standards, money income is often used as a rough measuring rod. As incomes rise people can afford to buy more; income changes therefore normally indicate movements in living standards. To obtain a more accurate picture allowance must be made for variations in the prices of goods and services. A sharp increase in prices may entirely eliminate the benefit from a rise in wages. The adjustment is made by means of a price index which indicates the real value of a wage or salary—the goods and services it will buy. For practical purposes a permanent change in real income can be regarded as a measure of the change in living standards. But it is difficult to measure changes in living standards over long periods because the quality and type of goods consumed may alter considerably; e.g. an automatic cooker cannot easily be compared with an old-fashioned kitchen range or a television set with a pianola. Moreover, personal consumption by itself gives an incomplete measure of living standards, which must take account of less measurable but important factors such as welfare services, educational facilities, the conditions of work, opportunities for recreation and so on. [11]

Standards, where laid down by law, constitute one of the three main methods of state intervention in the economy, imposed in the hope of improving its performance or overcoming its inadequacies. (The other two methods are direct provision of services and financing of low incomes.) It can thus aim to ensure that if competition is weak the consumer is not exploited; that what is produced satisfies generally accepted opinion on minimum requirements; and that individuals provide themselves (even against their wills) with services generally considered desirable. Hence minimum school-leaving ages, compulsory motor insurance, seat-belts and safe lighting in cars, etc.

The economic difficulty is that ensuring standards in what is produced may influence the amount produced. Safety and health regulations raise the costs of producing goods or services. If the costs can be passed on in higher prices, the demand may fall. If not, the supply may be reduced because revenue does not cover costs. There may be a "trade-off" between high standards and cheapness. Parker-Morris standards for houses (named after a government committee headed by a chairman of that name) are desirable in a technical sense but may prevent some people from acquiring a house. The choice may be between lower standards and more houses. In economic analysis there can therefore be such things as standards that are too high. [10]

State, Welfare. *See* Welfare State.

Static Analysis, the branch of economic method which studies the relationship between the factors determining an equilibrium position (the "conditions" of equilibrium) without reference to the process of adjustment by which it was reached. "Comparative statics," as the term implies, compares various positions of equilibrium achieved by attaching different values to the determinants without regard to the process by which change is effected. It can be contrasted with dynamic analysis, which studies the process of "time-path" of adjustment between one equilibrium position and the next. If, starting from an original "no change" position of rest or equilibrium at a price which balances supply of and demand for a commodity, consumers' tastes change so that at each possible price more of it is demanded than before, forces will be set in motion which will eventually result in a new equilibrium position in which a larger quantity will be bought and sold at (possibly) a different price. Comparative static analysis compares the new with the old equilibrium: dynamic analysis examines *how* price and quantity get from the old to the new position. Static analysis thus rests upon the device of assuming important determinants to be fixed so that the influence of other (variable) determinants on the equilibrium position can be isolated and studied. Despite their simplicity, such methods can be fruitful. [14]

Stationary State, one in which income per head remains unchanged because individuals have no incentive to undertake activities that promote the economic growth that would increase it. In the early phases of modern economics, some classical economists such as Ricardo thought that capitalism might move into a stationary or mature state if technical advance did not offset diminishing returns. In the next phase of economic thought, at the turn of the century, economists refined their analysis of the conditions of stationary equilibrium; the work of Walras and others represented a substantial advance over earlier discussions and was enlightening in, for example, analysing the distribution of a given income. But economists since Adam Smith have always been concerned with economic development—*increasing* income per head (now referred to as economic growth)—and attention for fifty years has increasingly turned to the economics of growing or dynamic states. Hence the discussion and debate about steady state growth and the notions of equilibrium at a point in time (static) or over a period of time (dynamic). [11]

Statistics, Relation to Economics. *See* Economics.

Statistics, Vital. *See* Vital Statistics.

Steady State, describes an economy in which the rates of growth in the main elements—consumption, investment, national income, etc.—remain unchanged, although not necessarily the same as one another. The concept has been developed by the Cambridge School and has become the assumption in analysis of growth models.

The theory of economic growth is not new. It originated in economists' dissatisfaction with the confinement of economic theory to the Walrasian stationary equilibrium or statics. In 1911 or 1912 Cassel seems to have conceived the notion of a "uniformly progressive economy" in which labour, capital, output and incomes grow at a uniform annual rate, i.e. in which *relative* magnitudes remain constant. Output of all goods increases at the same rate and all prices therefore remain constant. This notion seemed to have been rediscovered by Harrod in the 1930's. The Cambridge (England) School and the neo-classical school (Cambridge, USA) refer to the "stylized facts" of the steady state growth model, i.e. their artificiality or theoretical abstraction, although Solow of the neo-classical school has argued that "divergences from steady-state growth . . . in the advanced capitalist economies . . . appear to be fairly small, casual and hardly self-accentuating."

The concept of steady state growth has been criticized by L. M. Lachmann as fictitious, inadequate as a concept of the theory of growth, and irrelevant in understanding the movement of a growing market economy. He has argued that, unlike Keynes, the analyses of steady state growth stemming from Cambridge (England and USA) virtually ignore expectations and therefore the possibility that intentions may not be realized. Joan Robinson assumed (*The Accumulation of Capital,* 1956) that if there is change expectations are immediately adjusted to it and no further change is to be expected. Later (*Economic Heresies,* 1971) she allowed for expectations, though in the mass, not on the part of individuals, whose expectations could *differ.* The English neo-classicist John Hicks held there could be no tendency to equilibrium over a period. Lachmann went further and argued that *divergent* expectations undermined the concept of steady state growth itself, because in a world of uncertainty only some men can be right while others will be wrong. Since universal realization of expectations is impossible, some investment will fail, and growth equilibrium is also impossible. [14]

Sterling Area, term first officially used in 1940 to describe the free association of countries based on the use of sterling as an international financial medium. In the 1960's it comprised all Commonwealth countries (except Canada), Burma, Iceland, Eire, Jordan, Kuwait, Libya, South Africa, South West Africa and Western Samoa. The members embrace a quarter of the world's population and account for about a fifth of world trade.

The commercial and financial supremacy of Great Britain made sterling the key currency in world trade before 1914. Countries trading mainly with Great Britain found it convenient and helpful to link their currencies with sterling and keep their reserves of foreign exchange in the form of sterling balances in London, the dominant financial centre. The importance of these links with sterling became apparent in the financial crisis of 1931 when Great Britain left the gold standard. Rather than link their currencies to gold or to the dollar, or follow independent policies, the sterling satellites followed suit and by and large depreciated their currencies in step with sterling, thus forming a recognizable sterling bloc. Although Commonwealth countries formed the core, many other countries joined the bloc during the economic upheavals of the 1930's.

Up to 1939 sterling was freely convertible into other currencies. Exchange control, introduced at the outbreak of war, preserved the free circulation of sterling within the sterling area but limited its convertibility into other currencies.

The sterling area was defined by statute in 1947 as embracing countries pursuing a more or less common policy of exchange and import control designed to conserve supplies of scarce foreign currencies. The UK managed the gold and dollar reserves of the whole sterling area: members who were on balance earners of foreign exchange banked their surplus in the London common pool, and net spenders drew on the pool.

These arrangements continue, but in a looser form more akin to the pre-war pattern when sterling was freely convertible. Relaxation of import and exchange controls in recent years has restored to sterling area members complete freedom of action in the use of sterling balances to finance current transactions with other countries. But the periodic weaknesses of sterling have necessitated rescue operations by international organizations and assistance by individual countries. The chief justification for the continuation of the sterling area remains that it facilitates world trade and payments. Some economists doubt its value to Great Britain because with inadequate gold and dollar reserves she has to bear the strain of excessive demands of other members for foreign currencies. Others think it desirable or essential as Britain's standard of living depends on her exchanging a fifth of her product with the world and she remains an important international financial centre. [4]

Sterling Balances, the UK's short-term or liquid sterling liabilities—bank balances, Treasury bills and short bonds—to countries, persons and institutions overseas. In 1938 they amounted to £760 million, roughly equal to the UK's liquid assets of gold and dollars. They were increased by British wartime credit spending abroad to £3,700 million (1945). Despite some reduction since in the overseas holdings of certain countries, those of sterling area countries have increased: these, plus the growth of new liabilities to non-territorial institutions such as the International Monetary Fund, the United Nations and the International Bank, maintained the total at high figures in the 1960's and 1970's.

About three-quarters of the territorial liabilities represent the sterling assets of colonial governments, currency boards, banks and marketing boards, plus the external reserves of central banks and the working balances of commercial banks in the Commonwealth and other sterling area countries. Some of the latter balances such as those of India, Pakistan and Sri Lanka, were much inflated by British wartime spending, and in the post-war period were "blocked" by agreement to forestall pressure on sterling from large-scale withdrawal. Later agreed "releases" and the growing need of these countries for larger permanent reserves of sterling as world trade and prices rose substantially reduced this danger. (The need for capital for the internal development of the emergent ex-colonies has also led to heavy rates of withdrawal.) Similarly the remaining quarter of balances held by non-sterling area countries now mainly represents working balances for financing trade and for other purposes. Since 1958 the sterling balances have been virtually free of restraints on their convertibility into other currencies for financing current transactions and mainly reflect the convenience of holding a currency in which half the world's trade is conducted. Although still large relative to the country's liquid assets of gold and dollars, the total of sterling balances is likely to remain manageable unless economic instability in the UK were to provoke a "flight from sterling." [4]

Steuart, Sir James (1712–80), Scottish economist. He studied law at the University of Edinburgh and after some years' practice took up the cause of the Young Pretender. He lived in exile for eighteen years after the battle of Culloden Moor and during his enforced leisure studied political economy. His major work, the first in the English language to bear the title *Principles of Political Economy* (1767), was an early attempt to systematize knowledge on the subject. It was overshadowed by Adam Smith's *Wealth of Nations* published less than a decade later. His importance lies mainly in his discussions of finance and in his theory of population, which anticipated that of Malthus. [2]

Stigler, George Joseph (1911–91), American economist. He was educated at the Universities of Washington and Chicago, and has been Charles R. Walgreen Distinguished Professor of American Institutions at the University of Chicago since 1958. He is an eminent analyst of economic theory, particularly in resource allocation and pricing (*Production and Distribution Theories*, 1940). His work on *The Theory of Price* (1946) is an outstanding contribution. He has clarified and developed monopoly theory, notably in his critique of the theory of monopolistic competition as presented by Joan Robinson and Edward Chamberlin in the 1930's ("Monopolistic Competition in Retrospect" in *Five Lectures on Economic Problems*, 1949). Probably his most important contribution is in testing the validity of theories and commonly held assumptions by statistical or other empirical studies: "the sole test of the usefulness of an economic theory is the concordance between its predictions and the observable course of events." In his essay, "Competition in the United States" (in the *Five Lectures on Economic Problems*) he examined the view that competition had been declining steadily for fifty years. This statistical analysis of changes in the relative importance of industries classified by a measure of degree of competition showed the contrary: the share of competitive activities had been increasing. In *Capital and Rates of Return in Manufacturing Industries* (1963) he tested the theory that highly concentrated (and therefore presumably monopolistic) industries have higher profits than more competitive industries: he found no significant relationship between the degree of concentration in an industry and the rate of return on capital.

Stigler's most outstanding work is probably his study of the production and distribution theories of Jevons, Wicksteed, Marshall, Edgeworth, Menger, Wieser, Böhm-Bawerk, Walras, Wicksell and J. B. Clark. Few historians of economic theory have cast their net so wide, or been so meticulous in their comparative analysis. This is probably the best survey of the leaders of economic thought during this period. Stigler has also done valuable work on the early American pioneers of marginal analysis. His command of geometrical technique is considerable, and he has employed it to contribute to the study of production under conditions where the trend of average costs is not a continuous series. [2]

"Stochastic" Models. *See* MODELS, ECONOMIC.

Stock, (*a*) in a specialized financial sense, a type of security or method of holding capital. Unlike shares, which cannot be transferred in fractions, stock may be transferred in any moment, subject sometimes to limits. A company may convert fully-paid shares into stock; but stocks are issued mostly by public or semi-public utilities: local authority stocks are an important example. Stocks are always "registered" (so that their sale has to be made by deed of transfer) or "inscribed" (they can then be transferred only by the personal attendance of the owner or his appointed representative at the office where the list of stockholders is recorded). Stock transfers require much less work from the issuing body than share transfers: for this reason (all other things equal) stock is a more convenient form of security.

(*b*) in its general everyday sense of an accumulation of a commodity, stock is important in several economic theories on the rate of interest. The notion of a stock is often important in economic theory. Where stocks are large in relation to current flows of supply on to and off the market the latter may have little effect on price. For example, the price of houses is largely determined by the demand for the existing stock, not by the cost of erecting new ones. [8]

Stock and Flow Analysis, The Relation Between, for most goods and services, supply and demand analysis is concerned almost wholly with the mechanisms by which a balance is achieved between *flows* (i.e. quantities per period of time) coming on to the market from suppliers and being taken off the market by consumers. If the existence of *stocks* is recognized at all, their significance is assumed (usually implicitly rather than explicitly) to be negligible. Given the demand of consumers for additional supplies, attention is thus focused on cost of production of additional units of supply as the key factor determining price—the flow-balancing mechanism. Analogously, if a reservoir were tiny compared with the daily water flow into and out of it, water management would be concerned almost wholly with balancing inflow and outflow rates. For most goods and services, this approach is realistic and analytically meaningful. For some, however, it is unrealistic, analytically unhelpful and can mislead policy. Such goods are typically long-lived and the stock of them in existence at any time (accumulated over many years) is very large in relation to any flow of additional supplies in the form of new production. The price of such goods tends to be determined wholly by the intensity of demand for the existing stock: cost of production of new additions to supply plays no proximate part in price determination. An important example is housing, new supplies of which in any one year amount at most to only a few per cent of the total stock in existence at any time. The standing stock of housing dominates the market and the price of housing at any time is determined by demand conditions. Builders' costs do not determine house prices; they determine only the quantity of new building that builders will find profitable to erect at the going level of house prices (or the level which they expect to realize on completion)—which is demand-determined. Similarly, increases in the cost of building land cannot be said in any way to be the cause of higher house prices, for the price of building land depends on builders' (and others') bids; and these in turn will depend on construction costs (including builders' profits) in relation to what builders and others think buildings will realize when completed. This realization price will be governed by expectations about the extent of demand for the standing stock. The causal chain thus runs from housing demand to cost of new production and thence to the price of building land, not the other way round. Housing and land policies that fail to recognize these important analytical distinctions are often misconceived.

The price of income-bearing securities is similarly determined by the extent of demand for the existing stock at any time—which in turn depends upon the public's preference for holding wealth in the form of either income-bearing assets or in (non-income-yielding) cash. This is the essential difference between Keynes's theory of interest (a "stock" theory) and earlier theories of the rate of interest, which tended to regard the rate of interest as the price which equated (flows of) Saving and Investment. [7]

Stock Exchange, a market in which members trade in securities, both on their own account and on behalf of others. A stock exchange makes investments liquid and therefore reduces the price of (long-term) capital. Keynes was critical of stock exchange speculation for being based not on expected prices but on other people's speculations: by increasing the risks of investment, speculation could raise the price of capital.

In Britain the London Stock Exchange, in Throgmorton Street, is the main security market; there are also some twenty provincial exchanges, mainly in the large industrial cities.

Although the history of stockbroking in Britain goes back to the seventeenth century and the formation of a large number of joint-stock companies engaged in foreign trade (such as the Hudson's Bay Company), most of the trading in stocks was carried out in coffee-houses in the City. The profession of stock-broking was first organized and acquired premises, called the Stock Exchange, in 1773; the present site was occupied in 1802.

Management of the Stock Exchange is in the hands of its Council, consisting of twenty-six members, which controls the election and conduct of members, rules, rates of commission and so on.

There are about 3,500 members, belonging to about 500 firms, of which about two-thirds are brokers and the rest jobbers. Brokers act as agents for investors and buy from and sell to the jobbers. Every transaction in securities is known as a bargain, which, though noted in the books of both broker and jobber, is conducted and completed by word of mouth without written confirmation. (Hence the Stock Exchange motto "My word is my bond.") A broker who concludes a bargain may have the price "marked" or recorded in the official list for the day, but is not under obligation to do so: the marking system is the only record of turnover. Economists have criticized the conduct of stock-broking for restrictive practices which produce very high earnings.

Securities are not transferred on the floor of the exchange where the business is transacted; the staff of brokers and jobbers attend to the transfer.

Dealings in gilt-edged securities are for cash, all other deals are settled on the fortnightly Account days fixed by the Council. There are twenty-four Accounts in a year (of which four run for three weeks). The advantage of the Account is that it provides time for changes in the value of securities before payment is required.

Prices are quoted on the Stock Exchange only in recognized fractions of £1 (½, ¼, ⅛, 1/16, 1/32 and 1/64). [8]

Stock Exchange "Bargain." *See* JOBBER.

Stock-jobber. *See* DEALER.

Stock-turn. *See* TURNOVER.

Stockpiling, the process by which some part of current production is not consumed or put into use but is added to stocks. The term is most frequently applied to primary products, mainly raw materials, stocks of which may be built up to meet an emergency or may accumulate as a result of a decline in demand to which current output cannot adjust quickly enough. It is more usual for the term to be applied in a situation in which stocks are built up intentionally because, for example, of an outbreak or threat of war. In such circumstances stockpiling can take place as a result both of an increase in production in excess of current requirements and of a diversion of raw materials from non-war use or exports.

Abnormal stockpiling of raw materials is an addition to normal demand: one likely result is thus to increase, sometimes considerably, the market price of the commodities stockpiled. Frequently after an emergency considerable stockpiles become available for normal commercial use; such a sudden and substantial increase in supply depresses prices and can lead to drastic reductions in current production. Even if surpluses are not released immediately their likelihood influences "forward" transactions (for delivery at a future date), and thus current prices. [10]

Stocks (of commodities). *See* INVESTMENT.

Stocks, Buffer. *See* BUFFER STOCKS.

Stop-go, the oscillations in British Government policy in the 1960's between restrictions and relaxations in the effort to avoid overheating and stagnation. Owing to the difficulty of assessing the state of the economy (not least because statistics are imperfect, over-simplified and necessarily outdated) stop-go in practice sometimes seemed to make the oscillations more rather than less marked by overshooting the target ("over-kill" in the vernacular). The fixed exchange rate between sterling and other countries was also blamed for hampering government in its efforts because it limited the freedom of manoeuvre of the British government in offsetting the fluctuation.

The "stop" phase of stop-go required suppression of expansion, and the clumsiness of national measures could constrict expansion even where desirable in order to reduce costs or for long-term improvement. In the early 1970's the view developed that stop-go should be replaced by concentrating on growth, which was achieved for a short time by expanding the money supply but was soon followed by inflation, less growth and finally no growth.

Some economists have argued that the attempt at close and frequent regulation of the economy ("fine-tuning," "the finger on the tiller") is too ambitious, not least because the economic indicators are not sufficiently refined or precise, and over-reaction is unavoidable. Gradual and more general control by expanding the money supply to keep pace with the underlying rate of growth, likely in the modern world to be about 3 to 4 per cent, may therefore, some economists argue, stimulate growth without being accompanied by disturbing oscillations of inflation and deflation. [10]

Streeten, Paul Patrick (1917–), Austrian-born British economist. He was educated at the Universities of Vienna, Aberdeen and Oxford (Balliol College) where he has been a Fellow since 1968. He was Professor of Economics and Deputy Director of the Institute of Development Studies at the University of

Sussex from 1966 to 1968, since when he has been Warden of Queen Elizabeth House and Director of the Institute of Commonwealth Studies at the University of Oxford.

Probably his main contribution to the economics of development consists of questions to his fellow economists, arising out of his wide experience of development planning throughout the Commonwealth, particularly in India: how far economic concepts which have grown out of the experience of developed countries can be applied to the life of communities with a different social structure, history and scales of value; whether the same terms can be used without risk of misinterpretation—unemployment, for example; whether technologies can be transplanted, or new ones must be invented.

His main publications are (ed.) *Value in Social Theory* (1958); *Economic Integration* (1961); *The Teaching of Development Economics* (1967); (ed. with M. Lipton) *Crisis in Indian Planning* (1968); *Frontiers of Development Studies* (1972); (ed.) *Trade Strategies for Development* (1973). [2]

Strike, temporary withholding of labour in the hope of raising its price, by improving payment and conditions. In recent times withholding labour has been supplemented by "sit-down" or "stay-in" strikes to expedite settlement. The power of employees organized in unions is economic and legal. Economic power varies in different industries. It is strongest where the capital is specific (cannot be used for any other purpose) or the product is perishable (so that orders cannot be accumulated and met after the strike); in these conditions, as in newspaper production, the employer's bargaining position is weak. Legal power depends on the law on closed shops, picketing, etc. The economic case for legal privileges for trade unions in the famous Acts of 1871 to 1906 was that labour's bargaining power was weaker than the employers'. [5]

Strike-threat System. *See* HUTT, W. H.

Structure, the main framework of an economy, determined by consumer preferences and attitudes, population growth, technical change, government policies. Changes in these structural elements cause growth, structural unemployment or other fundamental, long-term changes. The task in empirical economic studies is to identify the structural causes of consequential symptoms like unemployment and to analyse them separately from medium-term and short-term (i.e. temporary) causes. Thus in diagnosing unemployment and policies to deal with it, the causes have to be identified because the solutions will differ. Structural long-term unemployment cannot be met by short-term palliatives like subsidies to prop up declining industries, except at the ultimate cost of seizures affecting the economy as a whole. [10]

Sublease. *See* LEASEHOLD.

Subsidies, government grants of money to industries to raise incomes in it or lower the prices of its products (as in British agriculture), or encourage exports, or enable local authorities to let Council houses at rents below the free market level, etc. Subsidies to British agriculture have equaled or exceeded the contribution of agriculture to the national income. Subsidies are usually given for "social," military, political or other non-economic reasons. In the mid-1970's it was argued (by Professor A. R. Prest) that the official statistics under-stated the extent of subsidies. [10]

Subsistence Wages, Theory of, originated in the late eighteenth century, was reinforced by Malthus's theory of population, and was expounded thus by Ricardo: population expansion outruns food production and wages settle down at the amount required for subsistence, because if wages tend to rise population will grow faster than supplies and wages will fall back to subsistence. The evidence of a continued though intermittent rise in real wages, especially after about 1840, discredited the theory. It is appraised by the British economist Henry Smith in the *Economic Journal* (1965). [5]

Substitution, one of the processes by which apparently insatiable and changing tastes are satisfied as well as possible given the scarcity of factors of production and of goods and services. All economic activity may be regarded as substitution: production involves the substitution of factors of production for one another to secure their most efficient combination; consumption involves the substitution of goods for money income and substitution between goods to maximize satisfaction.

The degree to which one factor (or commodity) can be substituted for another without loss of output (or satisfaction) measures the extent to which the two are perfect substitutes. The market price of perfect substitutes will tend to be equal, given perfect competition and factor mobility; if factors of production are imperfect substitutes for one another their prices will be different. A consumer distributes his expenditure between competing uses so that the ratios of prices to the satisfaction derived from the last unit of each good purchased are equal, that is, until the marginal rate of substitution between any pair of goods is equal to the ratio of their prices. This position is achieved when the quantities bought of all goods for the last small amount of money spent on each yield equal satisfaction. Similarly an *entrepreneur* will substitute the factors of production for one another until the ratios of their marginal products to their prices are equal, that is, until the marginal rate of technical substitution between any two factors is equal to the ratio of their prices. When this position is reached at any given level of outlay on factors of production no further economy can be secured by additional substitution between them. [7]

Substitution Effect, another name for price effect, seen in the change in demand when a price has risen or fallen. [7]

Substitution, Elasticity of. *See* ELASTICITY OF SUBSTITUTION.

Succession Duty, a tax on property, principally freehold and leasehold, passing at death. It was imposed in 1853 so that all inherited property not liable to legacy duty became liable to succession duty. The rates of duty were similar to those of legacy duty. The succession duty was abolished in 1949. [12]

Sumptuary Tax, a medieval levy designed to discourage the consumption of luxuries, then considered harmful. The nearest modern equivalents are taxes on wine and spirits (beer not being classified as a luxury) and tobacco (although here similar definitional doubts arise about the meaning of luxury). Modern taxes on luxuries tend to be justified by the argument that they are mostly bought by people who can pay higher taxes. [12]

Sunk Costs, outlays on permanent or durable equipment which by definition cannot be avoided. If the equipment is specialized and can be used for only one purpose (such as a blast-furnace), then whether current revenue is high enough to cover amortization of the original cost does not matter in deciding whether to use it or not since nothing is saved by not using it. [7]

Superannuation. *See* PENSIONS.

Supermarket. *See* MARKETING.

Supplementary Costs, those to which a firm has been committed by past decisions and which cannot be avoided by varying current output. Broadly they refer to the overhead costs incurred by a firm producing nothing but remaining in business, e.g., local rates, loan charges and cost outlays on fixed equipment that has been "sunk" into the firm and that are being "written off" or amortized over a period of time. Supplementary costs may be contrasted with the *prime costs* of production, viz.: those which vary with output and which can be avoided by reducing output, e.g., electric power, raw materials, labour.

The economic significance of the distinction between supplementary (unavoidable) and prime (avoidable) costs is that although all costs must be covered in the long run by the revenue received for its output if a firm is to stay in production, there may be shorter or longer periods (depending on the character of the supplementary costs in each case) during which a firm will continue to produce as long as prime costs are covered by revenue from sales and a contribution, however small, is made to supplementary costs. Since even if it reduced output to zero there is no way in which it can "avoid" supplementary costs it may as well produce as not so long as prime costs are covered. In some lines of production, e.g. small-scale farming, most costs are unavoidable during a season; therefore prices paid to producers might fall severely without much reducing the supplies they are willing to put on the market. [7]

Supply, the quantity of a commodity or service coming on the market at a price in a given period of time. The price and time qualifications are necessary because normally the higher the price offered the larger will be the quantity supplied, and the longer the period of time the more suppliers are able to adjust production to take advantage of changes in price.

Economic analysis distinguishes three periods. In the very short run supply refers to the stock of a commodity at that time, which will be fixed. This period, in which supply cannot be increased by new production, may be long in terms of clock-time; for example, the stock of houses can be increased in quantity only slowly. Fixity of stocks does not, however, mean that supplies coming forward on the market will be the same regardless of price, since the holders of stock will vary in attitude: some will not sell at any price, some will be eager to sell at relatively low prices, some only at relatively high prices. The supply coming on to the market will therefore normally increase with rising prices and decrease with falling prices (unless current prices are expected to go on rising or falling, in which case rising prices may *decrease* supply for a time).

Secondly, in the production short-run period supply refers to the flow of goods coming on to the market per period of time from the plant and equipment in existence. Again this period may be short or long in terms of clock-time; a tinker's equipment can be more readily varied in quantity than an oil refinery. The supply of a commodity in the production short-run period will depend on its price and its cost of production. With fixed amounts of equipment, cost per unit of output is likely eventually to rise as output expands because of scarcity and rising prices of labour or raw materials or because of diminishing returns, or both; higher prices may therefore again be necessary to call forth larger supplies. But where supply comes from very large units, it may be highly responsive to increases in demand even without an increase in price: relatively large increases in supply can therefore be sustained before cost per unit begins to rise. In every case the responsiveness of supply to changes in price will depend on the way in which costs change as output expands. In this context cost means that which could be avoided by not producing (or producing less). Thus supplies may not fall much as price falls so long as producers' current costs are covered: costs sunk into fixed equipment cannot be avoided by varying output, so the fixed equipment might as well continue to be used so long as prices cover current running costs.

Thirdly, in the production long run, both equipment and the number and character of the firms can change. Methods of production can be varied, production processes integrated or split into specialist parts. The supply of a commodity will then depend upon the rates of return to be obtained from the investment of new capital in that line of production compared with others. But the relationship is no longer simply between price and cost, for the character of the productive processes themselves, and therefore the nature of the commodities they produce, will change if the period is long enough. For example, motor cars in the 1980's cannot be regarded as the same commodity as the motor car of the 1920's. In the long run both the cost of production per unit and the price may fall although supply is increasing.

At any given point of time, supply and price in the real world will be related in a way which reflects the working of both short- and long-run influences. Some producers will be young and aggressive expansionists, some established and staid, some weak and able to maintain only a precarious foothold in the industry. Again, the industry may be in transition from many to a few large firms or from a more to a less competitive organization. The supply coming on to the market will reflect all these influences and tendencies. [7]

Suppressed Inflation. *See* OVERLOADED ECONOMY.

Surplus, Consumer's. *See* CONSUMER'S SURPLUS.

"Surplus Value." *See* MARX, KARL.

Surtax, a tax on higher incomes. It was first introduced as "super tax" in 1909. It applied to all incomes exceeding £5,000 per annum and was levied at a flat rate of 6*d.* in the £ on the income exceeding £3,000 per annum. In 1914 the exemption limit was reduced to £3,000 per annum and the tax was levied at rates increasing with the amount of income. By 1918 the exemption limit was £2,000. The tax was renamed "surtax" in the budget of 1926–7. Income tax and surtax are essentially part of a single progression, and from 1974 they were merged. [12]

"Sweating" (coins). *See* DEBASEMENT (OF COINAGE).

Sweezy, Paul Marlor (1910–2004), American economist. He was educated at Harvard University, where he taught from 1934 to 1946. His *Theory of Capitalist Development* (1942) is probably the most compact and authoritative restatement of the economics of Marx (and of the neo-Marxists) in English. He is a consistent Marxist in the strict sense that, in addition to accepting the economic sociology of Marx, as do many other economists of the Left, he also considers Marx's technique of economic analysis superior to that now commonly accepted, which they mostly do not. But Sweezy is not enclosed in Marxism, and brings to his exposition a wide knowledge of contemporary controversy and an extensive acquaintance with the history of economic theory. Schumpeter suggests that he attempted to make Marx into a Keynesian; Sweezy qualifies the pure orthodox attitude slightly by accepting Bortkiewicz's revision of Marx's theory of prices, but that is the limit to his willingness to synthesize Marx and Keynes. His most recent book (written with Paul A. Baran) is *Monopoly Capital: An Essay on the American Economic and Social Order* (1966). [2]

Syndicalism, a doctrine of workers' control of industry. It was developed in France in the late nineteenth century and spread to other countries. Its advocates believed that the capitalist must be overthrown by revolutionary means and that the workers in each industry, organized in trade unions, should govern industry. The general view has been that workers' control is impracticable since as demand changes employments become *redundant;* but if it accepts the risks of change in market conditions it need not conflict with the interest of the community as a whole as consumers. [5]

Syndicated Bid. *See* Discount Market.

T

Tableau Économique, an early model of the economic system, produced by the French Physiocrat F. Quesnay and first published in 1758. It has two aims: first, to explain how the total product of a society circulates between the broad social groups typified by landowners, tenant farmers, merchants and artisans; secondly, to show how the national product is reproduced each year. The key proposition is that only agriculture can produce a surplus. The *tableau* is important as an early model of a system of exchange and because it stimulated thought on the influences determining prices in exchange. [9]

Take-home Pay, the sum remaining after deduction of income tax and national insurance contributions, private pension and health insurance contributions, etc. It is often used to indicate the "private wage" in contrast to the "social wage," i.e. government welfare and other services paid for by taxation. Strictly this is misleading, since some deductions are for private welfare benefits like occupational pensions. The term is also used to indicate the earnings left to meet the cost of living, which is again misleading if deductions pay for the widening range of state services that enter into the cost of living such as education, medical care, etc. In practice the tendency in collective bargaining is to refer to take-home pay as the criterion for wage-settlements; on this ground some economists have argued that falling take-home pay, as the concomitant of rising tax and social insurance contributions, was an element in the accelerated inflation beginning in 1969. [5]

"Take-off." *See* Industrial Revolution; Rostow, W. W.

Take-over Bid, an effort to obtain control of a company by an outsider through purchase of its shares. In post-war Britain it was a symptom of the free market reacting against government controls, high taxation of incomes and inflation.

There were several contributory causes. (1) Changes in demand accompanying rising incomes and redistribution of incomes and changes in supply following new techniques and scientific invention made it necessary for business men to adapt their methods and ideas rapidly and fundamentally. Those slow to do so presented targets to outside interests prepared to adapt their assets more quickly and so make them more profitable. (2) Increased company taxation and tax relief on undistributed profits induced directors to distribute only a small amount of the profits to shareholders and to plough back the remainder into the business; such ploughed back profits could often have been used more profitably elsewhere. (Shareholders tend to be influenced primarily by current and expected dividends; the stock market usually looks about six to twelve months ahead.) (3) Companies were urged by post-war governments to observe "dividend restraint" in order to avoid inflationary wage demands. (4) Many companies held cash (or securities quickly changeable into cash) with which to replace worn-out or out-of-date plant and machinery at higher prices. A bidder who obtained control thus had access to large cash holdings which replaced the cash he had paid for the shares. (5) Owing to rising prices properties, particularly shops on good trading sites, were worth far more if sold than they were shown in the books or than they were currently earning. (6) The development of site properties by the existing owners was impeded by the restrictions on raising new capital for re-development. The Capital Issues Committee could veto new issues until 1959; intermittent post-war credit squeezes, designed to halt inflation, limited the amount of working capital that could be borrowed from banks. (7) Some companies postponed revaluation of their assets in order to make their earnings appear a higher proportion of their capital. (8) Shareholders were tempted to accept the bidder's offer because income tax and surtax made a tax-free capital gain more inviting than the prospect of highly taxed dividends. Although dividend distributions became more generous after about 1953 (partly in order to ward off take-over bids), they were still not large enough to outweigh the attractions of capital gains. Some economists argued that the remedy was to tax capital gains, others that it was to reduce taxation on income. Capital "gains" could be regarded as a belated compensation for the poor returns on the shares.

The take-over bid has been aptly described by two British economists as "a short circuit in an electrical system where the load was unevenly distributed" (George Bull and Anthony Vice). It has been widely criticized as an effort by outsiders with no interest in the activities of a company to snatch a quick profit, dislocate its trade, disturb its staff and denude it of its profitable assets to the detriment of its earning capacity in the long run. Two replies have been made. First, if the assets are undervalued, removing the surplus will not impair their earning power. (A common method, selling freehold properties and taking out leaseholds, yields capital sums, and the new rents can be written off against profits.) Secondly, a firm that joins a large group may gain rather than lose from the resulting diversification.

Take-over bids have been outnumbered by other forms of association that form part of the normal process of development and expansion. In a flexible free economy change is inevitable and desirable, particularly to keep pace with a changing world economy, and directors and employees risk losing their jobs and shareholders their money if market conditions alter. But such upheaval or distress has been exceptional in the post-war take-over bids. In most, although inefficient people have been dismissed or retired, the business has been expanded and additional people employed. The danger that take-over bids could lead to over-concentration of power by monopoly is common to all forms of industrial association.

The case for take-over bids is that they result in fuller use being made of economic resources. Whether this is so or not depends on the attitude to the life of a company's assets taken by the sitting board and by the bidder. The bidder's views are usually shorter than the board's: he will probably make the assets more profitable in the short run. If his view is *too* short, the general interest will suffer because the assets may be worn out too quickly, and he will not replace or augment them. If the board's view is *too* long, and the assets will not pay for themselves in the period envisaged perhaps because market change makes them out of date, again the public interest will suffer. The bidder's short-term views have probably caused boards of directors to review their generally long-term attitude and work their assets more intensively. In a rapidly changing world economists generally would argue that this is probably on the whole in the public interest.

The rights of shareholders as a class can be prejudiced (even though they make a capital gain or receive higher dividends) if the bidders use voteless shares to gain control, or if they make a bid for part of the shares so that those holding the remainder lose authority over the board, or if the board raises the dividend in the effort to keep the bidders out and thus weakens the company's resources.

Take-over bids, and even partial bids, which have been frowned upon as ruthless devices used purely for financial gain, were given a new respectability when in 1958 the joint-stock banks bought control or large interests in hire-purchase finance companies hitherto regarded as engaged in business of doubtful propriety.

Take-over bidders were not always successful. The firm which resisted them successfully did so by showing the shareholders that they were capable of using the assets no less profitably than the bidders. Making use of the assets profitably in the interests of the shareholder by and large meant making the best use of them in the public interest, since in competitive conditions they could be made more profitable only by offering services for which the public were prepared to pay.

In 1959, following several take-over bids which attracted widespread public interest and some criticism, the financial institutions, led by the Bank of England, published a code of conduct for bidders designed to remove the element (or impression) of secret negotiation or collusion between directors. The code was designed in the interests of the shareholding community and to remove public disquiet. But it approved the principle of take-over bids, and in helping to remove its abuses, real or supposed, it made them more reputable and therefore a probably growing feature of British industrial development. [3]

"Taking Work to the Workers." *See* DEVELOPMENT AREAS.

"Taking Workers to the Work." *See* DEVELOPMENT AREAS.

Tap Issue. *See* TREASURY BILL.

Tariffs, originally the official list of taxes paid on goods imported, now applied to the goods. Tariffs are customs duties. They are "ad valorem," as a percentage of the value of the goods, or "specific," as a stated amount per unit of weight (pound, ton) or volume (gallon, cubic yard).

Tariffs are used to yield revenue for government or to "protect" home industries from the competition of imports. When the purpose is revenue, an excise duty is levied on the home product.

Tariffs were raised by many countries in Europe and America during the great depression of the early 1930's in the effort to maintain employment at home. They have tended to come down in the period of trade liberalization since the end of World War II, e.g. in the General Agreement on Tariffs and Trade (GATT), the Common Market and the European Free Trade Association. [4]

Tâtonnement, French for continuous groping, the name given by Walras to his theory (or vision, conception) of the free market as a mechanism in which there was a permanent tendency towards equilibrium by successive approximations. If at a point in time demand in some markets exceeds supply, and in others supply exceeds demand, prices will tend to rise in the former and fall in the latter; by the time they will have equated demand and supply in all markets, the conditions of demand (taste, knowledge, income, etc.) or supply (information, efficiency, etc.) may have changed, so prices move again, still under the influence of unequal demand and supply and with the effect of equating them.

The modern metaphor for tâtonnement would be a computer, although a market is fed by information far beyond the capacity of a computer. The two conclusions from the Walrasian conception of a market are, first, that there is no need for a human mind to solve the equations of excessive demand or supply, and, second, that it is doubtful whether they can be solved by human or electronic "minds."

Tâtonnement describes a tendency or *movement* towards equilibrium, which may never be reached, so that the movement is perpetual. The theory of tâtonnement thus rests on a theory of economic dynamics, which can itself be seen as the process of tâtonnement envisaged by Walras. [7]

Taussig, Frank W. (1859–1940), American economist. He was educated at Washington University and Harvard and spent several years in Europe, studying at the University of Berlin. In 1882 he returned to the United States and began his long academic career at Harvard. In his earlier works, *Wages and Capital* (1896) and *Principles of Economics* (1911), he tried to combine factual and theoretical analysis, and later specialized in the problems of international finance. From 1917 to 1919 he was chairman of the US Tariff Commission, and in 1919 he was called to Paris to assist in drafting the post-war commercial treaties. His *Aspects of the Tariff Question* (1915) and *International Trade* (1927) contain his major contributions to international economics. [2]

Tautology, a form of pseudo-reasoning in which the "conclusions" merely restate the original assumptions, although sometimes they create an impression of having achieved fuller understanding. By their nature tautologies are irrefutable. An example is: "Commodities which have many effective substitutes have elastic demands." If substitutability is defined in terms of the ease with which purchasers shift between commodities when their relative prices change, the existence of good substitutes necessarily implies a high elasticity of demand: both are thus defined in similar terms. [14]

Tax, Consumption. *See* Consumption Tax.

Tax, Direct and Indirect, a direct tax is levied directly on the taxpayer, e.g. income tax, surtax, estate duty, private car licence, local rates; an indirect tax is levied indirectly, e.g. the excise duty on beer and spirits, the valued-added tax, the customs duty on imported textiles, cameras, clocks, cars. This distinction is administrative rather than economic; thus the motor tax is administratively direct but economically indirect since it must be paid if the consumer is to use the motor car.

The important economic distinction is between taxes that directly affect the demand for and the supply of goods and services and therefore their prices, and taxes that do not. This turns on the distinction between their immediate impact and their final incidence. Income and capital taxes cannot be avoided, so that the ultimate incidence is the same as the initial impact. Indirect consumers' expenditure (or outlay) taxes can be avoided to an extent depending on the elasticity of the demand for and of the supply of the product, that is, the degree of competition in its markets. If the demand is relatively elastic the price cannot be raised to pay the duty because consumers will buy the nearest substitutes which are not taxed; if demand is relatively inelastic buyers will not easily go elsewhere if the price is raised and the producer can pass at least part of the tax to the consumer. If the supply of the factors used for the product is relatively inelastic and they cannot readily find other employment, the producer may be able to shift the tax back in lower wages, salaries, interest, rent, etc.; if it is elastic it will be less easy to reduce these factor prices. Broadly, direct taxes tend to be progressive (by intention), indirect taxes to be regressive (in effect rather than by intention). [12]

Tax, Income and Capital, includes income tax, profits taxes, estate duties. These taxes were formerly raised mainly from the richer classes, but the increase in the number of income tax payers has dispersed income and capital taxes much more equally throughout the community. In the nineteenth century economists argued that income taxes were preferable to outlay taxes because they evened up net incomes and did not disturb consumption and production. But when the marginal rates of income and profits tax (the additional tax on increased earnings) are high, effort and output may be affected: savers may not save, and *entrepreneurs* may not undertake risky ventures; managers may not exert themselves, and workers may absent themselves from work; men may prefer security or (untaxed) leisure to a little more (taxed) income. [12]

Tax, Indirect. *See* TAX, DIRECT AND INDIRECT.

Tax, Outlay. *See* OUTLAY TAX.

Tax, Poll. *See* POLL TAX.

Tax Price, the cost in taxes of services supplied in the political process, or, at the margin, the tax required for an additional unit of a state service. The contrast is with the market price. If an individual as a consumer of private services thinks one more unit is worth paying for at the market price, he will *buy* it. If an individual as an elector of government that provides state services thinks one more unit worth the tax price, he will *vote* for it. The market price is shown in the market; it is generally the same for all consumers. The tax price for an additional unit is more difficult to calculate: if the state service is expanded and one more unit supplied to each individual, his tax price will depend on the size of his income, which determines his income tax, and the way in which he distributes it on purchases, which determines his indirect taxes, and on saving, which influences his capital taxes. The tax price thus differs between individuals, and it is easier to charge lower tax prices to people with low incomes. Market prices are regressive; tax prices can be progressive (in practice in Britain they have been roughly proportional, except at the upper and lower extremes of income). A major difference is that tax prices depend on collective voting decisions rather than on individual buying decisions. Since votes are cast for or against an increase in expenditure on a large number of services rather than on each service separately, the link between payment for and receipt of an additional unit of state service is remote. The vote is also ineffective unless it is a part of a majority; and votes can be used not only to indicate increased willingness to pay for services but to transfer the cost to minorities (other voters with relatively high incomes, or voters thought to be receiving income undeservedly or unwisely consuming goods such as tobacco or alcohol, etc.). Referenda or plebiscites on single state services might operate to refine public choices. The interesting economic question is whether tax prices are more or less efficient than market prices in ensuring the supply of desired services.

The economics of electoral processes as methods of making decisions on the use of resources have increasingly attracted the attention of economists, notably in the economics of public choice developed by the Virginia School. [13]

Tax, Profits. *See* PROFITS TAX.

Tax, Progressive. *See* TAXATION.

Tax, Proportional. *See* TAXATION.

Tax, Purchase. *See* PURCHASE TAX.

Tax, Regressive. *See* TAXATION.

Tax, Shifting and Incidence, the study of the ways in which the burden of taxation is shifted among persons and institutions in the economy. It thus amounts to a study of the general and particular effects of different taxes on the allocation of resources and the distribution of income. Nothing precise can be said about the *amounts* of tax that can be shifted, but the *tendencies* can be established fairly clearly.

Taxes on income, particularly progressive taxes, have effects on incentives to work and save. There may be possibilities of tax shifting where the demand for scarce ability is inelastic, that is, permits pre-tax incomes to be raised to offset high tax rates, or where some people have more opportunities for switching to non-taxed occupations or sources of income than others. These effects, however, are essentially long-run and conjectural, since the effects of a general tax on income may be offset or reinforced by the economic effects of government spending of the tax proceeds. The effect on saving is equally uncertain: it is difficult to assess the net effect of income tax on saving, and the effect on the economy of a change in saving depends in any event upon the general level of activity in the economy.

Taxes on the owners of productive resources are not confined to labour. They include taxes on land ownership (such as site value taxes), on long-term improvements to land (such as local rates on property) and on less durable goods (such as motor taxation). The theory of economic rent suggests that the total earnings of non-reproducible resources in fixed supply such as land will be entirely determined by demand. Taxes on the owners of such resources cannot be shifted because the owners cannot alter demand, reduce supply to raise price, or sell the land except at a price reflecting the tax liability. Such a tax in theory stays where it is levied and thus constitutes an "ideal" tax from the viewpoint of knowing its economic effects. This conclusion ignores difficulties of estimating site value where sites are developed. If the estimate is incorrect the tax may fall partly on income from improvements, investment in further improvement may be discouraged; as a result their prices may rise and the burden of the tax will be partly passed on to buyers and users of the improvements.

Taxes levied "indirectly" on commodities are paid initially by businesses. Their effect is to drive a "wedge" (the thickness depending on the size of the tax) between the price paid by the buyer and the price received by the seller. Which of these two gives way most depends upon the relative elasticities of demand for the product and supply of factors used in the production of the commodity. In the short run such taxes may be borne entirely by the business, but this is not likely to persist. A business is essentially an intermediary between consumers and factors of production. It will either pass on the tax to buyers if it can or it will find output less profitable and reduce it and so reduce also its demand for the factors of production. If the factors have few or no alternative uses their prices will fall and thus some of the burden of the tax will be passed on to them: if they are versatile (so that their supply is elastic) they will move to other uses and carry little or no share of the tax.

The shifting process is essentially circular since in the end all taxes are paid by persons who are both owners of factors (their own labour) and consumers of products. If taxes are shifted by sellers on to consumers in higher prices, consumers as sellers of labour can in turn shift burdens forward again in higher wages. Or if taxes are shifted backwards on to factors in lower rewards, factors (as consumers) can shift the burden back again in lower demands for products. One of the tasks of tax shifting studies is to indicate the "weak links" in the chain where the circle may be broken and the ultimate incidence of a tax may lie at least in part and for a time. The importance of the analysis is that it shows that people may not pay all or even part of a tax levied on them but that they may pay all or part of a tax not levied on them. The incidence is often very different from the immediate "impact." [12]

Tax, Specific. *See* AD VALOREM.

Tax, Value-added. *See* VALUE-ADDED TAX.

Tax, Wealth. *See* CAPITAL LEVY.

Taxable Base. *See* TURNOVER TAX.

Taxation, charges on income, property, commodities or services made for the conduct of government and the supply of services such as defence, transport, fuel, communications, education, health, housing, pensions, etc. They are usually levied at the point of purchase, sale, import or export, and paid by persons, partnerships or companies to the central government, when they are called "taxes" or social insurance contributions, or to local authorities, when they are called "rates."

Taxes may be progressive (the tax rate increasing faster than the taxable income base, as with income tax and death duties), proportional (the rate varying in the same proportion as the tax base), or regressive (the effective tax rate increasing as the taxable income base decreases, as with indirect taxes on drink, tobacco, cars, etc.). Taxation affects the economy differently according to how far it is progressive or regressive.

When the income tax was introduced in 1799, it was proportional (above the exemption limit). J. S. Mill, Sidgwick, Bastable and other economists were opposed to progressive taxation (*see* below). But in time, as people with smaller incomes were given the vote, progressive taxation acquired advantages for politicians, who could promise to benefit the relatively many by heavy taxation on the relatively few.

Economists and political theorists (Dalton, Tawney, and others) have adduced four main arguments for making taxation progressive: that the benefits of government expenditure vary more than proportionately with income; that the sacrifice is less among people with higher incomes; that progressive taxation can reduce economic fluctuations; that it lessens economic inequality.

Other economists have produced counter-arguments. First, benefits cannot easily be related to income or property; the public benefits that bear a rough relation (such as police protection or fire-fighting services) form only a very small part of the whole. Secondly, although it seems common sense that the better-off should pay a higher proportion of their income than the less well-off, the argument does not rest on the "diminishing marginal utility of money," once widely accepted as the economic justification for progressive taxation, for it supposes that personal needs and the capacity to satisfy them can be compared. There is nothing in economics which enables us to measure the satisfaction derived by different people from different incomes. It does not say that the "last" £50 of an accountant's £8,000 a year adds more or less satisfaction than the "last" £50 of a bricklayer's £3,000. Nevertheless, on other grounds, progressive taxation may be desirable because it seems to equalize "sacrifice."

Thirdly, by leaving a larger proportion of income with taxpayers when incomes are falling, and a smaller proportion when they are rising, progressive taxation may help to reduce fluctuations in expenditure and so help to avoid booms and slumps. But this does not require taxation to be progressive; the same "compensatory" effect over the trade cycle could be produced by changes in the rates of tax.

Fourthly, the view that progressive taxation lessens economic inequality because governments spend money in more desirable ways than do rich individuals (e.g. they build hospitals before hotels) is "static." In time, the number of hospitals might be increased by allowing the exceptionally gifted to have hotels. Further, incomes are now less unequal than in the past. Nevertheless, since the distribution of income reflects monopoly, chance, fraud, changes in the value of money, and inequality of opportunity, progressive taxation could reduce the differences. But a progressive tax cannot distinguish between *sources* of income: it takes a higher percentage of large incomes whatever their origins—whether merit or chance. The remedy is to prevent fraud, control monopoly, maintain the value of money and remove other distortions. Luck and chance are ingrained in human nature and the organization of society. Differences in inherited environment, upbringing and education result in part from the institution of the family; they may be weakened but they cannot be eradicated by taxation alone.

In recent years arguments against progressive taxation have been urged by some economists. They claim, first, that it complicates the structure of the tax system, encourages avoidance, creates problems of equity between taxpayers and impairs respect for the law. Secondly, it can encourage political irresponsibility, because in a democracy the higher rates of tax on the minority are fixed by the majority. Thirdly, progressive taxation, if taken far, lessens productivity: it increases the attractions of leisure, reduces the willingness to embark on risky enterprises; it may increase economic instability by encouraging investment in safe ventures that do not respond to general economic change, and reduces savings and the capital required to raise living standards. Fourthly, by discouraging the creation of private wealth based on work, energy and enterprise, it reduces the scope for economic, social or cultural initiative independent of the state. Fifth, as incomes are equalized by the spread of opportunity, the case for progressive taxation becomes weaker.

In Britain progressive taxation had increased the proportion of net national income paid in taxes, national insurance contributions and rates to central and local government to about 50 per cent by the mid-1970's. This is a higher proportion than is raised in taxation in some other western countries. The British economist, Colin Clark, has argued that when taxation exceeds about 25 per cent of the national income it inhibits production by impairing incentives, it is inflationary, because taxpayers react against attempts to reduce their spending by dissaving, it weakens the inducement in industry to keep down costs, and politicians are tempted to raise revenue by increasing the supply of currency and thereby debasing it. [12]

Taxis, Greek for a social order produced deliberately by an organizer putting the elements into their place: in economic policy a centrally planned society. The contrast is with *cosmos*, a social order which exists (or has formed itself) spontaneously, i.e. independently of human will. Economists have long been divided about the extent to which an economic system could be made more efficient (or humane, or just) by conscious direction instead of by the interplay of market forces. Probably the best-known economic thinkers, extending from American New Dealers through social engineers to Marxists, have favoured some form of taxis. The other economic school, holding that order resulting from the interplay of human action is not necessarily the result of design, goes back to Cournot and von Thünen. More recently F. A. Hayek has emphasized the necessity of clear terminology to denote the two broad kinds of economic order. [14]

Taxonomy, a classification of taxes. [12]

Taylor, F. M. *See* CALCULATION, ECONOMIC.

Technical Elasticity of Substitution. *See* ELASTICITY OF SUBSTITUTION.

Technology, Relation to Economics. *See* ECONOMICS.

Teleocracy, an order of arrangement or organization corresponding to a taxis. [14]

Teloi, the ends or hierarchy of ends of a taxis or teleocracy. The teloi of a planned society may be national strength, or social justice, or equality, or some other end. [14]

Tender Issue. *See* TREASURY BILL.

Terms of Trade, a measure of the purchasing power of exports in terms of imports. When import prices rise relatively to export prices the terms of trade are worsened; when export prices rise relatively to import prices the terms of trade improve. The usual measure of the commodity terms of trade is an index calculated by dividing an index of export prices by an index of import prices. A rise in the index in one year compared with previous years means a favourable movement in the terms of trade and a fall means an unfavourable movement. The British Board of Trade constructs its series for Britain's terms of trade as the import price index as a percentage of the export price index. Thus in British terms of trade statistics a rise in the index means a worsening and a fall means an improvement.

For some years there have been fears of a long-term trend in the commodity terms of trade against the under-developed countries. The evidence is difficult to establish by statistical analysis and is so far not conclusive, but it seems to suggest that they have moved in this way. To generalize on the effects of a change in the terms of trade on the real national income of a country requires information on the *causes* of the change. A rise in a country's export prices does not necessarily mean it is better off because the price rise might have been caused by a fall in output. For example, if disease strikes the cocoa trees in Ghana, cocoa prices will probably rise, but not necessarily in proportion, so that Ghana's export earnings from the smaller cocoa crop are lower than before; instead of high prices enabling her to buy more imports, they buy less. Equally a fall in export prices need not mean a worsening of the exporting country's situation, because the fall in prices might be due to improvements in productivity in the export industries which enable it to produce more exports at lower real costs. It could then buy a larger quantity of imports at lower real cost (in terms of resources required) than before; its national income would be increased and its inhabitants better off.

For Britain changes in the terms of trade mean mainly changes in the prices of manufactures relatively to raw materials and foodstuffs. Such changes have tended to be in Great Britain's favour during slumps, as in the 1930's, and against it in the booms, as in the 1920's and early 1950's. This is because commodity prices tend to swing more violently over the cycle than do the prices of manufactures. In the long period Britain has had the benefit of an improvement in its terms of trade. [4]

Territorial Division of Labour. *See* COMPARATIVE COST; DIVISION OF LABOUR.

Tertiary, Greek term applied to the luxury or semi-luxury products of a developed economy. Primary products are agricultural (wheat, etc.) or mining (leads, etc.), secondary are the simpler man-made tools. The developed countries have passed through historical stages when the bulk of consumption was of primary and secondary goods. The developing countries of Africa and Asia are in one of these stages or the other, although there are beginnings of tertiary production in some as a result of their possessing scarce natural resources (gold, oil) or receiving overseas aid. [9]

Test Marketing. *See* MARKETING.

Thesis, the kind of rule laid down in a taxis (directed economy) for particular groups of people or to serve the ends of the directors of the economy; they thus shade into commands. An example is the hire purchase regulations or other physical controls that apply only to a particular kind of transaction, contrasted with monetary or fiscal policy that comprises general rules or regulations applicable to the economy as a whole. [14]

Third Best, Theory of. *See* SECOND BEST.

Thornton, William Thomas (1813–80), English economist. After extensive travels he entered the London branch of the East India Company, and in 1858 he was appointed First Secretary of Public Works to the India Office. Despite an active business life he spent much time studying economics. He was a close friend of John Stuart Mill, but despite a general adherence to Mill's doctrines he became a sharp critic of the method of the classical economists. His first publications were *Overpopulation* (1846) and *Plea for Peasant Proprietors* (1848), but it is *On Labour* (1869) that is of most interest. It contains detailed criticisms that largely destroyed the concept of the "wages fund." [2]

Threshold, the name given in Britain to the arrangement by which wages were raised automatically when prices, as measured by the official cost of living index, had risen by a stated percentage. The threshold was a method of compensating for expected inflation by indexation. It was intended to be a way of moderating inflationary wage demands based on fears of unknown large rises in prices. Some economists argued that, if used in conjunction with a long-term strategy of *anti-inflationary* monetary and fiscal strategy, it might slow down the wage-price spiral; but in the mid-1970's it was used as a last-minute addition to a prices and incomes policy in a period of *inflationary* monetary expansion, and in these conditions it was likely to speed up the wage-price spiral. [5]

Threshold Analysis, a cost-based analysis to explain disparate rates of growth between cities. The explanation is in terms of the barriers in the form of higher levels of costs (e.g. in the provision of public goods such as roads, sewerage networks, urban re-development, etc.), which must be passed through before growth can proceed. Hence the term threshold analysis. It was developed in Poland in the early 1960's by B. Malisz. Threshold analysis alone constitutes an insufficient theory to explain differential rates of city growth since it largely ignores demand and locational patterns. [6]

Thrift, the disposition to be "economic," to make the most of available income, to avoid waste, to husband resources, to postpone consumption by saving. It is thought to have been a Victorian virtue and the term is unfashionable, but the practice or tendency is general, if unconscious. Thrift in saving is undermined by inflation, which tends to reduce the real value of money saved for future consumption. Rising interest rates would offset the fall in the value of the principal (sum saved) but they tend to lag behind partly because of the "money illusion." [1]

Thünen, Johann Heinrich von (1783–1850), German agricultural economist. Son of a landowner in Oldenburg. He bought estates in Mecklenburg and established a model farm there. Though his main interest was agricultural economics, his approach was highly theoretical and he believed in the use of mathematical techniques. In his main work, *Der Isolierte Staat in Beziehung auf Landwirtschaft und Nationalökonomie* (1826–63), he is mainly concerned with the principles determining the best system of cultivation, especially in terms of distance from the market. In this sense he was a fore-runner of modern theories of industrial location, but his analysis caused him to build up a theory of rent very similar to that of Ricardo. Because of his denial of the subsistence theory of wages and his use of marginal analysis he played a large part in developing modern economic theory. [2]

Tie, an arrangement that links independent buyers and sellers, or traders and borrowers, for a defined period. In Britain the best-known is the brewer's tie, in which a public house licensee agrees to buy beer (or other supplies) from a brewer in exchange for financial assistance by grant, loan or mortgage. Unless there is an element of compulsion on one side or the other, the agreements benefit both: the supplier is assured of continuity of orders and so can reduce costs of production, and the buyers receive finance and can engage in small-scale retailing with a financial stake (as opposed to working as salaried managers). The tie has been applied to arrangements between petrol companies and garages (gas stations) and in some cases to film producers and cinemas. [3]

Tied Lending, international loans in which the borrower agrees to spend the money in the lending country. This restricts the borrower's freedom of action and amounts virtually to lending by truck (goods). [4]

Tight Money, another name for dear money. [8]

Time, an important element in much economic analysis. Economic phenomena take time to show their effects. Many economic propositions are true "in the long run," but often in personal, industrial and public affairs what matters is what happens in the short run. Keynes once said: "In the long run we are all dead." If "in the long run" consisted of a continuous chain of "short runs" in which economic causes and effects never had time to work themselves out, many economic propositions might be interesting in theory but irrelevant in practice. But in so far as human beings learn by trial and error, "short runs" do not merely repeat themselves but show successive differences, each based on the experience and the lessons learned from previous ones.

In many economic activities the important period is the long run and not the short run. Thus in the short run firms will continue to produce as long as price covers only prime ("marginal") costs, but sooner or later all equipment must be renewed and the price must therefore cover the full average costs of the product if firms are to continue to produce.

It is possible to regard time itself as a factor of production since without it there can be no production of goods or services. In this sense time is necessary for the production of capital (through "abstinence" from consumption) and of labour (in training, acquiring experience, learning judgement, etc.).

There is much discussion about the power of the "laws" of supply and demand. For a time the "forces" of supply and demand can be controlled or suppressed by fixing prices, licensing producers and suppliers, rationing consumers, limiting entry into an industry by producers' monopolies or government decree, restricting entry into the professions by unnecessarily high standards of qualifications or into manual occupations by closed shops, demarcation rules and so on. In time the refusal to accept restrictions and the spontaneous tendency for people to come together in exchange as buyers and sellers leads them to find ways round the restrictions through the "working of market forces." Sooner or later restrictions on prices or supply or demand of goods and services produces "black markets." Rationing of consumer goods is bypassed by private arrangements between shopkeepers and customers. Licensing and other means of restricting entry into an industry produces unlicensed suppliers which provide essentially the same service or a near substitute; e.g. the licensing of public houses has helped to produce an increase in the number of clubs supplying alcoholic drinks; restrictions on the number of workers who may perform given tasks may sooner or later stimulate the introduction of labour-saving machinery; heavy taxation of income leads people to evade tax by asking for payment in kind or in cash.

Some of these devices, such as "black markets," are commonly regarded as immoral. Another view is that they are a symptom that controls and restrictions have gone too far and have alienated the moral allegiance of the community. Whatever the ethical issues, the economic significance of such consequences is that they are means by which the "forces" of supply and demand and "the laws of the market" reassert themselves and re-establish free exchange. In the short run they can be suppressed but in time they find a way round efforts to suppress them. The length of time depends on the political system, whether liberal or authoritarian, the character and temperament of the people, the ability of politicians to create and maintain a situation or atmosphere of emergency, such as war, economic crisis or "social purpose," in which restrictions will be accepted. For such reasons "supply and demand" can be suppressed for shorter periods in western countries than in under-developed or communist countries. [7]

Time Deposit. *See* DEPOSITS (BANK).

Time Discounting, the allowance made for the superiority of present contrasted with future command over resources. Uncertainty about the future (not least about the continuation of life) and more knowledge about the opportunities of the present create a difference between values over time. £1,000 now is worth more than £1,000 next year, and even more than £1,000 in five years. Conversely £1,000 in five years is worth less than £1,000 now—perhaps £900, or £800 or £700. This discounting of time is a basic reason for a rate of interest, which *ceteris paribus* would equalize values over time. In normal times a man in good health and middling years might discount at 4–5 per cent a year, an older man in poor health at 15–25 per cent a year. During inflation the rate of discounting accelerates because of the additional depreciation in future real values (inflation at 25 per cent a year would halve real values in less than three years). [7]

Time-lag, the interval between a cause and its consequence. In economics empirical study has revealed time-lags that could help in prediction and forming policy. Thus research into monetary history has revealed that an injection of money raises output about six to nine months later and prices in roughly a further six to nine months. The time-lag between monetary expansion and price inflation is thus around twelve to eighteen months. W. Stanley Jevons in 1882 said it was one to two years. [14]

Time Preference. *See* INTEREST.

Time Series, a succession of statistics of production, prices, sales, exports, etc., for a sequence of periods such as a day, week, month or year. Commonly used by economists in the effort to discover relationships, if any, between different categories. For example, a time series of prices and sales for a sample of people may yield conclusions about the elasticity of demand for a commodity or service. In practice the difficulty is that economic phenomena cannot be isolated and studied separately, as chemical or physical phenomena can be in a laboratory. Thus the demand for a commodity may change not only because the price has changed but also because the conditions of demand (incomes, taste, etc.) may have changed in the period being examined. A second difficulty is that the sample may not be representative of people in general, so that deductions drawn from their economic behaviour may not necessarily apply to others. Time series can sometimes be checked by cross-section analysis. [14]

Tinbergen, Jan (1903–94), Dutch economist. He was educated at Leiden University as a physicist. After working on the staff of the Central Bureau of Statistics at the Hague from 1929 to 1936 and from 1938 to 1945, and as a business cycle research expert with the League of Nations at Geneva from 1936 to 1938, he became Director of the Central Planning Bureau of the Netherlands Government from 1945 to 1955. He was also Professor of Development Planning at the Netherlands School of Economics, Rotterdam University, from 1933. He has been Chairman of the Board of the United Nations Research Institute for Social Development, and was joint winner of the Nobel Prize for economics in 1969.

Tinbergen is outstanding for his contributions to the development of econometrics, the application of econometric methods to practical research, and the training of practitioners in the method, particularly for work in developing countries. His wide experience has caused him to be regarded almost as the father-figure of econometrics and has led to invitations to advise on such subjects as the functions and operational efficiency of bodies like the United Nations Development Planning Committee.

Tinbergen's publications include *Business Cycles in the USA 1919–1939* (1939); *On the Theory of Economic Policy* (1952); *Economic Policy: Principles and Design*

(1956); *Selected Papers* (1959); *Shaping the World Economy* (1962); *Development Planning* (1968). [2]

Tithes, originally the tenth part of the profits of the soil paid to maintain the parish priest. The Tithes Commutation Act of 1836 changed all tithes in England and Wales into a rent payable in money. In 1936 the Tithes Act replaced the rents by sixty-year redemption annuities payable to the Crown, which issued government stock to the tithe-owners. Tithes were thus separated from the Church. In 1996 the annuities will cease and all tithes will be abolished. [6]

Tocqueville, A. de. *See* INDIVIDUALISM.

Token Money (coinage). *See* COIN.

Toll, a charge or tax levied for use of public property. Tolls were used in the early nineteenth century to raise finance for roads; they are now used for long-distance motorways in Europe and America. Some economists have advocated their use more generally, but Professor E. Victor Morgan has argued that British roads are mostly too short to justify the administrative costs. Tolls are also used for bridges, ferries and tunnels. Their economic interest is that, although sometimes called a tax, they are a direct market price rather than an indirect tax price. [7]

Tolstoy, Leo. *See* ANARCHISM.

Tooke, Thomas (1774–1858), English economist. He entered business at a very early age and acquired practical experience. Later he became an authority on finance and banking. His first contribution to economics was made in 1819 when he wrote the *Merchant's Petition* protesting against protective tariffs. The rest of his life was devoted mainly to monetary and statistical problems, giving evidence on several parliamentary committees, and writing pamphlets. His researches were embodied in the six-volume *History of Prices and of the State of Circulation during the Years 1793–1856* (the last two volumes were written in collaboration with W. Newmarch). Tooke maintained that price fluctuations were caused by changes in general conditions of supply and demand for commodities rather than by changes in the supply of money alone. [2]

Torrens, Robert (1780–1864), English economist. He spent his early career as an officer of Marines and saw active service during the Napoleonic wars. After a short period as a novelist he became interested in political economy. For some time he was the Member of Parliament for Ipswich and Bolton. His first contribution to economics was *The Economist Refuted* (1808), followed by an anti-bullionist tract entitled *Essay on Money and Paper Currency* (1812). His *Essay on the External Corn Trade* (1815) established him as a leading political economist. It was followed by *Essay on the Production of Wealth* (1821) and *Letter to Lord*

Melbourne (1837), which contained the first published suggestion that the Bank of England should be separated into two departments. Torrens was a leading exponent of the "currency principle" which led to the Bank Act of 1844; and as a founder of the Political Economy Club he was, with Malthus and Ricardo, the originator of some of the more characteristic doctrines of classical political economy. [2]

Town Planning, rationing and controlling the use of land space by official regulation rather than through the market. The central economic argument for it is that it enables longer-term and wider community interests to be taken into account rather than short-term commercial profit. The main economic criticism raised is that it often fails to achieve in practice what is claimed for it in theory: it is implemented by (local or regional) government, which can only be advised by other bodies concerned with long-term or wider interests; it has often produced colossal errors (as in high-rise flats and tower blocks); and it takes short-sighted decisions under political pressures. Professor F. G. Pennance has proposed that better results might be obtained if land use rights were auctioned to builders or developers who stood to lose or gain by correct assessment of the demand for land. [6]

"**Trade and Navigation Accounts.**" *See* SOURCES, STATISTICAL.

Trade Associations, organizations of firms in the same or similar industry or trade (or a section of it). They developed rapidly during World War I when the government found it could negotiate more easily with one trade association than with numerous firms. Their activities have ranged from collection of statistics and exchange of information to agreements in restraint of trade. In Britain the 1956 Restrictive Trade Practices Act made illegal the collective enforcement of resale price maintenance, e.g. by members of a trade association who threatened to withhold supplies from a retailer who "cut" the maintained price of the goods of a member of the association. [3]

Trade, Balance of. *See* BALANCE OF TRADE.

Trade Creation. *See* CUSTOMS UNION.

Trade Cycles, alternating periods of rising and falling levels of economic activity with similar characteristics in fluctuating output, prices, etc., from one "cycle" to another. Such cyclical variations can be traced back to the end of the eighteenth century and possibly earlier. A typical cycle consisted of a period of expansion, a downturn or recession, a period of contraction, and an upturn or revival. The whole cycle lasted generally from five to eleven years. During the contraction ("depression") national income, employment and prices fell: during the expansion ("prosperity") they rose. The cycle was most evident in the durable goods industries such as iron and steel and shipbuilding. In the UK the last normal "peak" of prices and employment was in 1937. Thereafter they began to fall, but rearmament in and after 1938 pushed them further up into the war-time and post-war inflation. Since World War II the "cycles" have been shorter—at some periods in alternate years—but much less in amplitude. Even in the "troughs" the whole economy has been at a much higher level of employment than before World War II.

There have been numerous and varied theories of the business cycle: the whole subject has been one of lively debate among economists. A "composite" explanation might proceed as follows: Whenever total demand for goods and services is less than necessary to maintain output at its existing level, the level of output and its associated employment will also fall. This could arise because of a chronic tendency for the economy to over-save (under-consume), or to develop a shortage of investment spending to fill the shortfall in aggregate demand caused by planned saving (under-investment). Whatever the reason, reduction in output is likely to be cumulative and to be reinforced by falling prices: stocks tend to be run down, capital replacement to be deferred, consumption out of reduced incomes to decrease, and so on. At some stage, however, stocks and equipment can be run down no further: some replacement of stocks and durable equipment becomes necessary if even low levels of consumption demand are to be met. As a result of the increase in investment, output, income and consumption tend to grow, in turn making further investment attractive, and so on. The expansion may ultimately drive the economy into boom, with its usual bottlenecks, rising prices and problems of maintaining a balance in external trade. In this stage there may be under-saving or over-investment, and attempts to correct the inflationary tendencies cause business men to reconsider their profit expectations and to reduce investment, which initiates a stage of contraction in economic activity.

Since no two cycles are identical in all respects, most explanations advanced by economists are valid to some extent and probably none is wholly wrong. In a general way, fluctuations of this kind are probably best regarded as a symptom of long-term economic growth, reflecting the imperfect ability of the many parts of technical and economic organization to adapt themselves continuously and smoothly to change. [9]

Trade Diversion. *See* Customs Union.

Trade Gap, the difference between the value of exports and imports of visible goods. More generally it can be used for the difference in value between all exports and all imports including invisible services (but excluding capital items). [4]

Trade Mark, a method of relating a commodity to the person or firm owning, producing or distributing it. The method may be a brand, heading, label, ticket, name, word or other device. (It is distinguished from a *trade name,* which denotes the commodity.) It is protected by Trade Marks and Merchandise Marks Acts from being copied by competitors.

Economic interest in trade marks is twofold. First, by being used to *identify* a commodity they enable consumers to buy with more certainty and knowledge and thereby help in one sense to make markets more perfect. Secondly, they *distinguish* or *differentiate* a commodity from other physically similar commodities, and so enable partial "institutional" monopolies (resting on name or repute) to be built by advertising, branding and distinctive packaging, etc., and this fragmentation of markets by "product differentiation" makes them more imperfect. Except where consumers' freedom of choice is limited, one brand dominating the market, or by agreement among producers to limit competition among themselves, the degree of monopoly power exercised by an individual producer is not likely to be large. [7]

Trade-off, the terms on which one objective is exchanged or sacrificed at the margin for another. Thus it is argued by some economists that the environment is not an absolute to be saved at all costs, but that there is a trade-off between a "little" environment and "a lot of" economic growth. [14]

Trade Union, an organization of employees, wage-earning or salaried, whose principal object is to negotiate on the terms and conditions of employment of its members. British trade unions can be divided into several types: those based on craft or skill whose members have some degree of training; those based on an industry or occupation, such as the National Union of Railwaymen; white-collar or professional unions, such as the National Union of Teachers; and the two huge general unions, the Transport and General Workers' Union and the National Union of General and Municipal Workers, each with members, often semi-skilled or unskilled, from many branches of industry.

For some time there have been over 600 trade unions in Britain with a total membership of around ten million. Trade union power is concentrated in relatively few unions. The strength of unionism varies between industries. Some are highly organized, as in the railways, docks, mines: in others, such as engineering and road transport, the majority of workers are union members; in some, including those with a high proportion of female labour (as in catering and distribution), trade unionism is comparatively weak.

The Trades Union Congress is the central co-ordinating body of the movement. Though the TUC acts as the movement's spokesman and can adjudicate disputes between unions, it has little power to discipline its members and can lead only by persuasion. But the presiding body of the TUC, the General Council, is made up of officials of the largest unions, and its decisions reflect the opinion of the bulk of the trade union movement.

Some economists have recently argued that the power of trade unions in Britain is excessive in the sellers' market for labour created by full (or over-full) employment. Unions are accused of other defects: apathy allows extremists or sectional interests to influence or dictate policy; some unions, especially in declining industries, are still haunted by the forty-year-old spectre of mass unemployment and insist on wasteful restrictive practices to ensure work for their members; often internal discipline is faulty and activists in the factories can provoke unofficial strikes. Not least, it is said that the "image" of the movement as a responsible institution is tarnished by the insistence of some trade union traditionalists on the fight against "capitalism" and their apparent reluctance in some cases to consider the national interest. An opposite view of some economists is that the unions cannot be asked to exercise "restraint" if the economic circumstances enable them to gain advantages for their members, and that if such advantages are obtained at the expense of the community in general the economic circumstances should be changed (e.g. inflation may enable employers to acquiesce in wage demands they can pass on in higher prices) or the legal privileges that enable the unions to enforce their claims should be withdrawn. [5]

Trades Union Congress. *See* TRADE UNION.

"Trading on the Equity." *See* LEVERAGE.

Trading Stamps, coupons given by shopkeepers, garages, etc. to customers in proportion to the value of retail purchases and redeemed by goods or in cash from the issuing company. They were developed in Britain in the 1960's largely by a British company in competition with an American company. They were widely criticized by some retailers and general observers as an irrelevance that unnecessarily raised costs and distracted retailers and customers from real values. In the early 1960's they were encouraged by resale price maintenance, which prevented retailers from passing on economies to consumers by lowering prices. Later they developed as a method of invigorating the retail market by competition as an alternative to other methods which were presumably more costly and less effective in attracting and maintaining custom. They were analysed by British economist Christina Fulop in several studies. Like other methods of publicity they could make markets less perfect by creating loyalties or more perfect by stimulating competition. [7]

Transaction Costs, the time, effort, etc. used in arranging an exchange, sale, contract; e.g. finding buyers (by advertising, etc.), transporting the goods to the market (place of sale), preparing the documents, transferring the cash or other payment, and assuring the buyer that he has acquired the property rights he desires in the goods he has bought. Transaction costs are clear in sales of property rights in buildings and land, but they are also present, though newer and more difficult to define, in, for example, air space for aircraft, sound waves for broadcasting. [13]

Transactions Motive. *See* QUANTITY THEORY OF MONEY.

Transfer Earnings. *See* ECONOMIC RENT.

Transfer Incomes. *See* TRANSFER PAYMENTS.

Transfer Payments, payments other than those made for productive services, particularly transfers of money made by the government in grants, allowances, pensions, etc., from taxpayers to people in need such as pensioners, widows, sick or unemployed persons, and others with little or no other income. The development of social insurance, National Assistance and the Welfare State has considerably increased the amount of individual transfer payments and their national total. Transfer payments form part of personal income but not national income since they redistribute wealth by reducing some personal incomes as much as (or less, by the costs of transfer) they increase others. [10]

Transfer Pricing. *See* INTERNAL PRICING.

Treasury Bill, the means by which the British government borrows for short periods. It is a promise by the government to pay a stated sum within a period not exceeding one year, but in practice Treasury bills are not issued for periods of more than three months. Between 1955 and 1962 special seasonal bills were issued for two months but did not prove popular. Treasury bills originated in 1877 and are issued in multiples of £5,000. They form the largest part of the floating debt.

Treasury bills are sold in two ways: by invitation to the public to "tender" for a stated amount of bills, or by issue at a fixed price, the "tap" issue, mainly to government departments or agencies (such as the Exchange Equalization Account and the National Insurance Fund) which have surplus funds. The rate of discount paid on the tap issue is not made public.

The demand for the tender issue comes from discount houses, from overseas central banks and occasionally from large industrial and commercial firms. The joint-stock banks do not tender direct; by an understanding with the discount market they buy bills in the market. This procedure enables the banks to select bills maturing on the dates they require. The banks also lend to the bill brokers on the security of Treasury bills. Shortly after the applications for "tender" bills are received, the Bank of England announces the lowest figure at which bills have been allotted and the percentage allotted (the amount applied for normally exceeds the amount offered). The marginal figure at which tenders are allotted is invariably the agreed rate of the discount market.

Some economists have criticized post-war governments for using Treasury bills to build up the floating debt, so maintaining inflationary pressure by adding to the general liquidity of the economy. [8]

Treasury Deposit Receipt, a wartime expedient, introduced in Britain in 1940, by which the Treasury could borrow directly from the joint-stock banks. Treasury deposit receipts largely replaced Treasury bills during the war; the banks were told each week the amount of Treasury deposit receipts they were required to take up. In 1944 outstanding Treasury deposit receipts amounted to some £1,700 million; they were gradually reduced to nil by the beginning of 1952. The Treasury deposit receipts enabled the authorities to control bank credit through direct action on the liquid assets of the banks. Since Treasury deposit receipts were not negotiable on the money market, an increase in them reduced the liquid resources of the banks and so curtailed the volume of other bank lending.

In 1958 the Chancellor of the Exchequer introduced a special deposit system to restrict bank liquidity. This system bore a strong resemblance to Treasury deposit receipts since it would give the monetary authorities more direct control over the liquid assets of the joint-stock banks. [8]

Treasury Notes. *See* FIDUCIARY ISSUE.

Triangular Trade, international exchange between more than two countries. Most international trade is not simply between two countries (bilateral) except in barter deals, where there are blocked currencies, as a result of tied loans, etc. A exports to B and may use the proceeds to buy in C or D, which then buys in B. World trade is thus mostly triangular or multi-angular. It would be surprising if all or most trade were bilateral because, like barter, it would require a double coincidence of wants: country A which had shirts to export and wanted shoes would have to find country B which had shoes to supply and wanted shirts. Triangular or multi-angular trade thus offers wider opportunities for profit through indirect exchange. [4]

Triffin, Robert (1911–93), Belgian-born economist. He was educated at the University of Louvain and at Harvard. He has been Professor of Economics at Yale since 1951. Triffin's first impact on the world of economics was made with *Monopolistic Competition and General Equilibrium Theory* (1940), in which he clarified market theory by tidying up the terminology and subjecting most of what had been written on the theory to fundamental criticism. His objection was based upon the proposition that the main focus of competition is not so much between firms in the same "industry" as between firms selling different products to the same area or income group. He is critical of economists drawing ethical or political judgements from economic analysis; he has argued that economic theory cannot say anything about the real world (not even about the facts, let alone about the value of the facts in terms of economic welfare). But he has become one of the leading authorities on the structure and problems of the world monetary system, and his vigorous polemics, particularly in *Europe and the Money Muddle* (1957), indicate a more normative attitude to the applicability of economic logic to the real world. [2]

Troika, a trio of advisers to the US President on economic policy: the Secretary of the Treasury, the Director of the Office of Management and Budget, and the Chairman of the Council of Economic Advisers. They meet weekly on average. [10]

Truck, the payment of wages in kind. It was commonly used and often abused in the eighteenth century: employees were either paid partly in kind or were required to spend part of their wages at a shop owned by the employer and charged exorbitant prices. The result was that real wages were lowered. In many employments, especially in coal mining, employees were forced by need to take advances on future wages, so that they were tied to the particular employer. In 1831 the Truck Act halted the worst exploitation and two further Acts extended protection by providing that the whole wage must be paid in cash unless the employee agreed to deductions (or to be paid by cheque). The 1961 Committee on the Truck Acts considered that they often prevented the employer from providing services that would benefit his employees and recommended that, in view of the changed industrial background and the adequate representation of employees by trade unions, the Truck Acts should be repealed and replaced by more modern legislation. [5]

Trust Busting, the policy, adopted originally under the US Sherman Anti-Trust Act of 1890, of breaking up monopolies formed by mergers into their constituent units. For example, in 1911 the Supreme Court ordered the dissolution of the Standard Oil Company of New Jersey, which had acquired the stock of more than seventy oil companies in order to monopolize the trade, and of the American Tobacco Company, which had acquired the assets of more than sixty companies. But other mergers were held by the courts to be legal under the "rule of reason," which considered unlawful only "unreasonable" restraints of trade. This interpretation by the courts focused attention on whether the competitive activities of combinations were "unfair" or "unreasonable" rather than on the fact of combination itself. The change of emphasis was confirmed in the Clayton and the Federal Trade Commission Acts of 1914, which sought to establish further control of monopoly based on "unfair" competition and discriminatory practices.

The dissolution of large combinations does not so far appear to have proved a successful means of dealing with monopoly problems. The firms that succeed combinations may be too few for active price competition, and they may be monopolists in their own regions. Some economists believe that trust busting should be persisted in, probably more vigorously; others believe that partial or short-lived monopoly is best tolerated and that the most effective method of keeping it partial and short-lived is to remove man-made causes such as patents, copyrights, tariffs, trade union privileges, in order to keep markets open to new firms which will weaken or destroy monopoly. [10]

Trust, Fixed. *See* Fixed Trust.

Trusts, originally referred to as a form of monopolistic combination in the USA. Control of the constituent companies was vested in the hands of a board of trustees, the companies' shares being exchanged for trust certificates. The first combination to adopt this form was the Standard Oil Trust established in 1882. In 1890 the Sherman Act declared trusts illegal, and other types of organization, especially holding companies, were employed. The term trust has survived as a general derogatory name for large combinations exercising monopoly power. In law trusts refer to arrangements such as family settlements. [3]

Tullock, Gordon (1921–), American economist. He was born in Rockford, Illinois, and was educated there and at the University of Chicago. He taught at the Universities of South Carolina and Virginia. In 1967 he was appointed Professor of Economics and Political Science at Rice University and from 1968 Professor of Economics and Public Choice at Virginia State University. He is, with J. M. Buchanan, one of the founders of the new political economy of public choice and of the Virginia School. He has developed into a fertile thinker and writer who applies economic theory to new subjects with illuminating results. His first major work was *The Calculus of Consent* (1962; with J. M. Buchanan), a path-breaking book on the new economics of politics. His other books include *The Politics of Bureaucracy* (1965) and *Private Wants, Private Means* (1970). [2]

Turgot, Anne Robert Jacques (1727–81), French statesman and economist. He studied theology at the Sorbonne, but in 1750 took up a legal career. He held several judicial posts, and in 1761 was made Intendant (general administrator) of Limoges, where he improved the roads and tax system and organized improved facilities for the trade in grain. His success at Limoges led to his appointment as Secretary of State for the Navy in 1774 and thereafter as Comptroller of General Finance. But his attempts at a programme of reforms provoked much opposition and he was dismissed in 1776. He came into contact with the Physiocrats at an early stage and was much impressed by Quesnay's theory of "produit net." His contribution to economics lies in his best known work. *Réflections sur la formation et la distribution des richesses* (1766), in which he discusses concepts, such as the division of labour, the productivity of labour and the effects of competition, that had much influence on Adam Smith and the classical school. [2]

Turnover, (*a*) generally, the total value (price multiplied by number of units) sold or "turned over" by a firm in a year (or other period). (*b*) more specifically, the rate at which goods are sold or "turned over." Turnover, or stock-turn, is important in an economic sense because it indicates the amount of capital locked up in stock and adding to costs by requiring interest to be paid on it. In retailing, some goods like food turn over much more quickly than others like furniture. An increasing turnover reduces the amount of capital locked up in stock. Whether it is better to have a higher than a lower rate of stock-turn depends on the costs of raising it, e.g. by advertising. An increase in turnover may be achieved by reducing the retail margin (the gross profit added to the wholesale price) and therefore the retail price. A lower margin will reduce the earnings on a unit sold but may increase total earnings by raising stock-turn and thus causing the capital used in holding stock to turn over more quickly. [3]

Turnover Tax, one on gross sales revenue from business transactions. Unlike a sales tax, which is levied only on gross value at the point of retail sale, a turnover tax is levied on all intermediate transactions between businesses leading to and including the final sale. A shirt may sell for £4, representing £1 worth of services contributed each by the spinner, weaver, manufacturer and distributor who helped to produce it. But if each was a separate business entity the sum of gross sales transactions at all stages of production would be £1 + £2 + £3 + £4 or £10. The taxable base (£10) of a turnover tax is thus much larger than that of a sales tax (£4), and the rate of tax will be correspondingly lower. Its economic disadvantages are that, even when levied at a uniform rate on all commodities, it raises the price of some disproportionately (depending on the number of intermediate transactions) and thus distorts the pattern of production and consumption. A uniform rate sales tax (if everywhere fully passed on by sellers) would not have this effect. Also, attempts to avoid tax payment might tend to lead to the integration of production processes and firms even when it lowered economic efficiency. [12]

Two-part Tariff, a price in two parts, frequently found in the charges made by public service undertakings supplying electricity, gas and telephones. The essence of a two-part tariff is that the consumer pays a fixed charge and a charge varying directly with the quantity of the service consumed; thus, the Post Office charges both a quarterly rental for the use of a telephone irrespective of the number of calls made by the consumer and a price for each call.

This method of charging is used by undertakings which require considerable plant and equipment with high costs of installation and maintenance. The demand for the services fluctuates over the day, the week or the season, with periods of concentration at peak hours. Since they cannot (except gas) be stored, the plant and equipment must be large enough to cope with peak demands. At other times the undertaking will be working at less than full capacity. Costs of supplying additional units of the service are considerably higher at the peaks than at slack periods. The fixed costs of the undertaking are related to the amount the consumer takes at the peaks, and are allocated in the form of fixed charges (rentals) to consumers. The charge per unit of the service consumed covers its direct or prime costs (the materials employed in producing it).

Two-part tariffs aim to cover fixed costs while keeping the charge for additional units of service low, thus encouraging maximum use of equipment and spreading fixed costs. A single price would result in a lower output and possibly a loss. An alternative to a two-part tariff would be to charge discriminating prices on the principle of "what the traffic will bear" to different consumers, in order to cover fixed costs and encourage consumption. Similarly, the fixed charge in a two-part tariff can differ for different users. To this extent the two-part tariff is also a form of discriminatory pricing the purpose of which is to spread overhead costs and promote the most extensive use of the service. [7]

Two-tier Price, is strictly impossible in a market with unimpeded knowledge and movement into it and is therefore possible only where there is government control or private monopoly, as in price discrimination. A two-tier market for US gold operated before 1961 and after 1968: the official price referred to transactions between governments, the free price was allowed to occur in other transactions. The fixed price was designed to prevent speculation. [7]

U

Unavoidable Costs. *See* Supplementary Costs.

Uncertainty, term used by economists in its everyday meaning of unpredictability or imperfect foresight. The concept of uncertainty is still in the process of being incorporated into economic theory. Much analysis is in terms of static conditions and perfect knowledge, so that problems arising from the existence of uncertainty are assumed away. For example, in much of the theory of the firm the individual *entrepreneur* is assumed to know all the circumstances necessary for him to maximize profits or minimize losses. But in the real world *entrepreneurs* do not know how much of their goods will sell at different prices, what will be the effects on sales of different advertising methods and costs, how their rivals will react to changes in their policies, and so on; their policy has therefore to be based on estimates and guesses. When uncertainty enters the analysis, simplicity and precision disappear along with many of the conclusions of static analysis.

The existence of uncertainty means that the outcome of an action cannot be known beforehand, i.e., what happens may be different from what was expected. Individuals frequently have to choose between several possible actions for each of which there are a large number of possible outcomes. The problem is to determine how, in such a situation, an individual reaches a decision. The traditional solution is in terms of the theory of probability. If the actions, being repeatable, have been undertaken a large number of times, it is possible to calculate the chances or probabilities that various possible outcomes will result from each of the possible actions. In this way ignorance and uncertainty are reduced, and comparisons can be made of the various possible actions open, of which the best is that which offers the largest (statistical) probability of achieving the desired result.

Probability theory does not help if the actions cannot be repeated. For choosing between several possible unique actions, for each of which there can be a large number of possible outcomes, the British economist Professor G. L. S. Shackle has developed a theory of which a bare outline is as follows. The individual who has to make a choice focuses his attention on the best and the worst possible outcomes for each of the possible actions. He may think that some outcomes are more likely than others. The best and the worst possible outcomes for each possible action can be converted into values corresponding to the outcomes that seem equally likely. For each set of converted best and worst possible outcomes, a point can be plotted on a gambler's indifference map for each possible action. The point (or points) falling on the highest indifference curve then indicates the best possible action (or actions). A point on a higher indifference curve is preferable to a point on a lower curve, because for the same loss a larger gain is possible.

An earlier theory of uncertainty, developed by the American economist Professor F. H. Knight, is of particular interest for the theory of profit. Profits are said to be earned by the *entrepreneur* for bearing the risks of uncertainty. Since the future is unknown and the outcomes of actions are uncertain, there are risks that the *entrepreneur* may have to meet unexpected costs and, as a result, suffer unexpected losses. The probable frequency of thefts, fires, floods and so on can be calculated from the evidence of experience, and *entrepreneurs* can relieve themselves of these risks by insuring against them, thus converting them into a known cost. With many actions, however, it is not possible to derive a "probability rating" of the possible outcomes, and so it is not possible to insure against the risk of undesirable outcomes. It is for bearing these uninsurable risks that Knight argued the *entrepreneur* receives a profit when his actions prove successful.

The existence of uncertainty raises the "supply price" of *entrepreneurs* by what is in effect a risk premium which the *entrepreneur* must expect to be paid if he is to be persuaded to undertake production. This expected "pure" or "normal" profit is thus a true cost of production, and profit realized in practice would tend in the long run (and in the absence of restraints on competition) to be equal to it. [14]

Undated Securities. *See* IRREDEEMABLE SECURITIES.

Under-consumption. *See* TRADE CYCLE.

Under-developed Countries, literally countries capable of economic development. Countries well endowed with resources not yet fully utilized could then be described as under-developed; but this would include wealthy countries like the USA, Canada and Australia. Normal usage confines the word to poor countries. The currently accepted economic meaning is countries in which the income per head falls below a more or less arbitrary stated level, such as one quarter of incomes per head in the USA. It is thus a synonym for poor, undeveloped or economically backward nations.

The term is strictly economic, implying nothing about political or cultural standards. The under-developed include most of the countries of Latin America, Africa, the Middle and Far East. Their chief common feature is extreme poverty.

Other characteristics of under-developed countries are a high proportion of the population engaged in agriculture, often over 70 per cent compared with around 10 per cent in the USA, or 5 per cent in Britain (an extreme case), or about 20 per cent in an advanced agricultural nation like Denmark; very little capital per head; practically no savings per head; agricultural output mainly in cereals and primary raw materials, with a low output of protein foods; heavy dependence on exports of a small number of primary products; high fertility rates and high mortality rates giving rise to risks of a population "explosion" if death rates are checked, as by improved medicine. These characteristics can be demonstrated by statistical measurement.

Other features are less easily shown and more controversial. Thus widespread under-employment of labour, especially in subsistence agriculture, is often said to be prevalent in such countries. Many economists have challenged this view. It seems to imply that some labour can be removed from its present occupations without causing a fall in output there and without a change in techniques. But much of the apparent idleness is due to seasonal swings in the demand for labour which may be fully occupied at sowing and harvest times. To use labour in new occupations that is free only at some seasons may be impracticable or expensive. [11]

Under-investment. *See* TRADE CYCLES.

Undervalued Currency, one whose exchange value in terms of other currencies is maintained below the level it would reach in a free market. Undervaluation usually arises because of an increase in the strength of a currency (based on improvements in a country's trading position and internal strength and stability) since the exchange rate was fixed. An undervalued currency may enable a country to widen its markets in other nations by making its exports relatively cheap. If a country wishes to bring its exchange rate into equilibrium with other currencies it may do so by revaluation. [4]

Underwriter, (*a*) specifically, an individual member of Lloyd's who joins with others to insure a marine risk, that is, damage to or loss of a ship or cargo. An underwriter writes his name under the insurance policy to indicate that he accepts a stated part of the risk. (*b*) more generally, underwriting is used in insurance of the other main classes of risk—life, accident, fire and other. For example, a pension scheme for a firm may be devised by a pension consultant who arranges for a life assurance company (or "mutual" office) to underwrite it, that is, insure that its benefits will be paid. (*c*) a financial institution such as an issuing house that commits itself to take up shares not bought by the public. [8]

Unearned Income, drawn from property (investments in company, land, etc.), in distinction to earned income, which is drawn from work (wages, salaries, fees, commission, profits, etc.). In Britain unearned income is taxed more heavily than earned income, part of which is not taxed at all (the earned income allowance) or at lower rates. The economic effect of this discriminatory taxation is to reduce inequality in income and, possibly, to discourage saving. It has been argued that the distinction between earned and unearned income is misleading, because to the extent that property embodies past labour the income from it is not "unearned" and should not be taxed at a higher rate than earned income. [12]

Unemployment, involuntary idleness of a person willing to work at the prevailing rate of pay but unable to find it. There can also be unemployment of capital, savings, land or other resources.

Unemployment of labour has been of six main kinds.

Frictional unemployment results when the demand for labour is not adjusted to its supply for lack of knowledge by employers that workers are available or by workers that employment is available. In Britain Labour Exchanges were established in 1912, largely because of the economic investigations and advocacy of W. H. (later Lord) Beveridge, in the effort to adjust supply and demand. In recent years advertising has been used increasingly to announce employers' requirements for employees. The lack of information about the demand for labour has been emphasized as a prime cause of unemployment that serves to provide a reserve pool of labour. (*See* INFORMATION COSTS.)

Seasonal unemployment is caused by seasonal fluctuations in demand. The ideal solution is to have more than one job in order to secure continuous employment: the ice-cream seller in summer turning to chestnuts in winter; the cricketer lecturing to schools in the winter (or, if he is very good, playing in Australia).

Structural unemployment results from a change in techniques in an industry or in the demand for its products which makes some employees redundant. Mechanization forced hansom cabbies to drive taxis; cotton operators have learned engineering and stayed in Lancashire or moved to other parts of the country which offered employment they preferred. In practice employers and employees have hoped for government support by preventing or reducing competition, especially by tariffs and other restrictions on imports, as in agriculture. If the employers are influential or the employees numerous they may be able to induce the government to restrict competition from new industries, as the railways have done in restricting the development of road transport by licensing. In the 1960's structural unemployment in shipbuilding and other staple industries led the government to extend the inducements to employers to establish factories in the north-east of England, Scotland and elsewhere. In the 1970's subsidies or other forms of assistance have saved "lame ducks" and maintained employment in older, declining industries or firms, docks, shipbuilding and engineering. Since there were shortages of labour in the Midlands and the South East this policy caused economists to debate the consequences of "taking work to the workers" as against "encouraging workers to go to the work."

General unemployment results from a general falling off in the demand for labour caused, for example, by a reduction in the total amount of spending in the economic system. Such a reduction may originate in structural maladjustments in the economy or may be brought about by government to avoid strain on sterling because high costs have reduced exports.

Cyclical unemployment was the most evident symptom of the downswing in the trade cycle before World War II. It was Keynes's argument that at such times the government should maintain the demand for labour by keeping up the supply of money and spending by low interest rates, tax reliefs and by undertaking "public works."

Institutional unemployment arises from obstacles put in the way of the mobility of labour by public or private policy: e.g. government restriction of rents induces older people to remain in homes that might be occupied by younger workers; local authority council housing gives the occupiers "squatters' rights" and makes them reluctant to move for fear of paying higher rents elsewhere; trade unions negotiate national wage rates that apply to all areas, including north-east England and Northern Ireland, from which high wages discourage movement and in which lower wages might reduce costs and increase employment; trade unions try to maintain closed shops, demarcation rules that reserve jobs to particular workers, unnecessarily long apprenticeship periods, etc.; nationalized industries and private firms in sellers' markets hold on to labour, or concede higher pay, in spite of large losses and a scarcity of labour elsewhere. [9]

Unfair, a question-begging term implying a judgement on a value, in the UK usually on values arising from the working of markets. When applied to markets where a buyer or a seller has a marked bargaining advantage over the other, the term has some meaning. If used about market values as such, the meaning is more obscure, since it implies that a lower or higher value would be more fair but does not define it. It thus begs the question. [14]

Unfavourable Balance of Trade, another name for passive balance of trade.

Unfunded Debt. *See* National Debt.

Unilateral, a one-sided action performed without reference to those who would benefit or lose from it. In modern economics it is mostly used to describe tariff changes. The central debate is whether unilateral tariff reductions benefit or harm the country making them. [4]

Unit Banking. *See* Banks, Joint-stock.

Unit Cost, another name for average cost.

Unit Trusts, organizations raising money (mostly) from small investors to reduce the risks of loss by investing in a spread of equities. In Britain unit trusts started in the 1930's but did not make much headway until the late 1950's, when financial restrictions were lifted and new trusts were created. They then expanded but were harmed by the Stock Exchange recession of the early 1970's.

The small investor benefits from the specialized experience of the trust managers. They are not free to invest where they like, but the tendency has been away from the fixed trusts, which held blocks of specified shares, towards the flexible trust, in which the managers have the power to invest in a wide range of securities.

A unit trust has to be authorized by the Board of Trade and its constitution embodied in a trust deed. The trustees are usually a bank or an insurance company, which is responsible for the custody of the securities and is often consulted on the investments. The trust deed must provide for the sale and repurchase price of units, the issue of units, advertising and management charges, audit and accounts.

The price at which unit trusts are offered to the public is based on the lowest market dealings of the underlying securities plus stamp duty, brokers' commission and a fixed percentage to cover management charges. It is thus disadvantageous to buy and sell units at frequent intervals, and encourages more permanent holding. The managers will buy back the units at any time and some unit trusts quote daily prices based on the value of the investments. Stamp duty and income tax at the standard rate (holders not liable at the standard rate have to claim repayment of income tax) discourage expansion of unit trusts.

"United Nations Demographic Year Book." *See* SOURCES, STATISTICAL.

"United Nations Statistical Year Book." *See* SOURCES, STATISTICAL.

Unproductive, yielding no utility, or yielding utility at disproportionate cost. The criterion is not the physical (objective) product but the consumer (subjective) judgement of it. Thus labour used mining coal is unproductive if it could have produced other goods valued more highly. [7]

Unrequited Exports, goods or services exported to pay interest on a loan or repay the capital. They are therefore not paid for by those to whom they are sent and so do not earn foreign exchange. In recent years they have referred in particular to the withdrawal abroad of money held in Britain (the "sterling balances"). [4]

Unused Capacity. *See* CAPACITY, UNUSED.

Urban Economics. *See* LAND ECONOMICS.

Urban Land Economics. *See* LAND ECONOMICS.

Urban Studies. *See* LAND ECONOMICS.

User Charge, payment for a state service made directly by charging a price rather than indirectly by a tax, e.g. tolls and licence fees, mostly for road or water transport. Economists are concerned to discuss how far user charges should cover only marginal cost or long-run average cost (to cover the replacement of obsolescent capital). [7]

Usury, charging "excessive" or "unreasonable" rates of interest on loans. Early laws of the Church and State prohibited or controlled usury. The usury laws were repealed in 1854 as part of the process of removing economic restrictions. In economics the term has little meaning unless markets are highly imperfect. If interest rates are high, then, unless the suppliers of loans have created a monopoly or the demanders do not know how much they are paying, the implication is that loans are scarce relatively to the demand for them. Allowing rates of interest to rise is therefore a method of removing the scarcity by stimulating the supply and/or reducing the demand. Much of the usury of which Shakespeare wrote, and moralists and churchmen of the Middle Ages complained, may have arisen from local monopolies caused by poor transport and lack of knowledge that loans could be obtained for lower rates of interest elsewhere. In more recent times poor people who borrowed money from pawnbrokers or moneylenders did not know how high the rate of interest was or could not easily borrow elsewhere. In our day many people who buy by hire purchase do not know that they are paying 20 per cent interest a year. Hire purchase laws require the information to be stated more plainly. "Personal" loans by some of the joint-stock banks to people with middling or lower incomes are also making the market for private borrowing less imperfect and thus helping to reduce interest rates. [8]

Utilitarianism, philosophical and political term originated by Jeremy Bentham for the theory of the means of ensuring "the greatest happiness of the greatest number." It had many followers among economists and political philosophers. [2]

Utility, in economics the power of a commodity or service to give satisfaction by meeting a want. Positive economics does not inquire into the morals of wants. Food, cigarettes, holidays have utility and are of economic significance if they satisfy wants. Positive economics does not distinguish between classical music and jazz, Shakespeare and Agatha Christie. This is because it analyses what is and does not judge what should be. Its interest is in the utility of a commodity or service *at the margin,* that is, the increase or decrease in total utility accompanying an increase or decrease in the supply, because this is where decisions are made and marginal utility (which usually diminishes as the quantity increases) enters into the determination of value and price. Thus fresh air is so abundant in everyday life that *at the margin,* i.e. a little more or less, it would make no difference and people are not prepared to pay anything for it. But in a submarine it may mean the difference between life and death and could command a high price. [7]

Utopianism. *See* NIRVANA APPROACH.

V

Value, in economics either value in use or value in exchange. The theory of value and the theory of distribution together form the theory of price. The theory of distribution deals with the determination of the prices of the factors of production; the theory of value deals with the determination of the prices of consumer goods.

The price of a commodity may be defined as its value in terms of money. The theory of value is therefore concerned with the relative prices or exchange values of commodities. Since goods are demanded because they have the power to satisfy human wants, they also have value in use. Water is valuable not because of the price it commands but because it has "utility," the power to satisfy a human want.

The concepts of value in use and value in exchange have sometimes caused confusion. Adam Smith's paradox of value stated that many "useful" commodities such as water had a low value in exchange, whereas much less "useful" ones such as diamonds had high exchange values. The solution to the paradox is that the supply of some goods is scarce relative to the demand for them. Water is normally plentiful and so commands little in exchange value or price, but diamonds are relatively scarce and so have a high exchange value or price. On the other hand water in the desert is invaluable, because it is scarce, but diamonds satisfy no urgent need.

Value in use is not an intrinsic quality of a commodity but rather its capacity to satisfy a human want. For a commodity to have exchange value it must have utility (or more strictly, it must give the promise of utility so that it is desired), and it must be capable of being exchanged.

Value in exchange expresses the amount of one commodity that can be exchanged for another: so many units of X can be exchanged for so many units of Y or Z. In a money economy these exchange ratios are not stated directly; the value of each good is expressed in terms of money and, given this knowledge, the exchange ratios of the commodities can be derived. If eggs cost 60*p.* a dozen and butter 60*p.* a pound, twelve eggs exchange for a pound of butter. The theory of value is therefore concerned with the determination of relative prices.

But it is not possible to analyse the price system in terms of the exchange ratios of commodities alone. Money and its value have to be considered because it is not "neutral." Money is not simply a technical device for converting the exchange values of goods into prices. There is an important difference between a barter economy, where value is determined purely by the exchange ratios of goods, and a money economy, where relative prices are influenced by changes in the value of money itself. The change in the price of one good may reflect either changes in its value relative to other goods, or changes in its value relative to money. A change in the value of money generally may change the relative prices of goods. Thus changes in the value of money and changes in relative prices are closely linked.

The theory of value has always held a key position in economic theory. In the early nineteenth century economists' explanation of the exchange value of (reproducible) goods emphasized the influence of relative costs of production (i.e. supply) in determining prices. The influence of utility (demand) was viewed largely as a condition necessary for the emergence of exchange value. Later in the century the marginal utility theory of value emphasized utility as the source and cause of an exchange value, and related exchange value to the marginal significance of additional units of a commodity. The influence of cost of production was allowed for in this more general theory, which explained the cost of a commodity in terms of the value (as again determined by marginal utility) of the alternative products that could have been produced by the land, labour and other factors employed. Alfred Marshall's "scissors" simile, in which both demand and supply were likened to the cut of the two blades simultaneously determining price, was thought misleading since both "blades" were derived from the single principle of utility. Nevertheless, the simile is useful because it emphasizes that, in the long run, the marginal utility principle will tend to equate exchange value to relative costs. Present-day economics regards price as determined by the interaction of supply and demand: given the conditions of supply and demand, equilibrium exists when the quantity freely demanded at a price is equal to the quantity freely supplied at that price. [7]

Value-added Tax (VAT), is levied on net turnover. It differs from a turnover tax in eliminating from the taxable "base" the cost of "inputs" of materials, labour, etc. For example, a shirt selling for £4 might include £1 worth of services contributed each by the spinner, weaver, manufacturer and distributor. A value-added tax is in effect levied on each of these £1 items and is thus similar to a retail sales tax levied on the £4 sale price. A turnover tax levied on *gross* turnover would by contrast be levied on £1 of the spinner's, plus £2 of the weaver's, plus £3 of the manufacturer's, plus £4 of the distributor's gross sales, that is on £10 in all. [12]

Value-judgement, a supposition or preference on which a proposition of normative economics is based. The value-judgement that the distribution of income is undesirably unequal underlies the proposal that taxes should be more progressive. The value judgements of economists *qua* economists have no more validity than those of other people, and they differ widely. Non-economists should therefore distinguish between economists' normative and behaviourist (positive) propositions. [14]

Variable, a quantity that can vary in size. In economics the basic variables are supply, demand, price and cost (micro-economic); income, expenditure, output (macro-economic). [14]

Variable Costs, those which vary with output. Some of the costs of a firm are independent of the output it produces, some are dependent on it. For example, the rent of a building or interest charges on borrowed capital do not normally change as output increases or decreases; but the costs of raw materials and the wages of labour used directly in production, such as engineers or mechanics in a car factory, alter with output. This distinction applies in the short run when the size of the enterprise is unchanged; in the long run all costs vary with output since the scale of operations can be increased or decreased by enlarging or cutting down the plant and equipment (down to nothing if the firm goes out of existence). Much economic analysis is concerned with the behaviour of cost as output varies; one of the basic ideas is that in the short-run period when a producer's equipment cannot be increased the *rate* at which total variable cost rises as output expands will first decrease and then increase (because of variable proportions). There is therefore for each firm an "equilibrium" level of output at which profits will be larger than at any lower or higher level. This will be the point at which the rate of change of total variable cost is just equal to the rate of change of total revenue (provided that total revenue is larger than total variable cost). [7]

Variable Proportions, Law of, the principle that describes the relationship between "inputs" of productive resources (factors) and the resulting "output" of product. Whenever increased output requires the combined services of different factors of production, one of which is limited in supply, any attempt to overcome its relative scarcity by combining it with larger amounts of other factors will eventually slow down the *rate of increase* of total output. More precisely, the law states that, as equal increases of a variable factor are added to a constant quantity of other ("fixed") factors, the successive increases in output will after a point decrease. The law applies to all forms of productive organization, provided one (or more) of the productive factors is fixed in supply, successive units of the variable factor added are all of equal efficiency, and the state of technological knowledge remains constant. The law rests on the common observation that factors are imperfect technological substitutes for one another. Diminishing returns are the physical effects of continuing the substitution of available for less available or unavailable (or fixed) factors.

It follows that up to a point the addition of equal increases of a variable factor to a fixed factor may result in *increasing* additions of product. One of the earliest formulations of the law, by the French economist Turgot, drew attention to this feature, but it was largely neglected in the development of the law by some of the English classical economists, notably David Ricardo, Sir Edward West and T. R. Malthus. They were concerned mainly with the application of the concept to the growth of population relative to agricultural land and the implications for the labour cost of producing additional food and therefore living standards. Their gloomy prophecies, based on the view that technological progress in agriculture would be insufficient to offset the effects of the law, were falsified by subsequent events. (This falsification has not prevented the emergence of similar prophecies about present-day world population growth and food supplies.) Later formulations of the law have tended to move away from this historical or prophetic treatment and have followed the earlier example of Turgot in emphasizing the analytical aspects of non-proportional (i.e. first increasing, then decreasing) returns of output when the proportions in which factors are combined are progressively varied under conditions of a constant state of technical knowledge. Hence the more general title (The Law of Variable Proportions) under which diminishing returns were often analysed in later writings.

In this form the law plays an important part in formulating the conditions in which output obtained from a given outlay is maximized or the cost of producing a given output is minimized. For example, the amount of additional product which a variable factor yields is a measure to a producer of its productive value. The law infers that this value in turn depends upon the quantity of the factor already employed with given amounts of other factors. Beyond a point, the larger the quantity already employed, the smaller will be the increment of product from a further unit of the variable factor. The optimum use of variable factors to maximize output thus requires them to be allocated among alternative uses so that the productive value of an additional unit of any one factor type is the same in every use. Similarly, where more than one type of variable factor is employed, the cost of additional product will be minimized when the various types are combined with the fixed factor(s) in such proportions that additional product per unit of additional outlay is the same for every type.

More generally, where a producer can obtain output only by the addition of variable factors such as labour or raw materials to a combination of fixed factors such as plant, machinery or management, the law infers that the addition of successive batches of variable factors will yield first increasing and then decreasing increments of output. If the cost of successive batches of variable factors remains the same, the cost of production per unit of additional output will tend first to fall and then to rise. The law thus throws light on the cost conditions of firms in the short run, that is when fixed equipment cannot be expanded. [14]

Variables. *See* COMPARATIVE STATICS; REGRESSION ANALYSIS.

Variance, a measure of the degree of difference between the individual items in a group and the arithmetical average. If all members of a cricket team scored 20 in a match the average would be 20. If their scores ranged from 0 to 100 the average might still be 20, but in this instance the variance would be larger than in the first (nil). The smaller the variance, the more informative the average. [14]

Veblen, Thorstein (1857–1929), American economist and sociologist. He was born into a large Norwegian immigrant family and began his education at Carleton College with a view to entering the Lutheran ministry, but decided on an academic career. He failed to obtain a scholarship to Johns Hopkins University but proceeded to Yale and Cornell, eventually becoming professor at the newly opened University of Chicago in 1892. His two main works, *Theory of the Leisure Class* (1899) and *Theory of Business Enterprise* (1904), with their scathing analysis of conspicuous consumption and other ideas led to his being called the Founder of "Institutionalist" economics. [2]

Vector, an arrangement of numbers. A column vector shows the figures vertically, a row vector horizontally. Vectors have assisted in the development of input-output analysis. [14]

Veil (of money), term used by Pigou and other economists to emphasize that thinking in terms of money obscures real values and real economic processes. Especially since the intensification of industrial fluctuations or trade cycles in the last century, economists have been increasingly concerned with examining the effect of the use of money on the real underlying structure of consumption and production. At one time they tried to discern a form of "neutral" money that would exert no independent influence on economic realities. For fifty or sixty years they have given increasing attention to the monetary causes of fluctuations in output and in prices (inflation and deflation). Until a neutral money can be devised economists will go on examining the independent effects on the working of economic systems. [8]

Velocity of Circulation, the number of times a unit of money is transferred between the money balances (bank deposits and cash) held by individuals, businesses and institutions in a given period. The velocity of *all* money units is an average of their average velocity. Coin and note balances circulate faster than bank balances, current account bank balances faster than deposit account balances. Some money may be held idle over the whole period. The more economically money balances are used, the larger the value of transactions which a given stock of money can support. This is implicit in the *equation of exchange* MV = PT, where

M stands for the stock of money,

T for total transactions occurring during the period,

P for the general level of prices, and

V for the velocity of circulation of money.

The degree to which money balances are so used depends on the forms of financial organization (in integrated firms book entries replace money), the frequency with which payments are made, changes in the general price level and business conditions, and the structure of interest rates (which reflects the "cost" of holding money balances idle). Economists differ on the extent to which velocity is steady or volatile. The Chicago School hold the former, the Keynesians the latter view. [8]

Vertical Integration. *See* INTEGRATION.

Viner, Jacob (1892–1970), Canadian-born economist (Montreal). He was educated at McGill University and Harvard. He went to the USA in 1914 and taught at the University of Chicago from 1916 to 1946, with intervals for public service, ending as Morton Hull Distinguished Service Professor. From 1946 to 1960 he was Professor of Economics at Princeton University.

Viner's name is associated with two major contributions to the development of economic theory. The first is embodied in his *Studies in the Theory of International Trade* (1937), which not only reviewed almost all that had been written on the subject (including some early works which his researches rescued from oblivion) but also reinterpreted them in the light of contemporary theory, separating what was permanently valid from what was not. In this book he introduced, *inter alia,* the distinction between the terms of trade measured in commodities and in units of the services of factors of production; the importance of the distinction was that the commodity terms of trade could move against a country or region even though the factorial terms of trade moved favourably, so that a lower price of a commodity in elastic demand could yield higher revenue to an unchanged amount of labour and/or capital services. The factorial terms of trade concept also showed that the theory of international trade is part of the general theory of distribution. Viner supplemented this work by a realistic analysis of Canadian foreign trade. From this he passed on to the theory of the firm, developing studies of cost conditions which tidied up much that Marshall had left unfinished, and providing material that was generously acknowledged by Joan Robinson to have contributed substantially to the theory of imperfect competition.

Apart from the 1937 *Studies,* Viner's main works were *Dumping: A Problem in International Trade* (1923), *Canada's Balance of International Indebtedness* (1924),

Studies in the Theory of International Trade (1937), *Trade Relations between Free-Market and Controlled Economies* (1943), *International Economics* (1951), and *The Long View and the Short* (1958), which contained "Cost Curves and Supply Curves" (1932) originally published in *Zeitschrift für Nationalökonomie.*

Viner was judged by Robbins to be the outstanding all-rounder among professional economists of his day in theoretical and applied economics, and *hors concours* in the history of economic thought. [2]

Virginia School, relatively new centre of thinking about the economics of public choice, founded in the 1960's at the (private) University of Virginia, Charlottesville, by J. M. Buchanan and Gordon Tullock, and transferred to the State University at nearby Blacksburg. [2]

Visible Exports. *See* BALANCE OF PAYMENTS.

Visible Imports. *See* BALANCE OF PAYMENTS.

Vital Statistics, (*a*) narrowly, the measures of birth rates, death rates, marriage rates, etc., relating to the population; (*b*) more generally, the key indexes of the economy—production, income, expenditure, prices, money supply, exports, imports, etc. Since the end of World War II there has been a vast increase in the collection of vital statistics. They are mostly measures of national totals (or averages) and form part of the increasing attention on macro-economics and are subject to its limitations: they supplement but do not replace micro-economics, the study of individual behaviour without which the meaning of macro-economics cannot be assessed. [14]

Voluntary Chain. *See* MARKETING; RETAILING; WHOLESALING.

Voluntary Liquidation, the method by which a (British) firm dissolves itself in order to cease activities. [4]

Voluntary Unemployed, people physically but not economically unemployed because they could find work at the going market rate of pay if they wanted it. Voluntary unemployment is thus a preference for leisure over income. Economists are more concerned with the analysis of involuntary unemployment. [5]

Voting, the method of expressing a preference between goods or services in the political process, in contrast to paying a money price in the market. Hitherto voting has largely been for large groups of policies at infrequent intervals. Switzerland uses referenda for single policies. The development of electronic computers might make it possible for each voter to record his preference on each policy and to instruct his representative accordingly. Differences between this and the market process are that experimentation is rare, that an individual voter has little influence over the decision unless he can persuade a majority to share his preference (and will therefore spend less on acquiring information than he would for a private purchase), that each decision requires large-scale investment, and that decisions may be irreversible for long periods. The study of the economics of voting is being developed, mainly in the USA. [13]

Voucher, a compromise between cash and kind. In terms of benefits, cash gives more choice, kind is more certain to reach the recipient. The method may be effective in habituating recipients of benefits in kind (e.g. education) to dispense cash. Experiments in education vouchers have been conducted in the USA. [10]

W

Wage-drift. *See* WAGES.

Wage-freeze, a (temporary) stand-still in wages in the effort to create a breathing space for a counter-inflationary policy, and perhaps a form of political shock-tactics to reduce expectations of continuing increases at a high rate. The method was tried in the 1960's and 1970's but not with substantial or lasting effect because the underlying inflationary pressures caused wages to resume their upward trend when the freeze became too politically unpopular to continue. [5]

Wage-fund Theory, a classical view, abandoned in the late nineteenth century, that wages could not rise beyond rates that would exhaust the "fund" created for them out of capital. Its weak theoretical foundation was that wages could be paid out of current as well as past production. It was essentially a more refined subsistence theory of wages and gave way to the theoretically more robust marginal productivity theory that in a free market wages were determined by the additional product of the marginal worker. [5]

Wage-squeeze, similar to a wage freeze but less rigid. [5]

Wage Systems, the methods by which wages are paid. There are two main ones. (*a*) In *time payments* the employee is paid according to the length of time for which he works, usually at a standard rate per hour. This type of payment does not depend on output (subject to a satisfactory minimum standard), and is therefore suitable where skill is required and quality is more important than quantity of output. An advantage of this system is that time payments are predictable and the employee can count on a known wage. Salaries are a form of time payment in which the unit of time is usually a month. (*b*) In *payment by results* the remuneration depends upon the quantity (and quality) of output. Incentive payment systems of this kind can work only where output is measurable. They are suitable when maximum output is the principal goal, as when standardized goods are being produced by unskilled or semi-skilled labour. To the employee an incentive system can be a mixed blessing: he can reach very high earnings, but as they depend on a high output they may be irregular. The possibility of variation in weekly earnings can lead to uncertainty and insecurity, although there is usually a minimum "fall-back" rate as a lower limit to wages. In practice the fixing of "piece-rates" and work bonus systems raises complex issues and has been the source of industrial dispute. [5]

Wages, in its broadest economic sense, the reward of the factor of production labour (including all income from employment, income from self-employment, fees and so on); in a narrower economic sense, only income from employment—the remuneration of operatives and the salaries of staff workers; popularly, the amount paid to operatives, and thus different from salaries (but mainly in the timing or form of payment—salaries are paid monthly, wages weekly—and the difference is unimportant in economic analysis).

The basic wage or *wage-rate* is distinguished from *earnings,* or the total amount of money paid; there is often a large difference, called "wage-drift," accounted for mainly by overtime payments (now common in many jobs), bonuses, etc. Since World War II many workers have often earned 50 to 100 per cent more than the basic wage. Much confusion about wage negotiations and comparisons of the attractiveness of various jobs has been caused by a failure to distinguish between wage-rates and earnings.

In economic theory, the wage in its broad sense (the real reward of human effort in general) is simply the price of labour, and like other prices it is determined in the long run by the interaction of supply and demand. The demand for labour is a "derived demand": labour is demanded not for itself but because it can produce goods which people wish to buy. The demand for labour therefore depends on the demand for the product it will help to make, on the productivity or efficiency of labour, and, not least, on the wage itself, since the number of workers an employer will hire is influenced by how much he has to pay them. The equilibrium wage for a given type of labour will be that which generates sufficient demand to clear the "market" of the supplies forthcoming.

The pattern of *relative* wages in different employments is also determined by supply and demand. The wages pattern in theory is such as to equalize the supply of and demand for labour in competing employments. In each sector of the labour market, wages will tend, unless prevented, to rise or fall until an equilibrium of supply and demand is reached.

In real life the theory is modified considerably. First, there is often confusion between *money* and *real* wages; in the *General Theory* Keynes argued that employees were influenced by the amount of money they received rather than by the amount of goods and services it bought, but especially in full employment and the inflation it stimulates the emphasis has been mainly on real rather than money wages. Secondly, it is not only wages which determine the demand for labour and the supply of it but the net advantages of each type of work. Thirdly, the labour market is far from perfect: many jobs require training or special aptitude; many employees are unwilling or unable to change jobs or even their place of work; trade unions restrict entry to some trades; housing difficulties discourage movements, etc.; a rise in the wages of some kinds of labour will therefore not necessarily induce an increased supply. Fourthly, trade union pressure through collective bargaining and governmental influence through wages councils have radically altered the conditions of supply of labour and thus affected wages. In many industries an employer must pay the same rate to all employees in a particular grade. Wages are therefore much less flexible than theory might suggest.

The result is that the wages structure is extremely complex. It includes conventional differences in pay between various groups of employees, including lower wages to female employees than to male. The existence of different rates of wages and earnings in different regions reflects the relative prosperity and the scarcity of labour (because of higher demand and/or smaller supply) in some of them. Differences in wages between occupations arise from such factors and, like differences between industries and firms, partly reflect prosperity or ability to pay and trade union activity. Differences between skilled and semi-skilled or unskilled employees are based partly on tradition, partly on the training of the skilled employee, and his relative scarcity. In recent years the high demand for labour in Britain has narrowed this difference, and the supply of skilled workers may become even more inadequate if recruits fail to regard the higher pay as sufficient to compensate them for the long period of training.

These complications qualify the theoretical explanation of wages as determined by supply and demand, but they do not impair the basic explanation of wages as the price of labour. In so far as they affect wages, the institutional, traditional and other influences do so through their effect on the supply of and the demand for labour. [5]

Wages Councils, statutory but independent bodies, comprising independent persons and equal numbers of employers and employees, that determine the minimum wages and other conditions of employment in trades where normal collective bargaining machinery is inadequate, usually because trade union organization is insufficient to arrange collective bargaining. Wages councils are composed of employer and employee representatives with up to three independent members appointed by the Department of Employment. They discuss wages and conditions of employment and submit their proposals, which may be unanimous or agreed by a majority vote, to the minister. He has power to reject a proposal, refer it back to the council for further consideration or, as in most cases, to confirm it, but he cannot amend it. When a wage proposal has been confirmed, a Wages Regulation Order is made, and all employers are notified of it and obliged to comply with it. Wages inspectors enforce the orders, and offending employers may be prosecuted.

If adequate machinery for collective bargaining develops, a wages council may be abolished. This has been the tendency in recent years. [5]

Wages Policy, a device developed in the 1960's to maintain a rate of rise in wages that would keep pace with the increase in output in order to avoid inflation. It required the co-operation of the trade unions as a whole through the Trades Union Congress, which found it difficult to resist the argument of some unions that changing market conditions had changed the *relative* value of groups of workers and that shortages in some industries could be met only by wages rising faster than the national average. The policy was refined by providing for exceptions, but this entailed a return to the pattern of differentials thrown up by the market. [5]

Waiting, in capital theory the postponement of consumption which helps to explain the rate of interest. [1]

Walras, Marie Ésprit Léon (1834–1910), French economist. He was trained as a mining engineer, but failed. He turned to journalism, again unsuccessfully. In economics his efforts bore more fruit, and he became Professor of Political Economy at Lausanne in 1870. He was an ardent social reformer, and his main works, *Éléments d'économie politique pure* (1874–7), *Études d'économie sociale* (1896) and *Études d'économie politique appliquée* (1898), divide his economics into pure, social and applied. In his first book he developed a marginal utility theory a few years later than Jevons and Menger but independently of them. His outstanding contribution to economic thought is his analysis of the conditions of general equilibrium. [2]

Want, a desire for a commodity or service. The desire may be to satisfy hunger, thirst, avoid cold or heat, to be cured of illness, be amused or entertained, earn praise, display generosity or kindness, or any others. Wants cannot be satisfied completely because goods and services are scarce relative to the wants they could satisfy. Resources are best used, that is, yield the maximum total utility, when wants are satisfied equally at the margin, so that the marginal utility of an additional unit or batch of resources in satisfying different wants is the same in all uses. This also means that wants can never be satisfied completely, for to do so would be to use resources where their marginal utility is less than in others satisfied less fully. The logic of this principle in practice is that the community's satisfaction of wants is likely to be achieved better by a system of allocating resources in which small ("marginal") adjustments can be made than by a system of centralized priorities that are difficult to adjust for local or individual preferences. [7]

Ward, Barbara (1914–81), British economist (married to Sir Robert Jackson). She was educated at the Convent of Jesus and Mary, Felixstowe, the Lycée Molière and the Sorbonne, in Germany, and at Somerville College, Oxford. She was a University Extension Lecturer from 1936 to 1939, and then worked on the *Econ-*

omist. She was appointed Schweitzer Professor of International Economic Development at Columbia University in 1968. She is an authority of considerable standing on the economic problems of the developing world. She has first-hand knowledge of the conditions from which they are trying to emerge and of the factors influencing their efforts, and brings common sense, a grasp of economic logic and practical sympathy to the task. Much of her writing is in anonymous journalism. Her signed works include *The West at Bay* (1948), *India and the West* (1961), *The Rich Nations and the Poor Nations* (with René Dubris; 1962), *Only One Earth* (1972). She is a strong advocate of aid to developing countries. [2]

Waste, in economics, the misuse of resources to produce goods or services that satisfy fewer or less intense wants than could have been satisfied by different use. Economic waste is thus concerned with maximizing the satisfaction of wants with the optimum use of resources: with demand, value, cost and price. It is fundamentally different from waste in the technical sense. For example, to close down a branch railway line "wastes" the equipment not yet worn out in the railway track, signaling equipment, trains, stations, etc. But in the economic sense it is wasteful to use additional human or material resources that can be used elsewhere to keep a branch line going if passengers prefer to travel by road or air, and show their preferences by refusing to pay prices sufficient to cover the cost of labour, materials and replacements necessary to maintain it. (This proposition would need to be amended if closing the branch line entailed "social costs" or the loss of "social benefits" that could not be expressed through the market mechanism of railway costs and fares. Economists differ on the extent to which social costs and benefits are covered in market pricing.)

Waste is therefore not to be judged by chemical, engineering, architectural or other *physical* criteria but by the *economic* criteria of value and cost and price. [7]

Wasting Assets. *See* SINKING FUND.

Watering (Stock), the process by which the nominal capital of a company is issued without the payment of money equal to its value. The purpose is to create the impression that more capital has been put into the enterprise than has been the case. This impression may be desired because it may lead to a higher value being placed on the shares of the company, particularly for purposes of a take-over offer or for determining compensation payments. Watering may also be employed to make it appear that with existing revenue the rate of return on the capital invested is lower than it is, so that, for example, exploitation of monopoly power may be concealed behind an apparently low rate of return. [8]

Ways and Means Advances, short-term loans by the Bank of England to the government. Part of the government's short-term or "Floating" Debt. [12]

Wealth, commodities (and claims to services) that are capable of satisfying wants. An individual's wealth comprises clothes, furniture, homes, motor car, savings in all forms, etc. A country's wealth is the total of all personal wealth (after cancelling debts between individuals) plus collective wealth such as municipal or state-owned transport, fuel services, mines, hospitals, schools and so on. Personal wealth can be regarded as including claims to the services of collective wealth. The total wealth of a community includes claims on the wealth of other communities. The total wealth of the world is the sum of the wealth of individual communities after canceling claims and debts between them. [7]

Wealth Tax. *See* Capital Levy.

Weber, Max. *See* Calculation, Economic.

Weights (in index numbers). *See* Cost of Living.

Welfare Economics, a term defined variously to refer to the efficiency of an economic system (behaviourist/positive economics) or its capacity to serve morally or politically-conceived purposes (normative economics). Much of modern economic writing is on welfare economics in these senses. Some economists believe it is welfare economics to show how the economic system can respond more sensitively and effectively to consumer preferences. Others think welfare economics is the use of economic mechanisms to solve problems of pollution, congestion, poverty, etc. [14]

Welfare State, one that provides minimum standards in education, health, housing, pensions, etc., when individual means are inadequate. Its origins are largely political and sociological. In Britain its early beginnings go back to the second half of the nineteenth century; it was considerably extended by the Liberal Government after 1906 and by post-war governments following the Beveridge Report on Social Insurance in 1942. In time it has become more comprehensive and universal.

The economic implications turn largely on the effects on production. By ensuring minimum standards, the welfare state can increase production, and to this extent is a good investment, that is, it can pay for itself by increasing the wealth of the country. The adverse effect is through incentive: high taxation to finance welfare sometimes limits the urge to increase earnings by risk-taking, enterprise and work; and the provision of free or subsidized services may blunt the urge to earn money out of which to buy them. There are three main limits to the minimum standards: the need (*a*) to permit those who work to have higher standards than those who do not, (*b*) to avoid making labour more immobile, (*c*) to keep the cost within national means.

Some economists have argued in recent years that as incomes rise it is wasteful to give equal benefits to all and that the education, health and other services should be confined to people in need, the remainder being freed to buy the state service or a private one if they prefer it. [10]

West, Sir Edward (1782–1828), economist and Fellow of University College, Oxford. In 1815 he published *An Essay on the Application of Capital to Land* which opposed restrictions on the import of corn. It has a place in the history of economic thought because it clearly states the law of diminishing returns and anticipates Ricardo's theory of rent (Ricardo acknowledged West in his *Principles*). West also published in 1826 *The Price of Corn and Wages of Labour, with observations upon Dr Smith's, Mr Ricardo's and Mr Malthus's Doctrines.* He was called to the Bar; when he died he was chief justice in Bombay. [2]

Whately, Richard (1787–1863), English ecclesiastic, logician and economist. He studied at Oriel College, Oxford, and was elected to a fellowship in 1811. He took Holy Orders, but after a short period as a parish priest he succeeded Nassau Senior to the Drummond Chair of Political Economy at the University of Oxford. His contributions to economics are embodied in *Introductory Lectures on Political Economy* (1831) and *Easy Lessons on Money Matters* (1833). On the whole Whately tended to follow the subjective theory of value, and is best known for applying the term "catallactics" to the study of economics. [2]

Wholesaling, buying from producers and reselling to retailers. It may reduce the costs of distribution because one commercial traveller can take orders from a retailer for the products of many manufacturers; manufacturers may send their goods to wholesalers in large consignments; the wholesaler on "breaking bulk" can make up relatively large parcels of several manufacturers' products for transport to the retailer; and the centralization of stocks held by wholesalers relieves manufacturers and retailers from carrying large stocks of their own. Wholesaling has declined in relative importance with the growth of large retail chains that place bulk orders with producers. In addition manufacturers have increasingly bypassed wholesalers in order to emphasize, direct to consumers by advertising, the merits of their brands at the point of final sale. Wholesalers have tried to compete more effectively by developing brands (in textiles), by more refined pricing based on better costing of sales of varying sizes, and by links with retailers who agree to buy stated amounts in exchange for assistance with display, stock-control, publicity, staff training and so on ("voluntary chains," especially in groceries). [7]

Wicksell, Knut (1851–1926), Swedish economist. He studied philosophy and mathematics at the University of Uppsala, but later became interested in economics and continued his studies in Austria, Germany and England. He became professor at the University of Lund in 1900. His first major publication was *Über*

Wert, Kapital und Rente (1893), in which he built up a theory of value and distribution based on marginal analysis. In *Finanztheoretische Untersuchungen* (1896) he developed these theories and introduced problems of public finance. His main contribution to economics came in *Geldzins und Güterpreise* (1898), in which he built up a theory of interest and the general level of prices which anticipated and informed a good deal of modern development in money and interest. His *Lectures in Political Economy* were published in 1901. [2]

Wicksteed, Philip Henry (1844–1927), English philosopher, theologian and economist. He was educated at University College, London, and spent the early part of his career as a Unitarian minister, becoming widely recognized as a medieval scholar. His interest in ethics and sociology caused him to read Henry George's *Progress and Poverty,* which led him to inquire into the nature of economic problems. Wicksteed soon became a university extension lecturer, and in 1897 he left the ministry and devoted his whole time to lecturing and writing. His *Alphabet of Economic Science* (1888) and *An Essay on the Co-ordination of the Laws of Distribution* (1894)—his most original piece of work—established him as a leading economist. His main economic work was *The Commonsense of Political Economy* (1910), which was the first comprehensive, non-mathematical exposition of the "marginal" theories of economics. In 1914 he published *The Scope and Method of Political Economy in the Light of the Marginal Principle.* [2]

Wieser, Friedrich von (1851–1926), Austrian economist and sociologist. After graduating from the University of Vienna he entered the service of the provincial government, but soon turned to economics. He continued his studies at Heidelberg, Jena and Leipzig, and became professor at the University of Prague. In 1903 he succeeded to Carl Menger's chair at the University of Vienna. Wieser was a leading exponent of the doctrines of the "Austrian" school. In his *Ursprung und Hauptgesetze des Wirtschaftlichen Wertes* (1884) he developed Menger's approach to value theory, introducing the term "marginal utility" ("Grenznutzen"). In his other main works, *Der Natürliche Wert* (1889) and *Theorie der Gesellschaftlichen Wirtschaft* (1914), he was mainly concerned with the concept of "natural" value. He gave his name to Wieser's law of costs—that the cost of a commodity was the alternative(s) foregone in producing it. [2]

Windfalls and Wipeouts, colourful title of a research study initiated by the US Department of Housing in 1973 and conducted by a team of lawyers and economists headed by D. G. Hagman, a University of California, Los Angeles, lawyer. The study examined the impact of land use controls and public activity in creating windfall gains for some landowners and losses (wipeouts) for others. The less informative English counterpart expression is "compensation and betterment"; "betterment and worsement" would be more logical. [6]

Winding Up. *See* LIQUIDATION.

Window Dressing, a practice used by joint-stock banks to disguise the true level of their cash reserves and their cash ratios. Before the Second World War joint-stock banks held to a conventional cash ratio of 10 to 11 per cent, but this was a minimum below which they were reluctant to see the ratio fall. If for any reason it seemed likely to do so the banks would "window-dress," most commonly by making up their weekly or monthly returns on different days of the week. Banks making up one day would call in loans from discount houses (thereby raising the item "cash" at the expense of "call money"), whilst the discount houses would pay off the loans by borrowing from banks who would make up on different days. Since 1946 a true ratio of 8 per cent has been established, and banks generally work close to it. [8]

Withholding Tax, American for a tax deducted currently from wages or salaries by the employer, and paid direct to the state. In Britain it was introduced in the Second World War on the advice of Keynes and became known as PAYE—"pay as you earn." The previous method of payment was by the (mostly salaried) taxpayer in arrears. The advantages are more prompt receipt of revenue by government, avoidance of the risk that tax money would be spent before it was due for payment by people with middling or lower incomes, and administrative convenience. The main drawback is the fiscal illusion which masks the taxpayer's consciousness of incomes taxes as tax-prices for government services: they tend to be regarded as a loss of income (hence the emphasis on "take-home" pay) rather than a disposal. [12]

Work in Progress. *See* INVESTMENT.

Working Capital, technically the excess of current assets over current liabilities, economically the funds available for financing current turnover from medium-long or long-term resources. It comprises the stock, cash in hand (or, equally liquid, cash at the bank on current account), and credits due in the short run. It is also known as circulating or floating capital. It varies fairly widely as a proportion of a firm's total capital according to the rate of turnover of the stock (a newspaper seller has almost no working capital, an antique shop a very large working capital), the kind of terms offered to customers (a cash supermarket will require less working capital than a department store offering credit), and whether the business is growing (when it will require more working capital than a department store offering credit), and whether the business is growing (when it will require more working capital to finance larger stocks) or declining (when receipts will not be put into new stock). [1]

World Bank. *See* INTERNATIONAL BANK FOR RECONSTRUCTION AND DEVELOPMENT.

Worsement. *See* WINDFALLS AND WIPEOUTS.

Write Down, recognition in the accounts of a firm that equipment, buildings, etc. are being worn out in current production or are becoming obsolescent because of changes in market conditions that outrun physical wear and tear. Economists complain that accountants have lagged behind them in writing down for the former but not always for the latter, which is the more significant for writing down the "book" value of a firm's physical (or other) assets. [1]

Write Off, recognition in the accounts that equipment, buildings, etc. have lost all their value, i.e. the final stage of writing down. [1]

Write Up, recognition in the accounts that in spite of physical wear and tear equipment, buildings, etc. have risen in current value owing to a change in market conditions. Accountants tend to be cautious or opposed to writing up because of the risk of abuse by firms anxious to make their profits seem larger or their positions stronger than they are, but in economic principle a firm's assets should appear in the books at their current value, not their value at some time in the past, which is of only historical interest. [1]

X

X-efficiency, the effectiveness with which profits are maximized by extending market opportunities. [7]

X-inefficiency, a term coined in 1968 by the American economist H. Leibenstein ("Allocative Efficiency vs X-Efficiency," *American Economic Review*) for the sub-optimal condition in a firm that results from market power. Absence of competitive pressures weakens the stimulus to minimize costs by continuous innovation, concentrating on the least-cost techniques, cutting out waste, etc. Instead firms may spend unnecessarily on prestige buildings, equipment, staff, etc. Costs will be higher than they would be in more competitive conditions, and so therefore would prices.

The idea has been discussed by economists for some decades in the less formal sense of "a quiet life" in which *entrepreneurs* might prefer a slower pace of business to lower costs and higher profits if there was no fear that a competitor would take their customers. In this general sense "a quiet life" is an accompaniment of any development that increases a firm's monopoly power: tariffs, mergers, assured government contracts that cover agreed costs, etc. And it could apply to organizations of all kinds that have a degree of protection from competition, from small shops through multi-national companies to non-profit-making organizations, public corporations and government departments. The concept has been developed by the British economist C. K. Rowley of the University of Newcastle. [7]

Y

Y-efficiency, the effectiveness with which profits are maximized by exploiting existing market opportunities. [7]

Y-inefficiency, a term coined in 1973 by the British economist M. L. Beesley ("Mergers and Economic Welfare" in *Mergers, Take-overs and the Structure of Industry*) for the failure to maximize profits by taking advantage of existing market opportunities. (It is thus a complement to X-inefficiency, which refers to the failure to *extend* them.) In both cases prices are higher than they otherwise would be, and some potential consumers are not supplied at all. In practice Y-inefficiency interacts with X-inefficiency because the product is affected by the production methods used (or neglected), and vice versa. [7]

Yamey, Basil S. (1919–), South African-born economist, educated at Tulbagh High School, the University of Cape Town and the London School of Economics, where he was appointed Professor of Economics, University of London, in 1960. His major work has been on monopoly policy. His book on *The Economics of Resale Price Maintenance* (1954) is a systematic analysis of the nature and effects of the practice of manufacturers prescribing the retail price of their product (RPM). It was published when the merits of RPM and the analysis of its consequences were widely disputed among economists and others; it rejected the argument for RPM in the interests of consumers. Yamey's views contributed to the movement of opinion which led to the abolition of RPM in Britain in 1964. In a series of papers on restrictive trade practices legislation in the UK, Yamey analysed the detailed provisions of the law and the implications of individual decisions. In *The Restrictive Practices Court* (with R. B. Stevens, 1965) he presented a comprehensive analysis of the weaknesses of a system of judicial judgements when applied to the resolution of economic issues. Yamey was appointed a member of the Monopolies Commission from 1966. His other main work has been on the economics of the developing countries, on which he wrote *The Economics of Under-Developed Countries* (1957) with Professor P. T. Bauer, and on the economics of commodity marketing. He is one of the British economists interested in the arts: he was appointed a trustee of the National Gallery in 1974. [2]

Years' Purchase, an expression used in valuation. The multiplier which is applied to an income flow to determine its capital value, is called the *income multiplier* or *Years' Purchase.*

Yield, of a security, is the percentage relationship of its income to its current market price. Except by accident it is unlikely to be the same as the nominal ("coupon") rate of interest which (for fixed-interest securities) is the contractual income expressed in relation to the nominal value of the security. Thus a 3 per cent bond has a nominal yield of £3 per cent of its £100 nominal value: if it can be bought for £50 the true yield is 6 per cent, that is ($^{100}/_{50}$) × 3 per cent. Similarly with securities yielding a variable income such as shares. The nominal yield of a share is the percentage dividend declared on the original issue price of the share, e.g. 20 per cent per £1 share. If the price of the £1 shares is £5, the true yield is 4 per cent, that is one fifth of 20 per cent. Yield is therefore indicated by dividing the par or nominal value by the current price and multiplying by the rate of dividend or interest. Other things remaining the same, the higher the price of a security the lower its yield, and conversely.

This is the "flat yield." With irredeemable securities flat yield indicates the rate of return on invested capital that a buyer will receive for all time as long as he holds it. This is not so with "dated" securities, which bear a date (or range of dates) for the cash redemption of their nominal or face value. The true rate of return on dated securities differs from the flat yield because of the prospect of repayment of the full nominal value of the security. The "yield to redemption" takes into account that if such a security is bought at a price below (or above) par value, the return will include capital appreciation (or depreciation) when it is redeemed. The yield to the redemption date is equal to the flat yield *plus* a percentage given by the formula: annual sinking fund required to accumulate to the difference between the purchase price and the redemption value divided by the purchase price. Without allowance for compound interest, the yield to redemption can be illustrated as follows: if the current price of a 3 per cent fixed interest stock repayable at par in eight years is £92, the purchaser of £100 nominal value will obtain an income of £3 *plus* an average appreciation of £1 per year on his investment as the stock rises from £92 to its maturity value of £100. If the capital value of the sum invested thus grows steadily over the whole eight years, the *average* sum invested will be £96 and the yield to redemption will be the percentage which the combined annual gain (£3 + £1) bears to the average sum invested of £96, i.e., 4.17 per cent. Similarly the current yield on shares, based on the last dividend paid, may bear little relationship to the benefits expected in the future. The "earnings yield" of a share is calculated by dividing a company's profits available for distribution by the value of its ordinary shares at the current market price: the relationship between available profits and dividends distributed enables an assessment to be made of dividend prospects.

Relative yields between different securities reflect the different degrees of risk and uncertainty, the costs of buying, the incidence of tax, transferability and marketability, given the pattern of holders' preferences (for liquidity, income-security, capital-security, etc.) in the securities market. At any time, however, there will be a *pattern* of yields such that, taking all these factors into account, yields are consistent with one another in the sense that differences between any two do not induce investors to switch between securities. Whenever yields are "out of line," the desire to sell relatively low-yield securities and buy relatively high-yielders will cause relative security prices to change until yields are once again in an equilibrium relationship to one another. [8]

Yield Gap. *See* Reverse Yield Gap.

Yield to Redemption. *See* Yield.

Z

Zero Price, economists' jargon for no price, or "free." Thus a private gift or a state service is supplied at zero price (the latter not strictly, since the tax-price, paid by most people, is paid indirectly, though there is no price at the time the service is performed). [13]

Zero Sum, a situation in which the gain to one party is wholly at the expense of the other, so that the sum of gain and loss is zero. This is a proposition of the theory of games which describes the diametrical opposition of two parties. If the sum is not zero but positive, the situation between the two is not of absolute conflict because the gain of one is not wholly at the expense of the other. [14]

Zollverein (*zoll* = toll; *verein* = union), a tariff or customs union of independent sovereign states establishing a common fiscal policy among themselves or against the outside world. The historic Zollverein was created in 1833 when Prussia agreed with four other leading German states—Hesse Cassel, Hesse Darmstadt, Bavaria and Württemberg—to withdraw tariffs against one another's goods and maintain a uniform external tariff. The first measure towards this end had been taken by Prussia in its customs law of 1818, which reduced a wide range of customs duties, eliminated Prussian internal provincial tolls and tariffs, ended the frontier system of tax-levying, and employed a fairly simple technique of assessment based on weight. In 1828 Hesse Darmstadt, as an independent state, accepted the Prussian tariff and established a precedent for the customs union between Bavaria and Württemberg and, later, for the Zollverein. By 1834, with the exception of three Hanseatic cities and three major states—Austria, Hanover and Oldenburg—Germany was for many purposes an economic unit. Uniform currency, weights and measures followed, virtually completing the economic unity. Similarly, the Benelux Convention of 1948 between Belgium, the Netherlands and Luxemburg is a customs union or Zollverein. So, also, was the Belgo-Luxemburg economic union of 1921.

An imperial Zollverein for Britain and the self-governing countries of the empire was advocated around the turn of the nineteenth century. It did not secure wide public support because the future dominions, being mostly committed to protectionist policies, did not want to offer the mother country more than preferential rates. The (European) Common Market and the European Free Trade Association, though radically different in many respects, may be termed Zollvereins. [4]

Zoning, a tool of land-use control. The economic arguments for and against zoning have been tested in Houston, Texas, which, in common with several other cities in the USA, has no land-use controls except for building lines and some minima for dimensions of buildings, off-street parking rules, restrictions on caravan sites, and by-laws on nuisances. The only other controls on land-use take the form of (voluntary) covenants between buyers and sellers or owners and tenants. The covenants are renewable at intervals and although they may be reversed by majority vote of the electorate of the town the evidence suggests this is rarely necessary. The main economic case for zoning is that government can take a wider and longer view of the use of land than individual owners or tenants. The main case against zoning is first, that within a framework of general laws, private covenants are capable of arranging the use of land to the indirect benefit of any third parties as well as of the parties to the covenants despite difficulties in separating individual rights over property in land from rights over property in adjoining land; and second, that zoning in practice tends to be applied for the benefit of the existing body of property owners in a city and to the disadvantage of others. [6]

Zoning, Euclidean. *See* Exclusionary Zoning.

Zoning, Exclusionary. *See* Exclusionary Zoning.

Zoning, Fiscal. *See* Fiscal Zoning.

The text for this book is set in Minion; the display type is Meta Plus Book. Both are relatively new faces, chosen to reflect Seldon's influence on and activity in contemporary social and economic thought. Minion was designed by Robert Slimbach for Adobe in 1990. In spirit and intent it derives from the Garamond tradition. Meta, designed by Erik Spiekermann in 1993, with open spacing for legibility at small sizes, has grown into an extended family and is now widely used.

Printed on paper that is acid-free and meets the requirements of the American National Standard for Permanence of Paper for Printed Library Materials, z39.48-1992. ♾

Book design by Barbara Williams, BW&A Books, Inc., Durham, North Carolina
Typography by Graphic Composition, Inc., Athens, Georgia
Printed and bound by Edwards Brothers, Inc., Ann Arbor, Michigan